THE PUBLIC PAPERS OF
THE GOVERNORS OF KENTUCKY

Robert F. Sexton
General Editor

SPONSORED BY THE
Kentucky Advisory Commission
on Public Documents
AND THE
Kentucky Historical Society

THE PUBLIC PAPERS OF

GOVERNOR KEEN JOHNSON

1939–1943

Frederic D. Ogden, *Editor*

THE UNIVERSITY PRESS OF KENTUCKY

Library of Congress Cataloging in Publication Data

Johnson, Keen, 1896–1970
The public papers of Governor Keen Johnson, 1939–1943.

(Public papers of the Governors of Kentucky)
Includes index.
1. Kentucky—Politics and government—1865–1950—Sources. 2. Johnson, Keen, 1896–1970. I. Ogden, Frederic D. II. Kentucky, Governor (1939–1943: Johnson) III. Title. IV. Series.
F456.J695 353.9769003'5 79-57562
ISBN 0-8131-0605-2 AACR2

Scholarly publisher for the Commonwealth
serving Berea College, Centre College of Kentucky,
Eastern Kentucky University, The Filson Club,
Georgetown College, Kentucky Historical Society,
Kentucky State University, Morehead State University,
Murray State University, Northern Kentucky University,
Transylvania University, University of Kentucky,
University of Louisville, and Western Kentucky University.
Editorial and Sales Offices: Lexington, Kentucky 40506-0024

CONTENTS

STATE ADMINISTRATION [82]

EDUCATION [121]

CONTENTS

CONTENTS

CONTENTS

FOREWORD

KEEN JOHNSON promised in his campaign to make a careful and frugal governor, and he was. His speeches often placed emphasis on democracy, and as governor, he never succumbed to dictatorial or autocratic methods.

He delegated responsibility for preparing the executive budget to the members of the Legislative Council and sat with them frequently through days of hearings, participating more as a member than as governor. He did not deliver his budget message in person. With the war operating to depress state revenues, his budgets were by necessity tight.

Despite his low-key approach to the problems of the state, Governor Johnson did not hesitate to speak out when his value concepts were involved. In urging the legislature in Extraordinary Session to redistrict itself, which necessarily involved changing the area of the districts of many members, he said, "When you have done that, you will have contributed to a noteworthy achievement which will be recorded as an outstanding episode in the legislative history of our Commonwealth." In the heated public debate in 1942 about Tennessee Valley Authority power, while urging legislation enabling cities to purchase and distribute it, he said, "The principle involved is as correct as the Ten Commandments."

During the Johnson administration, all eyes were on World War II and domestic interests were almost wholly concerned with the draft, war-related jobs, gas rationing, and the like. There was little demand for innovative state programs and Johnson pursued only those that were persistent or that appealed to him as being inexpensive and especially rewarding. He was a tireless traveler about the state, mostly by automobile, and often spoke in support of national efforts but not, as one observer suggested, because he had nothing else to speak of.

Though his speeches were filled with the rhetoric of economy, democracy, and patriotism, he frequently spoke to specific programs. Road improvement, education, penal institutions, hospitals, employment, welfare, taxes, public power, county debts, payments in lieu of taxes, tobacco research, teachers' retirement, and other current concerns of the government of Kentucky received attention in his public statements. In Louisville in 1940, he told the Kentucky Education Association, "We did not urge a program of spectacular reform or notable departure." But he also said, "It shall be my purpose to write the record of this administration through doing day by day, a careful, competent, administration job."

Improving mental health care was one of his principal concerns, and rehabilitating poorly maintained and outdated hospitals was a significant effort of his administration. He visited the hospitals, expressed hope to the patients individually, and personally knew how every dollar of contract money was being spent. In speaking to the Kentucky Medical Association in 1941, he wound up with pages of figures, as from an accountant's ledger, relating to hospital building rehabilitation costs. In this and other instances, sometimes he may have given his listeners more information than they wanted, but he viewed himself as the people's surrogate, and he told them what interested him.

Despite declining revenues in the first years of his administration, he was able successfully to carry out several important initiatives and accumulated a $10 million surplus. His achievements included rehabilitating state institutions and other buildings, a modest increase in old age assistance, establishing a teachers' retirement program, funding food commodities for the needy, completing the liquidation of the state general fund warranted debt, initiating a modest program for research into new uses of tobacco, construction of a new tuberculosis sanatorium, establishing an educational equalization fund, and advancing the road building program.

Significant legislative achievements included enabling the use of TVA power, soil conservation legislation, and legislative redistricting—the first in fifty years.

The rehabilitation of depression-ravaged county financial structures was substantially completed, Cumberland Gap National Historical Park was successfully sponsored, the sesquicentennial of the Commonwealth was celebrated with considerable interest, unemployment and workmen's compensation were revamped, and the number of state employees was sharply reduced. The latter was facilitated by not replacing employees who entered military service.

When it is considered that Johnson succeeded an unusually dynamic administration, that it was wartime, that state governments generally were earning a reputation for being the "last redoubt of the conservative," that Kentucky in 1942 was in some respects among the most backward of states, and that the man himself possessed relatively modest levels of ego and personal ambition, these were not mean accomplishments.

Perhaps because he was by profession a newspaperman, he wrote most of his own speeches, pecking them out on a typewriter that sat on a little steel table beside the massive gubernatorial desk. The drafts from which he spoke usually contained marginal notes and interlineation of anecdotes and stories. He was a great storyteller, and cabinet dinner parties at the Mansion typically ended in yarn swapping sessions. Some of his cabinet members, particularly commissioners Arthur T. McCormick, William A. Frost, and Vego Barnes,[1] were themselves great yarn spinners, and Governor Johnson had a knack for turning their stories to highlight his speeches. Many still treasure a favorite Keen Johnson story.

Privately and publicly Johnson was a gracious man who frequently lauded his associates and friends, and from his father he may have acquired some of the spirit of a Methodist preacher. In a speech toward the end of his administration, he admonished his listeners to conserve, buy bonds, be patriotic, read the Bible, uphold the government, disapprove of labor disputes, support the draft boards, and be zealous partisans of democracy.

By today's standards state government in 1939–1943 was small, general fund receipts were only about $25 million annually, and the governor had time to become personally acquainted with the administrative problems of the various departments. Johnson was a good counselor, but seldom gave orders. Henry Ward, a longtime state official and political leader, says Keen Johnson had a better grasp of the fundamentals and knew more about the details of state government than any governor he ever knew. Withal, his supervision of programs may have been spotted, for staff with responsibility for coordinating management, throughout the executive branch, was lacking.

Undoubtedly, he was proud of his administration and it was criticized relatively little, except for a vendetta waged by the attorney general, until the time approached to elect his successor. Then a suggestion of scandal in purchasing caused him to bristle with caustic reference to critics. He could be personal and biting in political controversy. When Rodes K. Myers and Ben Kilgore, candidates for the Democratic nomination for governor, criticized J. Lyter Donaldson, Johnson's choice as a successor, he dubbed them the Casanova of Bowling Green and the carpetbagger from North Carolina. He condemned the Republicans for trying to "magnify all the flyspecks they can find on a magnificent record" and pictured Judge Simeon Willis, the Republican candidate, as the handpicked vassal of isolationist and reactionary leaders. He said, "Willis is like an old owl—the more light I throw on him, the blinder he gets." But Willis won, and at the inauguration Johnson counseled him, "As soon as they swear you in, they start cussing you out." He concluded, "I make my exit from public service, smiling."

Johnson was enough of a historian to know that in fifty years three successive Democratic administrations had occurred only once and that, as a third-term successor, he might be the end of a line. Nevertheless, he was deeply disappointed with Donaldson's defeat and privately spoke of it as a repudiation of his administration.

Until after Johnson's time, Kentucky governors' offices were small operations, and his may have been smaller than many. Only two or three people assisted him, and they, only with the routines. This may explain why his papers are few and unorganized. Undoubtedly he did not look upon them as having great historical significance. To him rehabilitated buildings, increasing old age assistance, and cheaper electricity spoke for themselves.

It is hard to say whether Johnson was among the last of an old school or among the first of the new. The drought of documentation and the modesty of his programs compare in many ways with the pattern of most earlier administrations. Although state governments were at a low ebb in our federal system, Johnson built upon and expanded public services in a manner suggestive of the activist role seen today. It might be difficult to characterize him as a strong governor, but it is certainly easy to go along with the proposition that he was exceptionally well suited to the times he served.

H. CLYDE REEVES

---

1. Vego E. Barnes (1889–1962), b. Fruit Hill, Christian County. Commissioner, Economic Security, 1948. Chairman, Unemployment Compensation Commission. *Kentucky Directory, 1950,* compiled by Frank K. Kavanaugh (Frankfort, Ky., 1950) p. 125, and Louisville *Courier-Journal,* November 21, 1962.

GENERAL EDITOR'S PREFACE

THE Public Papers of the Governors of Kentucky is a series of volumes which preserves and disseminates the public record of Kentucky's chief executives. The need to make these records available was articulated by a number of persons interested in Kentucky history, government, and politics. In 1971 the Kentucky Advisory Commission on Public Documents, created by executive order, recommended the publication of the Public Papers of the Governors of Kentucky. The commission oversees and manages all aspects of the project in cooperation with the Kentucky Historical Society.

Approximately every four years the public papers of the last governor and one earlier governor will appear in separate volumes, each designed to provide a convenient record of that executive's administration. While the organization of the material may vary from volume to volume with differences in the styles of the governors, available materials, and historical circumstances, the volumes share an overall guiding philosophy and general format.

It is our hope that the series will prove useful to all those interested in Kentucky government, including citizens, scholars, journalists, and public servants. Not in themselves interpretations of Kentucky government and history, the volumes in this series will be the basis for serious analysis by future historians.

R. F. S.

EDITOR'S PREFACE

THIS volume is the fourth one in the series of *The Public Papers of the Governors of Kentucky*. It is the first one for a governor who is no longer living. I encountered different problems from those of the previous editors because of this fact and because the period covered (1939–1943) goes back further than the periods of previous editors.

Since consideration was not given to a collection of the papers of Keen Johnson when he left office, care was not taken to retain them. His widow, Mrs. Eunice Johnson, and his daughter, Mrs. Judith Jaggers, gave permission to search the attic of his residence in Richmond. Manuscripts of speeches were found along with cards containing outlines and notes for speeches and many newspaper accounts of speeches which he had made and of events in which he had participated. Apparently none of his public papers were deposited with the State Archives since the only materials which this office has are his executive orders and proclamations.

Many letters were written in an effort to obtain copies of the governor's speeches. Only a few speeches were found in this way. An appeal through the press for material on Keen Johnson was not successful. It was, therefore, necessary to rely on newspapers and to reconstruct many of his speeches from newspaper accounts and, in some cases, from his notecards. Principal newspapers used were the Louisville *Courier-Journal*, *Lexington Herald*, *Cincinnati Enquirer*, *State Journal*, *Kentucky Post*, and *Richmond Daily Register*. Local newspapers were consulted if Johnson had visited the particular area.

The material is organized by subject in twelve sections and chronologically within each section. I believe that this organization gives the reader easy access to related material. When the governor included more than one topic in a speech, it has been placed in the section of its major subject.

Some speeches have been edited to delete duplicate material. Where the duplication was slight or where removing it would effect the meaning of the speech, duplicated material was retained.

Where executive orders and proclamations seemed essential to supplement a speech or press release, they have been used.

Many speeches have been extensively footnoted to provide the reader with supplementary material. This additional information seemed necessary for a better understanding of these speeches. Explanatory headnotes have been used for a few speeches.

Information is included in the footnotes about individuals who are mentioned in the speeches. Particular attention has been given to Kentuckians. The task of obtaining data about individuals active in government during the Johnson period involved considerable correspondence and inquiries by telephone. Records for few Kentuckians of this period are available in the Department of Public Information biographical files. Persons mentioned are identified the first time that their names are cited. Several of the persons contacted expressed a sincere interest in the project to publish the public papers of Kentucky governors.

I am indebted to H. Clyde Reeves for his evaluation of the Johnson administration in the Foreword. Since he served as commissioner of revenue in this administration and since he has had a long connection with state government, he is especially qualified to evaluate the Johnson governorship.

The Appendixes include two campaign speeches made by Johnson while he was lieutenant governor and was campaigning for governor. They provide a background for his administration since he outlines his proposed program in them.

Finally, the Appendixes contain a complete list of all speeches, presented chronologically. The sources used when a speech was reconstructed are shown. Whether the item is a speech from a manuscript, a reconstructed speech or a summary of a speech from a newspaper or other sources, an executive order, a proclamation, a letter, or a press release is indicated. The list includes campaign speeches from October 9 to November 6, 1939, the period when Johnson was completing the term of A. B. Chandler as governor and also was campaigning for election to a full term as governor.

I have sought to present a full and accurate account of the administration of Governor Keen Johnson through this collection of his public papers. Editing them appealed to me because he was a resident of Richmond whom I had known slightly. I wish that I had known him better and had been able to edit his papers while he was still living.

Jessie Cupitt Ogden assisted at every stage in the preparation of these papers for publication. She served as a research associate, albeit a nonsalaried one. The completion of the project was aided immeasurably by her assistance. Typing assistance was provided by Nancy Botner, Kathryn Houser, and Charleen Tipton. Eastern Kentucky University provided office facilities, telephone, and mail service.

F. D. O.

GOVERNOR KEEN JOHNSON
October 9, 1939, to December 7, 1943

KEEN JOHNSON, the forty-second governor of the Commonwealth of Kentucky, was born on January 12, 1896, at Brandon's Chapel in the "Between the Rivers" section of Lyon County, Kentucky. He was one of four children born to Robert and Mattie D. (Holloway) Johnson. He was named for John S. Keen, a native of Adair County and a friend of his father.[1]

His father was a circuit-riding Methodist preacher and his earliest teacher. Because the administrative policies of the Methodist church required its ministers to move frequently, Keen Johnson became familiar with many parts of the Pennyrile and Purchase sections of the state.

Keen Johnson married Eunice Nichols of Higbee, Missouri, daughter of Robert Lee and Mary (Avery) Nichols, on June 23, 1917. Mrs. Johnson, through her father, is descended from a Barren County, Kentucky, pioneer who moved to Boone County, Missouri. Her father died when she was nine months old and she was reared among her mother's people in Missouri.

One daughter, Judith, was born to the Keen Johnsons on May 10, 1927. Now Mrs. Richard Jaggers, she is the mother of two sons, Robert Babbage, Jr., and Keen Johnson Babbage.

Keen Johnson received his elementary education in the public schools of the Commonwealth. He graduated from the Vanderbilt Training School, a Methodist preparatory school in Elkton in 1914. He entered Central College, Fayette, Missouri, a Methodist institution, and pursued academic studies there until he enlisted in the army.

With the United States' entry into World War I, Keen Johnson enrolled in the Reserve Officer's Training Camp at Fort Riley, Kansas, on May 15, 1917. He was appointed second lieutenant, Infantry, Officers Reserve Corps, on August 15, 1917, and assigned to active duty with the 354th Infantry, 89th Division, at Camp Funston, Kansas. He was promoted to first lieutenant, Infantry, National Army, on March 29, 1918, and embarked for France, June 4, 1918. He returned to the United States April 28, 1919, and was honorably discharged October 31, 1919.[2]

Following his discharge he edited a weekly paper, *The Mirror*, published in Elizabethtown. He purchased the paper with financial assistance from his father. After a brief time he sold the paper and entered the University of Kentucky where he received the A.B. degree in 1922 with a major in journalism. During his student days he was employed as a reporter for the *Lexington Herald*. After graduation he acquired a half-interest in the weekly *Anderson News,* Lawrenceburg, and became its editor and publisher.

In 1925 he moved to Richmond, Madison County, and became editor and co-publisher of the *Richmond Daily Register.* He purchased a half-interest in the paper from Shelton M. Saufley, Sr.

Keen Johnson was the first governor of Kentucky who had been a newspaper editor. Dr. Herman L. Donovan, president of Eastern Kentucky State Teachers College and later president of the University of Kentucky, said of him, "Our local paper soon took on a new life. Editorials worthy of a metropolitan paper began to appear daily."[3] He was noted for a 'Scrabble' column, an anecdotal column of events and comments on them.

Keen Johnson launched his political career when he became secretary of the Democratic State Central and Executive Committee in 1932.[4]

He became a candidate for lieutenant governor in 1935 and defeated J. E. Wise and B. F. Wright, the principal contenders in the primary, by a majority of more than 70,000 votes. On September 7 he defeated Wise in a runoff election. He defeated the Republican candidate, J. J. Kavanaugh, by more than 100,000 votes.

Johnson announced his candidacy for governor on May 17, 1939. After a strong primary campaign, he defeated John Young Brown on August 5 by a vote of 270,731 to 237,454. He opened his campaign for governor on October 7, 1939, in Mount Sterling.

United States Senator Marvin Mills Logan died on October 3, 1939, and on October 9, Governor A. B. Chandler resigned. Keen Johnson took the oath as governor and his first official act was to appoint Chandler to the Senate to fill the unexpired term of Senator Logan. Johnson was elected for a full term on November 17, 1939, having defeated King Swope of Lexington by more than 100,000 votes.

During the war years he was a strong supporter of President Franklin Delano Roosevelt.

At the invitation of President Harry S. Truman he served as undersecretary of labor, a newly created office, from 1946 to 1947. He attended cabinet meetings owing to the illness of the secretary, L. B. Schwellenback.

He was a member of the Democratic National Committee from 1940 to 1948.

In 1960 he campaigned for a seat in the United States Senate. He defeated his former opponent, John Young Brown, in the primary but lost to the Republican incumbent, John Sherman Cooper, in the general election.

Johnson joined the Reynolds Metals Company as assistant to the president early in 1944 soon after the end of his gubernatorial term. He served as a vice-president from 1947 and became a director in 1950. He held both positions until his retirement in 1961.

Over the years, Johnson served with various professional, fraternal, social, and military organizations. He was president of the Kentucky Press Association and of the Kentucky Social Workers Association. He served as president of the Louisville Advertising Club and the Louisville Safety Council during his active years with Reynolds Metals Company. He was chairman of the Kentucky Disabled Ex-Service Men's Board and campaign chairman for the Kentucky Crippled Children's Society. He was a board member of the Kentucky Heart Association, the Kentucky Chamber of Commerce, the Louisville International Center, and the Richmond Methodist Church.

Johnson belonged to many clubs and organizations including the Civil War Round Table, National Press Club, Metropolitan Club in Washington, D.C., Public Relations Society of America, Pendennis Club, Keeneland Club, American Legion, Veterans of Foreign Wars, 40 and 8, Masonic F. and A.M., Rotary, Elks, Sigma Alpha Epsilon, Omicron Delta Kappa, Sigma Delta Chi, and Scabbard and Blade.

The University of Kentucky awarded Johnson an honorary doctor of laws degree in 1940 and later a Centennial Award. He received a Distinguished Service Plaque from Eastern Kentucky University where he served for eight years as a member of the Board of Regents. He was president of the University of Kentucky Alumni Association. He served on the Kentucky Council on Higher Education for many years and for two terms on the Kentucky Board of Education.

Keen Johnson died February 7, 1970, in Richmond.

---

1. Paul Hughes, "Big Headlines Don't Tell the Story," Louisville *Courier-Journal Magazine*, July 23, 1950, p. 27.
2. Statement of Military Service, War Department, Adjutant-General's Office, Washington, D.C., E. T. Conley, Adjutant-General, April 14, 1938.
3. Speech by Dr. H. L. Donovan, January 3, 1936, in a ceremony to honor Johnson.
4. *Southern City* 7 (April 1943): 6.

INAUGURAL ADDRESS
Frankfort / December 12, 1939

IT pleases me immensely that you have assembled here in such numbers to witness the induction of myself and the Honorable Rodes K. Myers[1] into the exalted offices of governor and lieutenant governor. It delights me that virtually every county in Kentucky is represented in this vast throng. Much effort, ingenuity and expense has been required to make this, the supreme moment of my public life, a colorful and memorable event. So I want to express my appreciation to the members of the inaugural committee in Frankfort and to every individual in this great assembly, for their respective contributions to this, which will always be one of my most cherished memories.

But while I thank you for the honor which you pay to me by your presence here, I realize also that there is another more important aspect of this celebration. The greatest honor you pay today is not to me but to the office which I am about to assume, and to the form of government which is symbolized by this ceremony. Our celebration is not alone in honor of what we inaugurate; it is principally in honor of what we continue—the succession of power in the hands of the people through their elected representatives. You inaugurate me today as the governor of a sovereign people, and by that act, you reaffirm your own sovereignty. My own term is for a fixed period, after which I shall step aside and another shall take my place, but your rule will continue as long as we and our children shall be free Kentuckians and free Americans.

The sight of democracy being destroyed or threatened over wide areas of the earth makes many of us more keenly aware of how precious our own democracy is to us. Events in other lands demonstrate to us that we can not take democracy for granted.

When we see democracy under attack elsewhere, when we say to ourselves, "Thank God for America," we should renew our devotion to the welfare of our state and nation as a whole. Our democracy and its blessings are not individual possessions for our exclusive and selfish use. Democracy can exist only collectively. No man can take his share of it and go away from his fellows with it to enjoy it by himself. It serves all, or it ceases to exist and thereafter can serve none.

Our state constitution provides that no person may be elected as governor for successive terms. I have sometimes suspected that perhaps there were some, in crowds like this one here today, who had gathered, not to see that the new governor was inaugurated, but that the old one had left office.

By the intervention of death and resignation, I became your governor several weeks ago to serve out the short time remaining in the expiring term. Since I thus today succeed myself, I am happily spared any suspicion that any of you have come here today to make certain that I, the retiring governor, have gone back to private life.

It is my hope and my earnest, sincere intention to so administer the affairs of your Commonwealth that I will not need to entertain such a suspicion when another such throng gathers here four years hence.

But whether you and that other throng four years hence gather here to see the new governor inaugurated, or to see to it that an outgoing governor has really gone, you exercise in either case a privilege of citizenship. Whether your governor is going in or coming out, you speed him on his way. The new governor's responsibility begins on this day, but the responsibility of you who have installed a new governor does not end on this day. It is still your government. You are rightfully glad and proud today that you have reaffirmed your sovereignty by installing a new governor of your own choice. I could not have achieved this high honor without your support. Neither can I succeed for long without your continued help and support.

An administration is the civil machinery you have devised to serve you in your governmental affairs. You trade it in for a new model every four years. It is the vehicle by which you hope a certain amount of progress may be achieved within that time. Since it carries your hopes and welfare as its precious burden, it is incumbent upon me to use the utmost care in steering it. I ask all the citizens of Kentucky to help me keep it progressing, to help keep it in good running order, and to help get out of it all we can of mutual good and service for all our citizenship before we junk it for another model four years hence.

Four years ago I stood on this platform beside Governor Chandler and took the oath which made me lieutenant governor of Kentucky. In that subordinate role I tried diligently to perform as best I could those duties which were my responsibility. My principal pledge was that I would cooperate with the governor. I did that, and made whatever other contributions were within my power to that progress in government which has been made within the past four years. I feel reasonably certain that no official act of mine has been hurtful to the state. I shall be even more diligent and careful in the hope and determination that I may still be able to say this when my term as governor shall be over.

I am grateful to so many of you as voted for me, for having given me this opportunity to serve all of you as your governor. I shall try to justify your confidence by diligently endeavoring to make you a saving, thrifty, frugal governor. At the same time, with the funds available, I shall diligently endeavor to give you a constructive, progressive administration of your state affairs. I will not make you a spectacular governor, but I will try harder than did any of my predecessors to make you a good, honest governor.

We perhaps cannot foresee today all the problems with which your governor and your other state officials may have to deal within the next four years. After a long struggle to clear the chaotic wreckage left by the collapse of 1929, we have seen within the last few months very definite and substantial economic progress. But almost before this upswing was fully under way, forces were unloosed across the seas which threaten the moral foundations, and perhaps even the political foundations, of our civilization. What their ultimate effects on us will be, no man can foretell. For these reasons, it would be difficult indeed to attempt to tell you today what your state government may be able to accomplish within the next four years. We can only restate those principles by which I shall be guided.

First among those I would place the proposition that Kentucky consists not alone of one of God's most favored spots, not alone of fields and forests and factories and mines and mills, but that it is a community of some three million human beings. Many of these walk in the humbler paths of life. We must continue to see to it that the burdens of government do not weigh oppressively upon any class of our citizenship. Within the funds available, we must continue to place emphasis on the educational, health, welfare, and highway programs, which are of such direct benefit to such large numbers of our people.

Measured by her tax resources, Kentucky is a relatively poor state in the economic scale. We thus can afford less debt than our richer neighbors. So we are pledged to continue to keep the state's expenses within the state's income, and to continue to reduce the state's debt.

Increased public assistance to the needy aged, supported by an appropriation from available funds, will be proposed, with other detailed measures to put into effect the program we have advocated, at the session of the General Assembly in January.

There are many difficult problems with which your governor, the lieutenant governor, and the General Assembly will be faced. Many of these could be readily solved if there were public funds available in sufficient quantity. Unhappily, we may not employ that method of solution. I have a mandate from the people of Kentucky to operate the various agencies of your state government without increasing the burden of taxes. With the cooperation of the General Assembly, I shall faithfully respect that mandate.

There are many requests for increased appropriations of public funds. Most of the requested increases are for worthy and proper purposes. But increased appropriations cannot be made unless the burden of Kentucky taxpayers is increased. And I have repeatedly expressed opposition to that procedure.

That situation places on your governor the unpleasant duty of insisting that present appropriations cannot be increased in the aggregate, because present revenues are barely sufficient to meet existing appropriations. Yet within these limited revenues, we have the obligation of making as great an increase in old age assistance as is possible, and of providing funds to make the teachers retirement act operative. These are the major increased expenditures to which your new administration is committed. Obviously these additional expenditures can be made only by cutting down on other expenditures.

The total tax receipts of the state for the fiscal year which ended June 30, 1939, were approximately $2 million less than receipts for the preceding fiscal year, and $3 million less than receipts for the fiscal year 1936–1937. The decline is due principally to a steady decrease in the yield of alcoholic beverage taxes that has followed sharp curtailment of distillery operations. As pleas are pressed for increased appropriations, I am often asked why it is not possible to use the money formerly used to reduce the state debt. The answer is that the revenue which was largely used to reduce the state debt is no longer available, because of decreased income from taxes which no longer produce revenue in such volume as in the fiscal year 1936–1937. So it becomes apparent that in order to continue to operate our state without increased revenues, we shall be forced to get along without many things that would be desirable if we could afford them, and I have no doubt that the people of Kentucky desire that their state government should limit its expenditures sufficiently to keep within its income.

Fortunately, revenues of the highway fund have been well maintained and have shown a slight increase. This will make possible the continuation of the program of reconstructing those main highways in greatest need of modernization, extension of the road system into those regions most isolated, and continued aid to the counties in improving their secondary roads through the rural highway program. But this sane, sensible, and urgently necessary program would be destroyed if the road fund should be destroyed by diverting it to other purposes.

I hope there may be a wider acceptance of the fact that the best politics is good government and that politics reaches its highest justification as it advances better government.

In all problems that arise, I shall draw strength from the knowledge that we are a people who believe in God and liberty under the American flag.

It is our good fortune to live within a great and beautiful state, peopled by a splendid, intelligent, patriotic citizenship. I would not feel fit to be your governor it I did not feel a great love for Kentucky and her people. Love for Kentucky is with me a holy passion. I love her majestic mountains, her rolling Blue Grass. I love the Pennyrile, the Purchase. I have been in every one of her 120 counties and in each I have found something which makes me more genuinely devoted to the state I am privileged to serve as governor.

For many years our state was more noticeably divided into geographical sections. The people of one section were jealous and suspicious of those in other regions. Too often the progress of Kentucky as a whole was retarded when we were heedless of the fundamental truth expressed in our state motto, "United We Stand, Divided We Fall." Too often in the past we suffered from a lack of unity. While we have not fallen because of divergent viewpoints that were divisive, our advancement has been impeded by sectional misunderstanding. At times, one section of the state sought to advance at the expense of others.

In recent years, our geographical barriers have been overcome to a considerable extent as improved highways have linked the state together. As there has been increased commingling of the people of the Pennyrile with the people of the mountains, much of the sectional feeling has disappeared.

There was a time when there was a less friendly feeling than at present between the residents of rural Kentucky and those who populate our cities. That too has been dissipated as improved roads have brought rural residents and the urban population into closer contact.

It has taken years to overcome such real or fancied divisions among us. It is my high resolve to try always to be the governor of all Kentucky. It shall be the purpose of my heart to try to consider every legislative and administrative problem in the light of that which appears best for the entire Commonwealth. It is my earnest plea that all Kentuckians, state officials, members of the legislature, citizens alike, keep foremost in their minds the obvious truth that only legislation which advances the welfare of all the state is for the best interest of Kentucky.

I hope that there will not be a revival of legislation that seeks to help one section or group of Kentuckians at the expense of another section or group. I implore you to frown with displeasure upon legislative proposals that would take from one group of our people give to another to the detriment of Kentucky as a whole. I earnestly plead with you to support your governor as he insists that there be applied to all legislation the simple but accurate test: "Is it for the best interest of all Kentucky without operating to the detriment of my section?"

Let me urge you to encourage your representatives and senators in the General Assembly to subordinate selfish desires, to take a broad, statewide view of legislation. Let us place less emphasis on concentrating pressure to get something specific for our city or county, and be more concerned about supporting those proposals which seek to enhance the welfare of all Kentucky.

It is my earnest hope that the motto of our state may be emblazoned upon our hearts and consciences; that we may realize that enlightened self-interest may best be served by unitedly seeking to stimulate the advancement of all Kentucky.

"United We Stand, Divided We Fall" is more than an axiom. It is fraught with wisdom. It expresses a truth as self-evident as the noonday sun. How helpful it will be, as various groups seek to solve local problems through state aid, if they may but ponder the truth expressed in that motto, "United We Stand!" Not only shall we stand if we may be united in the great purpose of advancing Kentucky as a whole, but we shall steadily go forward to the fulfillment of our destiny as Kentuckians.

In the four years that lie ahead, I am glad that I will have the assistance of the gifted, intelligent, experienced, attractive young Kentuckian who stands by my side and who will take with me the oath of office. I have no doubt that Lieutenant Governor Myers will make an able, conscientious public official and I count myself fortunate that we are to be yoked up together in public service. The other state officials who are to take office January 2 will provide me with an official family that is honorable, conscientious, sincerely anxious as am I, that we together may perform as creditably our individual tasks as to merit the confidence you have imposed in us.

It is with deep humility that I approach the most solemn moment of my life, when there shall be administered to me the oath of the highest office within the gift of the people I love. I have made no effort to mislead you by posing as a statesman of great ability. I have told you frankly of my limitations. My only hope is that those deficiencies in ability and statecraft which are my misfortune may be made up for, in a measure, by a sincere devotion to Kentucky which will impel me to strive diligently, daily as I try to differentiate between the genuine and the counterfeit, as I exercise all the judgment I possess in an effort to reach correct conclusions in the many problems upon which it will be my responsibility to act.

I have a consuming desire to perform acceptably the important job for which you, the people, have chosen me. There could be no more abiding satisfaction than to feel, at the conclusion of my term, that I have kept faith with the folks I love, that through the years remaining I and my wife and our little daughter would be justified in feeling pride in the service I rendered.[2]

If I am to make a good governor, I shall need your help. It is not of great consequence personally to anyone except me, my wife, and daughter as to whether I succeed or fail in this task. But if I fail all Kentucky will suffer, progress of the state will be impeded. If I succeed in doing an acceptable job, the chief beneficiary will be Kentucky and her people. Thus, it is so important for Kentucky that I should succeed that I hope you will all realize the importance of helping me as much as you can.

I shall need your sympathetic understanding. I need so much your charitable tolerance when I make mistakes that are errors of judgment and not of the heart. It will be a great inspiration to me if I may have assurance that the people I am trying to serve and standing by me, justifying that loyalty by the belief that my impulses are correct and by my pledge that I will always strive to do right.

And now, Mr. Chief Justice, I am ready to take the oath of office.

---

1. Rodes Kirby Myers (1900–1959), b. Bowling Green. Lieutenant governor, 1939–1943; commonwealth attorney, Sixth Judicial District, 1933; state representative, 1934–1939, 1945; state senator, 1948–1950. *Who's Who in Kentucky, 1955* (Hopkinsville, Ky., n.d.), p. 243, and interview with Polly Gorman, secretary to Governor Bert Combs, June 19, 1978.

2. Eunice Lee Nichols (1895–), b. Howard County, Missouri. Married Keen Johnson 1917. Graduate Howard Payne College, Fayette, Missouri. Resides in Richmond.

Judith Keen Johnson (1927–), b. Richmond. Married Robert A. Babbage 1948; two sons, Robert A., Jr., and Keen Johnson. Graduate, University of Kentucky, 1948 with high distinction. Phi Beta Kappa. Married Richard E. Jaggers, Jr., 1970. Resides in Lexington.

LEGISLATIVE MESSAGES & STATEMENTS

ON RESIGNATION OF CHANDLER AS GOVERNOR
Frankfort / October 9, 1939

THE Honorable A. B. Chandler,[1] Governor of the Commonwealth of Kentucky, having resigned said office and reliquished all of his rights thereto, as appears of record on the Executive Orders of the Governor of the Commonwealth now on file in the office of the Secretary of State, came the Honorable Keen Johnson, the duly elected, qualified and acting Lieutenant Governor for the Commonwealth of Kentucky, and the Honorable Alex Ratliff,[2] Chief Justice of the Court of Appeals of the Commonwealth of Kentucky, and the Honorable Chief Justice administered the oath of office as Governor of the Commonwealth of Kentucky to the Honorable Keen Johnson[3] and the Honorable Keen Johnson thereupon assumed and entered upon the discharge of his duties as Governor of the Commonwealth of Kentucky at the hour of 10:30 A.M. Central Standard Time, on October 9th., A.D., 1939.

After reviewing the resignation of the said A. B. Chandler as Governor of the Commonwealth of Kentucky and his relinquishment of the office of Governor of the Commonwealth of Kentucky, it is now ordered by the undersigned, Governor of the Commonwealth of Kentucky, that said resignation of the said A. B. Chandler as Governor of the Commonwealth of Kentucky be and the same hereby is accepted and his relinquishment of said office is hereby confirmed.

---

1. Albert Benjamin ("Happy") Chandler (1898–), b. Corydon. Resides in Versailles. State senator, 1929–1931; lieutenant governor, 1931–1935; governor, 1935–1939, 1955–1959; United States senator, 1939–1945; candidate for governor, 1963, 1967, 1971; commissioner of baseball, 1945–1951; member Commonwealth party (formerly a Democrat). *Who's Who in the South and Southwest, 1971–72*, 12th ed. (Chicago, 1971), p. 105, and interview, Governor Chandler, March 13, 1978.

2. Alexander Lackey Ratliff (1884–1947), b. Ash Camp. Court of Appeals, 1932–1944, and chief justice. *Who's Who in Kentucky, 1936*, ed. Mary Y. Southard (Louisville Ky., 1936), p. 332, and *Lexington Leader*, August 24, 1947.

3. Johnson became the forty-second governor and the tenth lieutenant governor to serve also as governor of the Commonwealth. The lieutenant governors who also served as governors of Kentucky were Gabriel Slaughter, James T. Morehead, Charles A. Wickliffe, John L. Helm, John W. Stevenson, Preston H. Leslie, J. C. W. Beckham, James D. Black, and A. B. Chandler.

APPOINTS CHANDLER AS UNITED STATES SENATOR
Frankfort / October 9, 1939

IT appearing that a vacancy in the office of United States Senator from the Commonwealth of Kentucky has been created by the death of the junior Senator from Kentucky, the Honorable M. M. Logan;[1] and it further appearing that the Congress of the United States is now in session and has under consideration legislation of momentous importance not only to the United States of America but the entire world as well, and that it is highly important that the Commonwealth of Kentucky have full representation in the Senate of the United States during the consideration, decision and voting upon said measures; and that under the laws of the United States and the laws of the Commonwealth of Kentucky, the Governor of the Commonwealth of Kentucky is invested with full power to appoint a United States Senator to succeed the Honorable M. M. Logan; and it further appearing that the Honorable A. B. Chandler[2] possesses all the qualifications of a United States Senator, now, therefore, by reason of the powers vested in me, I, Keen Johnson, Governor of the Commonwealth of Kentucky, do hereby appoint the Honorable A.B. Chandler, of Versailles, Kentucky, to the office of United States Senator to succeed the Honorable M. M. Logan as a member of the United States Senate from the Commonwealth of Kentucky to fill the unexpired term of said M. M.

Logan and until his successor for the unexpired term shall have been duly elected at the regular November 1940 election, and qualifies and enters upon the discharge of his duties; and it is ordered that the said A. B. Chandler, of Versailles, Kentucky, be forthwith issued a commission in the manner and form provided by law as United States Senator from the Commonwealth of Kentucky.

---

1. Marvel Mills Logan (1875–1939), b. Edmonson County. Edmonson County attorney, 1902–1912; first assistant attorney general, 1912–1916; attorney general, 1916–1920; judge, Court of Appeals, 1926; chief justice, 1930–1931; United States senator, 1931–1939. *Who's Who in Kentucky, 1936,* p. 249.

2. Governor Chandler became the eleventh man to serve both as governor of Kentucky and as a United States senator from Kentucky. Only two other governors have resigned the governorship to go to the United States Senate.

LETTER TO VICE PRESIDENT GARNER
Frankfort / October 9, 1939

MY Dear Mr. Vice President:[1]

This is to certify that I, as Governor of the Commonwealth of Kentucky, have on October 9, 1939, appointed the Honorable Albert B. Chandler as United States Senator from the Commonwealth of Kentucky to fill the vacancy created by the death of Senator M. M. Logan.

In accordance with the provisions of the Kentucky Statutes, an Order has been entered in the Executive Journal in the Office of the Secretary of State of this Commonwealth, appointing and commissioning the Honorable A. B. Chandler as United States Senator from Kentucky.

There is attached a copy of the Executive Order, attested by the Honorable Charles D. Arnett, Secretary of State.[2]

---

1. John Nance Garner (1868–1967), b. Red River County, Texas. United States representative, 1903–1933, and Speaker, 1931; vice president of the United States, 1933–1941. *Who Was Who in America, 1961–1968* (Chicago, 1968), 4:346.

2. Charles Douglas Arnett (1879–1940), b. Hendricks. Attorney. State senator, 1913–1917; secretary of state, 1935–1939; unsuccessful Democratic candidate for governor, 1939. George Lee Willis, Sr., *Kentucky Democracy* (Louisville, Ky., 1935), 2:60-64, and *Louisville Times,* December 3, 1940.

STATE OF THE COMMONWEALTH ADDRESS
Frankfort / January 2, 1940

IT is a pleasure to greet you today at this convocation of the biennial session of the Kentucky General Assembly and extend to you a cordial welcome. It is a distinct honor to be privileged to serve as a member of the Kentucky legislature. It is an opportunity for fine public service which carries with it great responsibilities.

The Constitution directs the governor to advise the legislature of the state's needs and problems. It is your duty to legislate and I have no disposition to infringe upon your duties. It is the duty of the governor to offer for your consideration information and suggestions as to what seems to be necessary or preferable. The governor and your other elective state officials who comprise the governor's official family must stay here throughout the entire four years of our terms and administer the laws you have enacted, after you yourselves shall have completed your legislative duties and returned to your homes. So it is important that you leave us in a position where we may do acceptable administrative jobs.

I am sure that every member of the legislature joins with the governor and your other elected state officials in a common desire to render conscientious and valuable service to the people of Kentucky. Your problem is made difficult by the multiplicity of subjects with which legislation deals, and by the fact that your session is limited by the Constitution to a maximum of sixty days. After that time, and after you shall have returned to your homes, further legislative action can be obtained only by the great expense of a special session, or by waiting for two years until time for another regular session.

The pressure due to limited time has often resulted, in the past, in hastily drawn or hastily considered legislation. Bills intended to accomplish definite purposes sometimes are found later, when reviewed in the courts, to have had far different effects because of their interplay with older statutes.

There are already numerous laws on the statute books, and I think it is correct to state that Kentucky does not need many more laws. It is more important that all new laws enacted should be carefully drawn and carefully considered.

The staff of the Kentucky Statutes Revision Commission, the staff of the attorney general, and attorneys attached to several state departments have generously offered to give all the assistance possible to members of the legislature, consistent with their regular duties, to aid in drafting bills so as to make them conform to the Constitution and avoid unintended effects on existing statutes.

You who compose the legislature occupy a position comparable to the board of directors of a corporation. The position of your governor may be likened unto that of a president of a corporation. We are to work together for sixty days, concentrating all our efforts and thoughts upon the legislative needs of the Commonwealth.

Because of the great importance of your work, I shall endeavor insofar as possible to restrict all other demands upon the governor's time during the session, in order that I may be available to any of you when you wish to consult with me.

You of the General Assembly come from various sections of the state. Some of you represent rural regions and some represent urban communities. But I urge each of you to remember that you cannot advance the welfare of Kentucky by legislation which is helpful to your own district if at the same time it is hurtful to some other section of the state. I implore you to avoid legislation that would array one section or group within the state against another section or group.

We cannot treat the welfare of Kentucky as the Indian did his blanket in the story. His blanket was too short to keep him warm around the neck, so he cut a piece off the bottom and sewed it to the top. We can obtain only a false comfort for ourselves if it means shoving somebody else out into the cold.

The necessity and the wisdom of dealing with national problems nationally has been demonstrated under the leadership of President Roosevelt. We can and should apply this principle within our own field by dealing with state problems on a statewide basis.

The condition of Kentucky's government is much improved as you assemble here, contrasted with conditions that existed four years ago. The most marked progress that has taken place is in the reformation of the state's finances. Kentucky has lived within her income, and until recently made amazing reductions in the state debt. It has made this record in spite of the fact that it assumed, within the same period of time, the burdens of greatly expanded social service to its people. Among such costs may be mentioned the institution of old age pensions under the Social Security Act and the building of new prisons and hospitals to relieve long neglect.

A substantial part of the cost of these expanded services to the people was met by a reduction of approximately $1 million a year in interest charges on the state debt, and by the introduction of greater efficiency and economies resulting from the Reorganization Act[1] and budgetary control. Grants of federal aid have made a major and invaluable contribution to this progress.

The great reduction in the state debt was made possible principally by the high level of distillery operations immediately following the repeal of prohibition, when the state's five-cents-a-gallon tax on whiskey production poured a flood tide of revenues into the state treasury. This flow of revenue was augmented by the receipts from specialty taxes on soft drinks, ice cream, candy, and certain other items, which have since been repealed.

The distillery operations have now leveled off to an activity sufficient to meet replacement needs, and receipts from the whiskey production tax have consequently fallen off to a much smaller figure. The soft drinks–ice cream–and–candy tax is no longer on the statutes. Consequently, I must make it plain at the outset that there is no large volume of revenue available for spending purposes. There is no surplus of revenues being applied to debt reduction which the legislature might wish to divert to other purposes.

I want to emphasize also that the reduction of $1 million a year in interest charges on the state debt made a very substantial contribution to the newly assumed costs of old age pensions, to the costs of ending long neglect of our penal and charitable institutions, and to the routine costs of government.

This saving of $1 million a year was made possible in two ways: by a reduction in the amount of debt on which interest is paid, and by a reduction in the rate of interest which the state pays on the debt still outstanding.

This interest formerly was 5 percent; it has been reduced to as little as 1.5 percent on part of the remaining debt. This reduction in interest rate was made possible only by the fact that the state's budget was balanced and the debt being reduced. The financial markets will not absorb state warrants at such a low interest rate if an unbalanced condition in the state's budget raises any question regarding the definite prospect of payment of the state's obligations. Even when the state paid 5 percent interest, the financial markets at one time regarded the state's paper as being worth only about seventy cents on the dollar.

It is, therefore, urgently necessary that the state should continue to live within its income and continue to reduce the state debt, and it should do this without increasing the general burden of taxes. No more important duty faces you than to enact legislation which will assure that sound procedure.

Unless this is done, a rising interest rate will require additional money which could otherwise be used for more constructive purposes.

I recommend to you that you enact legislation which will increase the maximum payments which may be made for old age assistance from $15 to $30 a month. Under the present law, $15 is the largest sum an old age recipient may receive. That, of course, does not mean, as I have repeatedly said, that all persons who receive old age assistance will get $30 a month. Under both the federal and state laws, the amount of cash grants must be based upon the needs of the person to whom paid.

I ask that you mend the old age assistance act so as to eliminate the provision which requires old age assistance recipients to give the state a lien, or mortgage, on such property as they may own. Existing liens should be canceled. The General Assembly should make certain, when repealing this lien requirement, that there are adequate safeguards in the act to make certain that the old age assistance money shall go to those who actually need it.

I recommend that you submit to the people for a vote a constitutional amendment which, if adopted, would permit creating an educational equalization fund. Our state constitution now requires that state money for public education be distributed among the counties on the basis of the number of children of school age residing within them. These state funds are then supplemented by school funds raised by local taxation. Under this plan, the more prosperous counties provide adequate school opportunities without unduly burdensome taxes, but there are a number of poor counties which are still unable to provide adequate educational opportunities after taxing themselves to the limit. If the proposed constitutional change be submitted and approved, these inequalities of educational opportunity may be eliminated by increased state support to counties in greatest need.

I recommend that there be enacted legislation to create a Division of Markets in the Department of Agriculture. This agency should stress promotional market efforts and make available to farmers practical assistance in setting up farm cooperatives. You will note that I suggest in the budget bill that there be an appropriation of $15,000 each year for this activity.

I recommend that an appropriation of $7,500 a year be made to finance research in an effort to find new uses for tobacco. This appropriation you will find in the budget bill, which would make this money available for the University of Kentucky College of Agriculture, where I feel certain it will be most wisely expended.

I suggest legislation which would direct the creation of a nonsalaried commission to study the problems of farm tenancy relative to farm ownership, to assist farm tenants and farm laborers in developing a program for the purchasing and financing of farms.

Kentucky is rich in natural resources, is located near the center of population of the United States, and has an abundance of native labor that is available for employment. Employers and employees should be encouraged to realize that their interests are best served by a realization that the welfare of each is necessary for the success and the promotion of the best interests of the other. To aid in the development of these policies and in the accomplishment of these objectives some new legislation is both desirable and needed. Amendments to certain existing laws are also important to promote and protect the policies and objectives to which I have referred.

The Workmen's Compensation Law was enacted twenty-five years ago. At that time workmen's compensation laws were in their experimental stages. Since that time wages have increased and the cost of living has increased. I ask that this General Assembly give careful study to the present Workmen's Compensation Law and similar laws of other states; that there be enacted such amendments to the Kentucky Workmen's Compensation Law as will modernize it and remove any unfair and objectionable features; to improve the administration thereof, and to correct any inequities that now exist. I favor and ask that this General Assembly increase the benefits for injured workers in total disability cases and fatalities, in line with the general statement just expressed relative to increased wages and increased cost of living.

Employees are entitled to have the places in which they are required to work in a reasonably safe and healthful condition, and I recommend that favorable consideration be given to legislation that will require reasonably safe and healthful places of employment to be maintained by the employers, and to provide for adequate state safety inspection.

The Workmen's Compensation Law is intended to require that employers shall assume responsibility for compensating employees and their dependents for accidental injuries resulting in the course of employment. Under the constitution of this state, the Workmen's Compensation Law cannot be made compulsory and in some instances employers have neither elected to operate under its provisions nor to provide insurance or adequate indemnity for the discharge of the employer's liability for accidental injuries and death arising out of and in the course of the employment. I recommend and ask that this General Assembly pass legislation that will require employers who do not elect to operate under the Workmen's Compensation Act to carry liability insurance to indemnify their employees for injuries sustained in employment, and in cases of fatalities to protect and indemnify their families or dependents for any liability of the employers.

I am strongly in favor of peaceful and amicable conciliation, mediation, and arbitration of disputes between employers and employees. The employees' rights to organize and bargain collectively are rights throughly established as a part of the American system and with which I am in thorough accord. I ask your favorable consideration of and the passage of laws to empower the Department of Industrial Relations to investigate, conciliate, mediate, and to arbitrate disputes between employers and employees, and in that connection to vest exclusive jurisdiction of disputes between employers and employees in that department with the right of appeal by either party to the courts from the action or decision of that department. In so vesting that jurisdiction in the Department of Industrial Relations, injunctions should be prohibited and litigants required to submit to the orderly procedure, first, of conciliation and mediation, and, second, of appeal to the courts from the decision of the Department of Industrial Relations.

I ask your consideration of legislation to provide for the funding and establishment of prevailing wages on public works projects, with reasonable provisions for the enforcement thereof. It is my judgment that these provisions should be enacted in connection with other legislation relating to the Department of Industrial Relations, and jurisdiction and power of enforcing should be vested in that department subject to an appeal to the courts from the findings and acts of that department.

With the large number of persons now unemployed, there is a shortage of skilled labor, and I ask that you give favorable consideration to the enactment of a law to provide for a system of apprenticeship training.

I ask that you give favorable consideration to enactment of a law of general application to provide for one day's rest in seven for all employees, and extra pay at the rate of time and a half of the regular rate to employees who are required to work on Sundays and legal holidays when such employees are also required to work six other days in the same week.

The legislation which you pass on the subjects to which I have just referred should be carefully considered and a full opportunity given to representatives of organized labor and to representatives of the employers to be heard and when finally enacted, should be fair and reasonable both to the employees and the employers, and to the public generally.

The expansion of industries in Kentucky and the opportunity for new industries to be established here will largely depend upon the establishment and maintenance of a friendly and cooperative spirit between employers and employees and the absence of unfair practices on the part of either employers or employees. To insure and promote the accomplishment of these objectives will require your careful, thoughtful, and studious consideration of the legislation which I have requested that you consider and pass.

I recommend enactment of legislation that will exempt from the gasoline tax that gasoline used in farm tractors and stationary engines. It will be necessary to exercise extreme caution in this legislation in order to prevent opening a loophole that may result in evasion of the gasoline tax to such an extent as to reduce hurtfully the road revenues. I shall insist that you turn a deaf ear to all proposals which would divert the road fund for any other purpose.

I favor continuing the $2 million-a-year appropriation for the Rural Highway Department. This helpful program, and the work of improvement and maintenance of main highways, would both be jeopardized by any diversion of the revenues of the road fund. Any such diversion would make it impossible to match federal aid highway funds and result in the state losing up to approximately $3 million a year.

An important part of the legislative problems you face are financial in nature. If there was ample money available, our legislative tasks would be simple. Let me urge you to remember that it is not your money or mine which you will, by legislation, appropriate for various state functions. It is money collected from taxpayers, and by them earned by toil and sweat. There is no magic with which money can be plucked from the air with which to pay appropriations, regardless of how meritorious they may be. I covet your cooperation to the end that we shall be certain that there will be money made available with which to pay in actual cash every cent of the appropriations you make.

The state's actual general fund tax receipts in the fiscal year ended June 30, 1937, were 28,995,291; in the fiscal year ended June 30, 1938, they were $26,725,910; and in the last fiscal year ended June 30, 1939, they were $24,507,922. These figures reflect particularly the falling off in receipts from the whiskey production tax, and in general they illustrate also the variations in the state's income resulting from varying economic conditions. Two years ago, when the last budget bill was drafted, the Department of Revenue estimated that the tax laws would bring in, for the fiscal year ending June 30, 1939, income of more than $28 million. The decline from this estimate of $28 million to an actual income of $24,507,922 illustrates the limitations necessary to be imposed on appropriations.

The stubborn and inescapable fact is that revenues have shrunk, creating a situation which makes it necessary that we be as thrifty as possible. We must avoid an increase in general taxes by making readjustments in existing tax laws, strengthening these tax measures so as to assure provision of the money with which to meet the state's minimum needs. No new general taxes need be enacted.

From tax laws now in operation you can estimate with reasonable certainty that there will come into the state treasury in the next fiscal year, 1940–1941, $24,352,650 and about the same for the following year. In addition to tax receipts, the general fund may reasonably be expected to receive about $1,147,350 a year from miscellaneous fees, office sales, and rentals. So in round overall figures, under present laws, total state general fund income should be about $25,500,000 for each of the next two years. This will be a decline of more than $4,220,000 in general fund revenues as compared with the fiscal year of 1936–1937. That decline has resulted in part from the repeal of the tax on chewing gum, ice cream, and soft drinks, which produced $1.8 million a year, and a decline of about $3 million a year in receipts from the five-cent production tax on whiskey. The chain store tax has been held invalid as it was drawn, resulting in a loss of about $200,000 a year. There have been fluctuations in income from other sources of revenue.

In view of this decline, and in order that the essential services of government may be financed, it is your duty and mine to be cautious as by legislation we obligate the state to spend money. This situation makes it absolutely necessary that we be prudent and saving with the people's money. It makes it necessary to retain present tax measures. It places you and me in a position where we must face the facts and realize that we cannot repeal existing tax laws if we are to continue to make modest provision for financing present state agencies and activities. It becomes my duty to impress upon you that the first important consideration in dealing with the state's finances is to retain those laws which now produce the revenue with which to run your state government.

On December 12, 1939, when I assumed the duties of the office of governor for the ensuing four-year term, there was an actual cash balance of $2,586,684.70 belonging to the general fund, according to the official records of the Department of Finance. This amount included a cash balance of $68,862.49 held in reserve as a cold check fund, leaving a net amount of $2,517,822.21 on hand. Of this net sum $61,789.17 was temporarily held in a closed bank, but the state will get the full amount and for this reason it may be properly considered as cash available for the current year.

Against this cash balance, the Finance Department records showed there were immediate legal demands on cash as follows: encumbrance obligations approved against allotments, $3,006,013.92 (Of this sum of $3,006,013.92 that has been encumbered, $53,000 is being held for accrued interest on warrants, $438,000 is for building contracts already awarded, $1,385,000 is for school per capita for the current month, $220,000 is for free textbooks. The remaining $910,000 represents encumbrances or bills to be paid for salaries and current operating expenses and bills.); accrued interest in prior year warrants, $3,249.55; current warrants authorized but unpaid, $355,798.41; 3 percent interest-bearing warrants called for payment but not presented, $267,300.00; 5 percent interest-bearing warrants called for payment but not presented, $23,592.46. These immediate demands on cash amounted to $3,655,954.39, an excess of $1,138,132.18 over the net cash balance available.

In connection with this cash position on December 12, 1939, it is essential to consider the outlook for the entire year. Estimated receipts into the general fund for the present fiscal year amount to $25,312,238.35, while total appropriations amount to $26,296,387.23. From this it is evident that $984,148.88 must be withheld from appropriations to avoid an increase in the general fund deficit. But included within these figures is a sum of $500,000 set up as a revolving fund to aid in refinancing of bonded indebtedness of counties. Since the fund is not expended, does not deplete itself in preforming its function, the prospective actual deficit would only be $484,148.88, if steps were not taken to avert it. It will be necessary to practice rigid economy the last six months of this fiscal year to come within the budget.

This apparent discrepancy in balancing the budget for the present year has arisen since the budget adoption at the opening of the last regular session of the legislature and may well serve as a warning against similar conditions in the ensuing biennium. Receipts were estimated at $28,381,000.00 and total appropriations in the budget bill amounted to $24,715,131.10, leaving an estimated balance available for debt reduction of $3,665,868.90. However, since the adoption of that budget the estimate of receipts has been revised by the commissioner of revenue and is now only $25,312,238.35, or $3,068,761.65 less than originally estimated. In addition to this decrease in revenue estimates, appropriations were increased from $24,715,131.10 as included in the budget bill to $26,296,387.23, or an increase of $1,581,256.13. These appropriation increases were the result of special acts including appropriations or additions, separate from the regular budget bill.

Principal among these additional appropriations may be mentioned the funds provided to put into effect the provisions of the Chandler-Wallis Act[2] for improved service by the state hospitals. The providing of funds to improve the conditions of the unfortunates confined within these hospitals is clearly one of the most urgent demands upon the state, but I mention the effect of this item upon the budget to show you the conseququences when even the most urgent problems are added to the irreducible costs of education, operation of the courts, and other items in which few reductions are possible.

The combined result of increased appropriations after passage of the last regular budget act, and a decline of revenues under estimates, has created an apparent deficit of $984,148.88 in the budget of the present fiscal year, and this amount of appropriations must be withheld from actual expenditures in order that outlays for current operations may not exceed the estimated income as now reported by the commisioner of finance. This also means that any reduction in the state debt during the present year would require an additional withholding of appropriations, or increase in actual receipts above estimates.

On December 12, 1939, according to the official records of the Kentucky

Department of Finance, outstanding warrants unpaid amounted to $7,557,990.87 as follows: current warrants authorized, $355,798.41; interest-bearing warrants called for payment, $290,892.46; interest-bearing warrants not called for payment, $6,911,300.00. To liquidate the interest-bearing indebtedness of the state even during the ensuing four-year period would require approximately $1,750,000 per annum.

With the estimate of receipts for the next two years at $25,500,000 annually, slightly more than the estimate for the present year, to carry on the policy of further liquidation of the present state debt, it is impossible to increase the total expenditures for current operations above the amount authorized for the present year. To do so would surely run the state in the red. Your attention has been directed especially to the increase of the budget bill for the present year through subsequent acts carrying special appropriations and through requirements of general statutes. With the narrow margins between recommended appropriations and estimated receipts, such a procedure after the adoption of the proposed budget would most certainly run us in the red. Any substantial increases over recommendations in the aggregate would necessarily have the same effect. Under these conditions I urge that a policy of rigid economy be followed to the end that progress in the widened scope of state services may be maintained and yet a sound financial condition of the state treasury be assured.

The law directs that the governor submit to the General Assembly a prepared budget. Some of you are serving in the legislature for the first time and it is important that you understand that there can be no legal expenditure of state money unless it has been specified in the budget act.

The budget which will be laid before you has been carefully considered and thoughtfully studied by the state budget officer, the commissioner of finance, the governor, and the Legislative Council.[3] Heads of all state departments and institutions were invited to appear before the Legislative Council for hearings on their budget requests. Diligent effort has been made to make an equitable appropriation for each item.

Requests for appropriations were made by heads of departments and institutions which totaled $32,955,843 and $33,316,373 for the two years. If we had that much money available, the governor could present to you a budget bill in which each department or institution would have all the money requested. Unhappily such is not the case. The Legislative Council and the governor faced the painful and difficult task of cutting the budget down to make it fit the money available.

The budget which I ask you to enact into law totals $26,029,900.05 for the first year and $26,286,437.55 for the second year. That contrasts with actual appropriations for the current fiscal year in which we are now operating (1939–1940) which total $26,296,387.23. Two years ago the legislature passed a budget bill in which it appropriated $24,715,131.10. Later in the session and in extra sessions special appropriations were made which increased the possible total obligations of the state for this fiscal year to $26,296,387.23. Anticipated revenue had been estimated at $28,381,000.00 for the present fiscal year. However, altered conditions forced the commissioner of revenue to reduce his estimate to $25,312,238.35, a drop of $3,068,761.65.

I am repeating these figures previously referred to in order that I may point out to you what happened two years ago, with the hope that you will help me avoid the mistake of passing special acts which require money in addition to that set up in the budget bill.

In the budget I will submit to you there has been no reduction in the appropriation of any department or agency, with the exception of a cut in the appropriation for public buildings. Every function of your state government has operated reasonably well, your institutions of higher learning, your charitable and penal institutions have managed to get by fairly well the last two years on the appropriations they have had. While the increased money sought by these department chiefs and institutional heads would be wisely expended if it were available, I have no doubt that they can operate all right the next two years on the appropriations recommended. Our financial situation is such that we cannot grant the increases requested, although I have no doubt such would result in improved and increased services which would be desirable if we had the money with which to pay for them. We are confronted with a condition which makes it necessary for us to get along without many things and services we would like to have but cannot afford. In some instances extraordinary appropriations for capital outlay in the last budget have not been repeated but such appropriations which were made to construct new buildings or permanent improvements are never regarded as other than extraordinary.

The extensive building program of the administration just closed required an appropriation for the present fiscal year of $1,369,561.55. It has become necessary to reduce the money made available for this purpose to $600,000 for each year of the biennium.

Although this may appear to be an abrupt reduction in the appropriation for further improvement of these institutions, you should take into consideration the fact that the buildings already completed or in process of construction relieve the most acute building needs of the penal and hospital systems. The pace of further improvements may properly be slowed somewhat as buildings completed relieve the urgency of the needs. With the most acute phase of overcrowding now relieved, or in process of being relieved, it becomes possible to obtain further improvement with less expenditure by modernization of existing plants.

The provision of adequate trained staffs and personnel must be continued no less than the provision of physical facilities for the hospital system.

There are three major increases in the budget before you which are the result of the demands of the citizens of the state. The greatest increase is the addition of $1 million more to the annual appropriations for Social Security, the greater portion of which goes to pay old age assistance. This will provide funds to pay the increased maximum of $30 a month to those who qualify under the federal and state acts to receive this amount on a basis of need, and will permit increases also in the payments to those who legally qualify for smaller amounts. It will also permit the making of old age assistance payments to those persons who have already established qualification but for whom sufficient funds have not been appropriated.

I believe this additional $1 million is a reasonable and justifiable increase for this worthy purpose. But I am positive that it would be folly to try to appropriate more money for this purpose if we are to keep the state's finances on the solid foundation of solvency.

In setting the increase in this appropriation at $1 million, the governor, the Legislative Council, and the state officials familiar with this activity have taken into consideration the fact that federal old age retirement benefits became operative on January 1. This feature of the Social Security Act will provide retirement benefits to an increasing number of aged workers who have contributed to the retirement fund through salary and wage deductions, and will result in lessening from year to year hereafter the number of persons who will be qualified to seek old age assistance.

The second largest item which increases the total of the budget is a new appropriation never hitherto made, to finance a teachers' retirement plan. The law was passed two years ago to become operative in 1940. So it becomes our obligation to provide money with which to finance it. The governor and the Legislative Council have made careful inquiry into the matter and recommend that $500,000 a year be appropriated for that purpose, or so much thereof as may be required to match contributions of teachers made to the retirement fund. Amendments also should be made to the act passed two years ago to make it effective and workable.

Inasmuch as considerable time will be required to set up the machinery for a retirement system of this size, and further since it is desirable that each teacher who will benefit under the act should make some contribution toward its cost, I am recommending that the payment of benefits under the Teacher Retirement Act should be started July 1, 1942. This is in line with the policy of the federal government in setting up the old age retirement feature of the Social Security Act, where payment of benefits was deferred for a number of years until the system was soundly established.

This is a humanitarian piece of legislation and by starting benefit payments after two years, each teacher will be given the opportunity to contribute to a common fund which through the years will assure those teachers who have given a lifetime of service to the childhood of the Commonwealth a certain degree of safety and security in the twilight years of their lives.

It would be manifestly unfair to start paying retirement benefits immediately before any teachers had contributed to the building up of the retirement fund, because in that case many teachers would be paying into a fund presumably intended for their own security but which would be drawn upon by other teachers who had not made such a contribution. It was to avoid such an unfair procedure that the federal Social Security Act deferred old age retirement benefits until benefited workers should have paid something into the retirement fund.

A third item which represents a major increase in the budget is made necessary by recent demands of the federal government through the WPA[4] that the state contribute $10,000 a month to provide for the distribution of surplus food commodities among the needy of the state from food supplied by the Surplus Commodities Corporation.[5] That increases our expense $120,000 a year. In order to take care of this item the appropriation for Emergency Relief, which was $150,000 in the last budget, has been increased to $200,000 a year. It will be necessary to ask you to pass a deficit emergency appropriation so as to make $10,000 a month available for this food distribution from December 15 until the close of this fiscal year.

The budget carries funds sufficient to provide a per capita school fund of $12 for every child of school age in Kentucky on the basis of the estimated school census prepared by the Department of Education. Except for a minor variation of a few cents in the present year when the actual school census was found to be less than previous estimates, the level of $12 per capita is the highest that has ever been provided for the common school system in Kentucky. Together with the appropriations for institutions of higher learning, including the schools for Negroes, and for vocational education, this appropriation for the common school per capita means that the state will continue to spend approximately half its general fund receipts for education. This is properly placing the emphasis where the emphasis belongs, but it also leaves a relatively narrow margin to carry on all the other necessary functions of government. Any increase of the per capita above $12, consequently, cannot be provided at this time. A common school fund of $15 per capita, such as has been suggested by some, would require an increase of $2.4 million in this appropriation. Since we do not have the money, this increase obviously cannot be made. Relief for the most acute needs, where additional state support is desirable, will be provided if the proposed constitutional authorization for an equalization fund is approved.

There is another item in the budget to which I wish to call special attention, and that is the appropriation for interest on state warrants. It is necessary that you provide only $150,000 for this purpose. In the budget act four years ago it was necessary to provide $1.1 million for interest on the state debt. This large saving has contributed substantially to the increased assumption of social responsibilities by the state without necessity for tax increases. It is visible evidence of the financial progress made by the state during Governor Chandler's administration.

This budget provides for the spending of a big sum of money. Total expenditures of governmental agencies continue to increase. This is due primarily to the fact that we the people continue to demand that the government do more and more for us. The wants of the people continue to grow faster than the ability of the taxpayers to meet them. I feel that we should put the brakes on increased spending as tightly as we can. You will note that the three major increases in this budget come as result of increased wants and needs of substantial groups of the citizenship. That explains increased money for old age assistance, teachers' retirement, and food for the needy.

You will readily see that there is an apparent discrepancy between our estimated general fund revenues of $25,500,000 and $25,513,000 and a proposed budget of $26,029,900.05 and $26,286,437.55. I am determined, with your help, to keep Kentucky in a position where she will not spend more money than she takes in. I promise you that my chief concern will be to watch expenditures after you have finished the legislative job, and try to encourage saving as much money as is possible.

There are two large items in the budget over which the governor particularly may expect to exercise a large measure of control. One of them is the $600,000 for new buildings, repairs, maintenance, and equipment. The other is the $200,000 emergency fund. I promise you that a large part of these two sums, which total $800,000, will be expended slowly and only when it becomes apparent that the money is actually going to be available. This provides one element of leeway to narrow the apparent spread between estimated revenues and proposed expenditures. Another item of leeway to narrow this spread consists of the results to be obtained by those measures strengthening the tax laws which will be proposed.

The program of improved management started with passage of the Chandler-Wallis Act for rehabilitation of the hospitals for the mentally ill has made progress. In the last two years more money has been spent on these institutions than ever before in history. The same amount of money for operation would be again made available under the budget to be submitted.

The best medical thought available has been concentrated on the problem. The emphasis has been shifted from trying to operate the hospitals for the mentally sick as cheaply as possible and is now being placed on giving better care and treatment and increasing the medical and nursing staff and increasing the number and quality of attendants.

The year before the Chandler-Wallis Act the state expended in operating these three hospitals and the Feeble Minded Institute $120.26 for each inmate. The number of employees totaled 613. In this the present fiscal year the expenditure per inmate has been increased to $170.00 and the number of employees has been increased to 783 in accordance with expert psychiatric advice. Improved medical attention, better nursing and attendant care has been made available.

A modern psychiatric hospital is under construction on a state farm of 1,700 acres in Boyle County. Money is available to complete the first phase of its construction and make it a complete hospital unit. As result of counsel with a committee of outstanding Kentucky physicians, representing the Kentucky Medical Association, I am suggesting that our next chief concern be to completely renovate the buildings at each of the three hospitals for the mentally ill and the Feeble Minded Institute. I have requested estimates of the cost of doing over Eastern State Hospital, which is in a greater state of disrepair than the others. For an expenditure of $117,000, I am assured that the entire plant can be completely renovated, painted, plastered, and a general job of house-smithing done. Within that estimate it is contemplated to reduce the fire hazard by installing a sprinkler system, fire escapes, fire-proofing the stairs, and install needed fixed equipment such as a badly needed laundry plant. It is believed that the other institutions can be placed in first-class condition for an expenditure of approximately $100,000 each. I submit to you that this is the most imperative need of the immediate present.

Approximately $300,000 of the proposed $600,000 building appropriation will be sufficient to do that work which is most necessary, and the balance of the building appropriation would be spent for further improvements in the way of new buildings, repairs, and maintenance if the state's income provided sufficient funds.

Engineers, who have at my request examined the Capitol Building, report to me that it is unwise further to defer spending about $100,000 a year for two years in repairs on this structure.

Kentucky is fortunate in having one of the best health departments in the nation. The vital importance of the work of this department has been demonstrated in improved health conditions and in the fine record made following major catastrophes when epidemic sickness might ordinarily be anticipated. It is important that provision of necessary funds continue to be made for the work of this department to the fullest extent of the revenues available. The sum provided for this department in the budget was the most generous that appeared to be possible within this necessary limitation.

The Legislative Council, of which [Lieutenant] Governor Myers is chairman, has worked hard and has given valuable service to the state in helping to prepare the budget which I today hand to you, and in preparing various specific measures of legislation. I wish to acknowledge their invaluable and unselfish efforts.

The budget is an involved and intricate subject, in which is reflected the necessary activities of every state department and agency. Since it has been necessary to apportion the available funds as equitably as possible among all these departments and agencies, without being able to give any of them the increases which might be desirable if sufficient funds were available, it would be manifestly unfair to disturb the equity of these apportionments. Increases, if granted to some agencies, would be unfair to other departments whose needs are as great but for whom increased revenues are not available. I therefore ask you to pass the budget act without making any increase in any single item. I further ask you to send the completed appropriation bill to me promptly as your first act.

I am happy to be able to commend to you the elected state officials who share with me and with you the responsibility of the new administration. They have given evidence of their conscientious desire to help give to the governor, the legislature, and the people the cooperation and helpful service through which the cause of good government may be advanced.

You have selected able and experienced men to form your official legislative organization. Their opportunities for effective and valuable service to the state will depend in a large measure on the cooperation which the individual members of the legislature give them. I ask you to give them the same loyalty and support which you have evidenced to the administration of which they are a part.

There is nothing factional or partisan in the administration recommendations which I have presented to you. I repeat now what I have said repeatedly throughout the length and breadth of Kentucky, that I have no malice or bitterness in my heart against any man because of past political differences. I am today the governor of all the people of all the state, without regard to race or color or creed or political belief, and it is in that spirit that I have formulated my recommendations to you. It is in that spirit that I request your support and helpful cooperation in translating these recommendations into accomplished legislation.

If these recommendations are in furtherance of good government and of greater service to the people as I conceive them to be, there is a proper satisfaction to be enjoyed by all those who have a part in translating them into accomplishment, and credit for them should be shared by each of you. I have not proposed anything here which will bring any member of the legislature into disfavor with the people of his own district or with the people of the whole state in whose behalf you work here.

There will be a great mass of legislation considered by you outside of the administration's program, and in which the administration as such will not have any direct concern unless it obviously works against the general welfare of the people. I would particularly ask you to consider such legislative proposals in the light of the welfare of the state as a whole. I specifically ask you to bear in mind that we can best serve Kentucky by maintaining the principle of fair treatment for all and special privilege for none. By this attitude, by preserving a solid financial structure, and by maintaining stable and fair policies of taxation, we may over a course of years attract increased trade, business, industry, capital, and opportunities for employment within our boundaries.[6]

---

1. *Acts of the General Assembly of the Commonwealth of Kentucky, Extraordinary Session, February 24, 1936–March 7, 1936*, Chapter 1, p.1 (hereafter cited as *Acts of the General Assembly*). It was a major measure of the first Chandler administration which sought to streamline state government and to centralize control over spending in the Department of Finance.

2. *Acts of the General Assembly, Regular and First and Second Special Sessions, 1938*, Second Special Session, Chapter 1, pp. 1175-91. The act was named for Governor Chandler and Welfare Commissioner Frederick A. Wallis. It provided for an additional appropriation of $300,000 for 1938–1939 and an additional $500,000 for 1939–1940. This special session was called for the sole purpose of enacting this measure.

3. In his first meeting with the Legislative Council, Johnson said that he hoped present taxes would be retained, appropriations would be kept within available revenue, and the 1936 Reorganization Act would not be changed. The council consisted of sixteen legislators and five administrators. It was charged with formulating the legislative program. *State Journal*, December 15, 1939. It was limited by a budget of $3,100, but the governor provided an additional $10,220 by executive orders in 1940, 1941, and 1942.

4. Works Progress Administration, 1935; renamed Work Projects Administration in 1939. To provide work for needy persons on public works projects.

5. This corporation was established by Congress in 1935 to dispose of government food surpluses by distributing them to school lunch programs and welfare programs. The governor was faced with the need for funds for the distribution of these food surpluses early in his term of office. On December 15, 1939, he said that he had requested the Surplus Commodities Corporation to continue paying for distribution of the food until the 1940 General Assembly could provide funds for that purpose. "I asked for a period of grace until February 1 to work it out and pay

them back what we should have paid. I got the impression from a talk today with someone in Harrington's office [WPA administrator F. C. Harrington] my request would be approved." He stated that the corporation had been distributing surplus commodities to the needy for fifteen to eighteen months and that he had recently been told that "unless I started laying $10,000 a month on the line, they were going to stop it. I first offered the use of all Highway Department trucks and personnel they could use in distribution but they refused that. I offered them the $1,521 residue of a fund contributed to Governor Chandler for flood relief by private sources, but that was refused." He concluded that there was no other state money he could legally use to satisfy the federal corporation's demand. Louisville *Courier-Journal*, December 16, 1939.

6. The budget was read by Lieutenant Governor Myers, as Legislative Council chairman, before a joint session of the legislature. See *Journal of the House of Representatives*, 1940, 1:42-60.

ON HIRING AUDITORS
Frankfort / March 6, 1940

GOVERNOR JOHNSON appeared before the House Rules Committee to ask for favorable action on a bill to permit the governor to employ independent auditors.[1]

---

1. The bill was introduced in both houses by the administration floor leaders. Its introduction followed within a few days after a sharply worded report by David A. Logan, state auditor of public accounts, to the governor in which he criticized the condition of records in the Finance and Revenue departments. He asserted that an "elaborate cover-up" existed in the Finance Department's accounting methods. The report also asked Attorney General Meredith to determine the legality of payments made to Cotton and Eskew, Louisville accountants frequently employed by the state.

The measure was an early indicator of the factional political cleavage between Johnson and Meredith. The comissioner of finance, J. Dan Talbott, was a powerful figure in the Johnson administration.

The state auditor, an elective officer, is charged by law with the duty of making audits. Logan stated, "If any such legislation is passed, I think it ought to make certain that it does not limit or repeal the state auditor's authority to make post-audits. Otherwise there would be no need of having a state auditor." *Cincinnati Enquirer*, March 7, 1940. The bill became law on March 16, 1940. *Acts of the General Assembly, 1940*, Chapter 91 (S.B. 267), pp. 371-74.

VETO OF BILL TO LEGALIZE LIQUOR SALES
Frankfort / March 13, 1940

[HOUSE BILL 327 created exporter's licenses and provided for the sale and export of distilled spirits and wine. The House of Representatives passed it by a vote of 84 to 0 and the Senate by a vote of 31 to 3. Following its veto by the governor, the House reversed itself and sustained the veto 86 to 3. The General Assembly adjourned *sine die* on March 14. This veto message has been included because the veto was a courageous act by the governor since powerful interests supported the bill.]

It is with regret that I find myself in disagreement with you over a measure which received an overwhelming vote in both the House of Representatives and the Senate. I have a high regard for the composite judgment of the General Assembly. You have disclosed a sincere and conscientious desire to approve only that legislation which will be helpful to Kentucky. Your legislative acts have been singularly free from measures hurtful to the Commonwealth which you have sought sincerely to serve.

I am reluctant to take a position which might seem to you that I regard my judgment as superior to yours, and I desire to disclaim any such thought. There is, however, one measure, House Bill No. 327, which passed both houses, that I feel contains such possibility of being injurious to the state that I regard it as my duty to veto it. Executive disapproval of this bill should not in any way be construed as a reflection upon the judgment of the many conscientious representatives and senators who voted for the bill. I am certain that each of you felt that you were voting properly when you voted for it.

Since passage of the bill, however, there has come to me much information concerning this measure which you did not have when you voted your approval of it. I have tried carefully to analyze the situation created by passage of House Bill No. 327 and have arrived at the conclusion that to permit the measure to become a law would violate the "Good Neighbor" attitude which it is desirable that Kentucky maintain. Surrounded as Kentucky is by seven states, it is important that we maintain a friendly relation with the governments of these adjacent states. This I fear would be endangered should House Bill No. 327 become a law. I hope you will agree with me that it is unwise to take a chance upon this probable development by an act susceptible of being construed by our neighbors as unfriendly and disregardful of their welfare.

In vetoing this bill I wish to specifically state my reason as follows:

1. It establishes licensees authorized to sell distilled spirits and wine without payment of the Kentucky excise tax to residents of other states in violation of their alcoholic beverage control and tax laws. This fact has been brought forcibly to my attention by officials of other states and the Federal Alcohol Administration. Honorable Prentice Cooper,[1] governor of Tennessee, in a letter dated March 8, 1940, says: "Our Commissioner of Finance and Taxation and Attorney General's Office are of the opinion that if this bill is enacted into law that it will result in considerable loss of revenue to Tennessee because illicit dealers in dry counties will purchase whiskey from border dealers, and thus evade payment of tax to either Tennessee or Kentucky."

Honorable M. Clifford Townsend,[2] governor of Indiana, writes on March 9, 1940: "Unless we were to establish border patrols and sentries at all bridges and ferries across the Ohio River we would be faced with the problem of bootleg liquor. Similarly your other neighboring states would be faced with a like problem."

Captain W. S. Alexander,[3] federal alcohol administrator, writes on March 1, 1940: "It is, therefore, alarming to liquor control officials, including myself, who have applauded the Kentucky policy of interstate cooperation, to note from recent items in the press that the Kentucky General Assembly has recently passed a bill which, if approved by the governor, would reverse the existing policy and legalize out of state shipments of liquor intended for illegal delivery and use in other states."

There are no federal laws or regulations which condone this practice. Under a literal interpretation of the Twenty-first Amendment such operations may be conducted. However, no less authority than the Federal Alcohol Administrator wrote on December 20, 1938, that: "Such sales as your export licenses contemplate making are in definite violation of the Twenty-first Amendment."

Regulations of the Interstate Commerce Commission bar the transportation by public carriers of alcoholic beverages to persons not permitted by the laws of their state to receive such beverages. The federal occupational tax stamp which must be held as a condition to the purchasing of distilled spirits and wine from the licensees authorized by this bill is only a tax receipt, and does not convey any privileges to traffic in alcoholic beverages contrary to state law. The Twenty-first Amendment vests exclusive power in states to determine liquor control and tax policies, and the establishment of machinery to evade the laws of other states is inimical to sound public policy.

2. This bill would jeopardize the cordial relationships between Kentucky and neighboring states. The governor of Indiana in his recent letter cited above is quoted as follows: "The most deplorable feature of legisla-

tion conflicting with the interests of other states is that it invariably provokes retaliation, thus choking the channels of interstate commerce."

The governor of Tennessee wired March 13, 1940, as follows: "Respectfully urge that you veto House Bill 327 which I feel confident will fail in the end to be beneficial even to Kentucky since it is certain to be met by strong retaliating legislation in at least some of your border states. . . ."

The production of whiskey is a major industry of Kentucky. The United States Supreme Court has held that states may impose discriminatory taxes upon alcoholic beverages produced without the state. Indiana is a rival whiskey-producing state. Should that state and its neighbors retaliate by imposing discriminatory taxes upon Kentucky whiskey, the effect upon the industry would be disastrous.

Kentucky has experienced evils arising from the fact that Illinois has permitted its licensees to distribute distilled spirits in violation of our laws. This practice gained for Illinois the reputation of being an outlaw, and Illinois has officially abandoned it, thus establishing a milestone in recent efforts to establish more satisfactory relations between states.

Kentucky has agreements with many states to exchange information essential in tax administration. These understandings have in some instances been reached after considerable expense. The deliberate adoption of a permanent policy of exporting distilled spirits into other states in violation of their laws, and over their protests, would be invitation to terminate these useful arrangements.

3. This bill threatens Kentucky revenue sources. If other states supply dry Kentucky counties with distilled spirits as this bill specifically proposes to supply their dry counties, Kentucky alcoholic beverage tax receipts would decline several hundred thousand dollars annually. Certain Kentucky retailers sell quantities of tax-paid distilled spirits to the residents of a semimonopoly state. This bill provides a potential tax-free supply to such purchasers which it has been estimated would reduce Kentucky revenues by $100,000 a year. This Commonwealth receives millions of dollars from taxes imposed upon gasoline, alcoholic beverages, and cigarettes received from other states. If states in which these shipments originate fail to cooperate in identifying the taxable commodities, the administration of our revenue laws would be made difficult and tax receipts would decrease. Under export licenses tax-free distilled spirits may be consigned for delivery without Kentucky and returned to bootleggers in this Commonwealth. Thus, in several ways, this bill threatens our state government with an unbalanced budget.

4. The principle incorporated in this bill has been tried and abandoned. Prior to March 7, 1938, Kentucky law failed to provide for the orderly exportation of distilled spirits, and many wholesalers made a practice of selling into other states in violations of their laws and accumulated tax

liabilities which are uncollectible because assets have been concealed or withdrawn from the Commonwealth. The Alcoholic Beverage Control Law of 1938 restricted exports to common carriers which cannot deliver distilled spirits in interstate commerce to those unauthorized to receive such deliveries. This placed Kentucky in the category of states having thoroughly defensible alcoholic beverage control laws.

During the summer of 1938 the Department of Revenue found that distilled spirits ostensibly sold by southern Illinois vendors to illicit Tennessee and Mississippi dealers were being delivered in quantities to Kentucky bootleggers. The Alcoholic Beverage Control Board was strongly urged and finally persuaded that the Illinois business would be discouraged by establishing five export houses along the Tennessee border. These export licenses were, according to James W. Martin,[4] then commissioner of revenue and chairman of the Alcoholic Beverage Control Board, issued without opposition from Tennessee officials, and with the understanding that should Tennessee legalize the sale of alcoholic beverages they would be discontinued. In April of 1939 Tennessee legalized alcoholic beverages, and after conference with officials of that state the Kentucky Alcoholic Beverage Control Board agreed with the export licensees that they might continue operation until July 1, 1939, for the purpose of liquidating their stocks. On June 28, 1939, the Alcoholic Beverage Control Board annulled the regulation by which it had authorized the export business, and refused to reissue the licenses because, according to James W. Martin, "the substantial discontinuance of the Illinois border wholesale business in the vicinity of Cairo and Metropolis, and the change in legislative and administrative policy which took place in Tennessee, eliminated the legal and practical excuse for the border exporters."

5. The facts fail to indicate that the exportation of distilled spirits in the manner authorized by this bill would aid Kentucky distillers. During the six months following June 30, 1939, 47.2 percent of the merchandise sold by the two border exporters was secured outside Kentucky. During this period seventeen Kentucky distillers did not sell any whiskey to these two exporters, and only three Kentucky distillers did more than 8.7 percent of the business with them. The fact that approximately half of the sales made by the exporters was not Kentucky whiskey indicates that these places have made no special effort to distribute products of this Commonwealth.

Every legitimate effort not inconsistent with the propriety of other states should be made to encourage Kentucky business. Kentucky should not, however, interfere with other states seeking to regulate and tax the consumption of distilled spirits within their borders because we are confronted with a similar problem, and insists that if distilled spirits are secured through bootleg channels and consumed in Kentucky then our consumption tax should be paid. The people of other states educated to prefer and desiring Kentucky whiskey may secure it through the tax-paid channels without injury to the industry.

6. Finally, this bill is susceptible to the construction that it is mandatory on the Department of Revenue to issue a license to all applicants making a proper application. Furthermore, the language of subsection (c) of section 3 fails to definitely identify the states into which the exporters may sell to illicit dealers. Section 7 is ambiguous, and it is difficult to discern the exact status and functions of the Alcohlic Beverage Control Board. The powers of the board to conduct hearings under oath, suspend, revoke, or deny licenses are not clear. Court construction appears to be an inescapable incident of such ambiguity.

Expressions of disapproval of this bill have come to me from numerous citizens of Kentucky whose moral sensibilities are outraged by the suggestion that we are about to approve legislation which would give legal sanction to the practice of licensing exporters to bootleg liquor into dry territory beyond the borders of our state. I share their view that such action is reprehensible and unworthy of our Commonwealth, and sincerely believe that had the General Assembly been in possession of these facts this legislation would not have received its approval. I hope that upon calm reflection you will agree with me that it is improper for us to approve such an immoral practice.

For reason here set forth I feel that is my duty to veto House Bill No. 327. I shall be grateful to you of the General Assembly if you will accept this message in the spirit in which it is transmitted and will by your vote sustain this veto.

---

1. Prentice Cooper (1895–1969), b. Shelbyville, Tennessee. Attorney. Tennessee state representative, 1923; Tennessee state senator, 1937; governor of Tennessee, 1939–1945; United States ambassador to Peru, 1946–1948. *Who Was Who in America, 1969–1973* (Chicago, 1973), 5:150.

2. M. Clifford Townsend (1884–1954), b. Blackford County, Indiana. Governor of Indiana, 1933–1941. *Who Was Who in America, 1951–1960* (Chicago, 1960), 3:860.

3. Wilford S. Alexander (1878–1959), b. Eastport, Maine. Federal alcohol administrator, 1936–1940. Ibid., 3:20.

4. James Walter Martin (1893–), b. Muskogee, Indian Territory (Oklahoma). Resides in Lexington. University of Kentucky professor of economics, 1928–1948; distinguished professor, 1948–1964; emeritus distinguished professor, 1964– ; commissioner of revenue, 1936–1939; commissioner of finance, 1955–1957; commissioner of highways, 1957–1958. *American Men of Science: The Social and Behavioral Sciences*, 11th ed. (New York, 1968), p. 1056, and telephone interview, J. W. Martin, July 10, 1978.

MESSAGE TO LEGISLATIVE COUNCIL
Frankfort / November 24, 1941

GOVERNOR JOHNSON informed the Legislative Council that the state is now "Back on the Constitution" for the first time in more than twenty-five years. He said a call has been issued for the payment of $500,000 in warrants which will make the state's total indebtedness approximately $495,000 when the legislature meets.

"Our most difficult task is that of avoiding a spending spree. There is an insistent clamor from many quarters for more money for many things. It will be our unpleasant duty to decline to approve larger appropriations for many meritorious purposes. Kentucky's needs far exceed the money available to meet them. It is that circumstance which makes it impossible to consider the repeal or downward revision of existing tax measures."

Declaring that there is an equal chance for the revenues to fall below guesses or run above them, he urged that he be given the right to make a 10 percent blanket slash in the budget, excepting the school fund and offices set up by the constitution, and headed by elected officials, if revenues fall off.

He then asked that every cent over and above the amounts specifically appropriated be used for fulfilling the "second obligation of the state" to the mentally ill and unfortunates in the hospitals and the Kentucky Houses of Reform at Greendale. He asked that the School for the Blind and the School for the Deaf at Danville be included in this group.

Answering Senator Ray Moss's[1] question as to how much money he proposed to devote to institutions, the governor said, "Whatever the surplus is, it won't be enough. Why, you could spend $10 to $12 million to do it right.

"I am glad to be in position where I can say to you that no additional taxes are required, but it is my duty to advise you that it will be necessary to retain all tax measures from which we now receive revenue income.

"I believe you will agree with me that it is difficult to prepare a budget in January 1942 with such accuracy that it will fit the state's income through the two-year budget period for which the General Assembly is required to make appropriation. As we prepared the budget which was adopted by the legislature in January 1940, we set up a close budget with appropriations held to a minimum. It appeared that the revenue income would meet that budget comfortably. There was no way by which we could foresee the huge defense expenditures which have stimulated income and increased governmental costs.

"In that budget we provided $2,310,000 this fiscal year for the Welfare

Department. Had economic conditions which existed when that budget was adopted continued to prevail, that appropriation would have been sufficient to meet the minimum needs of the department and the institutions under its supervision. Of the sum appropriated, about $900,000 a year is required to buy food, clothing, and personal supplies for the inmates of the corrective institutions and hospitals for the mentally ill. Cost of food and clothing have advanced to such an extent that it will be impossible for the Welfare Department to operate through to the end of this fiscal year, July 1, on the sum which in January 1940 appeared ample. It is unavoidable that I recommend that you make an emergency appropriation of $250,000 for the Welfare Department to meet this unforeseen need. Thirty millions may not buy as much next year as 25 [million] bought in 1938–1939.

"Most of you are familiar with the imperative need for rehabilitation and enlargement of the charitable and penal institutions. The accumulative effect of decades of neglect has been to create a condition so frightful that we can no longer defer the expending of all money we can provide in an effort to correct conditions which reflect discreditably upon Kentucky. We shall visit some of those institutions so you may see what we have been able to do in the last two years and see for yourselves the necessity for accelerating this program of institutional improvement.

"Most of the agencies of the state government, educational institutions, and departments will present to you an urgent request for increased appropriations. Should we grant all requests that have been made for larger appropriations, it would require $32 million a year and we should have to levy heavy additional taxes. Many of the requests for increased appropriation are justified. The money could be wisely expended if it was available, but permit me to impress upon you the fact that the most imperative, the most impelling need is for the state hospitals, Houses of Reform, and other institutions. Therefore, I ask you to join me to hold the other appropriations at the lowest possible figure."[2]

---

1. Ray B. Moss (1889–1979), b. Pineville. State senator, 1931–1950; Republican floor leader in 1938. Director, Pine Mountain Settlement School, retired 1970; owner-manager Pineville Insurance Agents, 1930–1970. Letter, Ray B. Moss, May 5, 1978, and Louisville *Courier-Journal*, September 21, 1979.

2. Data on expenditures and revenues have been deleted. They appear in the 1942 State of the Commonwealth Address in this section.

STATE OF THE COMMONWEALTH ADDRESS
Frankfort / January 6, 1942

IT is a pleasant privilege to greet you at this the convening of the biennial session of the General Assembly of the Commonwealth of Kentucky. It is a high distinction to be permitted to serve as a member of the lawmaking body of our state. It affords an opportunity for important service. It is a position in which the honor is exceeded only by the responsibility.

The duty of advising the legislature of the needs and problems of the state is imposed upon the governor by the constitution. Enactment of wise and proper legislation is the duty of you who constitute the General Assembly. I have no desire to trespass upon your prerogative. There is enjoined upon the governor, however, the duty of presenting proposed legislation for your consideration.

One hundred and fifty years ago the Commonwealth of Kentucky was born to statehood in the American union. While George Washington was president of the United States, it was accepted into the Republic whose people are now united from ocean to ocean, under the flag which is the symbol of unity and freedom. That for a century and a half this binding compact has been kept stands as evidence that where honesty and integrity exist, agreements can be made inviolate.

In every war in which the United States has engaged, Kentuckians have shown their loyalty and patriotic devotion. For the first time in the lifetime of any of us, territory that is under the American flag has been invaded in an assault as treacherous and savage as the Indian attacks upon the settlements of those pioneers who at Boonesborough and Harrodsburg brought civilization to the wilderness in the early days when Kentucky was a frontier outpost. There has been no need to wait for the reply of Kentucky to the declarations of war against the United States by Japan, Germany, and Italy. Already, more Kentucky boys had voluntarily enlisted in the army and navy of the nation than from any other state in the Union in proportion to population. The Selective Service Act,[1] administration of which was imposed upon the governor, has functioned efficiently and smoothly. Kentuckians have died the death of heroes at Pearl Harbor. The fire of patriotic fervor has been rekindled in the hearts of our citizens.

The partisan and factional differences of the past are trivial. They have vanished in the face of a grim determination to meet the crisis, to stand by the president, defeat Japan, crush Hitler, and protect our cherished liberties. It is impossible for us today to foresee the demands that are to be made of the state in the next two years as we are called upon to do our part in winning the war. The first important step which you can take to place us in position to do our duty is to enact legislation that will create a State Defense Council[2] and provide for financing its activities.

It is essential that activities of the traitorous be restrained and guilty fifth columnists be punished. I am sure you will readily enact a sabotage prevention law, under which authority will be given law enforcement officers to bring to justice those who try to impede our march to victory.

President Roosevelt, in a recent speech, told of the prayer of a Chinese Christian who said, "Oh, Lord, reform thy world, starting with me." Kentucky has made a substantial start toward putting its own house in order. The wisdom of this will be increasingly demonstrated as our people are called upon to make the sacrifices that are necessary to make certain that the men who are fighting beneath the American flag have the guns and supplies required to lick Japan and Germany.

Had the legislative session started two months ago I would have placed great emphasis upon that which it has been possible to accomplish in advancing the cause of better government in Kentucky in the two-year interval since you last assembled. With the brutal blasting of Pearl Harbor by the pagan power of Japan, our national existence is threatened. Our state's achievements, substantial and constructive though they have been, pale into insignificance and are overshadowed by the peril presented by the slant-eyed Japanese and high-handed Hitler.

During the administration of my distinguished predecessor, Govenor Chandler, and within the past two years, a diligent, sustained effort has been made to get Kentucky out of debt and effect a reformation of the Commonwealth.

Six years ago Kentucky was in debt between $25 million and $28 million. Most of that debt was represented by state warrants bearing 5 percent interest. Today our state debt is only $495,000 and the warrants representing that debt bear only 1 percent interest.

Six years ago more than a million dollars was required to pay the annual interest on the debt. This year interest on the debt requires less than $10,000.

The Kentucky constitution was intended to forbid a state indebtedness in excess of $500,000 without a vote of the people. When it became possible recently to reduce the debt sufficiently to bring it within the constitutional limit, it was the first time since 1908 that indebtedness of the state had been in conformity with the constitution.

The General Assembly could perform great service by enacting legislation that would prevent the accumulation of another debt in disregard of the constitution. A bill will be presented which you are urged to enact, that will explicitly pronounce the legislative intent as an interpretation of the meaning of a state debt. As you vote for this bill you will vote to prevent Kentucky from again running into debt. Now that we have gotten our state government back on the constitution, let us take the precaution necessary to keep it there. You are the only legislature to which has been presented this opportunity.

Through issuance of revenue bonds with which to finance public improvements, some state educational institutions, many county and city schoolboards have increased the public debt in their enthusiasm to provide needed buildings. While these debts are not a direct obligation of the state, we should take cognizance of the fact that this method of financing has in instances been unwisely used. I suggest that there be legislation which will put the brakes on issuance of additional revenue bonds.

As an additional safeguard, I recommend that there be legislation which will require revenue bond issues to be submitted to the County Debt Commission and its approval be required before such bonds may be issued.

More than a year ago the governor was successful in a refinancing of state warrants that effected a substantial saving. With the cooperative aid of bankers it was possible to call in all warrants bearing 2.5 percent interest, amounting to about $3 million, and replace them with warrants bearing only 1 percent. This, the lowest interest rate in the history of the state, reflects the soundness of its credit. Six years ago state warrants were selling for as low as eighty cents on the dollar. Today they sell at a premium and are regarded as a gilt-edged investment. An incalculable saving results from correcting a condition in which we paid our bills with 5 percent interest-bearing warrants that were marketable only at costly discount.

We have been concentrating our efforts upon freeing Kentucky of debt with the hope that it would then be possible to make improvements in the charitable and penal institutions which are sorely needed. Just as we approach the goal of lifting the mortgage on the state, the catastrophe of war strikes us. Emphasis must be shifted from constructive activity to a plan in which our resources are concentrated upon a victory program.

Circumstances born of the crisis create a feeling of futility and frustration. We have striven to husband the resources of the state, spend the public money prudently, and in instances penuriously, in a determined effort to get out of debt. Then rulers of arrogant, aggressor nations knock cherished plans into a cocked hat, and threaten to thwart a constructive program.

But it has not been in vain—this prolonged struggle to restore the solvency of the state; to establish a reformation of its fiscal policies; to demonstrate that the state can be operated within its income; to infuse sound principles of finance into conduct of the state's business. It represents an achievement in financial state-craft of which we may be immensely proud. It is an accomplishment the full benefits of which may be obscured by the effects of war. Yet it is more fortunate than we can realize at this moment that Kentucky is better prepared than ever before to withstand the impact of war, to absorb the shock that is certain to come from economic dislocation. No contribution we can make to victory is more effective than that of keeping Kentucky on a solid financial foundation. Many of you contributed to the program which effected this amazing transformation in our state's fiscal affairs. You are justified in the pride you feel in this great service. It is important that we preserve the gains we have made. It is vital that the heights of good government, toilsomely reached, be tenaciously held.

We run into debt—and crawl out. There is nothing exhilarating or spectacular about paying off a debt. The fact it has been possible virtually to achieve that difficult goal, provide increased support for public education, old age assistance, and make some improvement of the state's institutions is due to the tolerant acceptance of the taxpayers who have realized that their money was being cautiously and wisely expended. Economy in spending the taxpayers' money must remain our dominant motive. I can assure you that extravagance and wastefulness in the spending of public money have been reduced to the minimum. Daily diligence has been exercised in an effort to be certain that full value is received for the taxpayer's dollar.

Our state's needs far exceed her revenues. Our difficulties have been complicated by necessity of concentrating upon destruction of despicable dictators that seek to enslave us. Effect of this altered world situation on revenue income of the state cannot be calculated. Prior to that day which altered the destiny of democracy at Pearl Harbor, it appeared that we might anticipate a cash surplus which could be expended in extensive improvement of the state institutions. Now we are confronted with a financial outlook both grave and uncertain.

Prior to Pearl Harbor I had repeatedly expressed the conviction that there would be no necessity for additional taxes. I contemplated with satisfaction the pleasure of assuring you of the legislature that you would be spared the disagreeable duty of voting to increase the tax burden upon our people. Today I am not so certain. The economic situation is changing rapidly. Events which have their genesis in the emergencies of war may create circumstances before you adjourn that make increased taxes inescapable. We can only hope that we may be spared such necessity.

It is vital that existing taxes be retained. Grim realities of the situation with which we are confronted drive us to abandonment of all hope that we may indulge in the satisfaction of repealing or reducing the taxes that are now levied. There are those who have advocated repeal of the income tax and various other taxes. They assert that since the state is virtually liberated from debt, this revenue measure which last year produced $5.4

million should be rescinded. Such an act would nullify the efforts of years to restore solvency of the state. It would intensify the precariousness of our financial structure. It would necessitate taxes on real estate for state purposes, a step which should be taken only when forced by dire extremity. I believe that those of our citizens who have sense enough to earn an income sufficient to be subject to income tax payment have sufficient sense to see the folly of repeal of this or any other tax at a time when the unprecedented future is so utterly unpredictable.

Our tax structure is highly sensitive to economic change. In the fiscal year of 1936–1937, all state revenue receipts to the general fund, including fees, totaled $30,143,229, as business boomed. The next fiscal year, 1937–1938, these revenue receipts declined to $27,931,527. The following fiscal year, 1938–1939, the same revenue receipts nose-dived to $25,745,385. In the next fiscal year, 1939–1940, income increased to $26,721,012. The past fiscal year, 1940–1941, reflecting the artificial prosperity produced by military activities, revenue receipts went back to about the 1936–1937 figure with a total income of $30,836,809.

This revenue fluctuation has been from substantially the same tax structure. The only tax measure that produced considerable revenue, which was replaced within the period, was the sales tax on ice cream and candy. I emphasize the variability of state income to impress upon you the fact that in this period of uncertainty, it is impossible to prophesy with accuracy the yield which will be received from esixting taxes. In the two-year period from 1936–1937 to 1938–1939 income dropped more than $4 million. In the following two-year period it went back up more than $4 million. These fluctuations occurred in a period of relatively normal stability. The next two years are certain to be abnormal, and more violent variations in revenue receipts are not improbable.

The commissioner of revenue has carefully examined all known factors that affect our revenue receipt. The unknown factors are what frighten us because they are beyond the range of conjecture. Commissioner of revenue, H. Clyde Reeves,[3] estimates that we may anticipate a general fund income in the fiscal year of 1942–1943 of $28,490,980. In the second year of the biennium for which you will make appropriations, he estimates our income will be $27,928,520. In addition there is ordinarily collected about a million dollars in fees, such as those which are earmarked for the Game and Fish Commission and the fees paid into the treasury from Jefferson and Kenton counties, 75 percent of which are returned to the counties by payments of county employees.

This past fiscal year the 3 percent tax collected on sale of new automobiles brought into the general fund $1.6 million. Production of new cars has been virtually eliminated, as automobile plants are diverted into making machines with which to destroy our enemies. Effect of that will all but wipe out this, a source of revenue which made a substantial contribution to our total funds last year. We are justified in anticipating with anxiety the effect of increased federal taxes on the state income tax revenues. The more federal income taxes our people pay the less state income tax they will owe us.

The production tax on whiskey contributed $3 million to the general fund this past fiscal year. That is abnormal. There is certain to be a decline in this source of income. The commissioner of revenue estimates a probable drop of $1.5 million, a 50 percent cut. These are the major factors which are regarded as likely to affect our income adversely. The storm signals are clear and unmistakable. We would be stupid, indeed, should we disregard their warning.

Necessity for rigid economy is intensified by the fact that the advance in price of all commodities essential to operation of the state government is increasing the cost of government. Purchasing power of the dollar which was appropriated by the legislature in 1940 has been so reduced that the dollar of two years ago will buy only eighty-three cents worth of commodities. Buying power of the dollar is certain to continue to diminish as a result of the upsurge of prices. So the increase in appropriations in the budget which is submitted to you is justified only because of advances in prices which increase the cost of governmental functions. The inexorable facts make it all the more imperative that we exercise extreme caution in the appropriation of money, in the spending of money, and in being certain that money is provided to meet the minimum needs as set forth in the budget bill which is presented to you.

In the last fiscal year we expended from the general fund for operation of all agencies of government a total of $25,230,457.80. Of the total expenditure of your state government from the general fund last year, 53.21 cents out of every dollar was spent for education, representing a total of $13,425,440.84. For the Welfare Department's operation of the charitable and penal institutions and old age assistance, we expended 23.03 cents out of each dollar, or a total of $5,810,371.39. We spent 7.28 cents out of each dollar for judiciary and court costs, which required $1,836,991.56. For general governmental administration, we spent 5.72 cents out of each dollar, the total for this item being $1,444,366.71. For reconstruction and repairs of state institutions, we spent 3.19 cents of each dollar, or a total of $805,240.00. For public health activity, we expended 2.42 cents of each dollar, a total of $609,466.86 for this purpose. For Jefferson and Kenton county fees, we expended 2.07 cents of each dollar, a total of $522,284.36. The law requires all fees collected by counties with a population in excess of 75,000 to be paid into the state treasury and directs that three-fourths of that amount be paid back to the counties in payment of salaries of county officials; so in reality the state profits from this source of income only to the extent of one-fourth. For combined services of the Department of Agriculture, Department of Industrial Relations, Department of Conservation, and Department of Business Regulations, we expended 1.89 cents of each dollar, a total of $476,855.91. We spent 0.58 cents of each dollar for Confederate pensions, a total of $146,027.74. We spent 0.33 cents of each dollar for the Military Department, a total of $83,824.35. We spent 0.25 cents of each dollar for interest on state warrants, amounting to $61,902.30. There was spent 0.03 cents of each dollar for legislative costs, amounting to $7,685.78.

The law directs that the governor submit to the General Assembly a prepared budget. It is important that you who are serving the legislature for the first time understand that no legal expenditure of state money may be made unless authorized in the budget act. The governor has no authority over expenditure of public money except that which you give him.

The budget act, which it is my duty to present for your approval, has been carefully considered by the state budget officer, the commissioner of finance, the governor, and the Legislative Council. Heads of all institutions, departments, and state agencies were invited to present their budget requests to the Legislative Council. Conscientious effort was made to equitably apportion the money available on the basis of need.

Department heads and institutional chiefs requested appropriations which totaled nearly $33 million. Had that much money been available, the governor and the Legislative Council could present to you a budget bill that would provide for every budget agency the amount of money requested. Since that much money cannot be provided without heavily increasing the tax burden, the Legislative Council, Lieutenant Governor Myers, and the governor were confronted with the disagreeable duty of cutting the budget to make it fit the money which we may reasonably anticipate.

The budget which I ask you to enact into law totals $28,554,917.56 for the fiscal year of 1942–1943. For the second year of the biennium, 1943–1944, the budget aggregates $28,774,207.56. The budget for the fiscal year within which we are now operating totals $26,218,437.55. The appropriation recommended for the fiscal year, beginning next July 1, exceeds the present budget by $2,336,480. The excess the second year is $2,555,770.01. The largest item of increase is $960,902 for education in the first fiscal year. In the second half of the biennium that figure is $100,000 higher, an allowance made for anticipated increase in the public school per capita as result of increase in the number of children in the school census and necessity of providing for the regular session of the legislature. The largest item in the budget is $9.6 million for the public schools. It provides a per capita of $12.70, the highest in history.

This school fund will be supplemented by an additional $400,000, to be set up as an equalization fund as authorized by the recently approved constitutional amendment. It will be used to supplement the money provided for public school education in those counties less favored financially, under provisions of legislation which will be submitted to you. I am sure that your approval of it will reflect credit upon the judgment of this legislature and greatly advance the school program.

It is necessary to increase the state contribution to the teachers' retirement fund $150,000 a year, making a total appropriation for this purpose of $650,000. The increase is necessary to keep the fund solvent in this the year in which paying of benefits to aged teachers is to be started as they retire from teaching. Teachers themselves have been contributing to the fund, matching the state money.

The state-supported institutions of higher education are confronted with a critical situation as result of the war. Not only have advancing prices increased the cost of fuel and many other essentials, but their revenue is being cut. Much of the income of the University of Kentucky and the state colleges is derived from fees paid by students. Activities incident to the war have reduced the student body in these schools to such an extent as to affect seriously their income. The increases proposed in the budget to meet the minimum needs of these institutions aggregate $497,900. Contained within that total is a proposed appropriation of $200,000 a year for capital outlay for the University of Kentucky. You will note that it is provided that this sum may be expended only with approval of the governor as to availability of funds and if conditions are sufficiently favorable to building as to justify the expenditure. Within the University of Kentucky budget you will note an increase of $25,000 a year for agricultural extension. This increased support represents the minimum need in maintaining the county agricultural agent and home demonstration agent programs in counties, and in stimulating the "Food for Freedom" endeavor. A new item is included in the university appropriation. It provides $7,500 a year for the College of Engineering and enjoins upon it responsibility for instituting research activity in coal, in an effort to develop smokeless fuels and profitable by-products of coal. The sums designated for the four state teachers colleges represent an increase of $15,000 a year for each of them and an increase of $20,000 yearly for the Kentucky State College for Negroes. The School for the Deaf at Danville would receive an increase of $15,000 in its appropriation, the School for the Blind at Louisville is increased $8,500 a year under the appropriations recommended. These last two institutions provide food for the children enrolled in them and advancing cost of groceries creates the necessity for these increases. The Mayo Vocational School, Paintsville, should receive an increase of $10,000 a year. Facilities of this school, which stresses instruction in industrial arts, are overtaxed as effort is being made to train youth for employment in defense plants.

It is proposed to increase the appropriation for vocational rehabilitation $18,619. This is matched by federal funds. This money is used in training those who have been crippled as result of industrial accidents, or have sustained debilitating injuries that make necessary acquiring new skills in order to become wage earners. Accelerated industrial activity has been attended by a 17 percent increase in injuries sustained in industrial plants. While this is due primarily to inexperienced workers being exposed to the hazards of industry, it is desirable that facilities be provided to help these crippled victims readjust themselves. It will not be long until Kentucky boys who have offered their lives a sacrifice upon the altar of freedom will be returning home maimed and mutilated by the cruel fate of battle. We should be prepared to provide training that will aid our heroic defenders to readjust themselves. This is another enlarged appropriation made necessary by war.

The second largest increase in the budget is contemplated for the Welfare Department and allied agencies. The minimum need requires an increase of $752,000. The largest item in that figure is $430,000 for operation of the state charitable and penal institutions. Steadily advancing costs of food and clothing for the 12,500 inmates in these institutions makes that increase unavoidable. It is recommended that $250,000 a year be added to the $4 million annual appropriation for Social Security, the major portion of which is expended for old age assistance. Two years ago old age assistance checks averaging $8.67 were being sent monthly to 45,198 aged, indigent Kentuckians. Last month we sent checks, which averaged $9.26, to 59,926 individuals. Kentucky ranks twelfth among the states of the union in the number of old age assistance recipients. It ranks eighteenth in the total money expended for old age aid.

You are requested to make available a civil and national defense emergency fund of $500,000 to be expended at discretion of the governor. This item was added to the budget by the Legislative Council after Japan struck at the Stars and Stripes at Pearl Harbor. The governor receives daily requests from Washington to perform services vital to winning the war, and has no money he can legally expend for that purpose. We have had to perform these requested services by utilizing existing facilities. It is desirable that money be provided for contingencies that are certain to rise. I pledge you that this and the Governor's Emergency Fund will be carefully guarded and no money expended from it except in a genuine emergency.

Increased demands upon services of the Public Health Department as result of military activity and development of defense centers in the state make more money for public health necessary. Laboratories of the Health Department are severely overtaxed because it is required to make the

Wassermann tests[4] for those called by the selective service boards. This unforeseen demand, together with the making of similar tests in compliance with provisions of the premarital examination law, creates imperative need for additional laboratory facilities. You are requested to approve an appropriation for the Health Department which is an increase the first year of the biennium of $119,895. Of that sum, $61,000 is added to the money with which to finance county health departments. Demands for establishment of county health units have run beyond money available. This increase will be matched by federal money. A sum of $20,000 is included in the budget to match WPA funds in enlargement of state headquarters of the Public Health Service Building and is included only for the first year.

Provision is made for expansion of the Highway Patrol, should such become necessary as result of conditions created by the war. The present sum of $300,000 a year is again provided for financing the patrol from highway funds. An additional $700,000 is made available which may be expended for enlarging the patrol if such becomes necessary.

The other major increases in the budget is for judiciary and court costs. To this appropriation is added $161,000. This is an uncontrollable expenditure. Whatever the unpredictable cost of operating the courts may be, we are required to pay it. Last year the actual cost of courts, including witness and jury fees, was $1,836,991.56. There had been appropriated only $1,753,600. But the costs had to be met. So there is no use to delude ourselves into a feeling that we are keeping costs of courts down or limiting the budget total by appropriating less than experience indicates will be required.

Increases in money regarded as meeting minimum needs of various departments were estimated in an effort to anticipate realistically additional costs of conducting the departments in view of steadily advancing prices for all sorts of office equipment, supplies, and services.

One increase about which you might raise a question is that for the Department of Mines and Minerals for which the appropriation is increased $17,000 a year. The acceleration in coal-mining activity in the state has brought into operation about 400 mines more than as of a year ago. Many of them are small mines and of meager equipment which should be frequently inspected in an effort to enhance mine safety. An expanded program of inspection becomes an imperious necessity as demands for fuel, stimulated by the Victory drive, intensify coal-mining operations.

I am frank to say to you that the budget total is alarmingly large. I believe you will recognize necessity as the justification for the increases. The budget suggested for next year is $2,334,430 greater than the budget for the fiscal year within which we are now operating. That is an increase of a little more than 8 percent. You well know that prices have advanced far more than 8 percent and that stern, severe economy will be required to operate under this budget. In fact, I anticipate it will be more difficult to perform essential functions under this budget than it was to live within the budget last year, and underspend it, as we did, $731,442.25.

Yet because of the uncertainty of the future it is requested that you include in the budget a clause which authorizes the governor to direct the commissioner of finance to reduce equitably the appropriation for any department if such becomes necessary in order to live within our income. The pruning provision provides that in order to prevent an overdraft or deficit, we may equitably reduce, according to need, without discrimination, the appropriation made to any officer, department, or division of the state government. It further provides that the authority shall not be so exercised as to reduce the appropriation to such an extent as to actually impair constitutional functions of any agency determined to be a necessary constitutional function in government.

You can realize how dangerously difficult it is to prepare a budget today that will fit the fluctuating economic future. That makes it vitally necessary that the budget you adopt be sufficiently flexible to be adjusted to the vagaries of a tax structure that is highly sensitive to economic change. With the emergency fund included in the budget with which unpredictable emergencies may be met; with authority given the governor to order a cut in appropriations if revenue receipts drop, you will have taken precaution to keep expenditures within income.

You will observe that no specific appropriation is included in the budget bill for improvement of the state's charitable and penal institutions, with exception of the $250,000 provided for lands and buildings. Greater portion of that will be expended on routine maintenance. I have been deeply concerned about conditions which prevail in the state institutions. For years we have neglected their ordinary maintenance. During those years when there was a mortgage on the state, when the Commonwealth each year expended more than it collected in revenue, conditions were unfavorable for improvement of these institutions.

My distinguished predecessor, Governor Chandler, made a gratifying start in correcting the deplorable conditions in these institutions. A splendid new prison was constructed at LaGrange. It is one of the best in the nation. But there are 1,200 men still living in temporary frame barracks. Additional permanent dormitories should be built to provide quarters for them.

A modern hospital for the mentally ill was envisioned by Governor Chandler. Its construction was started on a farm which skirts Herrington Lake. With a PWA[5] grant supplementing state money, one splendid building was completed. It has a capacity of 250 beds. Necessary utilities were built. The surgeon general of the United States requested that this plant be made available to the War Department for use in treating mentally ill of the army and navy. We regarded it as our patriotic duty to comply with the request. The property was leased to the army for one dollar a year. It is provided that the army may construct any buildings desired on the property. The army has the right under the agreement to purchase the property from the state for $856,000, the amount of state money invested in it, or return it to the state at termination of the contract with the buildings that have been built upon it. Already $700,000 worth of new buildings have been constructed there by the army.

A 600-capacity new, modern cell house was recently completed at the Eddyville penitentiary. It was started in 1938. It cost about half a million dollars. This mercifully relieves the crowded condition that existed in this prison.

Conditions at the Houses of Reform at Greendale have long been unsatisfactory. The plant was in a serious state of disintegration. Within the last two years we have expended $265,000 on improvements at this institution. A new superintendent has been placed in charge and is developing a wise program under which the school will be made increasingly effective in its rehabilitation of problem children. The most significant indication of improved conditions is to be found in the fact that only four children have run away in the month since the new superintendent, John DeMoisey,[6] has been in charge. In the month before he took command, twenty-nine children escaped from the institution. Improved conditions have had the effect of diminishing the desire to run away.

It is recommended that you enact a measure which will authorize the commissioner of welfare to transfer inmates of a corrective institution from one institution to another. This authority is needed so that boys of tender age who are committed to the state prison may be moved to the House of Reform or that incorrigible youth in the House of Reform may be transferred to prison.

Our major concern has been improvement of the three state hospitals for the mentally ill. The accumulated effect of decades of neglect of these institutions has been to create a condition of deterioration so acute as to require immediate attention. We have expended, or contracted to expend, $712,662 in improving the plants of these hospitals since you last met. Yet such is only a drop in the bucket. Effects of the expenditure can scarcely be seen. Much of the money was expended for boilers, restoration of heating plants, reconstruction of essential utilities, that had disintegrated as result of long use.

Particular emphasis has been placed upon improving and increasing the personnel in these institutions. Each major policy affecting the hospitals has been agreed upon only after the governor, Commissioner W. A. Frost, and Dr. A. M. Lyon, director of mental hygiene, have conferred with the Kentucky Medical Association's committee on state hospitals. Chairman of this committee is Dr. W.E. Gardner of Louisville.[7] Outstanding physicians compose the group. Their counsel has been helpful in formulating policies and no major decision has been made with which this committee was not in unanimous agreement. The hospitals are served by the best medical staff as has ever directed them. Increased difficulties have been experienced which result from frequent resignations of attendants in the hospitals to accept more profitable employment, opportunities for which have been stimulated by war activities.

It would require an expenditure of $18,458,000, according to engineering estimates, to place all these institutions in condition to provide properly for those wards who became the responsibility of the state. Obviously it will not be possible to provide that much money in the immediate future. But there are imperative needs in these institutions which must be met soon—cannot much longer be deferred. Meeting these needs is a duty we should no longer shirk. So in view of the uncertainty of our income and the necessity for an increased budget, no specific sum has been appropriated for these improvements so badly needed. Keeping in mind the important principle of budget flexibility, a new but sound provision has been written into the budget, approved by the Legislative Council. It would authorize surplus money in excess of the budget requirements, if any, to be expended in correcting the frightful conditions in the institutions under the Department of Public Welfare. Also included are institutions under the state Board of Education, School for the Deaf, and Hazelwood Tuberculosis Sanitarium. This money would be expended jointly, if available, by the governor, state treasurer, commissioner of welfare, commissioner of finance, and commissioner of revenue. I am certain this is the most practical plan by which we may adjust our spending to our income. I pledge you that in event there is a surplus which may be expended under this provision it will be prudently and cautiously used.

A month ago there was every justification for expecting that revenues for the Highway Department would be about the same as this year. With startling swiftness there came a bolt as unexpected as the attack on Pearl Harbor which contains possibility of cutting Highway Department income at least 33⅓ percent. Domination of the Pacific by Japan has resulted in cutting the United States off from 93 percent of its rubber supply. A harsh rationing of automobile tires has been imposed upon the nation. It is certain to have the effect of drastically reducing revenues from the gasoline tax. This is an example of the kind of disturbing developments which may cut sharply into our revenues as the drive for victory advances.

This administration has placed major emphasis upon road building.

Highway construction progress to date has been highly gratifying. Within the period from April 1, 1940, to December 1, 1941, there has been built 410 miles of high-type road; 437 miles of medium-type road; and 335 miles of low-type road. Contracts for bridges and grade separations have been let amounting to $4,308,486. Tremendous progress has been made toward building a modern highway system, with a total of $23,906,497 invested in that public improvement with the twenty-one-month period, exclusive of maintenance. All of it has been paid for in cash.

We have given complete cooperation to requests from the military authorities that we reconstruct roads that have been designated as strategic military highways. We have been able to complete half of that task. A magnificent construction program had been outlined for next year, beginning April 1. It has been as badly shot to pieces as was Pearl Harbor. At least a third of our highway revenue has vanished, which supplies another reason for our determination to crush quickly our foes, give the Axis the axe—right in the neck.

I believe you will recognize the wisdom of enacting into law a bill that authorized the Department of Highways to reconstruct and maintain streets within towns and cities which are a link in the state highway system.

Necessity for speedy freight movements for defense makes it expedient that we liberalize the law which places a limit on the load which may be transported by trucks operating over our highways. I urge that you speedily enact a measure which, for the period of the emergency, will permit trucks to carry a load not to exceed 28,000 pounds and extends the maximum truck length to thirty-three feet. The measure specifies the maximum weight on each axle. It directs the commissioner of highways to designate the roads that may be used for the larger load and imposes upon him the responsibility of excluding trucks with increased cargoes from roads when such may be necessary to prevent damage to a road or to bridges that constitute a part of it. This bill should contain an emergency clause so that it may take effect immediately upon its passage. As you expedite this legislation you will make a contribution to the extermination of Hitler and crushing of the Nipponese.

There is need for a law which establishes procedure by which designated representatives of the state may sell real estate and may buy real estate regarded as necessary for state use. This authority is specifically requested so as to permit purchase of a farm to be cultivated by inmates of the Eddyville penitentiary, in event money is available. Advancing cost of groceries makes this especially desirable at this time as a means by which food for inmates of this prison may be provided economically.

It is requested that you enact a law which would empower us to equip a State Militia. The present act forbids use of state money in the purchase of uniforms and equipment. This bill should be passed with the emergency clause that it may become effective at once. In a deficiency appropriation bill which will be submitted, you are to be asked to make available immediately money with which to provide uniforms for the patriotic Kentuckians who have voluntarily enlisted in the State Militia.

On the list of bills recommended by the Legislative Council, you will find a measure which makes it possible for counties to purchase voting machines if they desire to do so. This bill is required to implement the constitutional amendment approved at the last election.

A number of you have shared with me an interest in the endeavor to revise the Kentucky Statutes. The Statutes Revision Commission and staff have done a creditable service. At the last session you repealed a thousand useless and obsolete laws, clearing away the accumulated legal rubbish of a century. Because of the desirability of completing revision of our state law in time to present the revised statutes to the General Assembly for ratification, activities of the commission and its staff have been accelerated in recent months.

When the Statutes Revision Commission discussed the matter with the governor last summer, it was concluded that the staff should be expanded sufficiently to complete the revisal task prior to convening of the legislature. I took the responsibility for approving this procedure although it necessitated spending more money than had been appropriated for this activity. I expressed the belief to the commission that you would approve appropriation of $8,000 to cover the deficit incurred in hastening completion of the revision job. Had such not been done it would have been necessary to postpone for two years legislative approval of the revised statutes. That would have been more expensive than the plan which has been followed. There is in the budget a sum to finance printing of the new statutes. Money received from sale of the new law book will repay the state that which has been invested in this activity.[8]

There is commended to you a bill which establishes the Statutes Revision Commission as a permanent agency. It would be unwise to expend much effort and considerable money in clearing the rubbish from our law and then permit such legal deadwood to again accumulate. Staff of the commission can justify the expense of maintaining it by service to the General Assembly in checking proposed legislation to prevent conflicting and ambiguous laws from being enacted.

There is need for an amendment to the Kentucky constitution so as to authorize legislation that will make workmen's compensation insurance compulsory. I hope you will vote to submit such an amendment to the people for an expression of the public will. Should the law authorizing aid to dependent children and pensions for the needy blind be invalidated, we should submit a constitutional amendment to authorize these worthy social activities.

There are amendments to the Unemployment Compensation Act[9] which experience indicates are desirable. The Kentucky fund is sound and solvent. We are in position to liberalize the law so as to provide increased benefits for unemployed workers. This can be done without jeopardizing solvency of the fund.

It has been gratifying that there has been relatively little serious strife and discord in our state as result of angry conflict between labor and employers. There have been a few clashes which were disruptive of the peace. There has been conflict that caused us concern. But there are few states in which the loss of time from strikes has been less than in Kentucky. Numerous controversies between labor and employers have been amicably settled and the principle of submitting disagreements to the Department of Industrial Relations for arbitration has become more firmly established and has operated with increased effectiveness. The labor group in the state is composed in the main of genuinely patriotic Kentuckians. The attitude of labor leadership is that they and their people should make the maximum contribution to destruction of the enemy that seeks to enslave us. There is a disposition to call a truce on labor disagreements. This reflects creditably upon both employers and employees. I feel confident that strikes will not halt industrial plants in Kentucky that are engaged in producing materials essential in our drive toward victory.

The constitution of Kentucky makes it the duty of the Kentucky legislature to redistrict the state each decade so as to provide for equitable representation in the legislature of all the people. This mandate of the constitution has long been ignored. It is a problem we should tackle. I request that you immediately adopt a *sine die* adjournment date for March 3, twelve days in advance of the date on which the session would regularly be concluded. I shall then immediately call you into special session to consider redistricting legislation. There could be no better evidence that the administration of this legislature wish to set aside all partisan considerations in the present emergency.

The Reorganization Act, enacted in 1936, has functioned effectively and has been the instrument through which reformation of the state's finances has been possible. The system of financial control has proved invaluable in correcting abuses under which the state went into debt every year for quarter of a century. Wisdom of this legislation, to the enactment of which some of you contributed, has been proved. It would be a disservice to Kentucky to tinker with or weaken its provisions.

There are other legislative proposals which will be recommended by the Legislative Council. I join with the council in commending to you that constructive program. Under leadership of Lieutenant Governor Myers, the Legislative Council has performed a fine service. It has refined and prepared a program of legislation the wisdom of which you will recognize as you study it.

One of the most important measures which will be before you is an enabling act which will make available for Kentucky electric power generated by the Tennessee Valley Authority[10] at the Gilbertsville Dam. Communities in the TVA area whose citizenship desires to obtain TVA power should have the opportunity of doing so. The TVA enabling act should definitely and beyond question make provision for distribution of power within the state. It should be free from provisions which contain even a remote possibility of delaying use of that electrical energy which will become available early in 1944. It is necessary the legislation be passed now so that towns and cities will be authorized to contract with this federal power agency in advance of the day when the transmission lines are energized.

I am going to repeat a statement made in my message to the legislature two years ago which is as true now as then: "The budget is an involved and intricate subject, in which is reflected the necessary activities of every state department and agency. Since it has been necessary to apportion available funds as equitably as possible among all departments and agencies, without being able to give any of them the increases which might be desirable if sufficient funds were available, it would be manifestly unfair to disturb the equity of the apportionments. Increases, if granted to some agencies, would be unfair to other departments whose needs are as great, but for whom increased revenues are not available. I, therefore, ask you to pass the budget act without making an increase in any single item. I further ask you to send the completed budget bill to me promptly as your first act."

The course which the governor and Legislative Council have charted is one that advances good government. There is nothing factional or partisan in these recommendations which I have presented to you. Nothing in this the administration program will conflict with your conscience or your duty. It is a program which you can take pride in supporting. There is no proposal in it for which you will have to apologize and I anticipate your cooperation in a spirit of sincere service to our state.

The essence of distilled wisdom is contained in Kentucky's motto. For a century and a half we have officially recognized the logic of "United we stand—Divided we fall." Superimposed upon the Kentucky state seal is the figure of two tall, straight Kentuckians, firmly clasping hands.

During the 150 years of our history there have been times when there has been division among our people. Sharp conflict has cut across the Commonwealth and created discord within our state. Political warfare has at times created turmoil and bitterness. While we have not been so divided as to fall, there have been times when our progress as a state has been seriously impeded by division within our citizenship. There is less political strife in the state than at any time in our memory. Our people are unified by patriotic zeal and ardent support of the nation's activities.

Under normal circumstances, I believe that this legislature would have worked together more harmoniously than any that has ever assembled here. The support which you already have indicated is the most encouraging that has come to any governor in the midst of his term since the turn of the century. Your sentiment reflects the harmonious spirit of the entire citizenship of the state of Kentucky. The events that have taken place, however, completely overshadow our previously planned program.

Now we are at war. The flag has been attacked. The nation is in danger. The state must respond to the call to duty as it has done in every crisis of the past. Partisan politics is adjourned. All differences must be laid aside. We must work together, think together, and do our full share and more. I am sure that your action in this legislative session will add to the honor and credit of Kentucky.

Eyes of Kentuckians are upon us as we assemble here. We have an opportunity to perform notable public service for our state. United we shall achieve that exalted purpose—divided we fail. I anticipate with you a session in which we shall all derive satisfaction from high achievement. Let us by our action give new meaning to our long-cherished motto that united, we stand.[11]

---

1. The Selective Training and Service Act of 1940 was the first peacetime draft act in the history of the United States. It required compulsory military service for all able-bodied men except conscientious objectors who should serve in noncombatant duties.

2. A federal Office of Civilian Defense was created May 20, 1941, to assure coordination of federal relations with state and local governments, especially in the protection of civilians. Legislation was enacted to establish a state Civil Defense Council. The council in cooperation with the federal government handled matters arising as a result of military necessity.

3. H. Clyde Reeves (1912–   ), b. Scott County. Resides in Frankfort. Assistant to United States commissioner of education, Washington, D.C., 1935–1936; director of research and statistics, Department of Revenue, 1936–1938; commissioner of revenue, 1938–1942, 1948–1952; executive consultant, Kentucky Fair and Exposition Center, 1956–1960; president, Kentucky Independent College Foundation, 1960–1963; executive vice-president, 1963–1969, and professor, political and administrative services, University of Alabama, Huntsville, 1964–1973; Council of State Governments, 1973–1975; chairman, Special Advisory Commission on Electrical Utility Rates and Regulation, Kentucky, 1975–1976; chairman, Kentucky

Municipal Statute Revision Commission, 1976–1978. Letter, H. C. Reeves, December 18, 1977.

4. A test for the verification of syphilis.

5. The Public Works Administration was established by Congress in 1933 to increase employment and purchasing power through the construction of public works.

6. John Rivolette (Eugene) DeMoisey (1912–1963), b. Walton. Assistant superintendent, 1939, recreational director, 1939–1941, Greendale. Frederick A. Wallis and Hambleton Tapp, *A Sesquicentennial History of Kentucky* (Hopkinsville, Ky., 1945), 4:2270-72.

7. William Anderson Frost (1872–1954), b. Wingo. State senator, 1911–1919; chairman, Parole Board, 1936–1940; commissioner of welfare, 1940–1943. Managing editor, *Western Recorder*, a Baptist paper, Louisville *Courier-Journal*, July 25, 1954.

A. M. Lyon (1889–1941), b. Roscoe. Judge, Elliott County, 1923–1925; coroner, county health officer. Vice-president, Sandy Hook Bank. Superintendent, Feeble Minded Institute, ten years; superintendent, Western State Hospital, 1939–1940; director, state Hospitals and Mental Hygiene, 1941. Letter, Margaret Woll, March 23, 1978.

William Emmett Gardner (1877–1947), b. Sonora. Chairman, Kentucky Medical Association Committee on State Hospitals; superintendent, Central State Hospital,1910–1914; founded Louisville Neuropathic Sanatorium, 1915. *Who's Who in Kentucky, 1936*, p. 151, and letter, Margaret Woll, March 23, 1978.

8. The Banks-Baldwin Company of Cleveland published the revised statutes without authorization. Johnson said on July 30, 1942, that the state would not pay for the approximately 1,000 copies which the company had sent to state and county officials. The state awarded the contract for printing to the Kingsport Press of Tennessee. In October 1942 the Banks-Baldwin Company sought in a federal district court in Tennessee to enjoin the Kingsport Press from publishing the statutes. The governor employed a Johnson City, Tennessee, law firm to represent Kentucky. The case was dismissed and the revised statutes were delivered. Louisville *Courier-Journal*, July 31, 1942.

9. By the Unemployment Compensation Act of 1936, the legislature set up a plan to take advantage of the provisions of the federal Social Security program.

10. The Tennessee Valley Authority was established in 1933 by Congress to provide flood control, hydroelectric power, and the economic and social reconstruction of the Tennessee River Valley.

11. The governor then presented the suggested budget for the biennium 1942–1944, together with comparative analysis statements. See *Journal of the Senate, 1942*, 1:47-58.

TENNESSEE VALLEY AUTHORITY BILL
Frankfort / February 11, 1942

I WANT first to congratulate you of the General Assembly upon the wisdom with which you have been discharging your legislative duties. In the main, legislation which has been enacted has been constructive and helpful. You are especially to be commended upon preventing the enactment of laws that would be injurious to the state as a whole.

In my message to you on the opening day of the session, I expressed the opinion that legislation should be enacted which would authorize Kentucky cities and towns to enter into contracts with the Tennessee Valley Authority for electric power.[1]

For some time you have had before you in printed form House Bill 146. There has been no desire to press its passage until each of you could thoroughly familiarize yourselves with it. In the discussions that have taken place there have been objections raised to some features of the bill that had merit. In an effort to prepare the best possible act, a substitute bill has been drafted. It has been presented in the House as a committee substitute. It has been introduced in the Senate so that it might be printed and each senator have an early opportunity to study it. Every change in the substitute from the printed bill has improved it, made it more desirable legislation. I am convinced that the bill is in the best possible form. Now that every effort has been made to put before you the most acceptable bill, one that will actually enable towns that want TVA power to get it, I ask you to enact it into law without further delay and without amendments.

The discussions that have taken place on this subject have generated more heat than light on the question. I regard this legislation as being so vital to the welfare of Kentuckians and so important to the future development and prosperity of our state that I have sought the privilege of discussing it with you.[2]

Two years ago a TVA enabling bill was before the legislature in its regular session.[3] At that time, it was evident that TVA power would not be available for Kentucky before this session of the legislature. Court litigation was pending at that time in which the authority of a Kentucky city to contract with TVA was in dispute. Middlesboro had entered into a contract with TVA. Authority of the city officials to make such a contract had been questioned. The case was pending before the Kentucky Court of Appeals as the legislature assembled in 1940. There was a possibility that no legislation was necessary to permit a Kentucky town to use the cheap power of TVA. Since that time the court's decision has been rendered. It was held that the city of Middlesboro did not have authority to contract with TVA under existing law.[4]

As a result of that decision, Kentucky is forbidden the advantages of cheap TVA power until the Kentucky General Assembly passes an enabling act, delegating to towns of the state authority to make contracts with TVA for electrical energy. The situation that exists today is that a barrier stands along the Kentucky–Tennessee line which excludes Kentucky from the group of southern states that are enjoying the economic, industrial, and social advantages of cheaper electric power.

Two years ago, as we reached the conclusion that a TVA enabling act should not then be passed, there was no provision in the federal act creating TVA which permitted utility distribution systems, using TVA power, to make payments of money in replacement of taxes to the schools, city and county governments. Since then the federal law has been amended so as to permit communities to sell the power purchased from TVA at such rates as would make possible payments in lieu of taxes to local governmental units. Tax replacement is provided in the bill upon which you will pass judgment.

As TVA legislation was discussed two years ago and a decision reached to defer its enactment at that time, I gave assurance that if the court decision in the Middlesboro case created a condition that made legislation necessary to admit TVA power to Kentucky, that I would recommend such a law to this session of the General Assembly. These facts, which I have briefly reviewed, in my opinion not only make it my obligation to the people of Kentucky to recommend to you but your duty to your people to speedily enact the TVA enabling act now before you.

I ask you to consider carefully this fact. A vote against this TVA enabling act has the effect of declaring that you want to raise a wall along the Kentucky–Tennessee line and keep out of Kentucky the advantages of cheap electric power. People of our state cannot have the benefits and blessings of lower light bills unless you remove the barrier at our border which prevents cheap power from crossing into Kentucky.

The bill which I urge you to vote for does not force any town to take TVA power. But it does provide that they can get it when it becomes available if a vote of the people reveals that the folks want it.

The original bill provided that an election should be held to ascertain the wishes of the people if 25 percent of the voters signed a petition asking for the right to vote on it. In a sincere effort to meet objections that have been raised to the bill, that provision has been changed to make a referendum compulsory. Before a city may issue revenue bonds to finance purchase of the property in the town through which the private utility operates and enter into a contract with TVA for electric power, an election must be held. Unless a majority of those who vote express themselves as being in favor of their town contracting with TVA, the city council will have no authority to proceed. This provision provides home rule in the fullest sense. It provides by legislation that the question is to be decided by the folks who are to be affected by it. And after the people, by their vote, decide that they want their town to contract with TVA, that should settle the question. The town should not be required to come to the Public Service Commission and get permission to do that which the people declare they want. Critics of the bill insist that TVA should come into the state under regulations of the Public Service Commission. But I insist that the decision of the people should be final and that no certificate of convenience and necessity should be required from the Public Service Commission. I would caution you of the General Assembly not to vote against a bill which gives the people authority to decide by ballot whether they want their town to contract with TVA for power.

Critics place great emphasis upon the desirability of placing under supervision of the Public Service Commission those towns who set up municipally owned plants and buy their power from TVA. Our law does not require the dozens of other Kentucky towns that now own and operate their own electric power plants to come under the Public Service Commission and be supervised by it. By what strange logic do these critics justify the argument that municipal plants, using TVA current, should be under the Public Service Commission?

In an effort to arouse opposition to a TVA act, Kentuckians who have invested in public utility stocks have been frightened with the assurance that if this TVA monster gets into Kentucky, their investments will become worthless. That is typical of the misrepresentation which seeks to besmirch this legislation. There has been written into this bill specific procedure by which will be determined the value of the utility property which the town or city may decide it desires to buy. It provides every safeguard that any fair-minded person could expect. It provides for an equitable method of arbitration in an effort to fix a fair price of the utility property. In event negotiations are unsuccessful, and not until then, the municipality may condemn the property and go into court, there by judicial process to finally determine how much the city shall pay the utility for its property. Utility stockholders need have no fear that their investments will be rendered worthless. They can be sure that a fair price will be paid for the property which may be purchased by municipalities.

Critics of this legislation seek to create opposition with assertions that there is going to be a huge loss in taxes as municipalities acquire the property of utilities. There is a carefully considered provision in this bill which requires payments in lieu of taxes to the city and county and public schools. It is provided that rates charged for electric current shall yield a return that will be ample to make these payments of tax equivalents. The tax equivalent section has been so drawn as to prevent loss of revenue to the local subdivisions of government.

I am going to tell you frankly that there is some question as to the constitutionality of the provision in the bill which provides for tax replacement. Never before in the history of Kentucky has this question been before the legislature. The best thought of numerous good attorneys has been focused on the problem of devising a plan, not in conflict with Kentucky's constitution, by which electric power may be retailed by a city at a rate which would provide money for payments in lieu of taxes. I am convinced that the method used is the best approach to the problem, taking into consideration the constitutional difficulty. Mr. William C. Fitts, general counsel of the TVA, tells me that he regards the section of the bill which provides for tax equivalents as being the soundest method of approach and the plan which best meets the constitutional question.

But there is a possibility that this provision might be found by the court in conflict with the constitution. That uncertainty makes it all the more important that we pass this bill now, so that its constitutionality can be tested. Should it be held invalid, in light of the opinion of the court, the next legislature would have the responsibility of correcting the defect and providing a plan for tax replacements which would be valid.

Gilbertsville Dam, in western Kentucky, is well along toward completion.[5] Assurance is given that electric power will be available there by February 1944. This dam will have for distribution in Kentucky 90,000 to 100,000 kilowatts of power. The federal act specifies that the state within which the power-producing project is located shall have prior claim upon the energy it produces.

Municipalities in the vicinity of Gilbertsville Dam that may desire to buy power from this new generating plant will have no authority to make such arrangements until the General Assembly passes this enabling act. It is our duty to pass the bill at this session so cities that want to contract with TVA may be making their plans to do so. It will require quite some time for a town to ascertain by a vote whether its citizenship desires that it purchase TVA power. It will require much time to negotiate with the private utility serving the town, for purchase of its property and determining of a fair price. So it seems to me that it is imperative that we of the Kentucky legislature should clear away the first barrier between Kentucky and TVA power by passing an enabling act right now.

The population of Kentucky and Tennessee is almost identical. Yet in the year of 1940, the total light and power bill of Kentuckians was approximately seven million dollars greater than the total bill paid by Tennesseeans. And consumers in Tennessee used a far greater volume of power than was used in Kentucky because it was cheaper.

That great saving which left seven million dollars in the pockets of the people of Tennessee is the result of abundant TVA power. The average light and power bill of the average Kentuckians is approximately 42 percent higher than the average light and power bill paid by the average Tennesseean. Are you willing by your vote against this TVA enabling act to banish the hope that Kentuckians may profit from a reduction in costs of electricity? The people you represent do not want you to do that.

If TVA rates for electricity were adopted throughout Kentucky, the result would be a saving to residential consumers of approximately $3 million a year on their light bills. That is more money than was collected from the individual state income tax last year. If TVA rates were adopted in Kentucky, there would be an approximate saving to commercial users of electric power of $2.5 million a year. If TVA rates were in effect in our state, it would reduce the power bill of industrial consumers about $1.5 million a year. The saving to industrial and commercial users of electricity would be approximately $4 million a year. That sum is a million and a half dollars more than the total state income tax collected last year from corporations who are the industrial and commercial consumers of electricity.

You of the General Assembly have been told that if you would repeal the income tax, industries would come rushing into Kentucky. For the first 144 years of our existence as a state, an income tax was not imposed, yet there was no rush of industries into this Commonwealth. One of the greatest inducements to industry that can be offered is an abundance of cheap electrical energy. If you of the legislature pass this TVA enabling act, you will take the first and most essential step toward making available in Kentucky cheap, ample power. And that will give greater impetus to development of Kentucky industrially than would the repeal of the income tax or anything else you could do. If, by your vote, you make plentiful cheap power available in the future, you will have made a major contribution to Kentucky's social and economic advancement. It will mean that the convenience of electricity will be brought within the economic reach of many low-income Kentuckians who are now denied such benefits. It will mean that electricity will be used in increased volume to do more things, to take much of the drudgery out of life. The blessings of cheap electricity will tremendously enhance the happiness and prosperity of Kentuckians. And Kentuckians, as they enjoy those benefits, will be grateful to you of this General Assembly who removed the wall along the Kentucky-Tennessee line which now prevents our people from enjoying the benefits of cheap TVA power, no matter how much they may want it.

Opponents of the bill have sought to justify opposition on the ground that TVA electrical energy comes in competition with coal and since much TVA current is generated by waterpower, it cuts down the use of coal in steam-generating plants. The facts are that there has been more coal consumed in Tennessee since TVA has been distributing power than previously. Of course, considerable of that is due to the fact that coal-consuming industries have sprung up in TVA territory since cheap power became available. The industries, which I predict will be established in Kentucky when we create an advantageous power situation, will be large users of Kentucky coal.

Opponents of the bill have agitated the minds of those splendid competent Kentuckians now employed by utility companies. These persons are assured that they will lose their jobs if this TVA enabling act is passed. Competent, experienced employees will be needed, regardless of the source of power distributed in Kentucky. In Tennessee 75 percent of the employees of the private utility companies were employed after TVA went into operation. There will be increased employment opportunities for employees of the utilities as new industries come to Kentucky.

Those who seek defeat of this bill have sought to convince Kentucky towns that now own and operate their own electric plants that this legislation will be hurtful to them. That is a misrepresentation of the facts. Passage of this bill will not affect existing municipally owned plants in the least. They are not required to accept provisions of this act unless they prefer to do so. With TVA power made available, there will be instances in which it will be advantageous to municipally owned plants to elect to come under provisions of this act. But the municipality itself will be the judge of whether or not it is desirable that they do so.

Effort has been made to agitate those who are interested in Rural Electric Cooperatives. It has been suggested to them that municipalities contracting with TVA might invade their territory. Probability of that ever happening is farfetched. But to guard against such a contingency, there has written into this substitute bill a specific provision which eliminates that possibility.

An effort is being made by some critics of this legislation to create opposition by arousing prejudice against the TVA. Whether you regard establishment of the TVA as wise is not the question before you. It has already been created. The taxpayers' money necessary to establish the TVA has already been expended. Money paid into the federal treasury by Kentucky taxpayers has been used to build the TVA power system. The only way we shall get a return on our taxes invested is by using the cheap power produced. TVA is here on our southern border. It is building hydroelectric facilities within our state. You could not stop that if you desired. But now that TVA is here, it would be a distinct disservice to Kentucky should you of the General Assembly refuse to pass an enabling act that will permit our people to use the cheap power that is soon to become available. TVA has harnessed the waterpower of the Tennessee

Valley for the purpose of manufacturing cheap power. Now that these natural resources are being utilized to provide the most essential ingredient of an advanced social and economic order, cheap power, I am certain that it is our duty to take that action necessary to place these benefits at the disposal of our people, leaving to them the discretion as to whether they shall use the power facilities of TVA.

There are opponents of this bill who assail it as special privilege legislation.[6] I am frank to say to you that it is special privilege legislation—but it is legislation that will provide special privileges for the people of Kentucky. It provides the special privilege of cheaper power for every home, for every factory in Kentucky if the people indicate by their vote that they want it. It is special privilege legislation that will attract manufacturing plants to Kentucky to provide increased labor opportunity for our folks and enhanced prosperity for our people. It is because of the special privileges and benefits that this legislation provides for Kentuckians that I urge you to vote for it.

I have refrained from hostile criticism of the utilities companies. I have no disposition to recall to your mind unhappy incidents of a recent past. There are utility executives in Kentucky who have refrained from opposing this bill. I congratulate them upon their enlightened attitude on this, a problem which vitally affects the public. This bill is not presented with any desire to injure utility companies.[7] The sole consideration in urging your vote for this measure is that the best interests of Kentucky as a whole will be advanced by its enactment.

I am certain that there are conscientious Republicans in this legislature who will not be influenced to vote against this bill on the ground that TVA is a wicked New Deal measure. Wolf Creek Dam is under construction down in the heart of that section of Kentucky that is predominantly Republican. When that dam is completed, a considerable quantity of cheap electric power will be generated there. The region closest to that dam can be immensely benefited by the power which will be available right at its door. But the people in that area will be forbidden to use that cheap power and be denied all the conveniences that come with it unless you pass this enabling act.

Cheap TVA power will provide the stimulus that will accelerate the pace of progress in Kentucky. It is shortsighted to stand in the way of progress. It is stupid to stand in the way of labor-saving inventions. You cannot hold back the dawn. It is impossible to keep the sun from rising. It is just as impossible to expect to be able by legislative action to build a wall along the Kentucky–Tennessee line so high that it will exclude cheap TVA power from Kentucky forever. Should you make the mistake of trying to do that, or forbidding Kentuckians the right to decide by their own vote whether they want TVA power, the people will rebuke those who withhold from them electrical energy at rates low enough to make posible extensive use of it. I caution you against taking the attitude that the people shall not have the right by vote to make their decision as to whether TVA power shall be brought into their communities.

The opposition has sought to obscure the real principle involved in this bill. A smoke screen of controversy has been raised. Critics say, "I am for TVA coming in if it comes in the right way." But when you blow the smoke away, look at the matter clearly and without prejudice, it all boils down to this single vital issue—Are you in favor of permitting Kentuckians to enjoy the benefits of cheap electricity on the same basis with the people of Tennessee? Are you in favor of passing a bill that gives the people who want TVA power the authority to obtain it?

I have never had a stronger conviction on any question of public policy. No public issue has ever appeared clearer to me than this. The principle involved is as correct as the Ten Commandments. I am asking you to close your ears to the clamor of those who seek to persuade you that you should vote against this bill—close your ears to their importunities long enough to listen to your conscience and let it guide you to a correct conclusion. You are men of intelligence and judgment. You are capable of deciding between what is best for all the people and that which is not best. You are capable of deciding between right and wrong. And the question of whether Kentucky towns shall be permitted to buy TVA power, if they want it, is a question that will never be settled until it is settled right. I implore you in the name of the inarticulate masses of Kentucky who will be benefited in years to come to enact this legislation into law. It is a momentous question. If you solve it correctly, it will hasten the dawn of a new day, with new opportunities in which Kentucky will go forward to a richer fulfillment of her destiny.[8]

---

1. The governor promised the Murray Young Business Men's Club on February 10, 1941, that he would consider its request for legislation in 1942 to permit cities to acquire TVA power. Louisville *Courier-Journal*, February 11, 1941. On February 27 he said that his administration would cooperate in drafting legislation to enable municipalities to contract for TVA power. Representative Henry Ward said that the governor told him the Public Service Commission had been instructed to obtain information as a basis for preparing a bill. *State Journal*, February 28, 1941. In September 1941 the governor ordered a study of the operations, rates, economics, public regulations, and other aspects of TVA's dealings with municipalities and cooperatives in Alabama, Georgia, Mississippi, and Tennessee in preparation for the 1942 session of the General Assembly. He sent John S. Kirtley, chairman of the Public Service Commission, and three members of his staff to these states to make the study. *Lexington Herald*, September 30, 1941.

2. On February 6 the governor sent identical, terse messages to the Senate and

House in which he said "the one accurate statement" that Public Service Commission chairman John Kirtley made in criticizing the TVA measure before a House committee was that he was not speaking for the governor. "The only thing I'm concentrating on is passing the TVA bill and I'm going to pass it." *State Journal,* February 7, 1942. After the governor finished his address to the General Assembly, Kirtley announced his resignation as chairman of the Public Service Commission. *Richmond Daily Register,* February 11, 1942.

3. Representative Henry Ward sponsored it.

4. *City of Middlesboro* v. *Kentucky Utilities Co.,* 284 Ky. 833, 146 S.W. 2d 48 (1940).

5. The governor spoke on December 4, 1939, at a program to mark the progress on Gilbertsville Dam. Members of Congress, governors of surrounding states, and TVA officials attended. Johnson said, "All the help my administration can give to our representatives in Washington to bring this undertaking to a rapid completion" will be extended. *Paducah Sun-Democratic,* December 5, 1939.

6. In a letter to the governor, dated February 10, 1942, the Lexington Board of Commerce executive committee attacked the bill, stating it was "unfair and special privilege legislation which is neither in public interest nor for the good of our people." *Lexington Herald,* February 11, 1942.

7. R. M. Watt, president of Kentucky Utilities, asserted the bill would mean the eventual end of all privately owned electric utilities in the state. *Lexington Herald,* February 11, 1942.

8. The bill was introduced in the House of Representatives by Henry Ward, who stated that the governor had done as much work as anyone on the TVA enabling legislation. *State Journal,* February 5, 1942. See *Acts of the General Assembly, 1942,* Chapter 18 (H.B. 146), pp. 142-81.

CALL FOR REDISTRICTING
Frankfort / March 3, 1942

WHEREAS, in 1940, there was a national census, and

WHEREAS, Under Section 33 of the Constitution of the Commonwealth of Kentucky it is provided that the General Assembly shall every ten years redistrict the state giving due consideration to population and territory for the purpose of bringing about, as near as possible, equality of representation in the General Assembly, and

WHEREAS, the General Assembly has adjourned its regular session several days prior to the limitation of time for a regular session with the understanding that they could consider redistricting in a special session, now

THEREFORE, in order for the General Assembly to study and consider and adopt laws redistricting the Senatorial and Representative Districts, and according to the power vested in me by the Constitution of Kentucky to convene the General Assembly in Extraordinary Session, I do issue this, my proclamation, convening the General Assembly of Kentucky in Extraordinary Session at the seat of government at Frankfort, Kentucky, at eleven o'clock A.M. on Thursday, March 5, 1942, for the sole purpose of considering the following subjects:

To study, consider, and adopt laws dividing the State into thirty-eight Senatorial Districts and one hundred Representative Districts as nearly equal in population, with due regard to territory.

You will therefore in accordance with this proclamation assemble in Extraordinary Session at the seat of government at Frankfort, Kentucky, on the day, date, and at the time, above written, to consider the subject herein mentioned and only said subject.[1]

---

1. Section 33 of the Constitution of Kentucky requires that the legislature redistrict the legislative districts every ten years on the basis of population shown by the census.

By 1941, however, only three attempts had been made to redistrict the state since the act was passed in 1893 to create the districts after the present constitution went into effect. The first attempt, made in 1906, was held unconstitutional in *Ragland* v. *Anderson,* 125 Ky. 141, 100 S.W. 865 (1907), because the legislature did not create the districts in accordance with Section 33. The act pertained only to representative districts; no provision was made to redistrict the senatorial districts. The legislature attempted to redistrict the state again in 1918. The validity of this act was not directly questioned although the act was considered as to one district in Jefferson County in *Neutzel* v. *Ryans,* 184 Ky. 292, 211 S.W. 852 (1919). The legislature made another attempt in 1930. This act was declared void in *Stiglitz, County Clerk* v. *Schardien,* 239 Ky. 799, 40 S.W. 2d 315 (1931), on the grounds of "glaring inequities" which violated Section 33. The legislature passed two acts, one each for representative and senatorial districts. They were passed over the veto of the governor. These acts changed only the districts in Jefferson County, not the districts in the entire state. Since the act of 1918 made few changes, the legislative districts in 1941 were primarily the same as they were in 1893.

The nine congressional districts also did not conform to the equality of representation principle but the governor did not include congressional redistricting in his call. The state was redistricted after the 1930 census since it lost two House seats. Equality of representation was not, however, achieved. The 1940 census disclosed that the population of the districts ranged from 224,358 to 413,591. The average district for the nation had 301,000 persons. *State Journal,* November 10, 1940.

EXTRAORDINARY SESSION OF THE GENERAL ASSEMBLY
Legislative Redistricting
Frankfort / March 10, 1942

YOU may well take pride in the fact that you were members of the regular session of the General Assembly of Kentucky in the year of 1942. Seldom has there been a session so nearly free of legislation that is hurtful to the citizenship. For the first time in many years no legislation was passed which increased the tax burden upon our people. You enacted into law much wise and constructive legislation. You passed a budget bill under which it appears that the minimum needs of the state institutions and agencies can be met, despite the advance in prices of essential commodities. You passed legislation which requires the state to live within its income, keep its budget in balance. It is a prudent, cautious budget in which expenditures have been carefully apportioned on the basis of necessity.

You made provision to establish for the first time a public school equalization fund. You wrote into the budget act every possible provision to make it elastic enough to meet the economic uncertainties of the future. You authorized money to meet unforeseen emergencies which may be created as a result of the war.

You enacted legislation which established a state Civil Defense Council through which we may do our duty in cooperation with the national government in meeting problems which arise as result of military necessity. You appropriated money with which to buy uniforms and equipment for the State Active Militia, a new expenditure made necessary by military needs.

You passed an antisabotage law to deter subversive actions which would interfere with preparation for war. You passed legislation that permits the load limit on trucks to be lifted to 28,000 pounds on designated highways for the period of the emergency, so as to facilitate transportation essential to military preparation.

You enacted legislation that will prevent the accumulation of another state debt and which made available the Revised Kentucky Statutes in which the law of the state is simplified.

You authorized the Highway Department to maintain and reconstruct city streets over which pass state and federal highways.

You passed an act which permits a department head, with approval of the governor, to employ an attorney as legal counsel. This legislation has been misrepresented as being designed to provide jobs for a lot of lawyers. None of the abuses will take place under this bill that have been predicted and time will prove that it was wise legislation.

You passed an act which gives the Court of Appeals authority to employ additional commissioners from lawyers who have served on the court more than eight years. Critics have sought to create prejudices against the law by calling it a pension bill. I am certain that the court will exercise this authority with discretion. Only twenty-four justices could have qualified for such appointment in the last 150 years. There is a real need for additional commissioners to aid the court in disposing of appeals more promptly. In filling that need competent men should be employed. Men who have served on the court possess superior qualifications to serve as commissioners. I am confident that none of the abuses that have been forecast will take place under this act and wisdom of the legislation will be established.

The crowning achievement of the legislative session was enactment of TVA Enabling Act, under which it was made possible for Kentucky towns and cities to contract with the Tennessee Valley Authority for electrical energy if a majority of the people within the municipality indicates by vote that such is their desire.

Splendid though your accomplishments have been, one important legislative task remains for you to tackle. Under Section 33 of the Kentucky Constitution there is enjoined upon the General Assembly the duty of legislatively redistricting the state every ten years. That explicit mandate has been ignored for decades. Population changes in the state, coupled with failure of the General Assembly to make readjustments, has created a condition which results in glaring inequalities in legislative representation.

I suggested to you on the opening day of the regular session that legislative redistricting is a matter of such importance that it should be considered in a special session. You concurred in the recommendation that the regular session be cut short and that we attack the problem which has perplexed previous legislatures by concentrating entirely upon a task that has been too long deferred.

It is your constitutional duty to pass a redistricting bill that will provide equal representation in the General Assembly of all the people. The most vital principle in our democratic form of government is that the people shall have equal representation in the lawmaking bodies. It is a principle so fundamental that it is both unwise and dangerous to ignore it. In these critical days when this great republic is threatened by the armed forces of foes that scorn democracy as a form of government, we are rededicating ourselves to the exalted principles which have been written into the constitutions of our state and nation. Kentucky mothers smile through tears as with pride they surrender their sons, bid them answer the call of their country to follow the flag of freedom in the uncertainty of battle. Gallant young Kentuckians respond to the stern dictates of duty. They go to fight for the preservation of democracy—for the perpetuation of a government which is founded upon the principle that the people shall select their representatives and delegate to them authority to make their laws. But elemental justice dictates that there be equitable representation in the lawmaking body. It is inconsistent to proclaim allegiance to our democratic form of government and yet thwart its operation by nullifying our constitution in its mandate that inequalities of representation be adjusted each decade. It is inconsistent to fight for democracy and refuse to vote for it.

Disproportionate representation has become more pronounced as population has increased in metropolitan areas and in Eastern Kentucky. It was contemplated by framers of the constitution that the population figures revealed by the federal census every ten years should provide the basis for adjusting the legislative districts so as to keep them in conformity with equitable and fair principles of representation. That has not been done. To what extent any section of the Commonwealth has sustained injury as result of disproportionate representation is not susceptible of proof.

True it is that there has been no legislative discrimination against any area of the state. This is due to the composite wisdom of the General Assembly and is not a justification for evading the duty of redistricting. Fortunately sectionalism in Kentucky has been substantially eliminated in recent years. Improved highways have rendered all sections of the state readily accessible. As the people of the mountains have commingled with people of the Pennyrile, sectional suspicion has subsided to a marked degree. Kentucky has been unified as there has disappeared into the forgotten past those days when section was arrayed against section as a result of the mistaken belief that their interests clashed. The major portion of our important problems are statewide in nature. As legislation improves the school system in the Bluegrass region, it has the same effect in Northern or Eastern Kentucky.

The fact that solvency of the state government has been restored is as important to Paducah as it is to Pikeville. Paying off the state debt has been an achievement in which taxpayers of every section have participated. It is vital to the welfare of *all* that your state government be so administered as to live within its income, never again to permit the bad management under which for a quarter of a century more money was expended by the state government than was collected in revenue income.

The fiscal reformation that has taken place in the last six years is a major accomplishment in financial statecraft. But the high ground of achievement attained can be held only by rigid adherence to sound business practices and principles. It would be easy to slip back into the sloven, slipshod, extravagant method of state administration such as plunged Kentucky in debt more than 25 million dollars. That cannot happen unless the legislature permits it. The great gains in good government that have recently been made are beneficial to every section of the state. A legislature truly representative of the taxpayers should be a safeguard against a return of inefficiency and unbalanced budgets. Proper redistricting of the state should intensify the feeling of responsibility of the taxpayers as they select those that are to represent them in the General Assembly.

As sectional prejudice has subsided, there has been born a state consciousness. I have repeatedly visited every county in Kentucky. In each county one finds splendid, intelligent people who envision Kentucky as a whole. The better one knows Kentucky the more one loves her and her fine folk. There is a more pronounced feeling of unity in the state than ever before. There is less discord, more unity of thought and purpose. This fortunate fact should permit an open-minded consideration of legislative redistricting, free of sectional suspicion. It should be conducive to establishment of equality of representation. It should make it easier for you to draft a redistricting bill than it was for your legislative predecessors who failed to accomplish the task.

The principal thing that has prevented redistricting in recent decades has been unwillingness of a considerable number of legislators to vote for a bill which would eliminate their district or affect their tenure of office. There cannot be an equitable redistricting without abolishing a number of legislative districts. I urge you to permit your devotion to the vital tenet of democracy to transcend selfish desires to retain a district that is far below the population standard. I implore you to manifest a willingness to make that sacrifice necessary to restore equal representation. When you have done that you will have contributed to a noteworthy achievement which will be recorded as an outstanding episode in the legislative history of our Commonwealth.

EXTRAORDINARY SESSION OF THE GENERAL ASSEMBLY
Legislative Redistricting
Frankfort / March 30, 1942

WHEN I appeared before a joint session of the General Assembly on March 10, I requested that you concentrate upon a task which has been too long deferred—that of legislative redistricting.

I want to reiterate this point which I tried to impress upon you then: It is inconsistent to fight for democracy and refuse to vote for it. It is hypocrisy to laud democracy and then make it inoperative.

[The governor quoted the concluding paragraph from his address on March 10.]

I am now repeating what I said then because I want you to know that I meant every word of it. And I did not have my fingers crossed when I said it. I have been astonished to learn that there are those who are saying that I was not sincere when I asked you to pass a redistricting bill. It has been reported that opponents of redistricting have said that I was merely giving lip service to the cause of redistricting when I called the General Assembly into special session and delivered by address of March 10 on that subject. It has been suggested that I considered my responsibility at an end when I had done that.

I come to speak to you again in joint session so that I might dispel any doubt as to my sincerity as I insist that you must not leave here until you pass bills that will provide more equitable representation in the House and Senate. It is my duty as governor to insist that a fair redistricting bill be enacted. It is your inexorable duty to do that. It is my obligation to do everything humanly possible to assist in the enactment of such a bill. It is not a pleasant task before us. But we must not duck or dodge our duty. If we refuse to recognize our responsibility, turn our back on the constitution, we make a mockery of democracy; are recreant to a public trust and unworthy of the confidence the people placed in us as they elected us to public office.

No fair-minded person can study the situation that now exists without reaching the conclusion that redistricting is imperative. An analysis of existing representative districts reveals that more than half the people of Kentucky reside in forty-one large districts, while less than half of the people live in fifty-nine small House districts. The forty-eight members of this House who recently voted to kill House Bill No. 4, which was a pretty good redistricting plan, represent only 985,813 people out of the 2,845,627 inhabitants of the state. There are now thirty-one House districts with populations that range from 8,827 to less than 18,000. There are twenty-six House districts with populations that run from 36,000 to more than 200,000. Among the 100 House districts now existing, there are thirty-seven with populations below 20,000 each. Twelve have populations of between 20,000 and 25,000; thirteen of between 25,000 and 30,000; twelve of between 30,000 and 36,000; and twenty-six of more than 36,000. Thirty-seven members of this House of Representatives are from districts which have populations below 20,000. Twenty-eight counties with populations of less than 20,000 are in single county districts, which means that each has a representative, and one county with a population of only 36,587 has two representatives in the House. Ten counties with a representative in the House have populations of less than 13,000.

This situation exists in defiant disregard of an explicit command of the Kentucky constitution. It can be corrected only by the General Assembly. Destiny has decreed that you shall perform this important public service. You must correct this situation.

The legislative redistricting committee of the House is ready to report to you a bill with the expression of opinion that it should be passed. I am familiar with the provisions of this measure. Some of my suggestions have been incorporated in the bill. It has my emphatic endorsement. I think it should be passed in the form in which it will be reported by the committee.

I will also say to you quite frankly that it is not the best bill which could be drafted according to a purely mathematical formula. It is, in my opinion, the fairest and best bill which could be drafted and which can be passed.

Let me emphasize those last words—which can be passed. They deserve attention for the simple reason that it would be useless to present to the legislature a bill which could not be passed.

I have been amused at observations made by several who profess an interest in seeing a redistricting bill passed and who insist that it is a simple matter to prepare a bill that will redistrict the state in an equitable way. It has been suggested that the constitution contains a formula which, when applied to the problem before us, makes the whole task an easy one.

It is so simple to say that. And some persons have been misled by such observations from experts on everything who know better. But it is one thing to draft a bill which would be equitable from the cold mathematical viewpoint, and quite another thing to perfect one for which enough votes can be obtained to pass it in the House and Senate.

I know that some of you will vote against any redistricting bill which is presented. To ignore that fact would be folly. Since our obligation is not only to draft a redistricting bill but also to pass a redistricting bill, it is highly important that the measure presented to you be one that a majority of you will approve.

I would not be discharging my obligation to recommend to you a redistricting bill which would not be passed. That would be the surest way to sabotage the legislation. Those pious critics who gleefully point out defects in this bill are sinister saboteurs of redistricting. They smirkingly stick the stiletto of criticism into any redistricting bill with knowledge that this is the most adroit way to prevent redistricting. The bill which I have suggested that the House redistricting committee report to you is a bill which departs to some extent from what the theoretically ideal measure should be, but it is one which I am convinced can and will win the approval of the House and Senate and be sustained by the court.

This measurement makes great improvements over the present districting plan. Under its provisions, sixty-six of the 100 members of the House would represent districts with populations ranging from 20,000 to 36,000. Under the present plan, there are only thirty-six representatives from districts with populations of between 20,000 and 36,000.

The committee bill would leave seventeen districts with populations of less than 20,000. There are now thirty-seven districts in that classification. Under the committee proposal, eighteen representatives would come from districts with populations of between 20,000 and 25,000. There are only twelve representatives now from such districts.

At the present time, only thirteen members of the House represent districts with populations ranging from 25,000 to 30,000. The committee bill would send twenty-three representatives to the House from districts in that population group.

The committee proposal creates twenty-five districts composed of from 30,000 to 36,000 people. There are now only twelve representatives from districts in this population range.

Twenty-six members of the House now represent districts which have populations in excess of 36,000. The committee proposal would reduce that number to seventeen. The largest district under the present arrangement is one in Jefferson County with a population of more than 200,000. The largest district which would be left under the committee's bill would be Perry County, which has 47,740 people. Letcher County, which has a population of 40,592, is now in the same legislative district with Perry County. Under the committee bill, each county would have a representative.

There are now eleven House districts with populations of less than 14,000. Under the proposed bill, the smallest district would have 14,234. Two districts would have populations of between 15,000 and 16,000. There would be between 16,000 and 17,000 in two other districts. The populations in six districts would range from 17,000 to 18,000 and two others would have from 18,000 to 19,000. There would be from 19,000 to 20,000 in two districts. Thus, under the new bill there would be seventeen districts with populations of less than 20,000 people where there are now thirty-seven.

Many problems are encountered in an effort to draft an equitable House redistricting bill. If Kentucky counties were equal in area and population, the task would be simple. But one glance at a map and a chart of population figures shows why it is a difficult one. On population, the range is from only 3,421 in Robertson County to 385,256 in Jefferson. Little Robertson has an area of only 109 square miles, and across in Eastern Kentucky there is big Pike County with 779 square miles.

The arrangement of counties makes it impossible to prepare a redistricting bill that will provide exact representation on the basis of population. Consequently, in any bill there will be districts with both population and area greater than others.

In discussions which have attended consideration of redistricting, opponents seek to thwart redistricting by appealing to prejudices. They have tried to array the country against the cities. It is argued that redistricting takes representation from the rural areas and gives it to the cities and the coal-mining region.

It is true that any fair and just redistricting bill increases the city representation slightly. But we cannot, in all justice, accept this as an excuse to mock democracy and refuse to obey an explicit command of the constitution.

The purpose of the constiution was to provide that people shall be represented in the legislature—not miles of sparsely populated areas. This is a government of the people, by the people, for the people. We are at war to keep it that way. We must pass this bill to keep it that way.

People live in those urban sections, and in those coal-mining counties. They are human beings and Kentuckians, with a natural interest in their government and a right to be represented by those who levy taxes and make laws that have a direct effect on the lives and property of the people.

Those who hold that these people are not entitled to equality of representation voice sentiments that strike at the very foundations of our Republic. They scorn the sacred principles for which our forefathers fought and for which our gallant sons are now fighting.

The charge of opponents of redistricting that the effect will be to rob the rural sections of their influence in the legislature is a misrepresentation of the facts.

The truth is that those who prefer that rural Kentucky dominate the legislature need not be alarmed. An analysis of the House redistricting bill proposed by the committee reveals that at least sixty-five of the 100 representatives who would come to the House under its provisions would be from districts in which chief emphasis is placed on agriculture. Those districts would be dominated by the votes of persons who reside on farms or in small towns. They would guarantee that rural Kentucky would retain the voting dominance it now has in the House of Representatives.

The other thirty-five representatives would come from districts which might be regarded as being urban in character or in which coal mining is the outstanding industry. However, the majority of these districts would be composed of both urban and rural areas, and the representatives from them would come to the legislature with an appreciation of the interests of both and with a desire, I believe, to serve both fairly and honestly.

For example, under the proposed bill, two of the representatives from Jefferson County would come from districts in the country outside the city of Louisville. Two of the Kenton County representatives would be from the rural portion of that county. Fayette has one representative from the county district, and so does Daviess and Campbell. Each representative from McCracken County would have half the city of Paducah and half the county area. The Boyd County representative would represent the whole county, much of which is rural, not just the city of Ashland.

The bill prepared by the House committee is a country boys' bill. You will not be misled by the foes of the constitution who seek to becloud the issue by counterfeit contentions that redistricting will result in legislative control being placed in the cities.

Legislators who are honorable and conscientious do not confine their interest to the individual districts from which they are elected. They regard themselves as representatives of all the people of Kentucky and seek to do the best they can for the whole state.

I have sufficient faith in the people of Kentucky to believe that a majority of the members of the House and Senate will always be composed of men who are honorable and sincere, men motivated by an earnest desire to serve the Commonwealth, regardless of what particular section they may represent. Therefore, I believe that the proposed House redistricting bill is a fair and honest one and one which can be passed and ought to be passed.

The senatorial redistricting bill which has passed the Senate is before you. It is the best that can be drawn for which it appears possible to obtain votes needed to pass it. It passed the Senate 29 to 8. I urge you to enact it into law without amendment.

There is great inequality in the present arrangement under which the people of Kentucky are represented in the Senate. Three senators are from districts with populations of between 30,000 and 40,000. Four districts have between 40,000 and 50,000. Seven senators represent from

50,000 to 60,000 people each. Five have only from 60,000 to 70,000. Seven districts have populations ranging from 70,000 to 80,000, and three have from 80,000 to 90,000 people. There are six members of the Senate from districts with populations of between 90,000 and 100,000. Two have from 100,000 to 150,000 people in their districts and one senator repesents 202,000 people.

No fair-minded person can defend such an arrangement as that. It scoffs at democracy, sneers at justice. The Senate districts now in effect must be changed so as to be brought into closer conformity with the constitution.

The bill which has passed the Senate is not perfect, but it comes as close to approaching the ideal as is possible under the circumstances, and it is a vast improvement over the existing system. Under this measure, there would be twenty-nine senators from districts having from 60,000 to 80,000 people. Eight districts would have from 80,000 to 93,000 people, and only one district would fall below the 60,000 mark.

The task of preparing a senatorial redistricting bill is complicated by the fact that senators are elected for four years; half of them are chosen every two years. Consequently, in redistricting, it must be remembered that there are nineteen holdover senators who must be left with districts. This complicates the problem to such an extent that it is not possible to come as close to the ideal as we would like. The bill the House now has before it is the best approach we can make to that ideal, and it is my insistent request that the House pass it speedily and without amendment.

I have been astonished to hear that some of you are unwilling to vote for redistricting because you have signed a pact in which you pledged yourselves to vote against all redistricting legislation. I am unwilling to give credence to such a rumor. But if there be those who, in a misguided moment, signed a round robin compact, it is your duty to withdraw from such an unworthy commitment. Is it consistent to lift your hand aloft and take an oath to uphold the constitution of Kentucky as you did, and then sign a compact in which you make a secret pledge that you will not uphold the constitution of the Commonwealth?

That constitution to which you swore to adhere orders you to redistrict the state of Kentucky at this time into 100 legislative districts and thirty-eight senatorial districts. It is an order that you should obey. It is an order with which you should comply now—without further delay and expense.

You should face the issue squarely. You should not try to evade voting on a redistricting bill by resorting to parliamentary trickery. I get the impression that some of you shrink from obeying the mandate of the constitution because of a fear that such may hurt you politically. It has been my observation that seldom is a public official injured politically by doing his duty. Failure to do one's duty is certain to be hurtful politically and otherwise because to do so results in loss of respect of the people. And one who dodges duty has less respect for himself. "The path of duty is the way to glory," said Tennyson.[1]

Most of you have made up your minds to heed the command of the constitution. Some of you are vascillating between duty and that which you regard as expediency. Others have closed their minds and refuse to recognize their obligation to obey the constitution. They are in the attitude of a woman who hurried away to a political meeting and announced that "I am going with an open, unbiased, unprejudiced mind to listen to what I am convinced in pure rubbish."

But before you ignore the challenge of duty, let me remind you that the constitution whose command you are inclined to disobey is the same constitution which guarantees to you the right to worship God according to the dictates of your conscience; it is the same constitution that guarantees you the right of acquiring and protecting your property; it is the same constitution which guarantees you the right of peaceable public assembly; it is the same constitution which guarantees to you the right of trial by jury, established freedom of the press, protects you from unreasonable search and seizure. Are you going to enjoy the liberties, accept the protection the constitution gives you and then close your ears to the command given in Section 33 as it orders the General Assembly every ten years to readjust legislative districts so as to provide equality in representation?

We have had a notable legislative session. The majority of you have supported the legislative program which I have asked you to vote for. In doing that you have supported worthy and constructive legislation. Wisdom of those statutes will become increasingly clear with the passing of time.

We come now to the last legislation on my program. While it is the last to be considered, it is first in importance. Unless we redistrict now it will be another decade before this vital action may be taken. You must not shut the door of hope in the face of those who have a right to expect you to obey the constitution. You must not vote to perpetuate inequality of representation for another ten years. I challenge you to recognize the fact that duty brings to you an opportunity to perform a statesmanlike service for Kentucky.

We have recently paid off a state debt and gotten the state back on the constitution in a financial way. I urge you to join me in getting Kentucky back on the constitution by passing a fair redistricting bill. Such action will bring great credit to you. It will make right regnant and justice triumphant.[2]

---

1. Alfred Tennyson (1809–1892), b. Somersby, England. Poet. Named poet laureate of the United Kingdom, 1850. *World Book Encyclopedia* (Chicago, 1959), 16:7973. Tennyson wrote, "The path of duty was the way to glory." "Ode on the Death of the Duke of Wellington," *The Poetical Works of Tennyson*, ed. G. Robert Strange (Boston, 1944), p. 225.

2. By Executive Order on June 25, 1942, the governor transferred $15,000 from his Emergency Fund to the legislature. The regular and special sessions had exhausted its $220,000 budget. For the redistricting measures that passed, see *Acts of the General Assembly, 1942*, Chapter 1 (S. B. 4), pp. 1021-30, and Chapter 2 (S. B. 10), pp. 1030-53.

STATE ADMINISTRATION

DEPARTMENT HEADS OF STATE GOVERNMENT
Frankfort / December 8, 1939

FROM and after this date you will please advise Mr. J. Lyter Donaldson by written memorandum or letter, whenever in your judgment it is advisable to remove, release, or transfer any employee in your department, accompanying such advice with your reasons for recommending such action, and you will forward this advice to Mr. Donaldson at least ten days prior to the date you think it advisable to make such change in present employment, and you will furnish Mr. J. Dan Talbott, commissioner of finance, with a copy of such memorandum.[1]

Hereafter, whenever in your judgment it is necessary for the efficient administration of your department to employ additional men or women in any capacity, you will likewise communicate with Mr. Lyter Donaldson, by written memorandum or letter, of your desire to be furnished with additional employees, advising him of the nature of the employment, the necessary qualifications, and the compensation to be paid. Such information should be furnished to Mr. Donaldson at least ten days in advance of the need in order that he may have sufficient time to make recommendations to the governor.

In order that there may be proper coordination of the various departments of the state government in administering the personnel, I will appreciate your adhering strictly to these policies, herein before outlined.[2]

---

1. J. Lyter Donaldson (1891–1960), b. Carrollton. Commissioner of highways, 1939–1943; lost gubernatorial election to Simeon S. Willis in 1943 by 8,100 votes: chairman, Democratic State Central Executive Committee, 1944. *Who's Who in*

Kentucky, 1936, p. 114, and Polly Gorman, secretary to Governor Bert Combs, June 17, 1978.

J. Dan Talbott (1883-1950), b. Nelson County. Commissioner of finance, 1939 –1943; state auditor; regional field representative, War Manpower Commission. Letter, Mrs. Robert E. Willett, daughter, Bardstown, March 26, 1978.

2. Faced with the possible stoppage of federal funds, the governor appointed a Merit System Committee to work out acceptable standards. The members were Henry Henderson, director of personnel; James W. Martin, professor, University of Kentucky; and James T. Norris, Ashland publisher.

MERIT SYSTEM
Frankfort / December 10, 1940

THIS is to thank you for your letter of December 6 and the interest expressed in our problems. My interest in the matter about which you wrote me is comparable to yours and quite as sincere.[1]

I shall suggest to the commissioner of welfare that the director of mental hygiene be that individual on the list, submitted by the council of the Kentucky Medical Association,[2] which is recommended by the advisory committee of the Kentucky Medical Association. This committee was created in 1938 at the request of Governor Chandler. The chairman of the committee is Dr. Gardner. Other members of the committee are outstanding physicians and my contact with them has convinced me that they are just as interested in doing that which is best as are you and I.

---

1. This letter was in reply to a letter from the Louisville League of Women Voters, signed by Mrs. Cary Tabb, president. She urged the governor to protect the commissioner of welfare, Margaret Woll, from political pressure in appointing a successor to Dr. Joseph G. Wilson who was retiring as director of the Division of Hospitals and Mental Hygiene. He had charged the state administration with political interference in appointments. Shortly afterward the governor dismissed Woll with instructions that her service must cease immediately. Louisville *Courier-Journal*, December 22, 1940.

Mrs. Tabb stated, "We trust you are as sincerely interested as we are in the program and that you have the same confidence as we have in the principles and application of the merit system. We await your reply." The governor did not comment on the merit system. The league released a statement expressing concern over the principle of the merit system, "an obvious and unavoidable question confronts the public: Why are key positions in so important a department as welfare being vacated by resignations of admittedly qualified personnel?" *Louisville Times*, December 13, 1940. The merit system was introduced in the Department of Welfare in 1940.

2. As provided in the Chandler-Wallis Act, 1938, the council of the Kentucky Medical Association submits three names to the commisioner of welfare who appoints the director with the governor's approval. *Acts of the General Assembly, Regular and First and Second Special Sessions, 1938*, p. 1179.

REFINANCING OF OUTSTANDING WARRANTS
Frankfort / January 9, 1941

GOVERNOR JOHNSON announced arrangements had been made to refinance the state's $4,097,400 outstanding warrants and save $102,294 in interest during the next three years.[1]

He stated that about two-thirds of the unpaid warrants bear 2.5 percent interest and the remainder 2 percent, and that they would be exchanged for a like total bearing 1 percent interest.

"It is the lowest interest rate in the history of Kentucky, and we got agreements for the exchange after two days of maneuvering with the banks."

He added that Treasurer Ernest E. Shannon[2] said "advance requests indicate a minimum of 90 percent subscription for the new warrants" and that in addition commitments from insurance companies, banks, and other institutions made up more than "ten times over subscription" of the remaining balance.[3]

---

1. The debt had been reduced to $6,153,214 at the end of May 1940. On June 8, 1940, the governor said no more payments would be made until well into the coming fiscal year since a large cash balance would be needed for the schools and for old age assistance. *State Journal*, June 9, 1940.

On July 1, 1941, the state had its first surplus at the end of a fiscal year since 1907; the general fund balance was $4,879,012.17. Since there was a total of $3,037,478.72 in outstanding warrants and approximately $500,000 in encumbrances, the net surplus was $1,34,533.45. The budget was underspent by $1,228,000. During the first fiscal year 1940–1941, the state called for payment $3,060,000 in interest-bearing accounts. *Lexington Herald*, July 2, 1941. On July 1,

1941, the state called for payment $1,000,100 in noninterest-bearing warrants, and on August 15, $968,800 in 1 percent interest-bearing warrants. *Lexington Herald,* August 5, 1941.

Johnson announced the last interest-bearing warrants, amounting to $495,000, had been called for payment March 25, 1942. "It speaks for itself. There's nothing romantic or spectacular about paying off a debt. You run into debt and crawl out. We've been a long time crawling out." Technically the state had outstanding warrants after March 25 since warrants totaling $29,578 had not be presented. *Richmond Daily Register,* March 14, 1942.

2. Ernest E. Shannon (1873–1955), b. Kansas. State representative, 1920; offered first free textbook law; commissioner of purchasing, 1926; auditor, 1935–1939; treasurer, 1939–1943; candidate for auditor, 1943. *Kentucky Directory, 1940–1941,* compiled by Frank K. Kavanaugh (Frankfort, Ky., 1940), p. 144, and telephone interview, Mrs. E. E. Shannon, June 20, 1978.

3. At the end of his first year in December 1940, the governor commented, "Ninety percent of the effort of the present administration has been for administrative efficiency." It has not been personally or politically popular and has necessitated refusing many favors requested by friends. "It's been a pleasant year, but it's also carried a lot of tedious work. I guess I've acted like any country newspaper editor would in the governor's office. I've tried to look after a large volume of detail. I've tried to keep expenses down and at the same time get efficient administration by requiring full reports from department and division heads. And I've read them and tried to improve upon what was being done. I didn't like the idea of so much detail, but just show me how it can be avoided." *Lexington Herald,* December 12, 1940, and *Cincinnati Enquirer,* December 13, 1940.

CHAMBER OF COMMERCE
Somerset / February 20, 1941

GOVERNOR JOHNSON discussed the securing of more tourist traffic for Kentucky highways. It is the ambition of his administration so to improve state parks that they will not only be attractive to Kentuckians but will bring tourists from surrounding states.

He had long known that Somerset was one of the best towns in Kentucky and that there were many contributing factors, but its enterprising, energetic business and professional men of vision were the principal reason for its steady and sustained growth. "Nothing makes a greater contribution to a town or community than a strong Chamber of Commerce." Before taking up the question of state finances, he expressed his admiration for Mr. Williams and Mr. Ben D. Smith.[1]

In recent years the state's leaders have been making an effort to advance the cause of good government. "I am glad tonight to be able to truthfully say that the state's financial condition is better than it has been since 1834. I am not presenting these figures as a personal achievement but as an achievement of able Kentuckians sincerely interested in advancing the cause of good government.

"Efficiency and economy are not spectacular. Yet 90 percent of Kentucky's problems are financial in nature. The state is trying to pay its debts and get back on the constitution."

The reduction of the state debt from $26 million five years ago to a little over $4 million has made Kentucky one of the most attractive states in the Union from the standpoint of those who pay taxes. The financial condition has so improved that it was recently possible to refinance the debt at 1 percent, the lowest interest rate in the state's history. Interest charges have been reduced from $1.3 million to $40,000. "This is an indication of the fact that we are making substantial progress toward a strong financial condition which we hope will result in increased benefits and relief to those who pay taxes."

Cutting the expenditures of government is very difficult without jeopardizing some of the state's major activities. The major portion of expenditures each year, aside for the Highway Department, are fixed by appropriations. About $20 million of the expenditures are in the form of fixed charges, such as education, social security and old age grants, and the courts, and cannot be cut. This leaves about $6 million to which the economies must be applied. He had stressed economy and some progress had been made. There are 1,331 fewer persons on the state payroll at present than a year ago, representing a monthly reduction of $64,447 in salaries. Much of the money has been saved in the Highway Department and will be used to extend the road system.

"During the fiscal year 1939–1940, your state government sent into Pulaski County for all governmental agencies $229,951. This does not look like we are always taking money out of your county and giving you nothing in return. The public schools received $158,000, the largest portion of this amount; $25,475 was in benefits for the indigent and old aged; $13,537 for the circuit court; $2,568 for the county tax commissioner; $25,062 for the rural highway program; and approximately $5,000 for the truck license fund. Only 147 Pulaskians paid state income taxes last year and this amounted to only $3,652. We shall continue the careful, cautious, prudent expenditure of the taxpayers' money."[2]

---

1. Cecil T. Williams (1887–1942), b. Somerset. Commissioner of rural highways, 1936–1942. Editor, *Somerset Journal*. Louisville *Courier-Journal*, October 19, 1942.

Judge Ben D. Smith (1891–1977), b. Somerset. Attorney. United States commissioner. Willis, *Kentucky Democracy*, 3:73-74, and letter, Senator John Rogers, Somerset, June 30, 1978.

2. The Pulaski County Chamber of Commerce does not have a copy of the speech. Letter, Lester B. Abbott, executive director, February 23, 1977.

TO THE CABINET
Frankfort / May 23, 1941

BECAUSE of developments with which you are familiar, it has appeared to be proper that I prepare and present to the members of this group a statement for your consideration and as the first business of the Cabinet,[1] if you will indulge me, I shall present this statement as quickly as possible. Although it is a little longer than I would have preferred, it has been prepared for the record as well as for your consideration.

The Governor's Cabinet was created and its functions defined by Chapter 1, Article 26, Section 1, of the Acts of the First Extraordinary Session of the General Assembly of 1936. Members of the cabinet are the governor, who is chairman, the secretary of state, the attorney general, the state treasurer, the commissioner of agriculture, labor and statistics, the superintendent of public instruction, the adjutant general, the commissioner of finance, the commissioner of revenue, the commissioner of highways, the commissioner of welfare, the commissioner of health, the commissioner of industrial relations, the chairman of the Public Service Commission, who is ex officio commissioner of the Department of Business Regulations, the commissioner of conservation, the state librarian, and the commissioner of the Department of Mines and Minerals. The law provides that the Governor's Cabinet shall consider such matters involving general administrative policies and procedure, relations between departments and other agencies, and desirable measures of cooperation between departments and other agencies, as the governor or any member may place before it, and shall advise and consult with the governor at his request on all matters affecting the welfare of the state and relating to the several departments and other agencies. The governor shall be the chairman of his cabinet. For the purposes of this act, the cabinet shall be deemed to be attached to the office of the governor and not to constitute a separate department or agency of the state.

> The deliberative functions of the Executive Cabinet provided by Chapter one hundred and fifty-five (155), Acts of the General Assembly of 1934, are hereby transferred to and vested in the Governor's Cabinet.
>
> The administration of all functions heretofore vested in the State Planning Board, as set out in Chapter twenty-nine (29) of the Acts of the General Assembly of 1934, are hereby transferred to and vested in the Governor's Cabinet.
>
> The Governor's private secretary shall serve as secretary of the Governor's Cabinet and shall be paid Three Thousand Dollars ($3,000.00) annually for such services in addition to his salary as private secretary to the governor.

The Governor's Cabinet succeeded to all of the deliberative functions of the Executive Cabinet which was created by Chapter 155 of the Acts of the General Assembly of 1934, and the Executive Cabinet was abolished.

The Governor's Cabinet also succeeded to all administrative functions of the State Planning Board which was created by Chapter 29 of the Acts of the General Assembly of 1934. The State Planning Board was abolished by the 1936 Governmental Reorganization Act.

The functions of the Governor's Cabinet are advisory and the cabinet was designed to aid in correlating the administrative functions of the various state departments and agencies. Those functions have been effectively performed by frequent consultation and conferences between the governor and individual members of the cabinet and the governor's secretary, who is ex officio secretary of the cabinet. One member of the Governor's Cabinet has recently complained because I have not called a formal meeting of the cabinet at least once a month. This was the first intimation that I have received that any member of the cabinet desired a formal meeting of the cabinet. Had any member of the cabinet at any time requested that I call a formal meeting of the cabinet, I would have gladly complied with the request.

The Governor's Cabinet has functioned continuously and daily. I have been of the opinion that good administration could best be advanced by frequent consultation and conferences with individual members of the cabinet. I have followed that plan. Each of you has found the governor accessible for discussion of your problems. Each of you has found the governor's secretary accessible for discussion of your problems. In instances where matters of administration have arisen involving more than one department, I have conferred with you in groups of two or more in an effort to establish the best procedure, and in an effort to formulate the most effective and constructive program relating thereto. That method, I believe, has been more effective in improving administrative efficiency. I have been under the impression that the plan followed was more effective than referring such matters to a formal meeting of the full cabinet for discussion. I believe the cabinet can be more beneficially used day by day in discussions between the governor and individual members than by formal monthly meetings of the entire membership. In the future I propose that regular monthly meetings of the cabinet be held, but I hope that each of the individual members of the cabinet will continue the practice of consulting with the governor and the governor's secretary frequently on problems concerning their respective departments and concerning any constructive suggestions which may occur to any of you relative to improving the state service in any way.

The governor's secretary, who is ex officio secretary of the Governor's Cabinet, at the governor's direction has gone into the various departments from time to time and has spent much time in consultation with department and division heads in an effort to be helpful and in promoting and developing improved public service. The law specifies that this shall be the duty of the secretary and in my opinion he has performed all the services heretofore delegated by statute to the secretary of the Executive Cabinet. He has familiarized himself with department procedure, he has reported his findings and conclusions to the governor, and has made suggestions which several of you have told me were very helpful and constructive. The only other thing which the secretary could have done would have been to take and keep minutes of formal meetings of the cabinet had those meetings been held.

It is not practical to draw a line of differentiation between the duties performed or to be performed by the governor's secretary as secretary to the governor on the one hand and the duties performed or to be performed by the governor's secretary as ex officio secretary of the cabinet on the other. No definite line of division can be drawn because the very nature of those duties deals with the general administrative problems and policies which require the consideration of the governor, both as governor and as chairman of the cabinet.

I have followed the method of using the Governor's Cabinet which seemed to me to contain possibilities of making it most useful. One critical member of the cabinet has sought to convey to the public the impression that because we have not had formal monthly meetings of the entire cabinet, the functions vested in the cabinet and in the cabinet's secretary by law have not been performed. That is not true. Those functions have been performed and I think efficiently performed in the manner which I have outlined.

The governor and his secretary have at all times earnestly desired and sought the cooperation of each department and division head and the cooperation of each and every member of this cabinet. The governor has been pleased that he has had the cooperation and constructive assistance and suggestions of the department and division heads and all of the members of the cabinet with one exception. The governor needs your counsel, your cooperation, your constructive suggestions and advice, and I believe that you will all agree that the governor and his secretary have at all times demonstrated their desire and their readiness to extend to each of you their fullest measures of cooperation and to receive from you suggestions and advice. The governor is certain that there has been no injury to the state government because formal monthly meetings of the entire cabinet have not been held; and had any member of the cabinet at any time indicated a desire for such meetings, the governor would have called such meetings just as this meeting has been called because a member of the cabinet has expressed his view that such formal meetings should be held in technical compliance with the letter of the law.

I am sure that the state government is being carefully, efficiently, and economically administered. That is the result of the conscientious and competent direction which each of you is giving your department. Should there come to the attention of any of you any instance of improper official conduct or any instance of inefficiency or misconduct on the part of any employee of the state, I shall be grateful if you will give me the information that we, working in cooperation, may together correct it.

The duties of the Governor's Cabinet as the successor to the State Planning Board have been performed and are being performed with care and with thorough study and consideration under the direction of the members of the cabinet. We have sought to confine ourselves to research and planning, giving first consideration to the most pressing and immediate needs, but not to the exclusion of consideration and planning for constructive future development.

The planning as relates to highways is one of the most important phases. That planning has been done under the direction of the commissioner of highways in collaboration and cooperation with the United States Bureau of Public Roads and other federal agencies. In this manner has been assembled much useful information that has been used daily and is being daily used in the highway program. The state Highway Planning Survey has provided and is providing most useful information for modernizing, maintaining, and improving the state road system.

The greatest immediate need for buildings and capital improvements is in the Welfare Department. The planning of this program has been conducted jointly by the Welfare Department, represented by the commissioner of welfare, Dr. Frost, the Finance Department, represented by Commissioner Talbott and State Engineer Wyatt,[2] the superintendents of the respective state institutions and the Advisory Committee on Mental Hygiene of the Kentucky Medical Association.

A new cell block with a capacity for 550 inmates is nearing completion at the Eddyville prison, which will relieve the crowded condition in this institution. A water system adequate for the prison is the next important need. Plans for this improvement have been made.

A survey of the respective institutions to determine those improvements most needed has been made. Reconstruction of the boiler plant at the Western State Hospital could not longer be delayed; and contract has been let for the installation of three new boilers to assure adequate heating facilities. The water supply at this institution is uncertain, depending upon ample rainfall. Plans are under way to build an additional dam in the stream from which the water is procured in order to insure at all times an adequate water supply.

A pressing need at Central State Hospital was found to be refrigeration plant. The underground stream distribution system was found to be in a serious condition necessitating replacement. The water storage tank is not ample to supply necessary pressure. Plans to correct these most serious deficiencies are under way. Work has been started on complete electrical rewiring of the institution to eliminate fire hazards.

A girls' dormitory is nearing completion at Greendale Reform School which will greatly improve facilities at that institution. The sewage disposal plant at Greendale requires extensive repairs and such are planned within the coming fiscal year.

An additional boiler is being installed at Eastern State Hospital. Substantial improvement has been made in this institution as a result of the renovating program. The electrical wiring has been replaced, walls plastered and painted, and floors improved. A similar program of renovation is planned for each of the other state hospitals.

Reconstruction of the Capitol dome is nearing completion, and plans have been made for repairs of the Capitol along the northeast terrace.[3] This work will be started early in the next fiscal year. Most of the building problems are of an engineering and architectural nature, subject, of course, to the availability of money.

In the Department of Revenue a research program has been under way for several months which is seeking to assemble data on the industrial development and lack of it in Kentucky in the last quarter of a century. It seeks to analyze the entire industrial picture in the state. It is hoped, too, that this information will reveal what has been happening industrially in Kentucky and the causes thereof to the end that plans may be made for stimulating industrial growth.

With the National Park Service as cosponsor and with Commissioner

Clyde Reeves directing the work, a study has been made of parks, parkways, and recreational areas of Kentucky.

I recount these activities as evidence of the fact that the cabinet has functioned and has performed the functions contemplated by law. This planning has been done by members of the cabinet under the direction of the governor and the head of the department within which the responsibility lies. I have not undertaken to summarize or to recount all of the planning that has been done or to review the constant studies and plans which are in progress or which have been developed by your respective departments.

It has recently been charged by the attorney general,[4] who is a member of this cabinet, that the salary drawn by the secretary of the cabinet and the salaries drawn by two stenographers were illegally paid or drawn. The basis for that charge seems to have been that because there has been no formal meeting of the full cabinet, there technically could have been no duties performed by the secretary or by the stenographers. However, I am sure that each of you know and will agree that the secretary and the stenographers have daily and efficiently performed their duties and that they have performed the functions contemplated by law and contemplated by the appropriation made by the General Assembly of $4,000 per annum for the employment of administrative assistants to the cabinet. The statute specifically provides that "the cabinet shall be deemed to be attached to the office of the governor and not to constitute a separate department or agency of the state." The law specifically provides that the "governor's private secretary shall serve as secretary of the Governor's Cabinet and shall be paid $3,000.00 annually for such services in addition to his salary as private secretary to the governor." After payment of the secretary's salary, which is fixed by statute at $3,000 per annum, there is nothing in the law which prohibits the expenditure of the remainder of the $4,000 per annum appropriated by the General Assembly for clerical or stenographic services. In fact, that was the purpose for which it was appropriated, and those who have done this work have earned every cent which they have been paid. I am sure that each of you know that the secretary and the stenographers who have been paid out of the appropriation referred to have been on the job daily, that each of them has worked hard, that each of them has rendered efficient services, and that each of them has earned every cent which they have drawn. As governor and as chairman of the cabinet, I have been not only entirely satisfied with the services which they have rendered and with the work which they have performed, but I deeply appreciate the character of services and the efficiency with which they have performed these services.[5]

---

1. Members present were George Glenn Hatcher, secretary of state; Ernest Shannon, treasurer; William May, commissioner of agriculture; John Brooker, superintendent of public instruction; John A. Polin, adjutant general; J. Dan Talbott, director of finance; Clyde Reeves, commissioner of revenue; Lyter Donaldson, commissioner of highways; W. A. Frost, commissioner of welfare; A. T. McCormack, commissioner of health; John Kirtley, commissioner of business regulations; Charles Fennell, commissioner of conservation; Ethel Cantrill, librarian; Moss Patterson commissioner of mines and minerals.

2. Ralph C. Wyatt, director, New Land and Buildings Division, Department of Welfare. The division later was transferred to the Finance Department and given charge of engineering and construction plans of other departments.

3. On December 12, 1940, Johnson said, "While there has been a good deal of talk about repairing the dome of the Capitol, no one seems interested in the fact that at the same time we are also repairing the roof all over the Capitol building, a very necessary thing and a protection to the investment the state has in the Capitol building." *Lexington Herald*, December 12, 1940, and *Cincinnati Enquirer*, December 13, 1940. The first major renovation was completed in 1942 and cost $189,000. The building was constructed in 1910 at a cost of $1,820,000. Louisville *Courier-Journal*, August 31, 1942.

4. Hubert Meredith (1880–1957), b. Greeneville. Attorney general, 1937–1943; candidate for attorney general, 1943; commonwealth attorney, Seventh Judicial District, 1922–1928. *Who's Who in Kentucky, 1936*, p. 281, and Louisville *Courier-Journal*, January 1, 1957.

5. A discussion followed the governor's address. Talbott commented that the law only requires the governor to call special meetings of the cabinet if asked and concluded that Meredith was just as negligent as the other members because he had not requested one. May presented a resolution that approved Johnson's report and criticized the actions of the "critical member." Brooker served as chairman when the resolution was adopted. All members present signed it. Talbott stated that people had wondered what kind of governor Johnson would make. "Now you have been in some twenty months and . . . the people who are the thinking part of our population unanimously have come to the conclusion that in a healthy way you are making a good governor and . . . there is a genuine, fine affection and respect growing in your favor daily. . . . I can frankly say I always said Happy had the most loyal team any man ever had as governor, but I now want to say you have a better team than Happy had." Johnson expressed gratitude "for the kind expressions of Mr. Talbott and from others of you since this criticism developed" and said that no governor had ever had associated with him a finer group of competent, intelligent, and hard-working individuals.

IRREGULARITIES IN THE DIVISION OF PURCHASES
Frankfort / July 1, 1941

SOME of the complaints referred to in your letter have been brought to my attention and I have been investigating them.[1] I am extremely anxious to have any information or evidence which can be produced from any sources that may substantiate or tend to substantiate any complaints relating to purchases made by the state.

I appreciate your offer to furnish an attorney to aid in investigating the rumors, but as head of the legal department I insist that you participate with me in conducting the investigation and in producing all the evidence possible relative to the rumors and charges to which you refer.[2]

---

1. Johnson replied by letter to one from Attorney General Meredith concerning the Division of Purchases. Meredith wrote that he had "oral and written complaints of alleged irregularities" which included; Purchases are not always made by competitive bidding, but are split into small orders and bought on an emergency basis; Specifications are framed to shut out prospective bidders; Favoritism is shown certain bidders; Certain agents, employees, and receiving clerks have accepted favors from successful bidders and salesmen; Successful bidders are called upon to donate to "a so-called campaign fund," in proportion to the size of sales. The governor announced public hearings on the charges and said that he, the attorney general, and Commissioner of Finance Talbott would preside. No date was set for the investigation.

2. Executive Order, September 3, 1941, provided for an investigation of the Division of Purchases. Louisville attorney and former Appellate Court Chief Justice Richard Priest Dietzman was named to head the committee. Other members were Sam. W. Eskew, Louisville accountant, and Charles J. Cronin, Jr., Newport, hotel executive versed in credit and purchasing.

In a brief written statement, Johnson said, "Not only is there assured a thorough, impartial, unbiased and correct investigation of the activity of the Purchasing Division since my inauguration, but a critical examination of its operations will be made in an effort to find out whether there may be improvement in the function of the division." Louisville *Courier-Journal*, September 4, 1941.

The committee's report was released by the governor on February 16, 1942: "Your committee may at once clear the atmosphere by saying that it found no evidence of any dishonesty on the part of any member of the Division of Purchases, despite rumors to the contrary, none of which were substantiated by the evidence before the committee. However, the committee did find evidence of inefficiency, negligence, and favoritism as we shall more fully discuss hereinafter."

The committee recommended: That the division prepare fixed standards of quality and quantity so that "real competitive conditions may be obtained"; that the law be changed to require vendors' registration with the division rather than the secretary of state; that invitations to bid be "as broad in number as possible"; that "adequte procedure be adopted for checking goods when received" and that the University of Kentucky and the Highway Department laboratories be made available to the division for this purpose by legislation; that the division and the heads of all buying agencies exercise continuous effort to cut "needless use" of emergency purchases; that more detailed records be maintained by the division; that an attorney be provided for the commissioner of finance; that the division have at least two additional experienced buyers, preferably skilled in lines other than those in which the presently employed buyers are trained.

The governor said, "We are going to comply with the recommendations as far as possible. I have asked Judge Dietzman to draft legislation to carry out the recommendations." *Lexington Herald*, February 17, 1942.

CONSTITUTIONAL LIMIT ON SALARY
Frankfort / September 19, 1941

GOVERNOR JOHNSON ordered[1] a court test of whether the state Public Service Comission can continue to pay its principal consultant, Hugh B. Bearden,[2] more than $5,000 a year, the constitutional salary limit. He said that he did not know whether suits would be brought in behalf of some dozen others affected by Finance Commissioner Talbott's order, chiefly officers and professors at the University of Kentucky and the state teachers colleges,[3] whose salaries have been above the limit.

The governor authorized employment of Leslie W. Morris[4] to file the suit. He added that Morris's pay, to come from Public Service Commission funds, would be determined by the governor at the end of litigation. He pointed out that the attorney general, who advised Talbott against continuing to permit the salary limit to be exceeded, will oppose the suit and that he could not represent both sides.[5]

---

1. Decision to bring the suit followed Talbott's announcement on July 29, 1941, that he would adhere to the $5,000 limit in approving salary checks for state officials and employees.

2. Technical consultant to Public Service Commission since 1938. His salary in 1941 was $7,800.

3. On October 15, 1941, the governor authorized a court test to determine whether the University of Kentucky could pay its officers and teachers more than $5,000 a year. He employed J. Donald Dinning to bring suit on behalf of the university. Named in the suit were Dr. Donovan, president ($8,500), and ten other officers and teachers receiving salaries in excess of $5,000. Since the attorney general could not represent both the university and the finance commissioner, outside counsel was required.

Meredith was given permission by Circuit Judge William B. Ardery to include in the Bearden test case not only President Donovan and the ten persons on his staff but also President James H. Richmond, Murray State Teachers College, and three attorneys, Clifford E. Smith, Samuel M. Rosenstein, and Clyde L. Reed—all of whom Meredith said received more than $5,000 a year in state funds. He hoped that the suit would be decided in time for the 1942 General Assembly to submit a proposed constitutional amendment authorizing higher salaries if it desired. *Lexington Herald*, October 16, 1941.

4. Leslie W. Morris (1885–1961), b. Woodford County. Banker. President, Franklin County Bar Association. State senator for unexpired term and for a special session, 1917. Willis, *Kentucky Democracy*, 3:54, 57. Executive Order, November 25, 1942, commended Morris for service of a high order and the successful conclusion of the suit. It authorized the Public Service Commission to compensate him in the amount of $2,500.

5. On October 27, 1941, Judge Ardery ruled that salaries and commissions paid for professional services are exempt from the $5,000 a year limit. "Section 246 means exactly what it says—that it applies only to public officers—and it is just as plain in its terms as is the section that limits the public debt to $500,000 without a vote of the people. It [Section 246] could not be expanded to take in a class of people who were not public officers." Louisville *Courier-Journal*, October 28, 1941.

OUT-OF-STATE TRIPS
Frankfort / September 23, 1941

DESIGNATION of state officials whom he authorizes to visit other states as his messengers, under an 1893 act, has been started by Governor Johnson as what he terms a legal way to pay their expenses.

The new method was used in authorizing G. Moss Patterson[1] to attend a national defense conference in Washington designed to increase the nation's coal output. In approving Patterson's expenses up to a maximum of $100, the governor wrote: "I hereby appoint and authorize you to go in my stead and as my express in the attendance of this conference."[2]

---

1. G. Moss Patterson (1901–1968), b. Pineville. Head, Department of Mines and Minerals, 1940–1944; emergency coal mine coordinator, 1941; West Kentucky and Island Creek Coal Company, retired 1965. Letter, Edwin McGaw, Madisonville, April 11, 1978.

2. The governor acted under Section 345 of the Kentucky Statutes which authorized up to six cents a mile allowance when certified by the governor as necessary for any person employed by him "as an express to carry his dispatches to any place in or out of this state."

In December 1940 Attorney General Meredith had released a letter to the governor in which he indicated that state officials and employees had spent $40,000 to $60,000 illegally in traveling outside Kentucky in the previous four years. The governor replied that it was Meredith's duty to recover any "unauthorized or illegal payments."

The governor wrote Finance Commissioner Talbott not to approve for payment out-of-state travel expense accounts until they have been submitted to and approved by the attorney general, "except in such cases where the officer or employee or the head of the particular department certifies" the trip was on "official business." He requested Talbott to furnish copies of Meredith's letter to all state officials and to the heads of the state institutions and to advise them that "strict conformity therewith shall be required." Louisville *Courier-Journal*, December 3, 1940.

Meredith then sued Talbott to recover $45,000 spent by state personnel on conventions and conferences in other states during the four years ended June 30, 1940. His suit was based upon a Court of Appeals ruling that the state could not pay for out-of-state trips except for official business.

In November 1941 Talbott advised the governor that all state officers and employees should obtain a court order approving payment of out-of-state travel expenses "essential to the necessary performance of the duties of those state employees." He refused to approve any more out-of-state trips because of the attorney general's suit and because Meredith had given him conflicting opinions on individual cases. *Richmond Daily Register*, November 7, 1941.

On December 16, 1941, the Court of Appeals announced its decision in *Reeves, Com'r of Revenue* v. *Talbott, Com'r of Finance*, 289 Ky. 581, 159 S.W. 2d 51. Reeves filed the required forms for out-of-state travel with Talbott. Talbott did not act on the request because of Meredith's suit. The attorney general disapproved it. Reeves sought a writ of mandamus to require Talbott to approve his travel application. The circuit court denied his request. The Court of Appeals reversed the lower court and held that Reeves's request should have been approved. Joseph J. Leary was the attorney for Talbott in the suit by Meredith and the attorney for Reeves in his suit against Talbott. He advised Reeves to initiate his suit and delayed the Meredith one until the court had ruled on the Reeves case. Following the Reeves decision, Meredith withdrew his suit against Talbott since the case was now moot. Interview with J. J. Leary, Frankfort, November 3, 1978.

In November 1939 Johnson appointed Commissioner of Agriculture-elect William H. May as his representative to go to Virginia, North Carolina, South Carolina, Georgia, Tennessee, and Washington, D.C., to obtain information to create a Bureau of Markets. Executive Order, November 24, 1939.

ADMINISTRATIVE ORGANIZATION OF REVENUE DEPARTMENT
Frankfort / March 5, 1942

BY virtue of the authority vested in the commissioner of revenue and the governor of the Commonwealth by the Reorganization Act, the said commissioner with the approval of the governor, hereby modifies the previous organization of the Department of Revenue provided in the administrative order of May 19, 1939, so that on and after March 6, 1942, the said department shall be organized as follows:

1. The commissioner of revenue, aided by an executive assistant, shall be responsible to the governor for administration of the revenues of the Commonwealth and shall have full direction of the work performed by the several divisions herein authorized. The commissioner shall also exercise such supervision as he deems appropriate over administration of tax revenues which may, under the Reorganization Act, be entrusted to other departments.

2. The Division of Income Taxation, under the direction of the commissioner, shall administer the income, corporation license, franchise, bank deposits, building and loan association, inheritance and estate taxes. To facilitate this work the division is divided into three sections, one having charge of income and corporation license taxes, one of miscellaneous corporation taxes, and the other of death taxes.

3. The Division of Excises, under the direction of the commissioner, shall administer gasoline, oil production, other motor fuels, utility gross receipts, alcohol consumers', alcohol production and import, amusement, cigarette, racing, and store license taxes. To facilitate this work the division is divided into three sections, one having charge of gasoline, oil production, other motor fuels, and utility gross receipts taxes, one of alcohol consumers' and alcohol production and import taxes, and the other of amusement, cigarette, racing, and store license taxes.

4. The Division of Local Relations, under the direction of the commissioner, shall administer the motor vehicle operator's license, the motor vehicle registration tax, the motor usage tax, the property taxes (other than those on franchise corporations, building and loan association, and bank stock and bank deposits), and occupational license taxes. To facilitate this work the division is divided into three sections, one having charge of the administration of the motor vehicle operator's licenses, one having charge of administration of the motor vehicle registration and usage taxes, and one having charge of the property and license taxes

hereby vested for administrative purposes in the Division of Local Relations.

5. The Division of Research and Statistics, under the direction of the commissioner, shall perform the statistical and research functions contemplated by the Reorganization Act.

6. The Service Division, under the direction of the commissioner, shall perform such services for the other divisions of the department as the commissioner deems appropriate. The division includes the accounts and collections, property and miscellaneous, files, proving, back tax, and stenographic sections.

7. The Field Division, under the direction of the commissioner, shall be responsible for the execution of the activities of the department in the field as may be requested by the other divisions of the department.

LEGAL SERVICES
Frankfort / March 20, 1942

RECEIPT is acknowledged of your letter which came to my attention after having read it in the press. I am deeply grateful for your solicitude. Your continued practice of writing letters for the press before furnishing your advice to me or to other state officials is not at all convincing to me that you now have, any more than you have had in the past, either the desire or the inclination to assist us in rendering public service. In view of the persistent, constant efforts on your part to impugn the motives of practically every other state official, it is hard for them or for me to conceive of your attitude having so changed that you may now be willing to render . . . sincere conscientious and constructive legal advice or other legal services.

For a lawyer, even though he be an attorney general or an assistant attorney general, to be of service to a client requires that the lawyer demonstrate by his actions that the client is entitled to have confidence in his sincerity and purpose, and in the legal advice or services of the attorney.

So sacred, necessary, and important is this factor of confidence in the relationship of attorney and client that there is no better established principle of law then that this relationship be protected by law and by judicial decision in keeping inviolate all information obtained through such relationship by the attorney, who is not only legally but ethically charged with the duty of maintaining and protecting that confidential relationship . . . .

Being a newspaperman myself, no one recognizes more than I the right or desirability of the public to be fully informed through the press of all official acts of any officer or state employee. Nevertheless, I believe that any officer or employee is entitled to seek and obtain the advice of his attorney on any contemplated plan or program, or on any question, before acting upon such matter.

I believe such advice should be given direct to the officer or state employee, rather than through the press. If that advice be acted upon or not followed, then it is certainly a matter of public record, to which the press is entitled. . . .

It does not seem to me to be proper for the attorney to deliberately and designedly seek every opportunity to propagandize through the press his personal venom or prejudices, or to impugn the purposes or motives of the officer who, in good faith, requests the attorney's advice.

Your own personal attitude and conduct has been so constantly and so consistently at variance with the views which I have hereinabove expressed that neither I nor, I believe, any other state official is justified in believing that your personal or official attitude or intent has changed, or that confidence can now be placed in your expressed willingness to render unbiased, fair, and impartial official services in spite of your personal venom, prejudices, and desire to be recognized as a leader of all opposition to this administration.

The Department of Welfare was losing so much uncollected money that private attorneys were employed, as the law authorizes. Between 1929 and 1932, the sum of $16,471 was collected. In the next four years, from 1933 to 1936, collections increased to $106,225.

In the four-year period from 1937 to 1940, when services of Messrs. Reed and Rosenstein[1] have been used, net collections totaled $127,365, an increase over collections by the attorney general of 670 percent. In the year 1941 there was collected $26,669.

The Department of Welfare will not profit from saving the commissions paid for collecting this money if it fails to receive the revenue it anticipates from this source. The 25 percent commission paid for these collections is comparable to that charged by collection agencies.[2]

If your office will collect these claims and maintain the volume of income from this source that has been realized the last four years, Commissioner Frost and I shall be delighted.[3]

---

1. Clyde L. Reed (1905–), b. Brownsville. Resides in Louisville. Franklin County attorney, 1939–1945. At that time attorney in the firm of Smith and Leary. Telephone interview, Clyde L. Reed, September 12, 1978.

Samuel Murray Rosenstein (1909–), b. Frankfort. Resides in Miami, Florida. City prosecutor, Frankfort, 1933–1941. Acting county attorney, Franklin County, 1941–1942; at that time attorney in the firm of Smith and Leary; judge, United States Customs Court, 1968–1971. *Who's Who in Kentucky, 1936,* p. 347, and letter, S. M. Rosenstein, August 14, 1978.

2. In November 1942 the governor authorized the legal firm of Smith and Leary to collect these claims and to serve as attorneys in any legal proceedings connected with their collection. Meredith stated in February 1941 that the state was paying an average of $10,500 a year in commissions and that half of that amount could be saved. In a letter to Welfare Commissioner Frost, he said that Reed and Rosenstein had collected on their 25 percent contract $180,531.54 since July 2, 1936, and that their commissions totaled $45,956.89. *Louisville Times,* February 3, 1941.

3. The governor consented to accept the legal services of M. B. Holifield, first assistant attorney general, for himself and the Department of Finance, provided "General Holifield is authorized by you to exercise his own independent judgment in all legal matters referred to him." He agreed to a six-month trial period for the attorney general's department to collect board bills from solvent inmates of the mental hospitals or from families. "If it is demonstrated by your office that it is to the best interest of the department of Welfare that your office continue to handle the collection of those claims, this arrangement will be extended." The governor set the trial period to ascertain whether the attorney general's office could equal the four-year collection record of $127,365 set by Reed and Rosenstein. Louisville *Courier-Journal,* March 24, 1942.

LEGALITY OF 1942 APPROPRIATIONS
Frankfort / June 17, 1942

WITH reference to Attorney General Meredith's suit attacking the legality of an appropriation for $11,270,000 for emergencies and deficiencies for the current fiscal year,[1] Governor Johnson said: "It is very unfortunate and there is no necessity for it except for the interference of the attorney general. The record of what is done with these funds is on file and open to everybody. The cruelest thing about it is Meredith's claim that it will be used for a slush fund."

He said that out of the $200,000 civil defense fund for the current year, he had made only three transfers, naming them as $3,400 for fighting spring forest fires, $2,500 for accountants to carry out the salary deduction war bond buying program, and $15,000 to Morehead State Teachers College to enable it to buy material and take advantage of an opportunity for navy men to be trained there. He added that it was strictly a loan to be repaid out of the rent the government would pay Morehead.

He noted that the deficiency and emergency funds for civil defense and for highway patrol expansion were authorized by the legislature upon "insistence of the War Department," and took occasion to retort to Meredith's charge that many of the funds were intended for use in next year's gubernatorial campaign.[2]

---

1. Finance Commissioner Talbott announced that the June payrolls for the state highway patrol and the construction and engineering division of the Highway Department had been held up pending the outcome of the suit.

2. The Court of Appeals ruled on August 24, 1942, that the $11,270,000 appropriation could be spent at the discretion of the governor. The ruling, unanimous except for the absence of Judge W. H. Rees, declared there was no basis for Meredith's charge that such legislative delegation of authority to spend money was unconstitutional. The appropriation included $320,000 deficiency appropriation for 1941–1942, money for prison and hospital improvement, an athletic field house at the University of Kentucky, civil defense, expanding the state highway patrol, architects' fees, acquiring land for Cumberland Gap National Park, new buildings and land. *Commonwealth ex. rel. Meredith, Atty. Gen.*, v. *Johnson, Governor, et al.*, 292 Ky. 288, 166 S.W. 2d. 409 (1942). Johnson remarked, "It is fortunate for the administration of the state's fiscal affairs that the Court of Appeals has stricken the handcuffs which 'mouthing Meredith' tried to place on the state government." Louisville *Courier-Journal*, August 26, 1942.

The court dismissed a petition for a rehearing by Meredith in September 1942 on grounds that it was "disrespectful and contemptible" and not written in language "becoming a member of the bar." Meredith charged that the judges "expect the administration crowd to raise their salaries when the General Assembly meets in January 1944," and he asserted that "the court expects the limitations on state salaries ($5,000) to be removed next year by adoption of a constitutional amendment." Advised of Meredith's declaration, Johnson discussed the Meredith situation with newsmen but prohibited quotation. *Lexington Herald*, September 27, 1942.

On December 4, 1942, the court gave final approval for the governor's right to allocate emergency funds by denying another petition for a rehearing by Meredith. Johnson was represented by Joseph J. Leary of the firm of Smith and Leary. See Executive Orders, dated June 3, July 17, and December 9, 1942.

ASSESSMENT OF STATE EMPLOYEES FOR CAMPAIGN FUNDS
Frankfort / July 2, 1942

GOVERNOR JOHNSON declared state employees' contributions for the August primary elections were entirely voluntary. "Meredith's conscience was not so acute when contributions of employees were being expended for his political advancement."[1]

---

1. Meredith had obtained an order from Franklin Circuit Court restraining the governor and four officials from collecting, and state employees from contributing, campaign funds. The suit declared that a 2 percent assessment of employees' salaries had been started.

The order was a temporary one issued by the circuit court clerk. Circuit Judge Ardery permanently enjoined the governor and his four associates on July 9, 1942, from levying the assessment. He held, however, that nothing in the writ would prohibit the officials from "requesting" donations nor prohibit employees or citizens from contributing voluntarily. Louisville *Courier-Journal*, July 10, 1942.

The Court of Appeals sustained the injunction on July 14, 1942, and sent the case back to the Circuit Court to be heard on its merits. Joseph J. Leary represented the governor and his associates. Louisville *Courier-Journal* and *Kentucky Post*, July 14, 1942. The case was never pressed to a conclusion. Telephone interview with J. J. Leary, October 30, 1978. On July 16, 1942, Johnson charged that Meredith had withdrawn as a candidate for a seat on the Court of Appeals because he had failed to arrange a "deal" whereby he would discontinue attacks on the administration if the governor would obtain the withdrawal of Judge Gus Thomas as his opponent. "I regarded Meredith so unfit for service as a judge of the Court of Appeals that I did not entertain his dishonorable proposals for an instant." *Cincinnati Enquirer*, July 17, 1942.

The issue of assessing state employees was not new. In commenting on a report that state employees would be assessed for the fall election campaign, Johnson said on August 31, 1940, that he believed all should aid but that he opposed the use of "pressure." "I haven't even heard the report and don't believe it's being circulated," he replied to a query whether it was true that employees would be "assessed" 2 percent of their annual salaries. "I'm going to contribute to the campaign myself and I think all state employees should." Louisville *Courier-Journal*, September 1, 1940. On March 28, 1941, Meredith charged in a letter to Johnson that state employees were being forced to contribute 1 percent of their salaries toward a state administration campaign fund and challenged him to stop it. The governor declined to comment. Louisville *Courier-Journal*, March 29, 1941.

APPOINTMENT OF G. LAWRENCE TUCKER AS LEGAL COUNSEL
Frankfort / August 27, 1942

IN announcing the appointment of G. Lawrence Tucker[1] as legal counsel for Finance Commissioner Talbott and himself, Governor Johnson referred to the opinion of the Court of Appeals which upheld a 1942 act[2] authorizing state departments and agencies to hire counsel independently of the attorney general's office. He noted that, while the court regarded the law as constitutional, it commented that it was "fraught with opportunities for abuse and extravagance."

"There will be no abuses, and the authority given under the law will be used with caution and discretion. Where the legislative act authorized employment of a lawyer at $5,000, we have employed a good one at $4,000."[3]

He took exception to the attorney general's statement that the measure was a "ripper bill," passed in retaliation for his numerous attacks on administration policies.

"If we had wanted to 'rip' him, we could have 'ripped' him. We had the votes to do it. We could have simply appropriated $5,000 a year for his salary and no more. The constitution says nothing about assistants."

He added that at his own request the measure was worded to provide that it should not affect the pay or tenure of the assistant attorneys general or prevent any department calling on the attorney general for legal aid, and added, "We also gave him his regular appropriation."[4]

---

1. G. Lawrence Tucker (1907–   ), b. Cynthiana. Grant County attorney for four years; legal counsel to the governor, 1942–1944; commonwealth attorney, 1951–   . Letter, G. L. Tucker, March 22, 1978.

2. *Acts of the General Assembly, 1942*, Chapter 106, pp. 525-27. The Court of Appeals declared Kentucky's mother state, Virginia, in its first constitution created the office of attorney general without describing the duties and that all Kentucky constitutions have authorized the General Assembly to prescribe them. The court cited Sections 91 and 93 of the present Kentucky constitution to support this view. *Johnson, Governor*, v. *Commonwealth ex rel. Meredith, Atty. Gen.*, 291 Ky. 829, 165 S.W. 2d. 820 (1942). Tucker was the first one to be appointed following the validation of the act by the court.

3. The executive order, dated August 27, 1942, appointing Tucker stated that Talbott had requested an attorney for his department and added: "Whereas, the Honorable Hubert Meredith, Attorney General, in a statement before the Legislative Council, said that in his opinion the Commissioner of Finance needed the

services of a lawyer but that he was unable to provide such services; and "Whereas, much confusion has arisen by reason of the fact that the Attorney General of Kentucky has, in numerous instances instituted action and proceedings against various officials of the Commonwealth or selected, in a contest between officials, which of the two officials he would represent, leaving in many instances, elected or appointed state officials of the Commonwealth without legal representation."

It further added that many questions in the Finance Department need legal determination daily and that the department has funds to pay an attorney, that the governor had approved Talbott's recommendation for Tucker, and that he would serve as "legal counsel for the Commissioner of Finance and the Governor's Office."

4. On February 6, 1943, Meredith notified Johnson, "Notwithstanding you have your own employed attorney [G. Lawrence Tucker], it is still the duty of the attorney general to handle such legal matters as you may refer to him.

"You are advised that you should, when calling on this office for the handling of legal matters, address all communications to the attorney general, and not to one of his assistants.

"I make this request for the reason that I have the duty and responsibility of assigning work of the office to various assistants in such way as to provide something for all of them to do at all times. I cannot do this if heads of departments all select one or two of the assistants. This would leave some of them with nothing to do."

He added that he had instructed each of his assistants to refer to him any request from the governor or any department head for legal advise.

Johnson had called on Assistant Attorney General Holifield for advice as to purchase of rebuilt laundry equipment when Tucker was hospitalized. Louisville *Courier-Journal*, February 7, 1943.

ON KENTUCKY'S SOLVENCY
Lexington / January 19, 1943

KENTUCKY has never been better prepared to withstand the economic impact of war than at this time.[1] The long, toilsome trek from the brink of bankruptcy with an expensive debt of $25 million to the heights of financial solvency is an advance in sound government which the thoughtful citizenship should insist be retained.

As result of a war boom in business, the state's income has been artificially stimulated. The same tax sources, which produced a state income for the general fund of $33,580,948 last fiscal year, produced only $26,721,071 in the fiscal year of 1939–1940. When war-stimulated business activity subsides, the tax laws now in effect in the state will again produce an annual income with which to finance state activities of between 26 and 27 million dollars a year. If the citizenship want the state to stay out of debt, they should look with suspicion on those who promise to increase salaries of those paid from tax money, augment the rolls of old age assistance, and at the same time reduce taxes.

The impact of war is already adversely affecting the state's income. Last fiscal year the five cents a gallon production tax on whiskey manufactured in the state brought into the state treasury $4 million. Distilleries have been ordered by the War Production Board[2] to cease the manufacture of whiskey and devote all facilities to manufacture of industrial alcohol which is used in making smokeless powder and synthetic rubber. This means certain elimination of the $4 million in state income from this source.

The usage tax on automobiles, the 3 percent tax paid on purchase of a new car, brought into the state treasury $862,816 last fiscal year. With the sale of new cars virtually forbidden, this source of revenue is eliminated. These two items alone indicate certain reduction in state income of more than $4.5 million next year. It is impossible to foresee with certainty all other loss in revenue that may result from economic maladjustments which are born of war. It would appear to be a prudent policy to keep the state's finances in such a condition as to be certain to maintain a balanced budget and a solvent situation.

The state highway fund is separate from the general fund. Money collected from the gasoline tax goes into this fund and is expended in road maintenance and construction. We face the prospect of a reduction in the road fund of approximately $10 million a year as a result of gasoline and tire rationing, which has already reduced motor travel in the state 40 percent.

The major portion of the state's expenditures is fixed. Fifty cents of your general fund tax dollar is expended for education under the budget act. Ten million dollars of the education expenditure is distributed among the counties and cities to help finance the public school system. The remainder is expended for the institutions of higher learning, free school books, and teachers' retirement. Despite this considerable outlay of money for education, the largest in the history of the state, there are many public school teachers who are too meagerly compensated.

Twenty-five cents out of your tax dollar is expended for public welfare through the Welfare Department. Of this sum $2,740,000 is required for operation of the penal institutions and hospitals for the mentally ill and administration of the department. The increased cost of food and all other supplies essential to providing for the 12,000 inmates of these institutions is making it increasingly difficult to operate these institutions on the money appropriated.

The Welfare Department expends $4,250,000 a year for public assistance. From that sum a monthly check goes to approximately 54,000 aged indigent Kentuckians. Average amount of that monthly aid to the aged is $10.17. When I became governor, 44,000 were receiving an average check of $8.67. The advance in cost of food and other living expenses makes it desirable that the monthly grant be increased, but such can be done only as the legislature makes the money available.

Two other public assistance programs are now the responsibility of the state. The constitutionality of aid to the needy blind and aid to dependent children has been established by court decision. We are inaugurating these programs. They must be financed from the $4,250,000 appropriation referred to above. These two programs, if reasonably supported financially, will require more money than is now available.

Six and six tenths cents out of your tax dollar is required to finance the state courts. Two and a half cents of your dollar is required to operate the state's public health program, including treatment of crippled children and maintenance of tuberculosis hospitals.

This represents eighty-four cents out of your tax dollar for fixed expenses—expenses as fixed and definite as your telephone and electric light bill. The remainder of your tax dollar is expended for numerous miscellaneous items, including the Department of Conservation, Industrial Relations, military, Confederate pensions, and general governmental administration.

The state hospitals for the mentally ill and the Houses of Reform at Greendale have been among my major interests as governor. These institutions have been neglected for years. The result is that their buildings and equipment are distressingly inadequate.

During my administration we have expended nearly $2 million in rehabilitating these institutions, yet we have hardly started. That which has been expended has been for the restoration of the essential utilities, rebuilding of heating plants, electric rewiring to eliminate fire hazard, replacing of leaking roofs, and the doing of a general "house-smithing" job.

We have expended $264,000 in restoring the physical property at the Greendale Reform School to a state of adequacy. We have expended $500,000 in bringing the frightfully dilapidated plant at Eastern State Hospital to a state of decency and sanitation. But this expenditure has amounted to only a substantial start toward making these institutions habitable hospitals within which humane care and intelligent treatment is provided for the unfortunate Kentuckians to whom comes the tragedy of mental illness.

The type of rehabilitation which is under way at Eastern State Hospital is also going on at the other two state hospitals. The money we have expended on them has made it possible to continue to operate them. Had it been longer deferred distressing consequences would have been certain. The crowded condition in these hospitals will not be relieved until additional buildings are erected.

I am certain it will be unfortunate if the program of improvement in these institutions that has been started is not finished. It is a great disappointment to me that the major portion of the improvements we had planned cannot be carried to completion because of the war, which has resulted in scarcity of critical materials, requiring priorities which impose restrictions that make new building impossible. I wish every Kentuckian could go through these institutions and see the impelling necessity for correcting conditions within them that reflect discreditably upon our state. If such were possible, there would be an understanding of the imperative duty of the state to complete the program of improvement at these hospitals.

I have taken advantage of this opportunity to present as briefly as possible the story of the state's financial situation. I can assert confidently that finances of the Commonwealth are being prudently and frugally administered. Whether we shall maintain the state on the foundation of financial solvency or permit a situation to develop in the future that will put the state back in debt is the preeminent public question presented for the consideration of that thoughtful group of intelligent Kentuckians who are readers of the *Lexington Herald*.

---

1. Guest editorial, *Lexington Herald*.
2. The War Production Board replaced the Office of Production Management. It was created in January 1942 to direct procurement and production, conversion of manufacturing plants and plant expansion for war production. *The New International Year Book, 1942* (New York, 1943), p. 747.

CANCELLATION OF LAUNDRY CONTRACT
Frankfort / March 29, 1943

I HAVE undertaken to ascertain all of the available facts relating to the contract[1] which was made with E.H. Heilbron Company for the purchase by the state from E. H. Heilbron Company of laundry equipment for state institutions.

I am thoroughly convinced that W. Arch Bennett, commissioner of finance; W. P. Hogarty, director of the Division of Purchases and Public Properties; and Frank Tanner, assistant director of the Division of Purchases and Public Properties,[2] each and all acted with perfect honesty and good faith in the award of that contract.

Mr. Bennett, Mr. Hogarty, and I considered the bids, conducted the negotiations with Mr. Heilbron after the bids were received, and from the information which the three of us had, we thought the state was getting the equipment at a price favorable to the state.

I am now convinced that there may have been collusion between some of the bidders and that the procedure followed did not conform with the provisions of the law, and in this Messrs. Bennett, Hogarty, and Tanner agree, and the latter three will join with me in appropriate pleadings with the attorney general in asking that the contract be held invalid.

Mr. Ralph C. Wyatt was the engineer who prepared the specifications on which the bids were requested and furnished to the Division of Purchases the names of five persons to whom the invitations were sent. He was the technical advisor upon whom Mr. Bennett, Mr. Hogarty, Mr. Tanner, and I relied, and, without charging or imputing any collusion or misconduct to Mr. Wyatt, I have today entered an executive order suspending Mr. Wyatt from his employment by the state as engineer until all of the facts are fully developed and withholding final judgment with respect to Mr. Wyatt until all of the facts are fully developed.

It is my hope that all the facts will be thoroughly brought out in the pending suit and the attorney general will have my full cooperation, and I am sure the full cooperation of Mr. Bennett, Mr. Hogarty, and Mr. Tanner in searching out and presenting the full facts of the matter.[3]

---

1. On January 17, 1943, the government had announced that $285,000 had been allocated for laundry plants and expressed the belief they would be obtained despite wartime scarcities. They were to be installed at Central and Western State hospitals, Eddyville Prison, the State Reformatory, the Greendale Houses of Reform, and the Feeble Minded Institute. "Equipment at the institutions is in frightful shape in most cases," Johnson commented, "due to years of use without replacements. The laundries, except at Eastern, are so worn that they constantly tear clothes and bedding, and the machines have to be patched up because of breakdowns nearly every day." Louisville *Courier-Journal*, January 18, 1943.

On February 6, 1943, the governor said he acted on the advice of Assistant Attorney General Holifield in rejecting all bids when negotiating with the low bidder to save $30,000. He said the negotiations were conducted in the presence of an advisory committee of four laundrymen who assured him he was making a good trade. He noted, "No laundry equipment has been bought in more than twenty-two years, except some last year at Eastern State Hospital. Naturally, we could not get new equipment so we invited seven companies to bid on rebuilt equipment. Three bids were submitted. . . . The E. H. Heilbron Company, Lexington, was low with a bid of $190,780.

"All three bids were rejected as too high. I asked Mr. Heilbron to step from the room. The laundrymen examined his bid and told me he seemed about $30,000 high. I called General Holifield . . . who advised us that when all bids are rejected, we can negotiate for purchase at a price as low, or lower, than the lowest and best bid rejected. . . .

"We then . . . asked him [Heilbron] what he could come to. He said he would come down $15,000. . . . To make a long story short, the trading ended when Mr. Heilbron agreed to furnish the rebuilt machinery for $170,780 and allow us $10,000 for the old equipment. The net saving to the state was $30,000. General Meredith raised the question that the state won't know what it is getting in rebuilt machinery. Upon the advice of the laundrymen, we have employed Clarence S. Moore, of Lexington, a laundry machinery consultant of recognized ability and reputation. Mr. Moore . . . not only is to select the equipment Mr. Heilbron is to rebuild, but he will be required to . . . obtain a government permit to rebuild it." Louisville *Courier-Journal*, February 7, 1943.

2. W. Arch Bennett (1896–1966), b. Henderson County. Deputy welfare commissioner, 1937–1941; state supervisor, National Youth Administration, director, Accounts and Control, Finance Department, 1941–1943; commissioner of finance, 1943. *Lexington Herald*, January 10, 1943, and Polly Gorman, secretary to Governor Bert Combs, June 14, 1978.

William Paul Hogarty (1894–1971), b. Lexington. Purchasing agent, United States government, World War II; served in Highway Department, retired 1962. Telephone interview, Mrs. James G. Moore, daughter, Jacksonville, Alabama, September 25, 1978.

Frank Tanner (1889–1973), b. Louisville. Assistant director, Purchasing Division; mayor, Eddyville for twenty years. Telephone interview, Malcolm Tanner, son, June 22, 1978.

3. In issuing this statement, Johnson said that he would join with Meredith in seeking to cancel the laundry equipment contract. The statement was made after several days of investigation and with Joseph J. Leary present as legal adviser. He formally joined Meredith on April 3, 1943, the first time he became party to a state lawsuit on the side of the attorney general. Meredith's suit charged that the state would be swindled out of more that $132,000 and that the governor, the finance commissioner, and the purchasing director had been deceived by "collusion and conspiracy." In a petition filed in Franklin Circuit Court by G. Lawrence Tucker, the governor supported Meredith's pleading by charging "collusion between some of the bidders." He also charged that specifications on which bids were invited did not authorize the consideration of bids for reconditioned equipment or the rewarding of the contract. The governor was joined by Bennett, Hogarty, and Tanner.

Meredith's suit charged that Tanner, Wyatt, and Heilbron conspired to mislead and deceive the governor, Bennett, and Hogarty into awarding the contract to

Heilbron; that the invitation to bid specified new equipment but that Heilbron and two alleged Chicago confederates submitted three collusive bids on reconditioned machinery as part of a preconceived scheme to defraud the state. Using the premise that equipment now in use could be renovated for $38,022, Meredith calculated fraudulent loss to the state at $132,758 in event the Heilbron contract was not canceled. Tanner denied he was a party to any scheme of collusion, conspiracy, or deceit; that all he did was to mail out the invitations to bid. Louisville *Courier-Journal*, April 6, 1943.

The contract was canceled on April 21, 1943, by Circuit Judge Ardery. *Kentucky Post*, April 22, 1943.

On June 10, 1943, the state invited eighty firms to submit bids. Bids of six firms were opened by Hogarty on June 18, 1943. Three contracts amounting to $111,106 for new machinery and one for $400 for rebuilt machinery were awarded on July 7, 1943. Louisville *Courier-Journal*, June 19, 1943, and *Cincinnati Enquirer*, July 8, 1943.

CONSTITUTIONAL AMENDMENT ON $5,000 SALARY LIMIT
Frankfort / May 18, 1943

A SPECIAL Court of Appeals was named by Governor Johnson to decide whether the people could vote in November 1943 on the proposed repeal of the state's $5,000 annual salary limit.[1] Former Circuit Judge Lafon Allen,[2] Louisville, was appointed chief justice.[3]

---

1. The other members were Roy Shelburne, First Appellate District, Paducah; Allen P. Cubbage, Second Appellate District, Leitchfield; B. J. Bethurum, Third Appellate District, Somerset; Victor Bradley, Fifth Appellate District, Georgetown; Innes B. Ross, Sixth Appellate District, Carlisle; and Robert H. Winn, Seventh Appellate District, Mount Sterling.

The governor had previously appointed a Special Court of Appeals to decide the constitutionality of an act to provide pensions to the judges of the Court of Appeals. See *Acts of the General Assembly, 1940*, Chapter 131, p. 528. Joseph P. Goodenough, Kenton circuit judge, was named chief justice. Serving with him were J. Donald Dinning, Louisville; I. A. Faurest, Elizabethtown; C. C. Grassham, Paducah; Wilbur K. Miller, Owensboro; Frank C. Malin, Ashland; and William L. Wallace, Lexington. The court invalidated the pension act on January 17, 1941, by a 4-3 decision with the majority opinion written by Judge Faurest. The majority ruled that a pension would be additional compensation and that, therefore, the act was in violation of the $5,000 salary limitation. *Talbott, Commissioner of Finance* v. *Thomas et al*, 286 Ky. 786, 151 S.W. 2d. 1 (1941).

In 1942, the General Assembly passed and the governor signed an "Additional Commissioner" bill, termed by opponents as a "pension" bill. It provided that retiring members of the Court of Appeals may be retained as additional court commissioners at a salary of $5,000 a year. *Kentucky Post*, March 2, 1942.

2. Lafon Allen (1871–1952), b. Louisville. Republican. Judge, Jefferson Circuit Court, 1922–1931; president, Kentucky Bar Association, 1939. *Who's Who in Kentucky, 1936*, p. 6, and telephone inverview, Mrs. Garnett Cook, daughter, July 21, 1978.

3. On February 9, 1943, Attorney General Meredith had charged deception and fraud in the wording of the proposed constitutional amendment. As proposed by the General Assembly, the amendment would have repealed the constitution's salary limit section, substituted one authorizing the legislature to fix salaries, and made the change apply to officials and employees in office when the amendment was adopted. Meredith declared the proposed amendment was void because it attempted to amend more than one section of the constitution, not only that pertaining to the salary limit but also the one regarding penalties and the one prohibiting changing salaries of officials and employees during their terms of office. He added that the submission bill also attempted to amend certain statutes. Louisville *Courier-Journal*, February 10, 1943.

Circuit Judge Ardery upheld the attorney general and the case was appealed. On April 30, 1943, the Court of Appeals disqualified itself. *Cincinnati Enquirer*, May 1, 1943. On June 25, 1943, the Special Court of Appeals in a 5-2 decision approved placing the constitutional amendment on the ballot in November. In so doing the court ordered Meredith to prepare the wording for the ballots. *Hatcher, Sec'y of State, et al.* v. *Meredith, Atty. Gen.*, 295 Ky. 194, 173 S.W. 2d. 665 (1943). The salary limitation had withstood three previous referendums in 1925, 1927, and 1929. In the election of 1943 the amendment was defeated by a vote of 44,765 to 121,797.

RESIGNATION OF INDICTED STATE EMPLOYEES
Harlan / June 15, 1943

IMMEDIATELY after I received information of the indictments returned in federal district court at London charging the indicted persons with participating in irregularities in the Harlan County election in November 1942, I conveyed to members of the Harlan County election commission and to all of the state's employees who were indicted my conviction that they should immediately resign.

All of the state employees who were so indicted have resigned and their resignations have been accepted.[1] T. K. Watson,[2] the Democratic member of the Harlan County Election Commission, has resigned and his resignation will be accepted at the next meeting of the state Board of Election Commissioners.

Ray Rice[3] has returned the courtesy card issued him some months ago by the state highway patrol and courtesy cards held by persons other than regularly appointed and employed Highway Department officials and employees have been called in and canceled.

Directions have been given to the state highway patrol that no courtesy cards be issued to any person in the future except officials and employees of the Highway Department whose regular duties entitle them to such cards.

The attitude of the men who submitted their resignations and their willingness to resign from the state payroll pending their trials indicated a recognition on their part of the proprieties of the situation.

The election irregularities are deplorable and cannot be condoned. Fair and honest elections are vital to the preservation of the democratic form of government and the integrity of the ballot must be preserved not only in Harlan County but throughout the state. I shall exercise all the authority that I have as governor to protect and preserve the honesty and integrity of elections not only in Harlan County but throughout the state.[4]

I have given prompt attention to this matter and effective results have been obtained.[5]

---

1. The governor said that Clyde Saylor, a Harlan man employed as a file clerk in the Highway Department office, and eight highway maintenance men and laborers were among those indicted.

2. Probation and parole officer, Department of Welfare.

3. A political and business associate of Advisory Highway Commissioner Herb Smith.

4. In November 1941 a constitutional amendment to permit counties to purchase voting machines was approved by a vote of 176,596 to 70,017.

5. In discussing this situation, the governor commented that "few states have less election dishonesty than Kentucky" and that passage some years ago of the law requiring tabulation to be done at the county courthouse, instead of at the precincts, was designed to make it impossible to tamper with ballots. *Richmond Daily Register*, June 15, 1943.

ON CONVENING A SPECIAL SESSION FOR INCOME TAX REPEAL
Frankfort / November 19, 1943

YOU are doubtless aware of the fact that the regular session of the Kentucky legislature, which meets in January, will be powerless to relieve taxpayers of the obligation of paying the state income tax for the year 1943.[1]

The tax for the present year will have then become a fixed liability, a debt from which the legislature cannot relieve the taxpayer because of the constitutional inhibition contained in Section 52 of the Kentucky Constitution.[2]

The only way taxpayers may be relieved of paying the 1943 income tax is for a special session of the legislature to be called and repeal it before the close of the present calendar year. I have declined to call such a session.[3]

But I am taking the liberty of informing you that a decided majority of the members of the General Assembly are anxious and willing to vote for repeal of the 1943 income tax. They feel that they should help you carry out your pledge to the people of Kentucky that the state income tax would be immediately repealed in event of your election as governor.[4]

You will be inaugurated as my successor on December 7.[5] There will be ample time for you to call a special session of the legislature and relieve the taxpayers of having to pay the state income tax for the year 1943.

I can assure you that if you call such a session and ask for repeal of the income tax for 1943, you will receive the overwhelming support of the General Assembly, because the members are anxious to participate with you in relieving taxpayers of the necessity of paying this year's tax, which is due next April 15.[6]

---

1. Letter to Governor-elect Willis. Simeon S. Willis (1879–1965), b. Lawrence County, Ohio. Governor, 1943–1947; Republican; city solicitor, Ashland, Kentucky, 1918–1922; associate justice, Court of Appeals, 1927–1933; *Who Was Who in America, 1961–1968*, 4:1019.

2. Section 52 prohibits the state from "extinguishing or canceling" any obligation already incurred. Income Tax liability for 1943 was incurred by December 31.

3. The governor said, on May 19, 1943, that those who have been urging repeal should "keep in mind that as the federal income tax goes up, the state income tax goes down," due to provisions in the state law that federal payments may be deducted in computing what is owed on the state income tax. *Lexington Herald*, May 20, 1943.

4. On July 8, 1943, the Kentucky Tax Research Association stated that the income tax was no longer needed in Kentucky. It contended that the combination of income tax, intangible property tax, and inheritance tax kept industry from the state. The income tax was imposed in 1936 to pay off the state debt which had been paid. Seven states repealed or reduced state income taxes in 1943: California, Iowa, Maryland, New York, Oregon, South Dakota, and West Virginia. George E. Tomlinson, president of the association, said, "Kentucky would be wise to follow the example of these states." *Cincinnati Enquirer*, July 9, 1943. The association had notified its members in November 1941 that an effort would be made at the 1942 session of the legislature to repeal the income tax. *Cincinnati Enquirer*, November 22, 1941.

5. Willis was elected on a platform of income tax repeal without substituting another tax, at the same time promising a retroactive pay raise of $3 million a year to schoolteachers and pledging nearly $6 million a year additional to the common school fund.

6. The governor released his letter within an hour after a court order was served on his secretary, restraining Johnson from calling the session. The writ was issued by Franklin Circuit Clerk Kelly C. Smithers on petition of Attorney General Meredith. He described Meredith's injunction suit as a "futile gesture," saying the chief executive, by no stretch of the law, can be enjoined from calling a session of the General Assembly.

KENTUCKY GOVERNMENT, 1939–1943
Frankfort / November 27, 1943

[THIS statement summarizes the accomplishments that Governor Johnson regarded as the principle ones of his administration.[1]]

The complete rebuilding with modern fireproof construction of an 126-year-old building at Eastern State Hospital, Lexington, was the first major task the Johnson administration undertook in the campaign to modernize the hospitals for the mentally ill. So the report on the administration, which was made public today, indicates.

Then, Johnson reports, the bare outside walls of the old Pusey Building at Central State Hospital, Lakeland, provided the beginning of a sanitary, up-to-date structure with all modern hospital facilities and equipment. The construction program included extensive other improvements at these hospitals and at Hopkinsville and the Feeble Minded Institute at Frankfort.

The construction of a new building of reinforced concrete relieved overcrowded conditions at Eddyville State Penitentiary by providing 568 additional modern, sanitary, and well-ventilated cells. The new prison near LaGrange was occupied in 1940. Prison conditions have been relieved also, it is reported, by changes in management.The adult prison population in Kentucky today is approximately 25 percent lower than it was in 1939. More inmates have been paroled, and fewer have violated parole privileges. The probation law enacted in 1936 has also contributed toward lowering the number in prison. About 85 percent of persons the courts have placed on probation have proved to be good risks and never go to prison.

The Houses of Reform at Greendale have been improved through a new honor dormitory and recreation hall for girls, a new sewage disposal plant, and an industrial building for making concrete products. The inauguration of an honor system in 1941 and the addition of qualified personnel have greatly improved conditions at the Houses of Reform.

Improvements and additions to farm buildings, the buying of more livestock and farm machinery, and the purchase of approximately 700 more acres of land have greatly increased production of food on both hospital and correctional institution farms. An intensified agricultural program at all these farms supplies as much as possible of the food required for the inmates.

The governor reports that not only the building program but also the care and treatment of patients at welfare institutions have greatly improved. For example, the nursing personnel in mental hospitals has doubled. The penal institutions have intensified their health work through regular physical examinations and treatments which place emphasis on the control of tuberculosis. A result has been a marked decline since 1939 in the number of deaths from all causes.

More than 54,000 individuals were receiving public assistance in April 1943, as compared with 45,000 in December 1939, the report states. At the same time average payments for old age assistance increased from $8.66 to $10.27 a month; the needy blind received an average of $12.26 a month and needy children $23.01 a case. "The cost of operating the public assistance program in Kentucky is among the lowest in the nation," in spite of loss of personnel and an increased number of activities since the beginning of 1940.

In the carrying out of the program for aid to dependent and destitute children, emphasis has been placed on organizing one-county child welfare units totally supported by local funds. However, there are still eighty-eight counties in rural sections of the state without organized public services for aiding children.

Early in 1940 Governor Johnson's administration developed and published a policy of building roads where the traffic is heavy. As a consequence, it devoted nearly 80 percent of highway construction outlay in 1942–1943 to the building of high-type surface on those roads which carry the heaviest traffic, as compared with just over 50 percent in 1936–1938. This fact is illustrated in Governor Johnson's new report.

The administration has developed a long-range program for highway building designed to follow detailed planning and traffic surveys. During the war the report shows that this plan has been modified to place emphasis on relieving traffic conditions in the congested areas around war plants and on highways strategic for military purposes.

The department has made plans for construction in the areas around large cities where postwar unemployment difficulties are most probable. Already it has formulated and the federal people have tentatively approved definite plans for about 230 miles of such federal-aid highways.

The construction plans have also included bridges as a part of the general highway network, but no building can currently be undertaken because of the shortage of labor and war restrictions on necessary materials. Not yet completed is the Kentucky River Bridge at Clay's Ferry, which will tower 250 feet above normal pool when present plans have materialized.

The health of the general public in Kentucky has shown continued improvement during the last four years as the better public health service has been perfected. According to the Johnson report, "There have been fewer cases of communicable diseases in epidemic form during the past three years than during any other three-year period for the last twenty-five years."

The death rate for diphtheria in Kentucky is now among the lowest for any state. Progress in combating venereal diseases, particularly after enactment of the prenatal and premarital laws in 1940 and 1941, has expanded public health laboratory services. Widespread Health Department use of the sulfa drugs has lowered the mortality rate for pneumonia, and the decline for tuberculosis indicates that this disease has gradually yielded to organized public health work.

Plans and the contract for a new hospital building at Hazelwood Tuberculosis Sanatorium have been completed to provide facilities for 230 patients.

Specific industrial surveys have been made to determine proper illumination and ventilation, to detect presence of tuberculosis, and to find means of reducing industrial health hazards.

"Kentucky now has the largest number of full-time county health units of any state in the Union," the number having increased from 86 to 103 since January 1940.[2] Emphasis on public health education, public health nursing services, and the use of mobile units, such as those for dental work, have all operated for better health in Kentucky. A decline during the last twenty-five years of 28 percent in the maternal mortality rate and of 25 percent in the infant mortality rate has been due largely to the nutrition program and to organized maternity nursing service.

Opening the Oneida Maternity Hospital, after the governor had made funds available for repairs and installation of sewage and water systems, gave Kentucky the "only state-owned maternity hospital in the United States operated by the state with the assistance of federal funds."

The per capita grants for education have been greater than ever before, ranging from $12.19 in 1939–1940 to $13.49 in 1943–1944. Less prosperous school districts not having $30.00 per pupil in average daily membership, have received extra financial assistance under 1942 legislation, which implemented the constitutional amendment of 1941. Help has been extended to all schools through provision of free textbooks for grades one through eight and free supplementary materials in art, music, health, safety, science, and social science for grades one through four. In 1940 the present administration set up and secured an appropriation for an actuarially sound teacher's retirement system to provide old age and disability payments.

Transportation difficulties brought on by the war have been met to some extent through elimination of nonessential travel and stops. The Department of Education, with college and university cooperation, has established workshops and provided short work conferences to meet the need for teacher training and the problem of a shortage of teachers due to the war.

The Johnson administration has more than doubled efforts and achievements under the program of training handicapped individuals. The number of persons rehabilitated increased from 237 to 1,600 during the last four years. To meet the demand for workers caused by the war emergency, the administration has broadened the vocational rehabilitation program to include instruction for homebound physically handicapped children, and to provide courses for army rejectees.

Vocational training has expanded to include a larger number of students, particularly those in home economics education and in vocational agriculture. The program has placed emphasis on courses which are essential to the war effort, such as mechanics, aeronautics, home nursing, nutrition, and food production.

The state teachers colleges and Kentucky State College for Negroes have adapted their programs to war conditions. They have given instruction for civilian pilot training, Naval Flight Preparatory School, army air service, and regular soldier and WAAC training programs.

The University of Kentucky program is reported to include the Reserve Officers Training Corps, the enlisted specialist program for engineers, the army program for young engineers, and special courses for war industry workers.

The report gives examples of important research work which has been carried on by the university. The value of the burley tobacco crop has increased more than $8 million annually as a result of the work in developing a disease-resistant strain. The use of hybrid seed corn, bred by the University Experiment Station and introduced through agricultural extension work, has increased the corn yield from eight to ten bushels to the acre. The work of the College of Agriculture with marketing cooperatives has made some crops economically feasible and doubled the cash income of many farmers. In 1943 seven southeastern Kentucky counties marketed twenty-three carloads of onions and the equivalent of 178 carloads of Irish potatoes through cooperatives.

A special laboratory, under construction at the university, will help to determine whether or not it is commercially feasible—as university workers have already found it technically possible—to produce aviation gasoline from coal.

Under the governor's leadership the 1940 legislature authorized soil conservation districts. With the assistance of the federal Soil Conservation Service and the university College of Agriculture, the Kentucky Department of Agriculture has promoted the establishment of thirty-nine soil conservation districts in thirty-eight Kentucky counties. These districts are self-governing political subdivisions of the state for the application of soil conservation practices and for receiving any money, materials, or services made available by any public agency for this purpose. In soil conservation generally, the university has promoted the use of cover crops, of reforestation, and of other soil erosion control devices.

Additional activities in the conservation of Kentucky's natural resources, the report shows, have included preserving forests and protecting them from forest fires, providing game and fish and promoting development of wildlife through protection and provision of habitat and food, and improving state parks. Two important park developments have been the transfer to the United States in 1941 of the Mammoth Cave National Park area and the approval of a compact with Tennessee and Virginia for creation of the Cumberland Gap National Historical Park to include about 50,000 acres.

Out of each dollar spent for all the various activities of the state general government, the report shows that over fifty cents annually is spent for public education, about twenty-five cents for welfare, two or three cents for health, seven cents for the courts, four cents for new land and buildings, and the remaining ten cents for general administrative costs and for counties.

In recent years for the first time in Kentucky history, the financial control machinery has been made to work. The accounts have been modernized, purchasing centralized, and budgeting improved. Now, therefore, instead of the traditional deficit, the state has paid all of its warrant debt and has a balance of several million dollars. The administration in four years has averaged underspending appropriations by about $1.6 million annually. Revenues reached a peak in the spring of 1943, the increase since 1938 attributed by the report to greater prosperity, more effective tax administration, and better taxpayer cooperation. Wartime conditions have in recent months caused a sharp decline.

The state has assisted counties in child welfare work through helping to establish their local programs; it has helped local health units by both technical assistance and financial aid; it has supplied rural electric cooperatives with accounting, engineering, and administrative assistance; it has cooperated with county fiscal courts to construct rural highways; it has given financial and technical assistance to the common schools; and it has helped counties refinance debts and perfect budgeting and accounting plans. The report emphasizes the state's general policy of giving as much aid as possible in the form both of money and technical assistance but leaving the local government free to make its own policy decisions.

One important development in rural electrification has been the legislation in 1942 which enabled Kentucky municipalities and rural cooperatives to contract with the Tennessee Valley Authority for electric current.

---

1. News release.

2. The governor gave different numbers for the total number of county health units. On November 1, 1942, he reported that there were 100. On April 23, 1943, he approved the establishment of three units and stated that they would bring the total to 105. On May 24, 1943, he said that 105 counties had units. On October 22, 1943, he reported that 104 counties had full-time departments. It would appear that 103 was the correct number. See speeches from November 1, 1942, May 24, 1943, and October 22, 1943, respectively, in the Health and Welfare section.

EDUCATION

STATEMENT BEFORE TEXTBOOK COMMISSION
Frankfort / January 5, 1940

IT has been suggested that some of you would be interested in my thought as to the problems you confront as you undertake the important responsibility of making a textbook adoption. Your task is to determine how about $5 million shall be expended for textbooks. I have confidence in the integrity of members of this commission and have no disposition to question their judgment. My chief concern is that, when the adoption has been completed, you will have selected the best books available for our schools and at the most favorable prices to the Commonwealth. I have no doubt that you are in accord with that thought.

You know that there has not been a recent adoption of books in Kentucky that has not resulted in some undesirable developments. Court litigation has often resulted and there have at times been circumstances which did not smell right. I have no doubt you are anxious to avoid an unsavory aftermath. In the past the book companies and their representatives have contributed as much to the undesirable circumstances that have developed, perhaps more, than has the commission. You are dealing with cunning, adroit men who are trying to make money by selling books. It is your obligation to protect the schoolchildren and the state.

While the administration it is my responsibility to head is not responsible for the formation of this commission, the general public will regard the governor and superintendent of public instruction as being largely responsible for your action. Because of that inescapable fact, I am as anxious as you that the adoption square with your conscience and judgment in the appraisal of the books.

It seems to be proper that you seek conscientiously to determine the best books at the best price. When that has been done, it would seem proper that, if the best interests of the children and state not be jeopardized, the book business be apportioned among the Kentucky book representatives.

I suggest that by your procedure you try to create in the public mind a feeling of confidence as you establish the fact that you are trying to make an honest and proper adoption. For that reason I suggest that you not act hastily, because to do so would promote the thought that you had not been properly cautious. I believe that the finest way to protect yourselves as members of the commission and to establish the thought that every action is on the up-and-up, that every vote on an adoption be by open, signed ballot. I do not believe it proper to expend as much public money as will be spent by your action without subjecting your action to public scrutiny. I think that action will be conclusive evidence of your effort to act correctly and that it will forestall unjustified rumors that may reflect discreditably upon some member of the commission.

I have complete confidence in the integrity and judgment of Mr. Brooker,[1] superintendent of public instruction. I do not think it improper to suggest to you that in instances in which you may have doubt as to procedure that you regard it as proper to advise with him, because his will be the task of administering the textbook distribution after you have concluded your work.

---

1. John William Brooker (1899–1952), b. Newport. Superintendent of public instruction, 1939–1943. *Kentucky Directory, 1940–1941*, pp. 144-45.

EASTERN KENTUCKY STATE TEACHERS COLLEGE FOUNDERS DAY
Richmond / March 21, 1940

I AM so happy today to be back in Richmond and on the Eastern campus. It is the first time I have seen you friends since December 6 when numbers of you gathered to give us an expression of good wishes at a good-bye dinner as we left Richmond temporarily to reside in the Executive Mansion. That occasion will always be a cherished memory. Three and a half months that as been—and we have missed you so much. Then there is a feeling of relief that we have survived the first crisis of our responsibility as governor in cooperation with the legislature in a reasonably acceptable way. I find some satisfaction in the knowledge that no legislation was enacted that will be hurtful to our state and people. And just the joy of being back home with you for a day is a real delight. But it is especially gratifying to participate in this the most significant anniversary of the founding of Eastern in her thirty-four years of useful service to the Commonwealth.

In 1838, 102 years ago, Kentucky recognized education as a state function and there was created by legislative enactment a free public school system. In the same year there was created in Massachusetts the first normal school in America. Educational leaders of the state spent the next sixty-eight years advocating similar teacher training institutions for Kentucky. Private schools provided the only opportunity for training a teacher. The instruction was often inadequate. Private normal schools grew up in the state. They offered short courses designed primarily to help one pass the teacher's examination and obtain a certificate to teach. In 1880, there were sixteen of these private normal schools in Kentucky.

Educators continued to stress the fact that the first thing necessary to improvement of Kentucky's inadequate school system was an ample supply of well-trained teachers. In 1906, two normal schools were established, Eastern Kentucky State Normal School, Richmond, and Western Kentucky State Normal School, Bowling Green. These pioneer institutions gave impetus to improved instruction in the public schools. In 1922, the state legislature created two additional teacher training institutions, bringing into existence Murray State Normal and Morehead State Normal schools. As desirability of higher qualifications for teachers became apparent, these normal schools were advanced to the status of teachers colleges and raised to the level of four-year colleges. The development of public schools in the state parallels the growth of the normal schools. The improved quality of teaching in the common schools is directly attributable to better trained teachers made available by these teacher training institutions.

So the teachers college has evolved out of experience and necessity to meet the changing needs of education. It occupies a unique position. It partakes of the nature both of a vocational school and a liberal arts college. The teachers college must impart scholarship and at the same time develop skill in the profession of teaching. There must be developed scholarly young men and women who have acquired the fine art of instruction. It is as difficult a professional task to train good teachers as it is to educate lawyers or doctors; and of greater importance, because the teacher more vitally affects the lives of children in the formative period of life.

The teachers college is an important agency of national defense. It prepares those who are to teach the youth the duties of citizenship, imparts to them those ideals which are cherished by a democracy. The function of the teachers college is not unlike that of the Military Academy at West Point and the Naval Academy at Annapolis. The naval and military academies prepare the best of the nation's youth to meet the emergencies of war. The teachers colleges train those who are to instruct the youth of the nation, prepare these our children to meet the emergencies of peace.

There is no more effective program of national defense than to prepare the youth of each generation to face a crisis calmly, discharge the duties of citizenship under the stress of war, or intelligently analyze the problems of peace and find sane solutions for them. Adequate preparation of the younger generation for civic duty is vital to the perpetuity of this nation. This important phase of our national defense is a responsibility which we impose upon the teachers who instruct the youth. As are the teachers within a nation, so will be the defense of democracy against subversive influences from within or armed foes from without.

The fact that the American citizenship accepted the hard times of the recent years of severe depression, the privation of hunger and hardship, without succumbing to hysteria, without yielding to subversive influences such as provoked revolt in other nations, is in my judgment the finest tribute that has been paid the public school system of America. I am convinced that the advanced level of average intelligence of the masses of the nation proved to be a bulwark of strength in a period of peril. The seeds of radicalism and revolt sown in the nation fell on barren ground, never sprouted because the national policy of providing educational opportunity for all the people had prepared the citizenship to meet this major economic calamity with reasoned judgment. And those to whom we are most indebted for having created that mental attitude are the teachers of the nation, trained by the teachers colleges.

Popular education, as made available through the public school system, has proved to be a most effective antidote against disruptive influences such as breed in human misery and flourish on discontent. The patriotism instilled in the public schools by patriotic teachers, the faith in our system of government inculcated by public school training, the thought processes quickened by education were factors which restrained rash impulses in which disorder and revolution have their genesis. Education of the masses proved in the critical hour of our republic to be the great stabilizing influence which steadied the ship of state as it rode the most tempestuous sea of economic upheaval that has yet challenged our existence as a nation. We owe a debt of gratitude to the teachers of the nation for their contribution to a rational attitude toward the adversities of the depression. Since it is the function of the teachers colleges to prepare those who instruct the youth, instill in them the patriotism and wisdom to meet such emergencies of peace, I submit that comparison of the teachers college with the military academy as an agency of national defense is a proper analogy.

So the teachers college is a helpful ally of democracy. It provides the best possible training for those who are to teach in the public school system. As these teachers instruct the childhood of our state and nation in the duties and responsibilities of citizenship, they make a vital contribution to national defense because no other form of government is so dependent upon an enlightened electorate as is a democracy.

If we have accurately evaluated the teachers college as an educational agency, well may we rejoice today that Eastern on this Founders Day dedicates to public service these three magnificent buildings.[1] They are buildings in which beauty of architecture and practical usefulness are sanely combined.[2] They are buildings which enhance the physical equipment of Eastern and make possible increased advantages for young Kentuckians. They are buildings which stand as a monument to the vision and ingenuity of the superior educator under whose guidance as president Eastern has come to be recognized as one of the great teachers colleges on this continent. And as Dr. Dovonan's[3] genius has brought an enlarged physical plant for Eastern, he has here developed a high scholastic ideal, the result of which has been to stamp him as one of the nation's foremost educators.

So today as a resident of Richmond I am happy that these splendid buildings have been added to this campus. As a member of the Board of Regents of Eastern I am happy that this important building program has been completed. And as governor of the Commonwealth, to the enrichment of which Eastern has made notable contribution, I am delighted at this momentous moment to accept, on behalf of the state of Kentucky, these beautiful and useful buildings. Young Kentuckians will be inspired by their beauty and enjoy their conveniences as they find within them the educational aids which will make them better Kentuckians.

---

1. The buildings were the Student Union Building, the Fitzpatrick Arts Building, and a three-section dormitory for men (Beckham, McCreary, and Miller).

2. During the commencement exercises on May 29, 1940, President Donovan announced that the Student Union Building would be named the Keen Johnson Student Union Building.

3. Herman Lee Donovan (1887–1964), b. Maysville. Superintendent, public schools, 1910–1921; dean, Eastern Kentucky State Teachers College, 1921–1923; professor, George Peabody College for Teachers, 1925–1928; president, Eastern Kentucky State Teachers College, 1928–1941; president, University of Kentucky, 1941–1956. *Who Was Who in America, 1961–1968*, 4:258.

RED BIRD HIGH SCHOOL GRADUATION
Bell County / April 7, 1940

GOVERNOR JOHNSON told eighteen students in the graduating class that there are plenty new, unconquered frontiers for youth with the courage and the will to learn.[1]

---

1. This brief statement has been included because Johnson was the first governor to visit this isolated section of Bell County. He traveled by automobile, railroad car, and in the cab of a logging train locomotive. The school, operated by the Evangelical Church, was located about twenty miles from Pineville on land given by members of the Knuckles family. It was founded about 1920 and enrolled more than 250 students in 1940. *Pineville Sun,* April 11, 1940.

KENTUCKY SCHOOL FOR THE DEAF
Frankfort / April 17, 1940

GOVERNOR JOHNSON said he had no money available to aid the Kentucky School for the Deaf,[1] which announced it would have to close its school year May 1, a month earlier than usual.

"We recognized the needs of the institution and increased its annual appropriations from $110,000 to $115,000 in the budget bill. But there is no money in the emergency fund, except what is allocated to pay the cost of federal commodities distribution. The school knew what it had to spend during the past year."[2]

---

1. Founded in 1823, it was the first tax-supported school for the deaf in the country. John Ed Pearce, "Boyle County," Louisville *Courier-Journal and Times Magazine,* October 9, 1977.

2. Superintendent Madison J. Lee said that the school's $128,000 annual appropriation was cut to $110,000 in 1938 and that Governor Chandler gave $10,000 from his emergency fund in 1939 to maintain the regular school year. Governor Johnson visited the school on May 14, 1941, and said that he wished it were possible to appropriate more money but the budget did not allow it. *Danville Advocate-Messenger,* May 15, 1941. He allocated $2,500 from his Emergency Fund

in June 1941 to enable the school to operate for a full term. In April 1942 he authorized $9,500 for the purchase of 36.78 acres of land adjacent to the school and in September 1942 he reported that the state was spending approximately $11,000 for repairs. The school had 341 white and twenty-four black inmates. The annual appropriation for 1940–1941 and 1941–1942 was $115,000 for whites and $8,600 for blacks. In 1942–1943 and 1943–1944 the annual appropriation was raised to $129,500 for whites and $9,000 for blacks. *Danville Advocate-Messenger*, September 15, 1942.

KENTUCKY EDUCATION ASSOCIATION
Louisville / April 19, 1940

I AM delighted to come and express my appreciation for the fine service being rendered by the teachers of Kentucky in building an improved citizenship. I confess frankly that I am a little bit scared in the presence of scholastic wisdom in such vast quantity. You see a politician is not accustomed to speaking to such an intelligent audience.

As governor of the state to whose service you have consecrated yourselves, I feel justified in the assertion that you, the teachers of our children, may look to the future with increased confidence.

I want to publicly express my appreciation for the fine leadership in education which is being supplied by John Brooker as superintendent of public instruction. For the first time in several years, there is a feeling of understanding and cooperation between the superintendent of public instruction and the governor. John and I propose to demonstrate that the cause of education can be served better when the governor and the superintendent of public instruction are on speaking terms and working together.

I have confidence in John Brooker, in his ability and judgment. In the recent legislative session, the constructive school legislation enacted was prepared in cooperation with Mr. Brooker. I am convinced he has the qualities necessary to make one of the most successful superintendents of public instruction who has ever led the forces of education in Kentucky. And it shall be my purpose to give him every possible assistance in attaining that goal.

The appropriation act enacted by the General Assembly contained money necessary to maintain the $12 per capita, the most generous support of public schools in the history of our state. That bill appropriated half a million dollars with which to make operative the Teachers' Retirement Act.[1] That act made provision for the state institutions of higher learning. The appropriation act legalizes the expenditure of $26 million for each of the next two years. Of that sum, approximately one-half will be spent for education. That places the emphasis in the proper place.

One achievement of this administration of which I am proud has all but escaped your attention. It has passed unnoticed. A school textbook adoption has been made in Kentucky without the faintest intimation of scandal or impropriety. The Textbook Commission,[2] under the leadership of Mr. Brooker, made a textbook adoption that was highly acceptable. The job they did was untainted by suspicion, such as has been voiced in varying degree at every adoption since 1912. The best books obtainable were adopted. As the selection was made, the only motive of the commission was to choose those books which would best serve the needs of our children. When the task was completed, there was not the faintest justification for disapproval of the adoption. Because it was a job well done, it did not attract public attention. Had this important service not been properly performed, there would have been, as there has been in the past, nasty charges, court litigation, such as has marked many book adoptions in the last twenty-eight years. Mr. Brooker recently sent to my desk the front page of a newspaper published in a neighbor state, in which sensational headlines proclaimed the story of a scandal that had grown out of the textbook adoption. Appended to the newspaper was a penciled memorandum signed, "John," in which he said, "I am glad this did not happen here." We should all be glad it didn't happen here.Let's give an enthusiastic hand to John Brooker and the Textbook Commission for a clean, correct adoption.

The last legislature was composed of splendid Kentuckians, anxious to legislate constructively. Legislative approval was given to a suggestion from the governor that an equalization constitutional amendment be submitted to a vote of the people. The amendment, if adopted, would alter that provision of the state constitution which specifies that all state money for public schools shall be distributed on a per capita basis. It proposes to permit as much as 10 percent of the money appropriated for public schools to be apportioned to those poorer counties of the state, in addition to the per capita distribution.

Adoption of the amendment does not necessarily mean that 10 percent of the $9.7 million a year now divided on a per capita basis will be taken from that fund, reducing the per capita in the counties of greater wealth. As the legislation was discussed, there were those who assumed that would be the effect. The legislature will still determine the amount to be expended for public schools, and what portion of it may be used for an equilization fund, supplementing in poor counties the money available but inadequate for maintaining a good school system. The equalization process provided under the amendment does not propose to reduce the money available for the wealthier counties. It proposes to help the counties in greatest need by adding to the public school fund a sum of money which the legislature will determine, that may be used to give additional aid to the counties of inadequate resources.

There are a number of poor counties in the state which, after they levy the maximum tax rate, do not have money enough to provide as good a school system as they should have. The state could increase its aid to these counties by raising the per capita contribution if it had the money. It is estimated that, if the $12.00 per capita be raised to $15.00 these less favored counties could finance their schools. But there are about 800,000 schoolchildren in the state. An increase of $3.00 in the per capita would raise the public school appropriation $2.4 million. That would be an improved plan of meeting the problem if we had the money; but we do not have it. Our tax resources are about exhausted. There is no tax you would be willing to sponsor by which to raise $2.4 million. In my judgment it would be unwise to insist upon financial support for education that would be burdensome to the taxpayers. The increased tax load would be blamed upon the school system and would create in the minds of many taxpayers the feeling that our schools had become oppressively expensive.

But instead of raising the per capita $3.00 to equalize educational opportunity, it can be done by an increase of fifty cents per child. That increase will raise $400,000 a year. If that sum be wisely distributed among the poor counties, it will relieve their financial inadequacy. So, under the plan proposed in the constitutional amendment, instead of reducing the school fund for wealthier counties, there is provided a plan by which taxpayers in those wealthier counties may be taxed only to increase the school per capita fifty cents. Under the other plan of meeting the situation by raising the per capita to $15.00, they would have to pay taxes sufficient to increase the school distribution $3.00 for each child. This plan offers the most inexpensive, the most practical method by which educational inequality may be eliminated in the state. After that has been done, perhaps we can raise the per capita.

This is a problem we have had with us a long time. A census taker called at a humble home to take the census. She sought to get the information from a little girl. The child enumerated all members of the family. The census taker then asked, "How old is your grandmother?" The child replied, "I don't know, but we've had her quite a while."

The equalization amendment offers opportunity to solve the problem for all time to come. Just because we have always had the problem is no reason it cannot be solved.

A friend said to a young wife who was contemplating divorce, "Remember, dear, you took your husband for better or worse." The young wife said, "Yes, but I didn't take him for good, did I?"

There is no necessity for our taking this problem of unequal educational opportunity for good. We present a plan by which it may be solved "for good," and correctly.

The 1940 session of the Kentucky General Assembly left a record of notable public service. We did not urge a program of spectacular reform or notable departure. Our program was cautious and conservative. No legislation was enacted that will be hurtful to the state or its citizenship. Considerable legislation became law that is constructive and helpful. There is nothing spectacular about legislation that guarantees the financial solvency of the state; yet, there is nothing more vital. We enacted a cautiously sane budget bill in which reasonable provision was made for all phases of state government. Drafting of the budget would have been simple if there had been available $33 million with which to meet it. Requests of various agencies and departments for appropriations totaled $33 million. We could be certain of collecting from existing revenue laws only $25 million. We had the unhappy task of cutting the budget from $33 million to $26 million. We had the further disagreeable task of strengthening existing tax measures so as to raise an additional million dollars. That important task was accomplished. For the next two years Kentucky will live within her income. I hope that, by prudent, cautious conduct of the state government, we may be able to save a little out of the budget with which to make further reductions in the state debt. There is nothing in that prosaic accomplishment to arouse wild enthusiasm; yet, it is a major achievement.

There are those who assert that with adjournment of the legislature, the record of the present state administration was largely written. I disagree with that conclusion. It shall be my purpose to try to write the record of this administration through the doing, day by day, of a careful, competent administrative job.

The public school system of this nation has given us a highly literate citizenship. We are emerging from a disastrous depression. We went through that period of distress without serious disorder. This is one of the few nations in which depression brought hard times, that bloody revolt was not the tragic aftermath. It is difficult to reason with a hungry man; but it is impossible to reason with a hungry, illiterate man.

It is my opinion that the public school system did much to prevent disruptive revolt in this nation during the depression. I believe that those most adversely affected took a rational attitude toward their misfortune because their public school training had taught them to reason. The incendiary speeches of agitators did not inflame the minds of those that felt the pinch of hard times, because their intellectual level had been advanced by the public schools. Their sense of patriotism, taught in the public school, restrained them from rash action. Their more reasoned viewpoint led them to understand that revolution and disorder would only increase the chaos and defer the day of prosperity's return. Had a large percent of those thrown out of employment been illiterate, I shudder to contemplate how serious might have been a situation which was frightful at its best. A man of wisdom once said that no nation ever perished for lack of wise leaders; that there is greater danger from a lack of wise followers who have the good sense to choose wise leaders and to help formulate wise policies for the guidance of those leaders. And it is my opinion that the revolution, which was provoked by the depression in many nations, did not develop on this continent because a public school education had made wise followers of the citizenship.

If the public school system develops wise followers in abundance, the problem of leadership will solve itself. No leader of a subversive movement will get very far unless there be those who are persuaded to follow. Wise followers will not follow crack-brained, demagogic leaders. And when such individuals cease to have followers, they are no longer leaders.

There is no more important mission for the public school than that it develop millions of wise followers, men and women, who can differentiate the genuine from the counterfeit in leadership.

Such wise followers will have a sense of discrimination that will enable them to recognize "phony" propaganda. They will discriminate between the social usefulness of the idle rich, and the working, productive rich. They will discriminate between wise, able labor leaders and the walking delegate or radical agitator, between public welfare and private greed.

Kentuckians are eager for their children to have the benefits of good schools, be taught by properly trained teachers. They are willing to be taxed to pay the bill, so long as they are convinced that, as more money is provided for the schools, their children actually get better opportunities. I hope those to whom is delegated the difficult job of administering the financial affairs of the state will never be penurious with education. I hope educators will prove that more generous financial support of the public schools will make an adequate, tangible return on the investment. I hope educators will see the wisdom of refraining from demands for state financial aid that are out of proportion to the resources of the taxpayers.

There is a definite relationship between crime and illiteracy. The citizenship of the United States is the most literate in the world—and the most lawless. It reflects discreditably upon the schools (as well as the press, which is my major activity) that in this nation where the public school system has been most largely developed, crime is so widely prevalent. A strange anomaly that in this, the nation of least illiteracy, there is the most crime.

In no other nation has the press attained a higher development than on this continent. The sacred right of freedom of the press has been preserved inviolate in these United States, while dictators in European nations have banished this vital liberty. Yet, it is in this nation that crime is the most acute social problem. A search for the explanation leaves one baffled and confused. But the school and the press, representing potent agencies for advancement of good citizenship, dare not relax efforts to mobilize influences that are hostile to crime.

As we ponder the strange fact that in this, the most literate nation, there is also the greatest crime, the most lawlessness, we find facts, which, to considerable extent, absolve the public schools from the charge of being derelict in their duty.

There is a very definite relation between illiteracy and crime. Illiteracy unquestionably breeds crime. There is no more certain evidence of this fact than that those who constitute the prison population in Kentucky are in the main illiterate or have had meager educational advantages.

An analysis of the literacy of 2,378 inmates of the old Frankfort reformatory made a few years ago revealed that nearly a fourth of the population in the Frankfort prison had never attended school at all. There were 513 out of the 2,378 who had never been enrolled in school. There were 208 prisoners who had completed only the first grade; there were 335 who reached the second grade; there were 407 who only reached the third grade. The number who advanced to the seventh grade totaled 71 as compared with 407 who dropped out of school in the third grade. The number of prison inmates who reached the eighth grade totaled 106 as compared with the 513 who had never attended school. There were only 112 out of the 2,378 prisoners who claimed to have had any high school training.

These figures should provoke thoughtful consideration of the relation between crime and illiteracy. Crime is one of the costliest problems which confronts the state. The cost of maintaining a prisoner in the penitentiary is about $250 a year. I am under the impression that the average cost of keeping a boy or girl in school a year is less than $50.

These figures indicate that education is an effective antidote for crime. But you cannot inoculate children against crime if they never attend school at all, or if they drop out in the third or fourth grade. These data on inmates of the state reformatory suggest that greater emphasis should be placed on school attendance. One of the deficiencies of the school system may be ineffective enforcement of our attendance laws.

These data suggest the importance of the teacher so stimulating the interest of the child in school as to hold that interest, keep him in school, prevent him from dropping out. I fancy that many of those who quit school in the third and fourth grades did so because of an inferiority complex. They were ill at ease among other children. They did not develop self-confidence.

I realize that I have raised numerous questions and failed to suggest definite answers. Since I have occupied an official position in state government, I have been impressed with the fact that there are so darn many more problems than there are answers.

On one occasion, three city school superintendents leased a hunting lodge in the Canadian woods and prepared for an extended vacation. They agreed that two would stay at the lodge and read, and, the third would provide the game for the daily menu. The hunter the first day brought in a quantity of quail. The superintendent, whose job it was to supply the game the second day, returned with a deer. The third superintendent proceeded into the woods and unexpectedly was confronted with a lion. He was so frightened that he dropped his gun and ran. The beast pursued him. As he reached the threshold of the hunting lodge, the scared superintendent stumbled and fell. The lion ran over him and through the open door. The hunter jumped up and quickly closed the door, enclosing the lion within the room with his friends. He went around to a window and looked in. His companions were up on the rafters. He said, "Well, boys, you skin that one while I go bring in another one." Now I am suggesting that you solve these problems I have dragged in while I go and fetch in others.

The fine civilization which we have builded on this continent, and in which the public school system has been a major factor, has developed so many complexities as to make us dizzy as we try to untangle them. We are facing the crucial test of the American theory that every citizen should have an elementary education. If the emphasis we have placed upon creation of a literate citizenship is to justify itself as a national policy, it is necessary that this system of nationwide education develop leaders with the vision and resourcefulness to adjust the economic and social complexities that have created our most serious problems.

We must avert the tragedy of developing through education a splendid civilization which destroys itself because of complexities that develop within it; a social order that is unable to rectify the social maladjustments reflected in unemployment; an economic order that is unable to find the corrective for depressions; a governmental structure that fails to make itself responsive to the complex needs of the people.

I have faith in the composite judgment of the American people, because the influence of the public schools has made it a reasoned, intelligent judgment. But public education faces its most critical point in American history. Public schools must be so readjusted as to more adequately meet the needs of the nation that has for decades regarded education as a panacea for all national ills.

You, the teachers of the public school, face graver responsibility than any of your predecessors. But you are also confronted with a greater opportunity to demonstrate the wisdom of the American policy of providing a public school education for every citizen. If you measure up adequately to that responsibility, this nation will go forward to the heights of greater achievement. Should you fail, the disaster of that failure would be calamitous. The situation is a challenge to you and me. I have confidence that, together, we will meet that challenge.

---

1. When the Legislative Council met in December 1939, Johnson stated that the request for funds to put the teachers' retirement system into operation would have to be reduced from $750,000 to $500,000. Louisville *Courier-Journal*, December 20, 1939. He signed the teachers' retirement act on March 19, 1940. It provided for pensions ranging from $100 to $1,000 a year. No pensions were to be paid before July 1, 1942. *Acts of the General Assembly, 1940*, Chapter 192, pp. 742-50.

2. See speech from January 5, 1940, in this section. In 1935 the Textbook Commission adopted the Rugg textbook series in which Dr. Harold Rugg of Columbia University combined history, geography, and civics. The American Legion and the Kentucky General Association of Baptists charged that these books were "atheistic and pro-Marxist." In a speech to the Legion in Louisville on November 30, 1940, Johnson stated that he had no defense for the textbooks but that the state had a considerable investment in them. The Textbook Commission had taken them off the required list and made them optional for schools desiring to continue using them so that the investment would not be lost. Louisville *Courier-Journal*, December 1, 1940:

TRANSYLVANIA COLLEGE CONVOCATION
Lexington / January 8, 1941

I APPRECIATE this privilege of meeting with you at your convocation, having an opportunity to feel the fine spirit of this inspiring student body. I congratulate you upon the good judgment you have shown in selecting this splendid institution in which to better prepare yourself for a life of larger usefulness. One may live a life of satisfaction, make a contribution to the world, enjoy the financial and spiritual rewards of such a contribution, only if one prepares oneself to utilize innate abilities to the fullest extent. I commend you upon having the vision to realize this important fact, of availing yourselves of intellectual advancement here afforded.

There are those who are critical of our institutions of higher education. It is not difficult to find fault with our system of formal education. It is difficult to find the corrective for those things critics complain about. Will Rogers[1] once said, "College is a wonderful thing because it takes the children away from home just at the time they begin to argue."

The things taught in the schools are not an education, but the means to an education, said Emerson[2] more than a century ago. Such is as true now as then, and I hope you have made that discovery for yourselves. No royal road to learning has yet been found. No easy shortcut to an education has yet been discovered. Great as has been the progress in the science of teaching, prolonged, sustained mental effort is still necessary in getting an education. There have been many labor-saving devices perfected. But no invention has yet been stricken off by the brain of man which reduces the mental exertion necessary to reach the goal of graduation.

I heard of an aged, illiterate man who went into the office of an occulist and asked if he could buy a pair of glasses that he could read with. The doctor assured the man with certainty that such could be done. Testing of his eyes was started. As various lenses were placed before the eyes of the man, the doctor asked, "Can you read that line on the chart?" The patient continued to say he could not. Finally the exasperated doctor said, "Say, you can read, can't you?" The fellow said, "Thunder, no, that's what I want the glasses for."

Despite such defects as may exist, the colleges of Kentucky are meeting the responsibilities that are theirs in an admirable fashion. They are providing that training essential to leadership. There has always been a dearth of leadership. Never has there been a surplus of those prepared by adequate training to fill the positions of greatest responsibility. The foremost task of this college is to prepare men and women to assume the big jobs, to become leaders in various activities. Many of those who will be the leaders of educational thought in Kentucky in the next decades are within this group here assembled.

I regard it as especially fortunate that the morale of educators is being restored. During the bitter days of hard times, when governmental subdivisions, state, county, and city found it increasingly difficult to raise money with which to maintain educational standards, those engaged in the important job of teaching felt the cruel effect of an economy imposed by circumstance.

I can imagine that those of you who were preparing yourselves to become teachers could but wonder if you had not made a mistake in selection of your life's work. But this great nation, rendered prostrate by depression, is being restored to better times.

The distressing period of depression, from which we are emerging, has created a condition that is discouraging to youth. Many well-trained young men and women have found it impossible to secure employment despite training that has qualified them for useful activity. The fine enthusiasm of youth has been destroyed by discouragement. Failure to find a place in society has left these young folk with a feeling of futility and frustration.

The situation has been such as to justify young citizens, just out of college, in feeling that the period is past in which the door of opportunity stands ajar for every worthy youth. In this unhappy mental attitude youth is likely to conclude that there are no new frontiers, no oceans to cross, continents to explore, or poles to discover. The attitude of defeatism and futility has become distressingly prevalent. There is no more tragic victim of the depression than the youth who has had to breast this tide of defeatism, lost his enthusiasm.

It is difficult to encourage young Americans who face the cold realities of life in these days of restricted employment opportunity with words of hope. But there remain a succession of frontiers to be crossed such as have never faced youth. If I could wish but one thing for youth with assurance that the wish would be realized, I would express the desire that there be created a new attitude of expectancy, that you be encouraged to dream again, develop a sense of certainty and sustained enthusiasm.

Kentuckians who have been qualified for leadership have always found opportunity for exercise of their talents despite depression and adversity. You may well take pride in the fact that it is your good fortune to be a Kentuckian, share in the rich heritage of those who have made Kentucky history.

The first educational institution west of the Allegheny Mountains was built in Kentucky by Kentuckians who desired that their children have cultural advantages. Kentuckians have not only made the history of their state a colorful epic, but in every state of the Union they have left the imprint of their genius. Kentucky has furnished 105 governors to other states and territories.

Kentuckians, under George Rogers Clark,[3] extended the boundary of the United States from the Ohio River to the Great Lakes as result of the heroic campaign in which the frontiersmen captured forts Kaskaskia and Vincennes.

Kentucky furnished more soldiers in the war with Mexico than any other state, and it was a gallant young Kentuckian who scaled the walls of Chapultepec and planted the Stars and Stripes above the palace of the Montezumas.

The first steamboat was invented and constructed by John Fitch, a Kentuckian. The greatest ornithologist of the nation was John Audubon, a Kentuckian.[4]

One of the most gifted sculptors of the nation was Joel T. Hart, a Kentuckian, whose *Triumph of Chastity* is one of the masterpieces. One of the finest portraits painted by an American was that done by the brush of Jouett as he painted Henry Clay.[5]

Probably the greatest lawyer that has sat upon the bench of the Supreme Court since John Marshall was Samuel F. Miller, a Kentuckian, born in Richmond. The learned legal opinions of Chief Justice Robertson, of Kentucky, have been followed as legal precedent in the greatest tribunals from Washington to Westminster Hall. No greater journalist has arisen on this continent than Henry Watterson. Kentucky gave Lincoln to the North and Jefferson Davis to the South, and thousands of soldiers to both sides. There is abundant reason for Kentuckians feeling an intense pride in their state. Madison Cawein, a great Kentucky poet, it was who wrote:[6]

> This is Kentucky, turn and gaze;
> How fair the earth, the heaven so near,
> Where smile the stars, where glow the days
> More gloriously than here?

There are critics of Kentucky who charge that we place too great emphasis upon the traditions of which we are proud, live too much in the past, seek to recall and retain the glories of a forgotten era. They insist that the aristocracy of earlier days has sought to hold on to that past, perpetuate its customs, place undue stress upon birth and breeding in determining the worth of an individual. But this is true only in isolated instances and not to the detriment of Kentucky. There is arising a new aristocracy in Kentucky—the aristocracy of learning and achievement, the aristocracy that accepts those of obvious culture, finds companionship with those of vision, whose practical qualities have the faculty of translating that vision into action.

The accomplishments of these Kentuckians of a former day, men who achieved conspicuous success under circumstances no more favorable than exist today, have been no more notable than attainments of Kentuckians in recent decades.

The greatest single hero of the World War, so designated by General Pershing, was Sergeant Woodfill, a Kentuckian.[7]

A searching of *Who's Who in America* discloses scores of Kentuckians in varied phases of life who have attained eminence as result of superior accomplishments.

Elizabeth Madox Roberts[8] of Springfield, Kentucky, is recognized by literary critics as one of the foremost novelists of this continent.

Melvin Traylor,[9] a backwoods lad of Adair County whose ambition to do big things was first fanned by a sympathetic rural schoolteacher, attained a preeminent position in the banking system of the nation as president of the most powerful bank in Chicago.

Percy Johnson,[10] a Kentucky lad whose early advantages were meager, who faced the future with no more flattering prospect than lies before each of you, scaled the pinnacle of sucess, became a financial genius in the banking capital of the world.

Irvine Cobb,[11] whose youthful opportunities did not exceed yours, flashed athwart the literary firmament of the nation, attained international reknown and exceptional success.

Keats Speed,[12] managing editor of the *New York Sun,* is a Kentucky lad whose qualities of journalistic excellence lifted him to the heights of achievement.

An extended list of contemporary Kentuckians who have played a major role in important fields of endeavor could be presented, but it would not further illustrate the fact that there remain abundant opportunities for those who are prepared to seize upon them as they are offered. There are hundreds of young Kentuckians who have made their way forward despite adversities of the depression. They have had the ingenuity and vision that has impelled them forward.

Great as has been Kentucky's contribution to leadership of the nation, the supply of brains and courage has not been exhausted or even perceptibly depleted. Nor have all opportunities for large achievement been preempted. Your abilities may be circumscribed. You may not possess those innate qualities of greatness which when supplemented by educational training, qualify you for service of national conspicuity. But there is a position of leadership awaiting each of you in some useful activity, limited though it may be. The sphere of influence in which you radiate may be restricted to your immediate community or county. Yet large attainment is but a succession of smaller successes.

Our citizenship now faces a different situation, fraught with possibility of peril. Dictators with an unholy lust for power seek to enslave free peoples, destroy those governments in which freedom of the individual is the dominant ideal. It is a sad commentary upon the composite intelligence of the world that in this the most enlightened era of mankind, civilization is imperiled as never before.

Yet faced with the danger of subjugation by forces to whom our form of free government is obnoxious, peace-loving people that we are, we have no alternative other than to prepare as quickly as possible to defend our government, our way of life. Again I fancy that, as our citizenship faces this unhappy emergency, we shall face it grimly yet with reasoned judgment.

It is a time for genuine rather that jingoistic patriotism. A time for vital rather than vocal patriotism alone. A situation has again arisen which demands sacrificial devotion to this nation within which has developed, under a democratic form of government, the happiest and freest people in the world. We would be recreant to our duty as citizens did we not cheerfully make every sacrifice that may be required to maintain on this continent the freedom we cherish.

I doubt not that our people will face this crisis calmly, yet grimly. I anticipate that the rational, reasoned patriotism of our people, born of that knowledge acquired in this the finest educational system that has developed in any nation, will result in a national morale adequate to any demands.

The arsenals of our minds contain the information which guides logically to the conclusion that President Roosevelt was correct as he declared that our nation must become the arsenal of democracy. Ours will be a more fervent patriotism because it is based on information that is easily acquired as result of the free public school, a free press, and free facilities of communication. It is not intolerant as we insist that in America there shall be no Red without the white and blue. It is only elemental precaution that subversive forces not sabotage our freedom.

I sympathize and understand the troubled thought of many of you —the young men of military age especially. When the other World War broke out, I was a college student near the end of my junior year. I left school and voluntarily entered the army. I was disturbed that it interfered with my plans. Yet individual plans are unimportant when it becomes vital to the preservation of our freedom that we upset the plans of those who ruthlessly seek to put the shackles on civilization.

A man of wisdom once said that no nation ever perished for lack of wise leaders, that there is greater danger from a lack of wise followers. That thought suggests that those who fail to reveal the requisites for large leadership may become valuable members of society as prudent, patriotic, intelligent followers. If our educational system in the nation has prepared us for patriotic acceptance of our duty by developing wise followers, the problem of leadership will solve itself no matter what the emergency.

No leader of a subversive movement will get very far unless there be those who are persuaded to follow. Wise followers will not follow unpatriotic, demagogic leaders. And when such individuals cease to have followers, they are no longer leaders.

If there has been developed, as I confidently believe, through our educational system, millions of wise followers, men and women who differentiate the genuine from the counterfeit in leadership, we shall repel the foes of freedom.

An old Chinese philosopher once said, "Even in setting out on a 1,000 mile journey, you must start with the first step." So in preparation for life, with its uncertainty—whether you prepare for peace or war, the principle is the same. Do well today's job. And that after all is the age-old formula by which success is attained. A distinguished graduate of Transylvania was Professor Enoch Grehan.[13] As head of the Department of Journalism at the University of Kentucky, he greatly influenced my life. I recall an oft-repeated expression which fell from his lips—"Each day you have done your best, that in itself is success."

Yesterday is but a dream
And tomorrow is only a vision
But today, well lived, makes every
Yesterday a dream of happiness
And every tomorrow a vision of hope.

(From *Salutations of the Dawn*,
Translated from the Sanskrit)

Foremost thinkers of the nation say we are on the threshold of a new era. Youth is advised to prepare to meet a changing world. And none is there so blind as to be unmindful of changes that are taking place. But I see little that you can do about it other than try to learn to think clearly, develop an incisive intellect, be prepared to take the play as it comes to you.

The world will never change so much that the old virtues will not remain the yardstick by which we measure character. Honesty and courage, vision and intelligence, thoroughness and integrity are qualities you may cultivate without any fear that a changing world will render them obsolete.

There is an increased need for courage to face the uncertain future with minds clear, judgment unclouded, brain sane, head in the clouds, but feet on the ground. It is important that we recapture the resourcefulness and fortitude of the pioneer. There are unscaled heights to be reached in many fields of endeavor. They are going to be scaled by someone within the next quarter of a century whether war or peace prevails. Whether you are among the select company who cross these new frontiers is being largely determined by your daily attitude toward the student tasks before you.[14]

---

1. Will Rogers (1879–1935), b. Oklahoma. Actor and humorist. *Who Was Who in America, 1897–1942* (Chicago, 1943), 1:1053.

2. Ralph Waldo Emerson (1803–1882), b. Boston, Massachusetts. Philosopher, essayist, and poet. Leader in the transcendentalist movement. *Concise Dictionary of American Biography* (New York, 1964) pp. 271-73. His exact words were "accomplishments commonly taught children are not an education but the means of

education." From sermon "The Objects of Education," given September 23 and October 31, 1831. Kenneth Walter Cameron, *Index-Concordance to Emerson's Sermons* (Hartford, Conn., 1963), 1:144.

3. George Rogers Clark (1752–1818), b. Albemarle County, Virginia. Frontiersman and soldier who won important military victories in Northwest during the Revolutionary War. Lowell Harrison, *George Rogers Clark and the War in the West* (Lexington, Ky., 1976).

4. John Fitch (1743–1798), b. Connecticut. Came to Kentucky in 1778. Soldier, inventor, successfully operated a steamboat in 1787. *Biographical Encyclopedia of Kentucky* (Cincinnati, 1878), p. 407.

John James Audubon (1785–1851), b. Les Cayes, Haiti, of French parentage. Resided in Kentucky 1807–1819. Ornithologist, wildlife painter. L. Clark Keating, *Audubon: The Kentucky Years* (Lexington, Ky., 1976).

5. Joel T. Hart (1810–1877), b. Winchester, died in Italy. Sculptor, stonemason. *Biographical Encyclopedia of Kentucky*, pp. 58-59.

Matthew Harris Jouett (1788–1827), b. Mercer County. Portrait painter. Ibid., pp. 255-56.

Henry Clay (1777–1852), b. Hanover County, Virginia. Attorney, statesman. State representative, 1803. United States senator, 1806–1807, 1809–1811. United States representative, 1811–1821, 1823–1825; speaker, six terms; three times candidate for president. Ibid., pp. 7-10.

6. John Marshall (1755–1835), b. Germantown, Virginia. Fourth chief justice of the United States, 1801–1835. *Who Was Who in American Politics* (New York, 1974), p. 412.

Samuel F. Miller (1816–1890), b. Richmond. Doctor. Admitted to the bar 1844. Associate justice, United States Supreme Court, 1862–1890. Jonathan Truman Dorris and Maud Weaver Dorris, *Glimpses of Historic Madison County* (Nashville, Tenn., 1955), pp. 177-78.

George Robertson (1790–1874), b. Mercer County. Chief justice of Kentucky, 1829–1843. George Robertson, *An Outline of the Life of George Robertson* (Lexington, Ky., 1876).

Westminster Hall, London, England. Built by King William II in 1097. The Hall is connected with the Houses of Parliament, Palace of Westminster. Rulers of England held court in the Hall for nearly five hundred years.

Henry Watterson (1840–1921), b. Washington, D.C. United States representative, 1876–1877; editor, assumed management, *Louisville Journal*, 1868. *Who's Who in Louisville, 1912*, ed. Alwin Seekamp and Roger Burlingame (Louisville, 1912), pp. 231-32.

Jefferson Davis (1808–1889), b. Fairview, Christian County. United States representative, 1845–1846; United States senator, 1847–1851, 1857–1861; resigned at secession. President of the Confederacy, 1861. *Who Was Who in American Politics*, p. 183.

Madison Julius Cawein (1865–1914), b. Louisville. Lyric poet. *Who's Who in Louisville, 1912*, p. 83.

7. John Joseph Pershing (1860–1948), b. Linn County, Missouri. General, United States Army. *Who Was Who in American History: The Military* (Chicago, 1975), pp. 436-37.

Samuel Woodfill (1883–1951), b. Jefferson City, Indiana. Resided in Fort Thomas where an elementary school is named for him. Sergeant; Congressional Medal of Honor, 1918. Body moved to Arlington National Cemetery, 1955. Telephone interview, Howard Fischer,principal, Woodfill School, Fort Thomas, July 5, 1978.

8. Elizabeth Madox Roberts (1886–1941), b. Washington County. Author, literary critic. *Webster's Biographical Dictionary*, 1st ed. (Springfield, Mass., 1943), p. 1267.

9. Melvin Alvah Traylor (1878–1934), b. Breeding, Adair County. Attorney, banker. First National Bank, Chicago, 1919, president, 1925. *Who Was Who in America, 1897–1942*, 1:1251.

10. Percy Hampton Johnson (1881–1957), b. Lebanon. Chemical Bank of New York, 1917–1946; president and chairman of the board, 1935–1946. Frank Wilson Nye, *Knowledge Is Power: The Life Story of Percy H. Johnson* (New York, 1956).

11. Irvine Shrewbury Cobb (1876–1944), b. Paducah. Journalist, author, humorist, playwright, and screen writer. *Who Was Who in America, 1943–1950* (Chicago, 1950), 2:120.

12. Keats Speed (1879–1952), b. Louisville. Managing editor, *New York Sun*, 1924–1943. *Who Was Who in America, 1951–1960*, 3:807.

13. Enoch Grehan (1869–1937), b. Fayette County. Head, Department of Journalism, University of Kentucky, 1914–1937. *Who's Who in Kentucky, 1936*, p. 167, and *Lexington Herald-Leader*, December 12, 1937.

14. Remarks about the value of education in preserving the stability of the nation during the depression were deleted since they appear in the preceding speech.

KENTUCKY EDUCATION ASSOCIATION
Louisville / April 16, 1941

I AM glad to have this opportunity to express my appreciation for the fine contribution that is being made by the teachers of Kentucky in building a better citizenship. As governor of the state to whose service you have dedicated yourselves, I feel justified in asserting that you, the teachers of our children, may look to the future with increased confidence.

I have been greatly pleased that the school people of Kentucky have approved with enthusiasm other important changes in educational leadership that have recently taken place. Because the governor is chairman of the Board of Trustees of the University of Kentucky, he was especially anxious, as were all other members of the board, to obtain for president of the university the best qualified man available for that important post. Aside from my official responsibility in helping solve this important problem, I had the deep concern of an alumnus of the university that no mistake be made.

One of the unfortunate things about being governor is that there are so many more problems than there are right answers. But I am positive that the Board of Trustees of the university found the correct answer to a most important educational problem when Dr. H. L. Donovan was chosen as president of the University of Kentucky. That solution placed in the position of preeminent educational responsibility a native Kentuckian, a graduate of the university, for the first time in its history. Fortunately, there was available for the job one superbly qualified by training and experience. Under Dr. Donovan the university will have a dynamic, magnetic leader, a great administrator, a man of scholarly attainments, and one capable of building a greater university upon the foundation which has been laid under the direction of Dr. Frank L. McVey.[1]

Removal of Dr. Donovan from Eastern State Teachers College would have been a disservice to the cause of education had it not been for the fact that there was available as his successor one so admirably qualified as W. F. O'Donnell.[2] I have been delighted at the spontaneous, enthusiastic public acceptance of these changes which have strengthened educational leadership in Kentucky. And you of the KEA have contributed more to that favorable public acceptance than any other group because you know these men and their qualifications.

One year ago I expressed pride in the fact that an amended Teachers' Retirement Act had been enacted by the legislature on recommendation of the governor and the first appropriation of money made to put it in operation. During the year the teachers' retirement system has been strengthened by correct administration. The half million dollars appropriated by the state, together with contributions by teachers, have made the system sound as rock. It is actuarially correct. Confidence of the teachers in the system is indicated by the fact that 97 percent of all who are eligible to participate in benefits of the retirement act have availed themselves of its provision. It is important that we stand on guard to prevent tinkering with the system, keep it sound and solvent that teachers may have the security of retirement benefits after they have expended their lives in the service of the state.

I take pride in the fact that one of the achievements of this administration is that of providing a public school per capita of $12.33, the highest in the history of Kentucky. The budget act legalizes the expenditure of $26 million for each of the two years for which it makes provision. Of that sum approximately one half is being expended for education. That places the emphasis in the proper place.

I would call to your attention that the root of the local financial problems of the public schools lies in the failure of local authorities to properly assess taxable property. If all property was assessed, as the law directs, at 80 percent of its fair cash value, the needs of schools in many counties would be solved.

The governor has the responsibility of being head of the selective service in the state. I want to express my appreciation to the teachers for the substantial aid rendered in administering this important service. It is a fine compliment to the school system of the state that Kentucky boys have reacted to the present emergency so splendidly. I sympathize with boys whose plans are interrupted by necessity of military training.

You of the KEA are fortunate that you are to hear an address by a great American. Dr. Dykstra,[3] president of the University of Wisconsin, is one of the leading educators of the nation. He has distinguished himself as a great administrator. As the president looked the nation over for one to fill the important post of national director of the Selective Service Act, he drafted Dr. Dykstra for the job. He organized the selective service, had it functioning smoothly in every state within a few weeks. While he served in that position, he was my boss and I marveled at the speed and precision with which he created and set in motion the organization that is selecting our young men for military training.

Then as labor disputes produced acute problems, the president created a National Mediation Board. To this board is delegated the important task of settling labor controversies, settling strikes, preventing and minimizing loss of time in industries vital to defense. For this difficult and delicate job, the president selected Dr. Dykstra.

When a student in the university I recall a professor who said, "Wake up that fellow sitting next to you." The student replied, "You do it, professor, you put him to sleep."

Dr. Dykstra, I may have put this great audience to sleep but I am sure you will wake them up.[4] Ladies and gentlemen, I am delighted that I may present to you a great national leader, Dr. Dykstra.

---

1. Frank Le Rond McVey (1869–1953), b. Wilmington, Ohio. Fifth president, University of Kentucky, 1917–1940. *Who's Who in Kentucky, 1936*, pp. 278-79, and *Lexington Herald-Leader*, May 8, 1969.

2. William F. O'Donnell (1890–1974), b. Burnett, Texas. Superintendent, Richmond City Schools; president, Eastern Kentucky State College, 1941–1960. Archives, Eastern Kentucky University. At a dinner in honor of Donovan and O'Donnell in Richmond on June 24, 1941, the governor expressed confidence in both men. He referred to his effort to be a frugal governor and to the difficulty of resisting requests for more money. He commented that at dinner recently, "Dr. Donovan did a magnificent job of asking and I'm certain that the dinner we gave him didn't begin to atone for his disappointment at what I told him." *Richmond*

Daily Register, June 25, 1941. At a dinner given in honor of Donovan by the Lexington Board of Commerce on October 30, 1941, Johnson said that initially he had encouraged Donovan in his request for $900,000 for a field house but the need at the Houses of Reform at Greendale had greatly lessened the possibility of state assistance. Louisville *Courier-Journal,* October 31, 1941. The field house request was not new. In February 1940 the governor spoke between halves at a university basketball game and responded to cries of "We want a field house" by saying, "If it were as easy to pass tax bills and raise the money as it is to raise hell about a field house, we would soon get one." *Lexington Herald,* February 14, 1940.

3. Clarence Addison Dykstra (1883–1950), b. Cleveland, Ohio. City manager, Cincinnati, 1930–1937; president, University of Wisconsin, 1937–1945; provost, University of California, 1945. *Who Was Who in America, 1951–1960,* 3:246.

4. The speech has been edited. Parts apear in the speeches from April 19, 1940, and April 15, 1942, in this section, and a discussion of state finances appear in the speech from November 24, 1941, in the State Administration section.

GEORGETOWN COLLEGE CITIZENSHIP DAY
Georgetown / May 12, 1941

YOU are fortunate to be in Georgetown College. It is a great school, thorough, and has made a rich contribution. A college education enriches character, enlarges the individual's field of service, and broadens horizons of thought, but an A.B. or Ph.D. never makes any change in an a.s.s. I have no sympathy with those who feel our colleges are peopled with radicals. I personally believe that today's students are more mature and well rounded in their training and better prepared to accept leadership and citizenship than ever before. A small percent loaf awhile and disappear.

It is always a pleasure to be present and to have an opportunity to congratulate you who today attain citizenship.[1] You have the right to vote, the responsibility for your own actions, to pay your own bills, and to marry. You are becoming citizens of the greatest nation that has ever risen in the world—a nation full of happy, free, and liberty-loving people. Yet you must immediately become aware of the dangerous age in which you come to citizenship, aware of the serious dangers of curtailment of all these things we hold so dear. Liberties are taken for granted yet they are more highly valued when we face the possibility of losing them.

Only in the United States is there educational opportunity for all. The founders of the nation believed that a republic was the best form of government, but they were certain it could endure only if the citizens were literate and they emphasized education.

I sympathize with you young men. The war peril threatens to disrupt your plans. In 1917 I experienced the same anxiety. I left college and was in the army in three weeks after the war was declared. You face the probability of being called for military service. You who today attain the age of twenty-one become citizens with all its rights. You also must accept its responsibilities.

We have kept this fine social and economic order for one hundred and fifty years, and thus have kept our nation as a beacon light to the rest of the world. Whether we can keep it may be determined soon. It is your duty to help to preserve it.

Democracy emphasizes education for all. The dictator Hitler's philosophy, which he seeks to impose on the world, is different. In *Mein Kampf* [2] he wrote, "Universal education is the most corroding and disintegrating poison that liberalism has ever invented for its own destruction . . . . There must be only one possible education for each class . . . . We must therefore be consistent and allow the great mass of the lowest order the blessing of illiteracy."

You become citizens in a critical time—a time when forces hostile to this government we have inherited are at large in the world. Knowing this to be true, I appreciate the concern with which you must view acceptance of citizenship at this perilous time—a time of wars and near wars in all parts of the world. Adams, the historian, points out that democracies are born in unity and disintegrate in dissension, so, at this critical time, it is most important that our citizens have in their minds a unity toward the action of the leader of this great republic, our president.

It is a period of great challenge and opportunity. Dictators have an advantage in waging war; their orders are given. In a democracy a composite view of the people is considered. We must prove that democracy is not only the best form of government for peace, but is sufficiently virile to preserve itself in war. There have never been greater opportunities for youth. In becoming of age you must accept full responsibility for yourselves by being fully prepared, both in courage and fortitude of soul. That you will surely accept the challenge opening before you and will acquit yourselves like real men and women in facing the uncertainties ahead, remembering always that the responsibilities are ever greater than the rights of citizenship, is my deep conviction.[3]

---

1. The program was in cooperation with the National Education Association's observance of Citizenship Day to honor citizens who became twenty-one years of age during 1941.

2. In *Mein Kampf* Hitler sets down his political ideas, plans for German conquest, and his ideas on "race purity." It was the "bible" of the National Socialists in Germany and required reading in German schools.

3. A similar speech was given at Morehead State Teachers College on "I Am an American Day," May 15, 1941, and at Murray State Teachers College on the Fifth Annual Scholarship Day, April 28, 1942.

BOWLING GREEN HIGH SCHOOL GRADUATION
Bowling Green / May 22, 1941

I APPRECIATE the compliment of having been chosen to address this splendid group of young men and women who are being graduated from the Bowling Green High School. I rejoice with you of this fine community that there has been made available for these young Kentuckians the educational opportunity which comes to this happy climax today.

You fortunate members of the graduating class are to be congratulated upon having attained an important milestone along life's pathway. The diplomas which you receive today represent long years of studious effort. You are receiving these diplomas because this community and commonwealth made available for you the educational opportunity you have enjoyed. You are being graduated not only because of your own efforts, but because in instances devoted parents made sacrifices in order that you might utilize these advantages in preparing yourselves for lives of useful citizens. You in whose honor we are assembled on this happy occasion owe to those who have made possible the achievement we here commemorate a debt which you can pay only by using your training in promoting a better community, a greater state.

Nothing that is worth achieving can be accomplished without great effort, long years of toil. The individual who is looking for a soft snap, an easy way to get along in life, is certain to be disappointingly disillusioned.

You are graduating from high school at a critical time in the world's history. A vicious attack is being made upon the democratic form of government in the world. It is vital to our freedom and safety that this attack be repelled.

In these United States we believe that every boy and girl should have a chance to obtain an education. We place major emphasis upon a program of universal education. We expend more of the taxpayers' money for education than any other routine function of government. We believe that our form of government can justify itself only, and insure its continued existence only, by a program which develops an informed, literate citizenship.

[The governor quoted Hitler's statement on education.]

In that startling statement we find ample reason for being concerned about the threat from forces whose dictatorial leader boldly asserts that the masses should be kept in illiteracy. That philosophy of education and government must be thwarted in its effort to rule the world, destroy our form of government. And you of this graduating class are confronted with the stern duty of helping to crush that force which hopes to overthrow the kind of government under which this nation has grown great. It is vital to the future of civilization that we halt Hitler. The minds and hearts and will of the American people must be mobilized in a united effort to achieve that end.

Do not be deceived, my young friends, at the defeatist propaganda of the totalitarian states of Europe. Be not disturbed by the gloom of armchair tacticians at home. Democracy is still the most powerful form of government that enlightened people have ever devised. The self-governed peoples in the democracies will prevail over the brutal totalitarian forces of destruction. In a democracy the government obeys those whom it rules and the people rule the government which they obey. In dictator-dominated nations the people must obey the dictatorial decrees of an autocratic ruler or be shot without trial by a court of justice.

I readily agree that the first advantage in war accrues to dictatorships. The dictators have held the upper hand since Manchuria was invaded by the Japanese, since Nazi Germany remilitarized the Rhine, and Mussolini conquered ancient Ethiopia. They have had the decided advantage since September 1, 1939, when the Second World War began with Nazi invasion of Poland.

But dictatorship is geared to war, while democracy is geared to peace. The essence of dictatorship is destruction, while the heart of democracy is conservation. One tears down, the other builds up. The people of one lives in a dictated pattern, while the people of the other lives by self-administered law and order. Murder is the rule in a dictatorship, while democracy assumes that murder is the exception.

It is easy to see, therefore, how a dictated nation can create and maintain an efficient machine of destruction. The energy of every man, woman, and child is directed to a common purpose. Every pound of raw material, every industrial plant, every foot of railroad, every ton of shipping—even the museums, art galleries, parks, forests, theaters—are made the means to one end. Rational surprise lies not in the existence of such a machine, but in its inability to fulfill every whim of its masters.

Democracy, not being geared to war, necessarily is slow to arm itself for war. The wheels of democracy produce the instruments of peace, not destruction. The workers who turn the wheels are men of peace—men like your own fathers and their next-door neighbors.

We are slow to start, but once on the way, no force under heaven can prevail against us. Man for man, gun for gun, tank for tank, plane for plane, ship for ship, we are stronger than any dictator-driven force in the world.

The young man called to arms in a dictatorship knows only one thing, and that is how to fight under directions. He was born to fight, trained to fight, and taught that his sole destiny lies in the profession of arms.

The young man called to arms in our democracy knows more in a minute than a totalitarian youth knows in a month—and he will make a better soldier in just that proportion. He was born in a free state and all his life has known he has freedom of speech, worship, and initiative. He has been educated, rich boy and poor boy side by side, for all the pursuits that a free people have devised for their comfort, health, prosperity, and happiness.

A man will fight harder to preserve that which he knows is good than he will to seek what he has only been told is good. The passage of time has a way of distilling centuries of accumulated wisdom into short, simple sentences. The old expression "a bird in the hand is worth two in the bush" is no exception. It aptly illustrates the point.

The older men who have been charged with the responsibility of girding this democracy with armor, and making it invincible with arms, know more in a minute than the totalitarian worker does in a month—and they will make better workers and turn out better products in just that proportion.

The totalitarian worker already has worn his fingers to the bone making just one thing—arms and equipment for soldiers, sailors, and aviators. For nearly a decade now, he has been eating short rations, sleeping troubled sleep, and working long hours—week in and week out, month in and month out, year in and year out.

All this time our workers have been making the finest products in the world but dedicated to peace instead of war. They have been making automobiles, books, playground swings, homes, refrigerators, canoes, cameras, radios, surgical instruments, glass bricks, streamlined trains, civilian airplanes, toys, tractors, steam cookers, and electric fans. They have been making the accouterments of peace.

But now our workers, skilled in a thousand skills and fresh from the infinite variety of peaceful pursuits, are concentrating their vast pool of talents and inexhaustible source of energy on the production of armaments. They have had merely to readjust their lathes and tools and to set up new lathes and tools in new plants.

All this has taken time, and its passage has been cruelly long. Because we are a free people, we have fretted at the delay. We have been free to criticize the president, the army, the navy, the cabinet, Congress, capital, labor, and the weather. A totalitarian populace cannot criticize. That is their fatal weakness in the long run. We can. That is the secret of our prevailing strength.

But the wheels of industry have now been regeared, and new wheels are being set up with every passing hour. Our free, enthusiastic, capable, and willing concentration on the task of arming this nation will soon outstrip in quality and quantity the very best that can be produced by the weary industrial slaves of the totalitarian nations in Europe and Asia. But we must hurry.

A democratic force of free men, who know what they are fighting for and equipped with accouterments made by master craftsmen trained at the work benches of peace, in the long run can and will prevail against any force of driven men that can be held together by vicious masters.

Your future, and mark well my words, is bright with the prospects of work, service, adventure, and responsibility. This sorry conflict between the economies of slaves and free men will be over by the time you have reached the full stature of adulthood. This great nation will then be yours to run and to shape for the span destiny has allotted you. Looking to the future, I see this nation as the great beacon of hope for the weary survivors of a worldwide debacle of death and destruction. By precept and example, by the extended arm of sympathetic help, this nation will have to nurse a sick world back to health.

For you, I see a country where the extremes of wealth and poverty are to be drawn closer together. I see a country where work will be plentiful in a common effort to provide decent shelter, clothes, and food for all. I see a country of new frontiers in public service, in the extension of common comforts to the underprivileged millions who heretofore have been the by-products of an economy that makes the rich richer and the poor poorer.

The future will not be easy. It will not bring you great riches in gold and silver. But there will be work to do, plenty of it. There will be new frontiers of service for you to explore. I envy you your prospects for an eventful, full, satisfying future.

Let me urge you to seek increased preparation in institutions of advanced education. Prepare yourselves either for leadership, if such be your destiny, or to become wise and patriotic followers. A century and a half ago courageous pioneers trekked through the pathless forest into this land of amazing beauty. Here they established the first citadel of civilization west of the Allegheny mountains. They loved freedom. They were zealous crusaders for increased liberty and opportunity. Daniel Boone, Simon Kenton[1] and George Rogers Clark, together with their stouthearted followers, established in the wilderness this the Commonwealth whose glorious history has been a colorful epic.

The first constitution of Kentucky was framed at Danville 150 years ago. Those men of valor and intellect blazed new trails in government just as they had blazed new trails through the trackless forest. These lovers of freedom and democracy wrote into that constitution a guarantee of free manhood suffrage. They established the principle that every man should have the right to vote whether he owned property or not. It was the first time that ownership of property had been eliminated as a requisite to the privilege of voting. If we develop through the school system thousands of wise followers, men and women who can differentiate the genuine from the counterfeit in leadership, such will strengthen the national defense, give impetus to progress in peace.

It is vital that schools teach youth how to use the liberty that is their inheritance—impress upon them that with the rights of citizenship there are grave responsibilities. The right of freedom of thought can be abused —it should not be. Freedoms of speech and press can be abused to an extent as to be hurtful to the government which guarantees them.

As an individual you may or can exercise your constitutional right to freedom of speech. You may persist in the attitude that I am going to say what I please. In so doing you may condemn the leadership of the president. You may criticize his guidance. You have the right to do that. As you persist in doing that you will, if joined by sufficient number, prevent that unity of mind and heart necessary within the nation to resist effectively a type of government that denies its citizens any of these rights. By stubborn insistence upon these rights, you may create a situation that will result in you losing them.

It is our duty to demonstrate that an educated people understand and appreciate their government; that they have the perception to realize that it is emperiled; that they have the courage to repel that foe of freedom.[2]

---

1. Daniel Boone (1735–1820), b. Pennsylvania. Famous pioneer and explorer, first came to Kentucky with John Finley; colonel. *Biographical Encyclopedia of Kentucky*, p. 488.

Simon Kenton (1755–1836), b. Virginia. Indian fighter, pioneer. Ibid., pp. 781-82.

2. The same speech was given at Madisonville High School, May 22, 1942. Parts

of the speech have been edited. They appear in speeches from January 8, 1941, May 12, 1941, and June 4, 1941, in this section.

EASTERN KENTUCKY STATE TEACHERS COLLEGE COMMENCEMENT
Richmond / June 4, 1941

I APPRECIATE the compliment of having been invited to address this splendid group of young men and women who are being graduated from Eastern Kentucky State Teachers College. Eastern's brilliant record of contribution to the educational leadership of Kentucky is particularly noteworthy

Man's progress through the ages has been slow and laborious. In his march toward a better order, he has experienced frequent reverses. During certain periods of the world's history, man has established new outposts of civilization, far in advance of the maddening crowd. Athens is a classic example of such an outpost of civilization. Florence, under the Medici during the Renaissance, is another. But these examples are like the vanguard of an army that gets too far ahead of the main body of troops and finally is compelled to retreat before an approaching enemy. Athens in all of its glory was destroyed by the Romans who were not the equals of the Athenians in intellect and culture. Rome was finally captured by the barbarians. While the march of civilization has usually been forward, there have been many times when it was halted and the world has known its dark ages.

It may be that we are in such a period today. Civilization has once more been challenged. It has doubtlessly been halted. The world may be facing another dark age. Whether civilization is permanently halted by a fierce and warlike people who resort to the methods of barbarians will probably depend on the attitude of America in stopping these modern Huns.

The course of civilization must ever be forward. Education has, through the centuries, been one of the important instruments by which progress has been made. In former centuries, education was a privilege reserved for the scholar, the statesman, the diplomat, and the churchman. It was not regarded as essential to the welfare of the masses. If a favored few who occupied positions of honor and trust were educated, this was all that was believed to be necessary for the perpetuity of the state. All too frequently, the ruling class desired to keep the masses in ignorance because they were afraid of what might hapen if they were permitted to become enlightened.

Popular education received its first great impetus as a result of the Protestant Reformation. Luther and Calvin preached a gospel of personal salvation. They believed that if one was to attain eternal life, he must know the Scriptures; and to know the Scriptures, one had to be able to read. This doctrine constituted a powerful motive in advancing the education of the masses. If heaven was to be attained only by those who could read the Bible, the desire to learn how to read was naturally a passion with every individual who accepted this belief. Our Pilgrim fathers brought this Calvinistic concept of religion to our shores when they landed at Plymouth Rock, and because of their religious faith they established schools as early as 1648 so that their children might learn how to read the Scriptures and thus evade Satan. The motive for the establishment of public schools in the colonies was at first a religious motive.

The seeds of democracy were early planted in the thirteen original colonies. Slowly but surely, democracy developed. That all men were created free and equal before the law became an ideal in the New World. The philosophy of Voltaire, Rousseau, Paine, and Thomas Jefferson influenced the thinking of the leaders of our country. As a result of the growth and development of the spirit of democracy, we finally wrote our Declaration of Independence and fought the Revolution to establish on this continent a new nation conceived in liberty and dedicated to the ideal that all men are born free and equal. No sooner had we obtained our liberties and set up a government democratic in form than the founding fathers recognized that the very existence of this type of government depended upon the enlightenment of the masses. To learn how to read to save their souls was the first great urge that caused many to secure the fundamentals of an education. With the founding of the republic, it became evident to the leaders that the people should learn how to read and think to save their independence and freedom.

The founding fathers have left ample evidence of their great faith in the necessity of educating the common man. Let them testify to this fact.

First we shall call on the father of our country who said, "Promote, then, as an object of primary importance, institutions for the general diffusion of knowledge. In proportion as the structure of a government gives force to public opinion, it is essential that public opinion should be enlightened."

John Adams, explaining the New England point of view with regard to education, had this to say: "The instruction of the people for the proper practice of their moral duties as men, citizens, and Christians, and of their political and civil duties as members of society and freemen is a public responsibility which should extend to all, of every rank and class of people, down to the lowest and the poorest. . . . No expense for public education would be thought extravagant."

The author of the Declaration of Independence, the founder of the University of Virginia, and the author of the statutes of religious freedom, the outstanding philosopher of our democracy [Jefferson], said, "If a nation expects to be ignorant and free in a state of civilization, it expects what never was and never will be. There is no safe deposit (for the functions of government), but with the people themselves; nor can they be safe with them without information."

First chief justice of the United States[1] wrote: "I consider knowledge to be the soul of a republic; and as the weak and the wicked are generally in alliance, as much care should be taken to diminish the number of the former as of the latter. Education is the way to do this, and nothing should be left undone to afford all ranks of people the means of obtaining a proper degree of it at a cheap and easy rate."

The fourth president of the United States, James Madison, declared: "A popular government without popular information or the means of acquiring it is but a prologue to a farce or a tragedy, or, perhaps, both. Knowledge will forever govern ignorance; and a people who mean to be their own governors must arm themselves with the power which knowledge gives."

An examination of the speeches and correspondence of the distinguished leaders of this democracy would reveal that each of them believed that the perpetuity of the republic depended in a very large measure upon the intelligence of the citizens of the nation. America is the first great nation in the world to embrace without reservation the philosophy that the masses could be made sufficiently intelligent to determine the choice of their leaders and the policies of their government.

These are trying days in which we live. The nation has never faced a crisis so acute as we face today. Democracy is challenged. Many of the democracies in other parts of the world have perished before a ruthless and brutal totalitarianism. Democracy in our own nation is threatened. Our country, therefore, needs men and women who are highly intelligent and ready to repay their debt to society by being useful to the social order.

Has your education resulted in making you a more patriotic citizen of this democracy? Has it developed within you a high morale and a keen appreciation of what America means, not only to the citizens of our own country but to the world at large? Has it given you a better understanding of the nature and philosophy of democracy as a way of life? Are you willing to sweat, toil, suffer, and even die, if you are called upon to make this sacrifice, that this nation shall not perish from the earth? We know not the day when you may be put to the test. By your actions we shall then discover whether or not the state's investment in you has been wisely made. I have confidence, if that test ever comes, that you will quit yourselves as men and heroes, thus justifying the faith of your fathers in the validity of education.

If you are called upon to defend your freedom, I would remind you that you are not the first generation of youth that has been called to fight for its liberties. There were young men at Valley Forge with Washington. They walked barefooted in the winter and incarnadined the snow with their footprints so that this nation might be free. And again in 1917 and 1918, some of your fathers went to war and crossed the sea to make the world safe for democracy. Their fight for freedom, I maintain, was not in vain. The same diabolical forces of militarism that would have engulfed the world in 1917 and 1918 had we not gone to the rescue of the democracies of Europe are loosed again, and young men and older men are now called upon to preserve that freedom which we have so long known and so greatly cherished.

Democracy is not a thing that can be purchased once and for always. It would appear that we have to fight periodically to maintain our freedom if we would not lose it. It is probable that freedom would become a common and unappreciated thing if it did not have to be purchased at such a fearful cost. But we who know what it costs in blood and human sacrifice know how to appreciate its value.

If this education which you have secured over a period of sixteen years has so disciplined you in mind and body and has cultivated in you appreciations and values that make you willing to defend your country in time of peril, the state has not wasted any money on your education. I, as the governor of your state, believe that you are made of such mettle that you will not count the cost if you are called upon to dangerously serve your country and defend it against aggressors.

Has this education which you have obtained during these years in which you have been going to school developed in you a finer appreciation of moral values? Do you not only demand the precious freedoms guaranteed under the Constitution such as the freedom of the press, of speech, of religious worship, of assembly, and all other freedoms set forth in the Bill of Rights, but do you also appreciate the fact that there is resting upon you corresponding duties and responsibilities to be a good citizen? Has this education developed in you a keener appreciation of honesty in your dealings with your fellowman and in those transactions which you have with the state? Do you believe in justice and righteousness and will you work to see that they prevail? Are you interested in giving as well as getting? Are you conscious of the dignity of every personality and that the individual counts regardless of his station in life? If you have sentiments like these in your heart, the state has made a good investment in you.

Have we justified the faith of our fathers in the value of an education as a solvent for the ills of our republic? Has education contributed to the moral values of the nation? Are educated people more patriotic than those who are ignorant? Do they have a finer appreciation of their country and a greater love for it? Are educated people better prepared for leadership and responsibility? Is the educated man a better citizen? Is education a great national asset?

These are pertinent, pungent questions. It would be great if we could answer all of them with an unequivocal "Yes." An affirmative answer can be given to most of these soul-searching questions, but unhappily there are always exceptions. The thermometer is not the only thing without brains that is sometimes graduated. Yet the great experiment conducted on this continent for the last 150 years justifies the conclusion that education contributes greatly to our national well-being. And the nation's strength is in the strength of its people who are intelligent, righteous, upright, patriotic, and virile.

You have had eight years of elementary education, four years of secondary education, and four years of college education. At long last after sixteen years of study and toil, you are to receive a diploma signifying that you have earned a baccalaureate degree. This is no mean accomplishment.

As governor of the Commonwealth, I should like to remind you at this time that the entire cost of this education which you have secured has not been borne by you or by your family. A generous Commonwealth has provided you with a free elementary school, a free high school, and a state college where the costs of obtaining a higher education are extremely low. In all, the state has invested in your education a minimum of at least $1,500 to $2,000. This has been done by society on the basis that it would be good business to make this investment in you. You will, I have no doubt, render value received to the Commonwealth for the stake it has in you.

The account you give to society of your stewardship will determine in no small degree what future investments the state will make in the education of its youth. Our people believe today as much in education as the founders of the republic believed in it. They have demonstrated this faith through erection of the magnificent schools and colleges of our state and nation. Even in this period of great expenditures for national defense, they know the schools must function without interruption. Paul McNutt,[2] federal Social Security Administrator, testifying before a Senate committee recently, expressed the prevailing attitude of our people regarding the importance of this policy. He said, "The education of youth cannot await the end of an emergency of an indeterminate duration. We can defer building a road, a bridge or a building and catch up on its construction later. We cannot put educational opportunities for our children in cold storage for the duration of the war or even a period of financial stress, and restore it later."

The kind of world in which we live today requires an educated citizenship, if we are to survive, if we are to preserve here that form of government in which the government obeys those whom it rules and the people rule the government which they obey.

You of this graduating class are faced with the stern duty of helping to protect that kind of government. You will answer that call of duty, make the sacrifices it imposes, because of a fervent patriotism based on reasoned judgment.

My wish for each of you is that you may have the courage, the patriotism, the stamina and fortitude to vindicate the wisdom of those forefathers who committed this nation to the policy of providing an education for every worthy youth.[3]

---

1. John Jay (1745–1829), b. New York, New York. First chief justice, United States Supreme Court, served until 1795. Authored articles in *The Federalist*. Representative to First and Second Continental congresses; governor, New York, 1795–1801. *Who Was Who in America, 1607–1896* (Chicago, 1963), H:277.
2. Paul Vories McNutt (1891–1955), b. Franklin, Indiana. Attorney; governor, Indiana, 1933–1937; administrator, Social Security, 1939–1945; chairman, War Manpower Commission, 1942–1945; high commissioner, 1937–1939, 1945, and ambassador, Philippines, 1946–1947. *Who Was Who in America, 1951–1960*, 3:587.
3. The speech has been edited. Parts appear in speeches from January 8, 1941, April 16, 1941, May 12, 1941, and May 22, 1941, in this section.

CONSTITUTIONAL AMENDMENT ON SCHOOL FUND
Louisville / October 31, 1941

I AM delighted to speak briefly on this program in behalf of Constitutional Amendment Number 1.[1] This amendment will appear on the ballot at the regular election held throughout Kentucky next Tuesday.

Constitutional Amendment Number 1 is designed to make it possible for the General Assembly to appropriate additional funds for those school districts in Kentucky which levy the maximum tax rate and which still do not have sufficient money to offer an acceptable school program. At present all of the state school fund must be distributed on a census pupil or per capita basis. If the amendment is adopted, I shall recommend to the General Assembly that the amount of money made available for per capita distribution be retained at its present level and that an additional or supplementary fund be provided for distribution to school districts on the basis of need in accordance with laws enacted for that purpose. In this way there would be no reduction in the present per capita fund and no school district would be penalized in any manner.

Section 183 of the state constitution provides: "The General Assembly shall, by appropriate legislation, provide for an efficient system of common schools throughout the state." Thus education is a state function. All of the children in Kentucky are entitled to at least the minimum essentials of a good school program.

Kentucky has made great progress in the field of public education, especially in recent years. The adoption of the present educational code, provision for free textbooks for all elementary school children, increased state per capita, and the enactment of a sound teacher retirement system are outstanding accomplishments. Yet, despite this progress more than 200,000 Kentucky children have only a seven-month school term per year and have school facilities and equipment which are just as meager.

The General Assembly has made several attempts to remedy this situation. In 1930 an appropriation was made for "equalization" purposes, and in the school year 1930–1931 approximately $600,000 was distributed to certain school districts in the state for the benefit of children who were underprivileged, insofar as school services are concerned. In 1931 this plan was declared unconstitutional by our courts, as it violated Section 186 of the state constitution, which section we are seeking to amend next Tuesday. In 1936 and 1938 bills were proposed which would have placed a statewide real estate tax of from thirty to fifty cents on the $100 assessable wealth, for the benefit of the state per capita fund, with the further provision that the maximum local levies in all school districts would be lowered by a corresponding amount. One of these measures known as House Bill 204 was narrowly defeated in the House in 1938. This proposal, had it been enacted into law, would have been detrimental to many school districts in the Commonwealth that would have suffered great losses in revenue and would have been faced with the alternative of either drastically cutting educational services or greatly increasing the local tax rate.

The adoption of Constitutional Amendment Number 1 will provide a sound, sane, and sensible plan for the General Assembly to meet the needs of those children in Kentucky whose school services are substandard, without in any way injuring the fine educational programs in our wealthier school districts. Furthermore, these enriched and improved educational services may be provided at a minimum cost to the state as funds can be appropriated only where actually needed.

Schools are maintained at public expense for the purpose of training young people for the duties of citizenship in our great democracy. In these troubled times when the democracies of the world are being sorely tried, it is altogether appropriate that we should devote our attention to a measure of this kind which will make it possible to raise educational standards throughout our state and thus strengthen our American way of life.

It is my judgment that Constitutional Amendment Number 1 is one of the most meritorious proposals that has been brought before the voters of Kentucky in many years. Its adoption will ultimately guarantee to every child in Kentucky his sacred birthright of the opportunity for a good education.

Let me urge you to go to the polls on Tuesday and to vote "Yes" on Constitutional Amendment Number 1. I sincerely trust that it may be ratified by an overwhelming vote.[2]

---

1. See the speech from April 19, 1940, in this section for the provisions of this amendment.
2. The amendment was adopted by a vote of 312,986 to 53,924. It was passed by the Senate by a 27-7 vote on February 13, 1940, and by the House by a 71-21 vote on February 27, 1940. *Journal of the Senate, 1940,* 2:1503-7 and *Journal of the House of Representatives, 1940,* 3:3162-65.

KENTUCKY EDUCATION ASSOCIATION
Louisville / April 15, 1942

IT is a pleasure and privilege to have this opportunity to express my appreciation for the splendid public service being performed by the teachers of Kentucky. I want to express again my admiration for the able leadership in education of John Brooker, superintendent of public instruction. Two years ago I told you that John and I were going to demonstrate that the cause of education can best be advanced when the governor and the superintendent of public instruction work together harmoniously. Two years have passed and the only change that has occurred in the relationship between the governor and Superintendent Brooker is that the governor has an enhanced respect for the superintendent of public instruction. I find great satisfaction in the fact that in working together we have been able, with the help of the KEA, to significantly advance the cause of public education.

One year ago I expressed to you the hope that the educational equalization amendment to the Kentucky constitution would be approved by the voters. We all rejoice that it carried decisively. The recent session of the General Assembly enacted into law a measure which makes provision for distribution of the $400,000 equalization fund which was appropriated. I regard this as one of the most important advances toward improved educational opportunity that has been taken in Kentucky in half a century. There has been no accomplishment of my administration in which I find greater satisfaction. I am glad to have been able to help you of the KEA in performing this notable service for public education.

As result of this legislation, in the next school year, those school districts which make the maximum effort and are yet unable to provide as much as $30.00 a year for the education of each child enrolled in school will receive supplemental aid from this special fund.[1]

The teachers' retirement system has been securely established and the law enacted two years ago has proved adequate and workable. In the recently enacted budget law, the appropriation for teachers' retirement fund was increased from $500,000 to $650,000 a year. So we may find satisfaction in the fact that teachers' retirement has been perfected on a sound actuarial basis and adequate state money provided to make it financially solvent. We have provided money necessary to maintain the public school per capita at $12.70 which is the highest in the history of the Commonwealth.

I am glad I can report to you that Kentucky's state debt has been wiped out and that our Commonwealth is in the best financial condition in its history. The amazing financial reformation that has taken place in Kentucky in the last six years creates a situation that makes possible increased financial support for public education. In the budget act enacted by the General Assembly recently, the largest item of increased appropriation was that of $960,000 a year for education. Of that sum $400,000 is for the equalization fund, $150,000 for an increase in teachers' retirement, and the remainder for more generous aid to the institutions of higher education in our state.

Public education is a primary function of the state. The training of children cannot be postponed or delayed. Despite the war and the uncertainty of the future, the state has recognized this fact and has attempted within its ability to adequately finance a sound educational program during the present emergency. The first teachers' tenure law was enacted.

In addition to the progressive legislation which has been enacted in recent years, no laws have been passed that would tend to vitiate the splendid program that has been developed in the state. The integrity of the educational code has been maintained and no backward steps have been taken. No bad law was added to the statute books by the recent legislature.

Training for citizenship in our democracy is the function of public education. In these critical days of total war, it is the duty of the schools to reorganize and readjust their programs so as to make the maximum contribution to the winning of the war.To this task you as teachers have dedicated yourselves.

I want to take this opportunity to thank you, the teachers of the state, for your efficient helpfulness in the last registration conducted under the state Selective Service organization. Colonel Rash,[2] state director of Selective Service, said to me this morning that the help given by the teachers in mobilizing the manpower of the state was a very fine service, cheerfully and competently performed. I am sure you will give us the same kind of cooperation when the day dawns on which we are to register the elderly men of the state for classification as to military usefulness.

Soon your services will be requested to help us register the entire population as we prepare to work out the details by which the rationing of sugar and other essential commodities is to be perfected. I want to acknowledge with grateful thanks the considerable contribution you have made to these important war activities.

This is a very expensive war. It requires about a billion and a half dollars a month to finance our war activities. Most of that money can be obtained only by borrowing it from our citizens. In Germany the government seizes the wealth of its subjects when such is needed to sustain their war program. But in this great republic your government only asks that you loan your money with which to prepare an army that is to fight our battles and defeat our foes. We are asked to buy war bonds, loan our money and take the bonds of our government in exchange. If we win the war, those bonds will be redeemed and will be a good investment. Should we lose the war, you will not only lose what you invested in the bonds but everything else you have. Give your help in selling war bonds. These bonds are an investment in the future in America.

The schoolteachers of the nation are the shock troops of democracy. How well we are prepared mentally and spiritually to wage this war for survival has been determined to a great extent by the thoroughness with which the school system of the nation has inculcated in our citizenship a genuine and rational patriotism. It is too late to alter that situation. If the job has been well done, if love of our nation, an appreciation of this great republic has been instilled in our citizenship as they passed through the public schools, we are well prepared to meet the impact of war. If that which has been taught in the schools has developed a deep devotion and a fierce loyalty to the United States and its form of government, the arsenals of the mind have been well prepared for the supreme test to which we are being subjected as a republic.

I am convinced that the job has been well done in Kentucky. As the war governor of Kentucky, I am glad that I can say to you that the fire of patriotic fervor burns brightly in the hearts of Kentuckians. That is due to the fact that love of country was implanted in our hearts as we attended the public school.

The children of Germany have been dangerously but skillfully schooled. They have been taught to hate democracy. Their thinking has been regimented. Our children have been taught to love democracy. They have been encouraged to do their own thinking and develop initiative. Diametrically opposed philosophies of education clash in this war. The battlefront is the cruel testing ground upon which our system and ideal of education is being tested.

There are dark days of distress ahead. We shall have to do without many comforts of life. We shall have to give of our money in the purchase of war bonds—and you, the teachers, should be the leaders in your communities in that worthy activity.

We shall have to give our sons, whose lives will be offered a sacrifice upon the altar of freedom. We must suffer the anguish of broken hearts. We must mobilize the minds and the hearts and the wills of Kentuckians to make the maximum contribution to victory. We must understand that unless we win this war we lose everything we hold dear. Loss of the war would mean loss of our free public schools; loss of the right by our ballots to select our leaders; loss of the right to attend the church of our choice; loss of the right to criticize the conduct of public affairs. Loss of the war means economic and spiritual slavery for this free people.

As we consider the frightful consequence of losing this war, we come to an increased understanding of the vital importance of winning the war. You, the educators of Kentucky, represent the intellectual leadership of the state. It is your duty to become zealous evangels for freedom. It is your duty to paint the picture of the frightful consequences of losing this war. It is your duty to exert yourselves in stimulating our people to great sacrifice —sacrifice that must be made as a matter of patriotic duty—sacrifice that must be made to prevent the destruction of our nation, the enslavement of our children.

War is a frightful and ugly thing. The bloodshed, the starvation, the privation that war brings upon us is hideous and horrible. But frightful as is war the conditions that would certainly result from losing the war are far more ghastly and repugnant. And we can lose this war, unless the American people become so aroused as to the sinister consequences as to exert every ounce of strength, throw every resource in manpower and money into this struggle for survival. You, the teachers of the state, are the logical individuals to man the stations in the watchtowers, to perform the mission of a modern Paul Revere, warn of the danger that impends and stimulate our people to make the maximum effort in behalf of the liberty which you have taught our youth to cherish.

Let us unite our efforts to awaken every Kentuckian to the peril of this critical hour. Let us unite in prayer to the God of Justice and Mercy to sustain our nation in this period of travail and anguish. If we, as a nation, may be awakened to the grave dangers of these trying days, put our trust in God and our faith in the destiny of America, we can and will win this war, repurchase democracy, preserve our liberties and privileges which we may pass on to our children as the blood-bought heritage of a gallant, unconquerable people.

---

1. George L. Evans, Department of Education, announced on April 8, 1943, that an average of approximately $2.71 per pupil would be paid to thirty-seven poor school districts in the distribution of the 1943–1944 Kentucky Equalization Fund of $400,000. *Lexington Herald*, April 9, 1943.

2. Frank Dillman Rash (1878–1946), b. Saint Charles. Democrat; engineer; colonel, 149th Infantry, United States National Guard; lieutenant colonel, United States Army Reserve; mayor and city councilman, Erlington. Wallis and Tapp, *A Sesquicentennial History of Kentucky*, 3:1281-82, and *Lexington Herald*, April 19, 1946.

INSTALLATION OF HERMAN LEE DONOVAN
Lexington / May 6, 1942

DOCTOR DONOVAN, the program of the day reaches its culmination in the official induction of you into the presidency of the University of Kentucky. It is a matter of personal gratification that I, as governor of the Commonwealth and chairman of the Board of Trustees, have the privilege of taking part in this service.

You are taking this important place without reservation and you will give to it all the ability, strength, and purpose you have. My colleagues in this program of induction have commented on the responsibilities and burdens that a state university president must accept. I need not reiterate what they have said; however, as a friend of yours of many years I desire for you real joy in the services you can render to the state through the great university over which you preside. You can depend on the friendly advice and efficient help of the many who love the university. These will be yours in the days of hard going, as well as in the "ways of pleasantness and the paths of peace."

Knowing you as I do, I am sure you will maintain freedom of teaching and of speech on this campus; that you will hold scholarship combined with character and righteousness in the faculty and among the students as the major objective of the university. I can say to all those assembled here before me and to those in every part of Kentucky that you will be loyal to your profession of teacher, that you will maintain the purposes for which the university was founded, and that you will cooperate with all who work for further progress in the Commonwealth, for the advancement of knowledge and for the protection of the evidences of civilization shown forth in books, manuscripts, and materials.

On this occasion I now do ask if you accept the high office of president of the University of Kentucky with full knowledge of its obligations, of its requirements of duty, and of the service that may be rendered by sincere and devoted labor to the cause of education in the state and to the University of Kentucky.[1]

---

1. Donovan then accepted the office of president and the governor handed him the university seal as the symbol of office.

KENTUCKY SCHOOL FOR THE BLIND CENTENNIAL
Louisville / June 8, 1942

COMMENDING the Kentucky School for the Blind[1] on its century of "compassionate and worthy work," Governor Johnson said that the institution had always "been close to my heart."

He hoped to see improvements, "too long deferred," made at the school within the next eighteen months or two years. Priorities on building materials and the difficulty of obtaining clearances through the War Production Board were responsible, in part, for the delay.[2]

He paid tribute to the founders of the school, including W. F. Bullock, T. S. Bell, Samuel Cassedy, John I. Jacobs, James Pickett, Bryce M. Patten, Edward Jarvis, William Richardson, and Garnet Duncan.[3] "As a result of their united effort in 1842, this school was founded and has served its exalted purpose for a century."

---

1. The school is the third oldest institution for the blind in the United States. New York and Pennsylvania have older ones. The school has no record of the speech. Telephone interview, Will Evans, superintendent, June 15, 1977.

2. In January 1943 the governor assured officials that the old heating plant would be strengthened with a new boiler when the government released the necessary materials. Two new stokers had been recently installed. Louisville *Courier-Journal*, January 21, 1943.

3. William F. Bullock (1807– ?), b. Fayette County. State representative, 1839–1842; judge, Fifth Judicial District, 1846–1855; founder, School for the Blind, president of the board, 1842–1864, 1885–1889. *Biographical Encyclopedia of Kentucky*, pp. 268-69.

Theodore S. Bell (?), b. Lexington. M.D. received in 1832. Editor of medical journals; trustee, School for the Blind, eleven years president of the board. Ibid., pp. 24-25.

Samuel Cassedy (1795– ?), b. Lexington, Virginia. Louisville merchant. Trustee, School for the Blind, 1842–1849. Ibid., pp. 423-24.

John I. Jacobs (1777–1852), b. Baltimore, Maryland. Louisville banker, aided in establishing the school, trustee, 1842–1846. Ibid., pp. 321-22. *Memorial History of Louisville*, ed. J. Stoddard Johnston (Chicago, 1896), p. 291.

James Pickett (?). Trustee, School for the Blind, 1842–1843. *Memorial History of Louisville*, p. 291.

Bryce M. Patten (?). Superintendent, 1842–1871. Lula May Wash, *The Kentucky School for the Blind* (Danville, Ky., 1972), p. 9.

Edward Jarvis (?), M.D. Council member, Louisville, 1840–1841. Trustee, School for the Blind, 1842–1843. Became an eminent sanitary statistician in Massachusetts. M. Joblin and Co., *Louisville Past and Present* (Louisville, 1875), p. 26. *Memorial History of Louisville*, pp. 253, 291.

William Hall Richardson (? –1844). Chairman of obstetrics, Medical School of Transylvania, 1815–1844. *Some of the Medical Pioneers of Kentucky*, ed. J. N. McCormack (Bowling Green, Ky., 1917), pp. 52, 69; Wallis and Tapp, *A Sesquicentennial History of Kentucky*, 1:551.

William Garnett Duncan (1800–1875), b. Louisville. Attorney; law professor at Louisville. United States representative, 1847–1849. Moved to Louisiana. *Biographical Directory of the American Congress, 1774–1971* (Washington, D. C., 1971), p. 886, and Lewis Collins, *History of Kentucky, 1873* (Kentucky Historical Society reprint of 2d ed., 1966), 1:351, 582.

NAVAL TRAINING SCHOOL
Morehead / August 21, 1942

IT is with genuine joy that I, as governor of the Commonwealth, participate with you in these ceremonies which mark the induction of Morehead State Teachers College into the U.S. Navy for the duration of the war. In these anxious hours when our chief concern is the mobilization of all resources of the nation for the high and holy cause of defeating the dictators who seek to destroy us, we in Kentucky are happy as we make available the facilities of this fine institution as a training center for the nation's great navy. It is with a real thrill of pride that we witness the enlistment of Morehead State Teachers College in the service of our nation as a navy training center.[1]

We are glad that here are to be trained young Americans who will become important members of crews which will man the battle craft and aircraft of the navy. Although an inland state, Kentuckians have a deep pride in our navy. Many Kentuckians have served with distinction as naval commanders. In recent years three Kentuckians have attained the topmost rank of admiral. We rejoice that our navy has become the greatest in history of the world and entertain great hopes for its future.

Our comrades in arms, the British, take great pride in their navy. We as Americans are well on the way toward creation of a comparable pride in a navy whose exploits are destined to make a major contribution to winning of the war. I hope that superior personnel in the U.S. Navy, an exalted esprit de corps justified by heroic exploits of the navy, will result in such an attitude becoming widely prevalent on every battle craft in our fleet.

I had an inspiring experience recently. I visited the Great Lakes Naval Training Station. Governors of the midwest states whence come naval recruits who receive training at the Great Lakes Station were invited by Admiral Downes[2] to attend a Governors' Day program. We had an exhilarating experience. We had mess with the men from our states, had opportunity to get a glimpse of the training schedule which transforms recruits into specialists for varied assignments according to their aptitude and background. We were impressed with the intelligent plan by which the navy is mobilizing and training chosen personnel for the grim tasks ahead when shall come the opportunity to avenge the treacherous attack at Pearl Harbor.

This war requires many men of highly developed technical skills. It requires a higher order of intelligence and a higher degree of specialization than in any previous conflict. That has necessitated a vast system of navy and army schools in which men are given intensive training. It is that circumstance which prompted the navy in making use of the facilities at Morehead State Teachers College. We confidently expect that the men chosen for training here will acquit themselves with credit and uphold the high tradition of the navy.

Because the impression prevails in some quarters that Morehead State Teachers College has ceased to function as a college since naval training started here, I want to help dispell that impression. Morehead is only sharing its facilities with the navy. It has not ceased to function as a college in service of the Commonwealth. The advantages it offers for those of this section who seek higher education have not been curtailed in the slightest by sharing its facilities with the navy.

I am about to forget that I was assigned a subject. I was directed to speak about "Adapting the Educational Program to the Needs of a Nation at War."

The need for skilled workers in defense industries and for specialized posts in the armed forces has made large demands upon the vocational schools. In Kentucky the vocational schools, an integral part of the total school program, are training the persons employed by the NYA[3] and WPA. Superintendent Brooker and Dr. R. H. Woods, [4] director of vocational education, have so organized and readjusted vocational training facilities as to bring them to the maximum usefulness. More than 43,000 persons were enrolled in the regular program of vocational education the past year. In the War Production Training Program,[5] training has been provided to make 738 auto mechanics, 7,080 welders, 7,119 radio workers, 8,301 machine shop workers, 2,479 sheet metal workers, and hundreds of others whose instruction increases their efficiency in war industry. They have been promptly employed in war industrial plants.

Our schools in Kentucky have been asked to train more than 20,000 radio technicians for the Army Signal Corps. There are about 6,000 now enrolled in radio training courses.

For generations now our educational system has been training boys and girls to enjoy a richer and happier life. The schools have had as a first concern raising the standard of living of all the people. In this respect our school system has been a success and has added immeasurably to the created wealth of the land. This is as it should be, for ours has been a land of peace, where the creation and enjoyment of wealth has been without parallel in the history of mankind.

Now that all of this is in jeopardy and every other cherished concept of the American way of life is endangered, we must quickly adjust our schools to military needs. Most of us are only vaguely aware of the fact that every fifth person in the United States is in school or college. It is an understatement to say that the role of the schools in our national crisis is a major one. The power of the schools and colleges must be properly harnessed in the war effort.

Some of the services already rendered by the schools:

1. The schools were called upon to train mechanics for defense plants. Within the past two years, thousands of men have received special training that has fitted them to take their places in airplane plants, tank factories, and other war industries. In addition to this, stenographers, accountants, and other specialists have been trained in our schools to take specific places in the war effort. This is in itself a major contribution. Thousands more are being trained now for that service. Thousands of schools are open twenty-four hours daily preparing such workers.

2. The colleges and technical schools have trained thousands of officers for the armed forces. College graduates, schoolteachers, and other professionally trained men have been called into the army and navy in ever-growing numbers and they have proved to be good officer material.

3. Schoolteachers and school administrators have served efficiently and faithfully as rationing and registration agents. This service bids fair to increase as the war effort becomes greater.

4. The schools have labored intelligently and effectively in building morale. In this respect they have been "the men behind the men behind the soldiers and sailors that win the war."

5. Schools have introduced shorter terms in an effort to speed up the preparation of young men who plan to enter the war effort. Colleges and secondary schools have shortened vacation periods and introduced night classes for this same purpose.

While the services so far rendered by the schools are impressive, we have only begun to serve. The unfinished task so far surpasses the completed that we must turn to it.

Additional services that may be expected of the schools:

1. We must provide more technical and professional training. The machine age of which we are a part calls for an ever-increasing emphasis on technical and mechanical education. The schools must be reorganized to provide for more industrial and scientific education.

2. We must teach the "democratic faith." The American way of life is a great social faith. We have been prone to take our democracy for granted and have neglected to teach the duties and responsibilities of citizens.

3. The schools should be organized and equipped to cope with the propaganda campaign of the enemy. One of the most powerful weapons which the dictators are using today in America is false rumor and baseless propaganda. No other agency is in such a position to fight this battle for democracy as the schools.

4. The schools must enlarge and enrich their programs of health and

recreation. Such a program has a vital place in community life and in the war effort.

5. The schools should explore America's place in world affairs. We Americans today face a great decision. No other nation ever had such an opportunity for world leadership as America does today. Whether we will it or not, we must play the role of chief actor in one of civilization's greatest dramas. Are we prepared for such responsibility? Here again the schools must rise to the occasion. There must be new emphasis on foreign languages, world geography, international politics, sound economy, and world mindedness. The knowledge of the world must be brought to our classrooms. We have been too limited in our outlook and ideals. Tire rationing has taught us world geography that should have been common knowledge in a great and enlightened country. This is but one example of the limitations on our educational program in the past. In short, we need to know more about world conditions than we now do if we are to take our rightful place in world affairs.[6]

---

1. On May 1, 1942, the governor transferred $15,000 by executive order from the National and Civil Defense Emergency Fund to the college to help establish the Naval Training School (Electrical).
2. John Downes (1879–1954), b. Dorchester, Massachusetts. Admiral; commandant, Ninth Naval District, 1935–1936, 1940–1944; commanding officer, Great Lakes Naval Training Station, 1935–1936, 1940–1942. Retired, 1944. *Who Was Who in America History: The Military*, p. 141.
3. National Youth Administration. Founded in 1935 to provide job training for unemployed youths and part-time work for needy students.
4. Ralph Hickman Woods (1898–1973), b. Grant, Virginia. Director, Division of Vocational Education, Department of Education, 1936–1945; president, Murray State Teachers College, 1945–1968. Office of Alumni Affairs, Berea College.
5. This program presumably was connected with the War Production Board.
6. Parts of the speech have been deleted. See speeches from July 4, 1941, and September 25, 1942, in the World War II section. Johnson addressed the first group to complete the Women's Army Auxiliary Corps training program at Eastern Kentucky State Teachers College on May 19, 1943.

UNIVERSITY OF KENTUCKY CONVOCATION
Lexington / March 12, 1943

As Kentucky's war governor and an alumnus[1] of the University of Kentucky and a member of the Board of Trustees, I am glad to participate in this solemn, significant occasion.[2] Our hearts are stirred by mingled emotions as we assemble to express our appreciation of these fine young Kentuckians who are soon to leave the campus for army camps. While we are saddened by the circumstances that makes your going necessary, we are exultantly proud of you who calmly prepare to go forth to war.

You in whose honor we are today assembled have a rendezvous with duty. You have a blind date with destiny. As you depart to keep that appointment, you are prepared to offer your lives as a sacrifice upon the altar of your country. You represent the elite of Kentucky's youth. You have intelligence of a high order and physical fitness that superbly equips you for the grim experiences which lie ahead as you follow the flag as defenders of freedom. You have a fine attitude of accepting responsibility of citizenship.

I have a keen understanding of your mental attitude as you face the uncertainties of war. Twenty-six years ago I too quit the campus for an army cantonment. The two and a half years I spent in the army in the last war was an experience I am glad to have had. You will find an unexpected peace of mind in the army. You will be glad to be in it. There will be experiences that test your souls. The hardships and dangers of war are uninviting. But I doubt not that you will face them with calm courage and high fortitude.

Well equipped, well trained, and well educated, you fine Kentuckians know that only those are fit to live who are not afraid to die. Acquit yourselves admirably with calm courage and high fortitude; adapt yourselves to difficulties of the days ahead and fight with the valor of your fine heritage.

---

1. A portrait of Governor Johnson hangs in the Hall of Distinguished Alumni. He received an honorary degree in June 1940.

2. Almost 1,000 students facing early call to military service attended. President Donovan stated that between 5,000 and 6,000 graduates and former students already were in service, including sixty women.

UNION COLLEGE
Barbourville / May 11, 1943

It is with genuine joy that I participate with you, the friends of Union College, in this happy occasion. We are all here to reaffirm our faith in the ideal of Christian education as we dedicate this handsome Pfeiffer Hall[1] to constructive service. Within this building there is admirably combined beauty and usefulness. It will stand for decades as a monument to the generosity and vision of the great-hearted noble woman whose name adorns it. It enlarges the dormitory facilities for the young women who will seek in Union College the education that will equip them for a life of larger usefulness.

This is a proud day in the history of Union College. This great citadel of learning has enriched the lives of thousands of ambitious young Americans during its sixty-four years of fruitful service. It has held high the torch of Christian education, emphasizing spiritual values no less than intellectual attainments. I am proud to testify from personal experience as to the genuine worth of Christian education. I spent six years in schools sponsored by the Methodist Church. My father was a circuit-rider Methodist preacher. That godly man was a zealous apostle of Christian education. I shall always be thankful for the fortunate fact that I was educated in a Christian atmosphere in a spiritual environment.

An anomalous situation exists in the world today. Here in this beautiful, cultured town of Barbourville, within the shadow of the grandeur of the mountains, we consecrate this splendid structure to the exalted purpose of advancing the ideal of cultured womanhood. The joy of this occasion is diminished by the fact that sinister tyrants have unleashed in the world forces which seek to destroy those fine things for which Union College stands. We dedicate Pfeiffer Hall as an instrumentality through which education will be advanced; while beyond the oceans godless despots attempt to crush beneath a tyrant's heel the spiritual values which we here glorify and extol.

While we have the blessed assurance that the gates of hell shall not prevail against the church of God, we realize that it is our duty to exert the maximum effort to prevent such disaster—a calamity that would enshroud our Christian civilization in an eclipse of paganism. While we fight to prevent the triumph of the emissaries of evil, we here endeavor to expand the facilities of a college which promotes intellectual and spiritual perception.

Democracy is not a thing that can be purchased once and for always. It is a grim fact that we have to fight periodically to maintain our freedom if we would not lose it. It is probable that freedom would become a common and unappreciated thing if it did not have to be purchased at such a fearful price. But we who know what it costs in blood and human sacrifice know how to appreciate its value. That is especially true of the 153 patriotic young men who have left this campus to keep a rendezvous with duty.

As we fight to win, we fight to protect Union College and every other college on this continent from becoming subservient to the harsh decrees of Hitler, from an enforced curriculum which would exalt Hitler above Christ and expunge religious freedom from our hearts and minds.

The gates of hell shall not prevail against the church of God. Our brave armies shall thwart the combined might of the pagan Japanese and godless Germans. Then it will be our task to bind up the wounds of a broken and bleeding world, repair the ravages of an awful war. Consecrated, clear thinking leadership will be needed for that task. It is from institutions such as Union College that such leadership must come.

Women will exert increased influence in the postwar world. More of them may continue their education without the interruption of military duty. And this they should do. Women who are graduated from Union College in the future will be more adequate to the responsibilities of life because of the pleasant environment within which they lived in Pfeiffer Hall. As earnest, capable young women enjoy its facilities, they will bless the gracious woman who here has erected a memorial that will be a blessing and a benediction to young womanhood.[2]

---

1. The hall was named for Mrs. Annie M. Pfeiffer of New York whose donations to Union College amounted to $250,000. President Conway Boatman conferred the degree of Doctor of Humanities on her.
2. The speech has been edited. Similar parts appear in speeches from June 4, 1941, in this section, and April 20, 1942, in the Heritage section.

EXECUTIVE ORDER: TRANSFER OF FUNDS TO GOVERNOR'S EMERGENCY FUND
Frankfort / May 25, 1943

WHEREAS, the Appropriation Act of 1942 (House Bill #1) provides for the fiscal year of 1942–1943 (Part 1, Section 4, Item [d] 1) that there should be appropriated a General Emergency Fund for the purpose of meeting all ordinary recurring and extraordinary expenses which may be deemed emergencies by the Governor of the Commonwealth in the sum of Two Hundred Fifty Thousand Dollars ($250,000.00), and

WHEREAS, the said General Emergency Fund has of this date the sum of Twenty Six Thousand Three Hundred Thirty-Three Dollars and Forty-Two Cents ($26,333.42) as a balance therein, and

WHEREAS, the said Appropriation Act further provides in Part 1, Section

4, Item (d) 2 for a Special Emergency Fund and appropriates therefor the sum of Two Hundred Thousand Dollars ($200,000.00) for extraordinary expenses which may constitute a special emergency, and

WHEREAS, the said Special Emergency Fund has, of this date, the sum of Two Hundred Thousand Dollars ($200,000.00) as a balance therein, and

WHEREAS, the said Appropriation Act further provides in Part 1, Section 4, Item (d) 3, a National and Civil Defense Emergency Fund and appropriates therefor the sum of Five Hundred Thousand Dollars ($500,000.00) for the purpose of meeting extraordinary expenses which may be imposed upon the Commonwealth of Kentucky to meet emergencies created by the state of war existing between the United States and other countries, and

WHEREAS, the said National and Civil Defense Emergency Fund has, of this date, the sum of Four Hundred Ninety Thousand Six Hundred Dollars ($490,600.00) as a balance therein, and

WHEREAS, the said Appropriation Act further provides Part 1, Section 4, Item (d) 4, that the Governor of the Commonwealth shall be vested with the power to transfer any of the money provided in the three above emergency funds from one emergency fund to another, and the same may be expended for the recurring and extraordinary expenses provided for in the fund to which the said sum may be transferred, and

WHEREAS, there has in the Commonwealth of Kentucky arisen a widely recognized emergency facing the common schools, and

WHEREAS, the emergency is so acute that it is necessary to provide funds so that the adequate and efficient operation of the public school system may continue, and

WHEREAS, an acute emergency, in the opinion of the Governor, is thereby created and does now exist.

NOW, THEREFORE, I, Keen Johnson, Governor of the Commonwealth of Kentucky, by virtue of the authority vested in me as such, by this executive order hereby authorize and direct the Commissioner of Finance and the State Treasurer to transfer[1] from the Special Emergency Fund (Chapter 1, Part 1, Section 4, Sub-Section [d] 2, of the Acts of the 1942 General Assembly) Account Number 240, the sum of Two Hundred Thousand ($200,000.00) Dollars to the Governors Emergency Fund, Account Number 230, also, further authorizes and directs the Commissioner of Finance and the State Treasurer to transfer from the National and Civil Defense Emergency Fund, Account Number 250 (Chapter 1, Part 1, Section 4, Sub-Section [d] 3 of the Acts of the 1942 General Assembly) the sum of Four Hundred Ninety Thousand Six Hundred ($490,600.00) Dollars to the Governors Emergency Fund Account Number 230 so that said funds may be properly allocated to the Department of Education for the purpose of aiding the common schools of the state during the present emergency.[2]

---

1. On March 19, 1943, the governor had declined to transfer money from his Emergency Fund to raise teachers' salaries. He also told a KEA committee that he would not call a special session of the legislature for this purpose. "A special session probably would develop into organized pressure for repeal of the state income tax." The KEA committee was concerned about the loss of teachers to better-paying war jobs. Johnson told the members, "I know of no substantial approach to your problem until the regular session meets next January." He also said that he had been under heavier and more prolonged pressure to call a special session for repeal of the income tax than to provide aid for underpaid teachers. Louisville *Courier-Journal,* March 20, 22, 1943.

Lieutenant Governor Myers, in a radio address in Louisville on April 14, 1943, warned the governor that if he left the state, he would call the legislature in special session to provide financial aid for the schoolchildren and teachers. Myers was a gubernatorial candidate. Louisville *Courier-Journal,* April 15, 1943. In June he challenged the governor again to call a special session or to leave the state so that he could call one. He stated that the money provided by the governor from his Emergency Fund was not enough. The general fund, however, had a surplus. Louisville *Courier-Journal,* June 24, 1943.

The delegate assembly of KEA resolved in early May that, if the governor would call a special session to provide relief to underpaid teachers, it would give him a pledge signed by a majority of both House and Senate to adjourn at his request. KEA would also pledge not to ask him to include any other subject in the call. The governor acknowledged receipt of the resolution in a short letter which was noncommittal as to a special session. Louisville *Courier-Journal,* May 7, 1943.

2. The governor announced the transfer on the eve of a mass meeting in Louisville called to consider the loss of teachers to war jobs. He had been studying the matter for some time and had recently obtained an opinion from W. Owen Keller, assistant attorney general, that his Emergency Fund could legally be used for this purpose. He also announced that he would finance training courses to improve teaching standards. They were to be conducted during the summer in thirteen counties and were to be in addition to the usual summer schools for teachers. They were needed because recent high school graduates were being hired as teachers. Louisville *Courier-Journal,* May 25, 1943. By a companion order on the same day, Johnson allocated $126,806.16 to the equalization fund and $558,828.00 to the per capita fund, a total of $685,634.16. He said that the addition to the equalization fund would provide an average increase of $25 a year to the teachers in the school districts eligible for this aid; the addition to the per capita fund would mean an average increase of $31 a year to all teachers. He noted that the supplement to the equalization fund would bring the grant to $30 a year per child in these districts, the maximum set by law. The addition to the per capita fund would raise by seventy-five cents a year the per child amount paid to the school districts, from $12.88 to $13.63, the highest allotment in history. *Lexington Herald,* May 26, 1943.

EXECUTIVE ORDER: FEES FOR SUMMER TEACHER TRAINING COURSES
Frankfort / October 11, 1943

WHEREAS, the General Assembly of Kentucky, at its Regular Session in 1942, recognized that extraordinary and unusual conditions might develop as a result of the present War; and in recognition thereof, and to provide for such conditions and emergencies, appropriated money to be made available for such emergencies by the Governor of the Commonwealth of Kentucky, in his discretion; and

WHEREAS, because of the large number of teachers in the public schools of the Commonwealth of Kentucky who had entered the Armed Forces of the United States, and the large number who had accepted employment at higher compensation in industries engaged in war production, there existed an impending emergency in that the public schools of this Commonwealth were faced with a reasonably anticipated shortage of more than 2,000 teachers at the beginning of the current school year; and

WHEREAS, that situation was imposed upon the Commonwealth of Kentucky and was created by the state of War existing between the United States and other countries, and constituted a real, immediate, and serious emergency; and

WHEREAS, the welfare of the Commonwealth of Kentucky and its citizens required that every reasonable and proper effort be made to meet said emergency and to provide for the opening of all of the public schools in this Commonwealth; and that said schools be provided with the best qualified teachers that could be made available; and

WHEREAS, upon the recommendation of the Superintendent of Public Instruction, which recommendation was concurred in by the presidents of the various state institutions of higher learning, the undersigned, as Governor of the Commonwealth of Kentucky, authorized the Superintendent of Public Instruction to notify the respective county and independent school district superintendents to recruit teachers for the current school year upon the following procedure and upon the following terms, to wit:

1. That all persons possessing a minimum of high school education who desired to teach in the public schools might enroll in approved summer work shops and classes provided by the various institutions of higher learning,[1] with the understanding that the major portion of the fees required for such courses would be reimbursed by the Commonwealth of Kentucky, upon the following conditions, to wit:

(a) That a minimum of eight quarter hours of college training be earned by each such person in attendance upon such approved summer work shops or classes; and

(b) That such persons accept contracts of employment for teaching in the public schools of Kentucky during the current school year; and

(c) Upon fulfillment of the foregoing conditions (a) and (b), and after such persons shall have taught for at least one month during the now current school year, the aforesaid reimbursement will be made to each such person, upon proof, satisfactory to the Superintendent of Public Instruction, of the foregoing qualifications; and the funds for the payment thereof provided from the emergency fund appropriated to the Executive Department under Section 4, subsection (d) 3, page 30 of the Acts of the General Assembly of 1942; and

WHEREAS, the Superintendent of Public Instruction has certified in writing to the Governor that the amount necessary to meet the aforesaid obligations will be approximately $27,000.00,

NOW, THEREFORE, in consideration of the foregoing, it hereby is declared by the undersigned, as Governor of the Commonwealth of Kentucky, as follows, to wit:

I. That the emergency hereinabove recited did in fact actually exist and was imposed upon the Commonwealth of Kentucky or created by the state of war existing between the United States and other countries; and that as a result of the program which was adopted as hereinabove outlined, said emergency was substantially and in the most practical manner met; and as a result thereof, approximately 2,200 teachers have been provided for the public schools of Kentucky for the current school year, which schools otherwise would have been without such qualified teachers.

NOW, THEREFORE, IT IS ORDERED by the undersigned, as Governor of the Commonwealth of Kentucky, that the Department of Finance be and it hereby is directed to transfer from the emergency fund appropriated to the Executive Department under Section 4, subsection (d) 3, page 30, of the Acts of the General Assembly of 1942, to the credit of the Department of Education the sum of $27,000.00,[2] to be expended for reimbursing the teachers in the public schools of Kentucky, who were recruited and who complied with the conditions hereinabove set forth. Said funds shall be disbursed upon requisitions therefor approved by the Superintendent of Public Instruction; and when such requisitions shall be presented to the Department of Finance, they shall be approved by the Department of Finance and charged against the funds hereby transferred.

After a discharge of the obligations hereinabove referred to, any balance remaining in the fund so transferred shall be retransferred to the emergency fund from which the same was charged by the order of transfer, it being the intention that there shall be withdrawn from said emergency fund only such part of the $27,000.00 as may be necessary to meet and discharge the aforesaid obligations.

---

1. The governor and President O'Donnell of Eastern Kentucky State Teachers College inspected the summer program in Pineville, Hazard, and Hindman in June 1943. Centers were established in fifteen counties, all in Eastern Kentucky except for three in Western Kentucky. The governor said, "One of the most touching and gratifying things about the school situation is the eagerness of teachers attending the summer courses to make themselves better fitted for their work." *Richmond Daily Register*, June 30, 1943, and *Pineville Courier*, July 2, 1943. The centers were established because prospective teachers who needed the training programs had neither the money nor the incentive to attend traditional college summer schools. Allan M. Trout, Louisville *Courier-Journal*, July 4, 1943. They were operated by the University of Kentucky, Morehead State Teachers College, Murray State Teachers College, and Union College in addition to Eastern.

2. The fee for each person was $12. The teacher shortage continued to be severe. It was estimated that by the end of the 1943–1944 school year 3,500 to 4,000 teachers would be employed under emergency certificates. Louisville *Courier-Journal*, October 12, 1943.

EXECUTIVE ORDER: WEST KENTUCKY VOCATIONAL TRAINING SCHOOL
Frankfort / December 3, 1943

WHEREAS, the Appropriation Act of 1942 (House Bill #1) provides for the fiscal year of 1943-44 that (Part 1-A, Section 4, Item E) . . .

> For the purposes of repair, reconstruction and construction of buildings, and for the purposes of purchasing lands, buildings, and appurtenances, and for the purpose of equipping and supplying the penal institutions, the mental hospitals, the Feeble Minded Institute, the School for the Deaf, the state schools under the direct supervision of the State Board of Education, and Hazelwood Tuberculosis Hospital, there is hereby appropriated a portion of the unencumbered cash balance in the General Expenditure Fund at the close of the fiscal year ending June 30, 1943. This sum or amount shall equal the difference between the unencumbered cash balance at said date in the Treasury to the credit of the General Expenditure Fund and the amount

which shall be determined necessary as operating capital within this Fund preliminary to meeting the budgetary requirements for the 1943-44 fiscal year. The Governor, with the advice of the Commissioner of Finance, the Commissioner of Revenue, the Commissioner of Welfare, and the Treasurer, shall determine the necessary amount of operating capital as defined above and shall make direct approval of all expenditures from this appropriation. In no event shall the sum expended for these purposes exceed the total of the unencumbered cash balance in the General Expenditure Fund at the close of business June 30, 1943, nor shall the sum expended exceed Three Million ($3,000,000.00) Dollars.

WHEREAS, the above named Advisory Committee met with the Governor on Friday, December 3, 1943, for the purpose of considering the possibility and feasibility of purchasing certain real property and the nominal improvements thereon and hereinafter described for the use of the West Kentucky Vocational Training School[1] located at Paducah, Kentucky, and

WHEREAS, the West Kentucky Vocational Training School in the city of Paducah, McCracken County, Kentucky, has certain property used in the vocational training of its students, and

WHEREAS, the said property is situated on the west side of Atkins Avenue and extends westerly to Thompson Avenue with a portion thereof on the west side of said Thompson Avenue, and

WHEREAS, the said property of the West Kentucky Vocational Training School is part of the addition to the city of Paducah which is known as the Roland Place Addition, and

WHEREAS, there are privately owned tracts or lots in said addition which adjoin the West Kentucky Vocational Training School property, and

WHEREAS, there are certain tracts, parcels or lots of land extending through and dividing the property of the West Kentucky Vocational Training School, and

WHEREAS, the use and benefits derived from the use of the property by the West Kentucky Vocational Training School is materially affected because of the division of its property by privately owned tracts or lots, and

WHEREAS, it is necessary in the proper administration and utilization of the property to acquire additional lots or tracts so that adequate and proper facilities may be provided for proper ingress and egress to its buildings, and

WHEREAS, the acquisition of additional lots or tracts is necessary for the expansion of said West Kentucky Vocational Training School, and

WHEREAS, the lots or tracts in question are now available for purchase by the West Kentucky Vocational Training School, and

WHEREAS, the Board of Education has arranged for the purchase of

Thirteen (13) lots for the use and benefit of the West Kentucky Vocational Training School, and

WHEREAS, the said Thirteen (13) lots are described as follows, to wit:

Lot No. Twelve (12) in Block Seven (7) on the east side of Thompson Avenue and running in an easterly direction on the north side of Fourteenth Street, also, Lots No. Nineteen (19), Twenty (20), Twenty One (21) and Twenty Two (22) adjoin Thompson Avenue on the east and lying and being north of the present campus of the West Kentucky Vocational Training School, also, Lots No. Twenty Three (23) and Twenty Four (24) in Block Eight (8) on the east side of Thompson Avenue and lying between the boys' dormitory and the Mechanical Building, and also, Lots No. One (1), Two (2) and Three (3) in Block Nine (9) on the west side of Thompson Avenue and north of the girls' dormitory and extending to Thirteenth Street, also, Lots No. Eight (8), Nine (9) and Ten (10) in Block Nine (9) and lying on the west of Thompson Avenue and lying south of the girls' dormitory, and

WHEREAS, addition of the foregoing lots will greatly enhance the value, use and benefits of the West Kentucky Vocational Training School, and

WHEREAS, the state Board of Education has requested the purchase of the tracts or lots heretofore referred to, and

WHEREAS, the said State Board of Education has advised that the Thirteen (13) lots referred to in this Executive Order may be purchased for the total sum of Forty Three Hundred Dollars ($4,300.00), and

WHEREAS, the Governor's Advisory Committee has been advised that general warranty deeds could be obtained conveying fee simple title and having met for its final decision; giving proper cognizance to the $11,862,721.87 free, unencumbered balance in the General Fund at the close of business June 30, 1943, W. Arch Bennett, Commissioner of Finance of the Commonwealth of Kentucky, moved the following resolution, that:

> The Governor order and direct the Commissioner of Finance to allot $4,300.00 from the above quoted apropriation to the proper expenditure account in order to make possible the authorization of the expenditure necessary to obtain fee simple title of the Thirteen (13) tracts or lots of land referred to in this Executive Order and lying and being in the Roland Place Addition to the city of Paducah, McCracken County, Kentucky.

J. E. Luckett,[2] Commissioner of Revenue, seconded the adoption of this resolution and the vote being called for by Governor Keen Johnson, all the members present voted "Aye."

THEREFORE, I, Keen Johnson, Governor of the Commonwealth of Kentucky, and by virtue of the authority vested in me as such, and in accordance with the provisions of the Appropriation Act (together with the proper advice of the Committee specified in the Appropriation Act), by this Executive Order hereby order and direct the Commissioner of Finance to allot $4,300.00 from the Special Emergency Appropriation, Section 4, Part 1-A, Item E, Budget Bill 1942 to Department of Education, West Kentucky Vocational Training School, Account No. 2127-Capital Outlay Special, to be expended in conformity with the recommendation of W. Arch Bennett, Commissioner of Finance.[3]

---

1. This vocational school for blacks replaced West Kentucky Industrial College for Negroes on July 1, 1938. A.B. Chandler Papers, King Library, University of Kentucky. A new school that will replace it is under construction on the campus of Paducah Community College. Louisville *Courier-Journal,* July 10, 1979. In 1940 Johnson appointed a committee on Negro employment. It was recommended by a convention of white and black civic leaders called by Governor Chandler in April 1939. Lawrence A. Oxley, a field representative for the United States Employment Service, had also urged the governor to appoint one. The committee was to study the inroads made by white labor on occupations traditionally held by blacks, such as bell boys, waiters and waitresses, and elevator operators. The committee could direct black youth to vocational schools or recommend that vocational schools for blacks add courses to provide the students with necessary skills. Kentucky became the third state to establish a committee for this purpose. Missouri and North Carolina preceded it. Louisville *Courier-Journal,* April 7, 1940.

2. James E. Luckett (1910–), b. Morganfield. Commissioner of revenue, 1943–1944, 1955–1959, 1963–1967, 1967–1971; revenue official in Iran, 1944–1946; controller, city of Lexington, 1972–1974; commissioner of finance, Lexington-Fayette Urban County government, 1974–1980. Wallis and Tapp, *A Sesquicentennial History of Kentucky,* 3:1765, and letter, James E. Luckett, December 28, 1978.

3. The governor also showed his interest in vocational education when he transferred $4,000 from an emergency fund to the Department of Education on July 1, 1943, to match federal vocational education funds for training clerks and other employees for stores. He had authorized $3,000 in March, but, due to delay in starting the program, $2,000 had reverted to the general fund on June 30, 1943. The program was needed because the armed forces and war industries were drawing heavily on persons employed in distributive occupations. *Lexington Herald,* July 2, 1943. See Executive Order, July 1, 1943.

HEALTH & WELFARE

EXECUTIVE ORDER: ADMINISTRATIVE ORGANIZATION OF WELFARE DEPARTMENT
Frankfort / September 7, 1940

BY virtue of the authority vested in me by the General Assembly of the Commonwealth of Kentucky, under the provisions of the Reorganization Act of 1936, on recommendation of the Commissioner of Welfare with the approval of the Commissioner of Finance, I, as Governor of the Commonwealth of Kentucky, hereby authorize the establishment of the following administrative organization of the Department of Welfare. This order supersedes and nullifies the Executive Order No. 11, issued August 10, 1938, and becomes effective on the date signed by me:

1. The Commissioner of Welfare, assisted by a Deputy Commissioner and advised by the Board of Welfare, shall be responsible to the governor for the administration of all public welfare services, programs, and institutions which are under the control of the Department of Welfare.

2. For administrative purposes the Department of Welfare shall consist of the following divisions: Hospitals and Mental Hygiene, Corrections, Probation and Parole, Public Assistance, Child Welfare, and Staff Services, each of which shall be in charge of a director responsible to the Commissioner of Welfare for the administration and for supervision of all services, programs, and institutions charged to the respective division.

(a) The Division of Hospitals and Mental Hygiene shall be charged with the administration of all state institutions and programs for the care and treatment of the mentally diseased and feebleminded.

(b) The Division of Corrections shall be charged with the administration of all state prisons and correctional institutions, and state programs for inmate education and training, crime prevention, and criminal identification.

(c) The Division of Probation and Parole[1] shall be charged with the administration of the State Probation and Parole Act.

(d) The Division of Public Assistance shall be charged with the administration of all state public assistance programs.

(e) The Division of Child Welfare shall be charged with the administration of all state child welfare programs, the administration of all state institutions for children.

(f) The Division of Staff Services shall be charged with the administration of all special service programs performed for the department, including the services of: Fiscal Control and Office Management, Institutional Collections, CCC Selection, Surplus Commodity Distribution, Research and Statistics, Agricultural and Industrial Production, Informational Service, Personnel and In-Service Training, Home Economics, and such others as may become necessary for the efficient administration of responsibilities charged to the Department of Welfare.

---

1. Materials pertaining to the Division of Corrections and the Division of Probation and Parole are in the Public Safety section.

SOUTHERN MEDICAL ASSOCIATION
Louisville / November 12, 1940

SPEAKING as the chief executive of the Commonwealth of Kentucky, it gives me a great deal of pleasure to welcome the physicians of the Southern Medical Association to the homes and hearts of the people of Kentucky. I have the added distinction of representing Mrs. Johnson, herself a member, in extending an especially cordial welcome to the members of the Women's Auxiliary from the southern states.

We Kentuckians are very proud of our medical history and traditions. The first medical school in the south and west was Transylvania at Lexington and no institution in the country to date has made a greater contribution to the public health and welfare. We will be happy to have you visit its library, the nucleus of which was purchased by state appropriation more than one hundred years ago, where you will find the accumulated medical lore of the ages.

The first white men who came to Kentucky were under the leadership of a distinguished medical statesman and explorer, Dr. Thomas Walker.[1] You will find an attractive state park dedicated to his memory near Barbourville where the first human habitation was erected in the Commonwealth.

While the first settlers were still living, two events occurred in the medical history of the state which have profoundly affected the whole course of medicine since. Drs. Samuel Brown and Ephraim McDowell[2] were fellow students at the Medical School at Edinburgh. Dr. Brown heard that a country doctor, Edward Jenner,[3] had found a means for the prevention of smallpox. He walked one hundred miles of rough road through Scotland and England down to see this man. After having the method of vaccination explained to him, he was given a few scabs and threads impregnated with the vaccine virus which he brought back to Lexington in his pocket in balls of beeswax and while the rest of the world doubted, he vaccinated more than five hundred Kentuckians. Shortly afterwards an epidemic of smallpox decimated the frontier settlements of Kentucky and Ohio, but not a single one of those who had been vaccinated by Dr. Brown contracted the disease. At the time of his death, more people had been vaccinated in his neighborhood in Kentucky than in all the rest of the world.

While preventive medicine was thus developing at Lexington, his colleague at Danville, a few miles away, performed the first surgical operation on a woman for an abdominal tumor. Dr. Ephraim McDowell and his patient, Mrs. Jane Todd Crawford,[4] were thus immortalized and the McDowell Memorial Association and this Commonwealth have restored Dr. McDowell's home as nearly as possible to the condition in which it was on that Christmas day of 1809 when the operation was performed. Our Women's Auxiliary in Kentucky has begun the beautification of the highway which has replaced the sixty miles of buffalo trail over which Mrs. Crawford road horseback from her home in Green County to Danville.

In 1851 the legislature chartered the Kentucky State Medical Association. From that day to this, no legislation affecting medicine or public health has been written on the statute books of Kentucky without the approval and sponsorship of the organized medical profession of the state. More progress has been made in public health and medical service than in any other human activity in Kentucky. I am convinced that this is because the responsibility for it has been placed squarely on the shoulders of the medical profession. In 1878 the State Board of Health was created and county boards of health were developed. Members of these boards have always been selected by the profession itself; their policies have been developed from the increasing medical knowledge. Members of these boards of health have never received any other compensation than the thanks of a grateful people.

Much of the credit for the exceptional success of the public health program in Kentucky has been due to the wise leadership which has been supplied by our commissioner of health, Dr. A. T. McCormack.[5] Himself a direct descendant of Dr. Thomas Walker, the first white man to visit Kentucky, he has pioneered in the field of public health work as effectively as did his pioneer forebears. I regard Dr. McCormack as one of the most useful citizens of our Commonwealth.

In the last fifty years, the death rate has been reduced two-thirds; acute diseases have been reduced as much as in any other state; we have more full-time health departments than any other state. This organization has been entirely medical from its beginning and its principles have been determined and its activities controlled by physicians of the state. We realize fully that our doctors have made the largest contribution in value to the welfare of our citizens of any group and insofar as it has been possible for them to do so, they have given the same service to rich and poor alike. Seventy-five years ago the average age at death in Kentucky was thirty-two years; last year it was sixty-one years. This, of course, means that many more people are living into the older groups.

We must realize that this older average population presents us with a tremendous problem; we must make the same study and take the same care of chronic and degenerative diseases that formerly we have so successfully accomplished with the infectious diseases.

Opportunists talk very glibly about health insurance, the socialization of medicine, and the regimentation of physicians as the remedy for this situation. Such suggestions will receive no support by the people of Kentucky. We will continue to be guided in regard to public health and medical service by our doctors.

It was because professional control of medical service and public health had brought such beneficent results to its people that the legislature has recently determined to remove forever the stigma of inefficiency from our state institutions for the care of those who are mentally ill and the director of these institutions is now and will continue to be selected from nominations made by the medical organization of the state, and the scientific staffs and other personnel of these institutions will be selected on a basis of competency and merit with the sole view to the amelioration of the conditions of the state's most unfortunate citizens.

In Kentucky our own Dr. Irvin Abell[6] very happily expressed our feeling when he said that the organized medical profession of the state is the family physician of the state.

I am sure you will pardon me for having welcomed you by expressing the pride we feel in the members of the medical profession who, jointly with the people of this Commonwealth, are your hosts on this occasion. We are familiar with the medical and public health history of the Southern Medical Association and it would be a pleasure to say to each of you the things that would make you know how grateful we are for the contributions you and yours have made to the common welfare of our section and to the nation. We shall watch your deliberations with eagerness to learn the latest contributions which science has made to the betterment of humanity and we can all take pride that in a day when the major nations of the world are engaged in mutual destruction, we are gathered together to study the means of making men, women, and children healthier, happier, and better.

---

1. Thomas Walker (1715–1794), b. Virginia. Explorer in Kentucky; Virginia House of Burgesses, 1752. Wallis and Tapp, *A Sesquicentennial History of Kentucky*, 1:45.

2. Samuel Brown (1769–1830), b. Virginia. Founder of Transylvania's medical department. Ibid., 1:548.

Ephraim McDowell (1771–1830), b. Rockbridge County, Virginia. Resided in Danville. Noted surgeon; a founder and trustee, Centre College, Danville. *Who Was Who in America*, 1607–1896, H:346.

3. Edward Jenner (1749–1823), b. Berkeley, England. Physician, discoverer of vaccination. *Dictionary of National Biography* (London, 1922), 10:758-61.

4. Jane Todd Crawford (1763–1842), b. Rockbridge County, Virginia. Married Thomas Crawford 1794 and moved to Kentucky 1805; youngest son, Thomas Howell Crawford, became mayor of Louisville, 1859. *Filson Club History Quarterly* 6 (April 1932):109-23, and *Lexington Leader*, April 13, 1959.

On November 4, 1942, the governor issued the following proclamation:

WHEREAS, on the 13th day of December 1809, Jane Todd Crawford was first visited by Dr. Ephraim McDowell at her home and he diagnosed her condition as an ovarian tumor and recommended an abdominal operation—an experiment—for its removal; and

WHEREAS, on that date she decided to be operated on although she realized she would be compelled to ride horseback a distance of sixty miles over rough and treacherous roads, which are now known as the Jane Todd Crawford Trail, to the home of her surgeon, and further she fully realized that the operation was to be performed on a crude table of ordinary height and without the aid of an anaesthetic; and

WHEREAS, her great courage in submitting to this pioneer and hitherto unheard-of operation has been narrated and repeated by many Kentuckians and the account of this operation performed on Christmas day, 1809, has been translated into many foreign languages, thus becoming world famous, so Jane Todd Crawford, one of the brave souls of surgical history, helped lay the cornerstone to abdominal surgery, commemorated by the shrine at Danville, Kentucky, to Mrs. Jane Todd Crawford and Dr. Ephraim McDowell, the father of ovariotomy.

NOW, THEREFORE, I, Governor of the Commonwealth of Kentucky, do hereby proclaim Sunday, December 13, as Jane Todd Crawford Day in Kentucky.

And urge all officials of the government and all citizens of the Commonwealth of Kentucky to take cognizance of December 13 each year and to observe this day in schools, churches, clubs and other suitable places with appropriate historical and memorial ceremonies in honor of Jane Todd Crawford and the other courageous Kentucky women whose brave spirits have steadied the hands and steeled the hearts of Kentucky men.

A similar proclamation was issued on October 12, 1943.

5. Arthur Thomas McCormack (1872–1943), b. Howard's Mill, Nelson County. Chief Health officer, Panama Canal; assistant state health officer, 1900; secretary, state Board of Health, 1912–1943; special consultant, United States Public Health Service, organizer and dean, School of Public Health, University of Louisville. Wallis and Tapp, *A Sesquicentennial History of Kentucky,* 1:558-59.

6. Irvin Abell (1876–1949), b. Lebanon. Professor of surgery, 1908–1923; appointed clinical professor of surgery, University of Louisville, 1923. Ibid., 2:1106-9.

W. A. FROST APPOINTED WELFARE COMMISSIONER

Frankfort / December 30, 1940

I HAVE appointed you commissioner of welfare of the state of Kentucky.[1] You were not an applicant for this position. I accept full responsibility, officially and personally, for persuading you to accept this important post.

I have observed you as a member of the welfare board. I have been impressed with your administrative ability, your knowledge and experience in the work as chairman of the Board of Parole, your Christian spirit, your kindliness in your contacts with others, and your humanitarian impulses.

I have complete confidence in your ability to do a great public service in this position. I am certain that the administrative unity and morale essential to successful operation of this department will be established under your leadership.

I want to say publicly, as I said to you when I asked you to accept this place, that you will have complete control of the administration of your department. All contacts with your department by other administrative offices of the government and by me will be through you. You are authorized by law to select the heads of the divisions.

I desire each of them to know that your recommendations as to the retention or dismissal of the members of your official force will be approved by me. I expect their loyalty to my administration to be expressed through you and to be interpreted into loyal efficient public service.

Attention of the public has been called recently to the institutions under control of this department through the resignation of Dr. J. G. Wilson[2] as director of the Division of Hospitals and Mental Hygiene. At the request of the governor of Kentucky, the Kentucky State Medical Association appointed an advisory committee to the director of hospitals and mental hygiene composed of the following members: Dr. W. E. Gardner, Louisville, chairman; Dr. Ernest B. Bradley, Lexington; Dr. Irvin Abell, Louisville; Dr. Austin Bell, Hopkinsville; Dr. A. T. McCormack, Louisville; Dr. C. C. Howard, Glasgow; and Dr. A. C. McCarty, Louisville.[3] The council of the Kentucky Medical Association already has, in compliance with the law, submitted three names from among whom the new director must be selected. The advisory committee has made a specific recommendation with which you are familiar.

All of the superintendents of the state hospitals were named by Dr. Wilson before I became governor. Under the law no appointment can be made to any position in any of these institutions except by the superintendent thereof, with the approval of the commissioner of welfare. The superintendent makes the selection in accord with provisions of Article 10 of the Reorganization Act.

You will find some difficulty in recruiting competent individuals for the positions of attendants in the state hospitals. These workers receive $42.00 a month and maintenance. You will not be able to persuade college graduates to accept such jobs. I have sought to be helpful in assembling names of individuals to be considered for employment as attendants. Neither I nor anyone representing me has requested the employment of any specific person. Neither I nor anyone representing me has interfered in any way in the dismissal of any employee whom superintendents of the hospitals thought should be dismissed.

In an effort to create a reserve list of persons that would be acceptable prospects for employment as attendants, I have within the year I have been governor submitted to the commissioner of welfare for consideration lists containing the names of 698 persons. There were 136 of them that were employed to fill vacancies. Only seventeen of them were found unacceptable and they were dismissed by the superintendents.

During the year there were fifty-three dismissed out of a total of 776 employed in the hospitals. Thirty-six of them were employed before I became governor. There were eighty-three vacancies that resulted from resignations. Only twelve of those who resigned were employed after I was inaugurated. Seventy-one of those who resigned were on the payroll when I was inaugurated.

Those appointed from the total list of 698 to fill 136 vacancies were required to take the examination of the Division of Personnel Efficiency. It was presumed that none would be employed until interviewed by the superintendents. There was no official influence exercised to secure employment of anyone regarded by the superintendents as unacceptable.

Superintendents of the hospitals will, I believe, corroborate my statements that there has been no coercion in an effort to secure employment of incompetent persons and that I have sustained their action in each dismissal of an employee whose release they regarded as desirable.

Superintendents of the hospitals have authority to dismiss any incompetent employee and they have been sustained by the governor in each dismissal. Of the fifty-three employees dismissed since I have been governor, nine were released for intoxication. One of the nine had been employed since I became governor. I am sure that you are as anxious to keep drunks out of the state service as I am. I have asked the advisory committee of the Kentucky Medical Association to meet with the superintendents of the state hospitals and formulate recommendations for the selection of personnel which they believe would be helpful. Those recommendations I shall consider with you.

I particularly wish to repeat to you that political expediency shall not be permitted to enter into your consideration of these problems. No appointments shall be made in any of these institutions as a reward for political activities. All appointments will be made by the superintendents with your approval and based on the suitability of the applicant for the position to be filled.

You have my best wishes and I pledge you my hearty cooperation.

---

1. The governor read this statement after Frost took the oath of office in the governor's office.

2. Joseph G. Wilson (1874– ?), b. Smyrna, Ohio. Quaker. United States Public Health Service, 1906–1938; director, Division of Hospitals and Mental Hygiene, 1938–1940; left Kentucky in 1940. (Some newspaper accounts refer to

him as James G. Wilson, but the name was confirmed by Dr. Arthur R. Kasey, Louisville psychiatrist, who was assistant director of Hospitals and Mental Hygiene, in telephone interview, October 4, 1978.) Letter, Margaret Woll, April 4, 1978, and telephone interview, Mrs. Mersal, United States Public Health Service, Rockville, Md., September 27, 1978.

3. Ernest B. Bradley (1877–1948), b. Lexington. President, American College of Physicians, 1936–1937; regent, 1937–1940. William G. Morgan, *American College of Physicians* (Philadelphia, 1940), pp. 27-29.

Austin Bell (1874–1942), b. Bell, Christian County. M.D. Resided in Hopkinsville. Wallis and Tapp, *A Sesquicentennial History of Kentucky*, 3:1575-77.

C. C. Howard (1888–1971), b. Summer Shade. M.D. Resided in Glasgow. Telephone interview, Mrs. Carolyn McKinley, daughter, June 23, 1978.

Arthur Clayton McCarty (1897–1963), b. Henderson. M.D. *Who's Who in Kentucky, 1936*, pp. 167-68, and telephone interview, Mrs. A. C. McCarty, July 31, 1978.

A. M. LYON APPOINTED DIRECTOR OF HOSPITALS AND MENTAL HYGIENE
Frankfort / December 31, 1940

COMMISSIONER of Welfare W. A. Frost has recommended your appointment to fill the vacany in the position of director of hospitals and mental hygiene.[1] The law specifies that this appointment shall be made by the commissioner of welfare on approval of the governor. It affords me genuine pleasure to give that approval.

Your name was on the list of three submitted by the council of the Kentucky Medical Association along with two other highly capable men. The commissioner and the governor did not feel competent to make the choice. So the advisory committee on hospitals and mental hygiene, appointed by the Kentucky Medical Association, was requested to give advice as to which of the three were best qualified and adapted to the position of director.

I am authorized to announce that the advisory committee, composed of outstanding Kentucky physicians, arrived at the unanimous conclusion that you, Dr. Lyon, were the proper person to be appointed and so recommended. Your preferment over the other two able men is no reflection on them. The advisory committee further recommended that you invite Dr. Isham Kimball,[2] now on the staff of a United States Veteran's

Hospital at Gulfport, Mississippi, to accept appointment as superintendent of one of the state hospitals to fill the vacancy created as result of you being changed to the position of director. Dr. Kimball was one of the men on the list of three submitted for consideration as director.

Dr. F. K. Foley,[3] who has rendered fine public service as superintendent of Eastern State Hospital, was the third man on the list. So, if you follow the recommendation of the medical advisory committee, it will be Kentucky's good fortune to have it in its hospital service all three of those regarded as qualified for director.[4]

I want to assure you and the superintendents of the hospitals of the sincere interest which Commissioner Frost and I have in the sustained improvement of these institutions. As lieutenant governor I had a small part in the enactment of the Chandler-Wallis Act. I believed it to be good legislation then and my opinion has not changed. I shall continue to try to translate its provisions.

You as a superintendent of Western State Hospital and as former superintendent of the Feeble Minded Institute know the problems of the institutions from experience. You know that as governor I have not requested the employment of any individual. You know that I have sustained the superintendents in each dismissal that has been made of employees that they thought should be released. I pledge you a continuance of that policy.

As governor I have insisted on economy in all phases of state government—prudent economy under which it is sought to wisely expend available money. Neglected as our state hospitals have been for years, it will require much money, much wise guidance, and sacrificial service to bring them to the advanced position we desire. More money is now being expended in operation of the hospitals than ever before—yet it is inadequate to immediately correct the accumulated deficiencies of years. We have started a program of general renovating of the buildings at each of the institutions. It is proposed, as rapidly as possible, to do a complete house-smithing job.

You will find the work well advanced at Eastern State Hospital where there has been spent in the last year $101,077.50. This expenditure has resulted in rehabilitation of the refrigeration plant, installation of a new laundry, electric rewiring to eliminate fire hazards, rehabilitation of the antiquated plumbing, heating and boiler plant, installation of new kitchen equipment.

It is planned to replaster and freshly paint these buildings and place them in the best possible condition. I have concluded that this hospital should not be abandoned but should be renovated.

It is planned to perform the same type of service at each of the other hospitals as quickly as possible. Cost of these improvements is not being paid from the regular appropriation for the hospitals, but from an extra appropriation for buildings and repairs.

We have spent during the year at the Feeble Minded Institute $23,501.39 in replacing its boiler plant and making its heating equipment adequate. We have spent, as you know, $16,703 within the year at Western State Hospital, replacing the refrigerator plant and improving the waterworks system.

We have expended $11,437 in improvements at Central State Hospital, replacing the boiler plant smokestack and repairing engines and generators. This program of improvement will go steadily forward under your guidance.

I agree, gentlemen, that a smokestack does not seem important. But when the stack blows down at Central, it is the most important problem there until a new one is built.

More than a million dollars has been expended in starting establishment of a modern hospital on a 1,300 acre farm in Boyle and Mercer counties.[5] It is our desire to hasten the improvement of these institutions as rapidly as our limited resources will permit, keeping always in mind that money for even such worthy purposes can be obtained only by levying taxes upon our citizens.

Gratifying progress has been made in improving the hospitals since enactment of the Chandler-Wallis Act. Total expenditure on the hospitals in 1938 was $880,726. In the fiscal year which ended July 1, a total of $1,123,398 was expended. In accord with recommendations made by experts who conducted a survey of the hospitals, we have not only improved the quality of personnel employed in the hospitals but have increased the total number of employees from 613 to 776 as of today—an increase of 163.

Commissioner Frost and I desire you to understand that you will never be requested to sacrifice the welfare of these hospitals to political expediency. We believe you competent of doing this most important job. There is to be no interference, political or otherwise, with your performance of your duty as you see it. Neither you nor the superintendents will be coerced or importuned to employ anyone you do not regard as competent. Neither you nor the superintendents will be interfered with in the dismissal of those you regard as incompetent.

Regardless of what procedure may be followed in recruiting of personnel, there can be no serious disservice to the hospital inmates so long as superintendents know that they may dismiss any employee they feel should be released.

[The governor left his text and questioned Drs. Lyon, Foley, Summers, and Adams.[6]]

Have I coerced or importuned or asked you to hire anybody since I have been governor? Have I interfered with you in any way, shape, form, or fashion in your dismissal of any employee since I have been governor? [Each doctor answered in the negative.]

Commissioner Frost and I are certain that you will not permit partisan politics to interfere in any way with creditable conduct of these hospitals. And I would suggest that it is just as important to prevent personal politics, clique politics from interfering with performances of the type of public service which you have demonstrated you are capable of rendering.

You shall have my enthusiastic support in this important undertaking. You and I and Commissioner Frost shall work together in a zealous effort to improve the hospitals as rapidly as our resources will permit.

---

1. Before reading this statement, the governor said, "I feel a situation has now been created in which the governor can take an active interest in advancing our work in these hospitals without his motives being impugned. I contemplate, gentlemen, that all of us—Mr. Frost, Dr. Lyon, the three superintendents, and doctors from their staffs—will meet from time to time with the advisory committee on mental hygiene. By the exchange of ideas and the friction of intellects, I hope we will be able to work out sane, progressive programs for these institutions."

2. Isham Kimball, United States Veterans Administration Hospital, Gulfport, Miss., 1940; formerly staff member, United States Veterans Administration Hospital, Lexington. Superintendent, Central State Hospital, 1941. Returned to Alabama, 1952. Letter, Margaret Woll, Louisville, March 23, 1978.

3. Floyd K. Foley (1885–1957), b. Kentucky. Superintendent, Eastern State Hospital. Files of the Kentucky State Board of Medical Licensure, Louisville.

4. On December 9, 1940, the governor had asked Margaret Woll to resign as commissioner of welfare. Two days later he stated that he did not oust her because she had recommended Dr. Isham Kimball to succeed Dr. J.G. Wilson. He did not know of her recommendation until after he asked for her resignation. "I asked Miss Woll to resign because I wanted to put a competent administrator in that office. Miss Woll is a fine social worker, and I think all will agree on that point. But I have felt for some time her ability as an administrator is not all that the position requires." Louisville *Courier-Journal*, December 12, 1940. Woll resigned on December 10, 1940, effective January 1, 1941. *State Journal*, December 11, 1940. She was director, Field Operations, Department of Welfare, 1936–1938; commissioner of welfare, 1938–1940; director, Home Service, American Red Cross, Louisville, 1943–1961. Letter, Margaret Woll, April 4, 1978. An executive order, addressed to the secretary of state, reads: "For cause deemed sufficient by me as governor of the Commonwealth of Kentucky, the office of commissioner of welfare is declared vacant as of this date, December 12, 1940. I have this day appointed and you will please commission Dr. W.A. Frost, commissioner of welfare, for a four-year term, dating from July 1, 1940."

5. The hospital was taken over by the War Department in July 1941 before being used as a mental institution.

6. William Rankin Summers (1872–?), b. Webster County, Missouri. Assistant superintendent, Western State Hospital, 1922–1925, 1932; superintendent, Central State Hospital, 1940; superintendent, Western State Hospital, 1941–1944; returned to Missouri, August 1944. Files of the Kentucky State Board of Medical Licensure, Louisville, and Louisville *Courier-Journal*, February 23, 1939.

L. D. Adams (1880–1952), b. Livingston County. Superintendent, Feeble Minded Institute, Frankfort. Letter, Margaret Woll, March 23, 1978, and interview, Polly Gorman, secretary to Governor Bert Combs, July 28, 1978.

DIVISION OF PUBLIC ASSISTANCE, DEPARTMENT OF WELFARE
Frankfort / August 6, 1941

THIS month marks the first anniversary of the old age assistance program in Kentucky. In August 1936 the first old age assistance checks ever to be mailed to needy aged individuals in Kentucky were mailed to only 238 recipients and totaled $1,769. Compare these figures with the 58,325 checks mailed to eligible individuals totaling $520,865 last month. This indicates the tremendous progress which Kentucky has made in recognizing the needs of our destitute aged citizens and caring for them to the extent which our budgetary limitations will permit.

From the time Kentucky was admitted into the Union as a state until five years ago, no planned or effective method had been inaugurated to care for its aged citizens who, through circumstances beyond their control, had reached the last years of their lives without adequate means of support. Since that time, through the cooperation of the state and the federal Social Security Board, $21,672,678.95 has been distributed to needy eligible individuals in this state. It must be borne in mind that in distributing this large sum of money, the Division of Public Assistance has endeavored to fulfill a twofold obligation: first, to determine eligibility on the basis of a thorough investigation of each applicant and to make a grant on the basis of individual needs; second, to be cognizant of the responsibility to the taxpayers by preventing individuals who are ineligible or those who for selfish reasons desired to raid the public treasury by securing funds to which they were not entitled under the law.

It is evident that during this five-year period, many people have been misinformed concerning the real purpose and meaning of the old age assistance program. Various partisan individuals and groups have endeavored to mislead the old people in this state for their selfish purposes. Old age assistance means by the very nature of the phrase assistance to be granted to those eligible, to individuals in need and in proportion to the amount needed to provide a reasonable subsistence. It is now an old age pension, as the latter term would denote a uniform rate of pay to every individual without regard to their need of such assistance.

I would like to compliment you as supervisors and members of the staff in the Division of Public Assistance for this very fine five-year record. In addition to providing monetary assistance to these destitute old people, you have, through additional work, provided them with many services in connection with their domestic and financial problems in securing better living conditions for them, increased comforts, and a happier existence.

Since the beginning of my regular term of office in December 1939, a total of $8,557,371 has been distributed in grants to recipients of old age assistance. This represents a total of 969,568 checks which have been issued, or an average of 51,030 checks per month, over the nineteen months of my present administration. When you compare the old age assistance payment of $391,092.75 in December 1939 with the $520,865 distributed during July 1941, you will find that this represents an increase of $129,832.25 per month since my inauguration. We now have 12,669 more eligible individuals receiving old age assistance per month than were receiving assistance at the time of my inauguration.[1]

Every effort has been made by the Division of Public Assistance to complete a thorough investigation for all applicants for old age assistance as rapidly as possible. There is no need for me to tell you who are actively engaged in this program the many difficulties involved in connection with securing the proper documentary proof of eligibility concerning age, residence, citizenship, and other legal requirements. You are still receiving more than 1,000 new applications per month which must be investigated and receive final action as rapidly as is consistent with good work.

According to estimates from the Department of Welfare, you will have to deal with approximately 20,000 new and pending cases during the next year.[2] These estimates indicate that approximately 6,000 of this number will be denied, withdrawn, or institutionalized. Over 13,000 will be subject to approval as eligible to receive assistance. Of the number of individuals now receiving assistance, the department estimates that 4,800 will die within the year. It is, therefore, estimated that at the end of the next fiscal year 66,483 eligible individuals will be receiving old age assistance in Kentucky. By exerting every economy under our present budgetary appropriation, it is anticipated that approximately $6.66 million will be available for actual distribution during the current fiscal year. If this estimate is correct, then the department may be able to reach an average grant of approximately $10.00 per month during this fiscal year.

It is my intention, also, to request the next General Assembly to reappropriate the $500,000 previously set aside for the aid to dependent children and aid to the blind laws on an emergency basis, whereby it may become available for public assistance immediately upon passage. This sum, when matched with federal funds, will provide an additional total of $1 million available for old age assistance.[3] In the recent primary campaign, many candidates, in order to appeal to our aged voters, have advocated their interest in every old person in Kentucky receiving the full $30.00 per month.[4] Let us see for a moment what this would mean. It is estimated that there are 190,000 people over sixty-five years in the state. If each of these individuals could be paid the maximum of $30.00 per month, it would cost in actual grants $68.4 million per year or nearly three times as much as the cost of all the other functions of the state government exclusive of the Highway Department. Only a small proportion of this cost could be borne by the federal Social Security Board due to the fact that the federal law permits the matching of state grants only to the extent that the Department of Welfare can prove an individual's budgetary deficiency. Therefore, the major portion of this huge sum would have to be borne by the state government through greatly increased taxes.

Though Kentucky's fiscal condition is an envy of her sister states, though the day is in sight when our state debt can be completely paid off, we are faced with the necessity of paying for the rehabilitation of our state institutions whose physical plants have deteriorated through many years of neglect. It is also necessary to expand the facilities of these institutions to relieve overcrowded conditions that are now prevalent. Though we hope to do as much as possible for our aged population during the remainder of my administration, we must recognize the necessity for continuing our institutional building program and providing for these other groups of unfortunate individuals residing in our penal and eleemosynary institutions.

May I point out the greatly increased administrative functions of the Department of Welfare during the past fiscal year. Prior to that time, you were concerned almost entirely with the responsibility of administering the old age assistance program. In July 1940 it was necessary for the state adminstration to agree that the Department of Welfare would become the state referral agency responsible for the general supervision of the county referral agencies in making WPA, Surplus Commodity, and NYA certifications and the selection of CCC[5] enrollees. We were informed that unless the state agreed to assume this general supervision, the work of these agencies could no longer be continued in Kentucky. In order to cooperate with the federal agencies and provide for the benefits accruing from these programs to our citizens in Kentucky these functions were established under the Department of Welfare. Since then, a Division of CCC Selection and a Division of Commodity Distribution have been placed in the department and the Division of Public Assistance has been made responsible for the general supervision for the county referral or certification agencies.

In order to give you an idea of the increased work of the department in connection with these programs, may I point out as an example the increased certification and distribution of surplus commodities as part of the free school lunch program. During the entire school year ending in 1940, only eighty-seven schools were certified to receive surplus commodities as part of the free school lunch program. Only 3,544 children were benefited. During the past school year, 438 schools were certified and 25,773 schoolchildren were benefited by receiving surplus commodities as part of the school lunches.[6]

The supervision of the referral agents has now become an important function of the Department of Welfare. During the past year, the referral agents have selected 10,741 youths for enrollment in the Civilian Conservation Corps. Certifications for eligible individuals to receive federal surplus commodities has also been one of the major concerns of the referral agencies. At the beginning of June 1941, 84,114 cases, representing 348,051 families, were certified and receiving commodities. As compared with the case load of August of the previous year, there were 13,631 more cases certified and 66,921 more families receiving commodities. The increase was undoubtedly due in a large part to the prolonged strikes in the eastern Kentucky coalfield necessitating emergency certifications.[7] Such certifications were made in Harlan, Bell, Perry, Whitley, Floyd, Pike, Letcher, Johnson, Knott, Laurel, McCreary, Breathitt, and Knox counties. Besides determining family eligibility, the referral agents certify recreation centers on the basis of their enrollments, National Youth Administration Training Camps, and qualifying public schools. Twenty recreation centers, with a total enrollment of 2,813 children and forty-one National Youth Administration Training Camps have been certified by the department to receive surplus commodities.

It is also pleasing for me to note the increased productivity among the workers in the Division of Public Assistance. According to the records of the department, prior to my inauguration as governor, during 1939 it cost the department $10.45 for each completed case investigation report. During the calendar year of 1940, the field workers of this division completed 62,486 case reports, reducing the cost to $4.99 per report. During the first six months of 1941, these field workers completed 38,679 investigation reports and reduced the cost to an average of $3.90 per case for each worker. Though we desire to economize in every way possible, we must bear in mind the necessity for providing adequate service to these eligible recipients of public assistance in order to provide greater happiness and comfort. You are engaged in a great humanitarian work in helping many thousands of our less fortunate citizens. It is only through your acceptance of this great responsibility and conscientious efforts that we can achieve our goal of making Kentucky a better place in which to live.[8]

---

1. Removal of the lien clause from application requirements and increase of the maximum grant to $30 per month brought a large increase in the number of applications. The lien clause required old age recipients to pledge their property to the state for repayment of old age payments. *Richmond Daily Register*, March 29, 1941.

2. Commissioner Frost "froze" the old age rolls on March 1, 1942, because the necessity to set aside $500,000 for the new needy blind and dependent children programs made it impossible to add more indigent elderly persons. Attorney General Meredith, who advised Frost in the summer of 1942 that he should continue investigating old age applicants and add to his rolls those shown to be qualified, attempted later to get the federal Social Security board to require that action. Receiving no encouragement from that source, he filed suit in Franklin Circuit Court on December 9, 1942, for a mandatory injunction requiring the expansion. His petition declared that 10,000 applications were pending and that experience had shown that 60 to 70 percent of the signers would prove to be qualified. He charged that failure to investigate and to add qualified persons to the rolls since March 1, 1942, was discriminatory and in violation of the equal protection clause of the United States Constitution. On December 10, 1942, he stated that new applicants for old age assistance who proved their qualifications were as much entitled under state and federal laws to financial help as those already receiving monthly checks. The court granted the injunction in January 1943. (See *Commonwealth ex rel. Meredith, Atty. Gen.*, v. *Frost, Commissioner of Welfare*, 295 Ky. 137,172 S. W. 2d 905 (1943). Frost asked Meredith on December 14 to assign one of his assistants to defend him in the suit which Meredith had brought. On December 18, Meredith announced that he had employed Sam H. Brown to defend Frost and that he would pay him out of his own pocket. *Lexington Herald*, December 15 and 19, 1942. Declining to comment on the suit, the governor said a decision already had been made to increase state aid and that he had requested E. Lawrence Tucker, the attorney employed to aid him and the Finance Department, to draw up an order transferring $200,000 from the general emergency fund "for social security purposes and that included old age, the children and the blind." See Executive Order, December 11, 1942. The governor said the $200,000 would be added to the $4,250,000 appropriated by the legislature for the current fiscal year and that the federal government would provide an equal amount. *State Journal*, December 11, 1942. He disclosed on December 30, 1942, that new names had been added to the old age assistance rolls. *Lexington Herald*, December 31, 1942.

On May 25, 1943, Meredith attacked in Franklin Circuit Court a plan to give pensioners an extra payment. A large sum of the appropriations for old age assistance had not been expended and would revert to the general fund if not distributed before June 20. An equal amount would not be received from the federal government. Frost proposed to pay those persons (about 55,000) on the rolls a 30 percent additional amount for May and June. He estimated that about $235,000 of state money would be used plus an equal amount of federal funds. However, $350,000 or $400,000 would revert to the general fund. *Commonwealth ex. rel. Meredith, Atty. Gen.*, v. *Frost, Commissioner of Welfare*, p. 141. Governor Johnson said no greater effort was being made in 1943 to give additional money to the aged than had been made twice before unsuccessfully during his term in years when there were no statewide elections. *State Journal*, May 26, 1943. Franklin Circuit Court Judge Ardery upheld the plan to give old age pensioners an extra payment. *Lexington Herald*, June 9, 1943. Meredith petitioned the Court of Appeals. He asked to include those persons on the waiting list so that more of the fund would be used. He based his request on the authority of the state to obligate expenditures and pay for them as late as three months after the close of the fiscal year. The court ruled that the attorney general's plan was "neither feasible nor legal." It affirmed the decision of Judge Ardery. *Commonwealth ex. rel. Meredith, Atty. Gen.*, v. *Frost, Commissioner of Welfare*, pp. 147-48.

3. The governor had stated on June 27, 1941, that he would ask the legislature to reappropriate this $500,000 to the Department of Welfare. It could not be used because a test suit on the validity of the children-blind aid act was pending in the courts. Assistant Attorney General M. B. Holifield ruled that the money must revert to the general fund. Displaying emotion, Johnson said, "This money is going to stay right in the general fund—it's not going to be touched—and we'll ask the next legislature to reappropriate it to the Welfare Department." *Lexington Herald*, June 28, 1941.

Legislation to provide financial aid and other services for dependent children and the needy blind was adopted in 1940. Holifield ruled in May 1940 that the dependent children act was unconstitutional because all such children would not be treated equally since the act granted aid to dependent children living with their kin but not to dependent children living elsewhere. Louisville *Courier-Journal*, March 9, 1940. Judge Ardery declared the needy blind act unconstitutional in November 1941. His decision had the effect of voiding also the provisions which provided aid for dependent children. Louisville *Courier-Journal*, November 15, 1941. The Court of Appeals reversed Judge Ardery and upheld the constitutionality of aid for the needy blind in February 1942. *Bowman* v. *Frost, Commissioner of Welfare*, 289 Ky. 826, 158 S. W. 2d 945 (1942). This decision was announced after the 1942 legislature adopted the 1942–1944 budget and appropriated money for aid to dependent children and the needy blind despite the legal uncertainty. The act provided that it would be effective only if both the dependent children and needy blind statutes were upheld. Louisville *Courier-Journal*, June 11, 1942. Aid for dependent children was upheld as constitutional in December 1942. The court ruled that the limitation of aid to dependent children living with their kin was a reasonable classification. *Meredith, Atty. Gen., et al.* v. *Ray*, 292 Ky. 326,166 S. W. 2d 437 (1942). Frost announced on the same day that payments to the needy blind would start the next week and aid to dependent children by January 1943.

Lexington Herald, December 5, 1942. As a result of the delay, Kentucky was one of the last states to provide aid for dependent children and the needy blind.

4. The governor wrote early in March 1942 to the Newport Old Age Pension Club: "I regret so much that it does not seem possible or expedient at this time to increase pensions for Kentucky aged to a minimum of $30 per month. The all-out war effort of the nation will cut the income of our state government at least $5 million annually. The members of the General Assembly and the citizens throughout the state do not feel that it is wise to increase taxes some $10 million or $12 million in order to pay minimum pensions of $30. I believe that you will agree with me that our citizenship is burdened now with taxes that were not thought of in 1939.

"No one at the time predicted or dreamed of the situation as it is today. Whatever promises I made in 1939 were made in good faith with the intention of being fulfilled 100 percent, and while I did not say that I favored a minimum pension of $30 for everyone, I do regret that the state's income during the period of the emergency will be so limited that we cannot increase the pensions in line with the increased costs of living." *Kentucky Post*, March 4, 1942.

5. The Civilian Conservation Corps was created by Act of Congress in 1937.

6. On September 4, 1943, the governor transferred $6,000 from his General Emergency Fund to the Department of Education to be used in the administration of the Community School Lunch Program. The Food Distribution Administration of the War Food Administration provided up to $1 million for the school year. The program enabled the public schools to provide at least one good meal a day for the pupils. The federal government paid nine cents toward the cost of each full lunch, six cents for each meal of smaller quantity, two cents for milk only. The cost was twenty cents each for lunch for pupils able to pay. It was free for those unable to pay. The War Food Administration was created as an agency of the Department of Agriculture to handle food matters related to the war. The Surplus Commodity Corporation was dissolved. Louisville *Courier-Journal*, August 31, 1943.

7. Several thousand eastern Kentucky coal miners idled during these strikes submitted claims for unemployment compensation. Judge R. Monroe Fields of the Letcher Circuit Court upheld their claims. Similar suits were filed in five other circuit courts. The Court of Appeals denied the claims and reversed Judge Field's decision. It held that the miners' idleness was due to a "bona fide labor dispute" and, therefore, unallowable under state law. *Barnes et al.* v. *Hall*, 285 Ky. 160, 146 S.W. 2d 929 (1940). Certiorari denied, *Hall* v. *Barnes*, 314 U.S. 628. Although the case covered only those miners under jurisdiction of the Letcher Circuit Court, Vego E. Barnes, Kentucky unemployment compensation commissioner, stated that the decision would govern the commission's action in the other cases. *Richmond Daily Register*, December 20, 1940.

8. A temporary court order was obtained by Meredith on November 29, 1943, stopping a transfer of $478,430. The governor had planned to use $200,000 of general emergency funds for old age, child and blind aid; $275,430 for improvements at state institutions; and $3,000 for a civil defense deficiency. He said that but for his term ending December 7, he would fight the cases through and carry out the transfers. "There won't be enough money to match federal funds for old age assis-

tance, though, in December and the three months following, if the $200,000 transfer for that is held up." Louisville *Courier-Journal*, November 28, 30, 1943.

KENTUCKY STATE MEDICAL ASSOCIATION
Louisville / September 30, 1941

I CONSIDER it a very great privilege to address the physicians of Kentucky, the members of its auxiliary, and its honored guests on the occasion of the ninetieth anniversary of its organization. No other group of citizens of our Commonwealth have made greater contributions to its welfare and to the safety and security of its citizens than have you and your predecessors. It is tempting for one who has lived in and traveled in all parts of our state to dip into its glowing medical and surgical history and again place laurels upon the memory of these great men who have made contributions to the diagnosis and treatment of diseases by both medical and surgical means to the benefit of all mankind. But these immortals have been firmly placed on the proper pedestals by the historians and their lessons; yes, their very lives are your daily inspiration in your task of preventing and healing disease.

I like to think of the Kentucky State Medical Association as the family physician of the Commonwealth of Kentucky. There is no more hallowed nor honored member of any family than its family physician. No one realizes better the faults of the family and yet no other one is so kindly nor so tolerant in helping to ameliorate or cure their results.

It has been my privilege to read the minutes of many of your sessions and I have been impressed again and again with the breadth of vision and the constructive statesmanship which has illumined their pages. It was but a year after your organization was founded that, when led by your first president, Dr. Sutton,[1] the legislature registered its approval of the passing of the first vital statistics law. Even then your profession had the vision of the protection of human life and happiness and efficiency and your desire to make permanent records that you could continually study the vital facts of life and birth and death so that every possible safeguard might be thrown about us all.

It was not until 1863 that you succeeded in passing a medical registration law with a view to providing that the members of your profession might be better qualified for the essential services that it must render. The failure of these two laws to produce the beneficient results intended by the profession of the state was not your fault but was a failure which was due to the inefficient governmental organization which our individualistic forefathers builded for us. It was in 1878 under the guidance of one of the most illustrious of my predecessors, Governor Luke P. Blackburn,[2] himself an honored member of your profession, that the state Board of Health was created as the result of repeated epidemics of cholera, yellow fever, and smallpox, which diseases were soon proved to be first controllable, and then preventable. During successive years you so developed your agencies of government that such diseases as typhoid fever, diphtheria, and malaria have been robbed of their terrors. In 1888 your medical registration law was perfected and since 1910 vital statistics have shown us the relative importance of the several human problems to the solution of which your profession has given more leadership and more momentum than all of the others combined. It is but necessary to state that the annual death rate in Kentucky is less than one-fourth of what it was in 1879 and that the average span of life has been extended from thirty-two years to sixty-five during that short period.

And your interest has been as great in mental as in physical health. In 1824 under medical leadership the second institution for the care of the insane was built at Lexington—the second institution of its kind constructed under public ownership in our country. As the demand grew, similar institutions were constructed at Lakeland and at Hopkinsville, and the Institute for the Feeble Minded was developed at Frankfort. These were great institutions in their day and their medical superintendents were leaders among the psychiatrists of the nation. It never occurred to political leaders of the state of those days that the patronage of these institutions was a political asset. They were set apart as places for the restoration and care of the mentally ill. The buildings were the pride of the state and were considered a proper charge on the public treasury.

This bright period of Kentucky's history was suddenly darkened in 1896 when these institutions became the prey of partisan politics. Since that time they had become the stepchildren of the government and not only was the repair of their physical structure neglected, but the physicians and attendants were too frequently selected because of the political influence rather than because of their psychiatric knowledge and administrative efficiency. All of these changes for the worse met the constant criticism of the profession at the annual sessions of the Kentucky state Medical Association. Occasional abortive efforts were made to correct this wholly indefensible situation but there was no possibility of their real reform until the passage of the Chandler-Wallis Act in 1938 when the responsibility for their control was placed squarely upon the shoulders of the governor and the director of hospitals and mental hygiene, who is under the commissioner of welfare. Your association has appointed an advisory committee to the state director of hospitals and mental hygiene, and I desire to say to you tonight that no agency of government has ever performed a more valuable service than this able committee under the chairmanship of Dr. Gardner. I have had the privilege of meeting with them many times. No step has been taken in the rehabilitation or control of these institutions without the prior consideration and approval of this committee. We found the state hospitals for the insane and the feeble minded institution in a wholly indescribable state of neglect and approaching ruin. The professional staffs and their attendants and other employees were inadequate and the buildings in which the patients were housed were in a condition that defies description. Their essential facilities such as heating, lighting, water, and sewage, kitchens, and refrigeration systems had had little or no repairs for fifty years and no one of us who had knowledge of these facts went to sleep at night without the fear of one or the other of these essential facilities being destroyed during the night.

Conditions in the state mental hospitals are much improved. Inmates are receiving better treatment. They are being returned home in increased numbers. But the buildings which house the approximately 6,000 inmates are in horrible condition. They have disintegrated as result of years of neglect. Members of the Kentucky Medical Association committee have advised the governor and the commissioner of welfare that the most imperative need is to make these hospital plants habitable and sanitary and fireproof. We have been spending every available dollar in an effort to achieve that end. At the close of the fiscal year in June, I made available all of the governor's emergency fund for the improvement of the hospitals —$317,000. We have expended or have under contract improvements in these institutions which cost $475,162. A contract will soon be let for the beginning of complete renovating and fireproofing of the men's ward at Eastern State Hospital.

---

1. William Loftus Sutton (1797–1862), b. Scott County. First president, Kentucky Medical Society; secured law for registering birth certificates, 1852. C.R.T. Goldsborough and A.G. Fisher, *William Loftus Sutton, M.D., 1797–1862* (Lexington, Ky., 1948).

2. Luke Pryor Blackburn (1816–1887), b. Woodford County. State representative, 1843–1845; governor, 1879–1883; physician and surgeon. Democrat; served in Confederate Army during the Civil War; assumed general control of the yellow fever epidemic in lower Mississippi Valley, 1848–1854. *Who Was Who in America, 1607–1896,* H:58.

REHABILITATION OF STATE HOSPITALS AND OTHER INSTITUTIONS
Hopkinsville / October 16, 1941

GOVERNOR JOHNSON and Commissioner Frost, in a joint statement,[1] characterized Eastern State Hospital at Lexington and Central State Hospital at Lakeland as "old, worn out" hospitals and "almost falling apart" and in need of repairs and crowded far beyond their normal limits. Western State Hospital was described as the best of the three but in need of improvement of the physical property as well as more physicians.

Around $800,000 is spent yearly on state institutions, the governor pointed out, adding "you can hardly see what has been done." This sum was spent merely to keep the institutions going and did not include funds for badly needed additions to the plants and equipment.

About $125,000 is being expended on Western State Hospital alone for new boilers, a new dam to insure a safe water supply, and some other changes to the plant to keep the hospital going.

If the income tax law can be retained and demands from various state groups can be held within reasonable limit, Kentucky can start a program of rehabilitating state institutions now and look forward to a time when Kentucky will be proud of her hospitals and other agencies.

The board [Board of Welfare] believes that improvements and additions to the hospitals and other plants are necessary. The board discussed at length a general program for the hospitals but did not at this time intend to release any figures as to amounts to be asked from the General Assembly for this purpose.[2]

---

1. The statement was issued after an executive session of the Board of Welfare at Western State Hospital. Johnson was the first governor to make thorough inspections of the mental institutions. On June 12, 1941, he outlined a reconstruction program to cost approximately $435,000 at the three hospitals, Eddyville penitentiary, and the Houses of Reform. *State Journal*, June 13, 1941. On June 24, 1941, he announced that $322,000 of emergency funds would be used for these institutions. *Richmond Daily Register*, June 24, 1941.

2. Mental hospital problems were also discussed at an informal conference at the Pendennis Club, Louisville, on September 22, 1941. The governor met with the members of the mental hygiene committee of his advisory committee of the medical association and the hospital superintendents, Drs. McCormack, Frost, and Lyon. "I find it helpful just to talk over our problems, summarize what has been accomplished within the past few months and make tentative plans for the future," the governor said. Louisville *Courier-Journal*, September 23, 1941.

On November 27, 1941, a subcommittee of the Legislative Council was named to study the rehabilitation of state institutions. Members were Dr. B.F. Shields, chairman; Commissioner Frost; Senators Ray B. Moss, Pineville; W. E. Rogers, Sr., Guthrie; Elvis J. Stahr, Hickman; and Representatives C.R. Walden, Edmonton, and Faust Y. Simpson, Morganfield. *State Journal*, November 28, 1941.

RALLY FOR W. A. FROST
Mayfield / October 16, 1941

GOVERNOR JOHNSON praised Dr. W. A. Frost for outstanding work in one of the state's "most tangled and disorganized branches" and lauded him for his splendid work as head of the state Welfare Commission. Dr. Frost had "created order out of chaos in Kentucky's public institutions and has changed the whole attitude of the Welfare Department to where they are now all pulling together."

He had discovered Dr. Frost after a futile attempt to get someone to take over the commissionership of the disorganized welfare group. He inherited this welfare organization when he took office as governor. There was no cooperation in the organization and a great deal of jealousy. After a year that sorely tried his patience, he sought reorganization of the Welfare Department and after a great deal of study he selected a man for the post and asked him to take it. The man declined, and a few days later he asked another. This one also declined, and he was about to despair of getting the type of man he wanted for the post.

"Then one day at a meeting at Greendale, where the school of reform is located, I heard Dr. Frost clearly and intelligently describe the conditions of that institution. I suddenly pinched myself and exclaimed, 'Why Keen, you dumb ox, there's the man right there that you have been looking for for months.' " He then conferred with Dr. Frost, and after a few days the present commissioner decided to take the post.

During his ten months' work since his appointment, Dr. Frost had rendered one of the most outstanding pieces of work during the present administration.

FEDERALIZATION OF UNEMPLOYMENT COMPENSATION
Frankfort / October 18, 24, 1941

I AM vitally concerned about information which we have recently received regarding possible federalization of the Unemployment Compensation commissions—my interest, of course, being in the Kentucky agency.[1]

In a wire from Mr. W. O. Hake, president of the Interstate Conference, to the Kentucky commission, following a conference by him with Mr. Arthur J. Altmeyer,[2] Mr. Hake was permitted to quote Mr. Altmeyer as follows on the subject of federalization of state unemployment compensation commissions: "No conclusions have been reached with the president concerning federalization of state employment security agencies or any other social security matters. He further advised me that alternative plans have been discussed with the president in recent conferences but doesn't know when final conclusions may be reached."

You may rest assured that the secrecy which is surrounding this project is not likely to further the interest of the federal-state relationships. I am inclined to believe as governor of the Commonwealth of Kentucky that, if such plans are being formulated, I am entitled to some knowledge of them. I do not consider it too inquisitive on my part to inquire why the Social Security Board and other authorities of the federal government are advocating federalization and the accompanying confusion which must follow when the state agencies are taxed to their capacities to carry out the requirements of the national defense program. I am not able to speak, of course, for any of the other states except my own, but I can say to you that I am proud of the job thus far done by the Kentucky Unemployment Compensation Commission, which includes the Employment Service.

It is true that most of the state unemployment compensation laws were adopted as a result of the enactment of the Social Security Act. The states, however, were advised by those in authority at that time (some of those persons still being in authority) that the laws as adopted were to be administered entirely by the states. Certain standards, necessary to any appropriation, were attached and these standards have resulted in many prohibitions and regulations. Even under the most trying circumstances, however, Kentucky has never yet been found to be out of conformity. There, naturally, have been differences at times between the federal and the state administrators and between the federal administrators and myself. These differences were no more than to be expected, however, in such a large and entirely new program. As far as we know all differences were in no way personal but rather resulted because of the responsibilities under which each of the authorities were operating. These incidents have not deterred us in any way from doing all that was possible for those affected by the laws' administration. We have felt very proud of our accomplishments, even in view of the difficulties encountered, and, furthermore, we believe that we can do an even more commendable job as a result of the experience gathered during the past five years.

Will all of the accumulated experience of the state of Kentucky and of other states during this time be wasted? Cannot that same cooperation which has existed in the past be continued? Should not the states have some voice in the course to be followed? Why should the Social Security Board and others attempt a change, in this extreme emergency to our country, from a system which has proved itself to be workable to an experimentation which would only center more power in Washington and result in an employment security system which will take on the top-heavy, cumbersome, and lack of down-to-earth contacts which have characterized other federal agencies? We have too much interest in the welfare of the people of our state to desire such a situation.

The impact of the defense program upon the state agency has been tremendous. Our agency was so set up and people trained in such a way that it was possible almost overnight to switch from two types of work to almost one entirely—that of recruitment of labor. The Kentucky agency has been called upon to not only place many thousands of workers in Kentucky industries and industries on the borders of our adjoining states, but they have recruited for training thousands of workers that will be available to the more industrialized states. In fact we have hundreds of trained workers registered, waiting on a minute's notice to be transferred to other states. And it is probable that such transfers are being held up due to cumbersome methods set up by the Federal Security Agency. I know it is through no fault of the Kentucky agency. In every phase of defense work in which the Kentucky agency has been called upon to participate, I know definitely that they have responded immediately and have done the work efficiently. If this statement is not true, I am willing for facts to be presented which will prove the contrary.

In connection with the defense program we have, at the request of the Regional Supply Office and the Social Security Board, made numerous surveys of local labor market conditions in different areas of the state. The reports of the findings of these surveys have always been reported immediately and according to schedule. At the present time the agency is making a survey of the entire state which will show all available labor, the potentialities of every industrial plant in the state, power and transportation facilities of expansion, in every respect. This is a survey that was not requested, but one in which we have taken the initiative. A comparison of the results of this survey with the meager picture obtained by federal agencies will substantiate my contention that the only way a thorough job can be done in a program as large as employment security is through decentralization of power. There is not a single phase of the defense work in which Kentucky has not played a vital part and has met its responsibilities expeditiously and according to schedule.

I am firmly convinced that a change cannot be made during this emergency without a disruption and probably a collapse of the program. If I did not know the success with which the agency had been operating in this state, I would say to you that, for the benefit of those who are affected by this program, it should be taken over by the federal government. I believe at the present time, conditions being what they are, that new methods of cooperating, if that be necessary, should be in the making rather than new methods being devised which will result in disharmony in every aspect of the program. The federal government is dependent upon the cooperation of every individual and certainly every state in helping to build for the nation a defense that will be impregnable. I do not believe it is possible to do this in the face of the efforts of those who are determined to tear down. I do not believe five or six years is sufficient time to justify you or the Social Security Board in contending that this is not a state program if it was not one at the time the original Social Security Act became a law.

Much of my time and many of my efforts since becoming governor of Kentucky have been spent in assisting my administrators to do what I consider a good job. If I am correct, is it reasonable to ask that the federal government permit me and this state and the agency to continue as we have in the past? I am sure that by reason of our experience that we will be able to do even a more commendable job.

We trust that the common goal of social security towards which we are all working will cause you to see the folly of the selfish proposal of the board and that you will lend the influence of your office toward enabling us to continue forward rather than to take such a backward step as is now being contemplated.

[On October 23, 1941, the governor sent a second letter to McNutt.]

In my letter to you on October 18, I stated, "I am vitally concerned about information recently received regarding possible federalization of the unemployment compensation commissions." I am now even more concerned about a statement which I have now before me in which you are quoted by the Cincinnati press with reference to such proposals being made to Congress—"It may be today, it may be tomorrow."[3] In the various statements that have been made regarding this move by the federal government at the suggestion of the Social Security Board, I have yet to see mention made of what appears to me a barrier in enacting such legislation.

I am sure that you are familiar with a very important question which arose in Kentucky after the 1940 legislature had met and adjourned in regard to the amounts collected from railroad workers before the Railroad Retirement Board took over the administration of unemployment compensation to railroad workers. The Kentucky Unemployment Insurance law required a contribution from workers as well as employers; $1,077,593.32 was collected from railroad employees and because of a requirement of the federal law, the Kentucky legislature passed an act authorizing that the title be transferred from the state of Kentucky to the Railroad Retirement Board. The constitutionality of this legislative act was questioned and carried to the Court of Appeals and the court, by unanimous decision, held that this money so collected under a state law for its specific purpose, that of paying benefits to unemployed workers, could under no conditions be transferred to the federal government, but would have to remain state funds.[4]

In light of this court decision, I am unable to understand how Congress could, under any method of circuitous reasoning, pass a law which would permit the federal government to take over approximately $36 million from the state of Kentucky and over $2 billion from the other state commissions if it was not legal for them to require the state of Kentucky to pay over $1,077.593.32.

The Court has this to say in its opinion: "The root of the whole trouble is, it seems to us, in the federal act which, when carefully analyzed, appears to be a circuitous method of attempting to compel the making of a gift of the railroad workers' contributions to the federal government instead of permitting this money to remain to the credit of the commission for the payment of benefits to all covered employees."[5]

In this connection another problem vexes me greatly—how, in the face of the Kentucky Unemployment Insurance law, giving to the state of Kentucky right and authority to administer an Unemployment Compensation law, can the federal government advocate and declare null and void the Kentucky act?

I would like to add further—it has always been my thought, and I believe correctly so, that we live under a system of government in which the states retain specific powers and the federal government exercises specific powers. Under such a system there are bound to be differences. Some of the states have better schools than others but there has never yet been enacted by Congress a law to federalize all of our schools. Some of our states are richer than others but this fact cannot be changed, regardless of what steps are taken by the federal government or our state leaders. Some states choose to keep taxes on a lower level than others; that is their right and prerogative.

American democracy, as I think of it, does not mean equality of status, but means equality of opportunity. For Congress to attempt to seize the accumulations of some states to give benefits to the less provident states is not only a violation of the principle of our whole system of government but is an act of gross injustice.[6]

---

1. Letters to Paul V. McNutt, federal social security administrator. The letters are in Record Group 183, Bureau of Unemployment Compensation / Bureau of Employment Security, National Archives, Washington, D.C.

2. Arthur Joseph Altmeyer (1891–1972), b. DePere, Wisconsin. Entered federal government service, 1933; Social Security Board, 1935–1936, chairman, 1937–1946; United States commissioner, Social Security, 1946–1953. *Who Was Who in America, 1969–1973*, 5:12.

3. McNutt made this statement when he addressed a United Service Organizations meeting. He said that the necessary legislation would be introduced in Congress as soon as President Roosevelt recommended the change. Louisville *Courier-Journal*, October 21, 1941.

4. *Unemployment Compensation Commission, et al.* v. *Savage, et al.* 283 Ky. 301, 140 S.W. 2d 1073 (1940). Congress had provided in the Railroad Unemployment Insurance Act of 1939 that if a state Unemployment Compensation Commission did not transfer the money contributed by railroad workers, the federal government would not pay to the state commission a sum for administrative expenses (approximately $700,000 in Kentucky). In 1942 the Kentucky legislature attempted to solve the problem by authorizing the transfer of interest earnings from the unemployment trust fund to the railroad unemployment insurance account. The Court of Appeals also declared this act unconstitutional. Both acts were held to be in violation of Section 180 of the Kentucky Constitution. *Kentucky Color and Chemical Co., et al.* v. *Barnes, Executive Director of Kentucky Unemployment Compensation Commission, et al.*, 290 Ky. 681, 162 S. W. 2d 531 (1942).

Congress set a deadline for compliance of July 1, 1940. This deadline was first extended for two years and then in 1942 for an additional two years to July 1, 1944. In the second extension Congress authorized the use of interest earned upon contributions collected after enactment by a state of legislation providing for the transfer of funds from the state's account in the Unemployment Trust Fund to the railroad unemployment insurance account. 56 *Stat*. 465-66. This measure, sponsored by the entire Kentucky congressional delegation, was enacted after a representative of Governor Johnson told a House of Representatives subcommittee that the Kentucky Court of Appeals had hinted in the *Kentucky Color and Chemical Co.* case that this procedure would be legal. Louisville *Courier-Journal*, June 18, 1942. Kentucky did not adopt the procedure. In 1944 the General Assembly provided that the Unemployment Compensation Commission could use funds contributed after April 1, 1944, to pay administrative expenses. The Social Security Board began withholding funds to balance the railroad unemployment insurance account on this date. *Acts of the General Assembly, 1944,* Chapter 37, pp. 80-83.

5. *Unemployment Compensation Commission, et al.* v. *Savage, et al.*, p. 313.

6. On December 1, 1941, at the request of the governor, Senator Chandler and eight Kentucky congressmen called on McNutt to express opposition to proposed federalization of unemployment compensation. The delegation sought to learn details of the plan, but McNutt said no public announcement would be made until the president sent the bill to Congress.

The Kentucky representatives acted in response to this wire from Johnson: "Would appreciate your leading the Kentucky delegation to call on Mr. McNutt to oppose federalization of Kentucky unemployment compensation law. Please make every effort to get a statement of federal security plans. As matter now stands it is very disturbing to the Kentucky commission. Would further appreciate you and each of the members assuring Mr. McNutt of my sincere desire that Congress in no way interfere with the Kentucky unemployment compensation law." Louisville *Courier-Journal,* December 2, 1941.

McNutt replied to Johnson on October 25 and December 5, 1941, stating that a decision had not been made and that Johnson's views would receive full consideration.

Johnson spoke to the Interstate Conference of Employment Security Agencies in Louisville on October 20, 1943, and commented that he hoped that the federal-state partnership in the unemployment compensation program would be continued. *Louisville Times,* October 20, 1943.

CENTRAL STATE HOSPITAL WARD BUILDING
Lakeland / March 24, 1942

THE governor thanked Mr. Ralph C. Wyatt, Dr. Isham Kimball, the contractor, and the medical advisory committee. He said the progress during the one year of Dr. Kimball's regime was gratifying. During the last two and a half years, the state has spent $1,602,000 on the mental institutions and the prison at Eddyville, largely in a rehabilitation program. "We hoped to spend at least $1 million more for this type of work on each of the three hospitals within the next two years. We have in effect a contract for $274,675 on Ward Number 2 at Eastern. It is the disappointment of my life that for a time we will be unable to go forward with the program illustrated by this experiment. I think we have proved that the rehabilitation plan is feasible and economical. It would have cost $150,000 to build a dormitory comparable to this." Last May it was decided to take this building as an experiment on rehabilitation at a cost of $93,000.

The governor noted that another discordant note to the celebration was the fact that the rehabilitated building, which will house 250 of the hospital's population of 2,500, was totally without beds, chairs, tables, or any other furniture.[1]

After he had contrasted the old building's shabbiness with its present modern, fireproof state, in a tribute to the staff he said, "We dedicate this building to a humane concept of public service for the mentally ill, dedicate it as a monument to awakened public conscience that manifests concern for the ill, dedicate it as a monument to consecrated service of Lakeland's staff, dedicate it as a monument to compassion—to the nobler impulses of the human heart—proof of concern for the ill."[2]

---

1. The governor promised $3,600 for beds before he left.

2. On an inspection in February 1941, the governor said, "I could remove all of the things the grand juries find objectionable for $10 million or perhaps $5 million, but first they would have to find some way to get me more taxes." He referred to a recent Jefferson County grand jury report which was concerned about fire hazards. He commented, "One of the faults most likely to make this institution a fire hazard is the wiring. Most all of the wiring system in the hospital has become defective through age and we are planning to have a new system installed. We sought electricians for the work from Louisville but were confronted with a shortage of men as a result of defense work." Louisville *Courier-Journal*, March 1, 1941.

On an inspection in November 1941, the governor said it would take $1 million to bring the hospital "into line with present demands. I'm going to ask the legislature to keep the budget as low as possible and to let me have any surplus revenue to spend on our hospitals and prisons." A building for Negro patients and a new dormitory for attendants and nurses were the priorities. "The nurses and attendants must sleep right in the wards with the patients. We could build a dormitory for approximately $100,000 and this would relieve some space in the wards for the patients." He noted the need for more staff. *Lexington Herald* and Louisville *Courier-Journal*, November 26, 1941.

VENEREAL DISEASE
Frankfort / April 3, 1942

I AM calling on the state Department of Health and all local health departments to intensify their efforts in finding and bringing to treatment all cases of venereal disease and to develop an intensive venereal disease educational campaign.[1]

I am calling on all courts and law enforcement officers in the Commonwealth to inform themselves on the laws concerning repression of prostitution and to enforce these laws.

I am calling on all welfare agencies to direct their efforts to the prevention of prostitution and the rehabilitation of prostitutes.

I am calling on every citizen in the Commonwealth to cooperate with both health officials and law enforcement officers in efforts to control venereal diseases and to suppress the vice of prostitution that goes with it.[2]

---

1. This appeal was in response to requests from the War and Navy departments.
2. The Johnson administration sponsored legislation in 1940 to require premarital and prenatal examinations in an effort to control syphilis.

OFFICIALS OF STATE INSTITUTIONS
Frankfort / September 22, 1942

GOVERNOR JOHNSON spoke to a conference of institution heads, Welfare Department and other officials of the plans to spend $907,000 in repairs and minor construction work on the institutions and of an additional $1,215,000 program when and if materials could be obtained. The biggest of the assured program was $275,000 for completely rehabilitating male ward building Number 2 at Eastern State Hospital. Work there also will include $75,000 for repairs and painting and $15,000 for a temporary dormitory.

War's demands not only are holding up institutional construction work but also are making it difficult to get food and other supplies. In many cases no bids can be obtained on food and supplies, but only agreements to sell from time to time as needed as long as the supply lasts.

The $907,000 program,[1] part of which already is under way, includes, in addition to Eastern State Hospital, the following:

• Central State Hospital, repairs and painting, $100,000; coal storage bunkers, $5,000.

• Western State Hospital, repairs and painting, $75,000.

• Eddyville Penitentiary, repairs, plumbing, heating, and painting, $50,000; installation of bakery equipment, $10,000; construction of refrigeration plant building, $25,000.

• Kentucky Houses of Reform, repairs, and painting, $62,000; construction of dairy pasteurizing building and plant, $12,000.

• Feeble Minded Institute, repairs, plumbing and heating systems, and painting, $60,000.

• Kentucky School for the Deaf, repairs, and painting, $60,000; resetting of boilers, new laundry floor, repairs to power plant smoke stack, $20,000; bakery equipment, $5,000.

• Kentucky School for the Blind, repairs, and painting, $35,000; repairs to plumbing and heating systems, $10,000.

• Kentucky Children's Home, repairs and painting, $10,000.

On the "remotely possible" program the governor listed:

• Central State Hospital, 100-bed nurses' home building, $125,000; Negro ward building for 400 men and women, $450,000; sewage disposal plant, $150,000.

• Western State Hospital, sewage disposal plant, and incinerator, $150,000; waterworks filtration and pumping plant, $85,000.

• Kentucky Houses of Reform, white boys' forty-bed detention dormitory building, $125,000.

• Kentucky Children's Home, sewage disposal plant, $50,000.

• Eastern State Hospital, storm and sanitary sewer system, $50,000.

• Eddyville Penitentiary, refrigeration plant equipment, $30,000.

The cost of the program will come from the general fund surplus of which the General Assembly authorized spending a maximum of $3 million.[2]

The repair work included repairs to gutters, roofs, plastering, flooring, joists, sills, floors, and other parts, and whatever wiring and plumbing can be done with the amount of metal obtainable.[3]

---

1. The governor announced on October 16, 1942, that the $907,000 would be used for "deferred maintenance" since new construction was not possible be-

cause war priorities prevented getting the materials. Louisville *Courier-Journal*, October 17, 1942.

2. In December 1942 the governor stated that equipment in the institutions was either worn or antiquated. He noted that the state had $3 million in its surplus, but the war made it virtually impossible to fill the needs. "We need more plain chairs, wheelchairs, iron beds which simply can't be bought; X rays, sterilizers, flour mixers, and almost everything else you can think of." *Kentucky Post*, December 24, 1942.

After an inspection of Western State Hospital in February 1943, the governor said that renovation and reconstruction were under way to eliminate "fire traps." Wooden staircases would be replaced with concrete and fireproof construction. An expenditure of $1 million would be necessary to put the hospital in proper condition to house 2,000 mental patients. *Louisville Times*, February 13, 1943. On May 21, 1943, he approved a contract for a waterworks filtration and pumping plant at Western and stated that the project was "the most critically necessary of any restoration and renovation" project at state institutions. *Kentucky Post*, May 22, 1943. He announced in September 1943 the granting of priority rights to this hospital for reconstruction of two ward buildings. Louisville *Courier-Journal*, September 17, 1943.

3. The governor was also concerned about employees' salaries. He announced a five dollars per month raise to employees in the lower brackets at a meeting of personnel at Central State Hospital on December 8, 1942. "I realize this is a small raise, but it is the best we can do. We have wanted to do something about your inadequate pay since the 1942 legislature increased our appropriation by $500,000. But food began to cost more and more, and we were afraid to go too far until we saw where it was going to level off." He reminded them that, in one sense, they had received the benefit of a 33 percent increase in the cost of food. Their maintenance was still figured at the old rate of $21.00 a month whereas it was costing the state a third more. The increase affected approximately 750 to 800 employees whose salaries were $71.50 a month or less. Louisville *Courier-Journal*, December 9, 1942. In March 1943 he announced that 600 employees in the lower pay brackets would receive increases of approximately five dollars per month. He said that the personnel turnover in most institutions had been more than 100 percent before the earlier pay raise. He expressed the hope that the additional money would "show in a little way at least our appreciation of the work of these cruelly underpaid and necessary workers" and wished it "might be possible to do even more." *Lexington Herald*, March 3, 1943.

DEDICATION OF HOSPITAL FOR MOTHERS AND BABIES
Oneida / November 1, 1942

GOVERNOR JOHNSON congratulated Eastern Kentucky mountain folks for "having continued to maintain, over many, many years, the highest birth rate" in the state. "In this area, large families and home ties have been the rule; in other sections they have been, unfortunately, too often the exception."

He dedicated the hospital[1] "to the mothers of the mountains and to the babies who shall hereafter be born, under what, we hope, will be better circumstances than are usually afforded in the isolated sections of this country.

"Too often our lip service has not been accompanied by practical evidence of real devotion to mothers. Mothers are entitled to every safeguard that science can throw around them and their children. If this hospital symbolizes anything, it symbolizes a benevolent government's interest in and recognition of its responsibility for providing the best facilities possible for making childbearing safe and guaranteeing the greatest measure of security to the bringing into the world of its future citizens. In the development of a 'sane and sensible' program for the protection of public health, Kentucky occupies first rank among the states of the Union."

He praised Kentucky's doctors by saying,"They have been giving day in and day out, the best possible service in relieving suffering and safeguarding all the people against the unnecessary spread of disease."

Doctors aided in creating the state Board of Health in 1878. In Kentucky was established the first full-time county health department in America, and today 100 of the state's 120 counties have full-time local health administrations. "This is the largest number of county health departments in any state in the Union."

The governor described the Oneida hospital as one able to furnish "the same conveniences and the same care for women as are now received in the larger cities."[2]

---

1. The thirty-bed hospital originally was owned by the Dutch Reform Church of Brooklyn, New York. Later it was acquired by the Oneida Hospital Fund Trustees who turned it over to the state in 1941. In August 1955 its operation was assumed by the Seventh-Day Adventist Church after it had been vacant for some time. The present administration does not have records for the Johnson period. Letter,

Carole Sheron, executive secretary, Memorial Hospital, Manchester, February 7, 1977.

2. Federal and state funds were used for repairs. The governor transferred $2,000 from his emergency fund. Executive Order, November 27, 1941. See also Louisville *Courier-Journal*, November 29, 1941.

CHILD WELFARE SCHOOL
Louisville / January 30, 1943

KENTUCKY is honored to be host to the [American]Legion Conference on Child Welfare. As a legionnaire governor, I am proud that you see Kentucky and that we see you. Your conference has been constructive. You have been concerned with saving life and building character instead of destroying both. No phase of the Legion program is more worthy than child welfare.

[The governor referred to Jesus in Judaea as related in Matthew 19.] Eager parents brought children to him that they might be blessed by the Holy Savior. They desired that Jesus place his hands on them. His disciples rebuked them from annoying the Christ. But Jesus said, "Suffer little children, and forbid them not to come unto me: for of such is the Kingdom of Heaven." For of such shall be the world tomorrow.

Health and education are the cornerstones of child welfare, and legionnaires owe it to themselves and their communities to assist in every way possible the public health and public education programs.

In this fight for freedom we are also struggling for increased opportunities for our children in a better postwar world. The advance of civilization has complicated problems of child welfare and child guidance, but programs must be measured by the care and attention given children by the social order.

I am proud that aid to dependent children under the Social Security Act is being started in Kentucky.[1] Aid to dependent children is now a question of how much money we are willing to contribute in taxes to support the program. The type of child welfare a community enjoys depends on the ability and intelligence and interest of its leaders, and their willingness to work for, and their real concern in the well-being of, the children of the community.

It is the duty of community leaders, among whom legionnaires must be numbered, to guarantee, so far as possible, that our children have sound health by assuring prenatal care and other general measures of infant health. To this end we must assist and help the public health programs in every way possible. Child welfare is more than that of aid for underprivileged; it is also for a wholesome environment for normal children.

In the last thirty years in the South as the result of expanded public health programs, the child death rate in the first twelve months of life has been reduced 75 percent. [The governor referred to the work being done at the Oneida Hospital, Clay County, for mothers and babies.]

Second on our program of child welfare, after we have children with sound health, must be a sound educational system, and a sound educational system demands the support of leaders for the public school program.

[The governor spoke of the leadership of the Legion and the Auxiliary in efforts to combat juvenile delinquency.] A happy childhood is a rightful heritage. Concern for children is the impulse of a noble heart.[2]

---

1. The American Legion sponsored legislation for aid to dependent children.
2. The Legion does not have a copy of the speech.

HENDERSON COUNTY PUBLIC HEALTH DEPARTMENT
Henderson / May 24, 1943

In every field of human endeavor, the last fifty years have been more fruitful than any period of similar or double length in all the history of human progress. Within its span, many marvelous scientific developments have occurred. The majority of us here present have seen happenings which would have seemed veritable miracles to our grandfathers and even to our fathers.

In the airplane, we have seen realization come to a dream which had abided with man since the first Hebrew shepherds tending their flocks on the desolate Syrian plains watched the eagles circling above the knarled cedars that sentineled the rocky crests of Lebanon. In the radio, we have seen fulfillment of the promise behind the voice which breathed over Eden, spake from the burning bush, thundered from Sinai, and is still audible to each and everyone, everywhere, whose spiritual and mental ears are attuned to the divine rhythm with which Providence moves its wonders to perform.

But tremendously important as have been these and the many other developments in the field of science, pure and applied, not a single one of them nor all of them combined are comparable, when judged by the only true criterion, which is contribution to human welfare and human happiness, to the progress in public health. To say that health is basic is but to state a truism. It measures the value of everything in life and of life itself. In proportion as we have it, in just that proportion may natural endowments, educational attainments, and material resources be made to contribute to the welfare and happiness of the individual, the community, the state, and the nation.

From the earliest times, thinking minds have realized that the greatest asset of the state lies in the lives and health of its citizens. The natural corollary to this has been stated succinctly by one of the most clear-sighted and far-seeing of English statesmen, who declared, a hundred years ago, that "protection and promotion of the public health constitute a prime function of government."

Kentucky was among the first states in the American Union to give practical recognition to public health as a governmental function. Its state Board of Health, created by act of the General Assembly in 1878, sixty-five years ago, was the third among such organizations established in the United States. During its earlier years, appropriations for support of the board were exceedingly small and its activities were consequently and correspondingly limited, being confined largely to improvement of sanitary conditions and the control of epidemics of the more devastating communicable diseases. By the turn of the century, however, even these meager investments had begun to return tangible dividends of such increasingly impressive proportions that succeeding General Assemblies were progressively ready and willing to enact legislation broadening and expanding the board's authority and provide more generously to appropriate funds for its support, with the result that Kentucky now occupies an enviable position in its organized services for application of the steadily growing medical knowledge and constantly improving procedures in public health administration.

In the sixty-five years of its existence, the state board has grown from practically a one-man affair into a huge organization, operating through two divisions and fifteen bureaus. Funds for its support have increased from $2,500 a year in 1879 to approximately $2 million in 1942. Of this $2 million total, about one-half comes from outside sources—United States Public Health Service, federal Children's Bureau, and other agencies, official and nonofficial.

Today 105 of the 120 counties in the state,[1] embracing approximately 90 percent of the state's total population, have full-time local health service —a service which originated in Kentucky and which is now recognized by the American Medical Association, the United States Public Health Service, and health authorities everywhere as offering the only effective means of properly protecting public health in rural communities. Every year visitors from other states and from foreign countries come to Kentucky to learn, firsthand, how this service is organized and how it operates. The gradual extension of full-time health units has been in response to popular demand and has kept even pace with public recognition of the cumulative dividends which it returns in promoting health, prolonging life, preventing unnecessary suffering, increasing productivity, and enhancing the general welfare and happiness of the people.

The tangible results from our investments in health are all about us —close, in fact, and so obvious that we are all too apt to accept them as matters of course and, so, overlook them. They are to be seen in improved environmental sanitation, improved water and sewage disposal systems, in safer methods of producing and handling milk supplies, in constantly enlarging prenatal and child health conferences, and in steadily multiplying and expanding clinics of various kinds. They are shown conclusively in declining morbidity and mortality rates.

Within the past half a century, the span of human life has been nearly doubled. The baby born fifty years ago could, on the average, expect to reach thirty-five years of age; the baby born today has a reasonable expectation to live to be sixty-one years of age.

In 1911, when the Bureau of Vital Statistics began to operate, three of the first four leading causes of death were communicable diseases; in 1942, none of the first four leading causes of death was a communicable disease.

The older members of this audience probably remember when county pest houses were almost as common as county courthouses; today everywhere in Kentucky the pest house is conspicuous only by its absence. It has become as useless as a sixth finger. Application of the growing knowledge of preventive medicine has virtually eliminated the diseases for which pest houses were largely designed. It is probably no exaggeration to say that fifty years ago the maintenance of pest houses was costing the people of the state more money than is now being expended for our entire public health program in Kentucky.

At the turn of the century, tuberculosis was taking an annual toll of between 8,000 and 10,000 people in the state. Last year deaths from this disease aggregated less than 1,800.

Fifty years ago typhoid epidemics of sweeping proportions were common throughout the state. Then, the death rate from this disease was well over 100 for 100,000 population. Today, it is approximately two per 100,000 population. Dividends from investments in community sanitation and improvements in water and waste disposal systems would of themselves many times compensate for all the money that has been devoted to public health within this generation.

Fifty years ago trachoma was every year blinding scores of people everywhere and so impairing the vision of hundreds of others as materially to lessen, if not totally destroy, their productivity. At the same time, ophthalmia of the newborn was causing scores of children annually to grow up partially or totally blind. Today blindness from trachoma has been reduced markedly.

A generation ago bovine tuberculosis, largely caused by drinking milk from tuberculous cows, was affecting the bones and glands of hundreds of children. Thanks to a concerted drive by health authorities and agricultural experts, bovine tuberculosis has been practically eliminated from Kentucky.

Other tangible results are to be found in lowered death rates of mothers in childbirth and among infants under two years of age.[2]

These are only a few of the tangible dividends accruing from public health investments. The intangible dividends are just as important. Among these intangible dividends none is more important than that resulting from health education, which has been largely responsible for a more enlightened citizenship and for the individual and community response to the efforts of the state and local agencies for better health conditions. Everywhere in Kentucky today a steadily growing percentage of the people are acquiring an increasingly better understanding of the importance of health, personal and community, and of what is necessary for its attainment and maintenance. This is of first importance because public health procedures and practices can become effective only in proportion as their application receives the cooperation of an enlightened citizenship.

Kentucky has every right to be proud of its investments in health and of the rich dividends which are constantly and cumulatively accruing from these investments. We should not, however, allow our pride in past accomplishments to dispose us to become weary in well-doing. The progress already made, marked as it has been, is but an earnest of what remains to be done. Not only must we keep our public health activities up to the present standard, but we should leave nothing undone to expand and accelerate them wherever there is need. Particularly is this true of efforts devoted to control of tuberculosis and the venereal diseases. One out of every ten inmates of our mental institutions is, we are told, there because of syphilitic infection which was not treated early enough or not properly treated. The cost of caring for these alone is more than the total expenditures for public health in the state. By the same analogy, tuberculosis is costing us, in increased deaths and decreased productivity, more money than would be required to provide the facilities necessary for reducing its incidence to an irreducible minimum.

Public health is public wealth. Investment in health is the best investment the individual, the community, or the state can make. It returns generous dividends.

---

1. The governor approved the establishment of health units in Estill, Garrard, and Montgomery counties on April 23, 1943. "This brings the total to 105 counties, an all-time high, leaving only 15 counties without them. It is practically impossible to do anything in a campaign against venereal diseases without a health unit. I believe, too, that war conditions, which have caused a shortage of doctors and nurses, have increased the need for health units." Louisville *Courier-Journal*, April 24, 1943.

2. Proclamations designating Child Health Day were issued each year. In 1943 the governor cited that examinations of young men for selective service had revealed serious defects which could have been prevented by adequate health and medical care. He urged concentrated efforts on better nutrition for children, lunches in every school, schooling for every child, baby clinics in every county, immunization against preventable disease, care for children of mothers in industry, and health protection for employed youth.

CENTRAL STATE HOSPITAL BUILDING DEDICATION
Lakeland / July 12, 1943

I GET a genuine thrill of satisfaction, as I am sure you do, from the fine job that has been done in rehabilitation of the Pusey Building. This structure was erected in 1878 and named for Dr. Pusey[1] who served for a time as superintendent of Central State Hospital.

It is impossible to picture to you the deplorable condition this building was in when its rehabilitation was started. During the sixty-five years it has been in use, it did not have that normal maintenance necessary to keep it in repair. It had deteriorated to the point of dilapidation. The roof was leaking badly. The floors were sagging dangerously. The plumbing was antiquated and inadequate. The electrical wiring, installed many years ago, was defective to the point that it constituted a constant fire hazard. Walls were disfigured, dirty, dismal, with plastering having loosened and fallen off to such an extent as to be beyond patching.

Wards in this building were foul-smelling and difficult to keep clean. The entire structure was infested with vermin. The condition was such as to nauseate an individual unaccustomed to this depressing environment. It was inhumane to confine mentally ill Kentuckians under such revolting conditions.

As you view this rehabilitated building today, it presents a contrast that is amazing. It has been converted into an attractive, clean, sanitary, habitable structure that conforms to a high standard of hospital facilities. The transformation which has taken place is so astounding that I confess I was unable to visualize the possibilities. These brick walls were found to be structurally sound. It would have been wasteful to have torn them down. So the inside of the building was completely torn out; the leaking roof was replaced and interior of the building entirely reconstructed. New and additional plumbing was installed. The defective electric wiring was replaced and new fixtures installed. Mortar between bricks had deteriorated and fallen out. That condition was corrected by pointing up the brick so as to prevent moisture soaking through the walls.

For an expenditure of $154,000, we have salvaged this building from the junkheap. Instead of tearing it down because of its dilapidated condition, we have reconstructed it, making it a new building in usefulness and in appearance.

The result is that this week 362 mentally ill patients will be moved into new, modern, and attractive hospital quarters—quarters which, when they were removed from them, were unfit for human habitation.

With completion of this building, about 750 of the inmates of Central State Hospital are now housed in quarters that have been completely renovated as the Pusey Building has been.[2]

When the nurses' dormitory is completed, which will be shortly, attractive living quarters will be available for 100 women members of the staff. These nurses and attendants now live on the wards with the inmates; live under conditions which make it impossible to get that rest and have the privacy they should have. The nurses' dormitory will cost, when completed, about $125,000, unequipped. Most of the furnishings and equipment have been bought at an approximate cost of $14,000. Within a few weeks this building will be occupied by women staff members, making available for them living quarters that are adequate and attractive.

A contract will be let in a few days for construction of a modern sewage disposal plant here at Central, which will cost approximately $45,000. For more than a year we have been trying to obtain a priority from the War Production Board which would enable us to make this sorely needed improvement. The application was once denied. We again filed the application and recently were given the required priority. For years the inadequate sewage disposal facilities have been recognized as a menace to health. This untreated sewage has been going into Goose Creek, dangerously polluting this stream. Finally we are in a position to eliminate this condition. Incidentally, at the same time we obtained priorities which will permit us to construct a sewage disposal plant at Kentucky Children's Home, another state institution, sewage from which has been adding to the pollution of Goose Creek. A priority was obtained at the same time to build a sewage disposal plant at Western State Hospital, Hopkinsville, where conditions exist that are just as bad as here at Central.

Architects' plans and specifications have been drawn for modernizing of the administration building here, recently damaged by fire caused by defective electric wiring. It is planned to reconstruct this building with fireproof construction and, since the building was damaged by fire, it is believed that we will procure the priority necessary for fireproof restoration. Contract has been awarded for rehabilitation of the administration building at $149,355, subject to obtaining required priorities.

Architects' plans and specifications for building of a new Negro ward building[3] are complete and have been filed with a request for priorities necessary to build them.[4] The Negro ward buildings were found to be structurally unsound. These buildings are in such condition that engineers regard it as unwise and uneconomical to try to restore them. A recent fire in the Negro ward, caused by defective electrical wiring, so damaged the structure that we are making an earnest appeal for priority to erect a new building which will cost more than half a million dollars. It will be a splendid structure, modern and adequate to provide ample quarters for the Negro inmates of this hospital.

Architects are now preparing plans for erection of a modern 250-bed reception center and treatment hospital here at Central, the cost of which will be more than half a million dollars. It is the purpose to provide here the best possible facilities for treatment of mental illness, under the most favorable conditions, in which will be used every known method for restoring those mentally sick.

During my administration we have expended $520,457.41 in an effort to rebuild Central State Hospital. The major improvements that have been made and their costs are as follows: Rebuilding, fireproof construction, Ward Building Number 10 (housing 240 inmates), $94,517; new boiler, $10,382; underground steam distribution system, $80,941; waterworks repairs, $13,325; restoration of Pusey Building, $135,000; nurses' dormitory, $125,000; rehabilitation of Wards Number 14, 15, 16, 19, $34,482. The remainder of the expenditures have been for general repairs.

This represents a beginning toward modernizing this antiquated hospital plant. I derive much personal satisfaction from this accomplishment.

It represents a good beginning. I have been bitterly disappointed that more could not be accomplished. We have been frustrated in completely rehabilitating Central and adding the new buildings sorely needed because of the war which brought severe restrictions upon public construction. We have had to make our program conform to the War Production Board's definition of repairs. It has been necessary to modify our plans to conform with building materials available.

Any governor who will regularly go through these mental hospitals, inform himself of the conditions that here exist, will get the unhappy plight of the inmates on his heart and conscience to such an extent that he will become obsessed with a zeal to correct these lamentable circumstances.

We have sought as earnestly to improve the treatment of the mentally ill inmates of these hospitals as we have endeavored to improve the physical plant. Particular emphasis has been placed on applying all known medical knowledge to the task of restoring to mental health every sick person that enters our state hospitals.

Each of the hospitals is staffed with well-trained doctors and nurses, experienced in psychiatry. Development of this program to its maximum effectiveness has been hampered by conditions created by the war, the effect of which has been to make it difficult to maintain a competent staff of doctors, nurses, and attendants. There was a turnover of 167 percent in the attendant personnel at Central last year. In an effort to stabilize employment we utilized all available money to raise salaries of those who work in the hospitals.

Dr. Isham Kimball, superintendent, is a nationally recognized authority on mental illness. He is doing an outstanding job under difficult circumstances.

Increased emphasis has been placed upon providing adequate and proper diet for the hospital inmates. Trained dietitians are on the staff of each hospital. A dietitian, experienced in institutional diet problems, has been obtained to supervise the diet in all the institutions. Inmates are better fed and better cared for and more mentally ill persons are being cured and restored to society than ever before, despite the handicaps created as result of the war.

During my administration we have expended $3,970,142 in rehabilitating dilapidated state institutions and improving public property.[5] In addition to this program of reconstruction, during my term as governor, we have built eight new, modern, commodious armories, providing adequate quarters for the Kentucky National Guard units when they return home victorious. They are now being used by units of the Kentucky Active Militia. These eight armories, constructed in cooperation with the WPA, were built at a cost to the state of $232,184 and a similar sum from the WPA.

I find much satisfaction in the fact that mine has been a building administration—one in which the frightful conditions in state institutions have been ameliorated to a substantial degree. But much remains to be done when restrictions on building materials have been relieved. I hope that my successor will become so zealously interested in these institutions and the unfortunates within them that the program of rehabilitation will be pushed with utmost vigor. I wish that the citizenship of the Commonwealth could be so aroused as to the imperative need of completing the institutional restoration program that there would be militant support of the program.

---

1. Henry K. Pusey (1827–1896), b. Garnettsville. Superintendent, Central State Hospital, 1884–1896. Louisville *Courier-Journal,* March 1, September 2, 1896. Dr. Pusey designed the building according to his theories of institutional care. It was demolished in 1969.

2. On January 19, 1943, the governor inspected a completely renovated ward building to house 325 patients. Another ward building, housing 250, was renovated in 1942. *Lexington Herald,* January 19, 1943.

3. The governor said on May 17, 1943, that plans had been drawn for Negro ward buildings at Central and Eastern State hospitals, a boys' detention building at the Kentucky Houses of Reform, and receiving-treatment buildings at Central and Eastern hospitals, but they may have to become part of the postwar program. He hoped to obtain priorities for the Negro ward building at Central since it called for a minimum of critical material.

"The Negro ward buildings are identical as to floor arrangements, and each would be a 400-bed, two-story brick building. The boys' detention building plans call for a two-story brick structure, designed as a complete unit with school, recreation, feeding, and other facilities for boys under discipline. These boys now are housed on the second floor of one of the dormitory buildings at Greendale. Plans approved by the Legislative Council and placed before the 1942 General Assembly called for $18,400,000 to be spent on Kentucky's hospitals and correctional institutions over a period of years." Louisville *Courier-Journal,* May 18, 1943.

4. The War Production Board authorized construction of the Negro ward building. Louisville *Courier-Journal,* September 22, 1943. The governor authorized a fund transfer on October 25, 1943, and construction began on October 27. At the ground-breaking ceremony, he said, "The building will stand as a monument to an awakened concept of Kentucky's obligation to her Negro citizens." He noted that upon completion of the construction now under way, more than half of the 6,400 patients of the hospitals will be housed in modern, sanitary quarters. "Rehabilitation of these institutions that had been permitted to deteriorate into such deplorable condition is the most pressing obligation upon the state. This

program should be carried to completion. But it cannot be completed unless Kentucky's state government is kept solvent. In fact, the whole future of Kentucky depends upon maintaining the solvency of the state so that pressing needs may be financed. The old Negro ward building is beyond renovation. It is a foul-smelling, vermin-infested building in which there have been two fires, indicating that it is a veritable firetrap. This new structure represents the most modern concept in a hospital for the mentally ill." Louisville *Courier-Journal*, October 28, 1943.

5. Data on expenditures have been deleted since more recent data are in the speech from August 24, 1943, in this section.

EASTERN STATE HOSPITAL BUILDING DEDICATION
Lexington / August 24, 1943

I GET a genuine thrill of satisfaction, as I am sure you do, from the magnificent job that has been done in rehabilitating this, Male Ward Building Number 2. This is one of the oldest brick buildings in Kentucky. It was built about 1817 to 1820 and provided Kentucky with the first and at that time the best institution for the mentally ill west of the Allegheny Mountains. As originally constructed, this building had fireplaces as a means of providing heat for the various wards.

For decades, this, just as all other buildings at our mental hospitals, deteriorated due to neglect. This beautiful, fireproof structure, which we so proudly commit to the merciful mission of providing advanced hospital facilities for the mentally sick, was a dilapidated old firetrap when we started work on it.

In June of 1941,[1] I figured up the amount of money that remained in the Governor's Emergency Fund. And most all of it was there because I had been saving it to expend on the institutions. I transferred that money to Eastern State Hospital. We let a contract which had for its purpose converting that frightfully dilapidated building into a modern hospital.

For an expenditure of $366,798, we have salvaged this building from the junkheap. Instead of tearing it down because of its dilapidated condition, we have rebuilt it, making it a new building in usefulness and in appearance. The result is that this week about 500 mentally ill patients will be moved into new, modern, and attractive quarters which, when they were removed from them, were unfit for human habitation. The capacity of the building has been increased from 431 to 500.

With completion of this building and with the finishing of other rehabilitation construction that is under way here, we approach a condition in which this hospital will be an institution to which we can point with pride. By the first of December approximately 1,600 of the 2,000 inmates in Eastern will be in clean, bright, sanitary, modern hospital quarters, which have been completely renovated. When I leave the governor's office, approximately one-half of the 6,400 patients in the mental hospitals will be quartered in habitable, attractive hospital wards.

We hope to let a contract this fall for completing fireproof reconstruction of the remaining male wards, just as this building has been rebuilt. Architects' plans have been drawn for the building of a new Negro ward building. It appears unwise to attempt to reconstruct the quarters now occupied by the Negroes. We shall push our application before the War Production Board for a new Negro ward building, both here and at Central State Hospital at Lakeland.

Architects are now preparing plans for erection here and at the Lakeland Hospital of a modern 250-bed reception center and treatment hospital, each of which will cost approximately half a million dollars. These treatment hospitals will relieve the crowded condition in Eastern by increasing the number of beds available. The primary purpose, however, is to provide here the best possible treatment of mental illness, under the most favorable conditions, in which will be used every known facility for restoration of the mentally sick who are committed to Eastern.

Another addition to the facilities of Eastern in which I take pride is the acquisition of additional farmland acreage so sorely needed. We bought 164 acres of splendid, productive land adjoining our farm for approximately $50,000, money for which was made available from the Governor's Emergency Fund.

During my term as governor, my major interest has been the rehabilitation of our state institutions. We have made much progress, despite restrictions on building which resulted when priorities for building material were imposed as a war measure. We have been able to do more for Eastern than any other institution.

The improvements which we have been able to make at Eastern State Hospital during my administration, up to the end of the fiscal year last June 30, have represented a total expenditure of $775,810.16. That is more money than has been expended on this institution in the last half a century. Much of that money has been expended for the restoration of vital utilities, for improvements that are not visible, such as the sewer system, new boilers in the heating plant, restoration of roofs.

One cold, winter night three winters ago, the old, dilapidated boilers in the heating plant here collapsed. That calamity left this hospital without either heat or light. We borrowed a railway locomotive, ran it in here, and hooked it up to take the place of the bursted boilers until they could be repaired. With a heating plant so deteriorated as that, it is obvious that our first expenditure here was for two new boilers and the rebuilding of the heating plant.

This [total expenditure] represents substantial progress toward modernizing this antiquated hospital plant. I derive deep personal satisfaction from this accomplishment, as do you who recognize the imperative need for it. It represents a good beginning. But much more should be done here and in each of the other mental hospitals and the Feeble Minded Institute.

Any governor who will, as I have done, regularly visit these mental hospitals,[2] go into every corner of the most remote ward, inform himself of the conditions that here exist, will get the unhappy plight of the inmates on his heart and conscience to such an extent that he will become obsessed with a zeal to correct these lamentable circumstances.

The major purpose of these hospitals is to treat the mentally sick and cure as many of them as is possible. We have sought earnestly to improve the treatment of the patients. Particular emphasis has been placed on applying all known medical knowledge to the task of restoring to mental health every sick person susceptible of being cured. Each of our mental hospitals is under the direction of able, experienced, consecrated doctors who are among the foremost authorities on mental diseases in the nation. Dr. Foley is superbly qualified to direct a treatment program here that will get maximum results. Dr. A. M. Lyon, director of mental hygiene, has disclosed great ability and rare aptitude in treatment of mental illness. Each hospital is staffed with well-trained doctors and nurses, experienced in psychiatry. Development of this program to its maximum effectiveness has been hampered by conditions created by the war, the effect of which has been to make it difficult to maintain an adequate staff of competent doctors, nurses, and attendants. In an effort to stabilize employment, we utilized such money as was available to raise salaries of those who work in the hospitals.

Despite the handicaps, gratifying progress is being made in treatment of the mentally ill. Year after year for decades, more persons have been admitted to the mental hospitals than were released. The result has been that year after year these institutions have become increasingly overcrowded. But we get great satisfaction from the fact that the intensive effort to cure and restore mentally sick Kentuckians is beginning to show results. At the end of the fiscal year last June 30, there were 157 fewer inmates in the three mental hospitals than at the beginning of the year. There were 88 fewer patients here at Eastern. Yet another gratifying development was the fact that there were 1,116 inmates of these hospitals who had recovered sufficiently to be paroled, permitted to go home. They had remained in the hospital, prior to parole, two and one-third months less than those paroled the preceding year. Of the 1,116 paroled, it was necessary to return 467 for further hospitalization, but these 467 patients stayed at home on an average of one month longer than those who were paroled the previous year. This means that 467 hospital months, or 38 hospital years, were cut from the hospital load at a saving of $7,000. The 1,116 patients paroled, who were released two and one-third months earlier from the hospital than the previous year, lifted from the institution 217 patient years. Getting these patients out of the hospitals earlier effected a saving to the state of approximately $40,000.

The same type of improvement that has been pushed with all possible vigor here at Eastern has been under way in the other mental hospitals, at the Kentucky Houses of Reform, the prisons, and other state institutions. During my administration, we have expended or have initiated plans for expenditure of $4.5 million in rehabilitating disgracefully dilapidated state institutions and in improving public property.

A striking transformation has been effected at the Kentucky Houses of Reform at Greendale. We have expended on this institution during my administration $422,545.16 in as fine a job as has ever been done of rehabilitating a rundown, neglected plant that was well advanced toward complete deterioration. Fayette County grand juries for a quarter of a century have been criticizing the revolting conditions at Greendale. By the end of my term as governor, this institution will have been completely rebuilt and the unfortunate children committed to this institution will be housed in pleasant, comfortable quarters.

The major expenditures at other state institutions during my administration are: LaGrange Prison, $344,473.22; Women's Prison, $52,363.03; Eddyville Penitentiary, $346,719.67; Central State Hospital, $590,463.73; and Western State Hospital, $343,198.79.

The children at Greendale are better fed, more sympathetically directed under a better staff than has ever directed this institution. The children are healthy, happy, and being skillfully guided. Superintendent DeMoisey and the staff he has assembled are doing an admirable job of salvaging unfortunate children, exerting a good influence upon them, instilling in them correct attitudes and ideals.

We had planned to install at Greendale that equipment necessary to inaugurate vocational training. This type of equipment became unobtainable as a result of the war. But we are making application for a quantity of equipment formerly used by the National Youth Administration. We have been encouraged by indications that we will get sufficient equipment from this source to start vocational instruction at Greendale. This will be a highly constructive development in providing a practical type of training for youngsters at this institution.

We are letting a contract today for the building of a modern 250-bed tuberculosis sanitarium which will be an addition to Hazelwood Sanitarium. One wing of this new hospital will be set aside for treatment of Negro tuberculosis patients. It reflects discreditably upon our state that there is not a single bed in a tuberculosis hospital in the state for Negroes. We plan to correct that condition.

There were 1,752 Kentuckians who died last year from tuberculosis. Most of them could have been saved if adequate hospital facilities had been available. With the new hospital, we will take a long step forward in combating this insidious disease.

I want to take this opportunity to express my appreciation to the contractor and crew of workmen who reconstructed this building, to the workmen engaged in the other renovating program here on the women's wards, and to the state's Engineering Division for their coordinated efforts in advancing this merciful program. State Engineer Preston Sinton and his associates, particularly Ben Ingels, who is superintendent of the work being done here, have become keenly interested in the work and derive much satisfaction from participating in this laudable activity.

I have been particularly fortunate to have associated with my administration as commissioner of welfare an able, sincere Kentuckian who has done an excellent job in directing this department. Commissioner Frost's contribution to this program has been invaluable.

The whole future of Kentucky's progress is dependent upon keeping the state solvent. The money which we formerly paid on the state debt is now being used for the worthy purpose of correcting conditions in these institutions which have long been a stigma on the state. I implore you as Kentuckians to support a program which has for its purpose the completion of this task.[3]

---

1. The governor made his first official inspection on March 6, 1941.
2. On an inspection in April 1943, the governor said that he was "tremendously thrilled at the progress we are making." He had brought Lyter Donaldson to see the hospital and reform school because anyone who desires to hold the office of governor should become fully acquainted with conditions at such institutions. "A governor should visit these places three or four times a year so that he will never get the need for improvements out of his mind." *Lexington Herald*, April 17, 1943.
3. The speech has been edited. Parts appear in the speeches from July 12, 1943, in this section and January 19, 1943, in the State Administration section.

TUBERCULOSIS SANITARIUM, HAZELWOOD
Louisville / October 22, 1943

For many years we have needed in Kentucky greater hospital facilities for the treatment of those afflicted with tuberculosis. Too long we have delayed in meeting that need. Today we lay the cornerstone of a modern state tuberculosis sanitarium which will provide an addition to Hazelwood's facilities of 230 beds at a cost of $537,000.[1] It is one of the proud moments of my life. I get a genuine thrill and an exhilarating joy out of the fact that destiny decreed that I should be the public instrument through which this sorely needed institution should be inaugurated.

Now that we have surmounted barriers which delayed this day, there are those who come forward to declare that we need three state tuberculosis sanitariums. That I do not dispute. But for years the medical profession has been agreed that we at least needed one. And we must first have one before we can have three. We have the money to build one and it is well on the way. As to whether we have three depends upon whether Kentucky's state government remains solvent. In fact, the whole future of Kentucky depends upon whether she remains a solvent state, keeps out of debt. I have no quarrel with those who assert we need three tuberculosis hospitals. But after this one is completed, we will need only two. A young married couple may properly decide to plan for a family of three children. But in the normal course of events they can expect them only one at a time.

Since we have been able to start construction of this hospital, there have been those who have raised the point that no provision had been made for financing its operation. There is no legal plan by which I could have provided money to operate the new institution. That will be the duty and responsibility of my successor and the legislature. It is not likely that they will fail to make provision for operation of the facilities that are here to be constructed. During my administration the appropriation for operation of Hazelwood has been doubled.

At the recent meeting of the Kentucky Medical Association, the following resolution was adopted, to which I deem it proper to call attention:

> WHEREAS, There seems some misunderstanding on the part of the public resulting from press notices regarding the development of the program for increased facilities at the state Tuberculosis Sanitarium at Hazelwood, through the construction of a new building for two hundred and thirty (230) additional beds:
>
> THEREFORE, BE IT RESOLVED That the House of Delegates of the state Medical Association extend to Governor Johnson our complete approval of his

> program for this great humanitarian institution and our deep appreciation of his official acts on behalf of the unfortunates in Kentucky suffering from tuberculosis, which acts were in keeping with expert advice and guidance.

Today there is not a bed available in a state hospital for Negroes afflicted with tuberculosis. That condition will be corrected when this institution is completed. It will be our purpose to set aside one wing of this building, approximately sixty beds, for Kentucky's Negro citizens who need hospital care.

I am proud of the fact that mine has been a building administration. We have expended more than $4.5 million in rehabilitating the state hospitals for the mentally ill, the Houses of Reform at Greendale, the Kentucky School for the Blind, the Kentucky School for the Deaf, and in expanding facilities of the state prisons. These institutions, so long neglected, had deteriorated to the point where they were a disgrace to Kentucky. Those buildings which were found to be structurally sound are being reconstructed within existing walls. They are being transformed from dark, dismal, vermin-infested, foul-smelling wards into modern hospital quarters that are clean, bright, sanitary, and habitable.

We are completing a new and attractive nurses' dormitory at Central State Hospital, Lakeland. A contract has been awarded today for erection of a new Negro ward building at Central State Hospital. The old Negro ward building is structurally unsound, cannot be rehabilitated. A new building is to be erected at a cost of more than $400,000 which will provide a 400-bed building for the mentally ill Negro patients. And the money is available, has been set aside and earmarked for no other purpose than to construct that building. The sum of $537,000 has been set aside to complete this sanitarium and can be spent for no other purpose. When construction at the mental hospitals now under way is completed, more than half the 6,400 inmates will be housed in rehabilitated quarters.

We commend those who have developed and put into practice the scientific formulas for care and treatment of sufferers of tuberculosis. Kentuckians have been, for many generations, the beneficiaries of a progressive public health program—one that had its origin and fruition under the extraordinary leadership of him whom we honor in the inscription on this cornerstone and who had his inspiration and tutorship from an illustrious, pioneering, and patriotic father. Neither the father nor the son ever lost sight of his responsibility in relation to a program for prevention and control of tuberculosis. They recognized it as a scourge that is not here today and gone tomorrow but rather as a constant, insidious menace, pandemic in scope. Always these two leaders recognized that to combat this disease successfully they must marshal all the forces of science and, at the same time, command public confidence for a continuing battle. To this end they kept Kentucky in the forefront of states that organized and made effective local full-time units of health service. From 1908, when Jefferson County [Health Department] was organized, until today, when we have 104 out of 120 counties with full-time health departments, there has been no letup in educational service programs to reduce the incidence and mortality from tuberculosis.[2] In 1911, when our vital statistics law was put into operation, there was recorded annually a total of 229.6 deaths for every 100,000 population; in 1941, the rate was 66.5 for every 100,000. Thus we have seen in little more than a quarter of a century the number of deaths from tuberculosis decrease from an annual total of 5,293 in 1911 to 1,934 in 1941. While we rejoice with pride in this result, which is comparable with the very best attained by any state, we nevertheless face the fact that we cannot hope to make much further gain without a more adequate hospitalization program.[3] We have probably reached the limit of attainment in prevention through education and improvement of living conditions and must now be prepared to capitalize on the progress made in medical science for treatment and cure of those cases found in the early stages. We have in operation the machinery for locating and diagnosing these cases and must have the facilities for modern treatment and relief. On these grounds, when this building is completed, there will be adequate accommodations for over 300 patients. From a study made by the Kentucky State Medical Association, this is little less than half enough to provide a satisfactory program of hospitalization, and that organization is definitely committed to making further studies and offering, at the close of the present war, a statewide plan for adequately meeting the need.

I am proud that it has fallen to me to lay the cornerstone for a really worthwhile and enduring structure—one that will lay the pattern, we all hope, for other structures to come. On this foundation are laid our hopes, our ambitions, and our prayers for a secure program looking to relief from suffering for hundreds and thousands of our fellow Kentuckians. We leave to the future what we believe is the proper basis upon which to build.

So today we lay the cornerstone for an institution that is to stand as a monument to compassion and a memorial to one of the most useful Kentuckians who has labored in this state. We carve upon this cornerstone the name of Arthur T. McCormack in loving tribute to one whose life was a benediction, whose days were spent in a zealous endeavor to alleviate the suffering and sick in Kentucky.[4]

---

1. After an inspection on January 18, 1943, plans to triple the capacity of the sanitarium were announced. They included the purchase of seven acres, several

staff cottages, and two new ward units. Louisville *Courier-Journal*, January 21, 1943.

2. Some state aid was provided for county tuberculosis hospitals. On October 6, 1942, the governor refused a request for construction funds for the Kenton County Tuberculosis Sanitarium. He pointed out that the Lexington Sanitarium with 103 beds got an annual state appropriation of $10,000, and Kenton County with only seventeen beds received $7,500. *Kentucky Post*, October 7, 1942.

3. At the ground-breaking ceremony on August 30, 1943, the governor said, "This is to be a monument to mercy." He praised Dr. Paul A. Turner, superintendent of the sanitarium, and his wife, the business manager, and commented, "With inadequate facilities they have worked splendidly to restore health to as many Kentuckians as possible. With these improved facilities they will be able to save twice as many lives." Louisville *Courier-Journal*, August 31, 1943.

4. An evaluation of Johnson's accomplishments in the rehabilitation of the state hospitals and penal institutions may be found in an article by Carl Saunders, *Kentucky Post*, November 20, 1943.

PUBLIC SAFETY

LA GRANGE PRISON DEDICATION
La Grange / October 9, 1939

SENATOR CHANDLER and Governor Johnson each praised the aid of the other during their nearly four years together.[1] Governor Johnson referred to it as "teamwork, with a mandate that designated Governor Chandler to pull in the lead position and I was to pull my portion of the load from the off side."

He said the new institution with its large administration building, nine dormitories, and its shops and farm was made possible by Chandler's "vision" and by the "awakened conscience" of the people and invited all Kentuckians to cooperate in carrying forward the work until "all institutions of Kentucky are adequately provided for."

He was unwilling "to promise you that I will make the best governor of Kentucky, but I do promise you that I will try as hard as any governor ever tried to make you a good governor."

---

1. Johnson was sworn in as the forty-second governor of Kentucky and then went to La Grange.

STATE HIGHWAY PATROL
Frankfort / June 14, 1940

GOVERNOR JOHNSON ordered a new statement of administration policy mailed to each member of the state Highway Patrol and posted in all district headquarters. The statement outlines the following four-point program of conduct and duties:

1. The patrol will be expected to reflect to the letter the administration's policy of strict economy and loyal efficiency.

2. The patrolmen will be expected to conduct themselves so as to reflect credit on the whole administration, and "in such a manner as will inspire and retain confidence of the public." "The patrolmen must be taught and made very definitely to understand that the administration will, under no conditions or circumstances, permit political expediency or preferment to interfere with the rigid enforcement of all orders and instructions issued by the head of the patrol."

3. Patrolmen will be expected to enforce the laws "as written and enacted by the legislature" and particularly to enforce the motor vehicle statutes. "These statutes are specific, certain, and unambiguous, and should be enforced as written, without favor to any individual, regardless of who he may be."

4. Patrolmen will be expected to understand that they are servants of the public, and be "courteous, respectful, and helpful to all law-abiding citizens." They further are directed to extend help to distressed motorists on the highways whenever the opportunity presents itself.

Instant dismissal is promised for any patrolman not possessed of integrity, morality, and respect of duty. "Without any one of these three qualifications, a peace officer becomes an enemy of the public instead of its servant."[1]

---

1. The statement originated with Highway Commissioner Donaldson who sent it to the director of the Highway Patrol, Jack Nelson. He was the former chief of police at Paducah and had just succeeded Major William H. Hansen as director of the patrol. The patrol was a division of the Department of Highways at that time. Louisville *Courier-Journal*, June 15, 1940.

STATE GUARD CAPTAINS COMMISSIONED
Frankfort / December 17, 1940

I WANT to express my deepest gratitude to you outstanding Kentuckians who have recognized the importance of what we are trying to undertake.

This is a fine, splendid public service which you are making voluntarily since there is no money with which to compensate you. You have particularly pleased me and members of the State Defense Commission, and I am sure the service you are rendering will meet with equal appreciation and approval at home.

I am sure that under your wise and discreet leadership it will be possible to recruit State Guard units which will be adequate to meet any emergency and which will be of such nature as to make both men and officers proud to join them.[1]

---

1. The governor presented commissions as captains to twenty-two reserve army officers. Commissions for thirty-two men were executed, but ten were unable to attend. These officers were to lead the first home defense units to be organized in the United States since World War I. The units were established since the Kentucky National Guard was to be inducted into federal service for one year. See Executive Order, December 16, 1940.

KENTUCKY BAR ASSOCIATION
Louisville / April 3, 1941

THERE is no more intelligent group within the state than those who compose the membership of the Kentucky state Bar Association. The legal profession provides civic and political leadership in far greater proportion than its number bears relationship to the total population. All of you, by virtue of your profession, occupy positions of responsibility and esteem in your communities. Yours is one of the oldest as well as most respected of professions.

I want to express my thanks to the legal profession for assistance given the governor in setting up the mechanism by which the Selective Service Act functions. The governor faced the responsibility of selecting local Selective Service Boards and District Boards to effectuate selected service. It was necessary to select about 1,500 men throughout the state to render an important patriotic service for which they receive no pay. Many lawyers accepted appointment as appeal agents and in other capacities. For their helpfulness I am grateful. I note that Colonel Frank Rash is to speak to you. When you hear him, you will realize how fortunate I was in obtaining the services of one so competent to direct the selective service.

You deal primarily with the law and the courts. As a result of your experience and your exalted code of ethics, you realize how important it is that there be a wholesome public respect for the courts. Maintenance of justice is vital to the preservation of the form of government that we cherish. Courts are respected increasingly when prevails the opinion that one can be assured of a fair trial, an impartial adjudication of legal controversy.

You, the attorneys of Kentucky, realize that enforcement of law is essential to the protection of rights and liberties of individuals. I have a profound respect for the courts of our state. And while there is no experience to which the governor is subjected which is more unpleasant than that of listening to pitiful pleas of heartbroken mothers and fathers seeking clemency for errant sons, I am certain that it is the duty of the governor to sustain the decrees of our state courts.[1]

Governors are criticized or commended for those acts which the public can see. Many of the most commendable things which a governor does are never revealed. Things he does for the state are usually visible. Things he prevents being done to the state seldom are publicly known. If a governor issues a pardon to a dangerous criminal who is restored to freedom and again becomes a menace to society, that action is condemned. But if the governor refuses to grant executive clemency, his adherence to his conception of his duty is known only to those who are disappointed and sometimes embittered.

There are those who have criticized your governor because he refuses to interfere with the decrees of the courts by granting pardons. I have never announced as a policy that I would under no circumstances grant a pardon. But it will be an exceptional case if I do issue a pardon. The pardon mill at Frankfort has been torn down and junked. In fact, I have issued orders that released two men from prison. One was a World War veteran who fell from a ladder and broke his back at the Eddyville prison. I pardoned him that he might be transferred to a veterans' hospital to receive the treatment which would save his life.[2] I commuted the sentence of one young boy. He had formerly been an inmate at Ormsby Village. Authorities agreed to readmit him to that institution if I would commute his sentence and parole him. Within two months he was arrested for stealing an automobile and returned to prison as a parole violator.[3]

My policy of granting pardons only in exceptional cases is not just a stubborn attitude. It comes as the result of reasoned judgement. In 1936, as lieutenant governor and president of the state Senate, I took a great interest in the enactment of a modern probation and parole law. The legislation had the hearty approval of Governor Chandler. Numbers of interested citizens participated in drafting of that law in which is embodied the best features of similar laws in other states.

That law provides that the circuit judge, before whom the case is tried, may probate the sentence of those that appear worthy of that consideration. The sentence may be probated in any case unless the sentence is life imprisonment or death. There is a probation and parole office in each judicial district. Individuals who are placed on probation, permitted to remain at home by the judge instead of going to prison, are visited at least once a month and frequently oftener by the probation officer who takes an interest in them, encourages them to correct conduct.

The law has been in effect five years. Because you, the lawyers of the state, are so closely connected with this problem, I believe you will be interested in a report on the results of this legislation.

In the five-year period, there have been 2,297 offenders convicted in the circuit courts that have been probated by the judge. Of the 2,297 that were probated, there have been only 190 cases in which the court revoked the probation order and sent the offender on to prison. Of those probated, in 795 cases the individual was given a one-year sentence. In 738 cases, the accused was given a two-year sentence. In 143 cases, it was a three-year term.

Had it not been for the principle of probation, all 2,297 of these offenders would have served a prison term. Only 190 out of the group betrayed the confidence of the judge who probated them and were sent on to serve sentence. Punishment best serves society when it serves as a corrective. More than 2,100 persons, convicted of wrong doing, avoided the stigma of a prison term, appear to be trying to live correct lives. It costs an average of $165 a year to incarcerate a prisoner for a year. It is much cheaper to make pre-probation investigation and supervise those probated than it is to keep them in prison.

The law provides that the judge may extend, release, or revoke probation at any time. There are thirty-three out of the thirty-eight circuit judges who have used the probation authority in varying degree. As an example of the possibilities of probation, conscientiously handled, let me point out the success attained in the second judicial district where the Honorable Joe Price[4] is judge. Judge Price has probated 181 offenders. Of this number twenty-seven violated the terms of the probation and were sent on to prison. Accurate records have been kept in this district. There has been close cooperation between the probation officer and the circuit judge. Of those probated 86 percent have readjusted themselves to society and only 14 percent have betrayed the confidence of the court.

The law provides that the probation officer shall, if requested by the court, investigate those who may appear worthy of probation and report to the court his findings. That report will include employment record, family history, criminal record, etc. If the individual is probated, he is under supervision of the probation officer. It is the duty of the officer to help the probated person get employment, if such is a need, keep a close watch on the probationer with reference to his conduct, associates, habits, and attitude. If he violates the law or terms of the probation, the officer reports such to the court. It, in my judgment, is an intelligent, merciful method by which the courts are making a fine contribution to the salvaging of thousands of youthful first offenders.

I want to commend the circuit judges who have recognized probation as an instrument which can be used in the best interest of society. The judges who have utilized probation have done a fine, conscientious job. They have, by their discretion, diverted many young offenders from a career of crime.

The probation and parole law of 1936 liberalized terms of parole. Briefly, as most of you know, a law violator becomes eligible for parole when half the sentence has been served if the sentence is less than ten years. An individual sent to prison for two years becomes eligible for consideration for parole when half the sentence has expired, provided conduct of the individual has been correct and proof is submitted that employment is available upon release. That paroled person will be required to report to and be supervised by the probation and parole officer in the district of residence. If the parolee's conduct is proper, he serves the second year of sentence outside prison walls. If the law is again violated, the offender is returned to prison to serve out the unexpired portion of the sentence.

From January 1, 1936, to March 1, 1941, the Parole Board has released from our prisons 5,381 persons. During that time there have been 332 paroled persons who have been arrested and returned to prison to serve out their terms as parole violators. The Parole Board in the Department of Welfare investigates carefully each prisoner eligible for parole, makes every effort to reach a conclusion as to whether it is safe for society and best for the individual to be paroled. Effect of parole is to encourage prisoners to correct conduct so they may shorten the period of incarceration. It has a good effect upon the morale within the prisons.

As experience indicated that the parole policy was working well and supervision was adequate, the Parole Board agreed with the governor to liberalize the use of parole. In 1939, for example, there were 848 paroled from La Grange and Eddyville prisons. In 1940 there were 1,291 paroled. The board has paroled 29.5 percent of the cases considered.

Since January 1936 there have been 1,213 children paroled from the Kentucky Houses of Reform. Of that number, 326 have been returned for violation of parole.

I might talk at length about the principles of social welfare and penology involved. But my chief desire is to impress you, the officers of the court who are connected with these criminal cases, with the fact that probation and parole is working well in Kentucky. It is the commonsense method of approaching the problem. But it is dangerous to abuse it. We are having better success both in probating and paroling offenders than is the average for the nation. That will continue only so long as caution is exercised in selecting those who appear likely to respond to probation and parole. I have chosen in the brief period allotted me to talk to you about a vital problem with the hope that I may stimulate your interest in helping to make probation and parole increasingly effective.

With a modern probation and parole system, the governor should grant very few pardons and only in exceptional cases. First, the judge before whom the case is tried, who is best able to judge the merits of the case, has authority to probate the sentence. Then, if, as is too often the plea, the offender receives an excessive sentence, the parole law makes provision by which incarceration may be cut in half. With those liberal phases for correction of inequalities in punishment meted out by the court, pardoning should cease in Kentucky as a general rule.

Abuse of the pardoning power by Kentucky governors has in previous years approached the point of scandal. My predecessor, Governor Chandler, did not issue a pardon. As acting governor when lieutenant governor with Governor Chandler, I did not issue a pardon. I hope for that intestinal fortitude which will enable me to resist the pressure for exercise of the pardoning power. If I can hold out to the end of my term, we will have had for the first time in the history of the state, an eight-year period in which no pardons were granted. We will have established the correct principle that the governor should not interfere with the decrees of the court.[5]

---

1. Johnson took a similar stand when he refused clemency to four Harlan County miners serving life terms following the 1931 "Battle of Evarts" when four persons were killed in a battle between deputized mine guards and strikers. Edward H. Weyler, secretary of the state Federation of Labor, made the appeal when he led a delegation to the governor's office. Johnson said, "It is the duty of the governor to sustain decrees of the courts. I have come definitely to the conclusion that I am unwilling to accept responsibility of determining whether or not the courts made a mistake." One spokesman cited clemency petitions signed by all the jurors and editorials from the *Courier-Journal* and the *Louisville Times* urging that the miners be pardoned. The governor replied, "Kentucky jurors have a habit of doing what they think is their duty, then signing a petition asking me, the governor, to undo what they have done. I have heard 500 or so pardon pleas

and the jurors have petitioned me in every case. As for the *Courier-Journal* and the *Times*, I wish I could delegate to them the authority to hear all these pleas for pardons." Louisville *Courier-Journal*, December 24, 1940.

When Johnson was attending the inauguration of President Roosevelt, Lieutenant Governor Myers, as acting governor, granted clemency to these miners. He granted a full pardon to one and commuted the life sentences of three to twenty-one years. On his return the governor said, "I've nothing to say about that. If the Parole Board recommends paroles for these men, I will sign them. I have signed the parole of every prisoner recommended by the board." *Cincinnati Enquirer*, January 23, 1941.

2. The pardon was issued on December 8, 1939, to Valley Soards. Louisville *Courier-Journal*, December 9, 1939.

3. Johnson commuted the three-year sentence of Robert Price, Louisville, age nineteen, to two years and five months, thereby making him eligible for immediate parole. He was paroled to Superintendent H. V. Bastin of Ormsby Village who was to keep him until he was twenty-one or had completed his high school education. Louisville *Courier-Journal*, November 28, 1940.

4. Joseph Llewllyn Price (1877–1949), b. Fairdealing, Marshall County. Judge, Second Judicial District for twenty-five years. Louisville *Courier-Journal*, January 2, 1949.

5. In March 1940 Johnson revoked a conditional pardon granted by Governor Laffoon in 1935 to Virgil Smith of Pikeville. Smith had been fined and jailed twice and had broken jail twice since his pardon. The right of the chief executive to revoke conditional pardons had been sustained by the courts in 1938. Louisville *Courier-Journal*, March 29, 1940.

The speech has been edited. Parts appear in speeches from August 24, 1942, in the Industry section, and July 4, 1941, in the World War II section. The governor discussed his support for the probation and parole system in a speech to the Parole Officers Annual School, Frankfort, June 11, 1941. *State Journal*, June 12, 1941.

STATE HIGHWAY PATROL EFFICIENCY
Frankfort / July 12, 1941

ONE of the best jobs in the state government during the past year has been the improved efficiency of the state Highway Patrol.[1]

Compared with 3,681 arrests by the patrol in 1939, there were 9,164 in 1940 and already 7,095 in the first five months of the current year.

Convicted persons paid $69,259 in fines in 1939, compared with $151,395 in 1940 and $113,608 for the first five months of 1941. Stolen property recovered by the patrol was estimated at $84,271 in 1939, $112,423 in 1940, and $58,984 in the five-month period of 1941. Only one-third of the arrests were for exceeding the state's 18,000-pound gross weight limit for trucks. Most of the rest were for violations of other traffic laws.[2]

---

1. The governor spoke at a luncheon given as a surprise to Jack W. Nelson on his sixty-third birthday. The Kentucky State Police does not have a copy of the speech. Letter, Greg Williamson, executive assistant, April 1, 1977. He spoke in Nelson's home community, Paducah, in November 1942 and again praised him. *Paducah Sun-Democrat*, November 9, 1942.

2. In September 1941 the governor sent personal letters to thirty-five state highway patrolmen who had been sent to Harlan County because of disorder caused by a coal mine strike. He expressed appreciation for their exceptional service. *Richmond Daily Register*, September 1, 1941.

HOUSES OF REFORM, GREENDALE
Frankfort / October 3, 1941

GOVERNOR JOHNSON issued an executive order providing for a survey and study of conditions at Greendale by Dr. Frederick C. Helbing and H. V. Bastin.[1] The governor said that these two men had been selected to make the inquiry and submit recommendations because they are among the nation's foremost authorities on institutions of this type.

"They are directed to examine the institution, inquire into all phases of its operation and make a report to the governor on their findings. They are directed to make recommendations which they believe will improve the operation of the institution, keeping in mind the necessity of conducting the institution with such resources as are available."[2]

Johnson said that he is deeply concerned over the needs of the Kentucky Houses of Reform at Greendale and has spent much time in considering how the problem may best be approached. Since Norman Braden[3] became head of the institution two years ago, a recreational director and a social worker had been added to the staff and every teacher there was qualified for a post in the public schools. When Braden went there, only one teacher was so qualified. In the last two years, $218,000 had been spent in improvements, most of it going to erection of a new dormitory for girls, but including new steam and water distribution systems, new boilers and other equipment.

---

1. Dr. Helbing was superintendent for forty-two years at the correctional school, West Coxsackie, New York. He retired in 1941.

Henley Vedder Bastin (1882–1976), b. Crab Orchard. Superintendent, Ormsby Village (formerly Louisville and Jefferson County Children's Home), Lyndon, from 1935. Formerly a state prison warden. *Who's Who in Kentucky, 1936*, p. 24, and letter, Dr. William K. Keller, Louisville, April 10, 1978.

2. The governor said on October 23, 1941, that the report was expected soon and that the investigators "found plenty to criticize" but they also had noted great improvement. Both Bastin and Helbing had told him they realized that to make the improvements they desired would take as much as ten years and three or four million dollars. Johnson said, "The situation there is the result of forty years of neglect. Many of the 600 boys and girls there are among the toughest in the state—those whose parents, school heads, and county officials could not control —and they present a serious problem in discipline and training." *Lexington Herald*, October 24, 1941.

3. Norman Adelbert Braden (1907–), b. Pennsylvania. Resides, Pullman, Washington. Director, Parole and Probation, 1936–1939; assistant welfare commissioner, August 1939; acting superintendent, Greendale, 1939–1941; General Extension Services, Washington State University, 1949–1971, director at time of retirement. Telephone interview, Mrs. N. A. Braden, September 25, 1978.

WESTERN STATE PENITENTIARY
Eddyville / October 17, 1941

GOVERNOR JOHNSON spoke of the humble shack near Brandon's Chapel where he was born and said he was bound to Western Kentucky by sacred memories.[1] "It was here that I greeted my parents when I returned from France and I remember the Eddyville camp meeting.

"We dedicate this building to public service and the humane and enlightened concept of the state's obligation to those who transgress the law. It has taken a long time to finish this structure and I hope in the next two years to accelerate the progress of building new state institutions which we sorely need. This building will relieve cruelly crowded conditions and later we hope to provide a farm.[2]

"Our mental institutions have been neglected for fifty years. But now that Kentucky is nearing solvency, we will be able to provide adequate institutions for our weak and sick. This program, of course, is only started. But we now are able to concentrate all of our efforts in completing it."

The governor stated that the new prison unit, which adjoins the old cell block section constructed in 1904, was erected "to relieve the cruelly crowded conditions in the penitentiary. It will take nearly 600 inmates out of the halls and corridors where they have been sleeping on cots."

Constructed of concrete and steel, he described the new unit as one of the most modern penitentiary sections in the nation. Work on it was started in 1937 and completed last month. It contains 568 cells, each equipped with running hot and cold water, a toilet, wash stand, and a cot. Each cell is ventilated by an automatic hot and cold air system. Each of the six floors contains three cell blocks and at the end of each cell block is a tiled shower bath with three shower units.

The main dining room of the prison is in the basement. It has facilities for seating and feeding 1,900 prisoners. At present 1,481 prisoners are in the penitentiary. While the new unit will relieve the crowded conditions in the old sections, the prison still will have to maintain a dormitory of double decker cots for some 375 inmates.

"Only through careful administration of the state's affairs has Kentucky been able to launch its institutional building program. Six years ago the state's debt was $28 million. Today it is only $1 million."

The governor said that he would recommend to the 1942 legislature that no new taxes be levied. "But it is vitally important that the present tax structure be retained in order to complete our building program, improve our institutions and restore and care for more than 12,000 persons in those institutions. La Grange reformatory has had to house 1,200 in temporary barracks." He commended Commissioner Frost, members of the Welfare Board and the legislature in their work with him to make the institutions sanitary, humane, and decent. This new building is a symbol of progress.

Touching on the current purchasing department investigation, the governor said, "There has been some talk about the purchasing department at Frankfort. I have appointed a committee to make a thorough and careful investigation and report to me how we can buy the maximum for the least money."[3]

---

1. Johnson spoke at ceremonies dedicating the new $570,000 addition to Western State Penitentiary. Kentucky State Penitentiary, Department of Corrections, does not have a copy of this speech. Letter, D. B. Bordenkircher, superintendent, February 14, 1977.

2. Following an inspection on February 13, 1943, the governor noted that crowded conditions had been relieved by the completion of the new cell block. He spent much of his time at the new 430-acre farm. He made another inspection on May 22, 1943. *Paducah Sun-Democrat*, May 23, 1943.

3. See speech from July 1, 1941, in the State Administration section.

CHANGES FOR HOUSES OF REFORM, GREENDALE

Frankfort / October 30, 1941

CURRENT action on fifteen recommendations made by his two-man committee[1] investigating the Houses of Reform at Greendale represents a beginning, Governor Johnson said, on the list of forty-one recommendations.[2] "The institution has not been neglected altogether. We have spent $218,000 there the past two years and that is more than was spent at any of the other institutions." Included in that sum were a new girls' dormitory, costing $82,900, and reconstruction of the heating plant and steam distribution system at a cost of $72,600. "It at least can be said that this winter, for the first time in fifteen years, all the rooms will be warm."

Acting Superintendent Braden had been ordered to comply with the following recommendations:

"ONE: That the indiscriminate use of the paddle be abolished at once, and that no corporal punishment be permitted except on approval of a committee consisting of the superintendent, the assistant superintendent, and the principal of the school. All rules specifying definite and specific punishment for any offense should be abolished, with each case to be handled on its own merits. . . .

"TWO: That the artibrary rule that inmates must remain in the institution for a minimum of fifteen months be abolished; that each case be considered on its own merits. . . .

"THREE: The immediate removal of all kerosene lamps and their replacement with electric wiring.

"FOUR: That full information be secured immediately . . . on the fitness of employees.

"FIVE: That all employees be examined to ascertain if any are suffering from contagious or infectious diseases. . . .

"SIX: That provisions be made to set aside a suitable room for Catholic services, which is to be used for no other purpose.

"SEVEN: That an immediate cleanup campaign be undertaken to remove from the buildings . . . lumber, old machinery, rags, debris, and other junk that have accumulated to produce fire and health hazards.

"EIGHT: That all useless shacks and outbuildings be removed . . . the premises cleaned up . . . and order restored; that lawns and flower beds be given proper care and weeds eliminated.

"NINE: The immediate erection of an appropriate pole for display of the American flag."

The governor cited four recommendations which either were in process of execution or had been in execution for some time. One of them would authorize the superintendent "to go beyond rolls of the Personnel Commission in the selection of employees."

"Braden has had the authority to go beyond the rolls ever since he has been there, and to hire and fire. The committee itself noted this fact on Page 26 of its report in these words: 'Your committee is . . . advised that both you and Commissioner of Welfare W. A. Frost have authorized Mr. Braden to go beyond rolls of the Personnel Commission . . . . Furthermore, that Mr. Braden has been authorized to remove any employee under him who cannot or does not properly discharge his duties.' "

The governor said that the committee recommended immediate repair of the water tower, when, as a matter of fact, the work is under contract and will be completed as soon as delivery can be made on steel for the riser pipe.

He commented that Braden has informed him that fire hose and extinguishers have been tested from time to time and that defective hose always is replaced with new hose.

As to renovation of the boys' kitchen and replacement of a burned-out stove, the committee apparently did not know that when two new electric ranges are delivered to the new dormitory for girls, good equipment in the present kitchen for girls will be used to replace the dilapidated equipment in the kitchen for boys.

A suggestion that the name of the institution be changed cannot be met without an amendment to the Kentucky Constitution.

The governor stated that the following recommendation will be submitted to the 1942 legislature: "That the law be changed so as to give the commissioner of welfare, with approval of the governor . . . power to transfer such inmates who do not respond to the training program . . . or who exert a dangerous influence over other inmates . . . and defy lawful officers in charge of the institution."

Improvement of the disciplinary barracks and immediate reconstruction of the sewage disposal plant will be financed out of the governor's emergency fund. The sewerage work is expected to cost around $46,000.[3] The disciplinary barracks will be moved from the top floor of the old school building to a room directly above the white boys' dining room. The move will "give a space reasonably safe from fire, but must be considered as temporary until a permanent unit is constructed."

He declined comment on the recommendation by the Fayette County grand jury that Norman Braden, acting superintendent, be discharged.[4]

---

1. Helbing and Bastin. See speech from October 3, 1941, in this section.
2. Heading the list were recommendations for a comprehensive building program, employment of competent personnel, and elimination of political influences. Making public the thirty-three-page report, Johnson said, "The committee . . . has done a splendid job of analyzing what has been a perpetual problem of the state. The institution has been surveyed repeatedly but very little has been done. Many of the things the committee has suggested can be done without a large outlay of money and our purpose will be to make as many corrections as possible with our resources." Louisville *Courier-Journal*, October 26, 1941.
3. The governor transferred $47,623.65 from his emergency fund to the Department of Finance on November 13, 1941, for the sewage disposal plant and a few small items.
4. On November 27, 1941, the executive committee of the Kentucky Conference of Social Welfare commended the governor "for his program in connection with the rehabilitation of the state institutions and especially Greendale." *Kentucky Post*, November 28, 1941.

JOHN R. DeMOISEY APPOINTED GREENDALE SUPERINTENDENT
Frankfort / November 19, 1941

APPOINTMENT of John R. ("Frenchy") DeMoisey as superintendent of the Houses of Reform and removal of Norman Braden as acting superintendent was followed by announcement from Governor Johnson that numerous changes would be made in policy. "We are going to clean that place up from top to bottom—scrub it thoroughly, for one thing. We are going to revitalize the recreation system, buy new playground equipment, and pay for it out of the emergency fund. We are going to concentrate on the food situation and reestablish the band."

He noted that in the last two years $265,000 had been spent in improving the building and equipment, including what is now under contract, such as the sewage disposal plant and the pipe that carries water to the elevated tank.

"Mr. DeMoisey was chosen by Dr. Frost because of the confidence he had in him. I am thoroughly convinced that he reached the right conclusion. He will have complete charge of the institution in personnel and in every other respect and will have the full backing of Dr. Frost and the governor. He will arrange for daily instruction for each of the children. Mr. DeMoisey knows every youngster over there by his first name and he has the respect and confidence of every one of them. We are certain that with the experience he has had, he will succeed. He knows it's his big opportunity and we know he'll take advantage of it. He wants to make institutional work his life work. Why, even when he ordered a paddling, there never was a complaint.

"I will ask the coming state legislature to authorize the welfare commissioner to transfer inmates from one state institution to another. Under that, we can send some of the older and more incorrigible boys from Greendale to the La Grange reformatory."[1]

---

1. Johnson was asked whether DeMoisey had taken any courses in institutional work and replied, "He got it in practical experience at Greendale." He referred to the Helbing and Bastin report which said, "Your committee is of the opinion that Mr. Braden has shown rare good judgement in the selection of Mr. John DeMoisey, the former director of recreation, to become the assistant superintendent. Mr. DeMoisey . . . is an exceptionally capable man." When touring welfare institutions with the Legislative Council on November 25, 1941, the governor said at Ormsby Village, "I brought you here so you could see what can be accomplished at the state institution [Greendale]." He noted that the yearly cost for each child at Ormsby Village was $556, against $325 at Greendale. *State Journal,* November 26, 1941.

CENTRAL STATES PROBATION AND PAROLE CONFERENCE
Louisville / May 26, 1942

THE way to develop a probation and parole system is to select the most competent people obtainable to direct its activities, to give them responsibility, to sustain them consistently in their efforts, and to permit them to choose their own personnel, Governor Johnson told the Central States Probation and Parole Conference.[1] "That has been the procedure we have established in Kentucky."

The chief justification for parole was its efficacy in salvaging social derelicts, and the degree of success attained depends on intelligence and understanding. "The officers must face realities, and take violators as you find them. You must work with what you have."

Stating that the pardoning power had been abused for years in Kentucky, he said there had been no pardons granted since 1936 as "Governor Chandler and I decided that the only method to release prisoners from custody was through the probation and parole board."[2]

Praising the work of Kentucky's forty parole officers, Governor Johnson said that eighty-five out of every hundred parolees developed into good citizens. Parole is not perfect; you deal with imperfect human beings, but it is the best system devised for returning prison inmates to society. He got satisfaction from the increased efficiency with which it is working. "We have been able to increase the number of parolees without a proportionate increase in the number of parole violators. It is better to be disappointed in the 15 percent that failed to take advantage of their opportunities than to keep the other 85 percent in confinement and deny them the chance to atone for their transgressions."

He commented on Kentucky's new parole law which permits minor offenders, who have been given sentences of less than ten years, to join the army. He said 847 had volunteered and 588 passed the physical examination. "When these men return to their communities, they will be ex-soldiers and not ex-convicts."

Complimenting the cooperation developed "through such organizations as yours," he said that approximately 200 Kentucky parolees were in other states and were being supervised by parole officers of those states. At the same time, Kentucky parole officers are supervising more than 200 parolees from neighboring states.[3] "Your convention here has been an inspiration to our probation and parole workers."

---

1. The governor attended the conference of this association in Milwaukee, Wisconsin, in May 1941.

2. Johnson contradicted a claim by the counsel of Robert H. Anderson in February 1943 that the governor had refused to consider a pardon plea for him. "I have never refused to consider petitions for pardons, but so far I have never been convinced that one was deserved. Whenever I am, I'll grant one. In Anderson's case, I listened to the plea for a pardon for him early in January and instead of giving him the pardon he asked, I gave him a commutation until January 22, so he could present his new evidence to the courts." *Richmond Daily Register*, February 24, 1943.

Anderson was one of three convicted in the robbery-slaying at Lexington of golf star Marion Miley and her mother. On February 25 the Court of Appeals and the governor refused a stay of execution for Anderson. However, the governor granted a stay to Thomas Bass, a black soldier, until March 26, 1943. Assistant Attorney General W. Owen Keller requested the stay because the attorney failed to appeal the case to the high court. The governor's order said the "oversight" might result in an injustice to Bass. *Cincinnati Enquirer*, February 26, 1943.

3. Attorney General Meredith announced on August 20, 1942, that he would investigate the release of prisoners by Welfare Commissioner Frost under this law and test the constitutionality of the act. On the same day a paroled convict was returned to prison on a warrant charging parole violation issued by Johnson and Frost. John Michael O'Hara of Louisville had been paroled to join the army. He failed the physical examination but his parole was continued so that he might be employed at the Kentucky Hotel. He failed to report for work. Louisville *Courier-Journal*, August 21, 1942, and *Lexington Herald*, August 21, 1942.

KENTUCKY FIREMEN'S ASSOCIATION
Danville / August 11, 1942

GOVERNOR JOHNSON said that this nation is now in a war of survival and that we are fighting against the most ruthless bunch of dictators the world has ever known. "We are in a war that is horrible beyond the imagination of us here in the Bluegrass and we are getting licked every day. There are many in our state who refuse to admit that bombs could be dropped in Kentucky." He added that he hoped none were dropped on our nation, but he warned that it would be "inexcusable folly and absolute foolishness if we failed to prepare ourselves for such an emergency. It is highly probable that bombs will be dropped in our state because of the important war industries and camps located in Kentucky." He told the firemen their work with the local civilian defense councils "would help to lessen the disaster caused by the enemy bombs."

He reviewed the work of the Kentucky Defense Council and praised the cooperation of the firemen's association with the group. He said that twenty-three schools attended by 498 firemen had been conducted throughout Kentucky under the direction of Captain V. A. Beam, of the Louisville Fire Department and secretary of the firemen's association, in cooperation with the Kentucky Defense Council. "In many cities more favorable insurance rates were obtained because of the improvement made in the various fire departments as a result of the schools. During the past year the state Fire Prevention and Rates Department for the first time in years inspected every school, picture show building and laundry and dry cleaning establishment in Kentucky which resulted in the elimination of many fire hazards, thus reducing the danger of loss of property and life by fire."[1]

---

1. The governor spoke at the beginning of a four-day course in wartime fire fighting on July 28, 1941, at the University of Kentucky.

CITATION OF MERIT FOR CIVILIAN DEFENSE COUNCIL
Lexington / April 14, 1943

GOVERNOR JOHNSON declared that the recognition given to the civilian defense council in Lexington and Fayette County was due largely to the conscientious efforts of the late Mayor T. Ward Havely.[1]

"Mayor Havely was one of the most conscientious men I have ever known. He always was proud of Lexington and was determined that Lexington should always lead. He saw in civilian defense an opportunity to take an important part in the war effort. That Lexington should be the first city in the state to receive such a citation is due to one who would have been proud to be here today—not that he would have wanted praise for his efforts, but that he would have been glad to see his city achieve its goal.

"As Kentucky's wartime governor, I am extremely proud of Kentucky's efforts in civilian defense activities.[2] I am extremely proud of Lexington because it has been awarded the distinction for being the first city to receive a citation of merit from the regional Office of Civilian Defense."

He characterized Mayor Havely as "a man of high character, integrity, ability, a good neighbor, father, and husband, who never at any time shirked his duty as a citizen or public official. No individual in this or any other city ever gave his services less selfishly. That Ward Havely succeeded was due to the high quality of his leadership. This presentation of the civilian defense council is a high compliment to our departed friend."

---

1. Theodore Ward Havely (1894–1943), b. Cynthiana. Businessman, civic leader; mayor, Lexington, 1939–1943; organized Civilian Defense Council in June 1940, one of the first to be organized in the United States. Wallis and Tapp, *A Sesquicentennial History of Kentucky*, 3:1278, 1280.

2. Johnson spoke at the opening of Kentucky's first civilian defense school at Murray State Teachers College in June 1942. Forty-three persons from seventeen Western Kentucky counties enrolled. He warned, "We are not safe from the enemy's bombs and we won't be safe until we perfect our home defense. It will be too late to meet such a crisis after bombs start falling." *Murray Ledger and Times*, June 25, 1942.

On April 19, 1943, he transferred $2,500 from the National and Civil Defense Emergency Fund to the Department of Military Affairs, Civil Defense, to cover the cost of printing regulations for handling air raid warnings. On November 23, 1943, he transferred $3,000 from the National and Civil Defense Emergency Fund to the Civil Defense Fund to be used by the state Civil Defense Commission for expenses.

AIRPORTS, BRIDGES, & HIGHWAYS

KENTUCKY DAM DAY
Paducah / December 4, 1939

"I ALWAYS enjoy coming to Paducah. It was the first town larger than Smithland I ever saw. I came here on the Cumberland river packet *J. B. Richardson* when my father brought our crop of dark tobacco to market. I saw here the first bright lights—first streetcars—first elevator in the old Palmer House. Here we bought the suit of clothes that had long pants. I rejoice in the development of Western Kentucky. There are no finer folk beneath the sun than those who reside in Western Kentucky. I promise you that as your governor I shall have a sympathetic, sincere interest in your problems.

"As a boy who went to a five-months school at Tuckers Temple and Groves Chapel schoolhouses in Livingston County, I shall always be anxious to do that which will provide better educational opportunities for the youth of today. As a lad who remembers only the dirt roads of 1906, I shall rejoice as I have opportunity to contribute to the extension of improved highways in Western Kentucky."

The governor announced that from December 11, 1939, through January 1, 1940, during a twenty-two day trial period, motorists may make round trips on the state's eight intrastate toll spans for the price of the present one-way fare of thirty cents.

He said that the Paducah-Brookport bridge, an interstate span, remains unaffected by the order. The twenty-five cent fare, in effect since March 1938 when the toll was cut from fifty cents, will remain unchanged.

Although the special round-trip rate will be in effect only temporarily, the governor said that it was planned to make it permanent if it was found during the trial period that traffic increased sufficiently to hold the bridge revenue near present levels. He hoped that it would yield sufficient revenue to obtain from bondholders permission to make it permanent. Bonds outstanding against the bridges, grouped together in one project for financing purposes, now total $3,125,000 and bear 1.75 percent interest. Originally the bonds totaled $5,101,000 with a much higher interest rate.

He discussed the condition of state finances and the financial problems to be faced during the next four years. Recalling that in his campaign for the governorship he announced that he was opposed to new taxes, he said, "I construe the result of the balloting to mean that the people gave me a mandate to operate the state government without an increase in taxes."[2]

---

1. The bridges were over the Tennessee River near Paducah and at Eggner's Ferry; over the Cumberland River at Smithland, Canton and Burnside; over the Green River at Spottsville; and over the Kentucky River at Tyrone and Boonesboro.

In July 1939 Johnson wrote to the Kentucky Free Bridge Association, Paducah: "In view of the tremendous interest in the possibilities of the benefits which would be brought to Kentucky through lifting of the tolls on its vehicular bridges and the activities in which the Kentucky Free Bridge Association has engaged in the past to promote this development, I believe the association and its members are entitled to know my attitude as a candidate for the Democratic nomination for governor on the matter.

"I have already advised the officers of the Kentucky Free Bridge Association that, if elected governor, I will work with them in trying to develop a sound and feasible plan for amortizing the existing bonded indebtedness of the toll bridges of the state, so that they may be freed in the immediate future. I also have pointed out that substantial relief has been given the traveling public by a cut in toll charges, with which you are thoroughly familiar.

"It is impossible for me to determine at this time whether a feasible plan for complete lifting of the toll charges can be worked out inasmuch as several technical problems are involved. However, I pledge myself to cooperate sympathetically and conscientiously with the advocates of free bridges to perfect a plan to eliminate the tolls.

"While this plan is being developed, however, I believe that additional relief from the toll charges can be given the traveling public. The reduction in tolls of approximately 50 percent applied to the intrastate toll bridges a year ago has demonstrated that the bridges actually have been barriers to traffic in view of the fact that travel over the bridges has almost doubled. I have been deeply impressed by the evidence produced by this trial, which shows that actual revenue from the bridges after the large decrease in tolls was almost as great as the amount collected under the higher charge.

"Therefore, I am of the opinion that a further reduction can be made, and, if elected governor, immediately upon my inauguration I will take the necessary steps to put into effect a plan under which a traveler who makes a round trip over the intrastate bridges within a twenty-four hour period would pay only the toll now required for one-way passage.

"I believe such a method of collecting tolls would greatly encourage and increase trade and travel in the territories of the state which heretofore have been retarded in their natural development. I believe that a general and widespread impetus would be given to all commercial activity with a resultant benefit to the citizens of the entire state.

"I believe this plan can be put into effect, and I pledge my assistance in making it possible immediately following my inauguration. This round-trip feature also would benefit the people who deserve the most consideration—the local citizens who must cross the toll bridges to reach their county seats or other towns in their district. I am sincerely interested in perfecting a solution for the toll bridge problem and invite any suggestions you or any other citizens might have to make relative to the matter."

2. The event celebrated excavation of the millionth cubic yard of earth from the site of Tennessee Valley Authority's Gilbertsville Dam.

DEDICATION OF BRIDGE ACROSS KENTUCKY RIVER
Irvine / July 26, 1940

CONTRASTING conditions in this country to those in war-torn Europe, Governor Johnson declared that while Americans are building and dedicating new bridges, the armies in Europe are interested in destroying bridges.

"With the exception of Arkansas, Louisiana, and Alabama, no state in the Union has as many miles of navigable streams along its borders and within its borders as Kentucky. The northern boundary of the state, approximately 652 miles long, is formed by the Ohio River. The western boundary, approximately 52 miles long, is formed by the Mississippi River. The eastern boundary is formed by the Big Sandy River, approximately 110 miles long. The Kentucky River rises near the eastern border and flows diagonally across the state, entering the Ohio near the center of the northern boundary. The Green River rises in the central portion of the state and flows into the Ohio River near its mouth. The Cumberland River rises in the eastern section of the state, flows down into Tennessee, and returns to Kentucky in the western end of the state, flowing into the Ohio River near its mouth. The Tennessee River crosses the state just west of the Cumberland River and in some places not more than two or three miles distant from it. These are all classed as navigable streams. There are altogether 743 miles of navigable streams along the borders of Kentucky and 681 miles of navigable streams within the state, making a total of 1,424 navigable miles.

"In addition to the rivers, classed as navigable, there are thousands of miles of streams not navigable that criss-cross the state from north to south and east to west. To form a connected system of highways, these streams must be crossed by bridges or ferries provided. During the past year there were completed or under construction eight major bridges which cost, or will cost to complete, approximately $1,463,500. In addition to these major bridges, there are a great many smaller bridges under construction.

"In addition to stream crossings, modern highways require the separation of highway and railroad grades where practicable. The program of construction of the Department of Highways for the year ending June 30, 1940, included grade separation projects and grade protection projects estimated to cost $356,846, and for the year ending June 30, 1941, projects are estimated to cost $534,074.

"As of April 1, 1940, the Department of Highways had under maintenance 2,748 bridges of twenty feet or more span.

"The Kentucky River Bridge at Irvine will eliminate a toll barrier and will provide a modern entrance to the city of Irvine from the west and south of the river.[1] This bridge alone cost approximately $153,000 and with the approaches cost approximately $240,700."

He recalled that as lieutenant governor he had worked to obtain the construction of this bridge and said that its completion gave him great pleasure.[2]

---

1. The bridge replaced a rickety toll bridge erected by private capital in 1909 above the site where an ancient ferry had plied the river. Joe Tuttle, the toll collector on the outmoded span, remained at his post on this last day, collecting twenty cents on each automobile that crossed the bridge. Louisville *Courier-Journal*, July 27, 1940.

2. On June 21, 1940, Johnson dedicated a bridge across the Green River at Munfordville and said that he "was glad to see this section get some of the gravy from the taxes its citizens had paid." The 1,400-foot concrete bridge replaced a narrow steel span built by private capital as a toll bridge in 1907 and later taken over and operated as a toll bridge until 1928 by the state. Louisville *Courier-Journal*, June 22, 1940.

DEDICATION OF BRIDGE ACROSS OHIO RIVER
Owensboro / July 30, 1940

WE have met here today to celebrate a more perfect union of our two great commonwealths and their peoples. We hope and anticipate that from this union may come a fruitful increase of neighborliness, of trade and good-will, and of mutual cooperation and service.

Blessed is the tie that binds; blessed is this tie between our common-wealths; blessed is any tie that brings together our people more closely in these times when we must stand together, share our blessings, aid one another with our strength, carry together our burdens, and face as one our foes.

What we celebrate today is the opening of a structure of steel and concrete, but what we honor is the vision of those who conceived it, the civic service of those who brought it about, the skill and the toil of those who designed and built it. The countless numbers who will enjoy the service of this span are indebted to all of these, and so likewise are we who are gathered here today. We wish also to acknowledge our gratitude to cooperating agencies of the federal government.

This is a day of joy, particularly for the people of Owensboro. I join them in their joy, and I do not take away anything from this by telling them that their joy is shared also by the people of Kentucky and Indiana generally. Your city throws open a magnificent and welcoming doorway, symbolic of the hospitable greeting that waits here for all who come. A span less beautiful would not be worthy of the city which it serves.

We are happy that this span brings us into more intimate relationships with our neighbors in Indiana. Our sister commonwealth has shown to us throughout her lifetime the same face that we as a nation today turn to all the world. She is a good neighbor, and Kentucky is happy in the privilege to proclaim it. She has reached out to clasp our hand in the building of this bridge as she did to help build the Henderson-Evansville bridge. Without her cooperation, her friendly willingness, her determined action, neither one would have been possible.

From far to the north and from far to the south, the restless and hurrying caravans of busy America will pass by here, their journeys made quicker and more pleasant by this structure. No matter which way you face, it is now easier to go from here to there or from there to here. Many of the distant cities that will be served by this bridge have sent their citizens here today to join us in this celebration. We are happy to have them with us. We ask them to take home with them a greeting from

Kentucky, the word that we have taken one more barrier out of the road to our hearts where no barrier has ever existed.

It is an honor, a privilege, and a pleasure to participate as governor of the Commonwealth of Kentucky in the dedication of this bridge. I came along just at that happy time when the hard work had been done and little was left to do but join in the celebration. So I stand here, not alone as governor, but as a spokesman for all those officials of Kentucky who have had a part in making this day possible.

There was some good-natured joking at the bridge celebration dinner last night, about the fact that the two states had joined hands to build this bridge, but that Kentucky had her other hand out to collect tolls. These tolls will be used to retire the bonded costs of the bridge, and when those costs have been retired, then the bridge will become absolutely free. In the meantime, those who use the bridge will be on the same basis on which we are operating Kentucky—you will pay as you go, just as we are doing.

But we look forward to the day when this bridge shall be free. In that connection, I would like to give you a little history. A few years ago, Lyter Donaldson was a district highway commissioner. There was a toll bridge across the Kentucky River in his hometown, Carrollton. He arranged to have the state buy it, use the tolls to retire the cost, and then make it free. Of all the toll bridges that were bought or built by that administration, in which he was just a district commissioner, his bridge was the first one to become free. He did such a good job on that, that I called him to serve the entire state, not just one district, and I am certain that with him as highway commissioner, there will be splendid progress toward making all our bridges free.

By strict and careful collection and supervision of tolls, we are making certain that every cent of bridge revenues is devoted to the payment of interest and principal, speeding the day when the remaining barrier of tolls will be entirely eliminated.

We want Kentucky to be that kind of fairyland that charms one's senses, no longer a ferry-land slowing the traveler's journey and slimming his purse.

This bridge, and the splendid civic spirit of those who conceived it and made it possible, are contributions to that goal. Its dedication and opening is a joyous occasion in which I am happy to have the privilege to join.

DEDICATION OF PUBLIC SQUARE
Lancaster / October 1, 1940

GOVERNOR JOHNSON congratulated the community on the acquisition of a deserved and merited public improvement. He outlined some of the accomplishments of his administration and paid tribute to Joseph Robinson[1] for his fine contribution in cooperating to carry out the policies of thrift and economy, and for his adroit and sagacious leadership as Speaker of the House of Representatives.

The governor's promise to "make a thrifty, frugal governor" was considered by him as a binding covenant with the people of the state. His promises that pertained to legislation had already been carried out, and the pledge of economy and efficiency in administration would continue to be fulfilled throughout his four years in office.

He paid tribute to the accomplishments of his predecessor, Governor A. B. Chandler, and said it was his purpose to consolidate the gains and to make increasingly efficient the reforms inaugurated by the Chandler administration.

It was a pleasure to dedicate the public square—honestly built of substantial materials and the best engineering design—for the service, enjoyment, and welfare of the splendid, patriotic Anglo-American citizenship of Lancaster and Garrard County. He dedicated it to the public service and foresaw that it would serve its fine public purpose for years—during the lifetime of those present and of their children and children's children.

---

1. Joseph Evans Robinson (1873–1942), b. Hubble, Lincoln County. Farmer; owner-editor *Central Record*, 1910; Garrard County attorney, 1904–1912; city attorney, Lancaster, 1912; Democratic National Committee, 1928–1932; state representative, 1936, Speaker, 1940. *Who's Who in Kentucky, 1936*, p. 343, and telephone interview, James R. Whitaker, *Central Record*, June 20, 1978.

DEDICATION OF U.S. 60 BRIDGE ACROSS GREEN RIVER
Rockport / October 21, 1940

"THIS bridge is a sign that the state is meeting the problems of modern transportation for this is the fourth such bridge dedicated this year.[1] This bridge not only serves the business and pleasure of the public in the time of peace, but it will serve the military needs of the nation if it becomes necessary. Public improvements such as this bridge are the result of government being responsive to the needs of the people."

The governor noted that the bridge would replace the ferry and commented that "bridges are playing thunder with ferries, but they eliminate obstacles to travel."[2]

---

1. On November 13, 1940, the governor dedicated a bridge across the Green River at Livermore. For an account of the dedication ceremony, see *Owensboro Messenger*, November 14, 1940.

2. Remarks relating to registration for military service and to enlistments have been deleted.

KEHOE VIADUCT OPENED
Maysville / October 25, 1940

"WE are gathered here to do honor to a great Kentuckian, but nothing we can say would be appropriate. The name and memory of James N. Kehoe[1] will live as long in the hearts and memory of the people of Maysville and Mason County as that plaque which bears perpetual testimony to your esteem of him as well as that of the people of Kentucky.[2]

"I have known Jim Kehoe for a great many years and I am well acquainted, as are you, of his great record of public service."

Governor Johnson stated that, in his first appearance in Maysville since a visit last year as a candidate for the gubernatorial office, he was pleased to dedicate the Kehoe Viaduct and to help to honor the veteran public servant whose name it bears.

"This viaduct is one of your most valuable community assets. I do not recall what expenditure was necessary for the erection of this passage, but, whatever it may have been, it was well worth the money.[3]

"This is not his first accomplishment for Maysville as you here in Maysville know and as we do outside of your city. Jim Kehoe played a prominent part in securing the Maysville-Aberdeen bridge, and while a member of Congress, he secured for his city the post office and . . . it is only fitting and proper that you and we here today meet and pay tribute to a great citizen of Maysville, of the state of Kentucky, and of the nation.

"This is just as momentous an occasion, and is a great and living example of the methods of our country as in contrast with those of foreign nations. While they are engaged in great wars of destruction, we are building up our nation, not only in its armed strength, but in transportation. Construction, not destruction, is our ultimate aim and goal."[4]

---

1. James N. Kehoe (1862–1945), b. Maysville. Attorney; United States representative, 1901–1905; president, Bank of Maysville. *Who's Who in Kentucky, 1936,* p. 224, and Louisville *Courier Journal,* June 14, 1945.

2. A bronze plaque mounted on a limestone rock weighing 8,000 pounds with the bust and profile of Kehoe in bas-relief was unveiled. Lyter Donaldson, state highway commissioner, promised that the Maysville-Aberdeen bridge would be toll free by 1945.

3. The cost was $154,000.

4. Johnson emphasized the same theme when he dedicated two resurfaced streets in Danville on May 14, 1941. MS and *Danville Advocate-Messenger,* May 15, 1941.

CYNTHIANA AIRPORT DEDICATION
Cynthiana / November 11, 1940

IT is a genuine joy to join with you of Harrison County in welcoming the Dawn Patrol[1] and uniting in this memorial tribute to those who offered their lives a sacrifice upon the altar of their country. Aviation was in its infancy as a weapon of combat in that war which ended twenty-two years ago. Developments in aviation have been remarkable in the intervening years. In the war now raging across the Atlantic, the airplane is playing a major role. In our program of national defense, larger emphasis is being placed on aviation. As an accepted agency of transportation, aviation has earned a place in the world. But there has not yet come that widespread public acceptance of aviation which is desirable. Members of the Dawn Patrol are the evangels who are making a fine contribution to a better understanding of and appreciation for aviation.

Twenty-eight nations participated in that war which was ended by the armistice. Nine-tenths of the population of the world was involved. It resulted in mobilization of 60 millions of fighting men. Direct expenditures of all nations involved the stupendous sum of $186,233,000,000. The total direct casualties were 9,818,000 with deaths among civilian population an additional five millions. It was a war in which we of these United States engaged with lofty idealism and patriotic zeal because we believed it to be a war to end war and prevent a recurrence of such destruction of life and property.

That war failed of its exalted purpose in that it did not end war. Europe and Asia are again aflame with battle, even more brutal and frightful. Efforts following the armistice to outlaw war have been unsuccessful.

We of this great peace-loving nation are faced with the grim realities of war. We are forced by events to recognize the wisdom of George Washington when he said that the best way to preserve peace is to be prepared for war.

So the observance of this the twenty-second anniversary of the armistice is saddened by the necessity of mobilizing all resources of the nation to hasten the strengthening of our defenses in an effort to preserve peace on this continent.

On this the sad, sweet, solemn anniversary of the ending of a cruel war, let us rekindle the fire of patriotic devotion in our hearts; let us revitalize the faith of our fathers and quicken the spirit of sacrifice which sustained them. Let us solemnly subscribe, as did they, to that compact to "mutually pledge to each other our lives, our fortunes and our sacred honor." When we as an awakened and united people subscribe to that covenant and enthusiastically support that immortal phrase of freedom, we shall have prepared ourselves to defend democracy and preserve our republic.

As we unitedly meet this challenge of citizenship, we shall keep faith with those of our gallant dead whose valiant spirits sleep in the Valhalla of heroes.[2]

---

1. The Dawn Patrol was composed of members of the Bluegrass Aviation Club, the Louisville Aero Club, and private plane owners of Cincinnati.

2. The speech has been edited. Similar parts appear in speeches from July 4, 1941, and July 22, 1941, in the World War II section.

HENDERSON-EVANSVILLE BRIDGE BECOMES TOLL FREE
Henderson / March 20, 1941

"INDIANA and Kentucky always have been good neighbors.[1] Today we are happy beyond words that the toll house has been removed and the last barrier between the two states eliminated."

The bridge would be "a benefit not only to Evansville and Henderson, Indiana and Kentucky, but to all Americans. It is a very happy day when we gather here to celebrate an accomplishment looked forward to for so many years. The effect is the elimination of a barrier between the states of Kentucky and Indiana by the joint and cooperative effort of their leadership.

"We appreciate the fine, cooperative attitude of Indiana. Indiana always has been a fine neighbor."[2]

---

1. A boundary dispute arose, however, between the two states during Johnson's term. It involved an area south of Evansville. Whether the Evansville City Waterworks pumping plant was in Indiana or Kentucky was at issue. In 1896 the United States Supreme Court (*Indiana* v. *Kentucky,* 163 U.S. 520) gave Kentucky title to about 250 acres of bottomland on the outskirts of Evansville which had been moved to the northern side of the Ohio River when it cut a new channel during a flood. The 1792 charter from Virginia specified that the northern boundary of Kentucky was to be the low-water mark on the north side of the Ohio River. In 1896 the Army Corps of Engineers determined the course of the river and laid the boundary. A line drawn from its terminal post to the low-water mark by the shortest distance placed the Evansville Water Company in Indiana, while a line drawn as a continuation of the 1896 boundary placed the company in Kentucky. On December 6, 1940, Johnson said that he had no objection to renewal of the 1896 survey to determine the boundary, but he opposed consideration of the transfer of title of any part of the 5,000 acres upon which Henderson County collected taxes. Louisville *Courier-Journal,* December 7, 1940.

Governor M. Clifford Townsend and Indiana officials met with Johnson and Kentucky representatives on December 19, 1940, in Frankfort and agreed to the appointment of a joint commission to decide the dispute. Johnson reminded the conferees that he had stated that there was "no occasion for a conference" if Indiana expected Kentucky to cede the land. He was willing to arbitrate the boundary line. The governors agreed that each would name two members to the commission and that its report would not commit either state. *State Journal,* December 20, 1940. Johnson named Highway Commissioner Donaldson and Highway Engineer Cutler as Kentucky's members on December 31, 1940. Louisville *Courier-Journal,* January 1, 1941. The commissioners agreed upon the boundary line. The legislature of each state accepted the agreement and Congress gave its consent. The resolution was signed by President Roosevelt, June 29, 1943. Public 100, 57 *Stat.* 248. See also Louisville *Courier-Journal,* February 17 and June 16, 1943.

2. Governors Henry Schricker, Indiana, and Prentice Cooper, Tennessee, participated in the ribbon-cutting ceremony with Johnson. *Henderson Evening Journal,* March 20, 1941. The bridge became the only free Ohio River bridge between Pittsburgh and Cairo. That tolls were no longer collected was due to the Murphy Toll Bridge Act of 1928 under which nineteen bridges were built or bought. It was named for L. B. Murphy of Scott County who introduced the bill in the General Assembly. Louisville *Courier-Journal,* March 23, 1941. The Henderson-Audubon Chamber of Commerce does not have a copy of the speech. Letter, Jean Breamer, secretary, March 8, 1977. The governor spoke at a banquet on March 19 in Henderson. See speech from March 19, 1941, in the Industry section.

NEW ENTRANCE TO STATE CAPITOL
Frankfort / May 15, 1941

GOVERNOR JOHNSON paid tribute to the great French patriot and "angel" of the American Revolution, the Marquis de Lafayette, in delivering the principal address for the dedication of Lafayette Drive.

He stressed the convenience of the roadway,[1] which runs directly from U.S. 60 eastward to the Capitol Building. The modernization of the historic roadway, at a cost of approximately $20,000 with WPA labor and state materials, was lauded by the governor as being an outstanding accomplishment and one for which the "WPA, Frankfort, Franklin County, and the state are to be congratulated."

He expressed the hope that "the fine understanding between city, county, and state of our mutual problems will always exist."

Citing the timeliness and the "intelligent cooperation" that brought together "all the agencies which could cooperate best to bring about construction of the road," he paid tribute to the "leadership of County Judge L. Boone Hamilton and his fine fiscal court."[2]

He thanked the State Guard unit for being present and praised Franklin County for being the "first county in the state to provide uniforms for its State Militia company."[3]

"The law authorizing creation of the State Militia specifically inhibited the use of state funds for providing either uniforms or equipment for the militia, but authorized cities and counties to provide them." He complimented the men on their "fine appearance," a tribute that he likewise bestowed upon the personnel of the band.

---

1. For years its rocky surface kept most travelers from using it.
2. Another major development concerning bridges in 1941 was the allocation of $650,000 of a sum of $2,585,600 for work on U.S. 25 to the Clay's Ferry bridge across the Kentucky River between Lexington and Richmond, a span stretching 1,736 feet from bluff to bluff and rising 280 feet above the river. *Richmond Daily Register*, February 6, 1941.
3. The detachment wore Confederate gray uniforms.

BEN WILLIAMSON MEMORIAL BRIDGE BECOMES TOLL FREE
Ashland / August 5, 1941

IT is with genuine joy that I come to Ashland to join with the citizenship of this splendid city and our neighbors of this region in freeing the toll bridge from Ashland to Coal Grove, Ohio.[1]

Surrounded as is Kentucky on the east, north, and west by navigable streams, the problem of spanning those rivers with adequate bridges has been especially difficult and costly. Construction of essential bridges has been financed by issuing bonds against the bridges, charging toll with which to raise money to retire those bonds. Tolls which have been paid by the traveling public for crossing the river on this bridge have been used to pay off the bonds issued against it. Sufficient money has been collected to liquidate those bonds. The traveling public henceforth will have the convenience of using this bridge which they have paid for without payment of further toll.

So it is indeed a happy day that we celebrate. It is a significant occasion that brings us together to lift toll collection from this bridge, discard the toll takers' house, and commit to unrestricted public service this span which will for decades to come serve the needs of those who come this way.

Freeing of this bridge will promote neighborliness between Kentucky and Ohio. It eliminates a barrier which has militated against neighborliness. Kentuckians are a hospitable people. Kentucky desires always to be a good neighbor. We are unhappy that our state can be approached from the north and east only by crossing toll bridges. But those bridges are far more adequate to modern travel needs than were the ferries which they replaced. We are eliminating toll bridges on our border and within our state as rapidly as is possible. Recently the toll bridge across the Ohio River between Henderson, Kentucky, and Evansville, Indiana, was freed of toll, enough money having been collected in toll to redeem the bridge from the bondholders. Today we rejoice that there has arrived that happy hour for which you have longed — the hour when this bridge which is so vital to this region will be freed from bondage and consecrated to free public service. We are grateful for the cooperation of the great state of Ohio.

Before the year is out, it will be possible to free the toll bridge across the Ohio River at Newport. So the day is not far distant when the rivers which form the boundary of Kentucky will be spanned by toll-free bridges.

This fine community is to be commended for its understanding attitude, for its acceptance of the fact that the bridge could not be freed until money had been collected from the traveling public with which to pay off the bonds issued to finance the building of this bridge. You have been very patient and cooperative. Your patience is today to be rewarded and you are to perpetually enjoy the advantages for which you have paid in tolls.

During the fall of 1930 and the year of 1931, the Ashland Toll Bridge was constructed by the Department of Highways at a total cost of $903,715.41.

This bridge crosses the Ohio River between Ashland, Kentucky, and Coal Grove, Ohio, and serves to connect U.S. Highway 23 in Kentucky with U.S. Highway 52 in Ohio, and replaced a ferry operated between these two points. It was opened for traffic on August 10, 1931, and has been operated as a toll bridge since that date.

To provide funds for the construction of this bridge, the Department of Highways on July 1, 1930, issued Bridge Revenue Bonds in the principal amount of $944,000, all of which have been retired with the exception of $10,000. This remaining $10,000 will be called for redemption on January 1, 1942, the next interest payment date. A sufficient amount of tolls now having been collected to redeem the outstanding bonds on January 1, 1942, makes it possible to free this bridge at this time.

The bonds issued for the purpose of financing this project do not actually mature until July 1, 1950. However, due to the fact that the citizens of the city of Ashland have been very patient, it has been possible to permit the original schedule of tolls adopted at the time the bridge was opened to traffic, to remain in effect to this time, which has made it possible to make this bridge toll free in a period of a little less than ten years, nine years ahead of schedule. The patience of these citizens has been well justified and they are now to be rewarded by having a free bridge.

This condition has not been true, however, with respect to many of the other toll bridge projects, in particular, Project No. 1, in that considerable pressure has been brought to bear on the department at various times to reduce the schedule of tolls on the intrastate bridges.

While this was permissible under the terms of the trust indenture securing the outstanding bonds, and while it has perhaps stimulated traffic over some of these bridges, the fact remains that by the reduction in tolls the date on which the bridges will be made toll free has been proportionately postponed.

It is estimated that the toll bridge operated by the Department of Highways between the cities of Newport, Kentucky, and Cincinnati, Ohio, will be made toll free on or about November 11 of this year. It is also estimated that the Covington-Cincinnati Toll Bridge will be made toll free on or about November 15, 1942, and that during the year of 1943 the Catlettsburg-Kenova Toll Bridge will be made toll free on or about January 1, the Paducah-Brookport Bridge on or about November 25, and the Calhoun-Rumsey Toll Bridge on or about December 1.

If the present schedule of tolls remains in effect, it is estimated that at the end of the calendar year of 1943 all [but five] of the toll bridges operated by the Department of Highways will have been made toll free.

The department has, during the past ten years, issued $17,280,000 Commonwealth of Kentucky Bridge Revenue Bonds for the purpose of financing its toll bridge program. Of this amount, it has redeemed $11,745,000, leaving $5,535,000 in bonds now outstanding.

Freeing of this bridge will stimulate business in this section, enhance the feeling of friendship which prevails in Kentucky for our neighbors across the river. It will stand as a monument to the vision of those who conceived this practical plan for raising money with which to pay for this vital link in the highway system.

We are building a greater mileage of high-type highways in Kentucky than at any previous time in our history. Inadequate bridges are being rebuilt to meet modern needs. And in contrast to many other states in the Union, Kentucky is not burdened with a heavy road-bond indebtedness which requires much of road revenues for debt service. Route U.S. 23, the Mayo Trail, we will build as soon as the right-of-way is obtained.

Few states in the Union are in better financial condition than Kentucky. Completion of a modernized highway system for our state is a pleasant prospect for the immediate future. The program has been given pronounced impetus under the wise administrative supervision of Commissioner of Highways Lyter Donaldson and an able staff headed by Chief Engineer Tom Cutler.[2]

So the freeing of this bridge today is striking evidence of the progress we are making in Kentucky as we strive steadily to eliminate toll bridges as rapidly as possible and build a system of highways that will be ample to meet the requirements of peace and enhance our safety in event of war.

One of the early advocates of the building of this bridge recently died. He was a highly useful Kentuckian. He had great faith in Eastern Kentucky and was one of the pioneers in promoting its development. He lived to see his vision of progress in Eastern Kentucky become a reality. I wish he might be here today to rejoice with us as tolls are lifted and this barrier between Kentucky and Ohio eliminated. We revere his memory. He will live always in the hearts of those who knew him. It is especially fitting that he be honored by naming this bridge for him. So, in honor of one worthy of the distinction, this bridge will henceforth be designated as the Ben Williamson[3] Memorial Bridge. Commissioner Donaldson entered executive order yesterday.[4]

I'm coming back in 1943 to free the Catlettsburg-Kenova bridge.

---

1. Associate Justice Fred Vinson of the United States Supreme Court also spoke. For an exchange of letters between Vinson and Johnson about the bridge ceremony, see Vinson Papers, University of Kentucky.

2. Thomas Henry Cutler (1882–1966), b. Fort Scott, Kansas. Missouri state highway employee, 1922–1936; chief engineer, 1936–1948, engineer-manager, 1948–1960, Department of Highways, Kentucky. Returned to Missouri. *Who's Who in Kentucky, 1936*, pp. 102-3, Louisville *Courier-Journal*, June 19, 1960, and Polly Gorman, secretary to Governor Bert Combs, June 19, 1978.

3. Ben Williamson (1864–1941), b. Pike County. Executive: coal, hardware, banking; United States senator, 1930–1931. *Who's Who in Kentucky, 1936*, p. 437.

4. The order directed the bridge department to design suitable name plates for the bridge. *Ashland Daily Independent*, August 6, 1941.

NEWPORT-CINCINNATI BRIDGE BECOMES TOLL FREE
Newport / November 11, 1941

IT is with genuine joy that I come to Newport to participate with the fine citizenship of Northern Kentucky and our neighbors of this area in freeing this toll bridge connecting Newport and Cincinnati.[1] We here participate in ceremonies which officially terminate the collecting of toll on this bridge.[2] But you of this region who have paid toll each time you have crossed this span since November 1935 are in reality the liberators of this bridge. The money you have paid for use of this bridge has purchased for you the privilege of henceforth using it without further payment for that convenience.

Surrounded as is Kentucky by navigable streams on the east, north, and west, the problem of spanning these rivers with adequate bridges has been difficult and costly. The acquisition and construction of essential bridges has been financed by issuing bonds against the bridges and charging users toll with which to raise money to retire those bonds.

This bridge was bought by the Kentucky Highway Department November 15, 1935. The transaction was negotiated by the Honorable J. Lyter Donaldson, then chairman of the Highway Commission, and the present commissioner of highways. The purchase price was $1.8 million; 3 percent bonds were sold to provide the purchase price. Maturity date of the bonds was July 1, 1950. However, it was specified that the bonds were redeemable prior to maturity at a designated price and date. All these bonds have been called for redemption with exception of $75,000 worth. Although enough money has been collected in toll to pay off the remaining $75,000 worth of bonds, this final payment cannot be made until January 1, 1942, which is the next interest payment date specified under the bond agreement.

When the Department of Highways took over operation of this bridge November 15, 1935, it adopted the same schedule of tolls as was in effect when it was operated under the supervision of the L. & N. Railway Company. This same schedule of tolls has remained in effect without alteration during the time it has been operated as a toll bridge.

Within the period from November 15, 1935, to November 1, 1941, during which time this span has been under state supervision, approximately 14.7 million vehicles have crossed it. That is an average of 6,750 vehicles daily. Average daily receipts have been approximately $960.

Now that you, the users of this bridge, have paid for it, you have liberated it from bondage. So it is a happy day that we celebrate. The toll taker's house is to be discarded as we commit this vital transportation link to unrestricted public service.

The citizenship of Northern Kentucky is to be commended for its understanding attitude. You have been very patient and cooperative. You have accepted the fact that the bridge could not be freed until money had been collected from the traveling public with which to retire the bonds issued to finance the purchase of this bridge. Your patience is today rewarded and you are to enjoy perpetually the advantages for which you have paid as you have contributed to the toll taker.

Of course, I hope that there will be no exasperating traffic jams on this free bridge as all of you try to cross on it at once. But in event such does occur, you should find a degree of satisfaction in keeping in mind that about one year hence the Covington-Cincinnati bridge can be freed of toll if the present rate of toll collection is maintained.

Freeing of this bridge will promote neighborliness between Kentucky and Ohio. It eliminates a barrier which militated against neighborliness. Freeing of this bridge will stimulate business in this area, enhance the feeling of friendship which prevails in Kentucky for our good neighbors across the river. Kentuckians are a hospitable people. Kentucky desires always to be a good neighbor. We are unhappy that our state can be approached from the north only by crossing toll bridges. But we are eliminating toll bridges on the borders of our state as rapidly as possible. Recently the toll bridge across the Ohio between Henderson, Kentucky, and Evansville, Indiana, was freed of toll. The bridge across the river connecting Ashland, Kentucky, and Coal Grove, Ohio, was freed a few months ago.

If present schedule of tolls remains in effect and collections are sustained at present volume, it should be possible in the year of 1943 to halt toll taking on three other important bridges. It is anticipated that the Catlettsburg-Kenova bridge can be freed about January 1, 1943, the Paducah-Brookport bridge about November 25, 1943, and the Calhoun-Rumsey bridge about December 1, 1943.

There has been a growing inclination to insist upon reduction of tolls charged at state-owned bridges. A reduction has been made in some instances. While lowered toll rate may stimulate traffic over some of the bridges, the fact remains that by reducing toll charges, the date on which the bridges may be made toll free has been proportionately postponed.

This unhappy world is again in the agonies of war — a war more destructive than any yet waged. The freedom for which we fought is again threatened. Liberty cannot be bought once and for always. Democracy must be bought again and again. Because that is true, this the twenty-third anniversary of the armistice has been designated by the president as the beginning of a national Civilian Defense Week. It has also been designated as the opening day of the annual Roll Call of the Red Cross. There is no more merciful organization than the Red Cross. Wherever tragedy brings human suffering, be it as a result of war or natural catastrophy, the ministrations of mercy through the Red Cross alleviates human suffering. Its record of service justifies enthusiastic support.

It is hoped that during Civilian Defense Week the citizenship may be awakened to an increased understanding of the danger which confronts this nation. It is hoped that the fire of patriotic fervor may be rekindled in the heart of every American. The time has passed within which it was proper to debate the course this nation should follow. We are irrevocably committed to the policy of doing everything we can to help lick Hitler. People in those nations which refused to take orders from their leaders are now taking orders from Hitler. We must quit fighting among ourselves and get ready to fight Hitler.

It is vitally important that the heart, the mind, and the will of America be mobilized in support of the program to which this nation is committed. We have only one choice. We must either follow the leadership of Lindbergh and Wheeler or line up behind Roosevelt and Cordell Hull.[3] Every individual who lives beneath the protection of the Stars and Stripes should love America or leave it.

During Civilian Defense Week, I hope the hearts of Kentucky's people will be quickened with a fierce zeal for unity. It is important that our people be enthusiastically united behind the president in this crucial hour. It is important that there be developed a virile, vigorous public opinion that will by its disapproval stop strikes in the defense industries. Many of your sons and brothers are in training camps, preparing to preserve our liberties. They are being paid $21 a month. They need guns and tanks, airplanes, and artillery. No industry producing these vital weapons should be closed down because of labor disputes. We must not permit strikes to sabotage the safety of America.

I hope it will not be necessary for the army, which we are training, to cross a submarine-infested ocean to fight on foreign soil. But we would be stupid indeed did we not prepare for the day when such may be necessary.

A moonshiner went into a hardware store in Eastern Kentucky and said he wanted to buy a rifle. As he examined the guns, he became fascinated with a beautiful high-powered gun. It could shoot a mile with great accuracy. As he caressed the gun the moonshiner soliliquized, "It costs $129. That's a lot of money. And I may never need it. But there's one thing certain. If I do need it and I ain't got it, I'll never need it again." That expresses the whole philosophy of national defense.

Every citizen of this great state and nation must realize the necessity of enthusiastic, united effort to crush Hitler and prevent the enslaving of free men. We must be prepared to make great sacrifice in order to prevent the destruction of our freedom.[4]

---

1. The history of the construction of this bridge discloses a long fight by Newport and Cincinnati interests from 1830 to 1872 before the bridge was completed. A contract was finally awarded for construction in 1868. The initial cost was $2.9 million but because of changes, the total cost was $3,250,792. Congress consented to the erection of a bridge in 1869 and provided that it was to be used as a post road for the transmission of United States mails. However, an act of Congress, approved March 1871 provided that it should be unlawful for the bridge company to proceed with the erection of the bridge it was then constructing unless the bridge should be constructed as prescribed in that act. The bridge had to have a wider span and higher elevations. Work was suspended and new plans were approved by the secretary of war in August 1871. The first train crossed the bridge in 1872. In 1893 and again in 1895, the secretary of war approved plans for rebuilding and widening the bridge to meet demands for increased traffic. The rebuilding was completed in 1937 by the Pennsylvania Railroad Company. *Kentucky Post*, November 11, 1941.

2. On November 20, 1941, the Cincinnati City Council explored the possibility of charging a toll at the recently freed bridge to raise funds with which to break a resultant traffic bottleneck. Assistant Attorney General A. E. Funk said he believed Cincinnati would need permission of both the War Department and the federal Bureau of Public Roads to impose tolls on the Kentucky-owned bridge. He said Kentucky had received authorization from the War Department to buy the bridge from the L. & N. Railroad and permission from the Bureau of Public Roads to collect tolls and subsequently to free the span. Louisville *Courier-Journal*, November 20, 1941.

3. Charles Augustus Lindbergh (1902–1974), b. Detroit, Michigan. Famous aviator; first solo flight across the Atlantic Ocean; spokesman for neutrality before United States entry into World War II. *Who Was Who in America, 1974-1976* (Chicago, 1976), 6:248.

Burton Kendall Wheeler (1882–1975), b. Hudson, Massachusetts. Attorney. United States senator, Montana, 1923–1947; unsuccessful candidate for vice president of the United States, Progressive party, 1924; isolationist prior to United States entry into World War II. Ibid., p. 433.

Cordell Hull (1871–1955), b. Overton County, Tennessee. United States representative, 1907–1921, 1923–1931; United States senator, 1931–1933; secretary of state, 1933-1944. *Who Was Who in American Politics*, p. 327.

4. The speech has been edited. See speech from July 4, 1941, in the World War II section.

PADUCAH AIRPORT DEDICATION
Paducah / November 8, 1942

IT is with genuine joy that I come today to participate with the progressive and civic-minded citizenship of Paducah in dedicating to public service this splendid, modern airport.[1] We celebrate this noteworthy event against a backdrop of war. The impelling necessity for making adequate provision for the national defense gave impetus to the construction of this, an airport which will facilitate air transportation so as to meet the needs of a nation at war. It will be just as important as an auxiliary of air transportation when peace comes again to the world.

War is hideous, brutal, and destructive. Seldom is there born of war anything that is constructive, anything that contributes to human happiness and progress. But aviation has been given an impetus by war that has accelerated its development. When Schickelgruber [Hitler] started his armies on the march, smashing nation after nation, swarms of airplanes, piloted by skillful flyers, delivered a punch from the air that could not be resisted. The ingenuity of the major nations was immediately concentrated on the task of designing the fastest, sturdiest planes possible. The industrial genius of the united nations[2] has been concentrated upon building destructive bomber and fighter planes in huge quantities. With major emphasis placed on aviation as a matter of military necessity, adequate airports in increased number became increasingly important. The result is that more airports have been built since the war began than then existed on this continent.

Paducah is strategically located for a major airport. The vision of your civic leaders, the united enthusiasm of the community properly placed before responsible authorities the wisdom of building an airport in Paducah. As to the nature of the use to which it will be placed, I dare not hazard a prediction. But the happy thing is that it is here; that it has been designed with an eye to the future. It will serve a useful purpose during the war. And after the war its presence here will assure Paducah an emphasized spot on the air maps of the nation. You are fortunate that in the era of expanding air transportation that is to follow the war, Paducah is prepared to participate in the advantages which will come from this spectacular phase of transportation.

Aviation's development has been both amazing and recent. A man named Sam Matlack of Louisville is said to probably have been the first Kentuckian to fly an airplane in Kentucky. The flights were made near Lexington. Glenn Curtiss, one of the pioneers in aviation, flew a pusher type plane at Churchill Downs, Louisville, June 18, 1910. Lincoln Beachey and Ruth Law flew from the State Fair Grounds, Louisville, in the summer of 1913. Miss Law was the first woman pilot to fly a plane in Kentucky. The first plane landed at Bowman Field, Louisville, in 1919. In January 1923 the Aero Club of Kentucky was organized and in August of that year Bowman Field was dedicated. Passenger service was started in 1924 by the Yellow-Taxi Air Line Company. Airmail service between Louisville and Cleveland was started August 1, 1928. Passenger service was added in June 1929. This series of dates and events indicates development of interest in and public acceptance of aviation as an agency of transportation. A small group of aviation enthusiasts sought constantly to awaken that interest and stimulate progress in aviation. They performed an important pioneer service. Every new, modern airport that is brought into the air transportation system is to a degree a tribute to the vision and enthusiasm of those who refused to become discouraged as they tried constantly to obtain a wide public acceptance of aviation as an agency of advancement.[3]

In 1940 the Aero Club of Kentucky sought my assistance as governor in enactment of legislation that would create the Kentucky Aeronautics Commission. The legislation was passed. Representative Henry Ward of McCracken sponsored the bill in the House and Senator Keenon in the Senate. Of the original Aeronautics Commission appointed by me, two are now in the air service. One of those was R. W. DaVania of Paducah who is now in the Ferry Command of the Air Force. The other is Al Near of Louisville who was chairman of the first commission. He is now a major with the Army Air Corps on duty in England. To replace these men, I designated E. J. Paxton, Jr., of Paducah and Roger Schupp, manager of Bowman Field. Charles Gartrell of Ashland is now chairman of the commission, Harry Bullock of Lexington is vice chairman, and R. E. Schupp, secretary. Other members are Addison Lee of Louisville and H. D. Palmore of Frankfort. At the 1942 session of the Kentucky legislature, I included in the budget bill submitted to the legislature an appropriation of $7,000 a year for the Aeronautics Commission which was approved by the General Assembly. This was the first appropriation of money from the state treasury for the purpose of promoting the progress of aviation in the state.[4]

When the war created the need for a greatly expanded air service, it was realized that a chain of airports must be built in Kentucky. As result of the aid of Senator Barkley, Senator Chandler, and the Kentucky members of the House of Representatives, money was provided for the construction of modern, hard surface runway airports at Paducah, Bowling Green, and Lexington. Work is just being started on an airport in Boone County, just across the Ohio River from Cincinnati, which will be one of the major airports of the nation. In the 1942 session of the legislature, we enacted legislation that permits counties to join with cities to establish and maintain airports and authorizes cities of the second, third, fourth or fifth class to establish and maintain airports.

The most aviation-minded enthusiast cannot with accuracy foresee the important role which aviation will probably play in our national transportation system after we have conquered the Axis powers and restored peace to the world. That role is certain to be extensive and far reaching in its effect. Paducah and Kentucky will be well prepared to participate in the advantages which come with an ever expanding aviation in which safety and speed of planes will steadily increase as inventive ingenuity concentrates upon peace time aviation just as it has upon aviation for war's grim necessity. So there is abundant reason for rejoicing in western Kentucky today as we dedicate to public service this magnificent airport which in years to come will be widely used by this western region of the state in the transportation of passengers and freight by huge skyliners and cargo planes. It is an event of greater significance than any of us today can comprehend. Generations yet unborn will be the beneficiaries of this noteworthy development.[5]

---

1. The outdoor dedication and air show were canceled due to weather conditions. The governor arrived late for the banquet and did not give his speech. His flight was canceled and he traveled by car.

2. The reference is to the allied united nations and not to the United Nations Organization established at the end of World War II.

3. According to Edward Peck, Jeffersonville, Indiana, the first powered flight in Kentucky was made by Matthew Bacon Sellers in Carter County in December 1908. Peck is writing a biography of Sellers. No information about Sam Matlack was found.

Glenn Hammond Curtiss (1878–1930), b. Hammondsport, New York. Inventor, pioneer aviator. *Who Was Who in America, 1897-1942,* 1:287.

Lincoln Beachey (1887–1915), b. San Francisco, California. Killed while exhibition flying. D. A. Pisano, reference librarian, National Air and Space Museum, Smithsonian Institution, August 16, 1978.

Ruth Law (Mrs. Charles A. Oliver), (1887–), b. Lynn, Massachusetts. Resides in San Francisco. Fifth licensed woman pilot in the United States. D. A. Pisano, reference librarian, National Air and Space Museum, Smithsonian Institution, August 16, 1978.

4. Henry T. Ward (1909–), b. New Hope. Resides in Howey-in-the-Hills, Florida. State representative, 1934–1943; majority leader, 1940, 1942; state senator, 1946–1948; commissioner of conservation, 1948–1955; *Paducah Sun-Democrat,* editorial staff, 1928–1948; publisher, 1968–1969, commissioner of highways, 1960–1966; Democratic nominee for governor, 1967; president, Kentucky Independent College Foundation, 1969–1974. Letter, Henry Ward, August 14, 1978.

Rodman W. Keenon (1883–1966), b. Mercer County. Attorney; state senator, 1940–1944; clerk, Court of Appeals. *Kentucky Directory, 1942-1943*, compiled by Frank K. Kavanaugh (Frankfort, Ky., 1942), pp. 166-67, and Centre College Alumni Records.

R. W. DaVania (1908–), b. Mayfield. Served in Europe, North Africa, and China, World War II. Group commander, 61st Troop Carrier group, Berlin Airlift. Retired from the United States Air Force, colonel, 1965. Letter, R. W. DaVania, August 2, 1978.

Albert H. Near (1897–1951), b. Petoskey, Michigan. Chairman, first Aeronautics Commission; director of airports, Louisville and Jefferson County; served World War I and World War II, lieutenant colonel at end of World War II. Telephone interview, Mrs. A. H. Near, June 30, 1978.

E. J. Paxton, Jr. (1912–), b. Paducah. Paducah-McCracken County airport board, 1941–1977 (chairman, 1952–1977). *Paducah Sun-Democrat*, 1932–1977, editor, 1961–1977. United States Office of War Information, South West Pacific, 1943–1945. Letter, E. J. Paxton, Jr., July 13, 1978.

Roger E. Schupp (1888–1968), b. Louisville. Secretary, Louisville park board; Kentucky Aeronautics Commission, 1928; secretary, Louisville-Jefferson County air board. Retired, 1948. *Who's Who in Kentucky, 1936*, p. 357, and telephone interview, Orville Schupp, son, Frankfort, September 29, 1978.

Charles Henry Gartrell (1914–), b. Boyd County. Stockbroker. Commissioner and chairman, Kentucky Aeronautics Commission until 1942; first director of aeronautics, 1945–1947; naval aviator, test pilot, 1943. *Who's Who in Kentucky, 1955* (Hopkinsville, 1955), pp. 127-28, and telephone interview, C. H. Gartrell, July 21, 1978.

Harry Elmer Bullock (1883–1948), b. Whitley County. Coal executive; vice chairman and chairman, Kentucky Aeronautics Commission. Telephone interview, Paul Reed, son-in-law, July 3, 1978.

Addison W. Lee (1885–1949), b. Louisville. Utility executive; chairman, Louisville-Jefferson County air board, 1927–1949. Telephone interview, Addison Lee, son, June 30, 1978.

H. D. Palmore (1886–1961), b. Persimmon, Monroe County. Commissioner of highways, 1944–1947; member, board of trustees, University of Kentucky, 1942; businessman, Kentucky Pipe Company, Frankfort. Interview, Jack Palmore, nephew, Richmond, July 17, 1978.

5. In July 1941 Johnson spoke at the dedication of the Lexington airport site, calling it a development of importance for Central Kentucky's peacetime commerce and for its defense in time of war. *State Journal*, August 1, 1941. In May 1943 he spoke at the ground-breaking ceremonies for the Kenton County airport. *Kentucky Post*, May 4, 1943.

EXECUTIVE ORDER: COVINGTON-CINCINNATI TOLL BRIDGE
Frankfort / November 12, 1942

THE Attorney General of the Commonwealth of Kentucky having on November 7, 1942, filed a petition in equity in the Franklin Circuit Court, styled, Commonwealth of Kentucky, on relation of Hubert Meredith as Attorney General of the Commonwealth of Kentucky, Plaintiff, versus J. Lyter Donaldson, as Commissioner of Highways of the Commonwealth of Kentucky Defendant, and the Governor of the Commonwealth deeming it necessary, expedient and proper to employ special counsel for the proper defense of said suit,[1]

Now, Therefore, pursuant to the said determination by the Governor, the attached contract between the Commonwealth of Kentucky and the law firm of Smith and Leary[2] has been entered into and hereby is approved by the Governor of the Commonwealth of Kentucky, and a copy of said contract shall remain upon file in the office of the Secretary of State.

Contract:

This contract made and entered into this 12th day of November, 1942, by and between the Commonwealth of Kentucky, acting by and through the Governor of the Commonwealth of Kentucky, hereinafter referred to as the party of the first part, and Smith & Leary, a partnership and law firm, of Frankfort, Kentucky, hereinafter referred to as parties of the second part,

WITNESSETH: THAT, WHEREAS, the Attorney General of Kentucky, on or about November 7, 1942, filed a petition in equity in the Franklin Circuit Court, No. 39149, on the docket of said Court, styled, Commonwealth of Kentucky, on relation of Hubert Meredith as Attorney General of the Commonwealth of Kentucky versus J. Lyter Donaldson, as Commissioner of Highways of the Commonwealth of Kentucky; and

WHEREAS, the Governor of the Commonwealth of Kentucky is specifically authorized and empowered by law to employ such skilled or professional services which, in his judgment, may be necessary, expedient, or proper to protect the interests of the Commonwealth; and

WHEREAS the Governor of the Commonwealth does deem the defense of the aforesaid suit to be important, expedient, and proper; and

WHEREAS the Department of Highways and J. Lyter Donaldson, Commissioner of Highways, are represented in legal matters by an Assistant Attorney General of the Commonwealth of Kentucky;[3] and

WHEREAS the foregoing suit presents a situation whereby the Attorney General of Kentucky as relator for the Commonwealth of Kentucky is the plaintiff in said suit and his Assistant assigned to the Department of Highways would be called upon to represent the Department of Highways and J. Lyter Donaldson, Commissioner of Highways; and

WHEREAS the Governor of the Commonwealth deems it important, expedient, and proper to employ other counsel to represent the Department of Highways and J. Lyter Donaldson, Commissioner of Highways, in said suit;

NOW, THEREFORE, in consideration of the foregoing and the mutual terms and considerations hereinafter set forth, it is agreed by and between the parties hereto as follows, to-wit:

I. The first party hereby does employ the second parties as special counsel to represent the Department of Highways, and J. Lyter Donaldson, Commissioner of Highways, in the above mentioned suit only. Second parties hereby are employed to represent the Department of Highways and J. Lyter Donaldson, Commissioner of Highways, in the Franklin Circuit Court and in any other court to which said case may be taken on appeal by either party.

II. First party agrees to pay the second parties the sum of Two Thousand Five Hundred Dollars ($2,500.00) for the aforesaid services, payable as follows, to-wit: One Thousand, Two Hundred Fifty Dollars ($1,250.00) on December 15, 1942, and the balance of One Thousand Two Hundred Fifty Dollars (1,250.00) when the aforesaid case is finally decided by the Court of Appeals of Kentucky; or if no appeal be taken to the Court of Appeals, when the time of such an appeal shall have expired; but if no appeal be taken to the Court of Appeals nor any final order or judgment is entered in said case in the Franklin Circuit Court on or before December 15, 1943, said balance of One Thousand Two Hundred Fifty Dollars ($1,250.00) shall be paid on December 15, 1943.

III. Second parties have agreed to and hereby do accept said employment for the consideration aforesaid and agree to represent the aforesaid defendants, J. Lyter Donaldson, Commissioner of Highways, and the Department of Highways in said litigation in the Franklin Circuit Court; and if the judgment of the Franklin Circuit Court is appealed to the Court of Appeals of Kentucky or to any other court whatever to represent the said J. Lyter Donaldson, Commissioner of Highways, and the Department of Highways until said suit is finally adjudicated.[4]

---

1. Donaldson had announced that toll payments would be stopped December 1, 1942. Meredith filed suit seeking to have the bridge freed immediately because

more than $53,000 in excess of the amount required to free the bridge had been collected. *State Journal,* November 14, 1942.

2. Smith and Leary were paid $3,000 for defending Johnson and other administrators in Meredith's suit attacking the constitutionality of a legislative act appropriating $11,270,000 and an act authorizing various departments to employ their own lawyers. The firm defended the governor and other administrators without fee in such Meredith-launched cases as two out-of-state travel suits, judges' pensions, the attack on state employees receiving salaries in excess of $5,000 a year, and others. *State Journal,* November 14, 1942. For more information, see speech from June 17, 1942, in the State Administration section.

3. Alvarado Erwin Funk (1895–1954), b. Bullitt County. Assistant attorney general, 1936–1944. *Kentucky Directory, 1948,* compiled by Frank K. Kavanaugh (Frankfort, Ky., 1948), p. 132, and letter, A. E. Funk, Jr., June 5, 1978.

4. Judge Ardery of the Franklin Circuit Court rejected Meredith's suit on November 16, 1942. *Lexington Herald,* November 17, 1942. Meredith petitioned the Court of Appeals which ruled on November 27 that tolls cannot be collected on a bridge after enough money has been collected to pay for it. *Commonwealth ex rel. Meredith, Atty. Gen.* v. *Donaldson,* 292 Ky. 267, 166 S. W. 2d 303 (1942). Donaldson announced that tolls had ceased shortly after the court's decision was announced. Louisville *Courier-Journal,* November 30, 1942. On December 3, 1942, Meredith petitioned Franklin Circuit Court to enjoin the payment of the $2,500 fee for Smith and Leary. *Lexington Herald,* December 4, 1942. The court did not issue the injunction. Smith and Leary were paid. Telephone interview, J. J. Leary, October 30, 1978.

On February 17, 1943, the governor spoke at a Chamber of Commerce banquet, Covington, held to express appreciation for the freeing of this bridge. *Kentucky Post* and *Lexington Herald,* February 18, 1943.

RICHARD G. WILLIAMS APPOINTED HIGHWAY COMMISSIONER
Frankfort / April 1, 1943

"A FEW days ago, I was puzzled to receive the resignation of Lyter Donaldson.[1] But the matter cleared up when I read the morning newspapers. There now appears to have been a substantial reason for the course he is taking . . . . He has our best wishes for his success. I believe you will agree that your governor was inspired when he selected Dick Williams[2] as a worthy successor to Mr. Donaldson."

The governor digressed briefly to comment on what he termed hindrance to his administration. "It is the fate of whoever is governor to be beset with individuals more concerned with hindering than helping. I am no exception to that rule. There are those who seek studiously to hinder, but in fairness I must say there are those who seek to help such as, for example, those of you in this group before me."

He praised the administration of Donaldson since his appointment as commissioner of highways in January 1940 despite drastic curtailment of road building on account of war. He concluded, "It is a source of bitter disappointment that the program agreed upon early in 1940 has been frustrated to a degree."[3]

---

1. Donaldson resigned to seek the Democratic nomination for governor.

2. Richard G. Williams (1889–1981), b. Mount Vernon. Resided in Somerset. Businessman and banker; vice-president and honorary chairman, bank board, Somerset. Telephone interview, R. G. Williams, July 3, 1978, and Louisville *Courier-Journal*, July 24, 1981.

On November 17, 1942, R. G. Williams succeeded his brother, the late Cecil T. Williams, as rural highway commissioner. Cecil T. Williams (d. October 18, 1942) became head of the Rural Highway Division in 1936. *State Journal*, November 18, 1942.

3. The 1940 program called for completion of trunk highways as its primary objective. It was founded on the belief that added gasoline tax revenue from a network of high-type trunk highways soon would finance a supplementary program for improvement of feeder highways. Louisville *Courier-Journal*, April 2, 1943.

KIWANIS TRAIL AT CUMBERLAND FALLS
Corbin / July 10, 1943

GOVERNOR JOHNSON spoke[1] on the progress of the government of Kentucky during the sixteen years intervening between the time the first auto trip was made to Cumberland Falls from Corbin and the naming of the modern highway there now, "The Kiwanis Trail."

He said that the progress of Kentucky depends upon the maintenance of the present financial stability of the state. With real personal pride he will be the first governor of the Commonwealth to turn the office over to his successor "free of debt." "Under the old system of operation when Kentucky paid her accounts with cold vouchers, the teachers and other holders of these vouchers were forced to shave their accounts from 5 to 15 percent in order to get them cashed. Now, Kentucky's credit is restored. The state is saving a million dollars a year in interest which it had been forced to spend under the old system, and this money is available for educational purposes, for rehabilitation of state institutions, and for increased support of the aged in the state.

Expressing deep regret over the fact that this nation should be embroiled in deadly war, he explained that his administration had been forced to drop temporarily its comprehensive plans for development of the state's highway system. But $1,329,000 had been spent on U.S. 25-E from Corbin to the Tennessee line, and $343,000 on the western branch of U.S. 25 from here to Jellico via Williamsburg. The plans for a great park-to-park highway from Mammouth Cave via Cumberland Falls to Cumberland Gap had been forced to wait on the war.

"The big job of the moment is to win the war. Already 200,000 of the finest of our young men are in the services of the nation at all fronts in the world. This is more than double the 84,000 who answered the call to colors in the last World War. The imposing problem at the moment is one of exerting the full force of the army on the home front for the support of the men on the battlefront."

He appealed to Kentuckians everywhere to bear with the inconveniences of wartime regulations in order that the great privileges of this people might not be permanently lost.[2]

---

1. The governor was introduced by Robert A. Blair of Corbin. Following the Kiwanis Club luncheon, Malcolm Shull, governor of the Kentucky-Tennessee District of Kiwanis International, unveiled the "Kiwanis Trail" highway sign. Governor Johnson made a second address at the site. Cumberland Falls Preservation Association does not have a copy of this speech. Letter, Robert A. Blair, chairman of the board, First National Bank and Trust Company of Corbin, March 22, 1977.

2. Material pertaining to old age assistance has been deleted.

PADUCAH-BROOKPORT BRIDGE BECOMES TOLL FREE

Paducah / November 24, 1943

GOVERNOR JOHNSON, attending the sixth free bridge[1] ceremony since his inauguration, said that the people should congratulate the citizens of the community, the people of Kentucky—the users of the bridge—for their patience and tolerance in paying tolls over a period of years, thereby making possible the revenue to pay off the bridge.

"It is particularly fitting that the span between our state and southern Illinois should bear the name of a Kentuckian who has brought such great distinction to Kentucky—Irvin S. Cobb.

"When fire crippled passage on the bridge last spring, we were afraid sufficient revenue would not come in so that we might pay off the debt and have this ceremony before December. But we made it, and we are grateful to have the privilege of participating in one of the red letter days of Paducah and Western Kentucky.

"In no other state in the Union are there so many navigable rivers and streams that have been, and must be spanned, but we are rapidly approaching the day when the rivers and streams that have been separating Kentucky from other states will be spanned and the people will be the ones who have made this possible."

In concluding, he expressed the hope that new legislators and the new administration will enact legislation to free Kentucky's intrastate toll bridges at the earliest possible date.[2]

---

1. Johnson spoke on July 15, 1943, at the toll-freeing ceremony for the Catlettsburg-Kenova bridge, the fifth interstate bridge freed from tolls during his term. *Ashland Daily Independent*, July 16, 1943.

2. On October 15, 1943, Massac County, Illinois, authorities renewed their annual threat to Kentucky to sell the Illinois end of the state-owned toll bridge for nonpayment of taxes amounting to $29,000. Kentucky refused to pay taxes on this or any other publicly owned bridge that crosses the Ohio river into other states. *Kentucky Post*, October 15, 1943.

CALHOUN-RUMSEY BRIDGE ACROSS THE GREEN RIVER
Frankfort / November 27, 1943

INDICATING abandonment of his plan to free the Calhoun-Rumsey Green River bridge because of opposition by Attorney General Meredith, Governor Johnson charged the attorney general changed his mind after having approved the project.[1]

The governor wrote Finance Commissioner Bennett that the attorney general gave Senator Lee Gibson,[2] Owensboro, and a McLean County group an oral opinion that taking $8,000 from the general emergency account to pay off the last bonds and stop toll collections on the bridge by December 1 would be "legal and proper."

He explained that if the final bonds are not retired by January 1, they cannot be paid off and interest ended until next July 1 and said the project appeared to be a good business deal.[3] Then, referring to Meredith's stand, he added: "I read in the newspapers that he has changed his mind now. In view of this development, it appears to be unwise that the transaction be completed."[4]

---

1. Meredith denied the charge. He challenged the bridge project and other fund transfers after concluding that state law prevents use of state funds to pay off bridge bonds. Louisville *Courier-Journal*, November 28, 1943. Other transfers were $200,000 for supplementing old age, dependent children, and needy blind aid; $3,000 for the state Civil Defense Council; and $275,430 to pay architects' fees for rehabilitating penal and mental institutions. Charging Johnson with "abuse of his discretion," Meredith wrote Treasurer Shannon and Finance Commissioner Bennett that they "should have a court judgment in each of these orders before transferring or laying out money under them, because you might otherwise be liable on your official bonds." Louisville *Courier-Journal*, November 27, 1943.
2. Lee Gibson (1868–1967), b. McLean County. McLean County attorney, 1892; state senator, 1932–1944. *Owensboro Messenger and Inquirer*, September 18, 1967.
3. Executive Order, November 26, 1943, transferred $8,000 to the Department of Highway Sinking Fund, Project Number 11, to amortize the final bonds.
4. The governor said later that but for his term ending December 7, he would fight the cases through and carry out the transfers.

AGRICULTURE

KENTUCKY FARM BUREAU FEDERATION
Louisville / January 11, 1940

"FARMERS are the finest citizens, individually, but it is often difficult to get concerted action and cooperation. It requires much intelligence to be a good farmer. There is a difference of opinion among farmers on farming. The best farmers are in the Farm Bureau. There are critics of the farm program and its national administration."

Turning to the national debt, Governor Johnson said, "Your part of the debt can now be paid with 1,000 pounds of burley—and in 1931 it took 3,000 pounds.

"Unity is necessary to prevent scuttling the farm program. There ought to be a stampede to join the Farm Bureau—25,000 farmers have come a long distance. There are too many 'know it all' farmers. A farmer said he knew more about it than the farm agent—but he had worn out three farms."

He expressed belief that "the excellent legislation promulgated by the Farm Bureau" would be approved by the state legislature.

In discussing farm to market roads, he said, "Rural highway expenditures had amounted to $2 million.

"We have adequate rural schools and free school books. We should cooperate with school consolidation and remember these things cost money.

"Although it is unwise to be against all taxes, Kentucky farmers are paying less state tax than ever before. It is five cents real estate, and the sales tax exempts farm-used gasoline.[1]

"The state debt has been cut to $10.7 million and the interest rate cut from 5 to 3 percent. Charitable and penal institutions are receiving attention. The Farm Bureau 4-H program develops farm leadership; it is important first to be good followers.

"Kentucky is primarily an agricultural state. I oppose any and *all* efforts to increase taxes on land. High land taxes affect not only the landowner but make it impossible for the tenant and farm laborer to acquire their own farms and homes. I am in accord with the farm program of the national administration, seeking parity prices for farm commodities.

"Rural electrification is revolutionizing living conditions on Kentucky farms. Twenty-two rural electrification cooperative associations have been organized to build 6,500 miles of line, to serve nearly 30,000 rural customers. We shall do our part as a state in encouraging the expansion of this program to a maximum number of farm homes at reasonable rates. I shall appoint a public service commission not only friendly to this movement but one whose personnel is dedicated to serve the best."

---

1. On February 26, 1940, the governor said he still favored exemption of farm-used gasoline from the five cents a gallon tax. "I made the promise during my campaign; I restated it before the legislature and I'm still in favor of it." In opposing a motion to force the bill authorizing the exemption out of committee, Joe E. Robinson, Democratic floor leader, told the House that Johnson had promised during his gubernatorial campaign "under pressure" of the Kentucky Farm Bureau Federation to support the proposal and asked the legislature, "Why should we carry out a promise made under such circumstances?" The move to force out the bill failed 40-49. Ben Kilgore, Farm Bureau executive secretary, denied the Farm Bureau had exerted pressure and called on the governor to state whether he had been so urged. Louisville *Courier-Journal*, February 27, 1940.

THOROUGHBRED CLUB OF AMERICA
Lexington / October 10, 1940

AT the present time, racing in Kentucky seems not only to be upon its highest plane, as evidenced by the splendid racing at Keeneland and by the Kentucky Derby and other great events, but also by the fact that racing enjoys popular support and public favor as it has never done before in the long history of racing in this state.

Kentucky is indeed fortunate in the beauty of her scenes, in the richness of her soil, and in the conditions that make possible the breeding of the fleetest of thoroughbreds. Even these advantages, however, would not bring supremacy without the added contributions of warmhearted and generous men, of skilled managers and owners of vision, and of real sportsmen and breeders who have studied the mysteries of bloodlines and pedigrees.

Beautiful Calumet Farm on U. S. 60 between Lexington and Versailles which leads to Keeneland is typical of the most magnificent of the bluegrass thoroughbred estates. Here the best planning of which man is capable has combined with the artistry of nature to fashion a paradise. Kentucky is indeed fortunate as is no other state in the Union in the horse farms which are open to the public, a most generous and hospitable favor of the owners. Official and public gratitude and appreciation of this gracious contribution to the Commonwealth seldom is expressed in any formal or authoritative way.

While I confess that I know little about thoroughbred horses, I do know a thoroughbred gentleman when I meet one. And it is because he is a thoroughbred gentleman and sportsman that I have such an exalted esteem for Mr. Wright.[1]

His high conception of sportsmanship, his understanding of the problems of the thoroughbred industry, his success as a breeder of thoroughbred horses have won for him recognition as an authority in this interesting phase of Kentucky activity. His opinions are respected because he is recognized as a superior citizen and a turfman who unselfishly endeavors to promote a sport that is as indigenous to Kentucky as is the bluegrass.

You have exercised good judgment in designating Mr. Wright for this deserved distinction. None you have chosen for this coveted honor more richly merits your homage. In honoring him, you reflect credit upon yourselves and the thoroughbred industry. You enhance the prestige of a sportsman whom the public has long respected and admired as a result of his extended association with racing.

As you make these annual awards to such men as Mr. Wright, Senator Camden, Desha Breckinridge, Mr. Widener,[2] and others of the small, select company who have been the recipients of this unique distinction, you raise an elevated standard of sportsmanship. You by this action announce to the public that it is this type of superior American who is exerting the greatest influence on racing. You declare to all connected with the thoroughbred industry that you admire and revere men who are thoroughbreds. You dignify the annual award, invest it with tradition. The effect of that will be to make this scroll and trophy highly coveted.

I am happy to see one so worthy as Mr. Wright admitted to the select coterie of sportsmen who have been the recipients of this award. I am sure that this occasion will always be to him a cherished memory.

---

1. Warren Wright (1875–1950), b. Springfield, Ohio. Corporation president. Started Calumet Farm in 1931; owner of Whirlaway, 1941 winner, Kentucky Derby. *Who Was Who in America, 1951–1960,* 3:943.

2. Johnson Newlon Camden (1865–1942), b. Parkersburg, West Virginia. Resided Paris, Kentucky. Chairman, Kentucky State Racing Commission; United States senator, 1914–1915. *Biographical Directory of the American Congress, 1774–1971,* p. 695.

Desha Breckinridge (1867–1935), b. Lexington. Democrat. Editor, *Lexington Herald.* Opponent of repeal of pari-mutuel. *Who Was Who in America, 1897–1942,* 1:134.

Peter A. B. Widener II (1895–1948), b. Longbranch, New Jersey. Owner, Elmendorf Farm, Lexington. Director, Belmont Park and Hialeah race tracks. Louisville *Courier-Journal,* April 21, 1948, and letter, Thoroughbred Club of America, May 2, 1978.

SECOND ANNUAL TOBACCO FESTIVAL
Shelbyville / November 1, 1940

THE legislature cooperated with my recommendation and appropriated $7,500 a year to start conducting a research program in an effort to find new uses for tobacco.[1]

Three chemists are giving their full time to the experiments. The activity is being directed by Professor J. S. McHargue,[2] head of the Department of Chemistry, Kentucky Agricultural Experiment Station.

Thus far tobacco has been grown in Kentucky primarily for the purpose of smoking, chewing, and as snuff. Any other uses made of tobacco have been more or less incidental to the chief purpose for which the crop is grown.

However, tobacco contains a number of constituents, only one of which, nicotine, has been shown to be of commercial value. There is considerable evidence which indicates that low grades of tobacco contain other important ingredients in addition to nicotine.

Research investigations have been under way in the Department of Chemistry of the Kentucky Agricultural Experiment Station since July 1, 1940, to ascertain the economical importance of ingredients contained in low grade tobacco other than nicotine.[3]

Five million pounds of pure nicotine will make approximately 12.5 million pounds of Black Leaf-40. This product retails at forty cents an ounce. Therefore, 100 pounds of burley tobacco containing 2.5 percent of nicotine would have a potential value of $40.00 for making Black Leaf-40. However, when Black Leaf-40 is marketed in a five-pound package, the potential value of the same amount of tobacco would be about $8.75.

The nicotine content of dark tobacco ranges from about 3 to 7 percent and will average about 5 percent. Consequently, 100 pounds of dark tobacco will produce five pounds of nicotine, whereas an equal weight of burley tobacco yields only 2.25 pounds of nicotine. Assuming the yield of 800 pounds of dark tobacco per acre, it would have the maximum potential value of $640 when used for making nicotine and retailed in the smallest package of Black Leaf-40.

Accordingly, I am of the opinion that the economic production and utilization of tobacco, which is an important crop in agriculture, affords a very promising field for further chemical research. We would expect the results of such research to increase the production and consumption of nicotine from five to ten times the amount used at this time. This increase in the production of nicotine would remove from the market approximately 100 million to 500 million pounds of cheap and unmarketable grades of tobacco. There is also a possibility of producing and marketing several very useful and valuable medicinal compounds from tobacco which could be sold at a price considerably less than the price at which they are quoted at the present time. Further chemical research on tobacco would probably result in revealing a considerable number of new and useful products to be synthesized from the organic constituents contained in tobacco.

Some of the ingredients which have economical possibilities include:

1. Chlorophyll—Range of chlorophyll found: minimum 1.28 percent, maximum found 3.64 percent, average for sixty-one samples 1.04 percent. The poorest grades of tobacco contained the largest amount of chlorophyll. Green or unripe tobacco contains approximately 10 percent of chlorophyll. The retail price of crude chlorophyll is $4.00 per pound; for highly purified chlorophyll the retail price is fifty cents per gram or $227 per pound. Chlorophyll is used commercially for coloring foods, including gelatin, candies, cakes, and is also used in medicinal and vitamin preparations.

2. Furfural—Sixty-one samples of tobacco gave an average of 3.5 percent furfural. The stems and stalks of tobacco contain approximately 5 percent of furfural. Furfural is used in the manufacture of plastics and is quoted at about seventy-five cents per pound.

3. Nicotine—Sixty-one samples ranged from 2.66 percent to 7.32 percent, average 4.72 percent nicotine. Nicotine in a pure form is quoted at $4.50 per pound. Nicotine can be converted into nicotinic acid, a vitamin product, which is used in medicine for the cure of pellagra. It is quoted by

the Eastman Kodak Company at $12.00 per 100 grams or $54.48 per pound. Accordingly, nicotine from low grades of tobacco produced in Kentucky has many economic possibilities for the preparation of medicinal and insecticidal products.

4. Sugar—The sugar content of tobacco ranges from 1.22 to 5.10 percent of the air-dry leaf. Volatile acids range from 0.10-0.22 percent in the air-dry tobacco. The sugar and the volatile acids may not afford any economic possibilities; however, it is important to know the amount contained in tobacco.

5. Volatile acids, fats, and resins offer economic possibilities. This phase of the investigation will be undertaken as soon as new extraction equipment is available.

6. Organic Acids—Tobacco contains malic, citric, oxalic, and acetic acids. The quantity of these acids contained in tobacco is said to range in decreasing order from about 10 percent of malic acid to about 3 percent of acetic acid. It seems possible that methods can be worked but whereby these acids can be extracted from tobacco on a commercial scale. These acids range in price from $1.25 per pound for malic acid to thirty cents per pound for acetic acid.

7. Cellulose—After the above products have been separated from low-grade tobacco, there still remains a large residue of cellulose materials from which it is possible to make wrapping paper or paper cartons.

---

1. The governor was scheduled to speak at the First Annual Tobacco Festival in October 1939 but did not attend because of his campaign for governor. *Shelby News,* November 2, 1939. On October 24, 1941, he lauded the Third Annual Tobacco Festival as an event that "encourages a splendid, wholesome, vigorous community spirit. This fall festival, as it becomes a fixed institution, will encourage a community spirit in Shelby County that is indeed admirable. It is this unity of spirit that our whole country needs. Kentucky is farming with increasing intelligence, and in no country has there been greater improvement in farming, nor with greater profit." *Shelby Sentinel,* October 31, 1941.

2. James Spencer McHargue (1878–1960), b. Boreing. Head, Department of Chemistry, Kentucky Agricultural Experimental Station; retired, 1948. Letter, Co-operative Extension Service, University of Kentucky, April 27, 1978.

3. The governor discussed this tobacco research in a speech to the Lexington Co-operative Club on the opening day of the tobacco market, December 2, 1940. *Lexington Herald,* December 3, 1940. In December 1941 he spoke to the club and declared that the previous day's high tobacco average was "the best news that could come to Kentucky." *Lexington Herald,* December 2, 1941.

TOBACCO DAY FESTIVAL
Hopkinsville / April 10, 1941

AS both a farmer and a newspaperman, I have always been interested in problems of the Kentucky tobacco grower. Since becoming your governor, this interest has continued and, as a result, my administration has and is making a sincere and determined effort to ascertain what by-products are obtainable from low-grade tobaccos, their possible uses, and the markets they might command.

The General Assembly at my recommendation gave its cooperation and made an annual appropriation of $7,500 to begin a research program in an effort to find new uses for tobacco.

At the present, three chemists are making such experiments under the direction of Professor J. S. McHargue, head of the Department of Chemistry at the Kentucky Agricultural Experiment Station. These experiments, of course, are in their early stages but already sufficient results have been obtained to give a general idea of what by-products may be obtained from tobacco, their uses, and the possibility of their utilization in the commercial field.

Briefly, I shall tell you of some of the things the research studies have revealed to us.

I do not pretend to be a chemist or a research expert. I am neither. But the things I will tell you about have been reported to me by the chemists who are making the study in possible commercial uses for by-products obtained from low-grade tobaccos and are suggested only as possibilities.

Tobacco has always been grown in Kentucky primarily for smoking, chewing, and making snuff. Any other uses of tobacco have generally been incidental to these three. Our chemists, however, have found that tobacco contains a number of elements which are most important and could be developed into useful products. Up to the present, the most important by-product extracted from low-grade tobaccos and other tobacco waste material has been nicotine. There is now being produced in this country about 1 million pounds of relatively pure nicotine which is used in efforts to control damage to important food crops and exterminate insects injurious to livestock.

Nicotine in its purest form is one of the most poisonous alkaloids known. Spray solutions containing nicotine have been exceptionally successful in controlling or exterminating plant lice, white fly, red spider, chinch bug, bean beetle, June beetle, army worm, coddling moth, and external animal parasites including bee, ticks, fleas, and mites. Nicotine has been used with exceptional success in a mixture with bentonite to combat the coddling moth. This has been of great importance to the apple industry as it lessens the hazard of possible poisoning of humans who eat fruit containing lead arsenate residue.

Fruit growers, vegetable gardeners, and florists agree they would use increased quantities of nicotine preparations if the price were not prohibitive. This is one of the problems we are attempting to solve through our research studies, for there is a real need for more and cheaper nicotine preparations for agricultural use.

Since the market for black tobacco has been declining in recent years, considerable study has been devoted to the use of this type of tobacco in making such preparations. Dark tobacco has been found to contain nicotine in commercial quantities and nicotine preparations derived from it have been on the market for years.

Low-grade tobacco leaves have been found to contain about 4 percent nitrogen, about 4 percent potassium, 2 percent calcium, and smaller amounts of other constituents of fertilizer value.

It has also been learned from chemical analysis that when tobacco leaves are stripped from the stalks, the stalks themselves are found to contain nearly as much nitrogen, potassium, calcium, and magnesium as the leaves. Tobacco stalks were found to contain about 60 percent cellulose which can be utilized as advantageously and perhaps more so than corn stalks, cotton stalks, or wheat straw in making rayon and other cellulose products.

Another important discovery made in the research is a tarry substance which furnishes the base for a stain which would aid in water proofing and preserving wood and cloth. This substance is highly penetrating and is comparable to some of the more common woodstains. It is possible, so I am informed, that this tarlike material may furnish the resinous base necessary in the preparation of plastic products.

Extraction of these substances from low-grade tobaccos has given rise to the belief that by the removal of nicotine and tarlike materials, the residual low nicotine tobacco would give a satisfactory cigarette tobacco. The extracted substance still retains satisfactory burning qualities and may also aid in reduction of the nicotine content of cigarette blends. The nicotine extracted by this process is a valuable by-product for insecticidal uses.

It has also been learned that stalks of tobacco that have been submitted to such extraction processes contain an average of about 30 percent cellulose, this being true in either dark or burley tobacco. This tobacco cellulose resembles sawdust. It is similar to wood pulp and can be used in the manufacture of plastics, paper cartons, pasteboard, or other products made from wood.

These briefly are some of the experiments that are under way to find such by-products that can be produced commercially from low-grade tobaccos and be of financial benefit to the tobacco growers of Kentucky.

In reports from the chemists now working on the experiments, I find a statement that "from this preliminary study . . . it is the opinion that it is possible to recover a number of useful and valuable products from low grade tobacco." Again the chemist reports, "It is my opinion that from our research we can expect new and useful knowledge."

I have attempted here today in this short time to give you an outline of some of the activity now being carried on by this administration to aid the farmer—and in this particular instance the tobacco grower.

It is my intention to recommend to the General Assembly this coming January that the $7,500 yearly appropriation for these experiments into the by-product field for tobacco be continued for another two years. I have the highest hopes that from this research and from these experiments will come findings that will aid the tobacco grower substantially in a financial way.

4-H CLUBS JUNIOR WEEK
Lexington / June 12, 1941

GOVERNOR JOHNSON said that coming to Junior Week is one of the "nicest things in my experience as governor." He recalled the fine audience last year; "their singing and enthusiasm thrilled me." He contrasted this with German Youth Camps.

He congratulated the juniors upon being selected to attend and said the hope for future leadership for this nation is in its farm youth.[1] We have come a long distance since scientific farming was first stressed. He recalled that old farmers laughed about getting an educated farm agent, and an old farmer said, "Why I've already wore out three good farms," and another said, "Why I already know how to farm better than I am a-doing."

The governor stated that the movement of 4-H clubs has been a fine influence on farm youth; it requires brains and training to farm well.[2] Farm boys and girls are smart, have habits of thrift, are diligent, wholesome in outlook, and the farm youth of today know the genuine from the counterfeit. "I remember when our hired hand went to Paducah, the first town of any size he had been in, and he came back wearing a brilliant diamond pin in his tie. The jewelry dazzled the girls and excited the envy of the men. A suspicious man asked him if it was a real diamond. He responded, 'Well, if it ain't genuine I've been skunt out o'd seventy-five cents.' "

"I hope you may go to college," though there is a difference of opinion as to its value. "Will Rogers said, 'College is a fine thing—takes children away from home about the time they begin to argue.'

"Different ones go to college for different reasons. A dean of men asked a boy, 'Why did you come to college?' He said, 'I don't know exactly myself. Mother says it is to fit me for the presidency; Uncle Bill says to sow my wild oats; Sis, to get a chum for her to marry; and Pa, to bankrupt the family.'

"But that boy was not entirely uninformed. On examination he found in a history quiz the question, 'Who was Talleyrand?' and his answer was, 'She was a fan dancer.'

"A dean of women asked a cross-eyed, uncomely girl why she had come to college, and her frank answer was, 'I kum to college to be went with—but I ain't been yit.'

"The day is gone when the farmer is looked upon as a hick and hayseed. There is great opportunity on the farm and in farm activity. You all are ambitious and want to succeed, and each day you have done your best, that is success. Do well your job daily—that is the prosaic but certain way to success.

"We are fortunate to live in a great republic. Democracy has bought freedom of speech, thought, and opportunity. We talk of democracy in generalities—but what is it? It is opportunity, where the humblest boy may attain the presidency. Maybe some of you think you would like to be governor of Kentucky. Not one of you but what has a better chance, brighter prospects that I had. Democracy cannot be bought once and for all; we have to fight periodically to maintain freedom. The nation again is threatened. The most genuine patriotism is on the farm.

"You can help in national defense—in the movement under leadership of the College of Agriculture to increase food production. Food for Defense is a fine, patriotic activity. You can live off the farm.

"Support the president—free speech can be exercised—but some may be unwise. Promote unity of thought—stimulate patriotism—love of the flag."[3]

---

1. In November 1939 Johnson praised the achievements of the Garrard County Baby Beef Club and said that back of every thoroughbred calf was a "thoroughbred boy or girl, and back of them were a thoroughbred mother and dad." *Lancaster Central Record*, November 16, 1939. He praised the club members again

two years later for the production of the finest purebred cattle in the nation. *Lancaster Central Record,* November 20, 1941.

2. In 1940 the governor said, "The effects of 4-H club work, reaching into every county in the state, are due to the initiative and vision of one man, Dean Thomas P. Cooper, now acting president of the university. As far as I'm concerned he can keep on acting." He lauded the soil conservation and restoration work of the agricultural experiment station. *Lexington Herald,* June 13, 1940. In 1942 the governor told the 4-Hers that "the inspired work of Dean Cooper and his staff has led to tremendous strides in agriculture in Kentucky during the past twenty years or more." *Lexington Herald,* June 5, 1942. The governor was given an honorary 4-H membership in 1943. *Lexington Herald-Leader,* June 6, 1943.

3. The Co-operative Extension Service, University of Kentucky, does not have copies of Governor Johnson's speeches. Letter, Conrad Feltner, assistant extension director for 4-H, March 11, 1977.

DAVIESS COUNTY FARM BUREAU
Owensboro / August 7, 1941

"THE time has come when every citizen of this continent should either love America or leave it. We need a united people to stand solidly behind the president and his cabinet in this critical hour in this nation's history. It is impossible for us to have the information on which to intelligently pass judgment on the foreign policy of the government. I urge you to support the president of the United States and have faith in his judgment.

"We cannot win a war unless every man and woman realizes the importance of preserving the type of government in America that has brought the greatest happiness and prosperity the world has ever known.

"The chief of staff cannot win the war alone. The president and his cabinet cannot win the war alone. The army being trained throughout the nation cannot win the war unless you, the people, stand solidly behind them and support them.

"A diabolical dictator is seeking to destroy the type of government we enjoy. How long we will enjoy the liberties and privileges no one can foretell."

The governor complimented the farmers of Kentucky on the progress they have made in the last few years in carrying out an intelligent agricultural program. As a result, Kentucky farmers are better prepared than ever before to provide food for the defense of the nation.[1]

He urged greater support of the Kentucky State Fair this year than in the past and announced that a reduced admission price has been arranged for the first three days to stimulate attendance.[2]

---

1. Johnson showed his interest in agriculture when he appointed a Farm Tenancy Commission on January 17, 1941. He directed it to investigate the problem of improving landlord-tenant relationships and to make recommendations for improvement in the tenure system. The commission was authorized by the 1940 General Assembly. Louisville *Courier-Journal*, January 18, 1941. In commenting on its report in November 1941, the governor said that the commission had made a thorough study of the problems of farm tenancy and that he would submit the report to the Legislative Council. *Lexington Herald*, November 13, 1941.

2. The governor addressed the Louisville Rotary Club on September 4, 1941, and said Kentuckians, especially Louisvillians, do not realize the importance of the State Fair. Renovation of fairgrounds and buildings has been pushed "so the plant will be adequate when Kentucky awakens to the fair's importance." He asserted that less than one-fifth of Louisville's inhabitants attend. He praised the 1941 program, saying it was "well balanced to give encouragement to all farm products vital to prosperity. The barriers of sectionalism have been greatly reduced in Kentucky in the last several years. There is no single agent that can go farther toward removing these barriers than the fair." *Louisville Times*, September 4, 1941.

FARMS AT STATE INSTITUTIONS
Frankfort / July 27, 1942

GOVERNOR JOHNSON stated that increased production by farms at Kentucky's hospitals and penal institutions not only is saving the state money but is a boon for the inmates. The value of livestock, farm and garden products, and milk produced during the first six months of 1942 was placed at $124,216 compared to $94,161 during the same period in 1941.

"We have pushed this production hard in the past two years. Not only is it proving economical, especially when many things are scarce, but it is a wonderful thing for patients to have something to occupy their minds . . . . Specialists declare work of this kind is the best thing for the mentally afflicted.[1] Certainly it is much better for the prisoners to have work of this nature instead of being penned up as in the past."

---

1. On May 14, 1942, the governor said the state would buy a farm of 432 acres at $35 an acre for the penitentiary at Eddyville, and a farm of 164 acres at $300 an acre adjacent to Eastern State Hospital. Three-fifths gross, and two-fifths net, of the annual food bill of $500,000 was supplied in 1942 by livestock and foodstuffs produced on 6,819 acres of state-owned farms operated by inmates of the state penal and mental institutions. Louisville *Courier-Journal,* May 15, 1942. He transferred $49,500 on June 25, 1942, to the Department of Finance for the purchase of farmland.

Following a conference of institution and Purchasing Division heads in December 1942, the governor ordered food production on the state farms increased to the limit during the coming year. "I firmly believe there will be a food shortage and regard it as vitally necessary to expand as far as we can go in production and provide storage for it." He explained that the greatest drawback to a really sizable increase is lack of storage, refrigeration equipment, and farm tools, items that cannot be bought during the war emergency. He noted that although the refrigeration plant at Western State Hospital was renovated last summer, those at the other institutions are as old as the buildings themselves. Although the state has funds from its surplus to purchase new equipment, it is difficult to get because of war priorities. In order to get more farm tools, he had instructed institution heads to buy up used ones if in good condition. Louisville *Courier-Journal,* December 23, 1942.

KENTUCKY JERSEY CATTLE CLUB
Lexington / August 20, 1942

OUR farmers are farming more intelligently, producing more from the soil, yet maintaining soil fertility.[1] Dairying requires an exceptionally high order of intelligence. Growth of dairying in the state should be stimulated by the distribution of the purebred sires that are being given to those worthy to receive them.[2]

---

1. Presentation speech when twenty Jersey bull calves were given to farms by the Kentucky Jersey Cattle Club and the Department of Agriculture in an effort to improve dairy herds in Kentucky. The College of Agriculture, University of Kentucky, does not have a copy of the speech. Letter, Charles E. Barnhart, dean, March 31, 1977.

2. The governor proclaimed June as Dairy Month each year. In 1941 he noted that Kentucky's dairy industry furnished full-time employment to 50,000 people. Louisville *Courier-Journal,* May 28, 1941.

TOBACCO PRICE CEILING
Frankfort / November 19, 1942

UNDERSTAND you have called meeting tomorrow to discuss price ceiling on burley and dark tobacco.[1] I desire to protest against imposing of price ceiling on this, the chief cash crop of Kentucky farmers. Farm labor is scarce and high. This has been an expensive crop to produce.

I urge no action be taken until representatives of Kentucky tobacco growers have opportunity to present full facts.[2] Dr. H. B. Price,[3] College of Agriculture, University of Kentucky, will represent me at the meeting.[4]

---

1. This telegram was addressed to Meredith Kohlberg, chief of the Tobacco Section, Office of Price Administration, Food Price Division. A similar telegram was sent to OPA Administrator Leon Henderson. Telegrams were also sent to Senators Barkley and Chandler and Kentucky's eight members of the House of Representatives "expressing hope that they could attend the meeting and join in opposing efforts to curtail tobacco prices."

2. The Kentucky Department of Agriculture was represented by Wesley Vick Perry.

3. Hugh Bruce Price (1888–1978), b. South Dakota. University of Kentucky College of Agriculture, 1929–1959. Head, Department of Markets and Rural Finance, 1929–1946. Letter, Co-operative Extension Service, University of Kentucky, April 27, 1978, and telephone interview, Mrs. Edwina L. Featherston, June 19, 1978.

4. On January 3, 1941, the governor had stated that "the federal government is doing the best it can to relieve the sitiation" and declined to call a special session of the General Assembly to consider legislation designed to boost tobacco prices on state markets. "The production of tobacco doesn't stop at state lines. It is a problem national in scope. . . . Furthermore, a large percentage of the crop has already been sold and by the time the legislature could enact the necessary legislation, the remaining tobacco would be sold. In addition, negotiations for a tobacco loan are under way. After careful consideration, it is my conclusion that it does not seem sufficiently certain that a special session would solve the problem." *State Journal*, January 4, 1941.

FARMER DEFERMENTS
Frankfort / December 14, 1942

I HAVE been informed of a formula for determination of essential workers in agriculture.[1] I wish to protest vigorously against it, inasmuch as the formula does not provide for situations in Kentucky. For example, no provision is made for tobacco, yet it is proposed that acreage be increased 10 percent. The conversion factor for hemp, a critical product, is too low. I call attention to allowances for farm flocks of sheep and beef cattle.

I believe that corrections must be made to enable Kentucky farmers to produce requirements. It is necessary to modify that ruling of sixteen units for essential agricultural workers so that a smaller number of units, for example twelve, may be considered.

It would seem desirable that the determining factor be the proposed 1943 crop rather than the 1942. Since tobacco has long been Kentucky's chief cash crop, emphasis has been placed upon its production. Our farmers willing and anxious to adjust their programs in order that food production may be increased. Without a modification of your rules, many men who cannot qualify as essential will be inducted this winter. I earnestly request that a review of the entire situation be made. There is every evidence that our farmers are confronted with a serious labor situation. Further withdrawal of key farmers will make impossible the attainment of production requirements.[2]

---

1. The same telegram was sent to Manpower Administrator Paul V. McNutt; Selective Service Director Lewis B. Hershey; Secretary of Agriculture Claude Wickard; Senators Barkley and Chandler; and Kentucky's eight members in the House of Representatives. It was prepared after a conference with Dean Thomas P. Cooper, University of Kentucky College of Agriculture.

2. In commenting on his plea, the governor said, "The farm labor situation in Kentucky is acute and is growing worse. As the deferment formula now stands, not one Kentucky farm boy in 500 would be deferred. It applies only to the huge farms of Kansas and other western states." Since tobacco cannot be counted in deferment, he explained that making 1943 crops the basis for deferment of men eligible for military service would enable Kentucky farmers to adjust their production and help avert any food shortage. He commented, "While tobacco may not be a food, it's important to the soldiers and is part of their government ration." Louisville *Courier-Journal*, December 15, 1942. In replying by letter, December 18, 1942, Major General Hershey stated that tobacco was inadvertently omitted from the list of essential farm products and that local Selective Service boards could grant farm workers approximately six months in which to increase their produc-

tion to the required sixteen units. He noted that farm work could be pooled; a farm worker who might not be producing sixteen war units of essential food on his own farm could help on another farm and count his production there toward the sixteen units. The governor wired Hershey December 18, 1942, that his ruling "meets the situation admirably. It will permit the local draft boards to help us maintain manpower on farms necessary to meet increased food quotas assigned to Kentucky, which we are advised is vital to the war effort." Louisville *Courier-Journal*, December 19, 1942.

SOIL CONSERVATION
Frankfort / April 3, 1943

KENTUCKY lands must be protected from the "scorched earth policy" of the last war, when so many thousands of acres were ruined in the effort to supply war demands.[1] With farm labor practically gone, machinery, fertilizer, and supplies rationed and limited, every drop of rainfall and ounce of fertility must be conserved and mobilized for food production.[2] The two million farmers in 793 soil conservation districts of America are demonstrating that through contour farming, use of soil-building crops, and community cooperation, this increased production can be achieved in spite of labor, fertilizer, and machinery shortages, and the land protected from despoilation at the same time. We have just made a start in this direction in Kentucky.

I am proud of having encouraged the enactment of legislation by the 1940 legislature enabling the organization of soil conservation districts in the state, and I honestly believe that in every county where muddy waters run downhill our farmers should be encouraged to organize themselves into such a district where their own leaders promulgate a program of cooperative effort in the conservation of our basic soil and water resources.

---

1. Letter to L. Boone Hamilton, county judge, Franklin County. Zellner Peal, executive secretary, said that similar letters were sent on February 4, 1943, to other county judges throughout the state.

2. On January 4, 1943, the governor proclaimed January 12 as "Farm Mobilization Day in Kentucky," stating, "The federal government's 1943 farm production goals call for increases in most of Kentucky's major farm products. Kentucky has furnished 100,000 fighting men, bought millions of dollars of war bonds, and

furnished workers and professional men for the war effort." He urged that the state do its utmost in providing food for "the armies and for civilians made homeless by gun and Gestapo." He said his proclamation was in line with one issued by President Roosevelt. In commenting on Agriculture Secretary Wickard's request to all governors for rural and small town schools to close early in order that pupils might help plant spring crops, the governor said on March 4, 1943, "We have been working on that for three months." Beginning in January, many Kentucky schools were in session six days a week to aid in food production by releasing pupils several weeks before the usual school-term ending in June. *Louisville Times*, March 4, 1943.

In response to an appeal by the Farm Bureau Federation on June 9, 1943, the governor told highway workers they could "lay off and help the farmers." He said he saw no legal way in which the state could pay crews for working for others. Crop planting had been delayed by heavy rains. Louisville *Courier-Journal*, June 10, 1943. He endorsed a plan, originated by the United States Employment Service, for state and federal employees to spend their summer vacations producing and preserving food. Louisville *Courier-Journal*, June 19, 1943,

OPPOSITION OF BEN KILGORE TO REA
Frankfort / July 23, 1943

GOVERNOR JOHNSON issued a statement charging that Ben Kilgore[1] opposed the REA legislation because it gave the state Public Service Commission surpervision over those cooperatives.

The statement asserted that letters boosting Kilgore and bearing the name of Howard Daniel,[2] president of the Green River Rural Electric Co-operative Association, Owensboro, were sent out under date of July 16 to farmer members of the cooperative which supplies electric current in that vicinity. The governor made public a mimeographed letter bearing Daniel's name urging votes for Kilgore and said he had "unimpeachable information" that the letter was sent to the cooperative's members, in separate envelopes from their bills but timed to arrive the same day. He declared that "similarity of stenographic work indicates that the campaign material was prepared by the REA staff, on REA equipment, and addressed to the REA subscription list," and asserted it was a "shameful misuse of REA, a federal agency."

"The REA act would have been passed if Kilgore had stayed in North Carolina. The record shows Kilgore's own admission that he opposed the bill because it vested control in the Public Service Commission. Senator

Chandler has written a letter stating that Kilgore came to the mansion and begged him to veto it. The record further shows that the last two administrations have been extremely helpful to REA, despite Kilgore's opposition to the original enabling act."

The governor asserted that the record showed Kilgore made the following statement before the Public Service Commission on January 28, 1941: "I want to back up Judge McGregor[3] on his statement that with the cooperation of the commission we have seen in Kentucky a rather remarkable development. . . . I think Judge McGregor knows that I opposed putting the cooperative under this commission at the time the law was drawn, and that I was assured . . . the object was not to hamper . . . but to give assistance in a program of bringing light and power to the maximum number of farm homes at the lowest possible rates. I can say that promise has been kept . . . and I have publicly admitted the same thing pretty generally over the state."

The governor said the Public Service Commission on its own motion and after a hearing fixed wholesale cost of current to cooperatives at eleven mills in the face of opposition from private utilities.

John M. Carmody,[4] federal REA administrator, wired Governor Chandler May 18, 1937, stating that the rate order "should pave the way for the rapid extension of the benefits of electricity to the farmers of your state." On January 29, 1941, V. D. Nicholson,[5] Washington, general counsel for REA, told the state Public Service Commission that "the thing I have liked about Kentucky has been this—that public officials of this state have shown the same interest that we have had in the major objective of this program; namely, bringing electricity to the very largest possible number of people."

"From the day the act passed," the governor concluded, "the commission has led the way in speedy and orderly extension of electric service to widespread rural areas."[6]

---

1. Benjamin W. Kilgore (1901–1951), b. Raleigh, North Carolina. Staff member, *Progressive Farmer;* associate editor of Kentucky and Tennessee edition of *Progressive Farmer* with headquarters in Louisville, 1928–1932; became executive secretary of Farm Bureau in 1933; candidate for Democratic nomination for governor of Kentucky, 1943. Wallis and Tapp, *A Sesquicentennial History of Kentucky,* 3:1638-40, and *Lexington Herald,* May 31, 1951.

2. Howard W. Daniel (1891–1958), b. Owensboro. President, Green River Electric Co-operative, 1938–1945; farmer. Telephone interview, Howard W. Daniel, Jr., June 14, 1978.

3. Thomas Burnett McGregor (1881–1965), b. Benton, Marshall County. Assistant Attorney general, 1908–1912, 1920–1923; attorney general, 1923–1924; judge Fourteenth Judicial District, 1930–1932; Public Service Commission, 1935–1945;

member, board of regents, Eastern Kentucky State College, 1957–1965. *Who's Who in Kentucky, 1936*, p. 274, and *Lexington Herald*, September 18, 1965.

4. John Michael Carmody (?–1963), b. Bradford County, Pennsylvania. Industrial executive. Administrator, Rural Electrification Administration, 1936–1939. *Who Was Who in America, 1961–1968*, 4:155.

5. Vincent Dewitt Nicholson (1890–1945), b. Azalia, Indiana. Attorney, National Recovery Administration, 1934–1935; general counsel, REA, 1935–1941; first deputy administrator, REA, 1942–1945. *Who Was Who in America, 1943–1950*, 2:397.

6. For additional information, see speech from July 30, 1943, in the Democratic Party Leadership section.

KENTUCKY LAMB VERSUS NEBRASKA HOG
Frankfort / September 9, 1943

As governor of Kentucky and in behalf of patriotic, war-bond buying Kentuckians, I have accepted the challenge of the Honorable Dwight Griswold,[1] governor of Nebraska, to a war-bond buying contest.

I have notified Governor Griswold that on behalf of Kentucky a fine purebred Kentucky lamb has been posted, which will be forfeited to him should Kentucky fail to exceed its war bond quota by a greater margin than does Nebraska. Should Nebraska exceed her bond quota by greater percentage points than does Kentucky, the governor of Nebraska will have the pleasant experience of eating a delicious Kentucky lamb.

I have chosen to wager a Kentucky lamb against a Nebraska hog because I welcome the opportunity to publicize the fact that Kentucky lambs are a superior product. I am grateful to Mr. Henry Besuden[2] for his offer of a lamb from his flock, but I have no thought of having to surrender the animal to the governor of Nebraska. I am certain Kentuckians will buy war bonds in such quantity as to guarantee that the lamb will not have to be sent to Nebraska.[3]

---

1. Dwight Palmer Griswold (1893–1954), b. Nebraska. Elected governor, 1940, 1942, 1944; United States senator, 1952. *Who Was Who in America, 1951–1960*, 3:350.

2. Henry Carlisle Besuden (1904–), b. Clark County. Owner-operator, Winewood Farm, Winchester. Elected, Hall of Distinguished Alumni, University of Kentucky, 1975. Member, board of regents, University of Kentucky. Letter, Cooperative Extension Service, University of Kentucky, April 27, 1978.

3. On October 16, 1943, the governor, like twenty-six other governors who accepted Governor Griswold's challenge, had begun to wonder about the hog he had won. "At least Treasury statements would seem to indicate conclusively that we did. . . . I've written to Governor Griswold asking about the hog." *Louisville Times*, October 16, 1943.

The governor supported the lamb industry by proclaiming "Eat More Lamb Month" each June. Lamb Month was initiated in 1939. While Kentucky raised 1,250,000 spring lambs in 1940 and was the largest producing state, Kentuckians consumed less than one pound per capita compared with twelve to eighteen pounds per capita in some western states. Louisville *Courier-Journal*, June 28, 1940. The breeders presented the governor with a dressed prize lamb in June 1940 and he responded, "This ought to cut expenses at the Mansion this week."

BURLEY TOBACCO PRICE CEILINGS
Frankfort / September 19, 1943

EVERY consideration of simple justice dictates that the ceilings be raised for the 1943 burley tobacco crop and set by grades for the marketing season opening in December.[1] The matter is vital to Kentucky farmers who produce an estimated 70 percent of the nation's burley tobacco.

High costs of production, lower yield per acre, and increased consumption of burley tobacco point to the need for higher ceiling prices during the coming marketing season.

At the opening of the 1942-1943 marketing season, the ceiling prices were placed on burley tobacco designed to result in a market average of about thirty-eight cents per pound.[2]

Tobacco growers and warehousemen protested this action on the ground that market conditions warranted higher prices and larger returns to growers. After the markets opened, buying competition soon resulted in several bids at ceiling prices for nearly every pile of tobacco.

Kentucky farmers have done a magnificent job in increasing production of those commodities essential in waging war. Despite shortage of farm labor and adverse weather conditions, farmers of our state have produced food crops in great quantities. Kentucky farmers, however, must depend largely upon tobacco for the principal profit from farming operations.

Returns to burley growers are dependent not only on prices per pound but upon yields per acre and costs of production. Yields per acre in 1943 are variously estimated from 5 to 25 percent lower than in 1942. With costs per acre running some 20 percent higher than last year, total costs per pound may be 30 to 40 percent higher than in 1942. Thus, if prices high enough to offset shorted production are to be permitted, ceiling prices considerably higher than those of last year are essential.

Since last year, too, use of burley has increased about 8 percent. Disappearance of burley—trade word for use in consumption—totaled about 412 million pounds in the year ended last July 1, compared with 380 million pounds in the year ended October 1942.

At this rate of use, production in 1943 will fall short of disappearance by about 40 million pounds, making it the third successive year in which production has been less than disappearance. Manufacturers' stock on July 1 amounted to 797 million pounds compared with 894 million pounds in 1941. Wartime demands for tobacco products make some further reduction in prospect.

Flue-cured ceilings were fixed at forty-one cents a pound, or about six cents a pound higher than in 1942, when the 1943 sales season opened last July. Although flue-cured prices so far have not equaled the ceiling, they have averaged from two to six cents a pound above last year.

---

1. Appeals made to officials of the Office of Price Administration and the Commodity Credit Corporation. The OPA was created by Executive Order of the president, April 11, 1941, and by the Emergency Price Control Act, January 30, 1942. OPA was to stabilize prices and to prevent unjustified rises in the prices of commodities and rents. The Commodity Credit Corporation was an agency of the federal Department of Agriculture, established in 1933, to make loans to farmers and to purchase products from farmers to stabilize agricultural prices.

2. Ceilings were set by OPA according to grades in 1942 in an attempt to arrive at the weighted average price of $38.00 a hundredweight, but a record average of $42.14 a hundredweight was attained. The maximum "weighted average ceiling price" established by OPA on the 1942 crop was $59.00 a hundredweight, with the weighted ceilings ranging downward among sixty-eight basic grades to $11.00 a hundred. There actually was no price limit for any particular sale, according to OPA. A buyer who exceeded any of the ceilings, however, had to average out within a week to stay within the "weighted average ceiling prices" for all tobacco of that grade he purchased. In practice, this resulted in buyers bidding the "weighted average ceiling price" in most instances. Louisville *Courier-Journal*, September 20, 1943.

PARKS & CONSERVATION

MEETS PRESIDENT ROOSEVELT
Newfound Gap, North Carolina
August 2–September 2, 1940

GOVERNOR of Kentucky accepted invitation to be a spectator while President Roosevelt dedicated the Chickamauga Dam, near Chattanooga, and Great Smoky Mountains National Park at Newfound Gap, N.C.[1] Keen Johnson, newspaper reporter, also went along as did Zellner Peal and Tom Underwood.[2] Zellner, as secretary to the governor, does most of the work at the executive offices. Tom is editor of the *Lexington Herald* and chairman of the Democratic State Central Executive Committee. Sergeant Dan Gray piloted the Buick bus provided by indulgent taxpayers for the governor.

Governor of Kentucky joined Governor Prentice Cooper, of Tennessee, and Governor Ed Rivers, of Georgia, as members of reception committee to greet the president. Train backed into Chattanooga railway station. Those permitted in station waited expectantly. Minutes passed. General Watson, Colonel Starling, Paul McNutt, Secretary Ickes, other members of presidential party got off. Mrs. Roosevelt waved acknowledgment of applause. Then the president appeared on rear platform of train. Spontaneous and genuine the greeting he acknowledged with a smile and wave of hat. Into an open automobile. Motorcade started to Chickamauga Dam.[3]

Streets lined for miles with people. Many had stood long while to get a glimpse of greatest American of our day. Attitude of throng one of respect and affection for nation's chief. Acres of folks at dam. Arrangements for handling crowd and traffic exceptionally good. President spoke from his car atop $36 million dam, a unit in the vast TVA program. Could but conjecture as to what must be the emotional thrill enjoyed by the man who in 1932 envisioned this plan of development of natural resources, soil conservation, flood control, and national defense. He stood today on one of those huge dams. In 1932 it existed only in his mind. Today he witnessed it as a blessed reality. Today his the pleasant duty of dedicating it to public service. Today the joy of conspicuous national achievement was the reward of Franklin D. Roosevelt. Beneficial effects of the project will be enjoyed by millions of Americans yet unborn—the result of the constructive imagination of the dedicatory speaker. We rejoiced with him and thought it possible to sense something of his feeling when he said, "As for me, I glory in it as one of the great social and economic achievements of our time." President Roosevelt dreamed a great dream and the TVA is the realization of that dream. Well may this nation thank God for her dreamers.

It was with pride that the president referred to his Dutch and Scotch ancestry. His forebears have long been associated with the building of America. Franklin D. Roosevelt has attained distinction as a builder such as reflects credit on those forebears. And the nation is the beneficiary.

Governor of Kentucky sat with notables of the South atop a towering eminence in Great Smoky Mountains as coming of President Roosevelt was awaited for dedication of this region of scenic splendor as a national park. Roads lined with people. Limited space available on the mountain heights crowded with folk. Many had waited hours to express esteem for nation's chief.

Automobile flying presidential flag and Stars and Stripes wound up the mountain side. It encircled the throng through narrow lane that had been kept open. Tumultuous the welcome. The radiant smile and wave of hat accentuated cheering.

The smiling face became serious as from the mountaintop was proclaimed by this great patriot the warning that Americans must make sacrifices to preserve liberties menaced by history's greatest attack on free men. It was the challenge of an informed leader to the people whose welfare is his responsibility—a challenge to meet and thwart the menace of might.

The dynamic American instilled confidence, gave encouragement to troubled folk. They felt more secure because his wisdom and vision shaped the course of the nation.

As the president arose to speak, he addressed Governor Cooper of Tennessee, Governor Hoey of North Carolina, and noted presence of Governor Maybank of South Carolina.[4] As the governor of Kentucky congratulated him upon a superb speech as we left the platform, the president said, "How stupid of me to overlook the presence of the governor of Kentucky." I hastened to assure him that he should not be concerned about it. But after he had entered his automobile for the return drive to Knoxville, General Watson brought the information that the governor of Kentucky was invited to ride with the president. I confess I was immensely pleased. Of course the invitation was in compliment to the people of Kentucky and not to Keen Johnson, reporter. And though unnecessary, it was magnificent recompense for omission of the governor of Kentucky from the presidential salutation as he started his memorable address.

Other occupants of the car were Mrs. Roosevelt and Governor Cooper. A Secret Service man occupied the seat beside the driver. We whizzed down the magnificently engineered mountain road, through a tunnel and looped back over it. Rugged grandeur of the Great Smokies stretched away to the horizon. The irregular, yet symmetrical skyline along top of mountain ranges appeared to be a vast drapery hung against the backdrop of clouds. An ethereal haze encircled mountaintops like a bridal veil. Governor Cooper explained that the haze had been so pronounced the Indians referred to it as the Great Smoke, giving the name to the mountain range.

Highway out of the 200,000 acre park lined with boys from the CCC camps in the park. Boys stationed about 100 yards apart enjoyed saluting smartly as the president passed. Apparently entire populace of villages lined streets to get a glimpse of the president, express by cheers their affection for him. At the Dam the guard of honor had been Boy Scouts.

That which the president said during the drive was meant for the governor of Kentucky and not for Keen Johnson, reporter. That enjoins caution upon me as I record innocuous though interesting bits of that conversation.

Governor Cooper expressed regret that Secretary Hull had not found it possible to accompany the president. "Tomorrow (Tuesday) at noon there will be made a most important announcement which will explain why Mr. Hull is not here. It will reveal the important business which kept him so occupied he could not come," said Mr. Roosevelt.

Governor Cooper, after a brief interval of contemplation, said, "I have no desire to insist upon disclosure of that important announcement but I do want to make a guess. My guess is that the announcement will be that the United States is to make a quantity of destroyers available for England." President Roosevelt laughed as he said, "You should remember that I am Scotch." I commented, "and in return for the destroyers you have obtained those naval bases you referred to in your speech." There was no hint from the president as to correctness of our speculation. But subsequent events revealed Governor Cooper had guessed correctly.

Tennessee is a beautiful state. The president and Mrs. Roosevelt commented on beauty of the countryside, especially noting unusually good fields of corn. Diminished evidence of erosion, washed hillsides as contrasted with four years previous was noted with approval by the chief executive. He talked with enthusiasm about possibilities of flood control, soil conservation, social and economic development in other river basins. Experience in the TVA will light the path.

Kentucky's governor reminded President Roosevelt that we anticipate with pleasure his visit to Kentucky during his next quadrennium as president to dedicate Gilbertsville Dam, another important link in the TVA development. He was also assured that he would be expected in Kentucky within the next year or two to dedicate Mammoth Cave National Park. The president expressed interest in both the dam and park. "It will give me much satisfaction to participate in their dedication," he said.

While he appeared confident of the outcome of the political campaign, the president talked little of politics. Large national problems of tremendous import were on his mind. Of these he talked. One got the impression that he knew what he was talking about. His confidence was reassuring.

Conversation was abruptly terminated as we approached a town, while the president acknowledged cheers from those that thronged the way. The radiant smile and friendly wave along entire journey was recalled when later as we talked at dinner with Tennessee's Senator McKellar,[5] he said of the president, "he has the best disposition of any man I have ever known. In eight years close association I have never seen him angry."

Into a lighter vein the conversation was occasionally diverted. "Jimmy and I have had an argument," said the president. "Jimmy insists that Chattanooga has prettier girls than Atlanta. I insist that Atlanta girls are prettier." I inquired of Mrs. Roosevelt as to whether she acted as referee of the argument. "No, indeed, I do not," said the nation's First Lady. She recalled her visit to Kentucky in the winter of 1938 to dedicate a school in Breathitt County. Especially did she remember the little boy who introduced her.

President said I am going to make a sentimental visit tomorrow (September 3). He explained that as assistant secretary of navy during World War, he was instrumental in establishment of an armor plate factory at Charleston, W. Va. It had just gotten into production, making armor for battle craft and type of armor that will be used in tanks, when the armistice was signed. When President Harding made the naval treaty in which we agreed to sink our fighting craft, production of the plant was halted. Someone had the foresight to give the machinery a heavy coat of grease. It has been sitting idle. Recently the president ordered the plant into production of armor plate. He anticipated with pleasure visiting the plant, now vital to the nation's defense, which he had the foresight to establish in 1918.

As approached, Knoxville street lights were on. It was dinner hour. But streets were lined with people waiting for a glimpse of the nation's leader. Through lanes of cheering folk we drove directly to the railroad station. President requested he be permitted to shake hands with Tennessee highway patrolmen who had escorted him. Governors of Kentucky and Tennessee said farewell and thanks for a memorable experience as took leave of charming, gracious Mrs. Roosevelt and had final handclasp from masterful, dynamic, democratic American who guides the destiny of this great nation.

Pleasant dinner with Governor Cooper, his charming mother, Senator McKellar, and a group of their friends. Although we were tired as result of strenuous day, the president and Mrs. Roosevelt appeared less fatigued than any of us.

Started for Kentucky early Tuesday morning. Soon our bus resumed its temperamental practices. Monday we thought once we would not arrive for the park dedication because the car continued to become overheated. An hour's wait at a garage appeared to correct it. Trouble returned as approached Kentucky line. We limped along, stopping at every filling station to cool off the heated motor. Finally reached Williamsburg. Left car at Highway Garage. Completed journey to Frankfort in Highway Patrol car. So ended an experience that will be a cherished memory for the fellow who happens now to be the governor of Kentucky, and a thrilling experience for Keen Johnson, newspaper reporter.

---

1. Article by Keen Johnson.

2. Zellner L. Peal (1905–1966), b. Ballard County. Banker; secretary to the governor, 1939–1943. *Kentucky Directory, 1940–1941*, p. 143, and *Lexington Herald*, August 2, 1966.

Thomas Rust Underwood (1898–1956), b. Hopkinsville. *Lexington Herald*, 1916–1956, editor and political writer, 1935–1956. United States representative, 1948–1950; United States senator in 1951 to fill vacancy created by death of Senator Virgil M. Chapman. *Who's Who in Kentucky, 1936*, p. 411, and telephone interview, *Lexington Herald*, June 1978.

3. Eurith Dickinson Rivers (1895–1967), b. Center Point, Arkansas. Attorney. President pro tem, Georgia Senate, 1927; Speaker, Georgia House of Representatives, 1933–1935; governor, Georgia, 1937–1941. *Georgia's Official Register, 1939–1943* (Atlanta, Ga., 1943), p. 6, and *Biographical Directory of the Governors of the United States, 1789–1978* (Westport, Conn., 1978), 1:318-19.

Edwin Martin Watson (1883–1945), b. Eufaula, Alabama. Military aide to the president, 1933–1941. *Who Was Who in American History: The Military*, p. 621.

Harold L. Ickes (1874–1952), b. Blair County, Pennsylvania. Administrator, public works, 1933–1939; secretary of the interior, 1933–1946; administrator, Solid Fuels for War, 1941–1946. *Who Was Who in America, 1951–1960*, 3:436.

4. Clyde Roark Hoey (1877–1954), b. Shelby, North Carolina. United States

representative, 1919–1921; governor, North Carolina, 1937–1941. *Who Was Who in America, 1951–1960*, 3:314-15.

Burnett Rhett Maybank (1899–1954), b. Charleston, South Carolina. Mayor, Charleston, 1931–1939; governor, South Carolina, 1939–1941; United States senator, 1941–1954. Ibid., p. 417.

5. Kenneth Douglas McKellar (1869–1957), b. Richmond, Alabama. United States representative, 1911–1917; United States senator, 1917–1953. Ibid., p. 400.

LEAGUE OF KENTUCKY SPORTSMEN
Lexington / May 12, 1941

GOVERNOR JOHNSON praised the work of Steve A Wakefield as director of the state Division of Game and Fish.[1] He stated, "The division is functioning with greater efficiency and better results than ever before." Not all of the credit was due to Mr. Wakefield as director, because the aid and interest of the sportsmen had a great deal to do with results. "You help in crystalizing public sentiment for observance of law. There is less regard for game law than any other." All money from fishing and hunting licenses goes to support the Game and Fish Division. "The deadwood has been weeded out of the division" and Mr. Wakefield is "destined to be the best game and fish division director the state has ever had. He knows he has our support for any action that increases efficiency. The problems of the division are being intelligently and energetically attacked and the program is on a sound basis."

The governor said that federal money was helpful. The state had received about $30,000 under the Pittman-Robertson Act.[2]

He lauded the work done by James J. Gilpin, publicity director of the state Division of Game and Fish.[3]

He invited the league to be the guests of the capital city in 1942. In closing, he remarked that a governor's greatest service is in what he prevents from happening to the state.[4]

---

1. The speech was presented at the league's annual banquet. Steve A. Wakefield (1901–1977), b. Shelbyville. Director, Division of Game and Fish, 1941; assistant director, 1948–1954; director, Division of Flood Control and Water Resources, 1954–1956, 1959–1966. Louisville *Courier-Journal*, December 30, 1977.

2. This 1937 act provided that funds collected under an 11 percent excise tax on

sporting arms and ammunition were to be appropriated by Congress for disbursement to individual states for wildlife restoration purposes. The United States Fish and Wildlife Service administered it. Public 415, 50 *Stat.* 917.

3. Gilpin wrote a handbook on conservation that was published in 1941: *Kentucky Units in Conservation of Wildlife and Other Natural Resources.* The governor's foreword states: "There has been a great need for a more wide spread educational program on conservation of the natural gifts by a bountiful Mother Nature that will get such information as is available into the minds of those who will use it or be influenced by it. This handbook on conservation which is now being presented to the teachers of Kentucky should go a long way in answering this cry for conservation education and, if rightly used, should bring to the younger generations the realization that a great heritage has been handed down to them and upon their shoulders falls the responsibility of protecting it for all time."

James J. Gilpin (1910–), b. Frankfort. Resides in Lexington. Served with Kentucky Fish and Wildlife Resources and its predecessor agency for thirty-eight years until his retirement in 1975. Telephone interview, J. J. Gilpin, July 5, 1978.

4. Johnson's interest in protecting wildlife and the environment is shown in a letter, dated July 14, 1942, which he wrote to Fred Vinson. Vinson, a former congressman from Kentucky, was then on the United States Court of Appeals for the District of Columbia although he was soon to resign and to become the director of the Office of Economic Stabilization. The governor requested Vinson's assistance in obtaining equipment to control pollutants being discharged in the streams by distilleries. He pointed out that the distilleries were operating at capacity to manufacture industrial alcohol for war purposes. They had been unable to obtain the priorities necessary to procure the equipment. The governor sent his letter by Steve Wakefield. On July 22 he wrote to thank Vinson for his helpfulness to Wakefield. See Vinson Papers, University of Kentucky.

CUMBERLAND FALLS STATE PARK LODGE
Corbin / May 9, 1942

I REJOICE with you on this pleasant occasion that the usefulness of Cumberland Falls State Park is to be enhanced with the dedication of this new, attractive DuPont Lodge. We were distressed when fire destroyed the original lodge. Conveniences of the park were curtailed as result of that misfortune. But we are happy today that out of the ashes of that calamitous fire there has arisen a new, more permanent lodge. The original inflammable lodge has been replaced by a stone structure of artistic beauty that will, for decades to come, provide comfortable facilities for those who visit this beautiful park.

The state park system has been revitalized under the direction of Mrs. Nellie Vaughn,[1] director of state parks. She has been sustained and supported by Commissioner of Conservation Charles Fennell.[2] I want to publicly acknowledge our debt of gratitude to Mr. Gerald Hyde, of the National Park Service, with whom we have counseled constantly and whose guidance has been followed as a sustained effort has been made to make the state parks increasingly attractive and useful.

The success of a state park depends largely upon the patronage it receives from the community in the immediate vicinity. The people of this region are to be congratulated upon the interest they have shown in Cumberland Falls State Park. Their generous use of the park has been a major factor in its successful operation. A park with such facilities as are here available with the rebuilding of DuPont Lodge should become the center of community activity in southeastern Kentucky.

The effort to stimulate revenue production of the parks has been quite successful and has increased the funds available for park improvements. Income of the parks last year totaled approximately $130,000 as contrasted with $90,000 the previous year. Attendance at the state parks last year from January 1 to September 1 totaled 293,744 as compared with 204,722 the previous year.

Last year we utilized the services of the state Highway Department to blacktop many miles of road in the parks. A lake was constructed at the Audubon Park at Henderson. Additional rest rooms at Pine Mountain State Park were installed. Reconstruction of DuPont Lodge, in which substantial aid was received from the WPA, has been the major improvement. Money has been provided in the budget bill enacted by the state legislature to finance rebuilding of the dam in Natural Bridge State Park so that the lake there may be restored. The NYA, the CCC, and WPA have been most helpful in the program of park improvement and their contribution is acknowledged with grateful thanks.

Mrs. Vaughan, director of parks, has done a highly acceptable job in advancing an intelligently conceived park program. Kentucky is to participate with Tennessee and Virginia in acquiring the land necessary to establish Cumberland Gap National Park under direction of the National Park Service. The budget bill contains an appropriation of $75,000 each year for the next two years for that purpose, matching similar appropriations in Tennessee and Virginia. Creation of this national park in the region of scenic splendor which centers at Cumberland Gap will make southeast Kentucky a region with an increased appeal as a vacation land. Cumberland Falls will profit greatly as a result of the widened appeal of this region as a vacation center. Progress on the Cumberland Gap park will be impeded as result of the war but we shall make such progress in acquiring land desired by the National Park Service that it will be possible to bring this project to completion immediately after the war. The value of a national park in attracting tourist travel has been established. Cumberland Falls will find its facilities used increasingly as result of the influx of vacationers brought into Kentucky by the Cumberland Gap park.[3]

One of the developments of my administration in which I find much satisfaction is in acceptance by the National Park Service of Mammoth Cave National Park. Our concentrated effort to remove all obstacles in the way of establishment of Mammoth Cave as a national park have been eliminated and it passed into the National Park system last July 1.[4]

While the history of Cumberland Falls is a familiar story to many of you, it seems proper on this occasion to review that interesting story.

Shortly following the Revolutionary War, Matthew Walton and Adam Shepherd, engineers who served with General Washington's army, left Virginia to seek land in Kentucky. Although Dr. Thomas Walker, who built the first house in Kentucky in 1750, and the Long Hunters[5] evidently had been in the region, it is believed that Walton and Shepherd were the first to view the "Great Falls" of the Cumberland River. Walton settled in Washington County and Shepherd founded Shepherdsville in Bullitt County. Seeing possibility in the falls, however, they returned to that vicinity, surveyed and patented in their joint names two 200-acre tracts of land, the upper one of which embraced the falls. The surveys were made in 1800 but patents were not issued until 1814 and 1828.

In 1850, title to these lands was transferred from the heirs of Walton and Shepherd to Louis Renfro, a pioneer preacher of the old Baptist faith. Renfro constructed a home on the land which was the forerunner of the old hotel still standing on the brink of the falls. Work of building was laborious, the timber being hauled to Williamsburg and floated back. The old preacher, who had scorned remuneration for preaching the gospel, became involved in debt and was sued by his creditors. Commissioners appointed by the court gave him title to a homestead of 200 acres embracing the falls, of the value of $1,000.

Here he lived and conducted his hotel from before the Civil War to the early 1880s. Renfro, before his death, sold his holdings to Socrates Owen, whose heirs, on August 7, 1899, sold their interest to the Cumberland Falls Company, which in turn sold out, in 1902,to Henry C. Brunson. Brunson and his two daughters managed the hotel from that time until 1931 under the name of Brunson Inn. In 1927 Brunson had conveyed his property to the Cumberland River Power Company, a subsidiary of Insull and Middle West. This company proposed to erect a hydroelectric plant by building a dam above the falls and tunneling through the mountain to a point below the falls, which would have permanently destroyed the scenic beauty of the region.

Conservationists of the state, desiring that the falls retain their rugged beauty, sought to save the falls. Senator T. Coleman DuPont,[6] native of Muhlenberg County, became interested and proposed to purchase the land of the power interests and donate it to the state of Kentucky with the understanding that it would not be named for him.

Proponents of the power interests and advocates of conservation fought bitterly for the region which now had been known for many years as Cumberland Falls, due to the name of the river. In the meantime, in 1927, the Corbin Kiwanis Club, realizing the value of the falls to Corbin, had been instrumental in building a road from Corbin to the falls which was dedicated by Governor William J. Fields[7] in September 1927. The popularity of the scenic spot was greatly increased each year. In 1928, acceptance of Cumberland Falls as a park did not have the support of the state administration and a minority report favoring acceptance of the falls was brought to the floor of the Senate and voted down.

In December 1929 the Federal Power Commission at Washington held a public hearing on the matter which was deferred to the next session of the Kentucky legislature. After a hard fight during the 1930 General Assembly, on the tenth day of March 1930, the House and Senate, over the veto of Governor Flem D. Sampson,[8] passed a bill accepting the DuPont offer, and Cumberland Falls was saved for the people. The ceremony of dedication, September 7, 1931, was attended by 10,000 people and nearly 3,000 automobiles from as many as seventeen states. During the following two months period more than 50,000 visitors from thirty-seven states saw the falls.

Cumberland Falls State Park became the seventh state park and at the time of its purchase for $400,000 embraced 593 acres which represents its area now. A total of $200,000 of the purchase price had been set aside by Senator DuPont, but he died November 11, 1930, before the deal was consummated and the remaining $200,000 was donated by Mrs. DuPont and their children.

Although Senator DuPont requested that no recognition be made of his generous gift, a bronze tablet was placed in the park to his memory and DuPont Lodge named in his honor. The first DuPont Lodge was built in 1935–1936 through the efforts of the Kentucky Division of State Parks in cooperation with the federal government which furnished CCC and WPA assistance. This building was destroyed by fire April 5, 1940.

Immediately the state Division of Parks prepared plans and estimates, presenting them to the WPA for project approval. Actual construction started September 26, 1940, and the lodge was completed November 25, 1941, at a total construction cost of $43,609.87, of which $25,337.00 was supplied through federal funds while the state funds amounted to

$18,272.87. The newly completed DuPont Lodge is almost a reproduction of the original, wooden exterior walls having been replaced with native stone.

During 1941 there was a paid attendance of 107,546 persons at Cumberland Falls. With those who came to the park but did not visit the falls, this figure might be estimated at 250,000. High month was August when a total of 31,286 paid admissions were registered.

In this Kentucky's sesquicentennial year, we review with pride the fascinating story of the development of Kentucky. Those audacious pioneers, who established the first citadel of civilization west of the Allegheny mountains, marveled at the beauty of that region which has become known around the world as one of the most beautiful regions on the globe.

We have sought to keep faith with those pioneers who were captivated by the loveliness of Kentucky by preserving as state parks the beauty spots of the state, consecrating them to the recreation and enjoyment of our people. It is significant that Matthew Walton and Adam Shepherd, as they explored Kentucky and came upon Cumberland Falls, were seized with an urge to own the area. They saw beauty in a waterfall. They were intrigued by the rugged grandeur of the region, the gorge of the Cumberland. So they surveyed and patented in their joint names lands within which was included the cataract whose roar resounded through the primeval forest.

On this the 150th anniversary of Kentucky's statehood, we are justified in rejoicing that the waterfall which thrilled our pioneer forebears has been preserved, that it will be forever preserved as a monument to those Kentuckians who saw beauty in a waterfall.[9]

So it is with rejoicing that we today dedicate the reconstructed DuPont Lodge to the comfort and enjoyment of those who seek rest and recreation at this lovely spot. We dedicate DuPont Lodge to the memory of Senator T. Coleman DuPont, a generous philanthropist, a native of Kentucky, who gave generously of his wealth that in this ideal environment there might be established a playground and vacation center for the people. We dedicate this picturesque lodge to the service of those who find peace in communing with nature, who here seek the solace of solitude. We dedicate DuPont Lodge in the name of all Kentucky and for the enjoyment of all Kentuckians.

DuPont Lodge and Cumberland Falls State Park will be here maintained through the years as a memorial to the practical vision of those Kentuckians who recognized a waterfall as a great asset which should be preserved as the central attraction of a state park, ideally adapted for recreational purposes.

The pioneer frontiersmen, Matthew Walton and Adam Shepherd, who first possessed this land were worthy forebears. We dedicate DuPont Lodge to their memory and to those simple virtues so pronounced in pioneer Kentuckians as we honor their dauntless daring, their disregard of danger, their defiance of hardship, their stalwart strength of character, their love of Kentucky, and their appreciation of its primitive beauty.

Our pride in Kentucky in this the sesquicentennial year is intensified by the fact that our sons today, descendants of our pioneer forefathers, are fighting as valiantly for the democratic ideal on the battlefields of the world as Kentuckians fought a hundred and fifty years ago as they wrested Kentucky from the savages. Kentuckians are fighting the Yellow men today with courage comparable to that of their forebears who, with flintlock, fought the Red men of the forest.

So as we today in this sesquicentennial year dedicate DuPont Lodge to the future enjoyment of Kentuckians, we also rededicate ourselves to the challenging task of solving Kentucky's problems of the present. Our hearts are filled with anxiety as we assemble here amid a setting of scenic loveliness and tranquil peace.

Ruthless dictators have perfected powerful armies and set out on the unholy mission of conquering the democracies of the world. It is the most sinister threat with which we have been confronted. If we lose this war, we lose every right and privilege that we cherish. We will not submit to that infamous fate. We must accept cheerfully every sacrifice we are called upon to make in this war of survival, prepare ourselves to triumph when comes the Waterloo of the world.

We shall be required to make sacrifices in the near future the extent of which we cannot comprehend. We shall soon have to abandon the comfort and convenience of automobiles as a method of transportation. We shall soon have to live on a limited food ration. Economic dislocations as result of war demands will inevitably result in closing of many private business establishments. Our daily lives will soon be rigidly regimented. We must accept such fate cheerfully and endure it temporarily in order to smash the enemies who seek to impose a regimented life upon us permanently. The lowered standard of living that will soon bring us a considerable degree of privation must be endured temporarily in order to lick Germany and Japan and prevent them from permanently imposing upon us a standard of living so low as to rob life in these United States of the joy of living.

We of Kentucky must be worthy sons and daughters of our valiant Kentucky progenitors. We must fight with the same courage as did Daniel Boone, Simon Kenton, George Rogers Clark. We must demonstrate that the virility and valor of the frontier has been transmitted through the generations that have come and gone in the century and a half of our glorious past.

As the war governor of Kentucky it is with glowing pride that I say to you that the fire of patriotic fervor burns brightly in the heart of Kentuckians. Gallant sons of Kentucky are fighting on every battlefront and every battlefield is stained with their blood.

With that heroic little army on Bataan Peninsula that held a huge Japanese army at bay for three months, Kentuckians fought bravely and died nobly. The Kentucky National Guard tank batallion from Harrodsburg fought fiercely on Bataan and in Corregidor against insuperable odds. But they fought on with invincible courage until they fell from exhaustion and hunger. In this the most sublime epic of heroism since Thermopylae, Kentuckians wrote their names high on the role of heroes.

Kentucky's soldiers will match that heroism on many battlefields before peace comes again. But we on the home front, we who constitute the civilian population, must prepare ourselves for hardships, inconvenience, and privations such as we have not known.

So as we dedicate DuPont Lodge, it is especially opportune that we rededicate ourselves to devotion to the American ideal; reaffirm our allegiance to the flag of the Republic and, as did the signers of the Declaration of Independence, "mutually pledge to each other our lives, our fortunes, and our sacred honor."[10]

---

1. Nellie Vaughan (Mrs. Robert Vaughan) (1885–1955), b. Glasgow. Director, State Parks, 1941–1943. Five times chairman, state Democratic Women; manager, Women's Division, 1939 campaign. Telephone interview, William Vaughan, son, Glasgow, July 6, 1978.

2. Charles Fennell (1884–1959), b. Cynthiana. Assistant United States district attorney, 1914–1921; highway commissioner, Sixth District, 1932–1935. Willis, *Kentucky Democracy*, 2:187-89, and Louisville *Courier-Journal*, January 5, 1959.

3. On August 28, 1943, Governor Johnson, Governor Prentice Cooper of Tennessee, and Governor Colgate W. Darden of Virginia signed a three-state compact at Middlesboro for creation of the Cumberland Gap National Historical Park. Representatives of the three states, including Johnson, had approved the acquisition of 6,000 acres on August 12, 1942. *Lexington Herald*, August 13, 1942. Since Kentucky's $75,000 appropriation for 1942–1943 had to be returned to the general fund because it was not spent by June 30, the governor transferred that amount by executive order on November 19, 1943, from his Emergency Fund. At the compact signing, it was suggested that Kentucky, the host state, be given the original copy of the compact. Johnson was willing to "flip a coin" for it. A delegate had a pair of dice, and the governors "rolled high dice" for the privilege of taking home the original. Darden's roll was high. Louisville *Courier-Journal*, August 29, 1943.

4. The governor reported in September 1940 that the Kentucky National Park Commission had recommended that Mammoth Cave be taken over by the National Park Service. Louisville *Courier-Journal*, September 6, 1940. In October the

question arose of whether two other caves on the property would hold up operation by the Park Service. Kentucky wanted Great Onyx and Crystal caves to remain private. Louisville *Courier-Journal,* October 23, 1940. In June 1941 the question arose whether state and county roads in the area could be deeded to the federal government. Louisville *Courier-Journal,* June 22, 1941. Finally on June 23, 1941, Johnson said that Attorney General Meredith had signed an opinion removing this obstacle to the Department of the Interior's taking full possession on July 1. President Roosevelt and Secretary Ickes planned to attend the dedication of Mammoth Cave as a national park but a date was not set. Louisville *Courier-Journal,* June 24, 1941.

5. The Long Hunters, about forty in number, came into Kentucky with Colonel James Knox in 1770–1771.

6. Thomas Coleman Du Pont (1863–1930), b. Louisville. Engineer; coal executive. Republican. Resided Central City, 1883–1893. United States senator, Delaware, 1921–1922, 1925–1928. *Biographical Directory of the American Congress, 1774–1971,* p. 889.

7. William Jason Fields (1874–1954), b. Willard. United States representative, 1911–1923; governor, 1923–1927; commonwealth attorney, Thirty-seventh Judicial District, 1932–1935. Member, Workmen's Compensation Board, 1936–1944. *Who Was Who in American Politics,* p. 230.

8. Flemson Davis Sampson (1875–1967), b. London. Judge, Court of Appeals, Seventh District, 1916; and chief justice, 1923; reelected 1924. Republican. Governor, 1927–1931. *Who Was Who in America, 1961–1968,* 4:825.

9. Johnson demonstrated his concern for the preservation of Cumberland Falls in March 1941 when he requested topographical maps from the United States Army Engineer's Office in Nashville. A pamphlet about Wolf Creek Dam, which had been published by that office, stated, "Construction of Wolf Creek Dam will form a reservoir which will extend nearly 100 miles to foot of Cumberland Falls." Colonel W. A. Davis assured the governor that the upstream end of the reservoir would not destroy Cumberland Falls or reach the downstream boundary of Cumberland Falls State Park. Louisville *Courier-Journal,* March 30, 1941. In 1943 the directors of the National Conference of State Parks commended Johnson for his action. Louisville *Courier-Journal,* May 27, 1943.

10. The speech has been edited. A discussion of the state motto is in the speech from April 20, 1942, in the Heritage section.

EXECUTIVE ORDER: DEPARTMENT OF CONSERVATION
Frankfort / April 23, 1943

WHEREAS, the fire control problem of the Division of Forestry, Department of Conservation for and during the present National Emergency has become more extensive, and,

WHEREAS, it is evident that constant and vigilant supervision must be maintained over our state forests, and,

WHEREAS, the United States Government has by the Sixth National Defense Law approved a grant to the Division of Forestry, Department of Conservation, in the sum of Thirty Four Thousand Nine Hundred Ninety Three Dollars ($34,993.00), and,

WHEREAS, the Federal Government requires that the Division of Forestry, Department of Conservation, make all necessary expenditures and then submit reimbursement vouchers, and,

WHEREAS, the funds of the said Division of Forestry, Department of Conservation, are depleted and it has become necessary to obtain additional funds to enable said Division to conduct its program for the remainder of the fiscal year, and,

WHEREAS, said financial assistance may be reimbursed from the sum granted under the Sixth National Defense Law, and,

WHEREAS, the said Division of Forestry, Department of Conservation, has agreed to reimburse the General Emergency Fund on or before the Thirty-First (31) day of July, 1943, of the funds advanced to said Division, and,

WHEREAS, an emergency, in the opinion of the Governor, is thereby created and does now exist, and,

WHEREAS, by Chapter One (1) of the Acts of the 1942 General Assembly, the Legislature provided the Executive Department with a General Emergency Fund of Two Hundred Fifty Thousand Dollars ($250,000.00) to be used in meeting ordinary recurring and extraordinary expenses deemed emergencies by the Governor of the Commonwealth, and to be expended by the Governor in his discretion for any emergency that he may determine requires the expenditure of any part of said fund,

NOW, THEREFORE, I, Keen Johnson, Governor of the Commonwealth of Kentucky, by virtue of the authority vested in me as such, by this Executive Order hereby authorize and direct the Commissioner of Finance and the State Treasurer to cause to be set up out of the Governor's General Emergency Fund (Chapter 1, Part 1, Section 4, Sub-section (d) 1 of the Acts of the 1942 General Assembly) the sum of Five Thousand Five hundred Dollars ($5,500.00) to be transferred from said Governor's General Emergency Fund to the account of Division of Forestry, and known as Forestry Special #1029, to be used by said Division to meet current obligations and to be returned to the Governor's General Emergency Fund when the grant of the Federal Government has been received by said Division of Forestry, Department of Conservation.[1]

1. The governor issued several proclamations concerning the danger of forest fires.

EXECUTIVE ORDER: UNDERGROUND WATER SUPPLY
Frankfort / August 31, 1943

WHEREAS, the Appropriation Act of 1942 (House Bill #1) provides for the fiscal year of 1943-44 (Part 1-A, Section 4, Item D-3) that there would be provided a National and Civil Defense Emergency Fund, for the purpose of meeting extraordinary expenses which may be imposed upon the Commonwealth of Kentucky, to meet the emergency created by the state of war existing between the United States and other countries, in the sum of Five Hundred Thousand Dollars ($500,000.00), and

WHEREAS, the said National and Civil Defense Emergency Fund has of this date the sum of Four Hundred Ninety Six Thousand Dollars ($496,000.00), as a balance therein, and

WHEREAS, the War Production Board has determined that plants producing war materials in the vicinity of Louisville are faced with a serious reduction in the supply of underground water, and

WHEREAS, the operation of existing plants, together with the addition of many new plants, operating on a twenty-four hour basis have increased the water consumption, and

WHEREAS, the increased consumption of available underground water has lowered the static water table, and

WHEREAS, many of the wells from which underground water is drawn are now dry and the efficiency of others has been seriously impaired, and

WHEREAS, the said War Production Board, realizing the serious aspect of the reduction in the water supply has referred this matter to the United

States Geological Survey, the United States Corps of Engineers and the Department of Mines and Minerals, Division of Geology, of the Commonwealth of Kentucky, for study and report, and

WHEREAS, a meeting was held in Louisville, Kentucky, on Wednesday, July 28, 1943, to discuss the seriousness in the reduction in this water supply and its effect upon the production of war materials, and

WHEREAS, at said meeting on July 28, 1943, it was determined that a survey should be conducted by the United States Geological Survey, Ground Water Division, and the Department of Mines and Minerals, Division of Geology, of the Commonwealth of Kentucky, in order that the conservation and development of the underground water supply can be made, and

WHEREAS, the United States Geological Survey, by virtue of Acts of Congress, is empowered to make water resources investigation in cooperation with the state and to pay one-half of the expense thereof, and

WHEREAS, it will be necessary for the Department of Mines and Minerals, Division of Geology, to bear one-half of the expense of said investigation and survey, and

WHEREAS, it is determined that a complete investigation and survey can be made for a total sum not in excess of Fifteen Thousand Dollars ($15,000.00), one-half of which is to be advanced by the United States Geological Survey, and

WHEREAS, the appropriation made to the Department of Mines and Minerals, Division of Geology, is insufficient to permit said Division to expend the sum of Seventy Five Hundred Dollars ($7,500.00), and,

WHEREAS, an acute emergency, in the opinion of the Governor is thereby created and does now exist.

NOW, THEREFORE, I, Keen Johnson, Governor of the Commonwealth of Kentucky, by virtue of the authority vested in me as such, by this executive order, do hereby authorize and direct the Commissioner of Finance and the State Treasurer to cause to be set up out of the National and Civil Defense Emergency Fund (Part 1-A, Section 4, Item D-3 of the Acts of the 1942 General Assembly) Account #250 the sum of Seventy Five Hundred Dollars ($7,500.00) to be transferred from said National and Civil Defense Emergency Fund to the Department of Mines and Minerals, Division of Geology, Account #2843 to be used by said Division of Geology for the purposes set out herein.

INDUSTRY

LOUISVILLE BOARD OF TRADE
Louisville / January 1, 1940

GOVERNOR JOHNSON assured Kentucky businessmen that he intended to keep the state on a sound financial basis by practicing the most rigid economy. "My greatest ambition is to do as little to the state's business and to you as taxpayers as I can."

The budget soon to go to the legislature would contain three items of increase, one being $1 million for social security benefits, mostly old-age pensions. This could be regarded as insurance against the furtherance of unsound pension schemes. The other increases were $500,000 for a teachers' retirement plan which the governor termed desirable, and allotment of $10,000 a month for distribution of federal surplus food commodities to the state's needy.

In the past, Kentucky business leaders had feared sessions of the General Assembly because of new taxes which might be imposed. "You are not going to be forced to lay aside additional money for taxes." He knew from experience as a newspaper publisher the "very real problem" of meeting payrolls. "It is because of that that I'm determined, as far as the influence of the governor can be used, to urge curtailment of governmental spending so it will not need additional taxes."

The state's financial condition "has again become pressing" because of a decline in whiskey distilling revenue.

In a conversation with Senator Chandler, his predecessor as governor, while enroute from Frankfort to the reception, Chandler remarked that they were "breaking precedent." Johnson asked what precedent was being broken and Chandler said, "It's the first time a governor who went out and a governor who came in ever rode together after an inauguration."

KENTUCKY MINING INSTITUTE
Lexington / December 6, 1940

GOVERNOR JOHNSON declared that the state's finances at present are in better condition than at any other time for the past century.

"It is seldom that I have an opportunity to make a financial statement before a group representing the industry that provides some of the largest taxpayers in the state. I, therefore, think it appropriate to mention that the state shortly will make a payment that will reduce its debt to $4,097,000. Kentucky's former debt, which at one time reached $30 million, was contracted illegally in violation of a constitutional provision limiting its maximum financial obligation to $500,000.

"Once that indebtedness is paid off completely, the Court of Appeals would welcome a chance to overrule an opinion, handed down some years ago, that evaded the constitutional maximum and permitted some previous administrations to create such a heavy deficit." He recommended strongly that forthcoming administrations be "restrained from the unsound and uneconomic practice of spending for governmental expenses more than the income of the state."

He complimented the coal-mining executives for the progressiveness of their "far-reaching and ambitious safety program, undertaken in the interests of the workers. I especially appreciate the fine vision that is reflected in your keen sense of social responsibility, admirable attitude toward your associates, and the clear-sightedness that has resulted in your advanced concept of social ethics. Acquainted as I am with your efforts toward improvement, I boil with indignation when I hear uplifters deplore the 'horrible' conditions that are supposed to exist in the coal camps of Eastern Kentucky.

"I wish I were in a position to say the state's appropriation for this purpose [safety in coal-mining operations] would be twice as much, but naturally we are constrained by the tax income. We are making the best contribution to the program that seems to be possible under the circumstances."

He commended the coal operators for their work in this direction, and called attention to the fact that Kentucky for many years has been free of the major disasters that have beset mines in other states.

HAZARD COAL OPERATORS ASSOCIATION
Lexington / January 10, 1941

GOVERNOR JOHNSON stated that during the past year 1,290 persons had been dropped from the state payroll, effecting an annual saving estimated at $1.5 million.

Refinancing of the state's debt had been completed Thursday, reducing from 2.5 to 1 percent the interest rate on all but about one-tenth of the $4 million in warrants left outstanding. Contrasting the present situation with that which existed just a few years earlier, he declared that the two items mentioned represented a net yearly economy amounting to between $2.5 million and $3 million.

In explaining the "transformation that has taken place in the finances of the state in recent years," he stated that at one time the interest on the state debt was $1.35 million annually. Under the present refinanced setup, in which 2.5 percent warrants have been exchanged for 1 percent securities, the interest amounts only to about $40,000 a year. The analysis of Kentucky's financial condition and the exchange of the 2.5 percent securities for those yielding 1 percent were accomplished "with the splendid cooperation of the banking interests."

"The amount of money allowed for the Department of Mining and Minerals is inadequate," but "there is absolutely no chance for a reduction in taxes if there is an increase in the amount of money we spend.[1] Consequently, when the legislature meets next time, I've got to be against any increased appropriation for any department."

The governor praised the coal-production interests for the safety precautions they had put into effect, and said that despite the state government's low expenditure of $37,000 for its mining and minerals department, Kentucky's record is better so far as accidents are concerned than that of other states spending far more for industrial safety.[2]

---

1. At the association's annual banquet, November 28, 1941, the governor said that he saw no possibility for repeal of any of the tax laws in the near future. No additional taxes were indicated but those now in effect could not reasonably be repealed as long as state institutions remained in need of funds for construction and modernization. *Lexington Herald*, November 29, 1941.

2. The Kentucky Coal Association has no record of the governor's speeches. Letter, J. H. Mosgrove, vice-president, April 14, 1977.

GROUND-BREAKING FOR ARMCO BLAST FURNACE
Ashland / March 12, 1941

I REJOICE with you that the American Rolling Mill Company has decided to expend $5 million in enlarging the output of their plant here at Ashland. I am delighted as governor of Kentucky to join with you in an expression of our appreciation of this great industrial organization which demonstrates its faith in Kentucky and Ashland by this large increase in their investment here.

Mr. Verity[1] is one of the ablest industrial executives in America. He is a man of superior business judgment, and his decision to make here so large an additional investment is a high compliment to this community and Commonwealth. Five million dollars is a lot of money.

An acquaintance of mine relates his seven-year-old son rather irritated him one morning by dashing into the bathroom while he was shaving and asking, "Dad, how much is a million dollars?" The irritated father gave the lad a rather curt answer. That evening when the father came home, his small son crawled up in his father's lap and in a reproachful voice said, "Dad, you got me in bad at school today." The father was surprised and asked, "How did I get you in bad, son?" The lad explained, "Well, the teacher said, 'a hell of a lot of money' is not the right answer."

So we recognize $5 million as a lot of money. If you had that much money, you would be very cautious about where you invested it. Yet, the hard-headed business men who direct the destinies of Armco are of the opinion that this is a good place to make such an investment. We believe their judgment will be vindicated and as their neighbors, it shall be our purpose to help them to here realize a reasonable return upon their investment.

Twenty years ago Armco established its Ashland plant. During those years Armco has been a good neighbor. It has been a splendid, constructive citizen. As governor, I have come to have a sincere appreciation of our big taxpayers, and Armco has through the years been a big taxpayer. It has contributed substantially to the support of schools and government here in Boyd County.

Armco has been a generous contributor to the state treasury in taxes. This plant paid in taxes last year the sum of approximately $300,000. Armco has provided employment for as high as 3,200 men. Those men have received good wages and an opportunity to rear their children on a decent level of living.

So intelligent and enlightened have been the executives of this huge organization that they have not had a single stoppage in operation as the result of labor disputes. So there is abundant evidence to justify the statement that Armco has been a good neighbor and a splendid citizens. We appreciate Armco and the contribution it has made to the economic and social advancement of this fine community and to Kentucky. So since we entertain for Armco such high esteem, it naturally is most gratifying to have this manifestation of the fact that Armco likes Ashland and likes Kentucky. This organization has, after living here among us for two decades learning all about us—our faults as well as our virtues, decided to make this large expenditure in expansion of the great unit of their organization which is here located. We regard that as a high compliment, and by this action Armco places this community and this Commonwealth under increased obligation to continue to be good neighbors.

As governor of Kentucky, I take great pride in the fact that after twenty years of residence in our state, Armco executives have reached the conclusion that Kentucky is a good state in which to invest their money. And the facts justify that conclusion. There is not a state in the Union whose state government is on a sounder, more solvent basis than is Kentucky.

Six years ago Kentucky was in debt approximately $26 million. It was a debt for which we had nothing to show. It was a debt that had been contracted as a result of spending each year more money than was collected from the taxpayers. As a result of the wise leadership of my predecessor, Governor Chandler, his associates, and the legislature, the administrative mechanism of government was changed. The state's budget was balanced. The slow, painful process of paying off that debt was started. I am proud of the fact that as lieutenant governor I had a small part in that program. This is the first time I have had a chance to express to so large a group of Boyd countians my humble gratitude for their expression of confidence in me as expressed by their vote. In that campaign the one promise I made you, which I regarded as most important, was that I would make you a saving, thrifty, frugal governor. I am glad that I may truthfully say to you that I have tried earnestly each day to keep that pledge. And difficult though such a pledge is to keep, I am glad to be able to report to you that we have been getting along pretty well in fulfilling that most vital promise. As governor of Kentucky, I have tried to infuse into the state government the same principles of economy, efficiency, and good business that have made Armco so conspicuously successful.

Six years ago it required $1.25 million a year of your money to pay the interest on your state debt. Today the interest on your state debt can be paid with $40,000 a year. That debt of $26 million six years ago has been reduced to $4 million and prospects are good that it will be further reduced within the year. Kentucky now has the second lowest debt of any state in the nation. We collect from you in state taxes to perform all functions of government an average of $18 per person per year. There are only seven states in which the per capita tax payment is lower. Waste, graft, favoritism in tax administration, bad business have been eliminated from your state government, and we face the future with prospects of a situation so advantageous that I believe there is ample justification for the faith in the future of Kentucky which is expressed by the American Rolling Mill Company.

During those years when Kentucky was going steadily in debt, spending each year in excess of her income, the state's charitable institutions were shamefully neglected. I have visited each of the charitable and penal institutions, familiarized myself with their needs. Now that we approach the day when it appears that we shall be able to wipe out our state debt, the governor is receiving many suggestions as to what should be the future fiscal policy of the state. I am certain that our next most important duty is that of rehabilitating the state hospitals for the mentally ill. These institutions are sorely inadequate. They reflect discreditably on Kentucky. It will require a considerable expenditure to make up for the accumulated deficiencies that result from prolonged neglect of these important institutions. The conditions in them are much improved. They are being directed by highly competent superintendents, assisted by well-trained staffs. But the buildings within which these unfortunates are crowded must be extensively rehabilitated and expanded before we as a state have discharged our duty as an enlightened Commonwealth.

When that imperative obligation has been eliminated, Kentucky, debt free, living prudently within her income, her public institutions modernized, all agencies of public service modestly financed, we then approach the day when lightening of the tax load can be realized. In the meantime, Armco has assurance that it has chosen wisely in singling out its Kentucky plant for expansion. That expansion may proceed with the confident assurance that the state government and local governmental agencies are to be so economically administered as to eliminate the necessity for increased taxes.

The American Rolling Mill Company has been a great asset to Kentucky and Ashland. In these unhappy days when we face necessity of preparing for the defense of our country, Armco is a great asset to the nation. The modern facilities for production of steel that are here contemplated will make this great industrial operation one of increased importance as we proceed as rapidly as we can to help Britain in her gallant fight to halt Hitler.

And I have an idea that as the high command of Armco decided to enlarge the Ashland plant, one of the reasons was the fact that this plant is located in a region where reside a highly patriotic people.

[The governor discussed voluntary enlistments and the Selective Service Act.]

So as we look into the uncertain future, certain only of the fact that as Kentuckians it is our duty to render enthusiastic aid to the defense program, support our great president in his efforts to help Britain to halt Hitler, we pay tribute to the patriotic youth of Eastern Kentucky who will man the implements of war which will be forged from the steel that will be here produced by Armco. And we express our grateful thanks that in this great democracy there has developed, through private initiative, vast industrial organizations such as the American Rolling Mill, whose splendid facilities and efficient organization are made available for the defense of that type of government under which such industrial development is possible.[2]

---

1. Calvin William Verity (1889–1977), b. Newport. Steel and bank executive. Vice-president, American Rolling Mill Company. Resided Middleton, Ohio. *Who's Who in America, 1962–1963* (Chicago, 1963), 32:3221, and telephone interview, John Dryden, Armco, July 24, 1980.

2. In January 1941 the governor appointed an advisory committee to analyze the results of a survey of Kentucky's industrial facilities. The Associated Industries had sent out questionnaires at the request of Civil Defense Director J. J. Greenleaf. The governor said, "It will be the first time an accurate survey has been made of what Kentucky industrial facilities are and, in addition to aiding national defense, will prove valuable in other ways." He explained that national defense co-director William S. Knudsen had requested all governors to make such surveys. "The defense council wants to speed up the defense program by being able in letting contracts to primary contractors to tell them where they can sub-let part of the work. That means speed because existing facilities can be used instead of time being required to build new factories and plants. The data must be accurate to be of real value. We want to make ours such that it will not only speed up the program, but will bring more business to Kentucky. Data showing what Kentucky concerns already are engaged in metal work, chemical manufacture, and other projects necessary to national defense, or could turn to that or similar work, would be compiled from the questionnaires." *State Journal*, January 25, 1941.

The governor submitted the report on December 13, 1941, of Kentucky's capacity for national defense production to representatives of the Office of Production Management, army, navy, marines, and other defense agencies. *State Journal*, December 13, 1941.

HENDERSON'S INDUSTRIAL REVIVAL
Henderson / March 19, 1941

GOVERNOR JOHNSON extended congratulations to the Henderson Board of Trade and declared that Henderson's industrial rebirth is due largely to the united efforts of the board.[1]

He saluted the Associated Factories which employs 45 to 50 men, the Atlas Tack Corporation which expects work for 200 men, the Ohio Valley Soybean Co-operative, the Henderson Concrete Company, the Ice and Storage Company and the $15 million ammonia plant. "As governor, I am glad to welcome them to Henderson. These new industries have chosen wisely and selected a fine community in a great state." The new industries that have located in Henderson or will locate here soon "are to be congratulated upon their wisdom. They are certain of stability in the tax program. They are certain, and so am I, that there will be no increase in state taxes. I'm delighted that this community is getting a generous serving of gravy as it trickles from the defense kettle."

The governor commented on the state money coming back to Henderson during the last year and cited $15,379 for courts, $5,268 for county tax commissioner, $102,511 for public schools and free books, $78,483 for old age assistance, $19,477 for rural highways, $5,000 for truck licenses, $7,386 for Audubon Park, $56,196 for highway maintenance for a total of $289,700.[2]

---

1. The governor spoke at a banquet held to celebrate the end of a toll for the Henderson-Evansville bridge. See speech from March 20, 1941, in the Airports, Bridges, and Highways section.

2. Material about Kentucky's financial situation and the state hospitals has been deleted.

COAL FREIGHT RATES AND WAGE DIFFERENTIALS
Frankfort / April 14, 15, 1941

TELEGRAM to chairman, Southern Coal Operators' Wage Conference,[1] April 14, 1941:

Glad to comply with your request. Anxious to be helpful in preventing elimination of wage differential. Existing freight rate disadvantage on coal shipped from Kentucky justifies pay differential.[2] Explanatory memorandum:

The proposed increase in wages to a $7.00 base would amount to approximately 40 percent increase in cost in Western Kentucky and 25 percent increase in Eastern Kentucky. The Eastern Kentucky coalfields are on a $5.60 base; the Western Kentucky coalfields, $5.00.

The increase for the operators in the northern field amounts to $1.00 a day, or 16⅔ percent. Coal of a comparable quality is laid down at Detroit, for example, from the Western Pennsylvania coalfield, at present, for about fifteen cents a ton less than coal from Eastern Kentucky.

The proposed $7.00 wage rate would give the nothern operators an advantage of twenty-seven to forty-five cents a ton in the Lake markets and the bigger industrial markets of the Middle West.

In other words, a two-inch nut and slack shipped from Harlan to Detroit is delivered there for $3.62 on present price and wage setup, while a coal of similar quality from Western Pennsylvania delivers for around $3.47. Under the proposed contract, the same coal from Eastern Kentucky will deliver at Detroit for approximately $3.92, while the Pennsylvania coal can be delivered in Detroit for $3.64.

This same relationship will hold in other big industrial markets of the Middle West. These markets, combined with the Lakes, take the greater part of the production of Eastern Kentucky at present.

Western Kentucky on a $5.00 base is delivering run-of-mine coal in Chicago for $3.95. Illinois on a $6.00 base delivers a comparable quality of run-of-mine coal in Chicago for $3.55. The Western Kentucky coalfield is being undersold in its principal industrial market by forty cents a ton. Now under the proposed contract, $7.00 base in all fields, this same Western Kentucky coal would deliver in Chicago for $4.38 as against $3.75 for Illinois coal, increasing the difference to sixty-three cents a ton.

The price differential that will follow a contract based on a $7.00 a day all over the country will eliminate most of the Kentucky coal from the north. The southern coal market does not consume sufficient coal to keep the mines of Kentucky, Southern West Virginia, Virginia, Tennessee, and Alabama operating over 20 percent of full time.

The net result of this wage equalization and price increase will be the slow elimination of the majority of the producing mines in Kentucky with attendant unemployment of thousands of miners.

It is my opinion that less than 100 of the 270 railroad mines in Kentucky today could hope to survive this proposed adverse, economic setup.

Telegram to President Roosevelt, April 15, 1941:[3]

I respectfully urge you to suggest to the secretary of labor that she immediately certify to Mediation Board the pending coal mine dispute. I deem the situation with respect to suspension of coal mining in Eastern Kentucky most grave, causing deep concern to all our citizens, particularly to labor dependent on this production for livelihood, as well as impeding national defense in our greatest emergency.

Coal stocks are unevenly distributed, and while average supply apparently sufficient for twenty-eight days, most consumers' coal piles now reaching vanishing point. Kentucky miners want to get back to work, intensifying local problem. I am reliably informed that Kentucky coal producers joined with all other southern producers and offered wage increases of approximately 11 per centum, in agreement for mediation all further questions of wages and working conditions in order to get mines into operation immediately.

I believe there are sound economic grounds for the position taken by southern operators with respect to long established sectional differentials directly involved in controversy. Such differentials were recognized by NRA and in all national regulations. Freight rate differentials against southern territory are from thirty-five to ninety cents per ton to principal consuming markets, and price structures based on these rates necessitate wage differentials. These freight differentials amount to four times the wage differential. Acute competitive situation with respect to substitute fuel, such as oil and gas and hydroelectric power, bears most heavily on southern coal industry.

My judgment is that the situation calls for immediate action in the form of certification to the Mediation Board for realistic settlement in order that the mines may be started without delay, and I so respectively urge.[4]

---

1. Ebersole Gaines, Fayetteville, West Virginia. He had asked Johnson's aid in getting the case of the Southern Coal Operators before the National Labor Mediation Board. They had bolted the wage conference with the United Mine Workers and set up their own bargaining committee after northern operators agreed to a flat $7.00 a day base wage. Louisville *Courier-Journal,* April 15, 1941.

2. According to the governor, southern mines suffered from a thirty-five cents a ton freight rate differential. "That freight rate differential was recognized by NRA as imposing an inequitable differential on Kentucky coal operators. The prinicple of the wage differential was set up by NRA as a just and fair equalizing factor. Even with the wage differential, Kentucky coal is at a competitive disadvantage with Pennsylvania and Ohio coal, but they [Kentucky mines] are able to sell coal despite that disadvantage because of a superior fuel." Louisville *Courier-Journal*, April 15, 1941. The NRA was the National Recovery Administration, established in 1933 by the National Industrial Recovery Act as part of the Roosevelt New Deal program.

3. The governor sent similar telegrams to Kentucky's senators and representatives in Washington and asked them to join him in urging the president to get the matter before the Mediation Board. *State Journal*, April 16, 1941.

4. Violence erupted with the work stoppage. On April 2, 1941, the governor declared, "The Harlan slaughter must stop. Regardless of who is to blame, it cannot be permitted to continue." He telephoned William Turnblazer, Jellico, Tennessee, president, District 19, United Mine Workers, and appealed for peace. He told him that the operators had closed down their mines in an effort to reduce the possibility of violence. Turnblazer promised that he would direct Robert Hodge, secretary-treasurer, Harlan District, UMW to instruct the men to disperse, go to their homes, and refrain from activity. Louisville *Courier-Journal*, April 3, 1941. On April 15, 1941, four men, including the president and vice-president of a coal mine, were killed near Middlesboro and twenty-five miners were wounded. *State Journal*, April 16, 1941.

On May 7, 1941, an agreement was reached at a conference with the governor for an election to decide union jurisdiction at the International Harvester Company mine at Benham, Harlan County, and for union consent for resumption of work at twenty-three independent mines. The jurisdictional dispute concerned whether the miners were to be represented by the UMW (CIO) or the Progressive Mine Workers of America (AFL). The independent mines were in Bell, Harlan, Knox, and Whitley counties and employed 3,740 workers. Louisville *Courier-Journal*, May 8, 1941.

COAL FREIGHT RATES
Louisville / July 21, 1941

A PLEA that Western Kentucky coal mines be given a "fair share" of the big market in the Chicago industrial district by reduction in the freight rate advantages now favoring Indiana and Southern Illinois was made by Governor Johnson.[1]

In 1927, when Indiana and Illinois enjoyed only a twenty-five cents per ton differential on Chicago shipments, Western Kentucky produced 21 million tons of coal. In 1927 the difference in favor of Indiana and Western Illinois was raised to thirty-five cents a ton, and by 1940 Western Kentucky's production had dropped to 8.5 million tons a year.

The governor stated that Kentucky consumes "only a small part" of the coal it mines and Western Kentucky mines cannot ship east or southeast because of competition from Appalachian fields.

Coal consumption in the states south of Kentucky is "relatively small," and Indiana and Southern Illinois mines can ship into those states at the same rate as Kentucky.

The governor asserted that the Kentucky Railroad Commission, which requested the hearing, believed that the rates to Chicago were "unjust and discriminatory" against Kentucky.[2]

---

1. Interstate Commerce Commission hearing.

2. The Railroad Commission set no specific differential in its petition for the hearing, but Commission Chairman Robert E. Webb was understood to be seeking a return to the old twenty-five cents differential or even a lower one. The governor transferred $225 by executive order from his Emergency Fund to the Railroad Commission on June 3, 1941, to enable it to employ an additional rate expert to assist with the collection and assembly of data to present to the Interstate Commerce Commission at this hearing.

KENTUCKY MINING INSTITUTE
Lexington / December 5, 1941

REPLYING to recent demands for the repeal of Kentucky's income tax law, Governor Johnson declared that, while there was no need for additional taxes, "we cannot consider repeal until we have paid off our greatest debt—to our charitable, educational and penal institutions."

The governor rapped sharply those "pressure groups who come to Frankfort every day demanding more and more in appropriations and less and less in taxes. For six years we have been exerting every effort to get Kentucky out of debt. For the first time since 1908 we are back on the state constitution, which says that we cannot have a state debt of more than $500,000 without a vote of the people. Now, as a result of a fictitious prosperity caused largely by defense actifity, everybody wants taxes repealed. In consideration of the fact that the state income is highly susceptible to economic change and that in two years it may vary as much as $5 million, it would be stupid, indeed, now to begin the repeal of taxes and get ourselves right back into the debt we have been working out of for six years.

"We have been providing money for the bare minimum needs of our charitable and educational and penal institutions. Kentucky ranks discreditably low in support of them and of the many phases of its social program, and we have a greater debt to them now than ever before. That debt must be paid. Our public health program, the University of Kentucky, the Department of Mines and Minerals, all should have more generous appropriations, and they are going to get them. They'll have to get along on less than they are asking for, but they're going to get more than they have been getting."

The governor characterized the problem of smoke abatement as "a serious challenge and threat to the coal-mining industry of Kentucky. It is important that we unitedly begin trying to find the answer to the problem before metropolitan areas begin the passage of legislation which would seriously cripple the coal industry of this state. To anticipate any such action, an appropriation for research into smoke abatement, the distillation of coal and the utilization of its by-products will be made for the College of Engineering of the University of Kentucky. The initial appropriation will not be large, probably $7,500, but it will be a beginning to the solution of an important problem."[1]

---

1. The governor transferred $10,000 by executive order on September 4, 1943, from his Emergency Fund to the College of Engineering, University of Kentucky, to enable it to continue experiments on low-temperature distillation of coal and shale. In November 1943 he transferred $30,000 to the College of Engineering to be used in finding and defining metallic mineral deposits in Kentucky.

The Department of Mines and Minerals does not have a copy of the speech. Letter, Margaret Caywood, executive assistant to the commissioner, April 26, 1977.

TIRE RATIONING BOARDS
Frankfort / December 20, 1941

GOVERNOR JOHNSON announced that, at the request of federal officials, he would appoint a state tire rationing board and similar boards for each county and that after January 4, any person, firm, or agency wanting to buy a new tire must have a certificate of sanction from these boards.

"There just aren't going to be any more new tires for private or pleasure cars until the war is over. Mr. Alexander Harris of Knoxville, a field representative of the Office of Price Administration, has just told me that the United States has only 20 percent of its new tire needs on hand. There must be a good reason to get a new tire in the future.

"The new rationing boards must be ready to function by January 4, the date to which the federal government's outright ban on all new tire purchases has been extended. In the meantime, quotas will be set for Kentucky and other states and, in each state, the quotas must be broken down for the counties on the basis of their commercial vehicle registration.

"Sale of new tires after January 4 will be limited to persons or agencies needing them for the maintenance of industrial efficiency and civilian health. These will include the following broad classes: vehicles required for the maintenance of public safety and health; passenger transportation equipment, exclusive of private passenger cars; and a limited group of essential truck operators. Controls also are being planned for the sale of retreaded tires."

Harris had informed him that action to stabilize tire prices would be taken before the rationing plan started. Criminal penalties could be imposed on those violating the quotas or falsifying reports.

The governor said that the county boards are expected to have three members each although larger counties, such as Jefferson, probably would have several boards. Representatives of several large tire companies would confer with him the next day on the rationing plan.[1]

---

1. The governor stated on July 30, 1942, that the highway patrol would cooperate with the federal government's effort to prevent tire purchases by drivers who exceed 40 m.p.h. He said that he would instruct the patrol to report to George Goodman, state OPA administrator, the license number of all motor vehicle drivers seen traveling at more than the 40-mile wartime speed limit. This information would be transmitted to local rationing boards with a request that offenders' applications for tires be denied. *Cincinnati Enquirer*, July 31, 1942. Johnson had

issued a proclamation on February 16, 1942, putting the 40 m.p.h. speed limit into effect. On September 19, 1942, he reduced it to 35 m.p.h. In a proclamation, dated June 13, 1942, he urged full support for a nationwide Scrap Rubber Salvage Campaign, June 15-30, 1942, which the president had called for on June 12.

TIRE RATIONING BOARDS
Frankfort / December 29, 1941

GOVERNOR JOHNSON explained that Kentucky was attempting to discharge its defense program activities, as far as possible, with agencies and individuals already established or available since the state had no money with which to pay for outside aid in these activities. Tire rationing board members served without pay, and there was no provision for the pay of clerical help.

Pointing to tire rationing as the "first of severe and harsh sacrifices we will be called upon to make," he declared rubber to be the "one thing above everything else your government needs now. The Japs put their finger on the Achillean heel of these United States when they invaded, or attempted to invade, those areas from which comes 93 percent of the nation's rubber supply. With the Japs in temporary command of the Pacific, the situation as it affects the national rubber supply is extremely critical."

Tire consumption in the United States is approximately 4 million monthly, and there is now on hand only 8 million tires, or, roughly, a two-months' supply. Federal officials have "urged an immediate 80 percent reduction in civilian consumption of rubber." If Singapore should fall to the enemy, then the present situation would become even more serious, but if it did not, "it may be possible in the months ahead to relieve the seriousness of the problem."

The boards would be called upon to exercise very few "discretionary" powers. The rationing of tires would be handled by rigid rules and regulations. The governor stated that he would transmit orders relative to tire rationing as they come to him and obeying these orders is as important as obeying any military orders. "In fact, no military officer is contributing any more important duty than you will be contributing in helping conserve the nation's rubber supply.

"On the first of each month the state will be allotted a specific quota of tires for rationing or distribution and these, in turn, will be allocated to the various counties on the basis of the number of industrial vehicles registered in each county. This job will take all of your time for the first few weeks. You will serve without pay and there is no provision for supplying you with clerical help. It is a disagreeable job and I don't mean to discourage you, gentlemen, but these are the grim realities of the job with which we are confronted. There will soon be few tires to ration. May God have mercy on your souls."[1]

---

1. Johnson spoke to board members from the Sixth Congressional District. It was the first of a series of meetings in the nine congressional districts.

LOUISVILLE BOARD OF TRADE
Louisville / January 1, 1942

IT is a very great pleasure to come here this New Year's morning and to have this opportunity of again expressing to the members of the Louisville Board of Trade the gratitude of the governor of Kentucky for the fine contribution this splendid organization continues to make for the advancement of Louisville and the betterment of the Commonwealth of Kentucky. Two years ago I had the pleasure of assembling here with you. I had only shortly been sworn in as governor, and then on that occasion prophesized that having only recently been sworn in, I contemplated that I would henceforth be sworn at, and that prophecy has been fulfilled to some degree.

Kentucky six years ago as a result of prolonged periods of financial maladministration was in debt $26 million to $28 million. It required more than a million dollars of your money each year to pay the interest on that state debt. I am glad to say to you that today that state debt has been reduced to $495,000 and the interest on that state debt this year can be paid with less than $10,000 instead of more than a million that was required six years ago.

No one has contributed more to the financial reformation of Kentucky than you, the substantial taxpayers of the Commonwealth who have accepted with tolerance and patience a tax program designed to restore the solvency of your state. I am anxious to say this morning how much I appreciate the good taxpayers, those who have made possible the financial reformation of the Commonwealth, "United We Stand."

We have had great hopes and plans for the future that would permit, now that the state debt has been eliminated, that we might carry on a substantial program for the rehabilitation of our charitable and penal institutions. This is a program which was started under the administration of my predecessor. We still have hopes that we may be able to make some contribution to the improvement of that situation.

However, circumstances arising since bombs dropped on the Stars and Stripes at Pearl Harbor have completely altered our thoughts and thinking. It has completely changed the whole economic and financial picture. There can be no certainty that there will be from existing taxes sufficient revenue with which to do anything other than to meet the essential routine expected of state government and to adequately finance that program of defense which Kentucky must carry forward.

The certainty of an unpredictable future has altered serious plans and leaves Kentucky at first with a feeling of prostration and futility. For years we have striven to reestablish the solvency of the state in order that we might tell the folks of the payment of another debt, the debt which we owe the unfortunates in the institutions in Kentucky. The Louisville Board of Trade has always been interested in Kentucky's state institutions. Back in 1925, the Louisville Board of Trade pioneered as the advocate and sponsor of a state bond issue with which to raise money for construction of roads and with which to rehabilitate and reconstruct the penal and charitable institutions of this Commonwealth.

This organization has always had the vision, has always realized the necessity and the importance of our paying back this important debt. Now the picture has changed. There is no way to be certain as to whether it will be possible to carry forward that program or not. We cannot be certain that the revenue which appeared definite and specific will be available. We cannot be certain what incident, what unhappy economic dislocation overnight may result in its depletion.

As to the rationing of tires to which Mayor Wyatt[1] referred, I wish to express my gratitude to the mayor and other public-spirited citizens of Louisville for the fine service they have performed here in Louisville in formulating a setup by which tires here may be rationed as a result of the shortage of rubber created by Japan. Unless we ration the tires and rubber, unless we conserve tires and rubber and get ready to lick Japan, Japan will win the war and she will ration us.

But the economic dislocation that comes as the result of the rationing of tires already presents certain possibility of absolutely destroying a magnificent highway construction program well advanced for next year because of reduced consumption of gasoline. It means a reduction in our road income of at least 33.33 percent. President Wilson one morning closed all distilleries in the United States that the grain might be diverted for food. Should that happen in this war, and it is not an improbable thing, there will instantly more than $3 million in state revenue and state taxes go out the window.

The unpredictable, the uncertain future creates a situation that makes it necessary that your governor explain. A few months ago I was contemplating with great satisfaction the pleasure and happiness of saying to the Kentucky legislature, I have the distinction and honor to come before you as your governor and for the first time in the history of the state there is no necessity for increased taxes. I had hoped that I could say that.

Now I can only say to the legislature: I hope there will be no necessity for increased taxes. Before the legislative session adjourns, there may be an economic repercussion that affects our revenue so vitally as to necessitate the enactment of additional taxes. Not only is it necessary to retain existing taxes, but it is necessary to exercise extreme caution, care, and frugality.

It is going to be harder to live under a $28.5 million budget this and the next two years than it was to live under a $26 million budget last year. Why? The upsurge of prices, increasing the expense of all phases of your government, charitable and penal institutions, more than $1 million required last year to purchase food and clothing and personal services for inmates of your hospitals and your charitable, and penal institutions. Advancing cost of food, rising cost of groceries, has already created a situation so it is necessary to make substantial increases in your appropriations for those purposes. United may we stand, united may we see the necessity for that program.[2]

---

1. Wilson Watkins Wyatt (1905–), b. Louisville. Attorney; mayor of Louisville, 1941–1945; lieutenant governor, 1959–1963, member, board of trustees, University of Louisville, 1950–1958, chairman, 1951–1955; first president of the Young Democrats Club, Louisville-Jefferson County. *Who's Who in America, 1978–1979*, 40th ed. (Chicago, 1978), 2:3558.

2. A statement in the *Board of Trade Journal*, January 1942, notes that nine-tenths of the governor's address was on the national emergency. Because of interest in the state's fiscal policies at the 1942 session of the legislature, "and for sake of variety," that portion of his talk published in the *Journal* related only to proposed rehabilitation of state welfare and penal institutions and tax and revenue policies.

REYNOLDS METALS COMPANY
Louisville / May 23, 1942

IT affords me unusual pleasure to join as governor of the Commonwealth of Kentucky with those in high places in Washington to pay tribute to the Reynolds Metals Company and its loyal and faithful employees for exceptional and outstanding accomplishment at probably the most tragic moment in the history of the world.

We have many fine institutions in Louisville and throughout our great Commonwealth. We are proud of them all, but it delights me to meet with you in your number one "Battle Plant" because I understand this plant is an honored veteran of the last war.

We have met here today to award a Victory Pin for meritorious work to those who served this company for twenty years, fifteen years, ten years, and five years. From the record that is being made now, I am sure that every employee of this company will receive a permanent token for the devoted service being rendered the nation.

I am delighted to know that you men with your own funds have covered this great plant with the American flag. I am equally delighted with the cordial relations that exist between management and labor. I understand that for twenty-nine years there has been no authorized strike in any of the Reynolds factories. That is the spirit that has made, and will continue to make, America. We are all members of the team . . . fighting for our own liberties and freedom of the world.

I could talk longer on the record of this company, but after all, this company was born in Kentucky and reached maturity in Kentucky; therefore, I think it is far more fitting for me to read to you now speeches delivered on the floor of the United States Senate last Monday by three great senators paying high tribute to you and your company.[1]

---

1. Johnson read only one speech, that of Senator Lister Hill of Alabama. He said that, following Hill, Senators Truman and Mead added their praise. See U.S., Congress, Senate, *Congressional Record*, 88th Cong., pp. 4259-60.

STRIKE AT REYNOLDS METALS COMPANY
Frankfort / August 19, 1942

TELEGRAM to Philip Murray,[1] CIO president, Washington, D.C.

As governor of Kentucky I urge that you direct Cannon to order his men to return to work at the Reynolds plants in Louisville. This strike is halting production in plants engaged in producing aluminum used in manufacture of war planes. Merits of the controversy can be considered without halting production of vital defense materials. The action requested of you will reflect credit upon your leadership and be appreciated by me.

Telegram to Joseph D. Cannon, CIO regional director, Louisville.

It is a serious disservice to the nation in this critical hour to halt production. It is impossible to justify halting production because of a dispute over which union has the majority of workers.[2] You will render your organization and your flag an intelligent service if you will order the workers back to their jobs and keep them there. Facilities of the Conciliation Service Division of the state Department of Industrial Relations are available in helping to adjust differences.[3]

---

1. Philip Murray (1886–1952), b. Scotland. Entered United States in 1902. Vice-president, UMWA, 1920–1942; president, CIO, 1940–1952. *Who Was Who in America, 1951–1960,* 3:628.

2. The strike resulted from a dispute as to whether the workers were to be represented by the CIO or the AFL. Cannon contended that an election to determine the bargaining agent was in order since the AFL contract expired July 1. Edward H. Weyler, secretary of the Kentucky Federation of Labor, termed the strike "a shame if there ever was one in this town." *Kentucky Post,* August 20, 1942.

3. Cannon replied by telegram: "In reply to your telegram I will say that it is encouraging. Reynolds workers are anxious to return to work as soon as a discharged worker is returned to the job, no discrimination assured, and election provided. This is pretty much in line with your telegram, though it gives no assurance of this protection."

ARMCO BLAST FURNACE
Ashland / August 24, 1942

I AM glad to be here for this "blow out" at the blowing in of this huge blast furnace. The American Rolling Mill Company is today driving a spike in Hitler's coffin as it commits this great industrial machine to service. The tremendous output of steel which will be produced here will hasten the day of doom for the dictators that are trying to destroy us. It speeds the hour when the world will be liberated and right again becomes regnant in the world.

Well do I remember that interesting day March 12, 1941, as we gathered here for ceremonies which marked the breaking of ground for this furnace. While war clouds were spreading over the sky at that time, we hoped that the United States could avoid being drawn into the conflict. Within the seventeen months during which this furnace has been hurried to completion, startling changes have taken place in the world. Millions of our men are under arms. All resources of the nation are being mobilized to produce the guns and grenades, the planes and tanks with which to exterminate the mad dogs of Germany and Japan. Blood of Kentucky men has been spilled on every battlefront. Americans have fought bravely and died gallantly. But the day of triumph is yet far distant because of scarcity of materials from which to manufacture the weapons of war. This furnace, a modern marvel of industrial genius, will produce a thousand tons of pig iron a day. That will be converted into weapons with which armies of the united nations will conquer the Huns and the slant-eyed Japanese.

At the ground-breaking ceremony, I congratulated Mr. Verity and associates of Armco upon the vision and good judgment which led to the decision to so expand their Ashland plants as to double production. That decision was more fortunate than we could realize at that time. This plant comes into production at a time when there is an acute shortage of steel; at a time when steel is the preeminent need in this the most crucial period of world history. How lucky we are that Armco executives started this furnace seventeen months ago instead of waiting for Pearl Harbor. This vital plant goes into production nine months earlier as a result. The steel produced in that time will shorten the war, save the lives of many American boys.

I am delighted, as governor of Kentucky, to join with the people of Ashland in an expression of our appreciation of Armco, which has demonstrated its faith in Kentucky and Ashland by this large increase in their investment here. More than $6 million has been expended in this expansion. If you or I had that much money, we would be cautious about where it was invested. The hard-headed, successful businessmen who direct the destinies of Armco decided that this is a good place to make such an investment. I am certain their judgment will be vindicated, and as their neighbors it shall be our purpose to help them realize a reasonable return on their investment.

Twenty-one years ago Armco established its Ashland plant. During the years Armco has been a good neighbor and a fine citizen. As governor, I have a sincere appreciation of our big taxpayers, and Armco has through the years been a big taxpayer. It has contributed substantially to the support of schools and government here in Boyd County. This great organization has been a generous contributor to the state treasury in taxes. It has provided employment for as high as 3,200 men. Those men have received good wages and an opportunity to rear their children on a decent level of living.

So intelligent and enlightened have been the executives of the American Rolling Mill Company that they have not had a single stoppage in operation as result of labor disputes. So there is ample evidence to support the statement that Armco has been a good neighbor and a splendid citizen.

We appreciate Armco for the contribution it has made to the economic and social advancement of this splendid city and to Kentucky. Since we hold Armco in such high esteem, it is most gratifying to have this indication that Armco likes Ashland and likes Kentucky.

It is pleasing to me as governor of Kentucky that Armco executives concluded that Kentucky is a good state in which to invest money. Facts justify that conclusion. There is no state in the Union whose government is on a more solvent basis than is Kentucky's. At the ground-breaking ceremonies, I told you that Kentucky's state debt had been reduced to $4 million.

Today it is with pride that I boast of the fact that every dollar of the state debt has been paid, that Kentucky is one of the few states in the nation that is completely out of debt and has a substantial surplus in the treasury. That surplus places us in a strong position to meet the uncertainties of an uncertain future, maintain essentials of public service despite reductions in income that are resulting from economic dislocations and avoid an increase in taxes.

The artificial prosperity stimulated by the war resulted in state revenues being increased from existing taxes during the past fiscal year. But in the next fiscal year we face a certain drop of several millions of dollars in income. Revenue from the whiskey production tax will be lost completely. Manufacture of whiskey is to be stopped entirely as distilleries are converted to production of industrial alcohol required in making gun powder and synthetic rubber. This source of income produced about $3 million last year. The income from usage tax paid with the purchase of new automobiles will result in loss of $1.5 million. Automobile tire rationing is reducing the income from the gasoline tax substantially. But prospects for the next year are that we shall be able to operate the state government within its budget despite reductions in state revenue, maintain the financial solidarity of the state government.

A sincere effort is being made to administer public affairs cautiously and carefully. Favoritism in tax administration, wastefulness, and bad business have been eliminated. We face the future with prospects of a situation so advantageous to industry that I believe there is abundant reason for the faith in the future of Kentucky which is expressed by the American Rolling Mill Company. As they have made here this large expansion in plant, they have been justified in the hope that state and local governmental agencies are to be so economically administered as to eliminate necessity for increased taxes.

This new blast furnace definitely establishes Ashland permanently as an important steel manufacturing center. The result will be to attract other industries to this section to contribute to the development of this strategically located area and the advancement of Kentucky after the war is over and peace comes again. Ashland has long been associated with the production of iron and steel. It has been a pioneer producer of pig iron since Bellefonte furnace was built near Poage's Landing in 1823. This vast, modern furnace here committed to service marks the beginning of a new episode in the romantic story of the development of this vital industry—an episode in which will be recorded the high achievement of Armco. Fitting indeed it is that this new furnace is to have the distinction of bearing the name of Bellefonte. The original Bellefonte was doubtless as fine and efficient a furnace in its day as is this amazingly modern unit which is to have the honor of perpetuating the name of that plant which went into operation 119 years ago. Yet the contrast between the plants speaks eloquently of the development in the iron and steel industry within little more than a century.

This new Bellefont is christened in the most critical period of our nation's history. It is dedicated to the high and holy cause of producing the steel from which will be forged implements of war with which to defeat the foes of freedom. No doubt the high command of Armco, as they decided to expand the Ashland operations, considered the fact that this is a region where reside a highly patriotic people. Only from four states in the Union have more young men voluntarily enlisted in the armed forces than from Kentucky, and the population of each of those states exceeds Kentucky's many times. I am proud of the privilege of being governor of a state where the fire of patriotic fervor burns so brightly in the hearts of its citizens. Kentuckians have readily responded to every call for civilian participation in strengthening our armed forces. They are prepared to accept cheerfully any sacrifices that may be required to repel the threat of the sinister foe across the seas.

Here in Kentucky we have no patience with any group that slows down our effort to get ready to knock out our enemies. I am glad that labor in Kentucky is essentially patriotic. I am exasperated when an occasional instance occurs in which shortsighted labor leaders encourage strikes in war industries. When our army and navy desperately need the arms with which to fight for freedom, every factory engaged in producing those arms should be operated at capacity. Strikes should not be permitted to sabotage victory or impede the nation's effort to equip its gallant soldiers with the weapons they need. The crisis of this hour enjoins upon both labor and employer the duty to prevent such disagreements as will diminish the output of any plant engaged in war production. It is treason to strike when such action checks the making of war munitions. It is unpatriotic for industry to provoke discord by arbitrary action that infringes upon the rights of labor. The man behind the machine has no more right to strike in time of war than has the soldier on the firing line or the sailor at his battle station.

The supreme need of the nation in this period of grave peril is unity—unity of purpose, unity of thought and action, unity in sacrifice and service.

As we commemorate this important event in which this highly efficient blast furnace goes into production, let us thank God for it, rejoice because each day a thousand tons of pig iron will be produced by this blast furnace from which will be forged those instruments of death that our heroic armies need.

---

1. The speech has been edited. A discussion of the state motto is in the speech from April 20, 1942, in the Heritage section.

STATEWIDE DRIVE FOR SCRAP METAL
Louisville / September 17, 1942

GOVERNOR JOHNSON told the newspapermen that they had been challenged by the United States government "to prove the power of the press" and that he accepted the challenge in their behalf. [1] He designated H.M. McClaskey [2] as general director of the newspaper campaign and appealed to his own county scrap salvage leaders to "accept the assistance of the newspapers in this vital effort. The scrap metal situation is of such seriousness that we should talk about it very frankly." The newspapers have been called upon "as shock troops" to aid in locating and assembling Kentucky's scrap stockpiles.

"It has been difficult to convince the people of the seriousness of the scrap situation. The job has been presented to Kentucky newspapers to convince the people of the urgency of it. The press of Kentucky now has a chance to prove its leadership. The press must take over the task of dramatizing the need and use of scrap metal. The amount of scrap metal which Kentucky already has raised and the effort put forth by the citizens is not enough, but must be tremendously increased.

"During July, Kentucky poured 6 million pounds of scrap metal into the war machine. This amount was raised in thirty-one days. The October quota of the campaigns is forty-seven times this amount, to be raised in three weeks. "Kentuckians have been hunting for something spectacular, something big and important to do as a contributrion to the war effort. I have received many letters to this effect. Here is something they can do—pitch in and gather this scrap. It is as impossible to make steel without scrap as it is to make a mint julep without mint.

"Bravery and gallantry are not all it takes to win a war. They are ineffective against a mechanized army. We must help—Kentucky must help—forge a thunderbolt of power to hurl against our enemies. There is nothing more vital than assembling every ounce of scrap in this Commonwealth.

"I am delighted that Mr. Ethridge[3] and the *Courier-Journal* and the *Louisville Times* have accepted the leadership in this drive.

"Coupled with the tremendous response by the newspapermen of the state assembled here, I am certain our goal will be attained. The scrap drive is not only a challenge to the newspapers of Kentucky but a matter of vital concern to all. I am confident Kentucky will do a job comparable to any state in the Union."[4]

---

1. The campaign was announced at a luncheon at the Penndennis Club attended by representatives of virtually every newspaper in the state, county salvage chairmen, and war leaders. The goal was to collect 284,562,700 pounds of scrap metal from October 12 to 31. The governor was the keynote speaker. Louisville *Courier-Journal*, September 18, 1942.

2. Henry M. McClaskey (1892–1978), b. Boston, Ky. Promotion manager, retail advertising director, assistant general manager, Louisville *Courier-Journal* and *Louisville Times*, 1920–1958. Civic Leader. Telephone interview, Mrs. Henry M. McClaskey, Jr., June 14, 1978, and Louisville *Courier-Journal*, November 17, 1978.

3. Mark Foster Ethridge (1896–1981), b. Meridian, Mississippi. Vice-president and publisher, Louisville *Courier-Journal* and *Louisville Times*, 1937–1963; editor, *Newsday*, Long Island, 1963–1965; trustee, Ford Foundation, 1954–1967; lecturer, journalism, University of North Carolina, 1965–1966. Telephone interview, Willie Snow Ethridge, September 20, 1978, and Louisville *Courier-Journal*, April 6, 1981.

4. The governor wired Mayor La Guardia of New York on June 27, 1941, that he would "accept responsibility for a campaign to collect scrap aluminum in Kentucky." La Guardia was the national civilian defense director. Louisville *Courier-Journal*, June 28, 1941. On July 24, 1941, Johnson appealed through a one-minute radio statement for everyone to aid the nation by donating aluminum utensils and scrap. "We can express our love for America with scrap aluminum. Aluminum is a precious metal today—precious because it is vital in making airplanes for our national defense, the bulwark of American liberty." *State Journal*, July 25, 1941. In September he asked the bankers to finance the collection of scrap metal when it was not donated and where there was not a junk dealer. He expected 90 percent of the scrap to be donated. Louisville *Courier-Journal*, September 30, 1942.

McClaskey announced on November 2, 1942, that the goal had been exceeded. Johnson said, "I knew that patriotic Kentuckians would respond in this manner to the call of the government for their scrap metal, and I want to say that it has been the greatest demonstration of patriotic zeal and endeavor that I have ever witnessed." Louisville *Courier-Journal*, November 3, 1942.

On November 10, 1942, the govenor presented $5,000 in cash awards to the winners in the drive with a plea for all "to keep up the good work because the blast furnaces still need scrap for arms." The newspapers donated the money. Louisville *Courier-Journal*, November 11, 1942.

SCRAP METAL DRIVE
Louisville / October 2, 1942

I WELCOME the opportunity to speak to the teachers and young Kentuckians in the public schools. There is an important job to be done in which you can be of great help. Your nation needs every pound of steel that can be produced with which to make guns and grenades, tanks and planes with which to arm the brave men in our army. It is impossible to make steel without scrap metal. All steel manufactured contains one third to one half scrap iron. Steel cannot be made without scrap. It is as impossible to make steel without scrap iron as it is to make biscuits without flour, or to make an ice cream soda without ice cream. There is a dangerous shortage of scrap metal. It requires about 4 million tons of scrap a month to keep our steel mills running at full capacity. Steel mills are now dependent on incoming freight cars to furnish a supply of scrap for the day's run. The War Production Board has called on the schoolchildren of the nation to help meet this desperate situation. Every one of you want to do something to help win the war. You know that your brothers and friends in the army cannot defeat our enemies unless they have the guns and other armament with which to do the bloody job. So here is an important task which the 800,000 schoolchildren and teachers are urged to undertake. The scrap metal you assemble will go to the steel mills and be molded into steel from which will be made the guns and bullets our soldiers must have as they go into battle.

Our soldiers are men of valor and fortitude but this is a war in which raw courage is no match for cold steel. Modern warfare is highly mechanized. Thousands of our finest youth will be slaughtered if we send them into battle without tanks and planes and guns that are superior to the arms of our foe. We must have 17 million tons of scrap iron in order to keep the steel mills running at full capacity through the winter.

As your govenor, I urge you to jump into this job eagerly; get into this game with the same fine enthusiasm that you put into your football games. Remember that the victory you help to win in this nationwide hunt for scrap iron will hasten the day of victory over the mad men who brought upon us the misery of frightful war. If we lose this war, it will not be because our soldiers lacked bravery but because they did not have the guns and equipment needed. The guns will be provided for them if we keep the steel mills running by providing scrap iron. If we lose this war, there will be no free public school system in this nation. Hitler said in his book *Mein Kampf* that it is best to keep the masses in ignorance. Should he conquer us, he would instantly close every school house in the nation, rob American youth of the privilege of obtaining an education so as to make themselves useful and successful citizens. You can take a shot at Hitler by piling high the piles of scrap metal. You can prevent destruction of the public schools of the nation by hunting up every piece of scrap iron you can find and throwing it at Hitler and Tojo. [1]

Up until this time our people have been turning in the scrap iron for which there is no use or need. They have been keeping the things made of iron that they might find some use for in the future. The need for scrap has become so critical that every ounce of iron for which there is not an immediate use should be turned in to the junk dealer. We must win the war now. The need for scrap is immediate and imperative. And there is no more certain way to get the job done than to turn it over to the schoolchildren.

Kentucky has a magnificent group of superintendents, principals, teachers, and pupils in its schools. All are alert and energetic. Much has been done by the schools in the salvage drives already held. They have done so well and shown such tremendous energy that the War Production Board sent out the request that every school in the United States begin a scrap metal and rubber salvage canvass on October 5. The government and the nation is now calling on you to perform a great duty. You should be proud of the worthy place you hold in the estimation of our leaders in Washington.

The situation is so grave that the Kentucky newspapers have started a scrap metal drive. This drive will begin in Louisville on October 11 and out in the towns and counties of the state on October 12. The goal is 100 pounds per person for every man, woman, and child in Kentucky.[2] This means that our state goal will be 285 million pounds. Kentucky has a big quota to raise. Our tonnage of scrap for the last six months of this year is 306,000 tons. We stand fourteenth among the states in the size of our quota.

In the number of voluntary enlistments in the army, our state stands at the top. The same is true of our war bond sales. We must achieve the same result in gathering scrap iron.

The splendid effort now being made by the newspapers of Kentucky will help the school collection. The news stories and advertisements will make our people more conscious of the need. When you ask them to let you have scrap metal, they will know that you are working hard and seriously and they will be ready to assist you.

Tackle the job with all your enthusiasm and stay at it until every piece of scrap has been sent on its way to the steel mills.[3]

---

1. Hideki Tojo (1885–1948), b. Tokyo, Japan. Officer, Kwantung Army; minister of war, 1940; prime minister, 1941–1944. Attempted suicide, 1945; tried as a war criminal, found guilty, and hanged, 1948. *World Book Encyclopedia,* 16:8079-80.

2. The per capita collection was 114.7 pounds. Louisville *Courier-Journal,* November 11, 1942.

3. On October 3, 1942, the governor addressed a statement to "The People of Kentucky."

"Many of you have written me, asking what you can do to help win this war of freedom. I'm sure this question is in the mind and heart of every Kentuckian. Each one of us wants to share the burdens and responsibilities—yes, and the dangers—of those hours ahead on both the military and the home fronts. Each of us wants to look at some act, some accomplishment, and say to himself with pride: 'Here is something concrete, something I have done to defeat the enemy.

"I have an answer for all of you today. Do you want to know what you can do? You can collect and turn in every ounce of scrap metal on your premises. You can scour your attics and your basements and your stables and your garages for metal. You can comb through your homes and your farms.

"Then, having found and given all your own salvage, you can help your church, your school, your lodge, your club, your neighbor. Do you want a tangible sense of accomplishment? You can get it by holding a little piece of metal in your hand, then throwing it on Kentucky's great scrap pile.

"The newspapers and the radio and your own community leaders will tell you all about this campaign, its importance and its urgency. I only tell you this: If YOU want to help win the war, start this week to gather scrap metal." Louisville *Courier-Journal*, October 4, 1942.

Johnson proclaimed Monday, October 12, 1942, Columbus Day, a holiday so that all citizens not employed in hospitals, in serving food, on war contracts, or in necessary transportation could collect scrap metal. He directed all public offices and schools to close and requested private businesses to close. Later he excluded Louisville and Jefferson County at the request of labor leaders who pointed out that provision had been made for the collection on Sunday so as not to interfere with production in the plants producing materials essential to the war. Louisville *Courier-Journal*, October 9, 1942.

On December 9, 1942, Louisville and Jefferson County received the War Production Board "quota pennant" for the collection of 57 million pounds of scrap in the drive. The govenor said that Kentucky's drive was "tremendously successful" but warned, "We must not become complacent . . . for the need of scrap metal is continuing." Louisville *Courier-Journal*, December 10, 1942.

Johnson issued a proclamation on May 6, 1943, in which he urged all farmers and all county salvage committees to make special scrap metal collections during May. Kentucky's farm quota was set at 80,000 tons. On October 7, 1943, he proclaimed a "Victory Scrap Bank" campaign and declared October 18 and 25 as holidays to be used to collect scrap metal. Schools were to use these two Mondays for scrap collection.

AWARD TO TUBE TURNS PLANT
Louisville / December 18, 1942

MAYOR WYATT, this is indeed a proud day in the history of Tube Turns plant. I, as governor of Kentucky, am delighted to participate with you in this significant event. Every man and woman in this efficient, patriotic organization is to be congratulated that Tube Turns has attained such proficiency in production of vital war equipment as to earn the distinction of being awarded the "M" of the Maritime Commission. It is an honor in which each of you may share because each of you contributed to the production record which is recognized by this award.

Tube Turns was the first war industrial plant in Kentucky to win the army and navy "E." It now has the honor of being the first war plant in the state to earn the Award of Merit of the Maritime Commission and one of the few in the nation. These decorations are for distinguished service in defense of freedom. They mean that you on the production battle line are fighting valiantly and effectively so that the soldiers and sailors on the battle fronts of the world may have equipment with which to wage war. They mean that the fire of patriotic fervor burns brightly in your hearts, fires you with zeal and determination to produce the war products which come from your skilled hands in increased quantity. As you by your united efforts increase the output of this plant you drive a nail in Hitler's coffin and hasten the day of doom for the foes of freedom. While your job is less spectacular than that of shooting down an enemy airplane or sinking an enemy ship, yours is a job of importance. Because you have been doing well your job, our army and navy have been winning victories. You, the soldiers of production, have supplied the soldiers and sailors of the battle zones with the equipment they must have to win the war for us. Not a single one of these men shall die because we faltered.

I am especially proud of the fact that there has been no stoppage of work in this essential industrial plant because of labor disputes. Had there been a loss of precious man hours of labor, you would not today be celebrating this high achievement. The absence of discord reflects great credit upon both the workers and management.

On the battle fronts of the world where men fight and fall, no victories can be won unless the soldiers on the battle line of production provide the arms and munitions, the guns and grenades, the ships and submarines with which our brave men destroy our ruthless foes. In this war raw human courage is no match for cold steel. Men fighting under the Stars and Stripes have demonstrated sublime courage and fortitude. But in modern warfare the finest and bravest soldiers cannot triumph unless you provide them with weapons and equipment comparable in effectiveness to that with which our enemies are armed. That grim fact places upon the soldiers of the production front the responsibility of determining to a degree how many American men will be killed, how much blood will be shed, how long the war will last. Length of this bloody struggle depends to an extent upon how quickly we can produce the weapons of war and put them in the hands of our soldiers.

This "decoration" which comes to you of Tube Turns in recognition of your efficiency in production reflects great credit upon every man and woman in this fine organization. This significant "M" will be an inspiration to you to maintain the lofty standard here set. It will inspire workers in other industrial plants to strive to attain similar distinction. It is a badge of honor difficult of achievement. It admits Tube Turns into the select group of the nation's industrial war plants. It should be accepted by you as a challenge. It will stimulate you to try hard, not only to maintain the exceptional record you have made, but it is your duty to try every day to break your own records, increase production.

Apparently trivial things often have a big effect in determining the fate of battle. It is a serious responsibility which you have as you think of the fact that a battle may be lost, a ship fail to sail with needed war cargo, because on the production battle line there was not produced the equipment required. There must be no resting upon our laurels, no halting to pat ourselves upon the back. Little things determine victory or defeat.

You, my fellow Kentuckians, red-blooded patriots that you are, here thousands of miles removed from the battle line, are influencing the outcome of another battle of Marengo.[1] You have played well your part in this crucial struggle. You have shown high devotion to duty. May you be sustained daily by the same sublime courage as actuated the drummer boy. Remember, men and women, there must be no retreat. The command is always "forward."

---

1. The story about Napoleon at Marengo has been deleted. It appears in the speech from October 3, 1942, in the World War II section.

SAVE TIN, GREASE, AND HOSIERY
Frankfort / March 3, 1943

THERE are three salvage items which are of particular interest to the women and, to secure a successful collection of these items, the War Production Board has said many times that the women must do the job. These three salvages are tin cans, kitchen grease, and hosiery.

The War Production Board has asked all homes, hotels, restaurants, school cafeterias, and army camps to save all of their tin cans. America must salvage tin because the Japs conquered 95 per cent of the world's tin supply. With all shipments of tin shut off from that Pacific area which is in the hands of the Japs, it has become necessary for us to withhold tin from many manufactured articles that previously used it and to restrict the use of tin to food containers, bearings for airplanes, tanks and ships, and for medicinal purposes. The army is using more tin than it ever used before, and we have a demand for tin now that did not exist during the First

World War. In the first year of the last war it has been estimated that America used only 241 tanks in the combat area and only one American made airplane reached the fighting front in the first year of that war. But in the last month America made 3,000 tanks and 6,200 airplanes. Think then of the tremendous amount of tin that the army must have in order to make the bearings for these tanks and airplanes.

The present war has caused a demand for all metals which is unprecedented in the history of the world. A good illustration of this is the fact that in order to secure nickel we are withdrawing all of our present coins and replacing them with steel nickels. It is also shown by the fact that we are making all new pennies out of steel with a zinc coating, thus saving each year 4,500 tons of copper. We are saving 8,000 tons of zinc by changing the tops on mason jars from zinc to steel.

In order to secure as much tin as possible for our war needs, we are asking every housewife to save tin cans. Kentucky has twenty tin can shipping centers. The town of Frankfort shipped a car of cans this week. It is one of the centers. Lexington is also a shipping center and has shipped at least two cars. Danville will ship its second car this month. There is a shipping center within the reach of all Kentucky communities. The War Production Board, then, urges us to save all our tin cans.

A second important salvage is kitchen grease from which glycerine is obtained. The kitchen grease situation is so serious that the War Production Board is attempting to bring it to the attention of every home in the nation through advertising in newspapers and magazines and over the radio. The board has asked every community to have a house-to-house canvass for the purpose of asking every housewife to save her kitchen grease. Those Kentucky communities that have had these canvasses have doubled and tripled their collection.

Some communities are raising 156 percent of their quota, thus helping to make up for those communities that are doing nothing on this program. The quota for each community is a pound per person per year. Kentucky is asked for 202,000 pounds per month and at the present time is raising 54.5 percent of its quota and stands eleventh among the states. You might be interested to know that even with the rationing of meat the collection of kitchen grease is growing as more and more housewives become aware of the necessity for this salvage. America is raising over 7 million pounds per month, but this is too far below the goal of 17 million pounds per month. Unless we can collect this kitchen grease, our glycerine supply will continue to decrease, and our war effort may be seriously handicapped as glycerine is the basis of explosives and the army must have it.

Another important salvage is that of silk and nylon hosiery. The silk hosiery is used to make powder bags and the nylon is used for parachutes. You cannot make a powder bag out of cotton, wool, or rayon; therefore, the army must have this silk. It takes from fifteen to forty-three pairs of silk hose to provide enough silk for a powder bag, depending upon whether the bag is small, medium, or large size. It takes about 222 pairs of nylon hose to make a parachute.

Many people say that there is no silk hosiery in existence. We know, however, that this is not the case because 540 million pairs of silk and nylon hosiery were manufactured in the year before the restriction on these types of hosiery.

Since the salvage of hosiery began in November 1942, only about 17 million pairs have been collected. Kentucky has collected 10,773 pounds and the national collection stands at 1,250,000 pounds to date.

The War Production Board does not want any new silk and nylon stockings but it does want every used pair. Therefore, we urge every community to collect hosiery.

AWARD TO COCHRAN FOIL COMPANY
Louisville / March 16, 1943

THIS is indeed a proud day for the Cochran Foil Company and Kentucky rejoices with this efficient, patriotic war industry upon the signal honor earned as a result of consecrated service to our country.

I am especially proud of the fact that there has been no stoppage of work in this vital industrial plant because of labor disputes. That reflects great credit upon both the workers and management. There should be no strike in any industry that is essential to the war effort. I am glad there has not been a strike in Kentucky since Pearl Harbor.[1] I hope there will not be one.

I congratulate those of you who work in this plant that absenteeism is low on this vital sector of the home front. In these days when we must hurry to lick Hitler, every soldier on the production battle line should be at his or her post of duty daily. Each of you has a daily date with duty—a date you must keep here, making munitions needed by the united nations.

It is not possible to win the war on the home front. The final decision can be won only by the blazing battle line where our gallant men meet and master the brutal foe of freedom. We cannot win the war on the home front, but we could lose the war on the home front should we fail to do our individual duty. You of this efficient and patriotic organization are so performing your job that no American soldier will die in battle because you, the soldiers of production, failed.

All resources of this great republic are being mobilized for the high and holy purpose of destroying the conscienceless dictators who brought all this misery upon the world. In this the most gigantic struggle in history, we must build the biggest, best equipped, and best trained army that has ever marched to battle. We are engaged in a war in which the second best army is as worthless as the second best hand in a poker game. In this game of brutal warfare the nations with the second best army have all been destroyed, the people enslaved. Leaders of our nation are making every effort to get ready to shoot the works—and as quickly as possible. All we do is nothing if it is not enough.

I have been thrilled by the story of the founding of this infant industry, the Cochran Foil Company. It is a dramatic episode in which Mr. Cochran disclosed ingenuity, perserverance, and courage that surmounted obstacles which would have thwarted less determined men. I shall not recount that story with which you are familiar. But I do want to pay high tribute to Archie Cochran [2] and commend his resourcefulness. He refused to be licked by circumstances that would have crushed this industry had it not been for his ingenious leadership in adapting it to a nation at war. Those of you who have helped to build this organization should be immensely proud of that which has been here achieved by your united efforts.

On that battle front where men fight and fall, no victories can be won unless the industrial front provides the arms and munitions, the guns and grenades, the tanks and planes with which our brave men destroy our foes. In this war raw human courage is no match for cold steel. Men fighting under our flag have demonstrated courage and fortitude on every battle front. But in modern warfare, gallant men must be provided with weapons that equal in effectiveness those of their enemies. That grim fact puts upon the factories producing war equipment the responsibility of determining to a degree how much American blood will be shed, how many lives will be sacrificed upon the altar of freedom. Every day we can shorten the war saves the lives of many American men. The length of the bloody struggle depends primarily upon how quickly we can produce the weapons of war.

The superb efficiency in this plant that has been born out of a patriotic desire to help crush Hilter reflects great credit both upon the management of Cochran Foil Company and the skilled men and women whose diligence and competence have made possible attaining the high goal that merits the award of the Army-Navy "E." This emblem will be an inspiration to you workers to maintain the lofty standard here set. It will inspire workers in other industrial plants to strive for the distinction of an Army-Navy Production award, which is the Distinguished Service Cross for industry. Not a large percent of industrial plants have met the exacting standard of production necessary to qualify for this award. It is an honor difficult of attainment. It means the admittance of the Cochran Foil Company into the elite of the nation's war industry plants. It demonstrates that labor in a democracy produces at high efficiency when driven by the urge of patriotic duty as contrasted with the slave labor in Germany, driven by the lash of a tyrant. It hastens the day of Hitler's doom.[3]

---

1. See, however, speech from August 19, 1942, in this section.

2. Archibald Prentice Cochran (1898–1970), b. Louisville. Metal fabricator; president, Cochran Foil Company, 1939–1970. *Who Was Who in America, 1969–1973*, 5:139.

3. Similar speeches were given at the Porcelain Metals Corporation, Louisville, March 17, 1943; Stokes Industries, Covington, March 26, 1943; and the United States Naval Ordnance Plant (managed by Westinghouse), Louisville, June 22, 1943.

AWARD TO KELLY-KOETT MANUFACTURING COMPANY
Covington / April 15, 1943

THIS is indeed a happy day in the history of Kelly-Koett Manufacturing Company. As govenor of Kentucky I am delighted to participate with you in this significant event. I am proud of Kelly-Koett—proud of you who as members of this organization have had a part in making the fine record which is today recognized.

Every man and woman in this efficient, patriotic group of workers is to be congratulated that Kelly-Koett has attained such proficiency in the production of X-Ray equipment and other vital war materials as to become worthy of the distinction of being awarded the Army-Navy "E." It is an honor in which each of you may feel a personal pride because each of you contributed to a production record so noteworthy as to deserve this coveted distinction. Successful operation of Kelly-Koett provides ample evidence that industry can thrive and prosper in Northern Kentucky.

Here one finds conditions conducive to successful industrial operation.

The Army-Navy "E" is a decoration for distinguished service in defense of freedom. It means that you on the production battle line are fighting valiantly so that X-Ray equipment will be available for army hospitals and the fighting craft of the navy. This honor which you have won by your collective efforts indicates that the fire of patriotic fervor burns brightly in your hearts, stimulates your zeal and determination to produce the products which come from your skilled hands in increased quantity.

As you by your united efforts increase the output of this plant, you make it increasingly certain that no American fighting man shall die from wounds or disease because you failed to provide the X-Ray machine required to give intelligent care to the sick and wounded. Kelly-Koett is a unique war plant. It is producing equipment that is designed to save life rather than destroy it. Skill of a high order is required to fabricate these sensitive machines. Consecrated devotion to duty is as necessary as the critical materials from which this equipment is fashioned. You who work in the Kelly-Koett plant have attained the honor roll reserved for those of conspicuous achievement because of exceptional intelligence and an exalted concept of patriotic duty. You are making an important contribution to victory.

I regard it as particularly noteworthy that there has been no stoppage of work in this efficient plant because of labor disputes. Had there been a loss of precious manhours due to labor controversy, you would not today be celebrating this high achievement. In none of the Kentucky plants that have earned the "E" has labor strife raised its ugly head. I delight in the fact that not since Pearl Harbor has there been a serious strike in a Kentucky industry that is engaged in war production. That reflects high credit upon both management and workers. It provides proof of an unselfish patriotism that is worthy of the gallant Kentucky men who are fighting heroically on every battlefront on this globe.

Scores of Kentuckians have already died in battle. They fell with their faces toward the foe, following the flag of freedom, fighting for the liberty symbolized by that star-flecked banner. Many other Kentucky men are destined to fall before the gangster nations are conquered. Saddened though we are as comes the distressing story that they have laid down their lives for us, we are exultantly proud of our courageous men who died to keep America free.

The sublime sacrifice of these who have passed into the Valhalla of the nation's heroes is a challenge to us at home to so conduct ourselves as to be worthy of them. You who work in the plant over which the Army-Navy "E" pennant is today unfurled have earned the satisfaction of feeling that on the production battleline you are keeping faith with these, our immortal dead.

The "E" is a badge of honor difficult of achievement. It admits you to a small and select group of the nation's industrial war plants that have met the exacting requirements necessary to become eligible for this award. That "E" pin which you will proudly wear will be an inspiration to you to maintain the lofty standards which you have set for your organization by your united efforts. You will recognize the "E" as a challenge. It will stimulate you to try earnestly to break your own records, increase production. It hastens the day when the heroic MacArthur[1] will return to Bataan and the Stars and Stripes will fly again over Corregidor.[2]

---

1. Douglas MacArthur (1880–1964), b. Little Rock, Arkansas. Leading general of World War II and Korean War. Received surrender of Japan, August 1945. *Encyclopedia Americana* (New York, 1977), 18:8-9e.
2. The speech has been edited. Parts appear in speeches from June 5, 1942, and October 3, 1942, in the World War II section.

IMPLORES MINERS TO RETURN TO WORK
Frankfort / May 2, 1943

TELEGRAM to district presidents of the United Mine Workers of America: Ed Morgan, Madisonville, Ky.; Sam Caddy, Lexington, Ky., and William Turnblazer, president, District 19, Jellico, Tenn.[1]

As governor of Kentucky I implore you to heed the request of President Roosevelt to keep coal mines of Kentucky in operation. You will perform a fine patriotic service if you will direct members of United Mine Workers to return to work in the coal mines.

Appeal of the president for continued coal production is based on grim military necessity. I am certain the controversy between mine workers and operators can be settled fairly if submitted to the War Labor Board. You and the Kentucky miners who follow your leadership will deserve and receive the plaudits of all Kentuckians if the coal mines are quickly reopened. I urge you to get the miners back on the job and hasten the day when we can lick Hitler.

Telegram to Harold L. Ickes, Solid Fuels Administrator for War, Washington, D.C.

In accord with your telegram[2] I am designating William C. Burrow,[3] Kentucky commissioner of industrial relations, to represent me in conjunction with your representative. He can be reached at Lewellyn Hotel, Harlan, Ky. where he has been observing developments. His headquarters are Frankfort, Ky. Be assured complete cooperation from me in effort to reopen coal mines.[4]

---

1. Ed Morgan (?–1960), b. Iowa. President, UMWA District 23, Madisonville, for approximately thirty years. Telephone interview, Charles Head, UMWA District Office, Madisonville, July 20, 1978.

Samuel H. Caddy (d. 1959, age 75), b. England. Resided in Lexington. Sent to Kentucky by John L. Lewis in 1933; president, UMWA District 30 for twenty-five years; president CIO and Kentucky State Federation of Labor. *Lexington Herald-Leader*, January 5, 1959.

2. Telegram dated May 2, 1943, from Ickes: "To meet crisis caused by suspension of operation in coal fields, I have pursuant to presidential authorization taken possession of seven thousand bituminous and anthracite mines throughout country and appointed operating managers to operate the mines for the United States and to distribute and sell the products thereof. I have also appointed as regional managers to supervise this program the eleven field office managers of the bituminous coal division. Pursuant to presidential authorization and by cooperative arrangement with the secretary of war, all requests for intervention by the armed forces of the United States to protect working miners are to be referred to the regional managers and by them transmitted to me along with the recommendation of liaison officers assigned to work with the regional managers by the secretary of war. This cooperative endeavor offers assurance that intervention by the military will be restricted to minimum thereby avoiding unnecessary disturbance. In the interest of effecting best possible operating basis for insuring necessary protection and maintenance of public order, I suggest you may wish to communicate with me at Washington before taking any action beyond ordinary police protection. I should appreciate also your designating a member of your staff to be available for consultation with the regional managers for the area in question. Such an arrangement would assure coordination of all protective measures and would insure your having before you prior to making any decision to use state forces the benefit of any information available to me and the regional manager who will be in intimate contact with the situation at the mine. If this arrangement agreeable, please communicate the name of your designee and the address at which he can be located and I shall then advise you of the name and address of the manager in the region in which your state lies."

3. William Clark Burrow (1902–1974), b. Cadiz. First commissioner, industrial relations, 1936–1946; executive, Evansville Printing Corporation, Indiana, 1946–1971. *Who's Who in Kentucky, 1936*, p. 61, and letter, Mrs. Alma Burrow Mitchell, sister, Evansville, September 15, 1978.

4. The strike was serious. The *Lexington Herald* reported on April 30, 1943, that twenty-one of the forty-one soft coal mines in Harlan County were closed and

nearly 7,000 miners idle. The next day twenty-eight Eastern Kentucky mines were closed with 12,000 to 13,000 miners idle. Only small mines were in operation in the Harlan field. Two mines in the Big Sandy field were closed. Mines in the Hazard-Perry field and in Western Kentucky were open. On May 3, the *Courier-Journal* reported forty mines closed in the Harlan section with nearly 13,000 miners idle. In northeastern Kentucky all thirty-six mines were closed and 10,200 miners were on holiday. All thirty-two mines in the Hazard-Perry field were closed with 6,000 miners idle. In Western Kentucky 6,000 men were idle with five large mines and several small ones closed. By June 4, the *Courier-Journal* stated that 46,000 of the state's 60,000 miners were not working. Governor Prentice Cooper of Tennessee and Governor Chauncey Sparks of Alabama directed their Selective Service directors to order local boards to remove the occupational deferments of striking miners. Governor Johnson said that he would not follow their example. "I feel that the matter of removing draft deferment for striking coal miners is one involving such broad policy that it should be left in the hands of Selective Service officials in Washington." Louisville *Courier-Journal*, June 4, 1943.

KENTUCKY INDUSTRIAL SAFETY AND HEALTH CONGRESS
Louisville / July 28, 1943

DURING the last five years, 541 Kentucky workers were killed and 65,891 injured in plant accidents.[1]

In "hard-boiled" days, accidents were considered a natural hazard of the job, but modern safety ideas prove lives can be saved. The cooperation of employer and employee is necessary. After a company provides all possible safeguards, only 15 percent of the job has been done. Cooperation of the employee will prevent many of the remaining 85 percent of accidents. The employee can make the industrial plant safer than the community just outside.

Who pays the costs of accidents?

1. Cost to industry, as exemplified in some typical instances.
2. Cost to the injured employee and his family.
3. Cost to the community and to society.

Dividends to industry by stopping accidents.

1. Workmen's compensation payments and insurance costs.
2. Medical and hospital expenses.
3. Machinery repairs saved and spoilage of materials.

4. Employee personnel organization and morale preserved.
5. Production schedules maintained, higher efficiency.

Dividends to the uninjured employee.

1. A whole body preserved in full strength and vigor.
2. Wages kept intact for life's satisfactions and duties.
3. A good job preserved instead of a cripple's pay.
4. A contented home, children educated, increasing fortune.

Dividends to the community.

1. Steady production by a capable unit of society.
2. Charity expenses avoided for a part, at least, of a family forced down and out by disaster.
3. Conserved funds and ability to care for others who may need the community's help.
4. The continued satisfaction, dignity, and morale engendered in all citizens by knowledge of the attitude of an industrial organization that places safety of workers above other organizations.

---

1. On June 18, 1942, the governor proclaimed a safety campaign for Independence Day, stressing the prevention of accidents affecting war production.

LABOR DAY
Western Kentucky / September 6, 1943

KENTUCKY'S present Railroad Commission should be congratulated for its untiring efforts on behalf of the coal industry in Western Kentucky and for finally obtaining a reduction, against almost overwhelming odds, in freight rates in spite of the fact that certain interests have obtained a rehearing, but we are sure it will only mean a short delay before the actual reduction is put into effect. Following the loss of representation on the Interstate Commerce Commission in 1927, the commission increased freight rates on Western Kentucky coal from twenty-five to thirty-five cents a ton or 40 percent over that paid by mine operators in our neighboring states just across the river in Illinois and Indiana. As a result of this tremendous increase, 40 percent, coal shipments which were 12 million tons in 1927 dropped as low as 1.8 million several years later. Despite court attacks and other obstacles which were placed in their way, the commission has been able to reduce the rate to the former twenty-five cents, which we think is still plenty high. We are certain that, when this reduction is placed in effect, the coal industry in Western Kentucky will be revived and that you will not again face shutdowns as occurred during the long period in which this unfair freight differential was in effect.

An unfair rate can only result in damage to investment and in many cases complete destruction while on the other hand hundreds, yea thousands, of good Kentucky coal diggers are denied employment which in turn denies their families the necessities of life to which they are all entitled. Further, every businessman in Western Kentucky along with coal miners and the operators should back the Kentucky Railroad Commission in its great fight to restore a once prosperous industry. Unless wage earners receive regular wages and regular working time and a full work week, no community, county, or state can enjoy prosperity. Although Western Kentucky is possibly enjoying a good coal business because of the global war, we must fight to keep our Western Kentucky coal industry from being wrecked by unfair freight rates. Send a letter, all of you, businessmen, coal operators, coal miners, and public-spirited citizens to the Kentucky Railroad Commission, Frankfort, and let them know that you are 100 percent in back of them to keep the 40 percent reduction that has finally been obtained by the present administration, as this will be your just reward in postwar days which must come.

Since 1916 Kentucky has had on its statutes a workmen's compensation law which because of a court decision is a voluntary procedure, and we have no power to compel industrialists to protect their workers with workmen's compensation insurance; therefore, after many discussions during the 1940 and 1942 sessions of the legislature, it was decided to amend the constitution of Kentucky in order to extend this protection to all industrial workers. I am glad to report to you that this administration and your Workmen's Compensation Board which is headed by the Honorable Charles G. Franklin[1] convinced the legislature that this proposition should be placed before the people so that the next session of the General Assembly would have authority to enact into law a provision which would compel every coal operator and every industrialist in the state to carry workmen's compensation in order to pay benefits to those who are maimed and crippled because of unfortunate accidents in our mines, factories, and mills and also leave a substantial sum to the widows and orphans. This amendment will be voted on in November.[2]

We are well aware of two real catastrophes here in Western Kentucky during the past few years which snuffed out the lives of a number of good citizens. Neither of these operations were covered by the provisions of the compensation law; therefore, the state was powerless to compel the payment of death benefits to the widows and orphans or even to compel the payment of burial expenses. I understand that adjustments were made which is very fine, but that is a bad situation as there is no guarantee that the widows and orphans or the maimed and crippled will be taken care of after these unfortunate mishaps.

I do not hesitate to say to you that I am in favor of requiring the industrialists, whether it is coal, steel, timber, transportation, etc., to assume responsibility for the compensation for injuries and fatalities. Although the Guffey Coal Act[3] has not been renewed, when the prices were set by the coal commission, the costs of social security, unemployment compensation, and workmen's compensation were included in the price which was allowed to be charged to the consumer. So all in all, those who consume the product are the ones who pay the bill in the long run. It is unfair for coal operations or any other hazardous occupations in this county or any community which by the nature of the work exposes the workman to injuries or death to fail to assume the responsibility and compel the local citizens to assume the burden in the event of such injury or death. This is charity—not adequate protection to workers.

The Department of Mines and Minerals received a substantial increase in its appropriation for the purpose of assuring proper mine inspection in Kentucky. In fact, according to the latest reports, inspections have more than doubled, and 100 percent cooperation has been given to the federal Bureau of Mines. We are doing everything humanly possible to reduce accidents as well as to require protection of the worker by compelling the employer to accept the provisions of the Workmen's Compensation Law.

The Workmen's Compensation Law was amended at the 1940 session increasing death benefits from $4,000 to $4,800 and permanent and total benefits from $6,000 to $7,500. Prior to 1942, if an injured worker died after the expiration of a two-year period from date of accident, all compensation benefits stopped, as the injured person legally was not considered to have died as a result of such injury. An amendment passed at the 1942 session requires that dependents receive the balance due which would have been due to the deceased for such injuries up to the amount of death benefit.

It is a well-known fact that a state conciliation-arbitration law was passed at the 1940 session of the legislature which recognized the right of workers with respect to collective bargaining. This law sets out certain responsibilities for both employer and employee, and according to periodical reports from the head of the Industrial Relations Department, coal miners in Kentucky have cooperated 100 percent with that agency in the formal and proper adjustment of disputes, which have been few since the declaration of war.

The national mine problem is a matter which must be settled by authorized representatives of the coal operators and miners in Washington, and we know very little of the details and naturally in our position representing just one of the many coal-producing states, we can only be patient and hope for an early settlement of the national controversy. I am not informed as to the various details and will have to rely entirely upon national agencies to make proper adjustments. I hope that whatever settlement is made will be satisfactory to both parties.

However, there is one statement which I would like to make on behalf of Kentucky coal miners, not only Western but Eastern as well, and that is—certain propagandists have attacked the patriotism of the miners of this country. I can only speak for Kentucky, and I do not hesitate to say that although there may be misunderstandings with respect to proper wage rates, the number of hours which should be worked and the various conditions in the mines and on the tipple, I resent any attack on the patriotism of Kentucky coal miners. I know that this community and the entire Western coalfields have given many of its sons to the armed forces. No doubt many made the supreme sacrifice, many are listed as casualties and are now in hospitals while many are still in North Africa, Guadalcanal, Sicily, and wherever the American armed forces may strike next. Many of these fathers, sons, and even daughters come from Kentucky coal mining families and there can be no question in my mind or in the minds of all good Kentuckians when it comes to patriotism among the coal miners of Western and Eastern Kentucky. Their names can be found among those who served in World War I and all the other wars and that will continue to be true when defense of our freedom is necessary. The coal miners will contribute unstintingly their full share.

Prior to July 1, 1942, every employee whose employer was subject to the provisions of the Unemployment Compensation Law of Kentucky contributed 1 percent of his earnings to same and another 1 percent to the federal Social Security Retirement fund. Because the affairs of that department were carefully administered and there was no unnecessary expenditure of money, this fund has been built up to the strongest of any in the forty-eight states in proportion to the number of covered workers. Therefore, we reached an agreement with representative employers and employees, and at the 1942 session of the General Assembly repealed 1 percent of the assessment which is a saving to all workers as well as the coal miners in Western Kentucky.[4]

[The governor noted that the war bond purchases of miners have been fine and the man hours lost from work have been few.][5]

---

1. Charles G. Franklin (1883–1959), b. Charleston. County attorney, Madisonville; state senator, 1928–1932; head, Workmen's Compensation Board, 1939–1943. Telephone interview, Carroll Franklin, son, Madisonville, January 5, 1979.

2. The amendment was defeated, 78,466 to 82,305. An amendment for this purpose had been proposed by the General Assembly in 1938. It and one pertaining to aid for dependent children and the needy blind became known as "forgotten amendments" because the secretary of state failed to advertise them more than ninety days before the 1939 general election. He was enjoined from advertising them for a shorter period and they were not voted on in 1939. *Arnett, Secretary of State, et al.* v. *Sullivan,* 279 Ky. 720, 132 S.W. 2d 76 (1939). In February 1940 a suit was brought in Franklin Circuit Court to determine whether the workmen's compensation amendment could be voted on at the 1940 general election. The court held that it could not and the Court of Appeals affirmed. *Harrod* v. *Hatcher, Secretary of State,* 281 Ky. 712, 137 S.W. 2d 405 (1940). Since the General Assembly did not propose a workmen's compensation amendment in 1940, it was not proposed again until 1942. Johnson urged its approval when he spoke to the Legislative Council in December 1941. Louisville *Courier-Journal,* December 4, 1941.

3. This act was a federal law for the regulation of the bituminous coal industry. See Public 48, 50 *Stat.* 72.

4. This speech has been compiled from the governor's notes and a manuscript that was apparently prepared for him. No record could be found of where it was given although the content indicates it was presented in Western Kentucky.

Labor's support for Johnson was indicated at the thirty-sixth Annual Convention of the Kentucky State Federation of Labor when he was lauded by Edward H. Weyler. After reporting on the attainment of the legislative objectives of the federation in the 1940 General Assembly, he commented, "We are of the firm belief that had it not been for the cooperation of Governor Keen Johnson we would not have received the passage of any of this legislation, and we would have suffered the passage of anti-labor legislation. Each local union in this commonwealth should write Governor Johnson thanking him for his cooperation and assistance." *Lexington Herald,* October 17, 1940.

5. Johnson concluded by quoting the poem "Tearing Down" by Edgar A. Guest.

MENGEL COMPANY
Louisville / (date unknown)

LOUISVILLE is known as the safest industrial city in America. In a National Industrial Safety Contest started ten years ago, Louisville has won the trophy four times; no other city, regardless of size, has won this trophy more than once.

The employees of the Mengel Company have helped a great deal in bringing about this desirable result. Sixty-three plants in Louisville in 1928 had 1,058 lost time accidents, with 31,577 days lost. In 1938 these same plants with 7,000 more employees, had 260 lost time accidents, with 14,000 days lost. This proves that accident prevention work pays.

Compensation payments do not take care of all the results of an accident. In the event the injury is a total disability one, after a few years payment stops—then what? Not only will the man himself suffer, but his family along with him. Workmen have a responsibility, not only to themselves, but also to others.

It is known that a multiplicity of serious accidents have caused plants to close, throwing all the employees out of work. Some scoffers say it is company business. Well, in a measure it is, but what is company business is certainly your business. If your company doesn't prosper, you as one of its employees certainly won't.

Accidents don't happen—they are caused. Sometimes the person injured didn't cause the accident, but someone did. It cannot be disputed that this is a fact when we know that approximately 85 percent of all accidents come under the head of handling material, use of hand tools, falling objects and falls due to bad housekeeping. Good housekeeping is one of the fundamentals of any industrial safety campaign; so it behooves every industrial employee to keep his work place as clean as possible, and not throw things around carelessly and set traps for the injury of others. Your employer has safeguarded every possible danger point in your plant; see that these guards remain in place and use them. Can you imagine a catcher on a baseball team not using his mask and breast protector.

The American workman has done a remarkable job of safety work. Fatal accidents have been reduced from 35,000 a year down to about 14,000. Is this effort worthwhile? Safety is more a state of mind than anything else. Develop safe habits and you will be relatively free from accidents.

I'm not here tonight trying to tell you how to do your job safely. You know more about that than I do. I'm here to try to stimulate you to greater effort—to inspire or revive your safety consciousness.[1]

---

1. The present Mengel Company was unable to give any information about the speech. Telephone interview, April 23, 1978. The original Mengel Company went out of business in the mid-1950s. Louisville *Courier-Journal*, August 11, 1980.

WORLD WAR II

VETERANS OF FOREIGN WARS
Frankfort / January 6, 1940

GOVERNOR JOHNSON voiced disillusionment over the "war to end wars" in 1917 and urged that the veterans' organization lend its full influence in keeping "America from again crossing submarine-infested oceans to fight un-American wars." The veterans should take every precaution to see that "our sons are not subjected to the same experience we went through in that other war."

In outlining the work of the state Disabled Ex-Service Men's Board, he traced its accomplishments since its formation in 1921. Through its activities all but five mentally ill ex-servicemen, who were lodged in state mental hospitals, had been transferred to government hospitals "where they can enjoy better care and more advantages than can be provided in state institutions."

He explained the operation of the graves registration service whereby war veterans are employed in locating and marking the graves of all Kentucky's war dead.

A policy of providing work for veterans at the state arsenal had resulted in a complete roster of all Kentuckians who had served in the nation's armed forces during the World War, a roster lost for twenty years. "By means of this roster, approximately 150 widows and children of deceased veterans were supplied with data necessary to collecting their loves ones' bonus and war risk pay and were thus greatly benefited."

AMERICAN LEGION
Ashland / July 22, 1940

IT is a great pleasure indeed to come to you this morning assembled in this twenty-second annual convocation of the American Legion, Department of Kentucky. We are grateful indeed, as has been previously expressed by all of these people, for the cordial warm greetings and hospitality that has been extended to us by this splendid city of Ashland and its very hospitable people.

Jimmy Norris[1] told you about that picture of the Legion Convention when it assembled in Ashland in 1923, and he made a particular effort to obtain possession of that picture. Well, he confessed to me the principal reason that he wanted to obtain it permanently was because the picture showed him at a time when he had all of his hair. But it is an interesting contrast as you look at the picture of the Legion Convention here assembled in 1940 and that of the convention of 1923. When you look at us now, we are bald and gray and somewhat corpulent as compared with the youthful, slim fellows of 1923. So, I am frank to say to you that time seems to have dealt more kindly with the ladies than it did with the men.

Because the convention has reassembled itself here, it recalls memories of the earlier days of the Legion, memories of those experiences of 1917 and 1918, memories of the horrors and hardships and sacrifices of war, memories engraved upon the very soul, memories that we have sought through the years to forget, memories that have been recalled and rekindled as we read from day to day in the press and hear over the radio, the stories of ruthless bloodshed that come from across that same Atlantic which we crossed when infested with submarines to stand beside the Allies in an effort to thwart the autocratic might of an arrogant military foe in 1917–1918.

The Legion, since its organization, has been constantly dedicated to an exalted program, a program of very robust Americanism. It has sought constantly to properly emphasize the importance of a vigorous and adequate program of national defense. Now in this troubled time of world history, when there appears the unhappy prospect that this continent may become the last citadel of freedom, the wisdom and the necessity of a program of increased national defense such as that which the American Legion has contended for the last two decades become tragically apparent.

Now, I don't think that this is the time for flag waving. It is a time for intense, earnest, searching of our souls; a time for a reawakening of the same sincere devotion to our country and to its flag as actuated us in 1918 as we crossed that submarine-infested Atlantic to fight with the Allies; but in this particular period, I doubt that we can best serve our country by flag waving and we should keep that in mind. It is unwise to indulge in hysteria at this moment and at the same time unwise to stick our heads into the sand and refuse to be aware of the many forces of might that are being unleashed across the Atlantic.

It seems to me at this time, chaotic and confused as conditions are in the world in which we live, troubled and disturbed as we are, it is unwise for us to specifically commit ourselves to a program that is not sufficiently elastic to be varied to meet the changing conditions as they arise. I am not prepared to say this morning as to whether it would ever be wise for us again to fight on a European battlefield—and we all sincerely hope that that will never happen again and never be necessary. And I doubt if any of us are in position to forecast accurately the position that will be necessary for the nation that we love to take in the years that lie ahead in order to preserve her on this continent for that freedom and those liberties that we hold so dear. I am certain, and I believe you will agree with me, that the emphasis which the Legion has placed all these years upon a program of adequate national defense is correct and proper, and the Legion can make no greater contribution in this hour of peril than to approve and sustain, and interpret to our friends and neighbors, and interpret to the citizenship of our state and nation, the importance of the defense program upon which our national government has recently launched. None are better able to understand the necessity and the importance of that program than those of us of the Legion; none are better able to explain to those who do not have the proper conception of its importance; and none are better able to defend that program than those of the American Legion and those who followed the flag and wore the country's uniform in the last war.

We don't want to rush headlong into war, but at this particular hour we see the necessity and importance of hastening as rapidly as possible the mobilization of our material resources, the training of our agencies of national defense, to the end that these shores we love may be adequately defended and protected in event the mad maniac of Europe should turn in an hour of intoxication, in an hour of foolishness he would succumb to success of napoleonic accomplishments and turn in hostility toward our shores. Therefore, it is desirable that we at this particular time give support to the program of national defense—the program of the State Department as it endeavors to steer the course of the nation so as to avoid incurring additional enmity abroad, and at the same time to sustain and uphold the honor of this nation to the end that our national prestige may not suffer, and to the end that the influence of this great nation may continue to be felt throughout a war-torn world. It is desirable that we avoid making any new enemies and that is something for all of us to remember.

I think we all have great admiration for the statesmanlike and diplomatic manner in which the State Department has been handling the various situations that have arisen in order to avoid increased enmity and avoid making new enemies, and yet at the same time with such firmness, with sufficient appreciation of the importance and necessity of developing a real respect of this great nation.

Therefore, it seems to me especially important at this particular time that the program of the Legion should be a program of rational, reasonable patriotism; a program devoid of the jingoistic, and yet a program clear and specific; a program intelligently conceived and a program that undeviatingly supports the national defense program of this nation for which we have fought. It should endeavor at all times, however, to avoid, if possible, entanglements and involvements that might again embroil us in a frightful war.

It seems to me the policy of the Legion should be a levelheaded program of patriotism, a program of keeping our feet on the ground, a program dedicated always to undeviating loyalty and devotion to the nation that we love and yet a program of sane patriotism that seems to avoid emotional excesses that may carry us beyond our good judgment. This is the time we should be unselfish in our thinking, a time in which we should think first and always of the national good rather than the personal affect that it is going to have on me, on my beloved ones, in the event we are brought to the abyss of another ruthless and horrible war. It is time that the Legion dedicated again this great organization to the program of sacrifice, because each of you will recall that war exacts of every citizen in varying degrees perhaps, but of all citizens, a degree of sacrifice.

We talk of our democracy, of our opportunity in this great nation and on this continent, but there must in time of peril be a democracy of sacrifice. It is important that the Legion impress again upon those who have not shared their experiences in time of peril, the importance of approaching the period of peril with a willingness to sacrifice everything if need be for the maintenance of our national honor and preservation of the freedom and the liberties that we hold so dear.

It is important that we again be permeated with the spirit of sacrifice to the extent that we do not whimper when the perils of the moment exact from us personal service, increased taxes such as may be necessary for the accelerated program of national defense. It is important that we again be imbued with the same spirit of sacrifice that sustained us as we went on that last great adventure back in 1917. It is important that we seek to permeate our neighborhood with the importance of the American people being willing to accept again with a smile on their faces and with intense patriotism welling from their hearts, the necessities of such sacrifices as may be necessary and may be demanded in order that we all may have a clear conscience, and that the liberties, the freedom, that we enjoy in this, the last citadel of democracy in the world, may be preserved and passed on to the boys and girls in whose future our whole hearts are wrapped.[2]

---

1. James Thornton Norris (1893–), b. Augusta. Editor and publisher *Ashland Daily Indedendent*. President, Kentucky Press Association; director, Southern Newspaper Publishers Association. Hambleton Tapp, ed., *Kentucky Lives: The Blue Grass State Who's Who* (Hopkinsville, Ky., 1966), p. 390, and telephone interview, J. T. Norris, August 7, 1978.

2. The speech has been edited. For World War I stories see speech from July 4, 1941, in this section.

GREAT BRITAIN SUNDAY
Frankfort / September 24, 1940

WHEREAS, the people of Great Britain are suffering daily the horrors of a total war in which their cities are bombed without mercy; and

WHEREAS, Great Britain, the last great democracy remaining in the old World, appears in imminent danger of invasion by the forces of totalitarianism; and

WHEREAS, the sympathies of the people of the United States are always with a free people defending their freedom and their homeland; and

WHEREAS, the democratic institutions which our ancestors fought and died for on many a battlefield, and which we Americans hold so dear today, may be endangered if Great Britain succumbs to the attacks of the forces of totalitarianism; and

WHEREAS, Great Britain is fighting in defense of the ideals and the way of living which we Americans also hold most dear; and

WHEREAS, Americans of all walks of life, races, creeds, or political opinions are anxious to extend to Europe's last great democracy all the aid we can without violating our neutrality or involving our own country in war; and

WHEREAS, America from the beginning of its history has been a religious nation, believing in the omnipotence of Almighty Providence and invoking His aid in all projects which we deemed right and just,

NOW, THEREFORE, as Governor of the State of Kentucky, I do hereby proclaim Sunday, September the Twenty-Ninth as a Day of Prayer to be known as "Great Britain Sunday" and do hereby call upon the people of Kentucky to observe the day according to their respective religious convictions.

REGISTRATION FOR MILITARY SERVICE
Frankfort / September 25, 1940

GOVERNOR JOHNSON notified county clerks in Kentucky that they would be in charge of registration October 16 of all males between twenty-one and thirty-six for selective military service.[1]

His letter instructed them to conduct registration in each precinct at the regular polling place and to use election officers as registrars. At least three registrars, under the supervision of a chief registrar, must be on duty in each precinct. They are expected to serve without pay, and if additional registrars are needed, the county clerks will seek volunteers from civic clubs, the school system, or the American Legion.[2]

"If it is impossible to secure quarters for the registration without charge, such premises will be paid for at the rate charged for elections. Registration cards, certificates, and instruction placards are being mailed to each county clerk this week. These supplies are figured on the basis that one out of eight persons in Kentucky will be subject to registration."[3]

---

1. On October 1, 1940, the governor issued a proclamation calling all male persons (except those exempt under Section 5a of the Selective Service and Training Act of 1940) between twenty-one and thirty-six years of age to register for the draft on October 16. Employers were requested to give workers time off to register. Similar proclamations were issued June 17, 1941, January 15, April 3, June 10, and November 30, 1942.

2. The Kentucky Employment Service offered its services to the governor for the use of local draft boards. John B. Rodes, president, Kentucky Bar Association, instructed local bar associations to give free legal services and information to registrants on October 16. Louisville *Courier-Journal*, September 26, 1940.

3. The governor called on counties on October 7 to complete organization of registration machinery a week early to make Kentucky the first state to be ready for registration. He wrote the county clerk of Jefferson County, "Kentucky is proud of its record of leading all other states of the Union in volunteer enlistments as related to population. We are likewise proud of our record of 1917 when Kentucky was the first state to complete its quota of men under the initial draft of the World War." *Louisville Times,* October 7, 1940.

The governor announced on October 8, 1940, that state employees called into military service would be granted leaves of absence and would be reemployed when their military duty ended. His order did not cover employees who volunteered and said nothing of paying salary differences to those called into service. He had indicated previously that he would like to pay the salary difference of state employees in military service, but declined to make a specific comment. *Lexington Herald,* October 9, 1940.

DRAFT BOARD PERSONNEL
Frankfort / October 11, 1940

GOVERNOR JOHNSON countered Republican criticism of his draft board selections by stating that the general policy had been to give the dominant party in a county a majority on its draft boards and to balance that by choosing the appeal agents from the minority party, but "political activity" had not been a determining factor in the selections. "The practical result has been to give the Republican party far more representation in the state than its voting strength entitles it to, but the choices have not been based on political activities."[1]

The personnel of the draft boards has been recommended to President Roosevelt and is expected to be announced as soon as approved in Washington. "In selection of those to compose the draft boards caution has been exercised to be certain that outstanding individuals have been selected. Mr. Miller[2] has criticized the composition of the boards without knowing who composes them.

"The boards as recommended to the president are not composed of individuals who have been politically active and political considerations have not influenced the recommendations.

"Among those recommended for draft boards in Louisville and for appeal agents of the boards are such outstanding Republicans as W. B.

Harrison, J. J. Kavanaugh, Judge Richard Dietzman, Hubbard Petty, William A. Stoll, Frank Drake, and Jouett Ross Todd.[3]

"Mr. Miller might well have withheld his criticism of the draft boards until he knew who the members were. The boards do not represent the recommendation of any one person. Various individuals were requested to recommend outstanding citizens.

"A conscientious effort has been made to select boards composed of men of judgment and integrity, who will be impartial and careful to administer the act fairly. I am willing to permit the people to be the judge as to whether we have succeeded in that effort after the president announces the personnel of the boards. Members of these boards do not receive any compensation.

"The medical examiners for the draft boards were recommended by the committee on medical preparedness of the Kentucky State Medical Association. In most counties there were several equally good men to select from and the committee held back a number of names for the medical advisory and appeal boards that will be appointed later."

---

1. It was estimated that approximately 275 Democrats and 220 Republicans would serve on Kentucky's 165 local draft boards and that eighty counties would have boards predominantly Democratic and forty Republican. *Lexington Herald*, October 16, 1940.

2. Edward J. Miller (1881–1962), b. Louisville. Insurance executive; Jefferson County Republican chairman; member, Louisville Board of Public Works, 1917–1926; president, Louisville Water Company, 1926–1934. *Who's Who in Kentucky, 1936*, p. 283, and telephone interview, Miss Habenstein, Lincoln Insurance Company, Louisville, June 20, 1978.

3. William Benjamin Harrison (1889–1948), b. Louisville. Mayor, Louisville, 1927–1933; Republican nominee for governor, 1931. *Who's Who in Kentucky, 1936*, p. 181, and Louisville *Courier-Journal*, July 14, 1948.

J. J. Kavanaugh (1882–1951), b. Louisville. Louisville *Courier-Journal*, November 14, 1951.

Richard P. Dietzman (1883–1943), b. Louisville. Judge, Court of Appeals, 1924–1931; chief justice, 1931–1935. *Who's Who in Kentucky, 1936*, p. 112.

Hubbard R. Petty (?–1960), Died at age 72. Jefferson County sheriff, 1929–1933. Louisville *Courier-Journal*, September 16, 1960.

William Arthur Stoll (1896–), b. Louisville. Resides in Louisville; oil executive; president, Louisville Board of Trade, five years. *Kentucky Lives: The Blue Grass State Who's Who*, p. 529.

Frank M. Drake (1882–1960), b. Washington, D.C. Resided in Louisville, 1912–1960. Assistant commonwealth attorney, Jefferson County, 1921–1923; unsuccessful Republican candidate for United States Congress, Third District, 1934. Louisville *Courier-Journal*, September 17, 1942.

Jouette Menefee Ross Todd (1903–1967), b. Louisville. Attorney; treasurer, Republican National Committee, 1944–1946. *Who's Who in Kentucky, 1936, p. 404, and Louisville Courier-Journal,* January 27, 1967.

UNLIMITED EMERGENCY PERIOD
Frankfort / May 28, 1941

AS your governor, I conceive it my duty to address you on certain important matters. I am giving a direct message to the press, rather than a formal proclamation.

This date, May 28, 1941, is the first day of an unlimited emergency period, invoked last night by President Roosevelt in one of the most courageous announcements I have ever heard.

I sent the president a telegram early this morning. I commended his action in condemning disputes between capital and labor and in taking whatever steps are necessary to deliver the goods of war to Britain. I told him that Kentuckians approve his course and that we are ready to follow his leadership.[1] As Kentuckians, it is our solemn duty to ask ourselves one question: "What can I, as an individual, do to share my part of the load in the grim task ahead." We must ponder that question deeply. We must —and this is imperative—we must give it an honest answer. It is my purpose to make some suggestions that ought to help you, each one of you, to make an honest answer.

If you live on a farm, start immediately to produce and lay away enough foodstuffs for your own family. Write the College of Agriculture at Lexington, or see your own farm agent, for advice and suggestions.

If you live in a community where there is a local unit of the Active Militia still without uniforms, launch and support a drive to outfit these men who have volunteered without pay to substitute for the Kentucky National Guard while it is on active duty.[2] An unfortunate provision in the law prohibits the state from buying these uniforms.

You can conserve electricity. The southeast is in the grips of a great drought which has seriously curtailed hydroelectric production sorely needed for defense industries. Every kilowatt you conserve will help.

You can buy defense bonds at your Post Office and local banks. Investigate these bonds at once. Devise for yourself a systematic plan of purchase, suited to your own earnings and your own margin of savings.

You can uphold the hand of your governor who again states his emphatic disapproval of disputes between capital and labor which directly or indirectly retard the manufacture of defense goods.

You can nurture in your own hearts a virile brand of patriotism and a new resolution to bear cheerfully the sacrifices and hardships that inevitably will mark our transition from a peace economy to a war economy.

You can emulate the spirit of our Kentucky mothers who already have given up their sons for one year of active training. You can emulate the spirit of our Kentucky boys who volunteered in such numbers that only 25 percent of the draft quota had to be filled by selection. You can rejoice in the patriotism of Kentucky manhood that has set a national record, on the basis of population, for voluntary enlistment in the regular army and navy.

You can seek in your church a rebirth of spirit, of faith, and of good works. Read your Bible. Go to prayer meeting and Sunday school. Pay your debts. Get your own house in order. Read again some good history of the United States. Read again and again the Declaration of Independence. Try daily to become better parents, better neighbors, better citizens.

You can intensify your spendid support of local selective draft boards. These boards have done a fine job to date, but their duties will become more arduous as the emergency grows. They need your encouragement as well as your support.

Lastly, may I implore each of you to become a zealous partisan of democracy? Recount the blessings you have enjoyed as the free citizens of a free country which is governed by the free expression of your own suffrage. Contrast those blessings with the pall of human slavery that is our inevitable lot if Hitlerism prevails in this world. And let us unite enthusiastically in support of President Roosevelt and commit ourselves to a program of uncommon work for the common defense.

---

1. Johnson sent the president the following telegram on January 7, 1941: "As governor of Kentucky I send you fervent congratulations on your stirring message to Congress. You have translated the inarticulate feelings of our free people into a masterful plan of action that will be supported heart and soul by all. Kentucky, which is leading the nation in per capita volunteer enlistments for the army and navy, stands ready to follow your courageous leadership through the trying days ahead. The entire facilities of the state government and the citizenship of Kentucky are at your disposal. May God clear your head for thinking and steady your hand for action." *State Journal*, January 8, 1941.

2. On January 21, 1941, the governor issued a salute to the Kentucky National Guard when its members were leaving for a year of service and training. Louisville *Courier-Journal*, January 22, 1941.

KENTUCKY LEAGUE OF WOMEN VOTERS
Louisville / June 30, 1941

I WANT to congratulate the League of Women Voters upon their initiative in arranging this series of broadcasts and commend station WAVE for its cooperation in making available facilities for the discussion of the vital question of national defense.

"The Battle of Production" must be won. It can be won if we produce in the minds and hearts of the people of this nation the will to win. It is vital that there be produced a national attitude of determination to win the battle of production. It is important that our people understand that we cannot defend ourselves or aid our allies effectively until the full resources of the nation have been mobilized for the manufacture of airplanes, tanks, munitions, and the auxiliary accoutrements of modern warfare.

One of the foremost needs of the hour is a vigorous spirit of unity behind the leadership of President Roosevelt. The time for debate over the course we should take has passed. Ominous events in recent weeks indicate beyond any doubt that we must hurry our efforts to help halt Hilter.

Although Kentucky is not a state of great industrial capacity, the full facilities of industry have been made available for defense. More than four months ago an accurate survey of the industrial plants of the state was made in an effort to provide the Office of Production Management in Washington with reliable data as to the plants that could be used for making defense materials. It is estimated that 80 percent of the output of our large industrial plants is now being used in defense. The OPM in Washington has correct information as to the location and equipment of every factory in Kentucky that can be used to advantage. Defense contracts awarded to Louisville firms since July 1, 1940, total $39,174,618—total, including Fort Knox and Charleston, $200 million.

The "Battle of Production" cannot be won with mutinous soldiers. It can be won only through the enthusiastic help of every individual employed in the factories. Public opinion disapproves closing the plants engaged in defense production because of labor controversies. It is shortsighted to waste one precious hour in any factory in the nation because of labor disputes. Industry and capital have greater freedom of operation and opportunity in this nation than exists in any other country. Labor has greater protection and larger opportunity to earn generous wages in the United States than in any other nation. But these exceptional advantages are imperiled. If we lose the "Battle of Production," we shall lose these advantages. Labor will have no right to bargain collectively in a totalitarian state. Industrial employers will have no freedom in operation of their plants should we be conquered by the hosts of Hitler.

Because it is more important to win the "Battle of Production" than it is to win a labor dispute, it is vital that we eliminate lost time in industrial plants. We must vigorously disapprove of strikes which sabotage the safety of the nation. I congratulate labor leaders and industrial employers that labor controversies have been kept pretty well in bounds in Kentucky in industries which affect national defense. I urge that there be complete elimination of such controversies.

One of the needs in winning the "Battle of Production" is an increased quantity of trained personnel. There has been completed at the University of Kentucky a modern aviation laboratory. It is being used by the Army Air Service in research and in training carefully selected men through an intensified graduate course in airplane motors. Facilities of the College of Engineering, University of Kentucky, are being used in chemical engineering. This instruction in specialized subjects seeks to supply trained personnel to fill the vital positions in the army.

The "Food for Defense" program in Kentucky has resulted in greatly stimulated production of food, a vital factor in winning any battle. This has been carefully organized and promoted under the direction of Dean Cooper of the University of Kentucky College of Agriculture. There are approximately 100,000 farm families in Kentucky who are participating in some phase of the "Food for Defense" program.

Aluminum is a metal that is vital to the winning of the war. It is indispensable in the manufacture of airplanes. There is a shortage of this important metal. Defense needs have increased the demand for aluminum far beyond the capacity of existing plants to produce it. So the imperative need for aluminum must be temporarily met by collecting every bit of aluminum that can be spared and turning it over to our government. Mayor La Guardia[1] of New York, Civil Defense Commissioner for the nation, has requested that the governor of Kentucky assume responsibility for directing an organized effort to collect aluminum in Kentucky. July 21 is the beginning of the period within which our citizenship will be urged to help collect a vast quantity of aluminum.

Aluminum kitchen utensils that can be spared or replaced should be offered as your contribution toward defense of our country. Aluminum light fixtures that are outmoded, or can be spared, will be more useful on the wings of an airplane. Around garages it should be possible to collect a quantity of aluminum—such as discarded aluminum piston heads. This scavenger hunt for aluminum supplies a practical plan by which each patriotic Kentuckian may help in an important way to strengthen our national defenses. Within a few days a movement will be launched to organize our citizenship into a plan that will result in collecting every ounce of aluminum that can be spared to meet the needs of the nation. I am sure that each of you will realize that this is an important request which your government is making of you. Many of you are anxious to do something to help in the program of national defense. Here is something specific which you can do. I hope you will understand that this is an important request. The need for this precious metal is so serious as to create an opportunity for each of you to give to your government something that is greatly needed and is highly essential in winning the battle of production.

Under the direction of J. J. Greenleaf,[2] state director of Civil Defense, we are preparing in Kentucky for emergencies with which we hope we may never be faced. July 28 there is to be started at the University of Kentucky a Fire School. Every fire department from every city and town is invited to send men to that school for instruction in fire fighting and prevention. The aid of every citizen is enlisted in helping to prevent fires, to watch for evidence of fires of incendiary origin.

Steps have been taken to provide protection for the utilities services and the communications systems of the state. Railroad bridges and tunnels are being protected. Executives of these companies readily responded to suggestions that precautions be taken to prevent sabotage of these properties which are the natural target for enemies of the republic who would cripple our defenses.

A roster of 500 emergency highway patrolmen has been compiled. This roll contains names of men who are subject to call in an emergency for temporary duty. Squad leaders are being designated throughout the state to establish an airplane warning service. Cooperative plans have been worked out with the Red Cross by which disaster relief may be promptly organized in event of an explosion or other calamity. These activities have been organized because of the willingness of our people to cooperate in getting ready for the worst, if it comes.

I want to express my gratitude for the fine attitude which Kentuckians have revealed toward their duty as citizens. I have great admiration for the mothers of Kentucky for patriotic acceptance of the heartaches which come with the surrender of their sons for military training under provisions of the Selective Service Act. These mothers of our sons have smiled through tears as they have encouraged the lads they love to enthusiastically meet their military duty. I sympathize with these mothers who are separated from their sons. I share with them the pride they feel in the ready response of Kentucky's young men as they have realized that their country needs them.

Public acknowledgment should be made by the governor of the competent and conscientious service being performed by the organizations of more than 1,500 Kentuckians who are administering the Selective Service

Act. Colonel Frank Rash, who accepted appointment from me as state director, has wisely and efficiently administered this essential service. Members of the 165 local boards, the doctors, and all who have accepted responsibility in applying selective service in Kentucky are entitled to grateful thanks for their patriotic performance of duty. In no state in the Union has the Selective Service functioned more smoothly and with greater efficiency than in Kentucky. I am proud of that fact and congratulate these who have contributed to that fine record.

On Tuesday there is to be held throughout the state a registration of those young men who have become twenty-one years of age since the previous registration. I congratulate you who have attained citizenship upon becoming eligible for military duty. You are to have an opportunity to do something for the great nation that has done so much for you and your parents. That form of government by which we govern ourselves, the social order and economic system that has here developed, provides greater freedom of opportunity, more extensive liberties than have been enjoyed by any people. This democracy that we must defend cannot be bought once and for all. It must be bought again and again. It must be defended. And it is a proud fact in Kentucky's history that her men and women respond with heroic valor when the nation is endangered.

So, while I regret that mothers of the boys who are to be registered for military duty tomorrow are faced with the prospect of sending their sons to training camp, I am sure that there is pride in their hearts that those sons are unafraid, shrink not from treading the path of duty, uncertain though its end may be.

---

1. Fiorello La Guardia (1882–1947), b. New York, New York. Attorney; mayor, New York, 1934–1945; director, Office of Civilian Defense during part of World War II; head, United Nations Relief and Rehabilitation, 1946. *Who Was Who in American Politics*, p. 367.

2. John J. Greenleaf (1880–1961), b. Richmond. Attorney. Chairman, Public Service Commission; state campaign manager for Governor Johnson. Interview, Margaret Pryor, daughter, Richmond, March 28, 1978.

REDEDICATION TO AMERICANISM
Lexington / July 4, 1941

WE are assembled here on this the natal day of this Republic.[1] We come in compliance with the suggestion of the president of the United States that on this significant day we should reconsecrate ourselves to the preservation of the sublime principles boldly and defiantly proclaimed July 4, 1776.

The Declaration of Independence is enclosed in a glass case that has become a shrine. Millions of Americans stand in reverence before the sheet of parchment upon which is written in antique script the aspirations of those colonists who were unafraid of the unequal struggle as they risked their lives for liberty.

Fifty-six men, in powdered wigs and knee breeches, signed their names to that immortal document. By that act they became traitors to the king, subject to execution for treason.

On this the anniversary of the day when was signed the birth certificate of this nation, it is important that we revitalize the Declaration of Independence, reaffirm our faith in it, realize that intelligent self-interest dictates that we hasten in our efforts to halt Hitler.

The Declaration of Independence was a flaming document which reflected the desperate concern of our colonial forebears. Most of you recall the opening line of the Declaration, "When in the course of human events" and so on.

But it is important today that we refreshen our memory as to how it ends. There is reflected courage and stamina in the closing passage as is stated: "And for the support of this Declaration, with a firm reliance on the protection of divine Providence, we mutually pledge to each other our Lives, our Fortunes and our sacred Honor." Those words of ringing rhetoric have reverberated through the corridors of time. The men who put their names to that document realized that they might be required to redeem that pledge before a firing squad, as they pledged their life, fortune, and honor to support that Declaration.

Inhabitants of the colonies, who sent these the signers of the Declaration to Philadelphia as their representatives, understood the audacity of the deed. They knew it meant hardship and sacrifice as their poorly equipped, ragged armies faced the well-equipped troops of Britain. Already they had recognized the great odds against them as they fought gallantly at Bunker Hill and Concord. They were familiar with the cruel hardship of war with its mud and filth and flies—its hunger and suffering. They knew it would mean their property would be seized if the revolution was a failure.

Yet these colonists with a passionate zeal for freedom in their hearts responded to the call of duty as sounded by the Declaration. The Americanism which had its birth in those desperate days was a faith in the destiny of America—a zealous crusade for the establishment of this continent of a nation in which would be guaranteed the freedom and liberties essential to a happy people.

As writes a patriotic American, Robert Leavitt,[2] "To them, individually and as a people, certain ideals looked bigger than self-interest, safety of life." As news of action of the fifty-six patriots at Philadelphia spread through the colonies, the people were fired with a determination to win for themselves and for us the precious privileges demanded in the Declaration. They were determined to make that dream of freedom a blessed reality.

As years have passed the sheet of parchment on which was written the Declaration has turned yellow with age. Those who signed it live only in the memory of those who have been the benefactors of their vision and valor. The freedom of which they dreamed has been ours to enjoy. The rights which were purchased at such frightful sacrifice, we all enjoy. We have taken those liberties for granted. We have been inclined to feel that our democracy, bought with the blood of heroes, had been purchased once and for all.

But in the light of startlingly ominous events in Europe, we are shaken from our complaisancy by the harsh fact that great injustice and intolerable tyrannies have not been banished from the earth. We realize that democracy cannot be bought once and for all, that it must be purchased again and again and that the price may be very high. We realize democracy must be defended when assailed by dictators, that it must be preserved regardless of the cost when international hijackers trample justice under foot and enthrone ruthless might. We must understand that as we face necessity of repurchasing democracy that we can pay the price only if each of us willingly accepts the fact that the price of democracy is part of our individual and personal obligation.

Ruthless and brutal force has been unleashed in the world to destroy the ideals embodied in the Declaration of Independence. With fiendish efficiency it has savagely subjugated nation after nation. We would be stupid to close our eyes to the fact that Hitler's dream of world dominance imperils our safety. He had rather conquer us than any other nation and has definite plans to do that very thing. And those plans are progressing with startling success. It is vital to our safety that we hasten in our preparation to repurchase democracy—preserve this Republic which had its birth amid the uncertainties and vicissitudes of 1776. It is vital that there be a rebirth of that fierce and exalted patriotism which was manifest as this nation was born. It is vital that there be a resurgence of the spirit of 1776. It is vital that there be awakened in each of us a quickened sense of duty to our country.

It is not enough that we have declared that we will mobilize our resources to meet the mechanized might of a brutal foe of freedom. There must be a flaming resolve in every heart if we are to sustain that declaration.

Peaceful nations have been crushed. Their people were unwilling to believe that the international hijacker would conquer them. Their wishful hoping, their blindness to realities, made them easy victims. These nations were divided in thought, unprepared, tolerant of traitors. We must not be guilty of the folly of refusing to profit by their bitter experience. We must get ready to halt Hitler and we must do it in a hurry. It is wishful thinking to rely on distance and the protection of the Atlantic Ocean. There is protection from the Atlantic only if it is dominated by our navy. It is wishful thinking to believe that when Hitler has conquered Europe his appetite will be satiated. We must realize that as we help those who are fighting gallantly to halt Hitler, we are making America more secure, defending democracy.

For too long too many of us have been concerned about what we can get out of our government. In this critical hour our chief concern must be "What can I give to our government." There must be a rebirth of that unselfish devotion to the ideal of democracy which was born in the world 165 years ago.

One of the foremost needs of this critical hour is a vigorous spirit of unity behind the leadership of President Roosevelt. The time for debate over the course we should take has passed. We cherish the right of free speech but we can best protect it if we do not abuse it. Let us develop a virile public opinion that will not permit discord—that will unite the nation in its fight for freedom. That public opinion should refuse to sanction strikes in defense industries. There should be such disapproval of strikes which halt the production of airplanes, tanks, armaments, and munitions essential to defense, that shortsighted labor leaders and employers will not dare incur the displeasure of a patriotic people by halting production. Employers and employees must realize that the American people will not stand for strikes which sabotage the safety of the nation. It is unpatriotic to waste one precious hour in any defense factory in the nation because of labor disputes.

Every republic that has arisen in the world has been born out of a unified zeal of the people for improved government. Every republic that has collapsed has disintegrated because of discord and dissension. The lesson of history is clear and unmistakable. I wish the words of Kentucky's motto could be emblazoned before every citizen of the nation. "United We Stand—Divided We Fall" but reflects the distilled wisdom of the ages. The time has arrived to be intolerant of intolerance. The traitors who seek to weaken our defenses, who plot our destruction, must be driven from our shores. This crucial hour demands the love and allegiance of every citizen. We are justified in demanding that you love America or leave it. It is time that we show our colors, that we get rid of hyphenated Americans. The spies, renegades, and malcontents who abuse our hospitality should be treated as the traitors which they are. Freedom of speech should not be used as a cloak for speech and actions that are subversive to the ideals of our country and endanger her defenses.

As governor of Kentucky, I take great pride in the fact that in proportion to population more Kentucky boys have voluntarily enlisted in the army and navy than from any other state in the Union. My heart is thrilled by the fact that as we have called men for military training under the Selective Service Act, three out of every four required to fill Kentucky's quota have volunteered for training. I have great admiration for Kentucky mothers who have smiled through tears as they have encouraged their sons to follow the path of duty to the training camp. I have great sympathy for the mothers and wives who surrender their sons and husbands for military service and I share with them the pride they feel as they make this sacrifice for country. They exemplify the finest quality of Americanism. The fire of patriotic fervor burns in their hearts. There is no necessity of talking to them about a rebirth of Americanism or national unity. The same may be said for most Kentuckians. It is especially true of those who have accepted appointment from the governor of responsibility in connection with the Selective Service Act and Civil Defense. In no state in the Union has Selective Service functioned more smoothly or with greater fairness and efficiency than in Kentucky. This is a fine tribute to the patriotism of those who are serving without compensation in these places of importance.

I predict that as meetings like this are held throughout the nation on this natal day of freedom, our people will develop an increased understanding of the seriousness of the threat to our liberties. As they become aroused there will be born a virile, robust Americanism such as will sustain us as we make the sacrifices that will be required of us.

We have great admiration for the British and the gallant fight they are making to halt Hitler. We admire the unconquerable spirit of the British people. Ole Oleson, the celebrated comedian of "Hellzapoppin," relates that a British naval vessel sank a German ship and as soon as members of the German crew had been rescued from the sea and taken aboard the British craft, captain of the vessel issued an order in which members of the crew were ordered to be courteous and considerate of their prisoners. There was strict compliance with the order for a couple of days. Then a terrific fight broke out. A stocky, cockney Englishman soundly thrashed a big, phlegmatic German sailor. He closed both eyes, knocked out a few teeth, and almost tore off the ear of the German before bystanders pulled the Englishman off.

The British sailor was taken before the captain for reprimand and punishment. "Have you any explanation for this violation of orders?" inquired the ship commander. The sailor said, "Captain, when that bloody German said British sailors were cowards and the navy no good, I said nothing and kept my temper. When he called Mr. Churchill a windjammer and demagogue, I didn't say anything. When he called our king and queen vile names I took that—but when the bloody blighter spit in our ocean—I lost my temper."

There is greater danger of democracy being destroyed than many of us realize. We must mobilize the mind, the heart, and the will of America to prevent that disaster. It will require sacrifice from all of us. By our acceptance of those sacrifices, we will reveal the virility of our Americanism.

One of the most sublime examples of patriotism that came to my attention in the World War resulted from an incident in the winter following the Armistice. It was down in that lovely winter paradise of southern France—the Riviera. The majestic Alps mountains rose above the foam-fleck blue of the Mediterranean Sea. The warm sun bursted the rose buds. Orange blossoms perfumed the air. High up on the mountainside there was a magnificent French resort hotel that had been converted into a convalescent hospital for American soldiers. Amid this loveliness, medical science and surgical skill sought to repair the ravages of an awful war.

One day a distinguished French general came to visit the hospital and pay his respects to the American wounded. In the recreation room as the general entered, all stood at attention to salute the great French soldier —that is, all stood except one, a bright-eyed young lad who did not stand because both legs were gone. The general returned the salute, walked across the room and stood beside the maimed soldier. In a solicitous tone he inquired, "Where did you lose them, Lieutenant?" An indefinable light flashed in the eyes of the crippled youth and in a firm voice, surcharged with conviction, he replied, "I did not lose them, sir, I exchanged them for a clear conscience."

So on this significant day, as democracy is endangered, it is our obligation to so perform our duty as to keep our conscience clear. Let us begin by nurturing within our hearts a solemn resolve to preserve this Republic. Let us stimulate that attitude in the hearts of others until Americanism, zealous and virile, is regnant in the heart of every citizen. Let us recapture something of the faith and fire of those heroic Americans who signed the Declaration of Independence. Let us take the same pledge as did they as we "mutually pledge to each other our Lives, our Fortunes and our Sacred Honor." That unity and patriotism will keep the stars in the flag and we shall have no red without the white and the blue.

---

1. On July 1 the governor issued a proclamation to urge all Kentuckians to participate in the nationwide rededication ceremony which was to be broadcast on July 4 and was to include a brief address by President Roosevelt.

2. It is presumed that the reference is to a free-lance writer, Robert Keith Leavitt, b. 1895, New York, New York. One of his books, *Noah's Ark: New England Yankees and the Endless Quest* (Springfield, Mass. 1947), is about Noah Webster, but it does not contain the quotation that Johnson used. Frederick C. Mish of G. & C. Merriam Company could not identify the source of the quotation. Letter, July 31, 1978.

AMERICAN LEGION
Lexington / July 22, 1941

IT is a very great pleasure to be permitted to come and mingle with you, the comrades whose friendship I especially appreciate. I have an idea that there are some of you, who as a result of activities in which you have already engaged, would have a pretty good idea about a certain fellow I am going to tell you about. He was deputy sheriff in a certain Kentucky county and he had been sent out to this home to levy a tax on the furniture for the collection of a debt.

Well, when this deputy sheriff arrived at the home, nobody was in the house and the door was open, and so he walked in and he thought he might as well make a list of the furniture while he was there. He started out listing the furniture in the household and the first thing he wrote down was "one mahogany dining room suite, one mahogany sideboard, two quarts of bourbon whiskey, unopened." Then he decided to alter that and he wrote down "one quart of bourbon whiskey, unopened." Sometime later, the next entry was made and that was "one revolving oriental rug."

I know that you are having a fine time here in Lexington, here in Central

Kentucky. Lexington is indeed a hospitable city, and Man o' War Post has done a fine job in entertaining the convention. But, here in Lexington calls to mind an amusing incident that transpired and which was reported by our tourist activities last summer.

You know there is quartered here in Central Kentucky the great Man o' War, the greatest thoroughbred horse of all times, a great sire whose sons and daughters have contributed so richly to the advancement of the sport of the thoroughbreds. Man o' War is over here at Mr. Riddle's farm[1] and there is one of the finest, old colored fellows you have ever seen that has been Man o' War's groom all these years. His name is Will Harbut and I believe he thinks more of that horse than anything else and he is very proud of him and will tell you everything about him. Well, Man o' War has had unusual care taken of him and he has certain visiting hours. You can only see him from nine o'clock in the morning until four o'clock in the afternoon.

One afternoon last summer, there was a great, big automobile drove up there at four fifteen and some people got out and they walked over to Will and said they would like to see Man o' War. He said, "No, sir, you cannot see this horse until tomorrow morning at nine o'clock." This visitor said, "I have come quite a distance and I am disappointed that I cannot see him. I had no idea there was any restrictions on when I could see him." Will said, "I am sorry but you can't see him till tomorrow morning." The man turned away and walked toward his car and said, "My name is Dionne, [2] and I am terribly disappointed that I can't see him." When he got over to the car, it finally dawned on Will that this fellow had an unusual name and then he followed him over and looked at the license on the car, and then finally it dawned on him who he might be. He said, "Mister, what did you say your name was?" and the visitor said "Dionne," and then Will said, "Are you any kin of that fellow that had the quintuplets?" and the fellow said, "Yes, I am the father of the quintuplets." Then Will said, "Mister, you come on back here, please. I want this horse to see you."

I have no inclination or disposition to come before a group that I love and respect as much as I do my comrades of the Legion to do any bragging about what a good governor I am making, because I have an idea if I succeed reasonably well and do a reasonably acceptable public service, you will find out about it whether I tell you or not. But I am glad to have a chance to come and say to this representative group that the Legion leadership has been of considerable help to me, and I want to tell you how much I appreciate the help that has been given to me in my effort to make a good governor.

I never appreciated the Legion more and never have been more proud of my membership in it and association with you, than I have in the last year and a half, because from time to time there have been duties and obligations that have been imposed upon the governor that would have caused him increased concern had it not been for the fact he could instantly turn to the Legion and its leadership for the assistance so sorely needed.

For example, more than a year ago a representative of the War Department walked into the governor's office and said Congress has passed a Selective Service Act and now it is your baby. The responsibility for setting it up and for its organization and administration within Kentucky is the responsibility of the governor of this state, and I am going to say to you frankly, I was seized with a feeling of fear as a realization came over me of the delicate and important job that had been dumped on the governor's desk. The job of setting up the mechanism by which would be chosen those individuals who are to be called to the service for their country was a tremendous undertaking. When I think now how smoothly it is functioning and when I think of the fear and uneasiness and the anxiety which I experienced in the early phases of it as we approached the Selective Service organization, I realize that the reason that the anxiety and fear that I experienced has been dissipated as a result of the smooth operation of the organization is due primarily to the fine support and help of the American Legion, the Legion leadership, and the legionnaires throughout Kentucky.

One of the fortunate things that occured to me was that I had an inspiration when I searched for the leadership of that important service, as there came to my mind the name of Colonel Frank Rash for the state director of Selective Service. As a result of his wisdom and diligence and earnestness, together with the fine cooperation that we have had from the Legion in every community of the state, it has been possible to set up here in Kentucky a Selective Service organization that has functioned smoothly and fairly, efficiently, and has so administered that important act as to reflect credit on the state and all of our people, as well as the American Legion which has contributed so much to the fine job which has been done.

Nothing has thrilled me more than the fact that in accordance with her population, and in proportion to her population, more Kentucky boys have voluntarily enlisted in the army, navy, and marines than from any other state in the Union. We have filled Kentucky's quota under the Selective Service Act by 75 percent volunteers. About three out of every four Kentuckians that have gone into military service have volunteered rather than necessitating the formal routine of drafting them for service. I can't but feel, and I am sure you feel, that is an unquestionable indication that the fire of patriotic fervor still burns in the hearts of Kentucky and that our people are alert and awake to the danger with which we are confronted; that they are anxious to contribute to the defense of this great republic and only await the opportunity and are anxious to embrace the opportunity to do such as they can to contribute to the defense of the great nation that we love.

Selective Service has functioned splendidly because of a fine leadership and a great legionnaire, and because of the great helpfulness of the Legion members and the Legion itself throughout Kentucky, and I am glad to have a chance to say much obliged to you.

Then after the Selective Service and the responsibility of setting it up was imposed upon the governor, there came another duty that was very perplexing because of inadequate legislation. When the Kentucky National Guard was called into the service, the War Department called upon the several states to organize within themselves a comparable military group to supplant the National Guard. That necessitated the appointment of a civilian defense commissioner with the state. Well, we did not have any money with which to pay a civilian defense commissioner and it required a great deal of traveling and work, and so I called on my good friend Jack Greenleaf from Richmond, who was already on the state payroll as a member of the Public Service Commission, to assume the additional difficulties of the civilian defense commissioner. Jack Greenleaf and others have directed the defense activities particularly of the state militia. Then there are others, Commander Norris, Lee McClain, and others who have given of their time and effort to promote and effectuate the organization of a state militia until now their efforts have resulted in the creation of an outfit that reflects creditably upon their community and creditably upon their state.

Now, that has been done in the face of great difficulty, because when we were confronted with the necessity of the formation of an active state militia, we had no law or no legislation that fitted the situation perfectly. We were one of the few states that had a law which provided for the organization of a state militia. It was an act that was passed, as I recall, back in 1934. It authorized the formation of a state militia unit, but it specifically prohibited the state from spending any money in equipping it. It said counties or cities may spend money for the equipping of the state militia units, but that law specifically prohibited the state from spending any money for equipment of an acting militia outfit.

There we were then confronted with the unhappy situation of trying to obtain uniforms for the militia organization and such other equipment as they needed and the state forbidden even to make any expenditure for that purpose. Then again it demonstrated the enthusiasm and the vision of the American Legion in many communities of Kentucky. The American Legion posts took the initiative in raising a local fund the purpose of which was to buy uniforms for the state militia. Had it not been for the Legion, I am certain it would not have been possible to have made the progress that has been made. It has resulted in the recruiting of nearly two thousand men and ninety officers in the formation of a state militia that is a credit to Kentucky and that unit is being well trained and developing a proficiency that will make them extremely useful and effective in the event of an emergency. So again, I want to say much obliged to the Legion for their fine contribution to that program.

Then as the aluminum shortage developed, there was delegated to the governor the job of collecting all the scrap aluminum that could be found in Kentucky, so that it might be utilized in the construction of airplanes. I turned to Mr. Greenleaf, the Civilian Defense Commissioner, and we talked it over and I said the Legion will do that job for us. Mr. Greenleaf called on Commander Norris who assumed that responsibility, and again through the Legion and its leadership, another important defense activity is being directed. I am certain that with the result of its enthusiasm and cooperation of all Legion posts throughout the country, that the collection of scrap aluminum in the state will be such as to contribute tons and tons of this vital and important metal, making it available for the construction of airplanes, making it available that it may contribute to a hastening of the defense of our country.

Because of these things and many others, I feel especially appreciative and especially grateful to the Legion for the assistance that they have given to me as their governor. It makes me feel increasingly proud of the fact that I am a member of this fine organization. It makes me increasingly grateful to those of you who constitute the Legion for your fine sense of civic duty and responsibility, and the great helpfulness which you have given me in this period that needs a united effort of all of us so that we may hasten and facilitate the day when America may be sufficiently strong to defend herself against aggression from any foe.

---

1. Samuel D. Riddle (1861–1951), b. Glen Riddle, Pennsylvania. Owner of Faraway Farm, Kentucky. *New York Times*, January 9, 1951.

2. Oliva Dionne of Callander, Ontario, Canada. Quintuplets were born to his wife, Elzire, on May 28, 1934. *Webster's Biographical Dictionary* (Springfield, Mass., 1972), p. 422.

AMERICAN LEGION AUXILIARY
Louisville / October 27, 1941

WOMEN who are eligible to membership in the American Legion Auxiliary have much in common, are bound together by ties which provide abundant reason for creation and perpetuation of this splendid organization. [1]

Women of the Auxiliary share with each other the sad memories of the World War as they recall the heartache which was brought by tearful farewells to husbands, sons, and brothers as the call of duty disrupted happy homes, separated loved ones, imposed hardships and sacrifice.

Women of the Auxiliary have a common heritage in the memories of those stirring days when patriotic fervor sustained them in gloomy hours of loneliness as they waited with anxiety for news from across the Atlantic which carried assurance and calmed anxious hearts.

You recall those crucial days when through tears which could not be restrained you sent him away to training camp, later to surrender him for service in the hazardous adventure on the Western Front. You recall that despite the heartbreak of that bitter experience, there commingled with your grief a feeling of pride and lofty patriotism that you had sent your soldier where duty called.

Admirably as did the manhood of these United States acquit itself as in that perilous venture beyond the Atlantic, one of the most sublime phases of the World War was the courage, the patriotism, and fortitude of the women of America. Their fine attitude it was which sustained that high morale characteristic of the American soldier.

Striking evidence of the powerful influence of the woman behind the soldier in the AEF came under my observation as I read and censored the letters written by men of my company from overseas. Army regulations required that all mail be censored, in order to avoid dissemination of any news that might be helpful to the enemy. It was a drab and dreary task to read those letters in the flickering glow of a candle. Yet there was drama and heartthrob in those missives in which the men in khaki bared their hearts to mothers, wives, sisters, and sweethearts.

Well indeed do I recall the spirit of sacrifice expressed in those letters, the devotion poured out by heart-hungry men for the woman back home for whom they felt they were undergoing the hardships of war. Those letters gave me a new insight into the tremendous effect of womanhood upon the morale of an army, the stimulative effect of woman's encouragement, the inspiration of a woman's devotion to sustain a man through the hazardous experiences of battle.

Too there was humor revealed in some of those letters which men wrote to the girl that had been left behind. There was a tall, redheaded sergeant in my company who was a veritable Lothario, a sheik without much conscience. I could but smile as I ran hurriedly through Sergeant Red's letters. He wrote regularly, when conditions permitted, to three different girls. His letters were touching and tender in their expression of devotion. And he wrote the same letter to all three—merely wrote one letter and then carefully copied it for the other two. Only the names were changed in the letters to the trio. It was at times difficult to restrain the inclination to switch letters in the envelopes and expose the gay deceiver.

Women of the Auxiliary share in common the joy and relief from anxiety which came with the signing of the armistice, the restoration of peace, bringing the comforting assurance that loved ones would not again be subjected to the deadly spray of machine gun fire, the sinister zing of bursting shrapnel, or the noxious poison of hellish gas. Yet other women of the Auxiliary share the memory of a seared soul and broken heart as the star in the service flag turned to gold, as cruel fate exacted as a sacrifice upon the altar of our country the life of a loved one.[2]

One of the tragic incidents which I recall as having marred the hysteric joy of the armistice is but illustrative of the acute pain which that historic event brought to the hearts of many women in the world.

The French town in which I was stationed when the armistice was signed, enrolled as a student in the Army General Staff College, went into a delirium of joy as the happy news brought assurance that the war was over. People surged through the narrow streets, shrieking their gladness over termination of a struggle that for four years had bled France white.

A woman, dressed in black, sat by the window which opened on the narrow street. She was quietly sobbing as the hysterical throng swept past. My companion, who spoke French fluently, paused touched by the grief of the woman. "Fini la guerre" was the cry echoing through the air. "Why do you weep, little mother?" inquired my friend. "Oh, oui, Monsieur American, pour moi la guerre est fini trop tarde." For me the war is over too late. Then she told the tragic story. Two stalwart sons had answered the call of duty as did your sons and husbands. One fell at Verdun. Another was mortally wounded in the battle of Paris. Finally, as manpower was exhausted, her husband was called to the colors. And only a few weeks before had died in a hospital from wounds received in battle. For this woman, bereft of her husband and two sons, the armistice brought little joy—it only served to accentuate the feeling of loss and loneliness, as she could but ponder the severity of the sacrifice that war had exacted of her.

It is such bonds as these that unite women of the Auxiliary as they associate themselves for mutual helpfulness and companionship. Such memories, sanctified by the travail of anxious and bleeding hearts, are the common heritage of those women who with smiling courage sent their men to answer the stern call of duty, follow the flag on a foreign battlefield, in order that the autocracy of might be thwarted and the threat of German imperialism be turned back.

But there are more practical reasons why women who have experienced the grief and pain which war visits upon womanhood should associate themselves together. War exacts its most terrific toll in suffering and sacrifice from womanhood. Woman it is upon whom is visited the sorrow which is the inevitable byproduct of war. Women who have sent their men into the maelstrom of death know something of the soul-searching experience which war brings to womanhood. Women should hate war with an intense hatred because they are the helpless victims of its most hideous phases.

Women of the Auxiliary should be united in their love for peace, their hatred for war. The full weight of their influence should be exerted for preservation of peace, prevention of war.

Women of the Auxiliary should know that the toll of life taken of American troops was increased as result of this nation having been inadequately prepared for war. You should know that, despite the 30 billions of dollars spent by this nation to finance our participation in the nineteen months of the World War, when the firing ceased on the Western Front the first consignment of American manufactured artillery shell had just reached the front, too late to be fired.

Women of the Auxiliary should expend their influence in behalf of a program of adequate national defense, as a preventative of war. There is no finer objective for attainment of which women of the Auxiliary may expend their efforts than in promotion of reasonable legislative measures which will assure adequate protection and care for widows and orphans of World War veterans. It is a cause which is justified by every humane consideration, by every dictate of human justice.

So it is that there is abundant justification for women of the World War to unite themselves in this patriotic organization for promotion of causes which challenge their united and cohesive effort. I rejoice in the virility of this Auxiliary organization and am happy to render any service that will promote its spendid program.

---

1. This radio broadcast was arranged by the Women's Auxiliary of the American Legion.

2. When addressing the Kentucky Chapter of the American War Mothers at a tree-planting ceremony on the Capitol lawn on April 30, 1941, Johnson referred to the sad prospect of its membership being greatly increased. *State Journal*, May 1, 1941.

WAR PROCLAMATION
Frankfort / December 9, 1941

WHEREAS, the President of the United States has asked Congress to declare, and by Joint Resolution the Congress has declared, that a state of war now exists between the United States and Japan, and

WHEREAS, this action on the part of the President and of the Congress of the United States has been precipitated by the Japanese Empire, which, on Sunday morning, December 7, 1941, executed a most dastardly and unprovoked attack upon the enlisted forces, civilian population, ships, armaments, munitions, and possessions of this country, and

WHEREAS, the President of the United States by Executive Order on May 27, 1941, and I, as Governor of the Commonwealth of Kentucky, following the leadership of our great President, on May 28, 1941 issued an Executive Order declaring an emergency to exist, and

WHEREAS, a state of war now follows, it is imperative that our defense program be transferred into one of offense, and

WHEREAS, I have sent to the President a telegram[1] in which I stated that Kentuckians approve and endorse this act and that we, as a united people, are ready to follow his leadership,

NOW, THEREFORE, I as Governor of the Commonwealth of Kentucky, respectfully call upon every Kentuckian, whether he be old or young, rich or poor, humble or great, to take cognizance of the fact that we are at war, and I earnestly ask that all activities in our Commonwealth be immediately placed on a wartime basis. We must approach the problem with complete victory as our objective and to achieve that victory will require considerable sacrifice and effort on the part of all of us; therefore, I ask that all patriotic, freedom-loving citizens, both men and women, register as volunteers with local councils of defense.

I respectfully ask that capital, labor, and industry immediately erase differences of opinion that may exist and unite in a program that will result in the production of a maximum amount of materials for the prosecution of the war and the livelihood of our citizens. I call upon the farmers of the state to produce food and products to the limit of their properties. I request the cooperation of all ministers of the Gospel, all educators, members of all veterans' organizations, civilian defense councils, all officials of municipal, county, and state governments to direct their efforts toward the coordination and organization of our people in a united program for a righteous cause.

---

1. "The treacherous surprise attack by the Japanese on Pearl Harbor as a reply to your conciliatory message to the Emperor is an outrage which Kentuckians resent. As governor of Kentucky, I assure you that the people of this state are prepared to follow your leadership and to make any sacrifice you regard as necessary to meet the emergency." It was dated December 7, 1941.

DAY OF PRAYER
Frankfort / January 1, 1942

GOVERNOR JOHNSON spoke for the laity of the state in a stirring appeal that "we reconsecrate ourselves in the God of our fathers, the God of righteousness. We have not gathered here for the purpose of getting the Lord on our side—but to be certain that we do the things which will get us on His side."[1]

He expressed appreciation to Franklin County Judge L. Boone Hamilton[2] for the "thought which brings us here this morning to ask divine guidance."

"The words 'Happy New Year' fall glibly from our lips, but the happiness for the year which the words imply can come only from sacrifices—only when we throw all our vast resources into the conflict to achieve a vast and noble purpose."

One of the most memorable experiences of World War I was when Johnson visited his father, a Methodist preacher, in the latter's parsonage in Hardinsburg and heard from his father's lips the "inspiring story of Gideon" and his battles in which Gideon was aided and inspired by the Lord. On leave from an army camp at the time, Johnson said the story was one that had always remained with him.

"It is highly important now, therefore, that we turn to divine guidance for inspiration as we face the uncertain future which may be full with sorrow and travail."

---

1. Johnson proclaimed New Year's Day as a Day of Prayer on December 29, 1941, after President Roosevelt had so designated it.

2. L. Boone Hamilton (1888–1951), b. Benson. Judge, Franklin County, 1934–1951, serving fifth term when he died. Served six terms, state representative. *Who's Who in Kentucky, 1936*, p. 175, and *State Journal*, April 12, 1951.

DEDICATION OF POLIN NATIONAL GUARD ARMORY
Springfield / May 20, 1942

IT is with a mingled feeling of pleasure and anxiety that we come to dedicate this handsome armory—anxiety intensified by the fact that men of this county in the National Guard unit that this armory housed are on an unknown battlefront.

This armory was designed to house Troop I, 123d Cavalry—which became Battery C, 106th Battalion Coast Artillery. After training at Camp Hulen, Texas, sixty-six men and five officers sailed from New York for an unannounced destination.

This armory will provide quarters in the future for the National Guard unit. Two hundred and sixty five men from Washington County have been inducted and 524 men from Washington County were inducted in the last war. So Washington County has always contributed to the defense of the nation.

As we dedicate this armory, we officially designate it as the John A. Polin Armory in honor of a great citizen soldier, Adjutant General Polin.[1] You know of his useful life and service: Born on Possom Ridge at Poortown and educated at Springfield High School, Saint Mary's College, and the University of Louisville. From 1912 to 1916, he served in the state legislature. He served with the AEF in France from 1917 to 1919. One of my earliest official acts was to make Polin adjutant general. I am sure those men of old Troop I, could they be here, would rejoice that their armory is to bear the name of their former commander.

So today we dedicate this armory to the memory of every Washington County boy who has given his life for his country. We dedicate it as a monument to the heroism of those of old Troop I as we pray God for their safety. We dedicate the John Polin Armory as a token of appreciation for those 265 Washington boys who are in uniform. We dedicate this armory to the defense of our state and nation. We dedicate it to the democratic ideal of liberty and freedom. And we designate it as the John A. Polin Armory in honor of a soldier—a citizen worthy of the distinction.

As we dedicate this armory, we must rededicate ourselves to faith in America and our determination to defend her. As we pledge, as did the signers of the Declaration, "Our lives, our fortunes and our sacred honor."[2]

---

1. John Arthur Polin (1884–1965), b. Washington County. State representative, 1912–1916; lieutenant colonel, Kentucky National Guard; adjutant general, 1939–1944; president, First National Bank, Springfield. *Kentucky Directory, 1940–1941*, p. 143, and telephone interview, Mrs. J. A. Polin, July 31, 1978.

2. The speech has been edited. Parts appear in speech from July 4, 1941, in this section. On August 8, 1942, the governor dedicated at Saint Matthews the last of eight armories which his administration had decided to build two and a half years earlier. The others were at Carlisle, Harlan, Harrodsburg, Lexington, Richmond, and Williamsburg. The state spent $199,509 while WPA labor and material amounted to $232,381. *Democratic Campaign Handbook*, 1943, p. 20.

DEDICATION OF SIGNAL CORPS DEPOT
Lexington / May 29, 1942

I AM happy that it is my proud privilege as governor of Kentucky to give assurance to the Signal Corps of the army that we appreciate the fact that this major military plant has been located in our state. Kentucky regards it as a distinction that she was chosen as the home of this great depot of the Signal Corps. We commend the wisdom of those who selected this state and this site for the establishment of this highly specialized agency of the armed forces.

Kentuckians are genuinely patriotic. The fire of patriotic fervor burns brightly in the hearts of every citizen of this Commonwealth. We are anxious to make every possible contribution to hastening the day when we shall lick Hitler, crush the international hijackers who seek to rob us of our liberties. Through the Signal Corps Depot here at Avon, we are provided with an opportunity to make a definite contribution to strengthening of the army so that its triumph will be certain when comes the Waterloo of the world.

We of Kentucky are flattered that our state was chosen as the site of this type of military preparation. Technological advances in recent years developed numerous new methods of communication. It is necessary that the army adapt these new agencies to the new methods of warfare. While the Signal Corps is a relatively small branch of the army, it occupies an importance far out of proportion to numerical numbers in it. The Signal Corps is responsible for development of techniques which assure efficient and certain functioning of a communications system that makes possible the coordination of combined agencies of military attack.

Modern warfare, with its emphasis on mobility, is increasingly dependent upon the Signal Corps for the perfecting of methods by which rapidly moving mechanized equipment on the ground, fast flying aircraft in the air, and slower moving units on the ground may be so synchronized as to act concertedly against our ruthless, brutal, and cunning foes. We marvel at the advance in aviation, the development of mechanized equipment through the medium of tanks. These are spectacular advances. They are easily visible. But no phase of our army has made greater progress than the Signal Corps as it has with ingenuity and intelligence adapted every communication agency to the cruel purpose of battle.

In perfecting the Signal Corps so that it will function certainly and accurately as the nerve center and system of attacking armies, personnel of a high order is required. Individuals of exceptional intelligence are required in bringing the Signal Corps to its maximum efficiency. So it is that I repeat—we in Kentucky are flattered that this vital activity of the army has been located in our Commonweath, giving our citizens the exceptional opportunity of contributing their efforts to the holy cause of perfecting plans for the extermination of those who unleashed the dogs of war in the world.

We are glad that it has been our destiny in Kentucky to be given the opportunity of providing the location, becoming the guardian of a number of military activities.[1] We are glad to accept this duty with assurance that we shall seek always to ascertain means and methods by which we may facilitate the effective operation of the war instrumentalities entrusted to our guardianship.

Of the various military concentrations in our state, none is more welcome than the Signal Corps Depot. We appreciate it not only because of its great importance but we especially appreciate having it located here because it is primarily a civilian activity. It provides a close tie between the army and the civilian citizenship of Kentucky. It creates an opportunity for our patriotic civilians to utilize their specialized skills, give their technical knowledge to the perfecting of a communication system that will gear every branch of our armed services into perfect timing for the efficient and complete destruction of our foe.

We recall that Avon was chosen as the location for this depot before the declaration of war. We feel justified in anticipating that it is intended to be a permanent establishment; that it will become as much a part of our community as is Man o' War; that in the future we shall point out the Signal Corps Depot with pride; that we shall regard it as one of our important public institutions and zealously seek to guard its welfare.

We appreciate our leaders—the president, the leaders of the army and navy, Senator Barkley, Senator Chandler, and Congressman Chapman.[2]

It is a pleasure to be permitted to participate in this program and extend heartiest congratulations to Colonel Laurence Watts, Colonel Menger,[3] and associates upon the superb record of accomplishment here performed in bringing this plant to speedy completion and so quickly concentrating its facilities upon the important tasks assigned it.

I want to thank General Olmstead[4] for sending Colonel Watts to command this depot. We marvel at the speed and efficiency that has been daily demonstrated here. It encourages us, gives us renewed assurance that the army we are organizing and equipping to defend this Republic will be superior in intelligence, in fighting zeal, in valor and determination to any army that will be sent against it under the lash of tyrannical despots.

So it is with genuine joy that I take part in these ceremonies by which this Signal Corps Depot is dedicated to the high and holy purpose of winning this war. We dedicate this depot to the preservation of the democratic ideal, to the destruction of despotism. We dedicate this depot as a perpetual reminder to war lords of the world that free men are capable of concentrating their resources and energies to the purpose of preserving the freedoms they love with a passionate devotion. We dedicate this depot to the peace that is to come after the carnage of battle, after the crusading soldiers of this Republic have stopped the war which was started by despots and again made right and justice regnant in the world.

---

1. Johnson used his influence to have the Bluegrass Ordnance Depot located in Madison County. He talked with Senator Chandler who was a member of the Senate Military Committee and wired Congressman A. J. May, chairman of the House Military Affairs Committee. He urged the dean of the University of Kentucky College of Engineering who was on leave of absence with the War Department to support this site. *Richmond Daily Register*, June 30, 1941.

2. Alben William Barkley (1877–1956), b. Graves County. United States representative, 1913–1926; United States senator, 1927–1949, 1954–1956; thirty-fifth vice president, 1949–1953. *Who Was Who in America, 1951–1960*, 3:49-50.

Virgil Munday Chapman (1895–1951), b. Middleton. Attorney. United States representative, 1925–1929, 1931–1949; United States senator, 1949–1951. *Who Was Who in American Politics*, p. 144.

3. Laurence Watts (1887–1967), b. Fort Leavenworth, Kansas. Regular army officer in Coast Artillery and Signal Corps. National Personnel Records Center, Military Personnel Records, Saint Louis, Mo., July 8, 1978.

C. H. Menger, lieutenant colonel, area engineer, presented the keys to the depot to Colonel Watts.

4. Dawson Olmstead (1884–1965), b. Corry, Pennsylvania. Graduate, United States Military Academy, 1906. Regular army officer in Cavalry, Field Artillery, and Signal Corps, 1906–1944. National Personnel Records Center, Military Personnel Records, Saint Louis, Mo., July 8, 1978.

WAR BONDS
Louisville / June 5, 1942

OUR government is expecting us to invest in the war bonds and stamps making money available with which to supply our fighting men on the battlefront with the weapons they need.[1] The Treasury Department has informed me that every state must increase its monthly purchases two and one-half times in order to finance our war successfully through borrowing.

Now I know many of you have signed up, at the place you work, to buy war bonds and stamps on a regular basis every payday. I appeal to you to increase your investment in war bonds. Our government asks that we each voluntarily invest at least 10 percent of our income in war bonds or stamps regularly week by week. And I want to impress upon the thousands of workers who have not yet signed up in such plans or to whom no such plan for buying bonds is available, that it is their duty to buy shares in America. To you—the farmer, the merchant, lawyer, doctor, factory worker, office employee—to every worker or everybody with an income of any sort, I urge you as a patriotic duty to resolve to invest at least 10 percent out of each paycheck in war bonds.

Sign up with your company when it offers you a payroll savings plan. Or ask your bank to take a specified amount out of your account each month with which to purchase war bonds or resolve to buy them yourself, to the limit, on a regular and systematic basis.

The quota of $5,557,000 set by the Treasury Department for the state of Kentucky for the month of May has been met. The quota for the month of June is increased approximately $2 million and in July there will be a further increase designed to sell throughout the nation approximately $1 billion worth of bonds per month. And in order to meet these figures we must more than double our previous purchases of war bonds. Of course, we all realize that we are not asked to give this money to our government but to lend it at an excellent rate of interest. Every bond we buy for $18.75 will in ten years come back to us as $25.00 in good American cash. But more important, these investments do help to win the war. We all want to support our fighting men to the utmost, and there is no more effective way to help them than to provide guns and tanks and planes for them.

I am delighted to report to you that a Voluntary Payroll Deduction Plan has been promulgated and initiated by your state government.[2] While this proposal was submitted to employees of the state government less than thirty days ago, I am advised that more than 4,500 employees have authorized monthly deductions from their payroll for the purchase of war bonds and stamps.

In addition to the subscriptions of the employees referred to above, I find that a large percentage of the approximately 4,000 employees ordinarily termed state employees, but in reality employed by agencies of the state government, such as Jefferson, Kenton, and Harlan counties, your state educational institutions, and your state courts, have developed a similar plan and are participating almost 100 percent in the purchase of war bonds and stamps.

I am confident that the employees of your state government will continue to increase their purchase of these bonds and stamps until within a very short time we as a group will be contributing 10 percent of our income for this purpose.

The more sacrifices you make in order to invest in war bonds and stamps, the more weapons you put into the hands of our fighting men, the sooner we will lick Hitler.

And remember: the war program has brought many of us higher wages or better jobs or bigger incomes. Various war industries have increased the incomes of many communities by several fold. If we squander this extra income, we are sending prices higher and higher so that we and Uncle Sam get less for our dollars. But if we invest this money in war bonds and stamps, we help to prevent inflation prices and at the same time buy more weapons for our fighting men. Let us all resolve to meet these new quotas and set an example that the other states may follow. At the end of this month, I want to be able to report to our government in Washington that our people of Kentucky invested more money than we were asked to in the bonds and stamps that help speed victory. Let us show the nation that Kentucky and Kentuckians can and will do our part.[3]

---

1. Radio broadcast over WHAS and WGRC.

2. On April 30, 1942, Johnson requested that every state employee contribute part of his monthly salary to buy war bonds and announced that the treasurer's office would deduct from monthly pay checks whatever amount employees authorized. The treasurer's office estimated the record-keeping cost at $3,000 a year. The governor said it would be paid from his civil defense fund. *State Journal*, May 1, 1942.

3. On May 28, 1942, the governor urged Kentuckians to buy war bonds and stamps at theaters and proclaimed, "Until Final Victory Is Accomplished, Every Day Is Theater War Bond and Stamp Day." In accordance with a national program, he designated November 22-28 as "Women at War Week in Kentucky" and called upon them to assist in selling and buying war bonds and stamps.

ALEXANDRIA FAIR
Campbell County / September 6, 1942

HERE in this happy community, it is difficult to realize that this proud, peaceful nation is engaged in a frightful war. We are mobilizing all our resources in an effort to crush the pagan enemies that seek to enslave us. We had no choice in the matter. We have been treacherously attacked. We must fight to preserve our liberties and our self-respect as a people.

Ofttimes the question is asked: "What are we fighting for?" That question is difficult to answer specifically. We are fighting to preserve democracy is the most generally accepted generalized answer. We are fighting to preserve here the type of government in which the people are their own rulers. We fight to preserve a political and social order in which rights of the individual are the dominant ideal.

But let's look for another answer to the question: "What are we fighting for?" Let us consider what would happen to us should we lose this war; let us consider how this fine community and its intelligent citizenship would be affected should we be defeated by Hitler and Hirohito.

The right to trial by jury would be denied us. Our courts of justice would be abolished. Our system under which the humblest citizen has the right to utilize the courts for establishment of his rights would be destroyed. Your police force would no longer function solely as an agency to protect you and your property and enforce the law. There would be no law except the harsh decrees of a ruler who would be appointed by Hitler to rule over you. Your police force, efficient, fair, and friendly, would be replaced by a Gestapo—a police that would constantly spy upon you, report every act, tear you from your home, and throw you in jail on perjured charges.

Should we lose this war you would lose the right to freedom of worship. We exercise the right guaranteed under the Constitution of the United States and the constitution of Kentucky to attend the church of our choice, to worship that God about whom we were first taught at our mother's knee. The pagan foes who seek to conquer us are godless and cruel. They would take from us this cherished freedom—freedom of religion.

Should the despicable dictators triumph over us in this furious conflict, it would mean the end of the splendid free public school system in this country. Hitler in his book *Mein Kampf* states specifically that it is best for the masses that they be kept in ignorance. Such schools, as you might be permitted to maintain under the rule of Germany or Japan, would be allowed to teach only that propaganda which would indoctrinate your children with the false ideology of our pagan, totalitarian conquerors. Freedom of the mind would be destroyed. The right to think, to seek the truth, would vanish.

Should the Stars and Stripes be hauled down from the horizon of history, be supplanted by the German Swastika and the Rising Sun, emblem of Japan, your right to individual initiative would disappear. No longer would you be permitted to make as much money as your talent and toil will produce and keep it for the enjoyment of yourself and family. You would be fitted into a preordained system, required to do that work assigned you and your meager compensation would be determined for you. The high standard of living we now enjoy, under which more comforts and many luxuries are within the reach of all, would soon be only a memory.

Under the iron heel of Hitler, this free and happy people would lose their freedom; lose their faith in the divine right of man; lose the economic and social order which has brought to us the highest degree of civilization in the history of mankind.

If Hitler should win this war, you would immediately lose the right to free speech and a free press. You have always exercised the right of free speech, the right to criticize your public officials, the right freely to discuss public questions. You expect a free press to facilitate such discussion. But should Hitler get his fingers at your throat, the right of free speech would no longer be yours to enjoy. The Gestapo would listen to your conversation and hurry you away to jail, without a warrant being issued for your arrest, if your utterances were critical of Herr Schickelgruber. The free press would be pulverized beneath the ruthless heel of dictatorial government. The newspapers published in this community tomorrow would contain only that which a Hitlerite censor approved for publication. Your newspapers would soon cease to be sources of reliable uncolored news and information. It would quickly become a sheet for dissemination of distorted truth and officially endorsed propaganda. Best not abuse the right to criticize.

"What are we fighting for?" We are fighting to prevent dictators destroying these spiritual values that make us a great nation. We are fighting to prevent the destruction of these freedoms which we have so long enjoyed that we have come to take them for granted. We take them for granted much as we do the air we breathe, unmindful of the fact that they are essential to our existence.

"What are we fighting for?" We are fighting to prevent the desecration of Christianity on this continent; to prevent the destruction of courts of justice in this land; to preserve the freedom of our free public schools; to preserve the right of freedom of speech and freedom of the press; to keep for ourselves the right to govern ourselves through public officials that are our servants; to retain the right of the individual to find the best job he is capable of filling and keep for himself the money he earns as result of his industry and intelligence.

These rights and privileges constitute democracy—the democracy we are called upon to defend. These rights have been destroyed in Germany. But democracy is not all "rights." There are corresponding duties which are imposed upon every citizen who enjoys those rights. There is the duty to be a good citizen, the duty to pay taxes, the duty to vote, the duty to defend the nation against attack.

We have learned by bitter experience that democracy with all its precious privileges cannot be bought once and for all. It must be bought again and again. So it is the stern duty of us of this generation, descendents of the pioneers who established this republic and committed to us the responsibility of defending it, to again repurchase democracy. And democracy can be repurchased only with blood and tears and treasure and anguish and sacrifice.

When we win this war, we shall have preserved democracy for ourselves and our children. And we shall again have the opportunity to prepare a worldwide plan by which all peoples who desire the benefits of democracy may have it. Again will come to us the duty to devise a world order that will prevent the tragedy of constantly recurring wars—wars each of which is more frightful and destructive than the other. After we have triumphed over our pagan enemies, it will be our duty to perfect a plan by which we can enforce peace in the world.

But first we must win the war. We have enjoyed a life of comfort and plenty. We have been a self-indulgent people. We have been required to sacrifice some of our comforts. We will be required to do without many things. That is the contribution you must make to the defending of a democracy. The civilian citizenship will be asked to subject itself to an increasingly rigorous discipline of self-denial. More and more your liberties will be curtailed and your life directed for you. This is necessary in the systematic mobilizing of all our resources to win the war. We will surrender some of our freedom temporarily in order to preserve it permanently. We must accept cheerfully self-denial and inconvenience of doing without. It is the price of victory which you must pay.

Frequently letters are received at the office of the governor in which is asked the question, "What can I do to help win the war?" Those letters reveal that many of us are looking for something spectacular that we may do in winning the war. We cannot all be heroes. It is not possible for us all to be Major Doolittles and bomb Tokyo. We cannot all be Captain Colin Kellys and sink a Japanese battleship. Few of us can earn a citation for conspicuous bravery as was recently done by that Kentucky pilot, Lieutenant Dick Starks, of Midway, Kentucky, whose heroic action in a grim aerial battle over the North Sea was a thrilling story of audacious daring and courage.[1]

But there are many trite tasks each of us can perform that contribute to victory. Of course those fathers and mothers who give their sons make the major contribution. With admirable courage Kentucky mothers and fathers smile through tears as they send their sons to battle. It is a fine tribute to Kentucky's youth that they go so eagerly to don the uniform. In proportion to population, more young men have voluntarily enlisted in the armed forces than from any state in the Union. The fire of patriotic fervor burns brightly in the heart of all Kentuckians, and I am confident we shall gladly do everything required of us to lick Hitler.

You can help win the war by producing more food. But you are going to have to grow more and more food with less farm labor.

"How can I help win the war?" Such a simple thing as buying now your supply of fuel for the winter. The fuel authority in Washington is urging us to fill our coal bins during the summer. How many of you have done so? Those who have complied with the request have made a larger contribution to victory than is realized. Transportation facilities of the nation are overtaxed by the war effort. This winter every coal car will be needed to move coal to the war factories. Coal stored during the summer relieves the strain on our transportation system. You can help your local Civil Defense Council. This is an important activity through which plans are made to meet an emergency intelligently.

You want to help win the war? There is nothing spectacular about gathering up scrap iron, scrap rubber, or in saving the grease from your kitchen. But these are vital ingredients of victory. Blast furnaces at steel mills need scrap iron in huge quantities every day. Scrap rubber will help provide tires essential to preparing our army to deliver the knockout blow to the Japs and Germans. Limiting your driving speed to thirty-five miles an hour or less makes a contribution to winning the war and defers the day when you will be inconvenienced by losing the use of your car.

One of the most important things you can do to help win the war is to buy war bonds and defense stamps. Not only is this the most destructive war in history, but it is the most expensive. Billions of dollars are required with which to put into the hands of your brave men the weapons with which to defeat the enemies that have brought all this misery and sorrow on the world. Buy more war bonds than you can afford. If we win the war, those bonds will be a good investment in the future. If we do not win, nothing you possess will have any value. So there is no finer way to prove your patriotism than to buy bonds.

We are up against a cunning, ruthless foe. It is going to take everything we have to lick him. But unless we lick him, nothing we have will be worth anything. It is wise for us as a nation to shoot the works, throw everything into the struggle as quickly as we can. In so doing, we will shorten the war, save lives of our brave men.

The great need of the hour is unity of our people—unity of purpose, unity of mind and unity of heart—as we concentrate all we have upon the task of winning the war.

---

1. James Harold Doolittle (1896–), b. Alameda, California. Lieutenant general; army flier; bombed Tokyo, Japan, April 18, 1942. *Who's Who in America, 1978–1979*, 1:870.

Colin Kelly, Jr. (1915–1941), b. Madison, Florida. Navy flier killed in the bombing of a Japanese cruiser of the Haruna class, December 1941; first West Point graduate killed in action in World War II; awarded Distinguished Service Order posthumously. *United States Military Academy of Graduates Register, 1970*, and *World Book Encyclopedia, 1973* (Chicago, 1973), 2:211.

Richard Starks (1919–), b. Midway. Resides in Midway. Farmer. During the encounter the copilot was killed. Lieutenant Starks, although wounded, brought the plane back to its base. Telephone interview, R. Starks, July 30, 1979.

TWELFTH ARMORED DIVISION ACTIVATED
Hopkinsville / September 15, 1942

IT is with genuine joy that I participate with you in this significant ceremony which commemorates a notable military event. We today activate this the twelfth Armored Division of the United States Army. It is a thrilling experience to attend the birth of this division of armored might. It is a memorable day as there is added to the roster of the army of freedom this new and powerful fighting outfit. It means driving another nail in Hitler's coffin. It means that we are going about the grim business of getting ready to lick Hitler. That which we do here today will hasten the day of doom for the madmen who have brought upon the world the most frightful war in history.

As governor of Kentucky, it is with real delight that I assure you who form the nucleus of this armored division that we are glad to have Camp Campbell so located that considerable portion of it is in Kentucky. The War Department chose wisely when it selected this area for an army camp. Here on the boundary which separates, though does not divide, Kentucky and Tennessee, you will find that this military training center has been created in a region where the fire of patriotic fervor burns brightly in the heart of the citizenship. These folk are genuine Americans within whose veins flows the blood of a virile, patriotic ancestry.

This is Kentucky's sesquicentennial year. One hundred and fifty years ago Kentucky was admitted to the Union as the fifteenth state. This, the first citadel of freedom created west of the Allegheny mountains, was established by audacious pioneers. They wrested this region from hostile savages. The story of the heroism of the Boones, and the Clarks, the Harrods, the Kentons, and Shelbys, and their stalwart comrades of the frontier is an epic of valor without parallel.[1] It has been an inspiration to Kentuckians in every succeeding generation. The zeal for liberty which burned in the hearts of those intrepid men and women as they carved out this Commonwealth in the wilderness has not been diminished by passing years. In every war in which these United States have participated, Kentuckians have rushed to rally behind the flag of freedom.

So in this the darkest hour of our nation's history, I, as governor of Kentucky, feel a robust pride in the daily manifestation of the patriotism of Kentuckians. Quickly they responded to the call of their country. We are prepared to accept any sacrifice that may be required in order to hasten the day of triumph. Kentucky's sons are fighting gallantly on every battlefront of the world, acquitting themselves with high distinction.

One of the saddest towns in the nation is Harrodsburg, Kentucky. This pioneer community, where was cradled this Commonwealth, is sad though proud despite the anxiety which comes with uncertainty over the fate of nearly a hundred young men. These gallant young Kentuckians fought fiercely with MacArthur on Bataan and surrendered sorrowfully at Corregidor when overwhelmed by a numerically superior foe. These who composed Company D of the 192nd Tank Batallion, a Kentucky National Guard outfit, were decreed by destiny to participate in the first engagement of the war in which American tanks were committed to battle under the American flag. Those tanks commanded by Lieutenant Bill Gentry,[2] a farm boy of Harrodsburg—tanks driven by Mercer County men—tanks whose guns were manned by Mercer County men, destroyed six Japanese tanks and came through the engagement intact. It exalts our spirit that these Harrodsburg heroes, the first American armored outfit to fight, were worthy battle comrades of the heroic General MacArthur. In an hour of crisis when a ruthless foe assailed all the fine things for which Kentucky has stood, these boys, direct descendants of pioneer progenitors, were inspired by the spirit of their frontier forefathers to fight that foe with the zeal and fearlessness of men in whose hearts there burns a consuming love of freedom and a determination to preserve that freedom.

These Kentucky soldiers were all either killed or captured on Bataan. Fate decreed that they should play a leading role in the drama destiny enacted upon Bataan. It is the most sublime epic of courage since Thermopylae and the Alamo. Despite the fact that these men, commanded by MacArthur and Wainwright,[3] faced insuperable odds, they fought with inspired fierceness. Outnumbered ten to one, these heroes of the first engagement of America's armored force threw themselves with reckless abandon into a bloody battle that it was inevitable they lose. They killed Japs by the thousands. They so discredited the Japanese high command that the Jap commander-in-chief committed suicide. They so upset the military time table of the Japs that precious time was gained that our other defenses might be strengthened in the Pacific. These Kentucky soldiers and those who fought beside them have immortalized themselves, written a sublime story in the annals of military achievement.

I recount this story of the first participation of America's armored force on this occasion with the hope that it will be an inspiration to the Twelfth Armored Division. I have no doubt that when comes the opportunity for this division to hit the enemy that their action in battle will be as gallant and heroic as was the conduct of the first tank outfit which fought under the Stars and Stripes in this war.

I am glad that Major General Carlos Brewer[4] is to command this division. He is a Kentuckian of whom we are proud. He is a fine soldier and a great leader, superbly qualified to command this division in battle. This camp was named for a great Tennessee soldier, Major General William B. Campbell.[5] As you train here in a camp which honors his name, I have no doubt that the spirit of General Campbell will hover near and that the earnestness with which you tackle the task of forging this division into a thunderbolt of power and destruction will be worthy of his memory.

We in Kentucky are glad to share with our good neighbor Tennessee the distinction of being the site of Camp Campbell and the home of the Twelfth Armored Division. We shall take a deep interest in this division, regard it as our own. We shall follow its activities with pride. We are eager to render any possible cooperation to Camp Campbell and feel honored that we are to be hosts temporarily to those young Americans here assigned to military duty.[6]

Our arms are open to you; our hearts rejoice to greet you. And you have our ardent best wishes as you begin the job of preparing here a fine, effective unit of that great army which is to carry the flag to victory and again make right regnant in the world.

---

1. James Harrod (1741–1793), from Washington County, Pennsylvania, Founder of Harrodsburg, 1774; Indiana fighter and pioneer. Otis K. Rice, *Frontier*

Kentucky (Lexington, Ky., 1975), pp. 60-61, and Collins, *History of Kentucky*, 2:614.

Isaac Shelby (1750–1826), b. Maryland. Came to Kentucky in 1775; surveyor. Member, First Constitutional Convention, 1792; first governor of Kentucky, 1792. *Biographical Encyclopedia of Kentucky*, pp. 11-12.

2. William H. Gentry (1918–), b. Harrodsburg. Tank commander, Philippine Islands. Prisoner of war for thirty-three months after the death march out of Bataan. Plant engineer, Corning Glass Works, 1952–1975. Letter, William H. Gentry, Lakeland, Florida, July 15, 1978.

3. Jonathan Mayhew Wainwright (1883–1953), b. Walla Walla, Washington. Served Bataan campaign; Japanese prisoner of war in Manchuria, rescued August 1945. Retired, 1947. *Who Was Who in American History: The Military*, p. 610.

4. Carlos E. Brewer (1890–1976), b. Mayfield. Graduate, United States Military Academy, 1913; major general; commanding officer, Twelfth Armored Division, Camp Campbell. Telephone interview, Bernice Morehead, sister, June 23, 1978.

5. William Bowen Campbell (1807–1867), b. Davidson County, Tennessee. United States representative, 1839–1843, 1866–1867. Hero of Mexican War; Whig governor of Tennessee, 1851–1853. John T. Moore and Austin P. Foster, *Tennessee: The Volunteer State, 1769–1923* (Nashville, Tenn., 1923), 2:84-85.

6. Construction of Camp Campbell began March 18, 1942. Work progressed rapidly and the camp was activated on July 1, 1942. *Princeton Leader*, April 8, 1943.

HONORS CAPTAIN GEORGE (ED) KISER
Somerset / September 25, 1942

AS governor of Kentucky, I am honored to have the proud privilege of joining with the citizenship of Pulaski County in paying homage to Captain George Kiser[1] and in welcoming home this gallant son of Somerset. I imagine he is glad to have the opportunity of a brief visit home. There have no doubt been times when he has wished he could be back in Somerset.

The heroic exploits in battle of Captain Kiser fill our hearts with pride. The amazing achievements of this modest, virile young Kentuckian is a stirring story of audacious courage and patriotic devotion to duty. All Kentuckians rejoice with you, his home folks, that he has earned a place among the preeminent heroes of the American army, that he has become one of the immortals of history.

In this peace-loving nation, it is a fine tribute to the virility of our Americanism that this brave young officer, that you knew in this community as a normal, wholesome boy, has disclosed the cool, deadly courage that is reflected in his scorn of danger as he triumphed again and again over Jap flyers as they battled to the death above the clouds.

Captain Kiser is one of the most decorated fliers in the air service of the united nations. That is a distinction which he has earned in a career as an air fighter that is without parallel. He got his first Jap plane over Bataan as he pounced upon a Nipponese pursuit ship, engaged the pilot in a machine gun duel, and knocked him out of the air. He next participated in the naval battle for Java, where he escorted dive bombers. He shot four Jap bombers out of the sky, came through unscathed, and next went into action from an Australian base. This audacious ace flier soared athwart the sky and became a scourge of Japanese airfighters. This thunderbolt of the air sent his plane roaring through the clouds like an avenging demon and left Jap fighter ships falling like leaves in an autumn storm.

On August 23 Japanese aircraft attempted an attack on Port Darwin. American planes drove them off, shooting down thirteen craft. Captain Kiser in that engagement shot down one enemy bomber and four Zeros, Jap fighting ships. He is officially credited with having shot down eleven Nipponese planes. In recognition of this astounding achievement, this son of Somerset has been four times decorated. Lieutenant General Brett,[2] commander of the Allied Air Forces in Australia, pinned the Distinguished Service Cross upon this Kentucky king of the sky. He was subsequently twice cited for other conquests of the sky and in each instance was awarded the silver star with which to adorn the ribbon of his DSC.

In a few brief months Captain Kiser came to be recognized as one of the most skillful fighter pilots in the annals of aviation warfare. He was imbued with a zeal to blast Jap planes into eternity. He was in a state of constant eagerness for a fight. The anger of this peace-loving American youth had been aroused by the treachery of the Japanese at Pearl Harbor. From the cockpit of his plane, he faced the blazing machine guns of Japanese fighter craft, shot it out with them in deadly duels against the dome of heaven. This mild-mannered, peaceful youth found, it seems, a strange exhilaration in driving the enemy from the air.

The supreme honor conferred upon Captain Kiser was the award to him of the Distinguished Flying Cross by General MacArthur at the Australian headquarters of the American general. This citation was for carrying out a mission against great odds. And what was the mission? Captain Kiser led a formation of four Allied pursuit planes against a squadron of twenty-four Japanese bombers and twelve escorting Zero fighter planes which attacked Port Darwin. Despite overwhelming odds the four American ships attacked the Jap air fleet of thirty-six planes, forced the enemy to break formation and drove them off. Kiser personally shot down two of the bombers. Such an achievement sounds as miraculous as it was amazing. Accomplishment of so perilous a mission definitely marks this fearless flier as a child of destiny. He is one of those rare individuals decreed by fate to become a doer of great deeds in the most critical hour of our national life, one who faces death with laughing courage, dares the pick of the Japanese air force to face the devastating fire of his murderous guns.

The story of Captain Kiser is an epic of valor. His brilliant battle record is both an inspiration and a challenge to us on the home front. It makes us feel very humble and insignificant that we have done so little as contrasted with this superb soldier who has done so much. But we cannot all be Captain Kisers and acquire his superior skill as a fearless flier. However, there are many things we can do which will help win the war which Captain Kiser has waged with such bold and brilliant effectiveness.

Pulaski County has been doing her part admirably on the home front. Kentucky is pouring men into this fight by the thousands and money by the millions. This is the most expensive war yet fought. It requires billions of dollars with which to provide the guns and grenades, the planes and tanks our armies must have in order to crush our enemies. Aside from giving a son to the service, the most helpful thing you and I can do is to buy war bonds—buy more of them than we can afford. And Pulaski County has been doing that in such a way as to make Captain Kiser proud of you, his home folks, just as you are immensely proud of him.

Pulaski County in recent months has bought war bonds far in excess of its quota. In the month of May, this county was assigned a quota of $19,600 but bond sales to Pulaski countians more than doubled the quota with a total of $41,268. The quota in June was $29,800 but bonds bought totaled $53,327. In July, bond sales in this county totaled $112,937 although the quota was only $46,200. In August, the quota was $47,000 and sales amounted to $108,463. That money which you loan your government is being used with which to build planes for Captain Kisers to fly into battle on every front. It provides the machine guns with which intrepid airmen like Captain Kiser shoot hostile planes out of the sky.

Pulaski has sent many of her sons into service of the nation. While none has attained such distinction as has Captain Kiser, they are all acquitting themselves creditably. I recently had an interesting experience when invited to visit the thirty-eighth division at Camp Shelby, Mississippi. The Kentucky National Guard troops are serving in that division. There I met many Pulaski County boys, all fine soldiers, preparing themselves for the day when they shall engage the enemy. I witnessed a review of the division with the division commander, General Jones. I was especially proud when the 149th Infantry Regiment passed the reviewing stand. This regiment is composed of Kentucky troops and it is commanded by a great soldier from Somerset, Colonel Bill Taylor. It is a fine outfit, reflecting the excellent leadership of Colonel Taylor. General Easley[3] told me that the regiment had only recently completed firing the course on the rifle range. The result was remarkable. Out of 2,367 men in the regiment, all had qualified as marksmen except seventeen.

It calls to mind a story of an ambitious mountain boy who had completed grade school and was urging his uneducated father to help him attend high school in the county seat. They visited the superintendent and the father asked what would be taught his son. The superintendent said, "Why, we will teach him history, Latin, trigonometry"—and the father broke in—"That's it—take this boy and teach him triggernometry—he's the poorest darn shot up our holler."

It is a desperate situation we are called upon to meet. Bold air fighters of superior skill, such as has been demonstrated by Captain Kiser, have done remarkably well despite the fact they have been outnumbered. But it was a terrific handicap that was faced by Captain Kiser and three comrades as they took to the air to attack a Jap formation of thirty-six airplanes. Of course, our planes are good and our fighter pilots are superb. But four planes against thirty-six presents insuperable odds. We need thousands of planes with which to match the enemy plane for plane. We cannot build the planes without enormous quantities of steel. We cannot make the needed steel without scrap iron. That puts it right up to you and me—us on the home front.

We are glad Captain Kiser was permitted to come home for a well-earned rest and to marry the lovely girl whose heart has flown with him on each of his perilous adventures. We congratulate Mr. Bert Kiser, father of this illustrious hero of the American air service, that he has the signal distinction of giving to the nation one of its most distinguished heroes. Americans are a nation of hero worshipers. It is with exultant hearts that we acclaim the nation's No. 1 ace, the fearless flier and fine, wholesome Kentucky boy who has been destined to become the preeminent hero of democracy.

Your visit home, Captain Kiser, has been good for our morale. Your exploits have thrilled us because they surpass in daring and audacity any thriller story yet conceived. We see in you the embodiment of the finest in American youth. You have set a high standard of devotion to our flag.

Your visit home is an inspiration to us. It will make better soldiers of us, your countrymen on the home front. We shall accept cheerfully such hardships as must come as the nation is totally mobilized for war because you, one of our own Kentucky boys, have set for us a lofty ideal of patriotic service as you have repeatedly offered your life a sacrifice upon the altar of your country.

Our arms, our hearts are open to you. We adore and admire you and it is with joy and pride that I, as governor of Kentucky, proclaim you as the foremost Kentuckian of the war. I have not the authority to add to the military medals which have been awarded you in recognition of your exceptional service but I can give you a token of Kentucky's esteem that no other can bestow upon you. It is with mingled feeling of humility and exultation that I present you a commission as a Kentucky Colonel. Our prayers and best wishes go with you wherever the stern call of duty shall lead.[4]

---

1. George E. Kiser (1918–), b. near Pocatello, Idaho. Captain, Army Air Force; professor of business administration, University of Arkansas. Telephone interview, Eugene Kiser, brother July 3, 1978.

2. George Howard Brett (1886–), b. Cleveland, Ohio. Lieutenant general; deputy supreme commander, Unified Command, South West Pacific Area, 1942; commander, Allied Air Force, Australia, 1942. *Who's Who in America, 1954–1955* (Chicago, 1955), 3:28.

3. Henry L. C. Jones (1887–), b. Brokenbow, Nebraska. Major general; commanding general, thirty-eighth Infantry Division, 1942; served in Leyte and Luzon campaigns, 1944-1945. *Who's Who in America, 1952–1953* (Chicago, 1953), 27:1284.

William S. Taylor (1889–), b. Mintonville. Colonel, commander, 149th Infantry Regiment. Telephone interview, Adjutant General's Office, Boone National Guard Center, Frankfort, June 20, 1978.

Roy W. Easley (1891–), b. Frankfort. Resides in Bardstown. Chief of police, Louisville, 1926–1930; director of safety, Louisville, 1930–1934. President, Southern Liquor Company, fourteen years. *Who's Who in Kentucky, 1936,* p. 122, and telephone interview, R. W. Easley, February 19, 1978.

4. The speech has been edited. For remarks relating to scrap metal see speech from October 2, 1942, in the Industry section.

OFFICERS CANDIDATE SCHOOL GRADUATION

Fort Knox / October 3, 1942

THIS is indeed a happy hour for this fine group of young Americans who are today to be commissioned as officers in the Armored Force of our army. I rejoice with you who have persevered through the intensive training of officers candidate school and have earned the right and distinction of wearing the insignia of second lieutenants. It is an achievement in which you may well find deep satisfaction. You are lucky to have lived through it.

I am especially pleased to participate with you in this pleasant event because it brings back cherished memories. Twenty-five years ago I had the same experience as that which you are enjoying. I attended the first officers training camp in the last war at Fort Riley, Kansas, and was commissioned a shavetail. Nothing I have since achieved has thrilled me as much as did earning that commission. No lieutenant general was ever as proud of that third star as I was of that gold bar. I understand something of the emotions that stir in your hearts as you receive today the commissions you have worked so diligently to obtain. So I am going to talk to you as one shavetail to another.

You are glad that a tough course is finished. You are relieved that the suspense of wondering whether you were going to get a commission is over. You convinced your instructors that you have what it takes to make an acceptable officer in the Armored Force. You have earned your commission on your own merit as result of darn hard work. It opens an opportunity to you of making a greater contribution to the winning of the war. And it imposes great responsibilities. I hope you have enjoyed your temporary residence in Kentucky. You have doubtless been homesick at times.

You are to have a brief leave. I am glad you are to have this well-deserved period of rest and recreation. It will give you a chance to visit your family and friends—a chance to strut a little, to lord it over the fellows at home. Your officer's insignia will bring you preferred consideration of the girls. You will have a good time. Some of you will get married. That was what I did twenty-five years ago and I am still married to that same girl. That ten days will past quickly and you will report for your first assignment. So much advice has been given you as student officers that you may feel fed up on it. But as one shavetail to another, let me give you a few suggestions.

The noncommissioned officers under your command can do more to help you become a competent officer than anyone else. Try to win the confidence of your noncoms. Try to merit their respect. Make them feel that they are partners with you in the job of developing an efficient platoon. Praise them for a good job done and never express criticism of them before the men. Insist upon firm but just discipline and make the noncoms feel that you are relying upon them to develop a well-disciplined, hard-hitting outfit. It is not necessary that you be hard-boiled to get best results from your noncoms and men. Avoid exacting unreasonable things.

A story is told of an incident said to have occurred in the last war.

Breathitt County is a county in Kentucky that in bygone days was commonly called "Bloody Breathitt" because of the tendency of the men to kill each other. But Breathitt had the proud record of being the only county in the nation from which not a single man was drafted in the last war. The number of volunteers always exceeded the quota assigned the draft board. A Breathitt County boy became a good enough soldier to be promoted to sergeant of an infantry platoon. The company was deployed, advancing toward the front line near Grand Pre' on the Meuse-Argonne front, and suddenly came under heavy fire. The lieutenant in command of the platoon gave the command "lie down." Every man flopped flat except the sergeant. "Lie down, sergeant," the lieutenant ordered. Yet he only dropped to his knees. The lieutenant gave him a severe bawling out. The sergeant explained, "I can't lie down 'cause I got a bottle of cognac in my hip pocket and the stopper done come out."

Take it from me as one shavetail to another that you must work hard every day. You must spend every possible minute in study. Just because you graduated from this school doesn't mean you have learned it all. I observe that the best officers are not the most brilliant men, but the men who work hardest at the job of becoming proficient soldiers. If you are detailed to school, accept it gladly and be thankful for an opportunity to increase your knowledge of modern warfare.

If you have a sense of humor, be thankful for it. If you have not, try to develop one. As second lieutenants, you will be the butt of many jibes, allegedly funny, often crude. Accept them with a smile.

One of the stories which ran through the AEF in the last war that was especially enjoyed by the shavetails was about an American colored soldier who ran past a colonel back of the lines without saluting. The colonel called to him and inquired as to his hurry. "I'se gwine away from heah," said the excited soldier. "Where have you been?" the colonel asked. "I'se been up at dat front." "What's going on up there?" inquired the colonel. "Trees is falling 'thout nobody cuttin' 'em and holes is comin' in the ground without anybody diggin' 'em." "Do you understand that you are expected to salute officers?" the colonel queried. "Why you is uh officer, ain't you. Youse got them turkey buzzards on yo' shoulders. 'Scuse me, colonel, I had no idea I had run so fur back."

I realize that there is no necessity for giving you, the members of this graduating class, a pep talk as to your patriotic duty. You are intelligent men. Most of you are college and university graduates. You are familiar with the glorious history of this great Republic. As you trod the rugged path of duty, you will be sustained by a profound faith in the hallowed ideal of freedom which has been nurtured on this continent since 1776. In your hearts burns the unquenchable flame of patriotic fervor. Each of you has a rendezvous with destiny. You offer your lives as a sacrifice upon the altar of liberty. It is the greatest tragedy of mankind that, as civilization attains its zenith, the world is plunged into the most destructive and brutal war in history as result of the lust for conquest of the madmen of Germany and Japan. But a far greater tragedy it would be should they succeed in their diabolical designs.

You, the young Americans of this graduating class, are the embodiment of the finest of American youth. Your plans for a life of usefulness as you seek worthy careers have been cruelly shattered. The very existence of the nation is threatened—the nation that has provided every worthy boy with an opportunity through his own initiative and ingenuity to attain a degree of success commensurate with his ability. You are worthy sons of illustrious forebears. You are the descendants of those patriots whose lacerated feet incarnadined the snows at Valley Forge as they fought with sublime courage to establish on this continent a citadel of freedom. The liberties which were bought with the blood of those heroes have been handed down to us as a sacred heritage. From time to time they have been threatened. It is an exhilarating fact that the citizenship of this Republic has rushed to the defense of those liberties and defeated every foe that has imperiled them. You are following in the footsteps of those gallant defenders of the flag.

I am sure you take pride in the fact that you have earned the distinction of serving in the Armored Force. This new and mighty development of modern warfare offers possibilities of daring adventure and the certainty of high hazard in battle. Of your courage I have no doubt. But raw courage is no match for cold steel in these days of mechanized might. The bravest man is impotent against mechanized instruments of warfare unless he be similarly armed. This new arm of our fighting force requires that daring and boldness which is a characteristic of youth. Emphasis is being placed upon the preference for young men to command Armored Force outfits.

But history is replete with the exploits of youthful military heroes. Alexander the Great finished his conquests of the eastern world before he was thirty. Caesar became the leading spirit in Rome before he reached the age of thirty. Peter the Great exhibited marked military genius before he was twenty. Napoleon was only twenty-four when he distinguished himself at the siege of Toulon and laid the foundation for his future. George Washington was only twenty-three when he was made commander-in-chief of the forces of Virginia. General George Rogers Clark, at the age of twenty-two, at Fort Harrod, Harrodsburg, Kentucky, planned the conquest of the Northwest which was brilliantly carried out. I recently had the stimulating experience of participating with the citizens of Somerset, Kentucky, in welcoming home a heroic son, Captain Ed Kiser, American ace, who has shot down eight Jap planes in the Pacific and is twenty-four years of age.

So as you face the uncertainties of an uncertain future in this, the Armored Force, you have the assurance that your youth is an asset. You are to become an integral part of the thunderbolt of power and destruction with which we shall deal the knockout blow to Germany, hasten the day of doom for our enemies.

The lives of many men will depend upon your judgment. The outcome of battles may be determined by your leadership. You will meet a cunning, savage foe. You must make your command proficient in the cruel art of killing, because it will be a case of kill or get killed. Instill in your men a zest for offensive warfare. Fire them with an enthusiasm to beat the Boche; go get Hitler. Help them to forget that there is such a word as retreat.

At the battle of Marengo, the great Napoleon stared defeat in the face. He was discouraged as his army was repeatedly thrown back. He called a drummer boy and ordered him to beat a retreat. "Oh, sire, I cannot beat a retreat," said the troubled lad. "My marshall never taught me to beat a retreat. But, oh, sire, I can beat a charge—a charge so stirring that the dead will rise to form in ranks and fight again. I beat a charge for your troops at Lodi and at the Pyramids and in many other battles in which troops under your command have won victories. Oh, sire, let me beat a charge now," the youth entreated. "I will beat a charge such as has never inspired soldiers to advance." Moved by the zeal and earnestness of the drummer boy, Napoleon construed the incident as a good omen. He ordered the boy to beat a charge. The faltering ranks were electrified by the drummer boy's martial notes. They rallied, countercharged with dash and courage. The tide of battle was turned. And Marengo was added to the list of brilliant military triumphs achieved under the inspired generalship of Napoleon.

Young men, remember there must be no retreat. The command is always "Forward."[1]

---

1. Material about reasons for fighting has been deleted. See speech from September 6, 1942, in this section. A similar speech was given at the Avon Signal Corps Depot, December 4, 1942.

NAVY RECRUITING DAY
Louisville / October 11, 1942

THIS is a solemn though exhilarating occasion. We are assembled to witness the induction into the United States Navy of these 200 young Kentuckians. Of their own volition, they have volunteered to enter the service of their county. They will soon become members of the finest, most deadly fighting force that has ever sailed the seas. These men, who are today taking the oath of allegiance, take this step with grim determination. They are going to kill Germans and Japs. They are going to help destroy the naval craft of the enemies that seek to crush us. These patriotic young men are going to exert their energies in an effort to hasten the day when the United States Navy will sweep from the seas the naval might of the racketeer nations that have brought upon the world the misery and hardship of a cruel and needless war.

To the young Americans who compose this splendid group, I want to express my congratulations. You are doing a fine, patriotic thing. You are responding to the stern call of duty—the duty of every American to exert the utmost effort to defend the flag of freedom, to defend this great Republic under whose system of government a happy and proud people have enjoyed large liberties and precious privileges.

You, who are about to be inducted into the navy, face an uncertain future. You have a rendezvous with destiny. You are to know the joys of one who strives to do worthy deeds; who knows the great devotion to duty; who offers life as a sacrifice upon the altar of his country; who spends himself in a noble cause; who at the best knows in the end the triumph of high achievement in the supreme struggle to keep this nation free. You are to experience the hardships and hazards of battle. Should it be your destiny to fall in defense of your homeland, you will face that supreme sacrifice while daring greatly, sustained by the satisfaction that your place is not with those timid souls who know neither victory nor defeat.

Young men, as you are inducted into the navy, you become the heirs to and the defenders of the proud traditions of a navy that has always been worthy of the great nation it defends. While our navy has always been magnificent, it is today the greatest navy, the most powerful sea force that has ever done battle for humanity.

It is but proper that the navy to whose might you are adding your youthful strength and enthusiasm should have advanced standards, attain increased proficiency, because each new age is "heir to all the ages" and should improve upon the best and finest traditions of the past. You go forth to defend the flag wherever it may fly, wherever it may be attacked or wherever, as the president says, "its enemies may be found." Your parents, relatives, friends, and your state are tremendously proud of you. Your mothers smile through tears as they encourage you to don the uniform of your country's navy. You will always be in our minds and hearts and we shall daily pray that God may direct and protect you.

Captain Loftquist[1]—this fine class of young men is today available for the navy because of the energetic action of the Civilian Board of the Navy Recruiting Service, to which W. L. Lyons, Jr., has given dynamic and effective leadership as chairman. The Air Cavalcade has rendered great help in calling to our young men the opportunity for service which is afforded by the navy. Lieutenant G. E. Kincannon, head of the recruiting service in this region, has with sustained enthusiasm, coordinated and directed all effort with such effectiveness that I, as governor of Kentucky, have the high honor to present to you this group of eager, intelligent, patriotic young men who seek the privilege of serving in the United States Navy.[2]

---

1. E. A. Loftquist, captain, chief of staff, Ninth Naval District.

2. Johnson proclaimed October 11, 1942, as Navy Recruiting Day. He proclaimed October 27 as Navy Day each year. This day was the birthday of President Theodore Roosevelt who worked to establish a sound naval policy.

The governor attended the induction of eleven naval recruits at the State Capitol on June 7, 1942. The service was timed to coincide six months to the minute with the first bomb that fell on Pearl Harbor. He told the recruits that they were to become instruments of vengeance for the treachery of the attack at Pearl Harbor. *State Journal*, June 9, 1942. He attended Governor's Day, June 10, 1942, at the Great Lakes Naval Training Station. Kentucky sailors with outstanding records were selected to be his honor guests. *Louisville Times*, June 11, 1942.

370TH COMBAT TEAM ACTIVATED
Henderson / October 15, 1942

It is with genuine joy that I participate with you in this significant ceremony which commemorates a notable military event. We today activate this the 370th Combat Team of the ninety-second Infantry Division of the United States Army. It is a thrilling experience to attend the rebirth of this division of fighting Americans. It is a memorable day as there is added to the roster of the army of freedom this powerful fighting outfit. It means driving another nail in Hitler's coffin. It means that we are going about the grim business of getting ready to lick Hitler. That which we do here on this occasion will hasten the day of doom for the madmen who have brought upon the world the most frightful war in history.

As governor of Kentucky, it is with real delight that I assure you, who form the nucleus of this division, that we are glad to have you and Camp Breckinridge[1] located in Kentucky. The War Department chose wisely when it selected this area for an army camp. You will find that this military training center has been created in a region where the fire of patriotic fervor burns brightly in the heart of the citizenship. These folk are genuine Americans within whose veins flows the blood of a virile, patriotic ancestry.

We in Kentucky are glad this camp was named for a brilliant Kentucky statesman and gallant soldier, John C. Breckinridge.[2] He was elected vice president of the United States with President James Buchanan in 1856. Following that period of public service, he was elected to the United States Senate from Kentucky. He exerted all his great talent in an effort to avert the war Between the States. But when that conflict became inevitable, he followed the course of duty as he saw it, left the United States Senate to take command of the First Kentucky Brigade of the Confederate Army. On the field of battle he disclosed the same exceptional qualities of leadership he had demonstrated in the realm of statecraft. His memory and that of his illustrious family are revered by Kentuckians.

As you train here in a camp which honors his name, I have no doubt that the spirit of General Breckinridge will hover near and that the earnestness with which you tackle the task of forging this division into a thunderbolt of power and destruction will be worthy of his memory.

The ninety-second Infantry Division, a National Army Division composed of colored Selective Service men, was first organized in the last war at Fort Riley, Kansas, on October 24, 1917. In June 1918 the division arrived in France. From September 26 to October 3, 1918, the ninety-second Division participated in the Meuse-Argonne offensive as part of the reserve of the First Army Corps. Shortly before the armistice, this division participated in the attack of the Second Army and occupied the Bois Cheminot and Bois Frehaut. The division returned to the United States in February 1919 and demobilized, since which time it has remained completely inactive. This division is today activated and recommitted to the grim job of waging war upon the outlaw nations who have brought upon the world the misery of brutal armed conflict.

We in Kentucky are glad that Camp Breckinridge is located in our state. We shall take a deep interest in this division and other troops here, regard them as our own. We shall follow their activities with pride. We are eager to render any possible cooperation to Camp Breckinridge and feel honored that we are to be hosts temporarily to those young Americans here assigned to military duty.

You have our ardent best wishes as you begin the job of preparing here a fine, effective unit of that great army which is to carry the flag to victory and again make right regnant in the world.[3]

---

1. Camp Breckinridge was activated July 1, 1942, primarily for training infantry. Other army activities and a German war prisoner internment camp were located there. It is located in Webster, Union, and Henderson counties. *Lexington Herald,* July 4, 1943.

2. John Cabell Breckinridge (1821–1875), b. Lexington. Attorney; Confederate general; United States representative, 1851–1855; vice president of the United States, 1857–1861; United States senator, 1861. *Who Was Who in American Politics,* p. 109.

3. The speech has been edited. Parts appear in the speeches from September 15, 1942, and October 3, 1942, in this section.

GUEST OF PRESIDENT ROOSEVELT
Fort Knox / April 28, 1943

LAST Sunday a Secret Service man telephoned me for an appointment Monday morning. Two of them came to see me. They said the president had invited me to meet him at Fort Knox Wednesday morning.[1] They instructed me to arrive at the home of Lieutenant General Jacob L. Devers[2] at 9 A.M.

I already was scheduled to deliver the address at graduation of the WAAC class at Eastern, but I hurriedly made other arrangements. On Wednesday morning I arrived at General Devers's home a few minutes before 9:00. He and I drove to the depot. The president's train came in at about 9:30 o'clock.

Marvin McIntyre,[3] General Watson, and a few others got off the train first. We stood around talking, perhaps fifteen minutes. Then the president left his private car at the rear of the train and took his seat in an open car. I sat at the president's left, and General Devers sat on the folding seat at his left.

A sergeant drove the car. A Secret Service man sat in the front seat with him, one stood on each running board and two trotted along behind.

As we drove away, the presidential salute of twenty-one guns was given. We first drove to the vicinity of General Devers's office, down a street lined on one side with students of the Officers Candidate School standing at present arms, and lined on the other side with WAACs standing at salute.

We drove to the replacement center, where Major General Charles L. Scott,[4] commanding, reported to the president. He invited General Scott to take the other folding seat and we began our tour of the replacement center under his guidance.

There was no interruption to work as we drove along. We saw classes in flame-throwing, and the president remarked it was the first time he had witnessed it. We saw men learning to tear down and assemble machine guns, small arms, and the like. A class in hand signaling was in progress.

General Scott then left the car and was replaced by Brigadier General Joseph A. Holly,[5] commander of the Armored Force School. With General Holly directing, we then turned for a tour of his school. Where possible, the car was driven through buildings; where not possible, we drove by the side of them. Here we saw men at work on all types of armored equipment, engines of every description, and the like.

Everywhere we went, the men kept working. They undoubtedly knew in advance something out of the ordinary was in the air, and I suppose some of them had guessed the truth. The looks on their faces registered admiration and surprise as the president passed. But word quickly spread. For example, when we drove by the laundry, all the men and women stood waving at the windows nearest us. The children at school were waiting to wave at the president, also.

Mr. Roosevelt displayed unusual interest in everything he saw. His questions to the officers were incisive and directly to the point. He was dressed in a light gray, double-breasted suit, with soft gray hat. He sat on a big cape, which he pulled around his shoulders in the chill air. He smoked one cigarette after another in his long holder.

We left the Armored Force School and drove to OP6, where we found the grandstand filled with officers and the terrain in front cleared for a tactical problem.

The first feature here was a procession of mechanized and motorized equipment, with at least one vehicle of every type from light motorcycle to the heaviest tanks. The announcer explained for our benefit the characteristics and purposes of each. Then he announced the tactical problem, which follows: A German force has crossed Salt River and taken up position on Missionary Ridge opposite our observation point. Our purpose was to drive it off.

For forty-five minutes, there followed an amazing demonstration of firepower. All the equipment, from lightest to heaviest, was brought to bear against the enemy position. Every gun shot live ammunition, while bombers roared over and dropped live bombs. Every piece turned all the firepower it possessed on the enemy position.

For myself, the spectacle was one of the greatest I have ever seen at Fort Knox. And I am sure the president was deeply impressed by it, too.

We then drove to the Gold Vault, where the party disembarked and went inside the repository.[6] We boarded a small elevator and descended to where the gold is stored. The seal to one of the vaults was broken upon special permit from the Treasury Department. We stepped inside and looked around at the gold bricks. They are somewhat smaller than building bricks, and the guard said they are worth about $14,000 each. He took one of them down and held it close to Mr. Roosevelt, but I did not see the president touch it.

There were several reporters with Mr. Roosevelt's party, but only one of them was allowed to enter the Gold Vault with us. I don't know whether it was just his turn, but the United Press man came in while the others remained outside.

We next drove to the depot, where the president boarded his car. I presume he ate lunch soon after, for the train pulled out about 1 P.M.

The president, as it turned out, was not the only attraction at the depot. Fala was there. The dog did not go with us in the automobile, but one of the boys brought him out for play and exercise. I tell you, Fala is frisky and smart and can steal attention from even the president himself. Mr. Roosevelt was as fine as he could be, in a good and jovial humor. He and General Devers compared notes on their trips to North Africa, while the talk between him and me included topics of both state and national interest.

---

1. Johnson was the only one who was not a member of the president's party or the military.

2. Jacob Loucks Devers (1887–), b. York, Pennsylvania. Chief of staff, Panama Canal Department, 1939–1940; commander, Ninth Infantry Division, 1940–1941; commander, Armored Force, Fort Knox, 1941–1943; commander, Eastern Theater of Operations, 1943; commander, Armored Forces, North Africa, 1944; deputy supreme allied commander Mediterranean Theater; commander, Sixth Army Group, 1944; general, 1945; retired, 1949. *Webster's American Military Biographies* (Springfield, Mass., 1978), p. 100.

3. Marvin Hunter McIntyre (1878–1943), b. La Grange. Member, secretariat, President Roosevelt, 1933–1943. *Who Was Who in America, 1943–1950,* 2:361.

4. Charles L. Scott (1883–1954). Major general, commanding, Fort Knox Re-

placement Center, First Armored Corps, 1940–1942. *Who Was Who in American History: The Military*, p. 513.

5. Joseph Andrew Holly (1896–), b. Chicago. Commanding officer, Armored Force, 1940–1944; brigadier general, 1943; chief, Armored Section, Eastern Theater of Operations. *Who's Who in America, 1946–1947* (Chicago, 1947), 17:1105.

6. It was the president's first visit to the gold depository.

AMERICAN LEGION CONVENTION
Louisville / July 21, 1943

IT is always a pleasure to come and meet with the Legion in convention and see you collectively and individually and renew the friendships with this fine group that I cherish so highly.

I appeared before the various Legion conventions repeatedly since I have been governor, and I have made a good many speeches around the state. As a result, sometimes when I make a speech I find myself, without realizing it, repeating something that I said before and every once in awhile somebody complains about the repetition of some of my stale jokes and by way of apology and in anticipation of the fact that I might do that again, I am going to tell you a cow story.

There was a fellow running a dairy in Jefferson County that got short of help. He could not get anybody to work on the farm or in the dairy, and he came into town hunting for somebody to help him milk his cows. Well, he found a fellow who said he would like to go to the country and work in a dairy, and he took him out there and taught him the intricacies and the art of milking a cow. He was getting along pretty well one morning. The dairyman walked out there and the fellow was standing in front of the cow with a big bucket of milk and he had this milk pushed up to the cow's nose, trying to make the cow drink the milk. He said, "What in the world are you doing?" And this fellow replied, "Well, the milk was a little thin this morning, and I thought it was a good idea to run it through a second time."

The American Legion, because of the fine service it has performed, is a great civic and patriotic organization, but it has, of course, its greatest responsibility in times of war. I am sure that you all agree with me that we have been particularly fortunate this past year in having as Department Commander of the American Legion in Kentucky one of the most distinguished soldiers from Kentucky who served in World War I. In Ed Caldwell,[1] we have had that fine, dynamic, energetic and enthusiastic leadership so essential in these critical days when there is so much that the Legion might do. Under his leadership, I think we all agree, a superb job has been done in the meeting of the opportunities for service on the home front presented to the American Legion by these critical days.

I also enjoy coming to the Legion meetings just to see again the men in the group whose friendships I treasure. Ed, I agree with you and I am sure that you will agree with me that the American Legion in Kentucky constitutes the finest single segment of her citizenship. In the group that you find at the conventions representing the various posts of Kentucky, you will find that they also represent the elite of the leadership in their respective communities. I believe that you will find all of them to be outstanding citizens of the Commonwealth and that they are the individuals who energetically, diligently, and continually serve their communities and municipalities day in and day out and respond to every call of duty made upon them.

This is the last convention before which it will be my privilege to appear as governor of Kentucky. I take pride in having been the first overseas legionnaire governor of Kentucky. That honor and distinction, and that opportunity for public service, came to me very largely as a result of the support of those of you who constitute the Legion's membership. I owe to each of you a debt that I have sought to repay in a small way by diligently and conscientiously serving you. I have a genuine affection for the men of the Legion and shall always be cognizant of the fact that I owe them a tremendous debt of gratitude, not only for the support they gave me, which resulted in my being elected governor, but for the fine support that the Legion collectively and individually has given during the period that I have served in this important capacity.

I am glad to have been governor of Kentucky and to have been in the position to be helpful to the fine, splendid, constructive program sponsored by the American Legion in public assistance. The Legion has had as one of its outstanding projects for years the inauguration in Kentucky of pensions for the blind and aid to dependent children. We thought for a long time it was necessary to have a constitutional amendment and we submitted the amendment. The secretary of state forgot to advertise it, and, consequently, we could not vote on it.

In 1940 Bill Duffy[2] and a group of interested, intelligent legionnaires came to the governor's office and said, "We have become convinced that it is not necessary to have a constitutional amendment in order to inaugurate these public assistance programs." Well, we enacted legislation to make those programs possible and after they had run the whole gamut or gauntlet of the courts, our interpretations were sustained. A fine, thorough program is being steadily advanced.

I wish that the American Legion would take as one of its major programs the sponsorship for the program of the completion of the job of rehabilitation of the state's charitable and penal institutions. We have made a fine start toward the restoration of the institutions. I wish that the American Legion would recognize the importance of throwing its tremendous weight and power behind that program because the program is just getting started. During my administration, we have expended nearly $4 million for the improvement and restoration of these institutions that have been so long neglected.

I take great pride in the fact that during my administration more miles of highway road have been constructed than ever before and despite the restrictions that have come on building. There have been 1,446 miles of road of all types constructed exclusive of rural highways and of that number, 545 miles have been high type road.

I want to express my great appreciation to the American Legion for the tremendous help that they have given the governor in the operation, organization, and the functioning of selective service in Kentucky. That has been one of the most important jobs that has been delegated to the Commonwealth as a result of the wartime necessity. Under the inspired, conscientious, and sincere leadership of your distinguished legionnaire, Colonel Frank Rash, we have organized in Kentucky a selective service organization that has functioned smoothly and effectively and fairly and honestly. The American Legion has contributed more to that success than any other single segment of Kentucky citizenship. You will find legionnaires serving on practically every local board in Kentucky in one capacity or another. The fact that the boards have functioned so smoothly is due primarily to the interest that local legionnaires have taken in the performance of this important duty.

As was said a moment ago by the District Commander of the Fifth District, 200,000 Kentucky boys were inducted into the service as contrasted with 84,000 Kentucky boys who went with you and me into World War I.[3] That reveals something of the magnitude of this war, something of the tremendous job yet to be done. Those boys are in the service and they are doing their job splendidly and admirably and it is important that here on the home front, we steadily and earnestly and effectively support them, that victory may come more quickly.

The Legion has been so fine and helpful in so many things that it is impossible to name them all. You have been helpful in the organization of the civilian defense program throughout Kentucky, the organization of the Kentucky Active Militia unit, and many other outstanding programs, such as in the promotion and sale of war bonds in the Commonwealth.

The Legion has also done a fine job in your local ration boards and especially in interpreting to the people of your community the need and necessity for rationing. So many folks complain unthinkingly about the hardships that have been caused because they cannot get all of the gasoline they want or all of this, that, or the other thing. It is going to be necessary that you do that to an increased extent, because it is only going to be a matter of a short time until you are getting less gasoline than you now have.

Those thousand plane bomber raids over Germany with their increased activity, the enlargement of your navy, the increased activity of the convoys who are carrying American soldiers to the European and Pacific theaters of war are consuming an increased amount of gasoline. Consequently, that means that it is not going to be long until you are going to have to get along with less gasoline. It is important that the Legion and those of you who fought in the last war inform the people of that.

Now, those of you who have lived in foxholes and muddy trenches, those of you who have lived with cooties and lice and vermin, those of you who know the nausea and filth of battle, it is important that you interpret to the people in your community the need and the necessity of the sacrifices that are required of them and insist that they accept them enthusiastically and uncomplainingly. That has been one of the finest jobs that the Legion has done and it is necessary that you keep it up. It is necessary that you intensify your efforts on the home front to the end that the gallant, valorous, heroic Kentucky boys who are serving on every battlefield in the world may have the sustained support of the people at home.

It is important in the days that lie ahead that our people in Kentucky accept with a smile, zealously and uncomplainingly, the increased hardships and sacrifices that they are going to have to make. It is important that they have sand in their systems.

Now, that brings to my mind the story that ran through the AEF. Many of you fellows may recall an incident that happened on the beach down at Saint Nazaire in the spring following the signing of the armistice. There was a long, gawky, uncouth farm boy from the west who was down in that lovely vacation spot on furlough. He was having a good time and he was hunting for some fun. He did not have any difficulty in making the acquaintance of a very attractive and very sprightly and very lovely mademoiselle. They went swimming. They had a good time and they battered the waves and were playing in the salt water on the beach for some time. Finally they came out and got under their umbrella to rest. The attractive mademoiselle continued to make advances toward this young, bashful farm boy. Finally, when he continued to be embarrassed, she said, "Why don't you kiss me?" The bashful boy in American uniform said, "I got sand in my mouth" and the mademoiselle said, "You ought to swallow it; you need it in your system."

Well, these are days when we ought to have sand in our system on the home front. I do not know of any group of Kentuckians better qualified to inject that sand and that enthusiasm into the people on the home front than the men of the American Legion. There was a story related in France in the last war with which many of you no doubt are familiar. That is the story that happened in the raid upon the Meuse-Argonne. You will remember how they pulled off those raids on a localized area for the purpose of getting some prisoners and getting some information and for the purpose of reconnaissance. This company of American soldiers, the old Eighty-ninth Division, had been assigned the job of pulling off this raid. The barrage went out across No Man's Land. They followed closely and they carried out the mission and returned with prisoners. As they checked up, they found that a whole platoon had been cut off, surrounded, had gotten lost, and failed to return. The captain of that company called for volunteers to go out and rescue that platoon that had been cut off in the German trenches. There was a fine, alert, young lieutenant who stepped forward and called for volunteers. There was a timid officer in that group who was a close friend of the lieutenant. He whispered into the lieutenant's ear that the barrage was entirely too intense and that the machine gunning across No Man's Land was going to be curtains for anybody who attempted such a feat. He told the young lieutenant there was not a chance for him to come back. The young lieutenant said, with the fight of battle in his eyes and the valor of a hero in his heart, "We do not have to come back, but we have to go." That is the spirit of the American Legion. That is the spirit of the Legion as it has always been and the spirit of the Legion as it should be as we here on the home front seek to support the valorous 200,000 American Kentuckians who are fighting on the battle fronts of the world.[4]

---

1. Edgar Newman Caldwell (1897–1960), b. Glasgow. Department commander, American Legion. Colonel, United States Army. Telephone interview, Mrs. E. N. Caldwell, August 8, 1978.

2. William M. Duffy (?–1953), died age sixty-four, b. Louisville. Attorney; manager, Social Security Administration, Louisville, 1936. State representative, 1914–1918; state senator, 1924–1928. Active in American Legion. *Lexington Herald*, May 18, 1953.

3. On July 8, 1943, Johnson spoke in Louisville at a ceremony for the induction of the 200,000th Kentuckian into the armed forces, James Eugene Smith, an eighteen-year-old high school graduate from Liberty, Casey County. The gov-

ernor used the occasion to express appreciation to the men who were serving on the local Selective Service boards.

4. The speech has been edited. Parts appear in speeches from January 19, 1943, in the State Administration section, July 12 and August 24, 1943, in the Health and Welfare section, and May 20, 1942, in this section.

HOME FRONT PLEDGE
Radio Broadcast / August 26, 1943

As Kentucky's war governor, I have been extremely proud of the magnificent way in which Kentuckians have been contributing to the winning of the war. Kentucky mothers have smiled through tears as they have encouraged their sons to put on the uniform and follow the flag in defense of freedom. More than 200,000 of Kentucky's finest sons are in the armed forces. The fire of patriotic fervor burns brightly throughout Kentucky. I am certain that each of us is anxious to do everything possible to lick Hitler. The attitude of our people has been fine. I am going to talk to you for a few minutes about some things which you can do to help hasten the day of victory.

It is not possible to win the war on the home front. The war can be won only on the blazing field of battle where our gallant soldiers meet and conquer the enemies that are trying to enslave us. But we could lose the war on the home front. Actually the home front is you and your neighbor and the millions of other Americans.

The manner in which we conduct ourselves as citizens during wartimes and the kind of attitude we express toward our individual responsibilities determines the strength and effectiveness of the home front. We at home constitute the supply division for our armed forces and we must meet that responsibility. This is a war that requires the energies and the clear thinking and right action of every citizen. Men in our armies and navies on the battlefront are planning, working, fighting, and yes—dying every hour of every day to speed the moment of final victory. They are not fighting for the joy of combat; they are fighting to uphold the honor of our proud nation and to preserve for themselves and for you the heritage of a free people, a homeland of democratic ideals and liberties and for the privilege to continue to live as free men under a democratic system of government.

We at home have the same ideals to fight for but our weapons are different. We must take action in thoughts and words and deeds with intelligent planning and execution in the interests of maintaining our domestic economy on a rational and sound basis. During time of war, the stresses and strains on the internal balance of trade become terrific. Production for war takes first place and the production of goods for civilian needs is gradually reduced to bare essentials with limits upon the amount of production. Employment is accelerated; income soars; and surplus spending power begins to flood the market places.

Without definite price controls and the rationing of essential commodities to hold this money in check, a devastating economic collapse could occur. People with the most money would outbid those with less. Prices would rise under pressure of buying and scarcity. Wages and incomes would then be under more pressure for increases to meet the demands of price advances. From there on, inflation would set in; economic strangulation would result; and at the conclusion of the war, we would emerge a bankrupt nation with the purchasing power of our money destroyed.

We, the people on the home front, must realize that this is our war; that we have a job to do. It is true that we have not been bombed out of our homes. Our war plants have not been demolished by "block busters"; innocent women and children have not been the target of enemy dive bombers. We have not experienced the horrors of vast fires started by incendiary bombs nor the incessant cracking of antiaircraft guns as enemy planes zoom overhead, planting their seeds of destruction. We do not hear the low rumble of distant cannon nor stand in mute silence watching our land armies move up toward the front. In fact, we are so far removed from the actualities of war that it is difficult to realize that we are at war and it is easy to become complacent about it. That attitude could be disastrous.

War, total war, means harsh, sustained sacrifice. It means the subordination of individual or private rights and privileges to the collective good of all the people. A single objective, that of winning the war implemented by a concerted, spirited, and united public effort on the home front, is absolutely essential as we mobilize the nation to fight inflation. We must submit to regimentation temporarily in order to defeat foes that would impose regimentation upon us permanently.

We cannot, under war conditions of the magnitude of our present conflict, do business as usual nor can we conduct our individual lives as usual. It simply cannot be done. We Americans on the home front are battling today one of the most dangerous foes that our country has had to face in this war. That foe is inflation. Your and my concern at the moment should be primarily focused upon this enemy. Unfortunately there are some shortsighted Americans who put personal gain above duty and patriotism. If these few individuals are allowed to operate unhampered and without restraint, they will weaken our economic structure just as termites weaken the strongest of buildings. As a means toward checking and eliminating as much as possible such threats, President Roosevelt has aimed a powerful blow against these dangerous forces by directing the Office of Price Administration to establish definite controls against runaway prices. He has said again and again, "We must hold the line." But the main responsibility, ladies and gentlemen, for holding the line lies with the American people. They and they alone can smash the inflationary spiral and assure a fair share of food and other essential commodities for everyone. They and they alone can keep down the cost of living.

Rationing and price control have been in effect now for many months, and I am sure you will agree that even though some slight inconveniences may have been imposed upon you, they are trivial compared with the inconveniences suffered by our men and women on the battlefronts of the world. In fact, the suffering they experience brings blood, sweat, and tears. Yes, even death. So how can we then complain at home? Your government is seeing to it that you have adequate food as well as a fair share of other essential commodities, but, to do so, the government asks for and requires your cooperation. That, ladies and gentlemen, is not the condition that exists in many countries at war today. There hunger, devastation, poverty, and disease prevail generally.

I am convinced that the overwhelming majority of the people of Kentucky value their heritage and exalt their patriotism to such an extent that they want to comply with all rationing regulations. I am convinced that the majority of the people of Kentucky are so correct in their thinking that they understand the necessity for regulatory price and rationing measures designed for the high purpose of helping win the war.

Many sincere Kentuckians often ask, "What can I do to be certain I am doing all I can to advance the war effort?" There are two major things every citizen can do. One is to buy war bonds—buy more than you can afford. All surplus income should go into bonds as a loan to your government and as a saving for the individual. The other important thing you can and should do is to inform yourselves as to the details of rationing regulation; get an understanding of the necessity for compliance with these regulations; familiarize yourselves with price control measures and carefully comply with them.

The chief responsibility for holding the line, keeping prices down, lies with the American people. To more forcefully bring this to your attention, the Office of Price Administration is inaugurating a campaign in which special emphasis will be placed upon our responsibility in maintaining a solid home front.

As governor of Kentucky, I am taking the liberty, speaking for all Kentuckians, to pledge the Commonwealth's allegiance to that program and its worthy objectives. I urge you to give your support as individuals to this simple but important program. In a united effort to keep down the cost of living, hold rising prices in check, all Americans are being invited to join in a Home Front Campaign. You will be invited to make and keep this simple pledge: "I will pay no more than top legal prices. I will accept no rationed goods without giving up ration stamps."

Today groups of determined patriotic men and women the country over are making the home front pledge. The idea behind this pledge is sound because it goes straight to the heart of America's fundamental honesty. It makes an appeal to that honesty and to every American's sense of fair play. It is my clear conviction that the people of Kentucky will respond to that appeal.

All over the state, in each of our 120 counties today, a movement is being started to obtain the pledge of every citizen, and this drive will continue until every patriotic person has had the opportunity to step forward and pledge his allegiance to this program.

To do your part on the home front, to help distribute rationed goods fairly, to help hold down the cost of living, to help eliminate black markets, to bring violations to the attention of your War Price and Rationing Board, let me urge you to make this pledge. "I will pay no more than top legal prices. I will accept no rationed goods without giving up ration stamps." Let us, the people of Kentucky, be able to say to those who have gone to war, we are keeping faith.

HERITAGE

KENTUCKY DERBY
Louisville / May 4, 1940

NO one could stand here in the shadows of the historic steeples of Churchill Downs and see the marvelous sight we see here at this moment without a thrill of pride for things that are Kentucky's.

The thoroughbred has a particular place in Kentucky. And to all the world the Kentucky Derby[1] stands as a race full of the rosy memories of a great past and full of the drama and excitement of a great present. To win this race is a wonderful and proud distinction, both for the horse and for everyone who has had a hand in his victory, from the humblest stable swipe to the jockey who actually pilots him to this charmed circle over all opposition.

Such a horse, a horse capable of joining the equine great which have raised their names through dust and mud and sweat and rain and heat to the heights which are reached in a Kentucky Derby—such a horse stands before us today. He wears regally the garland of roses for he has defeated a crack field. It was a distinction for him even to be sent to the post in this race in which the competition was so stiff and so apparently one-sided. And now that he has won, it is a distinction multiplied a thousandfold.

I wish to congratulate the owner and I think that great assemblage of people from every state in the Union, perhaps, which is waving and talking excitedly across the track and on every side of us here, congratulates him too. The good horse Gallahadian is a popular and a gallant champion. Long may he reign! I congratulate the trainer and the jockey and the handlers. May they send this good horse on to further victories.

And now, as governor of Kentucky, a state whose flavor was never more lavishly represented than by the tradition of the Kentucky Derby, I am proud to present this trophy to Mrs. Mars.[2] On it will be inscribed the name of a truly great horse, Gallahadian. And in the hearts of all who saw this historic race today will be inscribed that name too. May it never be erased.[3]

---

1. The governor spoke at the Sixty-sixth running of the Kentucky Derby.
2. Ethel V. Mars, owner of Milky Way Farm, was absent because of illness. Trainer Roy Waldron received the gold cup for her.
3. The governor presented the cup to Warren Wright, owner of Whirlaway, on May 3, 1941. Louisville *Courier-Journal,* May 4, 1941. He made similar remarks to the ones above in presenting the cup on May 2, 1942, to trainer Gauer for Mrs. Payne Whitney, owner of Shut Out, and on May 1, 1943, to Mrs. J. Hertz, owner of Count Fleet.

STEPHEN COLLINS FOSTER PORTRAIT
Bardstown / July 4, 1940

THE title "Kentucky Colonel" is a unique distinction. Those upon whom it has been conferred have received this coveted commission because of noteworthy service to Kentucky or friendship for our state.

No single individual has rendered a greater service to Kentucky than did Stephen Collins Foster[1] when he caught into song the spirit of Kentucky which he feelingly expressed in that immortal melody which now is in the hearts and on the lips of every patriotic Kentuckian, that refrain we revere, "My Old Kentucky Home." It has been an inspiration to Kentuckians. It has quickened their devotion to be state, intensified their pride in this great Commonwealth.

While Stephen Collins Foster was not a Kentucky Colonel, none has ever lived that was more worthy of that preferment. He had those noble impulses of the heart, those fine attributes of mind which admirably qualify him for membership in the Honorable Order of Kentucky Colonels. So on this his natal day, as we pay homage to his genius and do honor to his memory, I, as governor of the Commonwealth for which he performed a notable service, have issued a posthumous commission as Kentucky Colonel to Stephen Collins Foster. This commission will hang near his portrait. It is evidence of belated recognition of our debt to him and testimony of the reverence we feel for one who contributed so richly to our state.

The Honorable Order of Kentucky Colonels in recent years has been alert in its efforts to be helpful to Kentucky. But it was a happily inspired thought indeed which resulted in procuring for My Old Kentucky Home the superb portrait of Stephen Collins Foster, produced by the creative genius of the gifted Howard Chandler Christy,[2] himself a Kentucky Colonel.

This magnificent portrait of the author of that song which stirs the hearts of Kentuckians will henceforth hang here in the stately mansion where Foster was a guest when the magic touch of the muse inspired him to write that sweet song. The Foster painting will enhance interest in this state shrine at Federal Hill. There is here provided for the portrait an environment as perfectly in accord with its symbolism as was the state anthem which was here inspired.

This portrait of the sweet singer on whose birth anniversary we are assembled is being hung today in My Old Kentucky Home as a result of the united efforts of Kentucky Colonels. Mrs. Anna Friedman,[3] secretary and keeper of the Great Seal, perhaps first conceived the ingenious idea. Under the energetic leadership of General Fred Miles, General Robert Barry, Mrs. Friedman, and Colonel H. H. Neel,[4] a plan was presented to the Kentucky Colonels which gave them an opportunity to make such contribution as they desired to the fund which was accumulated with which to acquire the Foster portrait. As governor of Kentucky and commander-in-chief of the Honorable Order of Kentucky Colonels, I want to express my sincere appreciation to whose who have made possible this singularly appropriate gift for My Old Kentucky Home. It is with genuine joy that I accept it for the Commonwealth of Kentucky.

---

1. Stephen Collins Foster (1826–1864), b. Pennsylvania. Song writer, folk music composer. *Webster's Biographical Dictionary, 1972,* p. 543.

2. Howard Chandler Christy (1873–1952), b. Morgan County, Ohio. Artist. *New York Times,* March 4, 1952, Sec. 1, p. 27.

3. Anna Friedman (Goldman) (1894–1981), b. New York, New York. Resided "The Forest," Anchorage, unofficial home of the Honorable Order of Kentucky Colonels since 1935. Married Samuel Friedman who was killed in 1946; married Melvin Goldman, 1955. Louisville *Courier-Journal,* May 8, 1966, June 22, 1981, and telephone interview, Mrs. Goldman, June 19, 1978.

4. J. Fred Miles (?–1963), died at age 79, b. Sheldon, Missouri. National general, Honorable Order of Kentucky Colonels. Came to Kentucky in 1917. Oil executive. Louisville *Courier-Journal,* August 23, 1963.

Robert Barry (1892–1956), b. Louisville. General, Honorable Order of Kentucky Colonels. Public relations director; president, Robert E. Barry Electric Company. *Who's Who in Kentucky, 1936,* p. 23, and Louisville *Courier-Journal,* December 3, 1956.

Harrell Herndon Neel (1894–1949), b. Louisville. Business executive; vice-president, National Dairy Products Corporation. Wallis and Tapp, *A Sesquicentennial History of Kentucky*, 4:2186-87, and letter, Neil O. Ewing, May 23, 1978.

KENTUCKY METHODIST CHURCH CONFERENCE
Wilmore / September 6, 1940

I AM the son of a Methodist preacher—a circuit rider Methodist preacher. During a lifetime in the ministry, he never had an assignment where his salary was over $1,200 a year. I recall when he served circuits of four and five churches for $600 a year. While I do not recall being hungry during those days of meager compensation, I used to get mighty tired of turnips and cornbread and sorghum molasses.

My father had a definite and real faith in God and a pronounced belief in the Democratic party. My mother was the most genuinely sweet and good individual I have ever known. She lived the religion that permeated her soul. She accepted everything as the Lord's will.

My father was not a highly educated man, but that education which he obtained was procured through privation and perseverance. He always insisted that I must have university training. As is often the case, he placed greater value upon a university degree than those who have it. Despite a lack of formal education, the Methodist preacher who was my father was an omnivorous reader, studied diligently, and attained much wisdom. He enjoyed arguing religion.

There are times when political associates become exasperated because of my refusal to sanction expenditures of public money which they regard as desirable. I acquired the habit of being saving and thrifty in a humble Methodist parsonage where such was a necessity. I was taught to avoid wastefulness. Extravagance was held up as a sin and I so regard it, regardless of whether it be in the expenditure of public money or private funds.

And I was never more sincere in my life than when as a candidate, I promised the people that I would make a saving, thrifty, frugal governor. The characteristic which results in me placing such emphasis upon that philosophy of public expenditure is the direct result of having been reared in a humble Methodist parsonage.

In that parsonage in which I spent my childhood, the family altar was a sacred shrine at which the family worshiped each evening. Family prayer was held each morning at breakfast. At evening prayer, father prayed first. He seemed to feel that he was talking directly to the God in whom he had implicit faith. He gave him a lot of advice, asked him for many things he never got. But that did not alter his belief in the God he worshiped. His explanation of the failure of those blessings to arrive for which he had petitioned was that God knew such would not be best.

I was a normal, mischievous boy. I resented the oft-repeated accusation that all preachers' boys are bad lads. I resented the condescension of the more prosperous members of the church toward the poverty of the parsonage. Yet with it all I do thank God that I was reared in a Methodist parsonage; that I was reared by godly parents; that reverence for religion was inculcated in me. I am certain that such traits of character as I may possess are the result of that environment.

My father was highly ambitious for me. As he demanded that I form studious habits, acquire the practice of much reading, he often insisted that I should be governor some day. It sounded preposterous to me and did not diminish my resentment over his insistence that I read and study instead of going fishing with the other boys. Strange as it may be, circumstances conspired to fulfill that prophecy made by my father. And as I stood in the presence of the multitude which thronged the state Capitol last December 8 to rejoice with me as I was inaugurated governor, there was deep regret in my heart that he had not lived to witness the fulfillment of his forecast. As I placed my hand on the Bible by which my father lived and took the oath of office, I realized suddenly the acuteness of my disappointment that the father and mother who had contributed most to advance me to that station of responsibility and public trust were denied the satisfaction of seeing the fulfillment of their dream. They would have enjoyed it far more than I, because I was frightened by the magnitude of the responsibility.

I approve of the more liberal attitude of the Methodist church that has come with the passing of the years. I am glad that our church no longer regards it sinful to have a little fun. My father was very stern and austere. He disapproved of everything that he regarded as worldly. Sunday was a solemn day. And I was required to keep it holy in accord with father's conception. Sunday school, Sunday morning service, and Sunday night service I was required to attend. And never was I permitted to miss. It became so much a habit that I did not mind it much. But I confess to you that I never did get so that I liked Wednesday night prayer meeting. It was the same dozen or more faithful, elderly ladies and a few men every Wednesday night. And for a restless boy it was extremely dull.

Well do I recall with what seriousness the parsonage prepared for

Conference. An all-summer campaign there was to raise the quota assigned the church for foreign missions—and with the shape the world is in I think there is some justification for the boyish skepticism I entertained to my father's horror, that the money spent for foreign missions could have served a more useful purpose. But the records of the Louisville Conference will reveal that Robert Johnson always went to Conference with his collections up, though in one instance I recall that he had to put in the money that had been saved with which to buy him a new suit to wear to Conference.

Then I recall the anxiety with which we at home in the parsonage awaited the verdict which determined whether we stayed another year or moved to another charge. Father and mother had a reverence for the bishop. They felt that he was the instrument through which God's will was expressed. Regardless of whether we moved or stayed where we were, father returned from Conference to plunge with zeal into revival meetings. He had a passion for saving souls. He believed in the mourners bench and, after he had finished a powerful sermon on "Where Will You Spend Eternity?" I have seen sinners come by the dozens to seek the experience of conversion.

My experience as the son of a preacher has convinced me that there is no group of men who make a greater contribution to the improvement of mankind than those who constitute the clergy. Though a humble servant of the Master, I am certain that my father influenced for good the lives of hundreds and hundreds of men and women. That is the experience of every minister. And it is a pity that they render such valued service at a sacrifice often of personal comfort of themselves and families.

There is no profession in which is required a greater variety of abilities or more extensive educational preparation than the ministry. I rejoice that the quality and cultural attainments of the ministry of our church has advanced to that high standard to which it has progressed today. A successful preacher requires the education of a university president, the executive ability of a financier, the craftiness of a politician, the adaptation of a chameleon, the hope of an optimist, the courage of a hero, the wisdom of a serpent, the gentleness of a dove, the patience of Job, the grace of God, and the persistence of the devil.

I am sure that you as learned men, men who are familiar with the distressing events that are transpiring daily in this troubled world, are deeply concerned as to the future of civilization. You are disturbed because of the apparent determination of civilization to commit suicide.

It is an anomolous situation that, in this the most enlightened period of the world's history, there is more crime, suffering, and bloodshed and oppression than ever before. We have placed great emphasis upon education in these United States. Vast sums of treasure have been expended in a prolonged effort to eliminate ignorance, create a literate citizenship. In Kentucky, half of the $26 million which will be expended this year from the state's general fund will be spent for public education. And I think that places emphasis in the proper place. Yet in this the most literate of nations, crime is most prevalent. Those who transgress the laws of God and man increase in numbers from year to year. I wonder why? Of course, our prisons are filled in the main with those who have not availed themselves of educational opportunity. They have come from substandard homes, been reared in an environment not conducive to good citizenship.

I recently visited the Eddyville Penitentiary where about 1,500 men are confined because of crimes committed. As I passed down death row there, I saw five men condemned to die for murders they had committed. I could but wonder wherein society had failed to avert this ignoble end for these young men. Perhaps if someone had paid more attention to these boys when they were in the high chair, they would not now face death in the electric chair. The governor would not face the grim duty of permitting the decree of the court to be carried out. I know it is easy to blame all our social ills on the dereliction of the church, the home, or the school. Yet neither of the triumvirate may escape major responsibility. A large percent of these who are being committed to prison are young men. I do not charge that the church has failed in its duty toward the youth. But I would point out that a youth program that seeks to divert youngsters from crime would make a constructive contribution to the state and nation.

War has again engulfed a large portion of the world. I know something of the frightfulness of war as result of service in the World War. War is hideous and brutal. It is destructive of everything for which the church stands. It ruthlessly disregards the teachings of the Christ. The forces of frightfulness have been set in motion by a godless creature who is devoid of the nobler impulses which the church seeks to develop in the human heart. He wages war upon that type of government for which our forebears made great sacrifice. He would destroy that type of government under which we have enjoyed the greatest freedom any people has ever known. His brutal hand has closed the church doors, denounced religion as a subversive influence.

Impossible it is to explain how it happens that, in this the most enlightened era of history, the most brutal of all wars has spread through Europe and threatens to engulf the world. Consequences are revolting to contemplate. It is inconceivable that such a peril to our free institutions has arisen.

History records that Benjamin Franklin said to George Washington after the signing of the Constitution, "Now we have a republic, if we can keep it." The wise Franklin knew, as said Adams, the historian, "Every democracy that has been created in the world has destroyed itself. Democracies are born in unity and die as result of dissension." That is a calamity which we must avert, and in this hour of danger the influence of this great church should be definitely exerted to preserve this Republic under which religious freedom has been one of our most cherished liberties.

For the defense of this Republic we need to mobilize the mind of America. We need to cease thinking as divergent groups and unite our minds, exercise our ingenuity to avert the peril which has become so pronounced.

We need to mobilize the will of America for her defense. We need a rebirth of that fortitude of our forefathers as they offered their lives a sacrifice upon the altar of freedom that we might enjoy the liberties which have made this the most favored and unique of nations. We need to mobilize the heart of America, awaken again that fierce patriotism which sustained our forebears at Valley Forge.[1] We need to rekindle the devotion of Americans to these United States.

We need to mobilize in defense of this nation the spiritual forces inherent in the church. We have assumed that as peoples of the world become more educated that probability of war would diminish. It has been our belief that intelligent, educated leadership in enlightened nations would avert war, settle differences by reason. But that logical theory has been knocked into a cocked hat.

I am beginning to wonder if it is not perhaps true that we have depended too much on education to reduce crime and banish war. I wonder if it is not probable that we have placed too great emphasis upon the development of mental process and neglected that spiritual development of the finer impulses of the human heart.

Hitler is mentally smart, crafty, and cunning. His is a mind of great power. But his heart is not right. He scoffs at God and sneers at religion. Perhaps it is being revealed that, as we have concentrated upon development of our mental capacity, we have neglected the spiritual nature and moral development of mankind.[2] Our intellectual advancement has outrun our spiritual growth. It may be that the church has failed in its mission as the spiritual teacher. It may be that mankind has refused to permit that spiritual cultivation necessary to a genuine culture. But I am suggesting that perhaps in this realm lies the immediate duty of the church.

Of course the church in the final analysis consists of the layman. Its leadership is powerless to lead into paths where laymen decline to follow. If the church has fallen short in its spiritual mission, it is not because of the clergy, but because of the influence of the membership as their thinking has been molded by economic change and material advancement.

Great as has been the progress of the world in mechanical and technological advance, no change has taken place which has outmoded the old-fashioned virtues of honesty and truthfulness. No progress has been made which justifies departure from the Ten Commandments or disregard of the teaching of the lowly Nazarene. No veneer of culture can long conceal the lack of character in the individual. And character is formed in the home. The church more than any other agency may accentuate its development. The school, left alone to do the job, is doomed to miserable failure.

The invitation to participate in this program pleased and flattered me. I am glad to have this opportunity to express my affectionate regard and exalted esteem for the ministry of the Methodist church. My father was a rather long-winded preacher. He had a contempt for sermonettes. I have sought to cultivate a brevity which was not characteristic of him.

I heard a story recently of a young bride whose husband was an usher in his church. She had left the roast for dinner in the oven and suddenly recalled that she had left the gas on. She wrote a note to her husband and sought to send it to him by another usher. But he misunderstood and delivered it to the minister, laying it on the pulpit. The preacher halted to examine the note and was met with this written injunction, "Please go home and turn off the gas."

I hope each of you get the assignment you desire.

---

1. Johnson addressed the Bryan Station Chapter of the Daughters of the American Revolution on Washington's birthday in 1941 and urged a rebirth of the spiritual concept and patriotism of Washington and his Continental Army. *Lexington Herald-Leader*, February 23, 1941.

2. The governor called Kentuckians on November 29, 1939, to unite on December 1, 2, and 3 with "men, women, and youth of more than fifty nations in a worldwide mobilization for spiritual and moral rearmament."

FIRST SUNDAY SCHOOL IN KENTUCKY
Frankfort / September 22, 1940

GOVERNOR JOHNSON drew a word picture of the Browns[1] of Liberty Hall and set the historical background for the observance. He told of Mrs. Brown's grief at the death of an eight-year-old daughter which turned her thoughts toward religious instruction of other children. He said that the cowbell's call to worship in 1810 was historically comparable with tidings of the Liberty Bell in Philadelphia in 1776.[2]

"As official representative of the citizenship of Kentucky, I am glad to join in this observance of the one hundred thirtieth anniversary of Kentucky's first Sunday school. Fitting indeed it is that we pay tribute to that noble Kentucky woman, Mrs. Margaretta Mason Brown, whose pioneer activity resulted in our first Sunday school. It is an inspiration to gather here today on this historic spot and worthily celebrate an event which launched an activity that has contributed so richly to the character of that vast company who in the intervening 130 years have been beneficently influenced by Sunday school training.

"Sunday school activity, launched here by Mrs. Brown, has been of great value.[3] It has given spiritual guidance to the multitude to whom religious instruction has been brought by this helpful auxiliary of the church. It has made better citizens of them. It has enriched their lives with a spiritual quality that strengthens character and makes life a more satisfying experience.

"So in recognition of the debt we owe to the pioneer spirit which launched the Sunday school as a vital and helpful religious activity, it is with genuine joy that I participate in this significant occasion to the extent of issuing an executive proclamation which reads as follows:

"WHEREAS, the first Sunday School in Kentucky was established in 1810 by Margaretta Brown, wife of the first Senator from Kentucky, and

WHEREAS, we are deeply conscious of and grateful for the spiritual influences and blessings this act has brought to succeeding generations of this Commonwealth, and

WHEREAS, extensive plans have been made for a state-wide observance of the 130th anniversary of the founding of this Sunday School,

NOW, THEREFORE, as governor of the Commonwealth of Kentucky, I do hereby proclaim Sunday, September 22, 1940, as the day for the celebration of the anniversary of Kentucky's First Sunday School."[4]

---

1. John Brown (1757–1837), b. Virginia. M. Margaretta Mason. Came to Kentucky in 1782–1783. First United States senator from Kentucky; member Virginia legislature from District of Kentucky. *Biographical Encyclopedia of Kentucky*, p. 14.

2. The two sons of Mrs. Brown ran through the streets ringing a cowbell as a signal that their mother's class was ready to begin. The bell rang during the governor's speech. Louisville *Courier-Journal*, September 23, 1940.

3. On April 27, 1940, Johnson proclaimed May 5, 1940, as "Go to Sunday School Day." On December 1, 1940, he endorsed December 8, 1940, as Universal Bible Sunday, sponsored by the American Bible Society.

4. The principal speaker was Russell Colgate, president of the International

Council of Religious Education and board chairman of the Colgate-Palmolive-Peet Company. In his speech Johnson noted that the Colgate family had eighty-two years of religious service.

STEPHEN COLLINS FOSTER BIRTHDAY CELEBRATION
Bardstown / July 4, 1941

IT is a very genuine joy to join you here today at this historic Kentucky shrine on the natal day of the nation and pay tribute to Stephen Collins Foster who has the same birthday as the Republic. Federal Hill has a wide appeal to the people of the nation as a symbol of the old Kentucky home of the romantic days of the old South. Its beautiful location and architecture combine to give it a loveliness of distinction.

But there transpired here an incident that so enriched the music of the world as to make this a hallowed spot. It is easy to understand how the genius of Stephen Collins Foster was stirred by the inspiration of this lovely home to immortalize into song the Old Kentucky Home.

All the songs produced by the gifted Foster have a sweet, simple charm that appeal to the noblest impulses of the human heart. But that song which makes the memory of Foster sacred to every Kentuckian is the plaintive melody which the beauty and charm of Federal Hill stimulated him to write here at Bardstown. "My Old Kentucky Home," with its elemental stirring of the soul, quickens the heartbeat of every Kentuckian. Its note of yearning creates a feeling of homesickness in the hearts of those native sons and daughters who find themselves "far, far away." It is a song which has an international appeal because in it the gifted, talented composer has caught into song the sob in the voice and the tear on the cheek of all who love home and the simple virtues of the fireside.

So because of the immortal melody stricken off by the artistic Foster here in this historic old Kentucky mansion, the melodious name of Kentucky and all it connotes as it conjures cherished memories from out of the past has attained imperishable fame, been sung about by multitudes around the world. They have been entranced and exalted by its sentiment and its melody. It is with reverence that I, as governor of Kentucky, express the appreciation of all Kentuckians for Stephen Collins Foster. We acknowledge our indebtedness to him for the song which has proclaimed Kentucky in every country and clime.[1] We revere the memory of this artist of the people who in 1852 while a guest of John Rowan[2] at Federal Hill sensed the tranquil spirit, the gracious living in this Kentucky home and translated it into the poetry of the people. The songs and music of Foster captivate our hearts and stimulate our imagination. Elvira Miller Slaughter's[3] lines on "Foster at Federal Hill" are strikingly appropriate as she pays tribute to "My Old Kentucky Home":

> It was a song of every day with its homely joys and sorrows,
> Of love and loss along the way and the heart break of the morrows,
> A song of home that hallowed place where the heart is ever turning
> Where heaven smiles from the mother's face and the fireside lights are burning,
> It linked Kentucky unto fame, a tie no years may sever,
> And made the lonely minstrel's name a household word forever—
> For there's magic in the strain that makes the bright tears glisten
> As we wake the dear old song again, the world draws breath to listen.

So it is easy to understand the allure of Federal Hill and Bardstown that draw thousands of travelers each year to this spot which holds hallowed memories. It is easy to explain why "My Old Kentucky Home" is known throughout the nation. And fitting it is that on the birth anniversary of Stephen Collins Foster, which is also the birth anniversary of these United States, we assemble here to do homage to the author of songs which have become the symphony of the Southland.

On the fiftieth anniversary of the signing of the Declaration of Independence, Foster was born. Father of the poet was presiding as master of ceremonies at a patriotic celebration near their home. As the cannon fired a salute of fifty guns at 12 o'clock, there was born the lad who was destined to launch a thousand songs and set millions to singing.

The people have been encouraged to celebrate this the one hundred sixty-fifth anniversary of the birth of freedom and make it a day on which is emphasized necessity for unity of the nation. Every democracy that has been born had its birth in the unity of the people, in their zeal for a government in which freedom and liberty would be ascendant.

The need of the nation in this critical hour is for a unity of mind and heart and will. A unity which recognizes the wisdom of the motto of Kentucky "United We Stand—Divided We Fall." We should unite behind the leadership of President Roosevelt—follow his direction, support him with enthusiastic patriotism as he steers the ship of state through treacherous waters.[4]

---

1. The governor made similar remarks at Bardstown on May 3, 1940, when he introduced Postmaster General James A. Farley on the occasion of the issuance of a Stephen Collins Foster commemorative stamp.

2. John Rowan (1773–1843), b. York, Pennsylvania. Member, Second Kentucky Constitutional Convention, 1799; secretary of state, 1804–1806; state representative, 1813–1817, 1822–1824; judge, Court of Appeals, 1819–1821; United States representative, 1807–1809; United States senator, 1825–1831. *Who Was Who in America, 1607–1896*, H:456.

3. Elvira Miller Slaughter (Mrs. W. H., Jr.) (1860–1937), b. Wytheville, Virginia. Came to Kentucky as a child and resided in Louisville. Poet, editor "The Tatler" column, *Louisville Times;* published "Songs of the Heart." John Wilson Townsend, *Kentucky in American Letters, 1784–1912* (Cedar Rapids, Iowa, 1913), 2:110-14, and letter, Paul Janensch, managing editor, *Louisville Times*, August 10, 1978.

4. The speech has been edited. Remarks pertaining to Stephen Decatur are in the speech from August 19, 1942, in this section. A discussion of the Declaration of Independence appears in the speech from July 4, 1941, in the World War II section.

JUSTICE BRANDEIS MEMORIAL SERVICE
Louisville / November 6, 1941

I AM glad to participate briefly in this memorial service in which tribute is paid to the memory of a great Kentuckian, Justice Louis D. Brandeis.[1] He reflected high credit upon his native state and rendered superior service to the nation. As a member of the Supreme Court of the United States, he humanized the law of the land. He interpreted the law with the clear and incisive mind of a great jurist. Yet the liberalism of his heart, the passion of his soul for social justice, was so rationalized as to breathe into the dead letter of the law the humanitarian impulses of one of the gigantic jurists of history.

With admirable modesty Justice Brandeis summed up his own career in one brief, cogent phrase when he said his philosophy of life was "high thinking and simple living."

No finer tribute may be phrased to this Kentuckian who so enriched jurisprudence than that voiced by President Roosevelt as, with sorrowful heart, he said on occasion of the death of Justice Brandeis, "The whole nation will bow in reverence to the memory of one whose life in the law was guided by the finest attributes of mind, heart, and soul."

As the herald of the concept of social justice, Mr. Brandeis was a pioneer. The cloakmakers strike of 1910, in which he acted as mediator, affecting 70,000 workers, stimulated his keen mind and responsive heart to formulate fundamental principles affecting employer and employee relationships that have in recent years been incorporated into the law of the nation.

When nominated for the Supreme Court by President Wilson, Justice Brandeis was bitterly assailed in the Senate and by presidents of the American Bar Association as a dangerous radical. Yet his serene spirit was unperturbed by that unjust vituperation. By his sound interpretation of the law, his unanswerable judicial opinions, he slowly won the respect of his traducers as he won the esteem and affection of the American people.

In connection with Justice Brandeis, there comes to mind an incident that I observed twenty-three years ago. It was in the winter of 1918 following the armistice which ended the last World War. I was on leave in Paris. In company with three other American officers, I visited the Louvre, one of the great art galleries of the world. Within the group was a young infantry captain who had a distinguished war record. He had served with one of the veteran divisions which had spent more days in the trenches than any other American outfit. Twice was he decorated for extraordinary heroism, miraculously escaping death when his command had been twice decimated. The frightful experiences of killing and butchery had left him a cynical, shellshocked, pathetic figure. All the finer qualities and nobler impulses seemed to have atrophied beneath the heavy barrages of the Western front. There was in the art gallery a magnificent painting of the Christ. In it was presented the artist's concept of the Christ as at the pool of Siloam he compassionately healed the maimed and crippled assembled about the pool. As my shellshocked friend intently examined that painting, it seemed to reawaken the humane impulses within him. His comment was, "Every time I see a picture of that fellow, he is helping somebody."

As one who extravagantly admired Justice Brandeis, you can understand why contemplation of his useful life, sublime character, and noble impulses recalled to my mind that incident in the art gallery in Paris. Certainly this great Kentuckian was always helping somebody. Whether it was as he encouraged and inspired an inconspicuous though worthy, ambitious boy, or whether in judicial opinion he humanized the law, emphasized human rights, made the law responsive to the needs of the humble folk, he was always helping somebody.

None more worthy of our veneration and esteem has been born in Kentucky. Through him our state made a great contribution to the nation. Though his useful life has ended, his successful career has been closed, he will live on in the hearts of those who love justice and courage. He will live through the centuries as a pioneer exponent of a rational liberalism. So it is on this sad, sweet, solemn occasion, with a sob in our voice and a tear in our eye, that we express gratitude to God for Justice Brandeis, for the fine man he was, the superb jurist that he was, the great American that he was. We shall be thankful always that he lived in a world which he made better. We shall always take pride in the fact that he was a Kentuckian. And we take a solemn, silent vow that we shall always revere his memory.

---

1. Louis Dembitz Brandeis (1856–1941), b. Louisville. Associate justice, United States Supreme Court, 1916–1939. Paul A. Freund, "Justice Brandeis," *Harvard Law Review* 70 (March 1957): 769-92.

SESQUICENTENNIAL YEAR
Frankfort / January 1, 1942

WHEREAS, in the year 1792, commencing on the first day of June of said year, the good people of the then District of Kentucky, after patient and prolonged effort and by their united action, won from the parent Commonwealth of Virginia fulfilment of the coveted right to establish a new and separate sovereign state of their own and, at the same time, gained admission into the Federal Union upon an equal footing with the original member states of that Union; and

WHEREAS, by the blessing of an all-wise God, both our state and the nation have survived the vicissitudes and crises of a century and a half and, in spite of all enmity and opposition, whether foreign or domestic, have enjoyed and still enjoy undiminished the rights and privileges of law-abiding freemen, and an unparalleled measure of material progress and prosperity; and

WHEREAS, it is fitting and proper that due recognition be accorded by our government and people to these momentous and memorable facts imbedded in the rugged structure of American character and history;

NOW, THEREFORE, I, Keen Johnson, Governor of the Commonwealth of Kentucky, in the name and by the authority of the good people of said Commonwealth, and in virtue of my office as Chief Executive, do hereby declare and proclaim that the year 1942 shall be observed by all the citizens and inhabitants of Kentucky as Kentucky's Sesquicentennial Year and that from time to time and at all seasonable times throughout said year it behooves our citizens, acting together and in unison with their relatives, friends, and guests from other parts of the world, to hold appropriate celebrations in their respective cities and communities in commemoration of the one hundred fiftieth anniversary of the birth and beginnings of Kentucky as a free and independent self-governing Commonwealth; and, on behalf of my fellow Kentuckians, both at home and abroad, I hereby extend a most cordial invitation to liberty-loving Americans and to free-born men and women everywhere to visit Kentucky during the sesquicentennial year, 1942, and to join with us in paying tribute and rendering homage to the broad-minded and farseeing patriots who, in times of stress and peril, not unlike those which confront our country now, were jealous and watchful of their individual rights and of their collective security, and laid deep and strong the fundamental principles of civil, political, and religious liberty, and the firm foundations of enlightened constitutional government, as set forth in the first and in all subsequent constitutions and Bills of Rights of Kentucky.

JOHN GILL WEISIGER MEMORIAL STATE PARK DEDICATION
Danville / April 20, 1942

WE are assembled today on this sacred spot to pay homage to the founders of this Commonwealth on the one hundred fiftieth anniversary of statehood. The splendid men and women whom I had the honor to appoint as members of the Kentucky Sesquicentennial Commission[1] started formulation of plans for a series of commemorative ceremonies two years ago. When we were plunged into war, it was realized that the program to celebrate the natal day of Kentucky should be modified. There were those who counseled that observance of the sesquicentennial be abandoned entirely. But the commission concluded, wisely I am convinced, that this significant year in our existence as a state should be commemorated. You know that it is not possible to put off one's birthday. And after all, Kentucky will not again have the distinction of celebrating her one hundred fiftieth anniversary.

The history of Kentucky is a colorful and inspiring epic. The Sesquicentennial Commission's activities should quicken our interest in the thrilling story of Kentucky's past and intensify in us today a determination to meet the duties of this critical hour with the same fortitude and courage as did those who created our Commonwealth. The story of Kentucky inspires us with a deep sense of duty, stimulates us to strive for high achievement. It increases our admiration for our ancestors, imparts to us the courage to face danger in these anxious days with the same calm fortitude as did these, the architects of Kentucky. Those Kentucky communities that organize a sesquicentennial celebration will experience a spiritual uplift. They will recapture something of the audacious disregard of their forebears for danger, their eagerness to fight for their freedom. As we read again the story of our state, we find that every battlefield where has flown the Stars and Stripes has been incarnadined with the blood of Kentuckians. Our brave young men will be inspired by the stirring story of Colonel William Logan Crittenden,[2] who, when about to be shot by Spaniards in Cuba, was ordered to be blindfolded and turn his back for the volley. He folded his arms across his chest and with defiant courage declared, "A Kentuckian kneels only to God and always dies facing the enemy."

It is particularly appropriate that the first sesquicentennial celebration should be held here in the historic and cultured city of Danville, where was framed Kentucky's first constitution at a constitutional convention which was here convoked April 19, 1792. It was the tenth of a series of conventions, the first of which was called to meet in Danville December 27, 1784, to discuss Kentucky's needs and plan for the eventual separation of Kentucky from Virginia. That first convention was called by Colonel Benjamin Logan,[3] the fearless warrior who had dashed through the gates of Logan's Fort to rescue a wounded comrade under a barrage of arrows from the Indians in 1775.

The Danville Chamber of Commerce and the Danville and Boyle County Historical Society are to be commended upon the initiative and effort which results in inaugurating the first sesquicentennial event here, where was born constitutional government west of the Allegheny mountains. As governor of the state whose first chief executive was the great soldier-statesman Isaac Shelby, I must express my grateful thanks to those citizens of Danville and Boyle County whose appreciation of the importance of appropriately marking this hallowed spot stimulated interest in the reconstruction of Constitution Square to here establish the Weisiger State Park. I am glad that, as the forty-sixth[4] governor of this state, I had the privilege of recommending to the legislature an appropriation for the restoration of Constitution Square.

We acknowledge with thanks the generous gift of Miss Emma Weisiger[5] who gave this property so that Constitution Square might be reproduced on the site where was cradled the Commonwealth. Miss Weisiger is the daughter of a beloved physician[6] who long resided in Danville. A monument is to be erected to the memory of the late John Gill Weisiger,[7] brother of Miss Weisiger. A plaque is to be put up which will forever proclaim the fact that Miss Weisiger donated this land. In due time, those requirements specified by the donor will be complied with.

Danville was designated as the seat of government west of the Alleghenies in 1785 by the Supreme Court of Virginia. The principal building erected, replica of which you see here today, was the pioneer courthouse. Here the conventions were held during the eight years of preparation and agitation for statehood for Kentucky. It was the building within which many important public meetings were convened, the gathering place of those early Kentucky leaders who fashioned the pattern of state government and established traditions which have influenced the lives of those to whom they bequeathed the responsibility for building a state upon the foundation they laid with clairvoyant wisdom.

A jail was also built here near the original courthouse within which were imprisoned those who transgressed the law.

A cupola-topped meetinghouse was built in which pioneer members of the Presbyterian denomination established a citadel of religious worship. Here radiated the blessed influence of the gospel as religion was recognized as an essential in the building of a new civilization. Here Dr. David Rice[8] was the dominant personality in the early work of the church. It was in his home here in Danville that Transylvania College, chartered in 1781, was actually founded in 1784 as the first seat of learning west of the Allegheny mountains. The Transylvania Presbytery, organized by Dr. Rice under authority of the Hanover (Virginia) Presbytery, held its first sessions in the courthouse.

Judge Samuel McDowell,[9] of the district court, served as president of the series of conventions which culminated in statehood for Kentucky and the drafting of the first constitution. Judge McDowell was a dominant figure in the early life of Danville. Dr. Ephraim McDowell, gifted pioneer surgeon, whose home across the street is a state shrine, was the sixth son and ninth child of Judge Samuel McDowell. Descendants of Judge McDowell have played a prominent role in the history of Kentucky. I am informed that a great, great, great, great granddaughter, Miss Louise McDowell,[10] is participating today in these ceremonies.

The first Kentucky constitution was a unique document. It was without precedent as a model for democratic government. It reflected the wisdom of those hardy frontiersmen, refined by hardships and danger. It was the first document of this character which eliminated the provision that only property owners should have the right to vote. It provided that all free men over twenty-one years of age should have the right and duty to vote. It was highly significant that those hardy, heroic pioneers were the pioneer exponents of the fundamental principle of manhood suffrage. The political ideal which they incorporated in their first constitution applied the principle that all men are free and equal. That ideal developed on the frontier where equality of men was established by grim circumstances. They were equal in the hardships shared, the privations suffered. As the defenders of Kentucky were hastily assembled to repel the attack of hostile Indians, they faced equal danger. There was more concern as to how straight a man could shoot than there was about the property he owned. So it was out of that equality of sacrifice on the frontier that there was born the conviction that all free men should vote. And that privilege was incorporated in the constitution as the pioneer trailblazers blazed new trails in the realm of government.

The governor and senators were elected by a college of electors. The representatives were elected by the people. Judges of the supreme court and also of the lower courts were nominated by the senate and appointed by the governor, and held office during good behavior. So, while the selection of public officials by direct vote of the people was still curtailed, the right of every man to vote was a significant espousal of a vital principle of democracy. And here it was, on this consecrated spot, that this political ideal was born. It is an ideal which has permeated the nation and been subsequently accepted from ocean to ocean.

So this state shrine, which we today dedicate in grateful remembrance of those who here wrought great deeds of statecraft, also marks the site of the birth of the basic principle of our national government which placed the ballot in the hand of every man and entrusted the destiny of the nation to the composite judgment of its citizens. I am glad we did not longer delay erecting here this monument which will stand through the years as a memorial to the practical vision of those pioneer statesmen who here on the outpost of civilization created the Commonwealth of Kentucky.

It is a proud privilege today to dedicate Constitution Square as a state shrine; to set it apart as one of the sacred spots in our state where transpired an important episode in our early history. We dedicate this shrine to the memory of John Gill Weisiger, brother of the donor of the land on which Constitution Square was laid out. We dedicate Constitution Square as a symbol of constitutional government and the democratic ideal. We dedicate this state park as a perpetual memento of the conspicuous service here performed by those who charted the course of our Commonwealth.

We dedicate Constitution Square to the service of our state so that as Kentuckians visit here, they may be inspired to emulate the exalted ideal of public service here demonstrated a century and a half ago. We dedicate Constitution Square as a monument to Kentucky's illustrious past, confident that it will kindle in us the determination to make Kentucky's present and future worthy of those who here laid the foundation upon which we have builded. We dedicate this shrine as a monument to the piety of those pioneers who here established the church of God, recognizing their dependence upon divine guidance. We dedicate this shrine as a memorial to the simple virtues so pronounced in the pioneer citizens, as we honor their dauntless daring, their disregard of danger, their defiance of hardship, their stalwart strength of character, their love of Kentucky, and their determination to obtain the status of statehood for her.

Our pride in Kentucky is intensified by the fact that our sons today, descendants of our pioneer progenitors, are fighting as valiantly for the democratic ideal on the battlefields of the world as Kentuckians fought 150 years ago. Kentuckians are fighting the yellow men today with courage comparable to that of their forebears who with flintlock fought the red men of the forest.

So, as we today dedicate Weisiger State Park to the future inspiration of Kentuckians, we also rededicate ourselves to the challenging task of solving Kentucky's problems of the present. In so doing, we shall make a contribution which will insure that Kentucky's future shall be as glorious as has been her past, adding new luster to the name and fame of Kentucky.

Our hearts are filled with anxiety as we turn from contemplation of the past and consider the uncertainties of the future. The infant Republic which accepted Kentucky into statehood a century and a half ago has become the greatest democracy that has arisen in history.

Ruthless dictators have perfected powerful armies and set out on the unholy mission of conquering the democracies of the world. It is the most sinister threat with which we have been confronted. If we lose this war, we lose every right and privilege that we cherish. We would become vassals of autocratic rulers whose chief concern would be to wrest from us our resources for the enrichment of their autocratic kingdoms. We will not submit to that infamous fate. We can escape that fate only by crushing those that seek to crush us. We must prepare quickly for the decisive struggle. We must willingly throw every resource into this war of survival, prepare ourselves to conquer when comes the Waterloo of the world.

By an act of the first Kentucky legislature, December 20, 1792, Kentucky's state seal was ordered "to be engraved with the device: two friends embracing with the name of the state over their heads and around them the motto, 'United We Stand, Divided We Fall.' " The necessities of those pioneer days had so welded together the interests and sympathies of the people that the state seal and motto were strikingly appropriate.

The distilled wisdom of the ages is expressed in that motto. In these anxious days it should be engraved upon the heart of every Kentuckian. We must mobilize the mind and the heart and the will of Kentuckians to make the maximum contribution to ultimate victory. There have been periods in our history when there has been division in our people. We have learned that united we stand, divided we falter. In this critical hour, it is vital that Kentucky and the nation stand united against the foes that seek to enslave us. So as we dedicate this state park, it is especially opportune that we rededicate ourselves to devotion to the American ideal; reaffirm our allegiance to the flag of the republic; and, as did the signers of the Declaration of Independence, "mutually pledge to each other our lives, our fortunes, and our sacred honor."[11]

---

1. The commission was created by the 1938 legislature. The members were appointed in 1940 and are named in the governor's speech of December 27, 1942, ending the sesquicentennial year. They threatened to resign in 1941 because of the lack of funds. Johnson declined to transfer money from his emergency funds and said that the 1942 legislature should provide the funds. The Junior Chamber of Commerce provided the money. Johnson praised the chamber and said, "The more young men you have out soliciting dollars, the more enthusiasm you will have for the program." *Lexington Herald*, July 27, 1941.

2. William Logan Crittenden, second son of Henry and grandson of John. Graduate, United States Military Academy; officer in war with Mexico; captured and shot in Lopez expedition against Cuba. Green, *Historic Families of Kentucky*, p. 249.

3. Benjamin Logan, b. Virginia. To Kentucky in 1775. Indian fighter, colonel. Member, First Constitutional Convention, 1792; member, Second Constitutional Convention, 1799, representing Shelby County. Died at an advanced age. *Biographical Encyclopedia of Kentucky*, p. 243.

4. Johnson was the forty-second governor.

5. Emma Weisiger (1859–1952), b. Danville. Wealthy real estate owner. Graduate of Caldwell College, forerunner of Women's Division of Centre College, 1876. *Danville Advocate-Messenger*, February 13, 1952. She donated the land in 1937.

6. John Rochester (Ross) Weisiger (1819–1873), b. Danville. Son of Dr. Joseph Weisiger. Acquired land and real estate in Danville and Boyle County. Calvin Morgan Fackler, *Early Days in Danville* (Louisville, 1941), pp. 218-19, and letter, John R. May, director, Grace Doherty Library, Centre College, September 18, 1978.

7. John Gill Weisiger (1849–1923), b. Danville. Farmer. Wealthy real estate owner. *Danville Advocate-Messenger*, September 3, 1923.

8. David Rice (1733–1816), b. Hanover County, Virginia. Came to Kentucky in 1783. Clergyman. *Biographical Encyclopedia of Kentucky*, p. 551.

9. Samuel McDowell (1735–1817), b. Pennsylvania. Moved to Virginia and progenitor of Kentucky branch. Eldest son of John, grandson of Ephraim of Londonderry, Ireland. Representative, House of Burgesses; member, Second Convention, 1776; judge, first district court held in Kentucky, 1783; judge, first county court held in Kentucky, 1786; president, Kentucky Constitutional Convention, 1792. Green, *Historic Families of Kentucky*, pp. 31-39.

10. Louise McDowell (1903–), b. Maysville. Editor-in-chief, *Book of Knowl-*

edge, 1934–1960. Resided in New York; resides Long Branch, N.J. Telephone interview, Keith McDowell, nephew, Fair Haven, N.J., September 22, 1978.

11. The speech has been edited. Remarks on Bataan appear in the speech from September 15, 1942, in the World War II section.

FLAG DAY
Murray / June 14, 1942

It is indeed fitting that citizenship of this proud, powerful nation should pause on one designated day within the year to pay tribute to the flag under which this country has attained a position of commanding preeminence in the world.[1]

That flag to which we today pay homage, to which we pledge anew our fealty, is symbolic of a nation that has attained the pinnacle of power and greatness through the sacrificial devotion of forebears who made of that inanimate banner the ensign that has come to be acclaimed throughout the world as the flag of freedom, under which liberty has come to full fruition in government.

The first flag, fashioned by the patriotic fingers of Betsy Ross, was viewed by the world as the radical banner of rebellious colonists. It was an impotent symbol, suggesting only the hopes and aspirations of those courageous men and women who had the audacity to assert their independence. There was no reverence or respect for that flag beyond the confines of the revolting colonies. But that infant Republic, born amid the uncertainties of revolt, cradled in adversity and hardship, whose only lullaby was the roar of cannon and the rattle of musketry, survived the crucial struggle, established its independence. And the flag under which those continental soldiers fought became the symbol of a new nation. That flag, sanctified with the blood of gallant men who had followed it to heroic death and glorious victory, came to command respect of other peoples as it was revered by those who had fought with rare fortitude to keep it unsullied.

With succeeding years, the accomplishments of those over whom floated the flag of freedom elicited increased esteem of the world. That nation grew in power and prestige as there was worked out on this continent an experiment in government unique in the annals of history. The flag became the star-flecked scepter, representative of a liberty-loving people within a nation where the fierce fires of freedom burned in the hearts of her patriots.

That impotent standard, first unfurled as the radical ensign of revolting colonists, has within the years attained supremacy in that collection of brilliant hued banners symbolic of the nations of the world. That flag which was the standard of a few hundred thousand colonists, scattered along the Atlantic seaboard, flies today over that vast domain whose western border is laved by the Pacific Ocean. That flag is enshrined in the hearts of 130 million people.

While the valor of American men and the fortitude of American women have invested that meaningless symbol of 1775 with a significance that is positive and potent through military conquest, the sanity of the citizenship over which Old Glory flies has restrained the nation from a militaristic policy. This nation has attained a material greatness without parallel because the ideals of those who first fought for that flag have remained regnant in the hearts of those who have succeeded them.

That flag which we today revere has become the symbol of peace and freedom. That nation over which it floats has come to be regarded as the land of opportunity, the haven where lowly birth and humble origin lays not its restraining inhibition upon genius, raises no interdiction against successful achievement of those possessed of the innate qualities of character and ability essential to achievement.

It is remarkable that this nation whose flag has ever been invincible, the flag which has emerged triumphant from every war into which it has been carried, has refrained from a policy of military conquest. Such has not been the inclination of other nations that have arisen and fallen. Military triumph has whetted appetites for acquisition of new territory, expansion of domain, attainment of new glory on the gory fields of battle.

But the Stars and Stripes has preferred to wave over a people that regard the triumphs of peace as preferable to victory by war. And under this same sane philosophy there has been brought into being a social order, a civilization that has reached the loftiest heights of government, amassed the greatest wealth, stimulated scientific and inventive genius to achievements which have enhanced the happiness of mankind, accelerated the pace of human progress.

It is a patriotic duty that we love and honor the flag as did our audacious ancestors, that we defend its honor with our lives as American men have done on hundreds of battlefields when those ideals of which it is the silent, yet expressive, symbol are imperiled.

---

1. Each year Johnson issued a proclamation designating June 14 as Flag Day. He issued a tribute to Old Glory in December 1942 in connection with a flag

pilgrimage in which the wife of each governor sewed a star on a flag as it was sent from state to state. *State Journal*, December 12, 1942. Each spring he proclaimed a Sunday in May as "I Am an American Day." He proclaimed September 14, 1943, as "Star Spangled Banner Day" in commemoration of the writing of the national anthem by Francis Scott Key 129 years earlier.

ANNIVERSARY OF HARRODSBURG
Harrodsburg / June 16, 1942

IT is with great pride that I, as governor of Kentucky, participate with the citizenship of this patriotic community in honoring all Mercer County men in the armed forces and in observance of the one hundred sixty-eighth anniversary of the founding of Harrodsburg in this, the Sesquicentennial Year of Kentucky. Here was established the first permanent settlement on the western frontier. That outpost became the first citadel of civilization west of the Allegheny Mountains.

George Rogers Clark, military genius of the western frontier, first visited Kentucky in 1775 as a surveyor when he was only twenty-three years old. His iron will and good judgment so impressed the pioneers at Harrodsburg that he was placed in command of the militia.

Clark convinced Governor Patrick Henry of Virginia that 500 pounds of powder should be provided to aid in protecting the settlements against Indians. Clark and Gabriel John Jones,[1] delegates to the Virginia Assembly, supplied the leadership that resulted in the creation of Kentucky County on December 7, 1776. That significant event occured exactly 165 years before the treacherous, infamous attack on Pearl Harbor.

George Rogers Clark explained to Governor Henry that the British were inciting the Indians to repeated attacks on the Kentucky frontier. On January 2, 1778, Clark received from Governor Henry private instructions to organize and lead a campaign to seize the northwest territory as a protection to Kentucky.

Here at Harrodsburg plans for that amazing military maneuver were perfected. Clark assembled his command at the Falls of the Ohio and set out on the perilous undertaking June 24, 1778. The astounding story of the successful capture of Kaskaskia and Vincennes prompted Bancroft,[2] the historian, to record that "the valor of the actors, their fidelity to one another, the seeming feebleness of their means and the great results of their hardihood, remains forever memorable in the history of the world."

On February 5, 1779, Clark and his little army of 170 men, most of them Kentucky frontiersmen, left Kaskaskia to march on Vincennes, a distance of 170 miles through uncharted country, across icy streams in midwinter. Bowman's[3] diary, under date of February 23, records that Clark's command "waded through water breast high."

The British commander at Vincennes, Colonel Hamilton,[4] was completely surprised and surrendered the fort without resistance February 25, 1779. The American flag was run up and the name of the fort changed to Fort Henry in honor of the Virginia governor.

The campaign added to the infant Republic a vast empire from which was later carved the states of Ohio, Indiana, Illinois, Michigan, Wisconsin, and a portion of Minnesota.

Those men who waded the ice cold water to follow Clark and seize Vincennes were the forebears of the gallant young men from Harrodsburg who fought with heroic valor under General MacArthur at Bataan and Corregidor. As we pay tribute to the fortitude of Colonel Clark and his band on this important anniversary, we lift our voices in gratitude for the fact that the courage of Clark and his comrades has been transmitted through succeeding generations of Mercer countians and that boys from this pioneer community have battled with the same audacious bravery to protect and preserve that liberty which Clark's men fought to procure for us.

The history of Kentucky is a colorful and inspiring epic. And there is no more glorious chapter than the story of Harrodsburg and its rich contribution to this Commonwealth.

The story of Kentucky inspires us with a deep sense of duty, stimulates us to high achievement. We today combine ceremonies which pay tribute to those who have gone before with an expression of homage to the Mercer County men of today who have thrilled us with their dauntless courage and to all Mercer countians in the armed forces. In so doing we shall recapture something of the audacious disregard of their forebears for danger, just as these sons of yours fought against the Japs on Bataan with a valor worthy of their brave pioneer progenitors.

So it is not only to the heroes who fought with Colonel Clark, our deceased heroes to whom we owe so much, that we pay tribute, but to the living heroes of Harrodsburg who have covered themselves with glory, that we pay grateful homage today. They will live forever. We shall draw inspiration from their sublime devotion to a lost cause. They will stand out in future history as a brilliant example of young Kentuckians who served their country with the last full measure of sacrificial service.

We shall have another public ceremony in Harrodsburg some day—and may God hasten the hour. That ceremony will be staged when these men of MacArthur's come home. What a happy day it will be when these modest, peace-loving heroes of Harrodsburg may again be taken to the hearts of their loved ones. What a heartwarming welcome it will be when the united nations triumph over the despots and these gallant men return to the homes they so nobly defended. What a happy day—when Hitler shall have been licked and the Rising Sun shall have gone into eclipse.

Until that day these, the men of whom we are so proud, will always be in our hearts. Our prayers will ascend for them daily. And we shall redouble our efforts to hasten the triumphant hour when freedom's foes shall have been crushed, when Old Glory is again unfurled over Corregidor and right once more is regnant in the world.[5]

---

1. Gabriel John Jones (1724–1806), b. Williamsburg, Virginia. Member, Virginia House of Burgesses, 1783; member, Virginia Conference to ratify the United States Constitution, 1788. *Who Was Who in America, 1607–1896,* H:284.

2. George Bancroft (1800–1891), b. Worcester, Massachusetts. Historian. Secretary of the navy, 1845–1846. Established United States Naval Academy, Annapolis. *Webster's Biographical Dictionary*, p. 97.

3. John Bowman, Indian fighter. Came from Virginia with 100 militiamen to Logan's Station (Stanford). Expedition against Shawnees, Battle of Old Chillicothe, 1779. Wallis and Tapp, *A Sesquicentennial History of Kentucky*, 1:95, 111.

4. Henry Hamilton (d. 1796), b. England. British army colonel. Captured at Vincennes, exchanged, later held administrative positions. *Who Was Who in America, 1607–1896*, H:230.

5. The speech has been edited. Remarks on Bataan are in the speech from September 15, 1942, in the World War II section.

ANNIVERSARY OF THE BATTLE OF BLUE LICKS

Blue Licks State Park / August 19, 1942

IT is with genuine joy that I join you here today at this historic Kentucky shrine to pay homage to the gallant pioneer forebears who were killed in the tragic battle of Blue Licks. I congratulate you whose initiative resulted in establishing here a shrine in commemoration of the valor of those whose blood incarnadined this sacred spot.

Observance of the Kentucky Sesquicentennial would be incomplete without ceremonies that appropriately memorialize the courageous frontier figures who here lost their lives as they sought to punish the Indian army which had invaded Kentucky. You who appreciate the significance of Blue Licks are to be commended that you have inaugurated the custom of assembling here on each anniversary to pay tribute to the memory of the gallant men who here lost their lives as they sought to make the Kentucky settlements secure and safe from savages of the forest. So it is today that we observe the one hundred sixtieth anniversary of the battle of Blue Licks in this the one hundred fiftieth anniversary of Kentucky's admittance to the Union as a state.

We had hoped that there might be an observance of the Kentucky Sesquicentennial which would be worthy of her glorious history. The splendid Kentuckians whom I had the honor to appoint as members of the Sesquicentennial Commission started formulating plans for a series of commemorative ceremonies two years ago. When we were plunged into war, it was realized that the program to celebrate the natal day of Kentucky should be modified. Yet despite adversities created by the war, the one hundred fiftieth anniversary of statehood has been appropriately observed. I want to express my appreciation for the intelligent, consecrated services of the Sesquicentennial Commission and thank each member for their laudable contribution to this worthy activity.

While it was unfortunate that the war interfered with plans for the sesquicentennial observance, as our attention has been focused upon Kentucky's colorful history, we have gained inspiration which is helpful as we face the sacrifices demanded of us by the present war. The sesquicentennial has quickened our interest in the thrilling story of Kentucky's past and intensified our determination to meet the duties of this critical hour with the same fortitude as did those who created our Commonwealth.

The story of Kentucky inspires us with a deep sense of duty, stimulates us to strive for high achievement. It increases our admiration for our ancestors, imparts to us the courage to face danger in these anxious days with the same courage as did those who fought and fell at Blue Licks on that fateful day 160 years ago. Those Kentucky communities in which a sesquicentennial celebration has been held have experienced a spiritual uplift. As we read again the story of our state, we recapture something of the audacious disregard of our forebears for danger, their eagerness to fight for freedom.

Free speech is one of the rights and privileges we cherish, but we can best protect it if we do not abuse it. When the nation was once confronted by a situation not unlike that which now causes us concern, Stephen Decatur[1] uttered a historic statement which should be the attitude of every American today. In proposing a toast Decatur said, "Our country—in her intercourse with foreign nations may she ever be right—but right or wrong—our country." Freedom of speech has been a shield for speech and action that are subversive to the ideals of our country. It is proper that we become intolerant of the abuse of freedom of speech by such treasonous persons as the infamous William Dudley Pelley.[2]

We as a people are jealous of our right to criticize those in public authority. There are hypercritical fault-finders who, in the exercise of free speech, impose cruel handicaps upon those who have the responsibility of public leadership. These captious critics pose as experts on everything. They regard themselves as foreordained to undermine confidence in public leaders. They become skilled as rocking chair strategists, dispensing advice based on misinformation.

There are those who clamor daily for a Second Front. Invasion of countries occupied by Germans so as to divert troops from the Russian front and relieve hard-pressed Russia is certainly much to be desired. The United Nations War Council is a better judge of whether we are prepared to sustain a Second Front than the critics who constantly clamor for such action. To launch an invasion before we are prepared would precipitate such a tragedy as here occurred at the Battle of Blue Licks.

You students of Kentucky history recall that at daybreak August 15, 1782, an army of four hundred British and Indians, commanded by the crafty Simon Girty,[3] attacked Bryan's Station. The surprise assault was repulsed. The Indians feared that reinforcements would come to the aid of the besieged force and withdrew in the night. News of the attack reached other settlements and armed men hastened to Bryan's Station. By night 182 horsemen had assembled. It was decided to give pursuit to the Indians without waiting for the arrival of expected reinforcements under Colonel Logan. The Indians had retreated leisurely, purposely leaving a trail easily followed, which Colonel Boone called "danger signs."

The pursuing party, led by Colonel John Todd,[4] came in sight of the enemy near Blue Licks on the morning of August 19. They halted and held a council of war. The Indians had crossed the Licking River and were believed to be planning an ambuscade. Colonel Boone, familiar with Indian tactics, urged that they wait until Colonel Logan and his troops arrived. His counsel would have probably prevailed had it not been for the reckless daring of one man.

Major McGary,[5] consumed by hatred for the Indians because a son had been killed by them, suddenly uttered a defiant cry and "spurred his horse into the stream, waved his hat over his head and shouted,'Let all who are not cowards follow me.' " The action produced an electrical effect. The horsemen dashed into the river, each trying to be foremost. The foot soldiers mingled with them in a disordered effort to cross the stream. The reckless Kentuckians struggled across the ford and charged up the riverbank. They re-formed ranks and advanced. As they approached the spot which Boone warned was favorable to an ambuscade, they found themselves exposed to deadly fire from a hidden foe. Officers rallied their men and fought gallantly against overwhelming odds. Soon their ranks were decimated, many slain. In a few minutes about seventy brave Kentuckians had fallen, twelve wounded and seven captured. Among the slain was Colonel John Todd, one of the most talented lawyers and fearless officers among the pioneers. Other leaders who fell were Colonel Trigg, Majors Harlan, and McBride and Boone's son.[6] The pick of the flock on the frontier had been wiped out. Colonel Logan arrived later with strong reinforcements. But the Indians had crossed the Ohio, and nothing remained except to bury the dead here to make hallowed this spot. The rash act of one man precipitated a needless tragedy.

The bloody incident supplies an apt illustration of what might happen should the high command of the united nations yield to the clamor of the rocking chair strategist for the immediate opening of a Second Front. A decision of such moment should be made by military leaders and they should reach that decision without nagging from impatient, imprudent critics. It requires eighteen tons of shipping to transport one soldier to a foreign battlefield together with supplies and arms to sustain him. It requires two tons of shipping to maintain the movement of essential war munitions. We may be sure that a Second Front will be established as soon as such can be done with reasonable assurance of success. Until then the greatest service that can be rendered by captious critics is to keep quiet.

The threat from Berlin and Tokyo presents the supreme challenge to Kentuckians and Americans. We must exert every energy, expend every resource to crush those that seek to destroy us. We must be worthy sons and daughters of our valiant Kentucky pioneer ancestry. We must fight with the same courage as did Boone and Todd and their comrades in the ill-fated battle of Blue Licks—fight for the preservation of the state and nation they handed to us as a land of liberty. We must demonstrate that the virility and valor of the frontier have been transmitted through the generations that have come and gone in the last century and a half.[7]

---

1. Stephen Decatur (1779–1820), b. Sinepuxent, Maryland. Naval officer; killed in a duel. *Webster's Biographical Dictionary*, p. 399. Decatur said, "Our country! In her intercourse with foreign nations may she always be in the right; but our country, right or wrong." *Bartlett's Familiar Quotations*, 14th ed. (Boston, 1968), p. 456.

2. William Dudley Pelley (1890–1965), b. Lynn, Massachusetts. Editor, pub-

lisher. Founder of Silver Legion of America (Silver Shirts) 1933. *Who's Who in America, 1942–1943* (Chicago, 1943), 21:1730, and *New York Times Obituaries, 1858–1968* (New York, 1970), p. 793.

3. Simon Girty (1741–1814). Rescued Simon Kenton from the Indians, Zanesville, Ohio, in 1778. *Biographical Encyclopedia of Kentucky*, p. 781.

4. John Todd (?–1782), b. Pennsylvania. To Kentucky in 1775. In 1780 was a delegate to the legislature of Virginia from the County of Kentucky. Ibid., p. 183.

5. Hugh McGary. Entered Kentucky from the Clinch Settlements with Daniel Boone; settled in Harrodsburg, 1776–1777. Wallis and Tapp, *A Sesquicentennial History of Kentucky*, 1:128-29.

6. Stephen Trigg (?–1782), b. Virginia. To Kentucky in 1779. Delegate, Virginia Assembly, 1775, 1780. Commanded Fort Harrodsburg, 1782. Green, *Historic Families of Kentucky*, pp. 200-201.

Silas Harlan (1752–1782), b. Virginia. To Kentucky in 1774. *Biographical Encyclopedia of Kentucky*, p. 107.

William McBride (?–1782). Wallis and Tapp, *A Sesquicentennial History of Kentucky*, 1:129-30.

Isaac Boone (?–1782). Son of Daniel. *Biographical Encyclopedia of Kentucky*, p. 488.

7. The speech has been edited. Parts appear in speeches from April 20, 1942, in this section, and from June 5, 1942, in the World War II section.

CELEBRATION OF KENTUCKY'S SESQUICENTENNIAL
Louisville / September 18, 1942

AS we approach the end of a series of community programs, the purpose of which has been to commemorate appropriately the one hundred fiftieth anniversary of Kentucky's admittance to the Union as the fifteenth state, I want to avail myself of this opportunity to thank Judge Samuel M. Wilson[1] and those who have served on the Kentucky Sesquicentennial Commission for the admirable service they have performed under adverse conditions.

Kentucky's sesquicentennial has been observed against a backdrop of war. The splendid men and women whom I had the honor to appoint as members of the Sesquicentennial Commission had envisioned plans for an observance of Kentucky's one hundred fiftieth birthday that would be worthy of the significant event. When we were plunged into war, it was realized that the program in honor of the natal day of the Commonwealth should be modified.

There have been numerous local celebrations throughout the state that have been worthy of the high purpose for which they were held. The history of Kentucky is a colorful and inspiring epic. The sesquicentennial observances have quickened our interest in the thrilling story of Kentucky's past and intensified in us a determination to meet the duties of these dark days with the same fortitude and courage as did those who created this Commonwealth. Those communities which organized a sesquicentennial celebration experienced a spiritual uplift. They recaptured something of the audacious disregard of their forebears for danger, their eagerness to fight for liberty, their cheerful acceptance of hardship and sacrifice in order to establish here the first citadel of freedom west of the Allegheny Mountains.

In all the wars of the Republic, Kentuckians have been in the forefront from the firing of the first gun to the last day of battle. In the beginning they came into the great meadow fighting Indians, and it was only a short step from redskins to scarlet-coated Britishers. Our first governor, Isaac Shelby, won his spurs in the Revolutionary War as one of the heroes of the battles of King's Mountain and Point Pleasant. It was his gallantry in the initial struggle for liberty that caused the people of Kentucky to name him as their first chief executive.

Henry Clay, perhaps the greatest Kentuckian in our history, dominated the War of 1812 and was sent to Ghent to negotiate the treaty of peace. Shelby was so wrought up over this second struggle with England that he left the gubernatorial chair at Frankfort, where he was serving for the second time, to again draw his sword in defense of his country. He did not go alone; thousands of Kentuckians followed him including that great old Indian fighter Green Clay, sire of the Lion of White Hall, Cassius Marcellus Clay, who was only two years old at the time.[2]

In the Mexican War of 1847, Kentuckians cluttered up the battlefield with their bodies. Too many other sons of the dark and bloody ground gave their lives at the battle of Buena Vista. Jefferson Davis and John Hunt Morgan got their first baptism of war in Mexico, and Old Rough and Ready, Zachary Taylor, who spent his boyhood in Jefferson County and who is the only president buried in Kentucky soil, went over the top of the Mexican General Santa Anna to the White House.[3]

It was in memory of young Clay, McKee, and a few others that Colonel Theodore O'Hara wrote at Frankfort,[4] perhaps sitting against Daniel Boone's monument and gazing out across the Benson hills and down at the river winding at his feet, one of the most famous war elegies in the world, "The Bivouac of the Dead," the greatest single poem written by a Kentucky hand.

In the War Between the States—which we best remember as the brothers' war because it was Kentucky brother against Kentucky brother—

the state declared its neutrality almost at the outset. Perhaps the definition of that neutrality is best symbolized in our giving to the North one of our greatest sons, Abraham Lincoln, and to the South, one of our greatest sons, Jefferson Davis, because that was the kind of neutrality it was. Both armies were filled with Kentucky Breckinridges, Buckners, Clays, Crittendens, Helms, Johnsons, Powells, Todds, and many other families just as able.[5] Like the good Kentuckians they were, they faced each other across the rock fences, from behind trees, and any other cover they could find and shot each others' ears off.

One of the great battles of the war was fought in Kentucky: Perryville. Certainly it was the biggest battle ever waged in this state. There boys on both sides fell fighting gallantly as Kentuckians have always fought and will always fight, and there many of them lie buried.

Into that struggle Kentucky poured her best, which included John C. Breckinridge, Mr. Davis's secretary of war when Grant so graciously received Marse Robert's[6] sword at Appomattox. Another Kentuckian, Albert Sydney Johnston,[7] born in Mason County, was one of the great leaders of the South, killed at Shiloh just as he was coming into the full flower of his military genius. Nor should we forget John Hunt Morgan, who was in Mexico on his twenty-first birthday fighting for the Stars and Stripes. All over our own and adjoining states, he fought under the folds of that finally conquered banner, the Stars and Bars, until he was brutally killed in a little town in Tennessee early one morning when he was trying to make his escape through a garden. To the North, Morgan is the rebel raider; but to the state that nurtured him, loved him, and knew him best, he will always live in our hearts as the Thunderbolt of the Confederacy.

General Morgan's brother-in-law, General Basil W. Duke,[8] who succeeded to his old command, should not be forgotten. I know he will not be forgotten in Louisville where he lived long and honorably after the war.

After Appomattox came thirty-three years of blessed peace. But Kentuckians were growing restless, oiling up the old blunderbuss and wondering why they couldn't go into action again. They didn't have long to wait; the Maine was sunk in Havana harbor and the country went wild with the spirit of war. The time was 1898. We were fighting the Spaniards with the Cubans' help. The first Roosevelt organized the Rough Riders, and as many Kentuckians joined him as he would take. Those that were left out enlisted with the Louisville Legion whose distinguished leader was that fine Confederate soldier, General John Breckinridge Castleman,[9] who sat his horse in a fashion that reminded Kentuckians only of Morgan. The Kentucky mountain boys were assembled in the Fourth Kentucky Regiment, and they languished for action in Lexington while the little war went merrily on. At the end they were no nearer the battlefield than

Alabama, so they cussed their luck and came home. It didn't amount to much, but a great many fine young Kentuckians died, some on the battlefield but more in the hospitals.

Kentuckians in World War I again occupied high places from the outset; and at the end, Henry T. Allen of Sharpsburg, who for a time commanded my division, the eighty-ninth, was in supreme command of the AEF in the Rhineland. General George B. Duncan of Lexington served with great distinction. Admiral Hugh Rodman of Frankfort was a mighty sea dog, hero of several major engagements. And there were others, many others, like Willie Sandlin, Sergeant Woodfill, and Jesse Creech, whose exploits were splashed over front pages from one end of the country to the other.[10]

Already in this war names of Kentuckians are being heralded in newspaper dispatches because of deeds of daring in the air, on the sea, and on the land. Company D of the 192d Tank Batallion fought gallantly on Bataan and was decreed by destiny to be the first armored force to fight in this war under the American flag. While we are anxious because of uncertainty of their fate, we are proud of their valor, proud of the fact that they were worthy battle comrades of the heroic MacArthur. Only in recent days we have been thrilled by the audacious daring of Captain George Kiser of Somerset and Lieutenant Dick Starks of Midway,[11] who triumphed over Jap fighters in stirring battles above the clouds. But time does not permit a calling of the complete roll. It exalts our spirits as there is demonstrated the fact that young Kentuckians of today are worthy of the fine traditions of the frontier, that they fight with the same dauntless courage as did their forebears—fight to preserve and protect the heritage of freedom of which we have been the happy beneficiaries for a century and a half.

Kentucky's contribution to the wars of the Republic is a record of proud patriotism. It is a glorious record, worthy of our first 150 years of statehood. This happy occasion is one of the last of a long list of dinners given in honor of our birthday. I congratulate the Louisville Board of Trade, the Louisville Sesquicentennial Association, the *Courier-Journal* and *Times* upon the successful sponsorship of this event. It was arranged to remind our people again that 150 years ago Kentucky joined the Union and has never left and never will. We are proud of our part in all the wars. But we are prouder of our progress in peace. We all fervently hope that this will be the last war in which our people will be called to engage. We want it to end quickly. We shall individually and collectively endeavor to hasten the day when comes the Waterloo of the world and the armies of freedom triumph. Then will the Stars and Stripes again be unfurled over Corregidor as vindication of the brave Kentuckians who died there, and right shall again become regnant in the world.[12]

---

1. Samuel M. Wilson (1871–1946), b. Louisville. Judge, Lexington. Chairman, Sesquicentennial Commission. Attorney, historian, writer. *Who's Who in Kentucky, 1936,* p. 439, and Louisville *Courier-Journal,* October 10, 1946.

2. Green Clay (1757–1826), b. Virginia. General, surveyor, farmer. Member, Virginia Convention, which ratified Constitution of the United States, 1789. *Biographical Encyclopedia of Kentucky,* p. 353.

Cassius Marcellus Clay (1810–1903), b. Madison County. Abolitionist. State representative, Madison County, 1835–1839, and Fayette County, 1840–1842. Minister to Russia, 1861–1869. Ibid., pp. 353-54.

3. John Hunt Morgan (1825–1864), b. Huntsville, Alabama. Civil War general. Ibid., p. 714.

Antonio Lopez de Santa Anna (1795–1876). President, Mexico. General of the Army. *Who Was Who in America, 1607–1896,* H: 463.

4. William Robertson McKee (1790–1847), b. Garrard County. Colonel, killed at Buena Vista, Mexican War; fought in War of 1812; graduate, United States Military Academy. State representative, 1806–1808, 1818–1820; United States representative, 1809–1817. *Biographical Encyclopedia of Kentucky,* p. 275, and Collins, *History of Kentucky, 1873,* 2:687.

Theodore O'Hara (1820–1867), b. Danville. Confederate colonel; captain, United States Army. Poet. Collins, *History of Kentucky, 1873,* 2:445.

5. Simon Bolivar Buckner (1823–1914), b. Munfordville. Confederate general. Governor, 1887–1891. Son of Aylette Hartswell Buckner who entered Kentucky at age eleven from Albemarle County, Virginia, in 1803. *Who Was Who in America, 1897–1942,* 1:162.

John Crittenden, b. Virginia. Major; representative from Fayette County in the Virginia House of Burgesses, 1783–1784. Four sons, John T., Thomas T., Henry, and Robert. Green, *Historic Families of Kentucky,* p. 247.

John L. Helm (1802–1867), b. Hardin County. State representative, 1826–1843; state senator, 1844–1848, 1865–1867; lieutenant governor, 1849; elected governor, 1867, inaugurated in Elizabethtown and died a few days later. Green, *Historic Families of Kentucky,* pp. 216-18.

Richard Mentor Johnson (1781–1850), b. Louisville. First native Kentuckian to serve in the state legislature, 1804. Established Choctaw Academy for Indians in Scott County. United States representative, 1807–1819, 1829–1837; United States senator, 1819–1829; vice president of the United States, 1837–1841. Colonel, War of 1812. William Emmons, *Authentic Biography of Colonel Richard M. Johnson of Kentucky* (New York, 1833), *and Biographical Directory of the American Congress, 1774–1971,* pp. 1196-97. (The biography differs from the *Directory* and gives the years as 1780–1852.)

Lazarus Whitehead Powell (1812–1867), b. Henderson. Governor, 1851–1855; United States senator, 1859–1865. Powell County, formed 1852, named for him. *Biographical Sketch of the Hon. Lazarus W. Powell* (Frankfort, Ky., 1868).

6. Robert Edward Lee (1807–1870), b. Westmoreland County, Virginia. General; commander, Armies of the Confederacy. *Who Was Who in America, 1607–1896,* H: 309-10.

7. Albert Sidney Johnston (1803–1862), b. Washington, Mason County. Secre-

tary of war, Republic of Texas; United States Army until 1861; Confederate general, killed at Shiloh. J. Winston Coleman, Jr., *Historic Kentucky*, 3d ed. (Lexington, Ky., 1967), p. 172.

8. Basil Wilson Duke (1838–1916), b. Scott County. Attorney. Confederate brigadier general. *Who Was Who in America, 1897–1942*, 1:344.

9. John Breckinridge Castleman (1841–1918), b. Fayette County. Confederate soldier, exiled. President Andrew Johnson allowed his return in 1866. Commanded the Louisville Legion during Spanish-American War and was made brigadier general. Member and chairman, Board of Park Commissioners, Louisville, for twenty-five years. In 1900 named adjutant general by Governor William Goebel when the governor was mortally wounded by an assassin. Louisville *Courier-Journal*, April 28, 1978.

10. Henry Tureman Allen (1859–1930), b. Sharpsburg. Commander, Ninetieth Division, American Expeditionary Force, 1917, in France. *Who Was Who in American History: The Military*, p. 7.

George Brand Duncan (1861–1950), b. Lexington. General, American Expeditionary Force, in France. Ibid., p. 145.

Hugh Rodman (1859–1940), b. Frankfort. Admiral; commander, United States battleships, April 1918. Ibid. pp. 486-87.

Willie Sandlin (1890–1949), b. Long's Creek, Breathitt County. Supervisor, Highway Department, Leslie County. Sergeant, 132nd Infantry; Congressional Medal of Honor, 1918; Croix de Guerre with Palm, 1919; Medal Militaire, 1919. Telephone interview, Mrs. Belve Sandlin, Louisville, August 7, 1978.

Jesse O. Creech (1895–1948), b. Harlan County. First lieutenant; World War I air ace, shot down eight German planes: Distinguished Service Order. Appointed to Aeronautics Commission, 1940; Republican; state representative; the airfield at the Lexington Signal Depot was named for him in 1959. Myron J. Smith, Jr., *World War I in the Air* (Metuchen, N.J., 1977), p. 258, *Lexington Herald*, February 17, 1948, and *Lexington Leader*, November 20, 1958.

11. Starks did not serve in the Pacific. See speech from September 6, 1942, in the World War II section.

12. The speech has been edited. Parts appear in speeches from July 4, 1941, in the World War II section, and October 2, 1942, in the Industry section.

CLOSE OF SESQUICENTENNIAL YEAR
Louisville / December 27, 1942

AS governor of our beloved Commonwealth, I today officially bring to a close the observance of the Sesquicentennial Year which has commemorated the one hundred fiftieth anniversary of Kentucky's admittance into the Union of the United States of America.[1]

Had we not been fighting a war, we would have presented a more fitting finale as a stirring climax which would fittingly mark the end of such an anniversary. As it is, today, it falls my lot as Kentucky's war governor to note the conclusion of the anniversary in this simple manner following a Sesquicentennial Year during which the patriotic citizens of Kentucky, although circumscribed largely by the effect of world affairs, have responded splendidly to the effort made to see that the year was observed with as great a degree of commemorative activity as was possible under circumstances in which our thoughts are monopolized by the war. In the course of these brief remarks, it will be my intention to give a summary of the activities of the Sesquicentennial Year which will reveal the extent of our efforts in observance of Kentucky's one hundred fiftieth anniversary.

Represented by the fifteenth star in the bright, blue field of the national emblem, Kentucky has been imbued with a spirit of patriotic fortitude. So it is that, confronted at this time by a world afire and by a state of national peril which has precluded a fuller observance of their Sesquicentennial Year, Kentuckians have sought to recapture the pioneer spirit of sacrifice and audacious disregard of danger and hardship. The reenactment of many of the stirring scenes leading up to and following June 1, 1792, which were emphasized in the limited program for the year, has rekindled in our hearts a determination to be worthy of our courageous forebears in these critical days.

I, as governor, appointed a Sesquicentennial Commission on May 27, 1940, to formulate and supervise a program which would fittingly commemorate Kentucky's one hundred fiftieth anniversary year. Even then there lowered the storm clouds of war which later enveloped the world, creating necessity for modification of ambitious plans for observance of our sesquicentennial. I wish to express appreciation to the eminent Kentuckians who accepted appointment on the commission. Each member of the commission entered upon the task imbued with great love for Kentucky. Each had a broad knowledge of Kentucky's history and an understanding of the importance of reinterpreting a glorious past in terms of the stern realities of war. The activities, which were stimulated under leadership of the Sesquicentennial Commission, inspired Kentuckians to face the sacrifices demanded by war with a courage and fortitude worthy of their pioneer ancestry.

At the first meeting of the commission held in Lexington, July 6, 1940, Judge Samuel M. Wilson of Lexington was named chairman; Mrs. W. B. Ardery of Paris, vice chairman; Mr. Harry V. McChesney of Frankfort, secretary; and Mr. Harry B. MacKoy of Covington, treasurer. Other members of the original group were Mrs. W. P. Drake of Bowling Green; Mr. John H. Hoagland of Louisville; Mr. Herndon Evans of Pineville; Mr.

Curtis Alcock of Danville; and Mr. Eugene Stuart of Louisville. Unhappily, Mr. Alcock, one of the most valued members of the commission, died during the year. Mr. Vernon Richardson, also of Danville, accepted appointment to fill Mr. Alcock's place. Mr. Stuart resigned during the year and his place was filled by Mr. R. C. Ballard Thruston of Louisville. Dr. U. R. Bell was chosen as executive director and was, upon his resignation, succeeded by H. I. Miranda.[2]

Patriotic organizations and public-spirited citizens of numerous Kentucky towns, notably Danville, Lexington, Harrodsburg, Paris, Frankfort, Covington, Louisville, Bardstown, Ashland, and Mount Sterling took early action to organize celebrations in which was emphasized the unique and colorful backgrounds of their localities. So, the Sesquicentennial Year, observed against a backdrop of war, was marked by a number of appropriate historical programs.

In addition to such celebrations in the various communities of the state, the commission inaugurated other phases of the sesquicentennial program which were statewide in their nature.

As early as February 4, 1941, the one hundred fiftieth anniversary of the date of the passage of the Act of Congress for admittance of Kentucky to the Union, one of the plans embraced in the program was the creation of a Hall of Fame, composed of ten outstanding Kentuckians. The state schools and colleges participated in the selection of our most distinguished citizens from a long list of nominations, and the following famous Kentuckians were selected for the distinction of being designated for Kentucky's Hall of Fame. In the order of their popularity, those chosen were Abraham Lincoln, Daniel Boone, Henry Clay, Jefferson Davis, George Rogers Clark, Zachary Taylor, Isaac Shelby, Dr. Ephraim McDowell, John Fitch, and John James Audubon. In compliance with plans of the commission, it is hoped portraits of these great Kentuckians may be procured by the Kentucky Historical Society and be hung in the Old Capitol, now the repository of many of Kentucky's treasured historic relics and mementos.

Another feature of the year, aside from various community celebrations, was the designation by college students of the state of Kentucky's chief attractions. Those receiving the highest number of ballots were My Old Kentucky Home, Mammoth Cave National Park, Cumberland Falls, the Abraham Lincoln Memorial, Cumberland Gap, the State Capitol, Horse Farms of the Bluegrass, Man o' War, Natural Bridge State Park, the grave of Daniel Boone, the home of Henry Clay, Saint Joseph Cathedral, Old Shakertown, Audubon Memorial State Park, the Ancient Buried City, Pine Mountain State Park, the Abbey of Gethsemane, Boonesboro, and the Pioneer Memorial State Park.

In a poetry contest the poem submitted by Mrs. Eugene Phillips[3] of

Paducah was selected as the official sesquicentennial poem. Mrs. Phillips was commissioned as the sesquicentennial poet laureate of Kentucky. A poster contest for the schoolchildren of the state was won by Miss Lyle Irvine of the Frankfort public schools.

Commemorating the sesquicentennial of Kentucky, the Post Office Department issued a souvenir stamp bearing a reproduction of the Gilbert White[4] mural over the entrance to the House of Representatives in the State Capitol which depicts Daniel Boone overlooking the site upon which Frankfort was built. First day's sales conducted at Frankfort on June 1, 1942, the anniversary date, saw the cancellation of approximately 300,000 of these stamps as a great factor in contributing to the success of the sesquicentennial.[5] Souvenir editions of the state's newspapers filled with historical data concerning Kentucky were widely distributed throughout the nation and radio stations over the state supplied facilities for the dissemination of information concerning the program of the sesquicentennial on numerous occasions.

Appropriately heralding the actual celebration of the anniversary, Danville, the cradle of the Commonwealth, was the scene of the initial observance on April 20 and 21, 1942. Here an artistically staged historical pageant portrayed the stirring scenes enacted during the constitutional conventions prior to Kentucky's statehood. As a feature of the Danville celebration, a memorial tablet was unveiled on historic Constitution Square, in the center of the old city, which was recently dedicated as the Weisiger State Park. On May 24, 1942, a statewide religious observance in commemoration of early Kentucky religious activities was featured by an address by the Right Reverend H. P. Almon Abbott, Bishop of the Episcopal Church of Kentucky.[6]

On June 4, 1942, a program at Lexington celebrated the one hundred fiftieth anniversary of the date upon which the legislature held its first meeting, and Governor Isaac Shelby was inaugurated as Kentucky's first governor in that city. At Frankfort, historic old capital of the Commonwealth, an observance on June 6 presented a résumé of the progress of Kentucky with particular emphasis on the important role Kentucky has played in the nation's affairs.[7] On June 7 in the same city, a religious service on the Old Capitol grounds was held, reminiscent of early religious services.

On June 16, 1942, Harrodsburg, oldest permanent Kentucky settlement, celebrated the founding of the town. In keeping with its valiant history, a recital of incidents of pioneer days in Kentucky was combined with a tribute to the heroism of Mercer countians in the present war.

An elaborate historical celebration at Covington on July 3, 1942, designated as "The Cavalcade of Kenton County," reviewed episodes in the lives of Boone, Kenton, Clark, and other noted pioneers. At Paris, on

September 2, commemorative ceremonies were completed with a community singing program in which members of the armed forces and many visitors took part.

On the evening of September 18, 1942, a dinner in Louisville, honoring Kentucky at War on the one hundred fiftieth anniversary of her statehood, attracted a large patriotic gathering. Numerous but less pretentious celebrations were held in various cities and communities over the state commemorating local events of historic interest. Many of these celebrations were held in connection with annual activities. Numerous commencement programs in high schools and colleges featured Kentucky's birthday.

Among organizations which made valuable contributions to the success of the year were the Kentucky Federation of Women's Clubs, the Daughters of the American Revolution, the United Daughters of the Confederacy, the American Legion, the Parent-Teachers Association, and similar patriotic, civic, and religious groups.

To increase interest in Kentucky's anniversary, the Sesquicentennial Commission issued and distributed timely publications of genuine historic value. One of these was a map, drawn by a member of the Kentucky Historical Society, showing Kentucky as it appeared in 1792, with county divisions,the location of early forts and stations. The border of this attractive souvenir carried illustrations of historic buildings of the state. A total of 4,000 copies of the map were distributed to schools, colleges, and libraries in Kentucky and over the nation.

The other publication is an attractive chronological history of Kentucky, entitled "Kentucky in Retrospect." Much of the data was assembled by Mrs. Ardery, Mrs. Drake, and Judge Wilson, members of the Sesquicentennial Commission. Artistically illustrated, the book has been acclaimed as a unique publication of exceptional merit. An excellent brochure dealing with the sesquicentennial, written by Mrs. Maude Ward Lafferty[8] of Lexington, was entitled "Sesquicentennial Stories" and was distributed among the schools, libraries, and clubs.

Kentucky's sesquicentennial has been a success. Although, of necessity, abbreviated in its scope, it has encouraged Kentuckians to rededicate themselves to the faith of their pioneer progenitors.

And so, as with these remarks, the curtain closes on the Sesquicentennial Year of our great state, it is not unlike the drawing of an imaginary tapestry across a brave scene in which the characters have been figures secure of their places in American history and in which the setting was one of charm and beauty. It has been a show worth seeing and one that will be encored certainly on a more propitious day.

As governor of Kentucky, I would like to pay tribute to the citizens of the state, who, regardless of the anxieties and duties created by the war, have labored zealously to make it a success, knowing full well that it was with troubled hearts at times that they carried on in the true tradition of Kentuckians. Enriched by the past and made resolute by the present, we may all look to the future with the hope that when another anniversary arrives there will be no war to cause our people distress and anxiety. And on that day when another half-century has been caught into the folds of the robe of eternity, Kentucky will again welcome all to her hearts and homes:

A green velvet dress she'll be wearing
With goldenrod caught in her hair,
A cloak made of radiant sunshine,
Perfumed by the flower-laden air.

Redbirds will render the music,
As she serves hospitality
With favors of natural beauty,
Enriched by history.

'Her receiving line—a retinue
Of elms and sycamores,
Who'll nod and bow in courtliness,
To all ent'ring her doors.

Her invitation to everyone
Will be—"Come to help me celebrate
My Bicentennial Birthday,
Yours truly, A Beautiful State."

---

1. WHAS radio.

2. Julia Hoge Spencer Ardery (1889–1976), b. Richmond, Virginia. Historian. Member, National Trust for Historic Preservation. Wife of Judge William B. Ardery. *Kentucky Lives: The Blue Grass State Who's Who*, pp. 14-15.

Harry Vernon McChesney (1868–1947), b. Caldwell County. Attorney. Fifteenth superintendent, Public Instruction, 1899–1903. *Who's Who in Kentucky, 1936*, p. 268, and *Lexington Leader*, August 16, 1947.

Harry B. MacKoy (1874–1952), b. Covington. Attorney. Committee member to revise Kentucky statutes. Telephone interview, Mrs. Harry S. Robinson III, daughter, Cincinnati, August 1, 1978.

Mrs. William Preston Drake (1895–1979), b. Bowling Green. Attorney; member, board of regents, Western Kentucky University. Telephone interview, Ray Lazarus, Office of the President, Western Kentucky University, August 3, 1979.

John H. Hoagland (1900–1962), b. Louisville. Promotion manager, Louisville *Courier Journal* and *Times* and Radio WHAS. Louisville *Courier-Journal*, January 14, 1962.

Herndon J. Evans (1895–1976), b. Morehead. Editor, *Pineville Sun* for thirty-two years. Editor, *Lexington Herald*, 1956–1968. *Who's Who in Kentucky, 1955*, p. 109, and telephone interview, Andrew Eckdahl, managing editor, *Lexington Herald*, June 12, 1978.

John Curtis Alcock (1881–1940), b. Glasgow. President, *Danville Messenger*. State representative, 1928. *Who's Who in Kentucky, 1936*, p. 4.

Eugene Stuart (1885–1960), b. Elizaville, Fleming County. Manager, Louisville Auto Club. Telephone interview, secretary, Auto Club, June 21, 1978.

William Vernon Richardson (1872–1952), b. Monticello. Attorney; journalist. *Who's Who in Kentucky, 1936*, p. 338, and Louisville *Courier-Journal*, July 13, 1952.

Rogers Clark Ballard Thruston (1858–1946), b. Louisville. Historian; geologist; president, Filson Club, 1923. Wallis and Tapp, *A Sesquicentennial History of Kentucky*, 3:1286, 1288, and *Lexington Leader*, December 30, 1946.

Urban Radcliff Bell (1889–1953), b. Versailles, Illinois. Minister, Disciples of Christ. President, Paducah Junior College. *Who's Who in Kentucky, 1936*, p. 29, and Alumni Records, Oberlin College, October 17, 1978.

H. I. Miranda (1906–1973), b. Ashland. Resided in Lexington. Businessman. Telephone interview, daughter, August 1, 1978.

3. Louise Scott Phillips (Mrs. Eugene) (1911–), b. Paducah. Now Mrs. Louise Sandow, Eddyville. The Kentucky Federation of Women's Clubs sponsored the contest. The poem was titled "Kentucky." Letter, William S. Murphy, mayor, Paducah, July 27, 1978.

4. Gilbert Thomas White (1877–1939), b. Michigan. Artist. *Who Was Who in America, 1897–1942*, 1:1334.

5. Johnson purchased the first sheet on June 1, 1942, and presented it to the Kentucky Historical Society.

6. Henry Pryor Alman Abbott (1881–1945), b. Halifax, Nova Scotia. Episcopal bishop of Lexington, 1929–1945. Wallis and Tapp, *A Sesquicentennial History of Kentucky*, 2:1000, 1002.

7. Johnson introduced the speaker, Colonel Edgar E. Hume, a native of Frankfort and a career officer in the Army Medical Corps.

8. Maude Ward Lafferty (1869–1962), b. Cynthiana. Lecturer, writer. *Who's Who in Kentucky, 1936*, p. 237, and *Lexington Herald*, December 1, 1962.

MOTHER'S DAY
Frankfort / May 9, 1943

WE pause today in every church, in every home on this continent, to pay homage to our mothers. Against a backdrop of a brutal and bloody war, we on this Mother's Day seek to do reverence to those who have built the civilization and Christian faith that war seeks to destroy.

Mother love is the most sublime of human emotions. The love of mother for her children is tender, compassionate, as enduring as it is strong. It is expressed in daily devotion in which mother expends herself in behalf of her children.

Because her children too often thoughtlessly neglect to express their appreciation of mother, we have set aside Mother's Day, a day which we have hallowed to the memory of mothers who have gone and dedicated lovingly in honor of those mothers yet living whose daily lives are a benediction and a blessing.

The hatred in which war has its genesis is the antithesis of the noble emotion of mother love. Hate corrodes the soul, blights the finer sensibilities of the human heart. Love enriches life, ennobles mankind.

The hearts of millions of American mothers are filled with anxiety today because the world is engulfed in a savagely ruthless war. We laud the valor of our fighting men whose deeds of heroism on every battlefront of the world thrill us with pride. But these our fighting men are gallant because they are the sons of courageous mothers.

The morale of our citizenship is virile and strong as we seek to mobilize all the resources of the nation to crush the godless despots that have brought this misery upon the world. But this fortunate fact is a tribute to the courage and fortitude of our mothers.

War, with its destruction and cruelty, brings greatest grief to mothers. As Kentucky's war governor, I have observed with great gratification the heroic attitude of Kentucky mothers as they have faced the grim realities of war. Kentucky has been near the top of states in the Union in the number of men voluntarily enlisted in the armed forces in proportion to population. Kentucky's quota of men for military service has been met promptly month after month. That reflects high credit upon the mothers of Kentucky who smile through tears as they send their sons to don the uniform of the nation and follow the flag of freedom.

We may all feel proud of the fact that in every phase of activity which advances the war effort Kentuckians are discharging their duty nobly. The irritations and inconvenience that come as result of rationing are being accepted without whining—because our mothers recognize it as the contribution we at home must make in sustaining the sons who are absent from home on this Mother's Day because of military necessity.

Kentuckians are doing without many things—cheerfully—because they realize that the things they give up will be used to crush our enemies and hasten the day when the sons of this Commonwealth can come home.

In every war bond selling campaign, the goal set for us has been exceeded. In the salvage campaigns, the collecting of scrap metal, kitchen grease, tin cans, our people are unitedly doing their duty. The mothers of

Kentucky's soldiers have been a stimulating influence. Their zeal and enthusiasm has been a vital factor in unifying our citizens in aggressive support of our armed forces.

So we pause today as Americans and as Kentuckians, in a world strewn with the debris of battle, to show our affection and esteem for mother. Words are inadequate to express our appreciation of her. This faltering tribute fails to convey the impulse of our hearts as we face the stern realities of that war in which we fight to preserve a world in which motherhood will continue to be exalted and sanctity of the home preserved.

A mother herself bares her heart in the bit of verse published in Allan Trout's[1] column "Greetings" in the *Courier-Journal.* Mrs. W. C. Bragg[2] of Irvine expresses in rhyme the thoughts of a mother who is lonely on Mother's Day:

Mother's Day in war times
  Is different from the rest,
For my boys and their daddy
  Have left the old home nest.

Instead of a family dinner
  And a gift from each one,
I'm doing the giving now,
  Like they have always done.

I'm sending each a Testament,
  The words of Jesus are in red,
Also, there is included
  What the psalmist said.

I'll spend this Mother's Day
  Like they would have me to,
I'll go to church as usual,
  Keep busy all day through.

I'll write the one who flies the sky,
  And the one who sails the sea;
And to their daddy at Pearl Harbor,
  All in service for you and me.

To all three I will remind them,
  If in danger they seem to be,
To remember the 91st Psalm,
  And be brave as they can be.

1. Allan Trout (1903–1972), b. Churchtown, Tennessee. Folklorist; newsman; columnist, Louisville *Courier-Journal*. Louisville *Courier-Journal*, December 10, 1972.

2. Florence R. Bragg (Mrs. W. C.) (1892–1970), b. Allentown, New York. Resided in Irvine. Interview, Mrs. Johnny Scrivner, daughter, Irvine, March 11, 1978.

BIG SINGING DAY
Benton / May 23, 1943

GOVERNOR JOHNSON paid high tribute to the custom of preserving the pioneer tunes through the annual "Big Singing," which he described as a "wholesome, fine, splendid thing." [1]

He declared that these old songs are of faith in God, in the church, and in religion. "It is appropriate that we sing the songs of our fathers at a time when we must have faith in the future and in democracy. Here today we hear songs expressive of the great truths of old which is most important that we uphold today. People who come here and sing these songs of heaven, redemption, and repentance surely have the American spirit."

The governor said that he is proud of the reaction of Kentucky to the war. In the Axis countries people are forced to sing the songs chosen by their dictators, not the simple ballads of their forefathers. He pleaded for united support of the leaders of the war effort.

---

1. Johnson was the first governor to attend the Old Southern Harmony Singing. The Big Singing was originated in 1884 by J. R. Lemon. The Old Southern Harmony ballads and sacred songs date from plantation days. The singers use shape-note music, a system of seven notes showing the musical scale by the shape of the notes, including triangular, rectangular, and half-oval.

DEMOCRATIC PARTY LEADERSHIP, 1939–1943

CLOSES GUBERNATORIAL CAMPAIGN
Richmond / November 6, 1939

I WANT to thank Senator Barkley, Senator Chandler, and your next lieutenant governor, Rodes K. Myers, for their fine contribution to our concluding campaign broadcast.

This is the last time in probably a long while I shall address myself primarily to the Democrats of Kentucky. Tonight I am a candidate and find my audience divided between those who are my supporters and those who are the supporters of a political opponent. But for more than four years after tomorrow, I will be the governor of all the people of Kentucky without regard to their political faiths or stations in life or race or color or creed.

The political division that exists tonight will continue in the form of two political parties, but every member of those parties, in his individual capacity as a citizen, will look to the state government as his government no matter whether he voted for or against those who will be chosen tomorrow to occupy, for a while, the offices of that government.

I and my official associates on the Democratic ticket, in turn, will be equally the servants of all.

Several weeks ago, through the intervention of death and resignation, I came to this most exalted office within the gift of the people of Kentucky in advance of the time when I had hoped to attain it. I am now serving as lieutenant governor become governor the brief time remaining in the present term, and you will decide tomorrow whether I may continue to serve you in a full, four-year term of my own.

Of your decision I have no doubt. It will be an overwhelming Democratic majority for the continuation of sober, respectable, sound, and progressive administration of state government, and for continued cooperation with the national Democratic administration.

These are the things for which you will vote when you vote the straight Democratic ticket, and I am humbly conscious that your vote is for these things and not merely for me, who happens to be the head of that ticket. I am only the instrument of your desires.

I approach humbly the responsibilities which I anticipate your decision will impose on me.

I have frequently told the people that I do not claim that I will be the best governor Kentucky ever had. I am aware of my own limitations. I have been preceded in this high office by forty-one illustrious Kentuckians, most of whom have served with great distinction. But I repeat now my promise that I will try harder than have any of these forty-one predecessors to make you a good, competent, honest governor.

I will not make you a spectacular governor. Good government is seldom spectacular. It may only seem to be spectacular when it follows a period of bad government. It is fortunate for the people that no condition of bad government now exists in the administration of your state affairs. Even the partisan opponents of the present state administration, both within and without the Democratic party, generously and frankly say that it has been, on the whole, a good administration. Consequently, there is no radical or spectacular change which I have proposed to make in the policies of your government.

Instead, I have proposed, and the Democratic party proposes, a steady and progressive improvement in the services the government performs for the people within the limits of the funds available and without increasing the burden of taxes. We propose to hold on to what is good, to improve it, and adjust it to changing conditions, and to keep always uppermost in our minds the democratic creed that the government is the servant and not the master of the people.

As your governor, I will need the tolerance, the patience, and the understanding of the people; standing now on the threshold of the responsibilities you are about to impose on me, I ask all of you for that tolerance, that patience, and that understanding.

There is nothing in the program we advocate and there certainly is nothing in my heart or mind which is calculated to stir turmoil and excitement or serious divisions among the people. I am hopeful that political divisions among the people may be minimized, and that such differences as may continue will be prosecuted without passion or bitterness. We already have signs that this hope may be realized, as evidenced by the subsiding of factional divisions within the Democratic party. We are, after all, Kentuckians and Americans first, and Democrats or Republicans afterward. I hope we may all live together and work together in this fashion.

For this final talk to the people of Kentucky before the balloting tomorrow, I have come once again (as I did at the end of the primary campaign last summer) to my modest little home in Richmond. I have continued to live here, even after becoming governor. It is only with a wrench at my heartstrings that I can contemplate leaving my own home, for an interval, to take up official residence in Frankfort with Mrs. Johnson and our daughter, Judy. They sit beside me now as I talk to you. We are just such a plain, average family as most of you to whom I talk tonight, and none of us has any ambition for the pomp and circumstance of high office.

A few minutes ago I came from closing my public speaking campaign before my home folks here in Richmond, where for many years I have been editor of the *Richmond Daily Register*. Even though the people of the whole state have honored me, I shall regret being taken, for a while, from these home folks who have been so generous of their support, their loyalty, and their affections to me and my family. They are the people who have had the opportunity to know me best, and I especially treasure the overwhelming vote of confidence they gave me in the primary last summer.[1]

I am grateful, also, to the hundreds and thousands of persons who have befriended me and encouraged me and helped me during all my life, since my boyhood as the son of a circuit-rider Methodist minister in Western Kentucky, along the path that has brought me to the highest office within the gift of our people. In the humble circumstances into which I was born and along the way I have come, few of the persons who have known me have been rich in worldly goods, but almost all of them have been kind and charitable and generous and sympathetic and understanding. These are the qualities by which I hope my administration as governor may be marked. They are the homely and everyday qualities of the people I love, the people of Kentucky.

I hope I may have the time and opportunity to go back into every county at some time during my term as governor, to thank the supporters who have so loyally helped me obtain my nomination, and all those who tomorrow will add still further to my obligation by helping to elect me governor. Until I may meet them face-to-face, I take this opportunity to thank them all, and I am grateful to every one, no matter whether he holds a position of large responsibility in the campaign organization, or is a precinct worker, or is only a loyal, individual voter.

Since the first days of the primary campaign, you men and women who have helped to present my candidacy and who have helped to present our party's program, have been the advocates of a cause rather than merely the partisans of a faction. Many of you have given your help at considerable personal sacrifice, and in numerous instances you have done this without ambition or desire for personal reward or recognition. To the fullest extent that your efforts may have advanced the cause of good government, the whole people of Kentucky may properly join with me in gratitude and appreciation for your work.

In saying this, I specifically include those of you who differed with me on the questions of the primary campaign, and who have joined wholeheartedly in the support of the Democratic ticket in the general election.

You, who have done so much for me and for the Democratic party, have one more day of work ahead of you, as you urge your friends and neighbors tomorrow to exercise their precious American right of suffrage. I ask all of you who hear me tonight to be especially diligent in your efforts to see to it tomorrow that everybody votes, no matter whether or not you are enrolled as a campaign official or precinct worker. I ask this not only as a candidate for governor but as your governor. I think it is especially important this year that everybody should vote. If we treasure our American citizenship, we should exercise it. Democracy is under attack in many places; it already has vanished for the moment from wide areas of the world; and we should demonstrate our determination to make democracy continue to work here. We can have a part in this as individuals by voting. Our government does not consist of just a few elective and appointive officials. It consists of the people themselves. It can only function in the mass if you perform your duties as individuals. Only then can it really be government by the people—by all the people.

It is your government, and you have not only the privilege but also the duty of participating in it. I ask you to do that, and this probably will be the last political request that I shall make of you in a long time. I have no political ambitions beyond my desire to make you a good governor. It is probable that I will not trouble you much in the next four years with political matters. Of course, I will do what I properly can next year to help elect a Democratic president. The fact that a presidential election is coming next year makes this present state election especially important. We are the only state that has a contest for governor this year. Our Kentucky election is the barometer by which the entire nation and the whole world will attempt to forecast the political trend toward the approaching national election. An increased Democratic majority would indicate to the nation and to the world that no serious defection from Democratic administration has developed among our people.

For this reason, it is important that the Democratic majority tomorrow should be a big majority, a decisive majority, even though victory is already assured.

I am happy to be able to say that the entire campaign has been singularly free from passion and hatred. I earnestly hope that this may continue to be the case, and that good feeling may prevail while the ballots are cast and counted and at all other times. There is no resentment or bitterness in my heart or mind against any person or group. I want those who support me to have no bitterness or resentment against anybody; together, we want to give no cause for resentment or bitterness among those who oppose us.

In that spirit, I now turn over this campaign to you, the people of Kentucky, for your decision tomorrow. In that spirit, I hope the victors and the vanquished may join again after tomorrow, not in the political debate of the campaign, but in an everyday, diligent endeavor to make Kentucky a better and more prosperous state, thankful to God for a form of government under which we all may have a part in doing this. In the words of our campaign theme song "God bless America" and Kentucky.

---

1. Johnson expressed his gratitude to his Madison County friends and neighbors when the Exchange Club of Richmond gave a banquet in his honor shortly before his inauguration. He commented that his election was a "doubtful experiment which may just ruin a pretty fair sort of country newspaper fellow." He stated that he intended to return in four years to reenter the life of the community as a private citizen and newspaperman. He hoped that he would grow with the responsibility of being governor and not just "swell up." *Richmond Daily Register*, December 7, 1939, and *Eastern Progress*, December 14, 1939.

STATEMENT ON ELECTION OUTCOME
Richmond / November 9, 1939

THE outcome of the election is not only a source of gratification to me as the party's standard-bearer, but the 100,000 majority, an all-time record, is significant in that it was attained despite a falloff in the total vote of more than 200,000 as compared with the governor's race four years ago.

A sectional analysis of the vote reveals that the Democratic trend in Kentucky continues upward, even in some of the heretofore rock-ribbed Republican strongholds. Our majority of Tuesday is certainly indicative of another great victory in next year's presidential race.

I am neither unmindful of nor ungrateful to the thousands upon thousands of Republicans and independents who, by their support, endorsed the policies of the present state administration and expressed confidence in the leadership of the Democratic party, both in the state and in the nation. I do want to thank every member of the Democratic organization, from those who manned the precincts to the state campaign manager, for their untiring efforts and loyalty to the party. They are responsible for the outstanding success attained by our party in the election.

I don't believe there was ever a more intelligent campaign conducted by the Democratic party in Kentucky than that of this fall and I wish particularly to recognize the generalship of J. Lyter Donaldson, whose alert and able leadership led to such a splendid victory.

JACKSON DAY
Louisville / January 8, 1940

WE are gathered to pay homage to Andrew Jackson on this the anniversary of his brillant military triumph at New Orleans and pledge anew our allegiance to the Democratic party under whose philosophy has been made most of those social and economic advances which have made our government responsive to the needs of the people.

As I sought guidance as to the kind of speech appropriate for this occasion, I consulted speeches made hitherto by gifted speakers at Jackson Day dinners. I found that slight attention had been given Jackson, that present-day political problems monopolized their attention. But it seems to me proper to talk about Jackson at a dinner in honor of his memory.

There has been no more colorful or potent personality on this continent than was the seventh president of the United States. He was just the type leader needed to direct the people toward a fulfillment of the destiny of America at that time. And it is singular that the Democratic party has always produced such a leader when such was needed.

Andrew Jackson was a commoner, and there were many in his time who considered him an uncultured ignoramus. But the story of his life, the achievements he wrought with honesty of purpose for the welfare of the common folk, is an epic.

Tradition relates of Rachel Jackson that she explained a family epidemic by saying, "The General kicked the kivers off and we all kotched cold."

That incident summarizes the career of Jackson whether we consider him as the conqueror of his country's foes or the defender of the people's right. Right lustily did he kick and right constantly.

He is the hero of the people, not the intelligentsia. The people delight in the legends of his prowess, of his lurid language, his dictatorial temper. The tale of his usurpations does not appall them but delights them, for Americans have always loved a masterful man, a courageous fighter.

There was bitter criticism because it was charged that Jackson was setting himself up as a dictator as he fought for the welfare of the common folk. The same cry is raised today by the same insincere interests, as it is charged that a dictator has been enthroned in the White House. But the people of the nation have indicated that they had rather be under the rule of a dictator in the White House than be ruled by a dictator in Wall Street.

When Jackson first went to Washington, certain senators, who had been critical of him, heard from friends that he had sworn to cut off their ears. They went into hiding. Americans have never been able to resist a man who could talk like a pirate and act like a Presbyterian preacher and Jackson could do both to perfection.

As the champion of the unorganized, inarticulate masses, Jackson destroyed a sinister alliance between politics and finance that was swiftly reducing these unimportant folk to economic serfdom.

Probability did not apply to Jackson. He conformed to no known rules. He refused to be bound by precedents, blazed new trails.

Jackson, as a lad of sixteen, comes reeling across the pages of history with a saber cut across his head, inflicted by a British officer. And as the years accumulated upon him, they glitter with steel and blood. As a soldier of the Revolution when cornered by a British detachment, a haughty officer ordered the Jackson lad to clean and black his boots. His insolent refusal provoked the saber cut that left him wearing a scar of honor for life and kindled in his heart a hatred for the British which steeled his courage and cleared his judgment as he decisively defeated the pick of the British army in the battle of New Orleans.

Yet with all the rugged exterior, he loved intensely. His devotion to his wife, Rachel, was sublime. When gossip, started by political scandalmongers, reached his ears, the author of the slander faced a duel with Jackson. He cut and slashed his way to power. But he had an exalted code of honor, included in which was fidelity to the rights and interests of the common people, and he lived up to that code. He hated and loved and swore with magnificence. But he did not cringe nor fawn. He did not carry water on both shoulders. When he lost, as frequently he did, and heavily, he paid without whimpering. Unlettered, uncouth, unskilled in the graces of polite society, he was nonetheless a courtly chevalier.

Jackson's Americanism was that of the masses. The man of no influence demanded what he thought America stood for—an opportunity, a chance to improve his station, rise above the station in which he found himself. It was a dream that the common man had dreamed since he fought for freedom in the Revolution. He realized that he had missed it, that the government had been monopolized by a coterie of influential individuals who were unable to dream the dream of the common man.

In Andrew Jackson, this disappointed citizenship sensed anew an opportunity to capture that for which they had dreamed, make it a reality. It was the beginning of the formation of that type of Americanism which is genuine, indigenous to the soil of this continent. And the shrine of that virile Americanism for which Jackson fought is in the heart of the common man.

The parallel between Roosevelt and Jackson is striking. Utterly different in their personalities, they are amazingly alike in their political philosophy, their sincere desire and burning passion to adapt government to the needs of the average folks. Singular it is that in President Roosevelt, reared amid culture and wealth, the bluest blue blood in America coursing through his veins, unfamiliar from bitter experience with hardship and suffering, the common folk find a champion as zealous in his crusade for government which will aid them, as was Jackson, who was a product of the frontier, of humble origin, whose whole life was a struggle.

Nicholas Biddle's[1] bank in Washington, as the result of being depository of the federal government, had come to be a financial power sufficiently strong to defy the government. All Jackson's closest associates were afraid to make a fight on the bank, but when Jackson's secretary of treasury declined to remove the government deposits from the bank, the president removed him and appointed a treasury head who would carry out his orders.

It was a prolonged and bitter fight—this the first struggle between that power represented by concentrated wealth and interests of the common folk as conceived by Jackson. The Senate passed a resolution in which the president was censured, but he stood resolutely by his determination to see that "the barnacles were scraped clean of the ship of state." He won the first pitched battle with the selfish financial interests of the nation and scored a triumph for the common welfare.

Jackson had the vision to see that mischief was certain to result from a coalition between the government and big business. He knew that eventually big business would become the dominant partner and the government would become subservient to selfish interests.

This invisible government had grown arrogant and defiant. Biddle summoned senators and congressmen by the peremptory command and they cringed before him. Through the National Bank, there had been established a financial despotism that was able to intimidate businessmen into doing its bidding.

Through its agencies of publicity, it tried to frighten the people into deserting their great leader by misrepresentation and falsehood. Jackson was pictured as a "Red" and socialist. It was charged that he had trampled on the Constitution, but they were unable to inflame the public mind against the defender of the people's rights.

When the insincere, selfish few charged that Jackson was tearing up the Constitution, the people knew that the squawk was provoked because they were being denied the right to exploit the people.

When they sneered at Jackson as a socialist experimenter, the people realized that his critics were disgruntled because the president was smashing the entrenched position of special privilege, restoring to the people their rights and freedom.

Nothing which the critics of Jackson said of him has not been charged against President Roosevelt. The same covert effort has been made to discredit his efforts to meet the emergency created by the depression, bring under subjection those sinister forces which have been subversive of good government.

It is important to elect a Democratic president so that the philosophy of Jackson will remain regnant in the nation.

---

1. Nicholas Biddle (1786–1844), b. Philadelphia, Pennsylvania. Director, Bank of the United States, 1819–1822, president, 1822–1836. *Who Was Who in America, 1607–1896*, H:55.

STATE DEMOCRATIC CONVENTION
Louisville / July 2, 1940

THIS great gathering of harmonious and united Democrats is an inspiring sight. The news reports from distant lands, that are not so happy and so fortunate as our own, tell of the insidious work of "Fifth Columns."[1]

Where there is a vigilant, active, strong, and united "First Column," the "Fifth Column" will not dare raise its treasonous head to undertake its destructive work of undermining the confidence of the people in the government they have formed and whose officers they have elected.

You are Kentucky's "First Column." As such I greet you here today. Spared the gruelling sacrifices and stark and harrowing tragedies of war, you as Democrats, as citizens, and as "First Column" defenders of free government have now a serious responsibility as we face the problems of this grave hour.

We are glad today that we are Kentuckians. We are glad that we are Democrats. And we are glad, above all, that we are Americans, and may God bless America.

We are glad to assemble here in the charming, hospitable city of Louisville for this important convocation and are grateful to Louisville Democrats for the cordial reception extended. It is the duty of you who compose this convention to select delegates that will represent Kentucky democracy at the National Democratic Convention in Chicago where will be chosen the next president of these United States. That will be a momentous decision. It will determine the leadership of this great nation during the most perilous period of world history. That leader should be a virile, farsighted American who will have the courage to defend our democratic form of government through preparedness instead of appeasement. I confidently predict that the nominees chosen as the banner bearers of our party at Chicago will win a decisive victory for democracy. I make this prediction despite the protest of the ninety-day wonder, Wendell Willkie,[2] who so recently fell off the Democratic bandwagon and backslid into the Republican party. The executive of an electric power company "electrified" the Republican convention. But he will blow a fuse and short-circuit the Republicans before November. The voters of the nation will not be willing to take a chance on this great electrifier, even though he convinced the Republican convention that the chance of a Republican victory would be enhanced by nominating a Democrat as the GOP candidate.

We gather harmoniously and united as a party without discord in our ranks. In the majority of cases the county mass meetings of last Saturday revealed a remarkable unanimity of purpose and of opinion. This is unusual. For years the party has looked upon convention calls as sounding the gong for a Golden Gloves tournament.

Today the Democratic party in Kentucky can make ready to submit its recommendations to the Democratic National Convention in Chicago with our own house in order. There are no "dummies" on the ballot and no "sleepers" on the payroll. There is no discord in our ranks. There is no extravagance with public funds. This is no jobholders convention. At this point, let me pay my respect and that of the Democrats of Kentucky, here assembled, to those to whom we may refer as "our absent brothers and sisters." I speak of those who are under the Hatch Act.[3] We miss them but we recognize that the duties of the offices that they hold should come first. I also wish to say that in the reorganization in Frankfort I regret any criticism that has been made of any public official. I have not instigated this. But the administration is determined, even though it means that we must ask for sacrifices to be made by many of our most loyal friends, to continue the reorganization of the state government in the interest of efficiency and economy and to handle the affairs of the state in a business-like manner. I appreciate fully the assistance that I have received in this and the other arduous duties of the governorship from all of those who have cooperated with me.

A year ago you honored me with selection as the Democratic nominee for governor of Kentucky. I made just as few promises as I could. Because of the splendid service rendered to the state and nation by the Democratic party in Washington, in Frankfort, and in the counties and cities of the state, a Democratic nomination in Kentucky is now almost equal to election. I hope it continues to be for many years to come. So I didn't make many promises. But I did make a few. Those that I did make I have earnestly endeavored to keep. One year ago I publicly declared in favor of a delegation to the Democratic National Convention instructed for Senator Barkley for president.

But Senator Barkley is unwilling that the Kentucky delegation be instructed to vote for him for the presidential nomination unless President Franklin D. Roosevelt makes himself unavailable for the nomination. In accordance with the wishes of Senator Barkley, I favor instructing Kentucky's delegation to the National Democratic Convention to urge President Roosevelt to again accept the nomination of the Democratic Convention as our candidate for president. In event President Roosevelt should decline to be drafted as the standard-bearer of the Democratic party, I favor Kentucky's gifted and able senior senator, the Honorable Alben W. Barkley, as the Democratic presidential nominee, and I hope the Kentucky delegation will be instructed by this convention to support Senator Barkley for president in event President Roosevelt should be unwilling again to carry the banner of democracy as its nominee.

At the Chicago convention, the committee on arrangements already has named Senator Barkley to act in the role of permanent chairman of the convention; a position of great importance because as permanent chairman he will preside when the president of the United States is nominated. Twice keynoter at Democratic National Conventions and now the Democratic floor leader in the United States Senate, he has been called, aptly, the "right arm" of President Roosevelt. No man in America has stood more loyally by the president and his program or is able more effectively to champion and proclaim it before the people of the United States.

We regret that the junior senator from Kentucky, Senator A. B. Chandler, has been called back to Washington to a meeting of the Military Affairs Committee of the Senate, of which he is a member. He had hoped to be present with us but was called back there for the meeting of that committee and to carry on in the fine spirit with which he has entered upon his duties as a member of the United States Senate.

The records of the two United States senators and of the members of Congress, some of whom we are pleased to have here, reflect credit upon the Democratic party and the state of Kentucky, and I think we all are gratified with the excellent work that they are doing in the world's greatest deliberative bodies. The Democratic party in this state is united behind the president and behind them. The solemn purposes of our harmonious get-together is to uphold the president's program for peace and preparedness, that the freest people on this earth may make their liberty and independence secure with the best government and the biggest navy in the world.

Most of the promises I made last year, as the candidate of the Democratic party for governor, pledged the enactment of various legislative proposals that seemed desirable. I am certain that we cannot legislate ourselves into a millennium. I am sure that we cannot solve all problems by passing a law. More important than legislation is the careful, conscientious administration of existing law and the daily doing of a good administrative job.

As we work daily at the task of trying to run your state economically, the policy to which we shall always try to adhere will be to require each individual on the state payroll to be competent and to do a useful day's work to earn his pay. There is nothing more pleasant than to be able to grant requests of loyal Democrats. We wish it were possible to provide a state job for all who seek it. Many of those applicants are worthy and competent. It is unpleasant to be placed in position where one must say "No" to many requests for jobs. But that promise I made you which is so difficult of fulfillment, the promise to make you a saving, thrifty, frugal governor can be redeemed only by sticking to the policy of holding the expense of government at the lowest possible figure. That makes it my unpleasant duty to decline to approve additions to the payroll unless justified by good business.

Two days from now throughout the United States, we shall commemorate on the Fourth of July the Declaration of Independence. That venerated document set forth principles involving human rights in which we all believe.

> When Freedom from her mountain height
> Unfurled her standard to the air,

She tore the azure robe from night,
And set the stars of glory there!
She mingled with its gorgeous dyes
The milky baldric of the skies,
And striped its pure, celestial white
With streakings of the morning light.

But the symbol of freedom's chosen land and the declaration made in the Declaration of Independence are of value only when they are coupled with the eternal vigilance of an active electorate.

The election that will take place this November may decide the future of the United States and will certainly determine the policies of government in the last remaining secure citadel of freedom and of peace throughout the world. The way to make democracy work is through the established methods of party government, set up as a means by which we can solve our problems, and through representative government as authorized by the Constitution and by Congress. Toward that end, let us now proceed with the business that is before this convention, and may God bless America.[4]

---

1. The term "Fifth Column" stood for undercover agents operating within a country to destroy it.
2. Wendell Lewis Willkie (1892–1944), b. Elwood, Indiana. Republican candidate for president, 1940. Attorney. *Who Was Who in America, 1943–1950,* 2:582.
3. The first Hatch Act, passed in 1939, prohibited civil servants from taking an active part in political activities. In 1940 the act was extended to state and local governmental employees who were paid in whole or in part from federal funds.
4. The governor delivered the keynote address. Material about the accomplishments of his administration has been deleted.

YOUNG DEMOCRATIC CLUBS OF AMERICA
Louisville / August 21, 1941

It is with genuine joy that I extend to the Young Democrats of America assurance of a warm welcome to Kentucky. You made us very happy when you selected Louisville as your convention city and we have never had the opportunity to welcome to our state more worthy guests than you who represent the youthful, vigorous leadership in the Democratic party.

We are proud of Kentucky, her glorious history, her traditions, her contribution to national leadership, and we are highly honored by your presence in our state. Kentucky is widely celebrated as the home of superior thoroughbred horses, beautiful women, and for the production of good whiskey. You will have opportunity to see our charming women. Since the races are not now in progress, you will not see our thoroughbreds in action. Those of you who have the inclination may have a chance to sample that third product for which Kentucky is noted.

Your presence here is indicative of your interest in good government. You realize that it is important that we as citizens interest ourselves in government. You understand that under a democratic form of government one may participate in government only through political parties. The citizen who assumes a superior attitude, disdains politics, does little other than criticize has a misconception of the duty of citizenship.

It would be fortunate if we might alter the attitude toward politics as a vocation, develop a public attitude that would encourage entering public service. You of this attractive group can contribute much to that more wholesome attitude.

In this critical period of our nation's existence, there is a need for national unity. We are not asked to surrender our democratic institutions and privileges. But we may best preserve the right of free speech, for example, by not abusing it. Time for debate over the course this nation should take in the world crisis has passed. Leadership of the nation has charted a course believed best for preservation of this Republic. A united nation should support that leadership, rally loyally behind President Roosevelt, accept his guidance, and enthusiastically follow his direction.

The time has come when there should be complete loyalty and allegiance to President Roosevelt as he strives to make America secure. The day has dawned when every individual on this continent should love America or leave it.

The need of the hour is not a leader. There has been raised up by destiny a great leader in the dynamic personality of Franklin D. Roosevelt. What is more imperative is that there be millions of followers of the leader.

No nation has ever perished for lack of wise leaders. That which is especially vital is that there be wise, intelligent followers—men and women who are genuinely patriotic—who have the wisdom to realize that in an hour of national peril the first duty of the citizen is to follow those upon whom have been imposed the responsibilities of leadership.

It is unpatriotic to try to make political capital out of national defense. The liberties and freedoms which we enjoy as Americans are shared by

Republicans as well as Democrats. Preservation of this Republic is as vital to Republicans as to Democrats. Republicans in the Congress should be as anxious that we hurry in our effort to halt Hitler as are Democrats.

Now that the need for a united people is imperative, it is inexcusable that Republican members of the Congress in such numbers oppose legislation essential to our national safety. Secretary of War Stimson, Chief of Staff General Marshall,[1] recently advised that it would be unwise to release those who have been called for military service at the end of one year. Their reasons for that conclusion are obvious. Necessity for legislation extending the period of military training was presented to the Congress by those best qualified to form an opinion on this important problem. Yet the majority of Republicans in both houses of the Congress voted against the wisdom of those who have the job in preparing our army to help destroy the ruthless Nazi dictator.

In the Senate, seven Republicans voted for the bill extending the period of training and thirteen against it. In the House, 21 Republicans voted for the measure and 133 voted against it.

On other measures vital to defense, the Republicans divided similarly. On passage of the lend-lease bill, under which we have been able to give help to those who are fighting the battle of civilization against Hitler and his hordes, only 24 Republicans in the House voted for the bill while 135 voted against it. In the Senate, ten voted for it and seventeen against it.

We would prefer to construe the position of the Republican opposition charitably. But we can only conclude that those who voted against these vital measures could not resist the temptation to do that which they regarded as politically expedient at the moment. It is unpatriotic to permit partisan political considerations to sabotage the safety of the nation. And that zealous, patriotic unity of our people so essential to success is difficult of attainment so long as the majority of Republicans in Congress are unwilling to contribute to it. Every member of Congress should be more concerned about the welfare of his country than about his own political welfare. Every individual should be more concerned about the defense of the nation than about avoiding personal sacrifice and inconvenience. We need a rebirth of the heroic zeal of those patriots who risked their lives and fortunes that this infant Republic might be established.

There is an opportunity for you, the Young Democrats of the nation, to become the evangels of a militant, unifying Americanism—an Americanism that places greater emphasis on the importance of giving to our government than in getting—an Americanism that will mobilize the will and the hearts and the minds of America in defense of this great Republic—an Americanism that condemns strikes in defense industries which impede the manufacture of guns and munitions for the army and navy.

It would hearten and encourage the president should you assure him of your approval and support of his foreign policy and his efforts to create an army and navy sufficiently powerful to insure our safety. A good army may not be good enough. Poland had a good army but not good enough. A second best army is as useless as the second best hand in a poker game.

I would again assure you that it is no perfunctory welcome that I here express—but that it is a welcome warm and sincere. We hope you will have a profitable convention and a visit to Kentucky so pleasant that it will leave only pleasant memories.

---

1. Henry Lewis Stimson (1867–1950), b. New York, New York. Republican. Attorney; secretary of war, 1911–1913, 1940–1945; secretary of state, 1929. *Who Was Who in America, 1951–1960,* 3:822.

George Catlett Marshall (1880–1959), b. Uniontown, Pennsylvania. Chief of staff, United States Army, World War II; secretary of defense, 1950–1951; secretary of state, 1947–1949. Announced the Marshall Plan for Europe after the war; Nobel Peace Prize, 1953. Ibid., p. 555.

DEMOCRATIC WOMEN OF KENTUCKY
Frankfort / December 1941

THROUGH the courtesy of your secretary, I have just been supplied with a copy of the resolution approved unanimously by your group at your recent meeting held in Lexington, Kentucky. I hasten to acknowledge this expression of patriotism and loyalty on the part of you, my fellow Kentuckians. Such an expression serves to encourage your chief executive and to prepare him for the uncertain future that lies ahead. I am gratified to learn that the state and nation will have the wholehearted support and loyalty of you and your organization.

Today the United States celebrated the one hundred fiftieth anniversary of the signing of the Bill of Rights. The principles as set out in that document have served as the foundation and cornerstone of our government. As we pause to revere and pay tribute to the memory of the brave men and women who founded this nation, and particularly to the authors and incorporators of the Bill of Rights, we must pledge and rededicate our allegiance, our lives, and our fortunes not only to that group of pioneers, but to the memory of those boys who have so recently given their lives and to those who will yet be called upon to make the supreme sacrifice in order that our nation and our government may survive.

If we are to conquer the forces that seek to destroy us, we must all contribute our share toward erasing from the face of the earth the enemies of free people and free nations. A great many of you no doubt will be called upon to bid a tearful goodbye to a dutiful son or a loving husband who may be unfortunate enough not to return. To give a loved one in the defense of our cause requires abundant courage. The people of this nation have ever been ready to fight in order to preserve the principles of democracy. I am proud to be the governor of a state which has always contributed more than its share for the defense of the nation. The United States has never lost a war because we fought only when it was necessary to do so in order to preserve freedom and our way of life, and we shall not lose this one regardless of what the cost may be because we are again fighting for the protection of our homes, our loved ones, and the right to be a freedom-loving people.

In acknowledging your resolution pledging support to your state and your nation, I am reminded of that poem in which the author so ably pays tribute to the fine women of this country in the following words:

The noblest things of thought or plan
Have not always sprung from the heart of man.
The grandest age must still unfold
That back of man stands the woman bold.
Back of might, of strength and power,
Back of achievements each day and hour
A woman's love, encouraging and hope
Keep men from falling as blindly they grope.
For back of it all—remember this—
Woman's heart is a chrysalis.

I extend my best wishes to each of you individually and express the hope that together we may enjoy a speedy victory.

SUPPORT OF SENATOR CHANDLER
Louisville / July 29, 1942

KENTUCKY is being well represented in the national capitol in these critical days. We have the distinction of contributing to the nation the majority leader in the United States Senate in Senator Alben W. Barkley. The junior senator from Kentucky, Senator A.B. Chandler, has grown rapidly in usefulness since he went to the Senate in 1939. The Democratic members of the House of Representatives have given their districts intelligent representation.

In these anxious days, our interests are monopolized by the war. Kentuckians are genuinely patriotic. They are united in their zeal for sacrifice and service such as will help meet the military needs of the nation. We are so absorbed in our endeavors to contribute to victory that we had hoped Kentucky would be spared the distractions of a primary election. We had hoped that we might expend all our energy in fighting our pagan enemies.

However, the opponent[1] of Senator Chandler ignored the fact that a primary election under these circumstances is inopportune. He has made exaggerated charges against Senator Chandler that reflect upon his integrity—charges based on misrepresentation which he has tried to magnify into the importance of a campaign issue. He hastened to place his accusations about a swimming pool before the Truman Investigating Committee of the United States Senate. An investigation was made and the committee found no action of Senator Chandler's that justified the charges made by his opponent. These charges by this chronic office seeker were referred by him to the War Production Board. An investigation was made and the War Production Board found no act by Senator Chandler that justified the vicious charges brought by his opponent. This chronic office seeker, who had demanded that these federal agencies conduct these investigations, now complains bitterly because their reports show him up as guilty of infamous misrepresentation. When these reports revealed this chronic office seeker as handling the truth recklessly, he squawked, "white wash."

This chronic candidate accused Senator Chandler of improper conduct because his wife bought some recapped automobile tires. This charge was investigated by the Office of Price Administration. It reports that there is no basis for charges against the Chandler family for violation of tire rationing regulations. Every accusation made by Senator Chandler's opponent has been disproved.

There was no necessity for a senatorial primary. Senator Chandler has served Kentucky so well in the Senate that his capable services should be retained. The man who precipitated this primary election pretends to be concerned about conserving our resources to advance the war effort. Yet he brought on a primary which he has no chance to win. That primary will cost the state and counties more than a hundred thousand dollars, a needless expense that should have been avoided. This unnecessary primary creates discord at a time when we should be united and harmonious as we exert every effort to help win the war. One whose action is such as to foment strife, seeks to discredit our public leaders, is guilty of a grave disservice to our state at a serious time. He should be rebuked by the voters. And a vote for Senator Chandler is not only a vote to keep him in the Senate, but it is also a vote which will express disapproval of the individual who forced this uncalled-for primary campaign based on malice and misrepresentation.

In this agonizing hour, it is important that Kentucky have able, experienced representation in the United States Senate. Senator Chandler has grown and developed under the impact of responsibility as a member of the Senate. He has faithfully and effectively supported President Roosevelt and the majority leader, Senator Barkley, in enactment of all legislation necessary to hasten the building of armed forces with which to smash our foes. Senator Chandler supported the president's program of military preparation and his foreign policy before Pearl Harbor just as zealously as he has since.

Senator Chandler has voted for every proposal which has helped the men in our armed forces. He voted for more generous pay for these defenders of the flag. He voted for a monthly allowance for dependents of those in the military service. He voted for free mail service for the soldiers. Every vote he has cast as senator has been for the best interest of Kentucky and the nation.

Senator Chandler has not only voted for the president's war program, but he has been in a position to exert helpful leadership in expediting war legislation. He is a member of the Senate Military Affairs Committee. With the nation at war, this is the most important committee in the Congress. The service of Kentucky's junior senator on this committee has been so constructive that President Roosevelt wants him returned to the Senate. In no public service is experience so vital as in the federal Congress. In this perilous period, it would be folly to discard the capable, seasoned services of Senator Chandler and substitute an individual incompetent and unfit to assume such large responsibilities.

The opponent of Senator Chandler served one term in the federal House of Representatives as result of a political fluke. During that term, he voted against legislation that established parity prices for tobacco farmers at a time when the farm population was suffering from the depression. This chronic officer seeker, who professes great concern for the soldiers, as a member of Congress, voted against the interests of veterans of the last war. Kentucky farmers and World War veterans should not forget these votes against their interests by one who now pleads for their support.

Senator Chandler's record of public service refutes charges that have been brought against him. As a member of the Kentucky state Senate, as lieutenant governor, as governor of this Commonwealth, he has sought always to advance the state's welfare. His honesty and integrity have been proved in the crucible of public service. Senator Chandler has performed his duties as a public official so well that not even his faultfinding opponent has had the temerity to criticize his official record.

His statesmanlike service in the United States Senate has been so noteworthy that President Roosevelt is anxious to have Senator Chandler reelected. Senator Barkley, majority leader in the Senate, says that it is for the best interest of Kentucky that the experienced services of Senator Chandler be retained.

Mayor Wyatt and the Louisville Democratic organization have endorsed Chandler. The Kentucky State Federation of Labor, the United Mine Workers, the Brotherhood of Railroad Trainmen, the Kentucky delegation in Congress realize the importance of keeping Senator Chandler in the Senate and have endorsed his candidacy. Only this lone critic and the dyspeptic, disgruntled attorney general have arisen to try to convince you that your senator, whose services have been highly acceptable to President Roosevelt, should be defeated and the responsibility of serving as Kentucky's senator be entrusted to this chronic office seeker.

I have great admiration for Kentucky fathers and mothers who have smiled through tears as they have sent their sons to don the uniform of our fighting men. I served two and a half years in the last World War. I understand something of the anxiety of you who have sons and brothers and husbands in the army. The opponent of Senator Chandler has sought to inflame your emotions, to play upon your anxiety, in accusations he has made. He has tried to create resentment in your hearts against Senator Chandler. I believe most of you will resent that. You should know that as a member of the Senate Military Affairs Committee, Senator Chandler has enthusiastically supported all legislation that will provide arms for your sons, give our fighting men the guns and planes and tanks they need. The opponent of Senator Chandler is trying to get your vote by telling you how interested he is in your sons in the army. He tells you he is a superpatriot. Senator Chandler's record as a member of the Senate Committee on Military Affairs is one of positive and effective action which proves his interest in your fighting sons and in giving them every possible help.

From every section of Kentucky, there comes evidence that the Democrats understand that it would be folly to dispense with a senator who has served our people with statesmanlike ability. The Democratic voters resent the campaign tactics of misrepresentation and intrusion that have been employed. They withheld judgment as to the besmirching charges brought against Senator Chandler until investigation had been made. When the Truman committee reported that it found no evidence to support the charges made by Senator Chandler's opponent, when the War Production Board reported that nothing was found to justify the accusations, Kentucky voters immediately concluded that it is their patriotic duty to give an emphatic endorsement to Senator Chandler. Not only will Senator Chandler be nominated in the Democratic primary August 1 by a majority of a hundred thousand, but his opponent will be rebuked for precipitating this unnecessary primary.

Since necessity for making a choice between Senator Chandler and his opponent has been created, it is our solemn duty as Democrats to go to the polls Saturday and vote to keep our gifted junior senator in Washington. When you have done that, you will have complied with the wishes of President Roosevelt and Senator Barkley. You will have voted for a man who will continue to uphold the hands of our commander-in-chief; you will have voted for a man who will continue to give Kentucky worthy and wise representation in the Senate of the United States.

---

1. John Young Brown, Sr. (1900–), b. Geigers Lake, Union County. Attorney. Resides in Lexington. State representative, 1930–1932, 1953–1954, 1962–1963, 1966–1967; Speaker, 1932. United States representative, 1933–1935. *Biographical Directory of the American Congress, 1774–1971*, p. 650.

ADDRESS TO STATE WORKERS
Frankfort / October 13, 1942

I THANK you for giving me an opportunity to talk to you about some of our problems and obligations. First, I want to express my appreciation to each of you for the contribution you are making to the cause of improved government. I feel a deep sense of pride in the good job that is being collectively done and to which each of you is contributing. We have striven constantly to improve the efficiency of the state government. I am certain that notable progress has been made. I get much satisfaction from the knowledge that higher standards of efficiency are being maintained and that the important day-by-day routine task of administering all phases of the state government is being economically and effectively done. I believe you too are proud of that fact because you, by your united efforts, have made possible this unspectacular, though important, accomplishment.

I am sure that each of you has a high conception of public duty. You realize that you have important duties to perform and take pride in performing them well. And for that admirable attitude, I want to say much obliged to you and tell you that I am grateful to each of you for helping to make this administration function efficiently in rendering effective service to the taxpayers whose servants we are. I believe each of you is proud of the record which we are making. If you believe in the job that is being done and the public service being rendered, then as members of a team which has collectively made the record of this administration, it naturally follows that you are proud to be members of that team and the Democratic party.

The Democratic party has functioned splendidly in Kentucky and in the nation in recent years as the instrument of good government. The Democratic party is dedicated to the high ideal of adherence to that which advances the welfare of this Commonwealth and the nation. There are always those who, through malicious misrepresentation, seek to besmirch Democratic administrations both state and national. For partisan or prejudiced selfish purposes, these critics try to tear down. Their thought and attitude is destructive. Their attitude and their status is well expressed in a bit of verse that recently came to my attention, entitled "Tearing Down."[1]

You, the members of this fine, enthusiastic team, are builders. But you must protect that which you are building from those who are content only with tearing down. The Democratic party as an agency of the nation's welfare is again under attack. The Republican party is trying to take control of the federal Congress. An occasional dyspeptic, disgruntled Democrat lends aid to those that try to wreck.

The governor ought to do a better job than he does because he gets so much advice. The president gets even more advice. But these so willing to volunteer advice disagree as to whose advice should be followed. Partisan critics are assailing the president and Kentucky's Democratic members of the federal Congress, trying to appeal to prejudice in an effort to increase the number of Republicans in Congress. These critics do not approach the point of comparison in ability and wisdom with the Democratic candidates they criticize.

President Teddy Roosevelt it was who said, "It is not the critic that counts; not the man who points out how the strong man stumbles or where the doer of deeds could have done better. The credit belongs to the man who is actually in the arena, whose face is marred by dust and sweat and blood; who strives valiantly; who errs and comes short again and again because there is no effort without error and shortcoming; but who does actually strive to do the deed; who knows the great enthusiasm, the great devotion; who spends himself in a worthy cause; who at the best knows in the end the triumph of high achievement; and who at the worst, if he fails while daring greatly, knows that his place shall never be with those cold and timid souls who know neither victory nor defeat."[2]

In these, the darkest days of the nation's history, attention of the people is so absorbed by the war that it requires greater effort to get our people to vote. Because interest in the November election is overshadowed by war and activities that grow out of it, it is of increased importance that we mobilize the leadership of the Democratic party and set it at the job of getting the vote to the polls. This is a tremendously important election. It offers an opportunity for the people of the nation to express their confidence in President Roosevelt, the commander-in-chief of our armed forces. Under his brilliant leadership, we have made amazing progress in creating an army and navy and in providing them with the guns and grenades, the tanks and planes they must have with which to crush our enemies. Yet despite the remarkable progress made in mobilizing the might of the nation, our commander-in-chief is harassed by critics who hope partisan gains may be made in the Congress. It is our duty to demonstrate to the president that we have confidence in him. We have an opportunity to do that. It can be done by reelecting Kentucky's members of the federal Congress by increased majorities.

Kentucky is represented in the United States congress by able, patriotic, and experienced men. Senator Barkley, as Democratic floor leader of the Senate, has reflected great credit on our state. Senator Chandler, in the three years he has been a member of the Senate, has proved himself to be an able, courageous, and clear-thinking representative of Kentucky. He is a member of the important Military Affairs Committee and other key committees. The Democratic members of Congress from Kentucky each have important committee assignments.

The reelection of Senator Chandler and each of the Democratic members of Congress by a big majority is important for the state and nation —important for the Democratic party in Kentucky. Should the lack of interest in the election result in these men being reelected by diminished majorities, Republicans would construe that as meaning that the faith and confidence of Kentuckians in President Roosevelt had waned. Republicans are making a hard fight on Congressman Jack May[3] in the Seventh

District. Congressman May is chairman of the Military Affairs Committee in the House. If, as a result of lethargy and indifference, Congressman May should be defeated, or be reelected by a reduced majority, Republicans would brag about it as a repudiation of President Roosevelt. It would make Hitler happy if his propagandists could proclaim that the chairman of the House Committee on Military Affairs had been defeated. Such would be interpreted as meaning the people of Kentucky did not want to fight Germany—were displeased with the war and its conduct.

Should Senator Chandler, member of the Senate Committee on Military Affairs, be reelected by a reduced majority, it would be hailed with glee by the Republican leadership as indicating diminished confidence in President Roosevelt and his leadership in waging the war. And there would be some justification for such an analysis because Senator Chandler and Congressman May and Congressman Chapman and Congressman Gregory and Congressman Vincent and Congressman Spence and Congressman Joe Bates and Congressman O'Neal and Congressman Ed Creal[4] have staunchly supported the president, have voted for the legislation he has requested as necessary in order to get the nation ready to lick Hitler.

The Republican National Committee is claiming that there is a swing of sentiment to the Republican party and that the Republicans will increase their membership in the Congress in the November election. In 1932 and in each succeeding election, the voters of Kentucky have demonstrated by their ballots that they believe in President Roosevelt and have confidence in his leadership. Since our president, as result of the war, is now commander-in-chief of our armed forces and the man to whom the united nations look for leadership in winning the war and the peace that follows, it is more important than ever that Kentuckians give the Democratic nominees a decisive majority—a majority that will say to the world that Kentuckians emphatically endorse the president, appreciate his wise guidance, and are glad to follow his leadership.

Ever since 1931, the Democratic party has won each state election by a substantial majority. The result has been that the Republican party has lost prestige and leadership. So long as the Democrats carry the state by a large majority, there is no likelihood that the Republican national organization will furnish money in an effort to rebuild the Republican party in this state. So it is not only important that Senator Chandler and the Democratic nominees for Congress be reelected by an overwhelming majority as an endorsement of their staunch support of the president in this grave emergency, but it is also important as a factor contributing to the success of the Democratic party in Kentucky next year and succeeding years.

It then becomes your duty and mine to actively and energetically get busy in behalf of the Democratic ticket. The collective, unified effort, the enthusiastic teamwork which you as members of this great team exert between now and November 3 can and will produce election results that will keep the Democratic party regnant in Kentucky to carry forward its constructive program of good government. If each of you, with a spirit of energetic leadership and active teamwork, will hit the line and hit it hard, encourage and inspire your friends to demonstrate their faith in the Democratic party, every precinct in Kentucky will be thoroughly organized and the vote registered at the polls despite the lack of interest. When you have done that, the victory achieved will be registered in a majority of such proportions that each of you will find satisfaction in duty well done.

This team of which we are members can perform effectively only when every member of the team performs well the job assigned. As the titular head of the Democratic party in Kentucky, as the one who has the proud privilege of being captain of this team, I urge each of you to get busy in an effort to overcome the lack of interest among the voters that is too evident. From this hour until the polls close, I urge you to do everything you can think of, do everything your ingenuity can devise, to quicken interest of Democrats in doing their duty on election day. Exert all your ability, expend your energies and enthusiasm to be certain that the precinct in which you vote is carefully organized and plans perfected to get the vote to the polls. Write to and call upon your friends and relatives and impress upon them the fact that this is an election of great importance. Get them to see that an adverse election result or even a reduced majority will hamper the president as he strives valiantly to lead our armies to triumph over our pagan enemies. Point out to them that this is one of the few nations left in the world in which elections are held, in which the people still have the right by ballot to influence the course of their nation's government. Impress upon them the fact that as we fight to prevent destruction of a government in which the people rule that they must not neglect the important duty of the citizen to vote.

As the man who has the responsibility of being captain of this team, let me insist that there be immediately awakened in our group a militant, aggressive attitude. The signal is that each member of the team hit the line with determination and zest and keep on hitting the line until the polls are closed and the votes counted. You know how to do the job; you know what is needed to be sure that the Democratic majority does not slump in your precinct. I am calling upon you to overcome lethargy and lack of interest by redoubling your effort.

I have every confidence that each of you will do your full duty, demonstrate again your leadership and effectiveness as Democrats. And when that is done, the results of the November election will give no comfort to the Republicans. We shall rejoice together upon results which reaffirm our faith in President Roosevelt, in Kentucky's members of the federal Congress, and the Democratic party.[5]

---

1. The poem by Edgar A. Guest has been deleted.

2. *Theodore Roosevelt Cyclopedia*, ed. Albert Bushnell Hart and Herbert Ronald Ferleger (New York, 1941), p. 2.

3. Andrew Jackson May (1875–1959), b. Langley. Prosecuting attorney, Prestonsburg, 1901–1909; United States representative, 1931–1945; member, House Military Affairs Committee. *Who Was Who in America, 1951–1960*, 3:564.

4. Noble Jones Gregory (1897–1971), b. Mayfield. Banker. United States representative, 1937–1959. *Biographical Directory of the American Congress, 1774–1971*, pp. 1032-33.

Beverly Mills Vincent (1890–), b. Brownsville. Resides in Brownsville. Attorney general, 1936–1937. United States representative, 1937–1945. Ibid., p. 1859, and telephone interview, Mrs. B. M. Vincent, July 31, 1978.

Brent Spence (1874–1967), b. Newport. Attorney. United States representative, 1931–1963. *Biographical Directory of the American Congress, 1774–1971*, p. 1734.

Joseph Bengal Bates (1893–1965), b. Republican. Attorney. United States representative, 1938–1953. Ibid., pp. 563-64.

Emmet O'Neal (1887–1967), b. Louisville. Attorney. United States representative, 1935–1947; ambassador to the Philippines, 1947–1949. Ibid., p. 1492.

Edward Wester Creal (1883–1943), b. Larue County. Attorney. United States representative, 1935–1943. Owner, publisher of a Hodgenville newspaper, 1918–1943. Ibid., p. 800.

5. The governor held a rally at the Executive Mansion on October 10, 1942, at which he urged more than a hundred state officials and department heads to "get out the vote." *Kentucky Post*, October 11, 1942.

SUPPORT OF J. LYTER DONALDSON
Louisville / July 30, 1943

AS governor of Kentucky, I deem it important and proper that the people of Kentucky be correctly advised of the accomplishments of the present state administration before casting their vote in the Democratic primary August 7.

There are those ambitious office seekers who, motivated by their own interests, scream to high heaven that "the governor is a dictator" when he undertakes to acquaint the people with some of the noteworthy achievements of his administration, and counsels a continuance of the program he has inaugurated. No one denies the right to criticize those in high public office; yet, by the same token, no one should deny the right of the officer to speak out respecting the things which have been accomplished.

Nearly four years ago the people of Kentucky, by an unprecedented majority, nominated and elected me as their governor. I have performed the duties of that office to the best of my ability. I have worked diligently at the job every day, trying to accomplish those things which would bring the greatest good to the greatest number of the people of Kentucky. I have kept faith according to the best understanding which I possess.

I do not propose now to see the accomplishments of my administration misstated and slandered by ambitious and irresponsible office seekers without placing before the people of Kentucky the true record. I do not propose to see the men and women in the state service, who have labored long and honestly to bring about great progress in Kentucky's government, slurred and slandered without stating to the people of Kentucky the facts as they exist.

I propose to review for you some of the things which have been accomplished under my administration. I suggest that you should not permit these accomplishments to be destroyed by your next governor. When I have laid the record before you, then you can make your choice.

If this be "dictatorship," then let my critics make the most of it. It would be an unfaithful architect, indeed, who designed a beautiful building, but saw it placed in the hands of irresponsible builders without advising the owner of the results which would inevitably follow.

The most vital phase of a sound state government is a solid financial structure. The most important achievement that has taken place in Kentucky in a quarter of a century has been the transformation which has lifted the state from the brink of bankruptcy to the solid, secure foundation of financial solvency.

[Material about elimination of the state debt, appropriation increases for 1942–1944, state institutions, old age assistance, aid for dependent children and the blind, the road building program, and major legislation of the Johnson administration has been deleted since it appears elsewhere.]

Much of this legislation was enacted despite the sternest opposition. The sole purpose of this kind of legislation was to advance the welfare of the people. "Corrupt politicians" would have had no interest in it. Scores of other needed and remedial laws were enacted. The absence of public criticism of legislation added to the statute books during my administration provides eloquent testimonial that it was acceptable to the people.

In those departments of your state government that are the responsibility of the governor, a thorough and efficient administrative job has been done.

The Department of Revenue supplies an example of high efficiency in collection of taxes. There are now 200 persons employed in performance of this service, as compared with over 300 prior to 1936. During the fiscal year ended last June 30, it cost less than one cent to collect each tax dollar. This is one of the lowest costs of collection in any state in the Union. Actually, in the fiscal year of 1941–1942, it cost 79 cents to collect $100 in taxes. That kind of efficient public service cannot be performed by a corrupt political regime, such as Kilgore charges is in power in Frankfort.

The Unemployment Compensation Commission furnishes striking proof of the gains brought about by good management. For the benefit of the worker, the duration for which benefits may be paid within any twelve consecutive months has been increased from fifteen to sixteen weeks; the waiting period has been reduced from three weeks to one week. The tax on workers was abolished, effective July 1, 1942. Discontinuance of this tax represents an annual savings to the workers of Kentucky of approximately $3.5 million.

For the benefit of employers, the maximum contribution rate of 3.7 percent was reduced one cent, effective January 1, 1942. This reduction directly affected 1,452 employers, who would have been required to pay the higher rate for 1942. The experience rating provisions of the law have been continued, and 404 employers, out of the 8,600 subject to the law, have built reserve balances by stabilized employment so that they now pay no contributions whatever for unemployment compensation. Twenty-eight hundred other employers are now paying contributions of only 1.8 percent to the state. Had it not been for our experience rating provisions, these employers whose rates have been reduced would have paid additional contributions of over $1.8 million during 1942, and a careful estimate shows that such employers would have paid additional contributions of approximately $2.5 million during 1943.

On June 30, 1943, Kentucky had to her credit in the United States Treasury for unemployment benefits, $58,109,684. A recent comparative table of the solvency status of the trust funds of the forty-eight states and of the District of Columbia, Alaska, and Hawaii, released by the Social Security Board, shows that Kentucky leads the fifty-one jurisdictions with a solvency percentage of 104.5 against 89.4 for the next highest state and an average solvency percentage for all states of only 45.9. Kentucky is the only state that is able to pay every potential benefit claimed in full.

Further emphasizing efficiency of operation is the record of the Workmen's Compensation Board. The cost of operating this board is met by contributions of those employers who have accepted the terms of the Workmen's Compensation Law. Shortly after I became governor, the force of referees employed by this board was reduced from thirty-three to eleven. The efficiency of this board has been maintained on a high level. Such economies were effected that last year—for the first time in history—no assessment was made against the employers in Kentucky to finance the board's operation.

The Division of Insurance presents another example of efficient, economical public service. The number of field men in the Fire Prevention and Rates Section has been reduced from thirty-four to seventeen. Expenses of the division were reduced $10,000 per year; yet collections were increased $45,000 per year. The net balance in the state Fire and Tornado Insurance Fund has increased to $750,000, making a saving in insurance premiums during my administration of $543,000.

Time forbids mention of many of the agencies of the state which have achieved notable accomplishments during my administration.

[Statistics on how the tax dollar is spent have been deleted since they are given elsewhere.]

My friends, when you hear a smooth-talking candidate promise "to cut the waste in expenditures," he is usually dishing out the same old campaign hokum which you have heard so many times before.

I have no apology to make for the record of constructive accomplishments of my administration. I am proud of it! It will compare favorably with that of any administration which has preceded me.

I recommend to you that the program of progressive government so splendidly launched be placed in the hands of an able successor in order that the gains so laboriously made shall not be lost. In making this recommendation to you, I cannot avoid some mention of the gentlemen who seek your vote in the Democratic primary.

One is from North Carolina. Now, North Carolina is a great state, but I do not believe the time has yet come when we must ask North Carolina to furnish Kentucky with a governor. He is undertaking to use the Kentucky Farm Bureau—which, at a good salary, he served as secretary for a number of years—to advance his own political fortune. The membership of the Kentucky Farm Bureau resent this effort to impair the usefulness of that agency by plunging it into politics. The Farm Bureau's purpose is to serve the farmers and not to advance the political ambitions of its former secretary. The Farm Bureau has paid Ben right generously for his services in the past. Now he undertakes to make a political machine of a nonpolitical organization which has been more than generous to him. He is a political adventurer and a phony farmer.

I had the opportunity many times as governor and lieutenant governor to be helpful to the Farm Bureau. I have guided and sponsored much of its legislative program through the legislature, and I have signed into law many of the bills sponsored by the Farm Bureau and passed by the legislature. This was done in spite of the paid lobbyist, Ben Kilgore; and not because of him. But Ben claims credit for all farm legislation passed in Frankfort. And he is no more responsible for it than he was for the abdication of Mussolini.

The favorite topic of this phony farmer is "rural electrification." He tells rural Kentuckians who are enjoying the conveniences of electricity in their homes that "Ben got it for them." This is nothing more than Ben's "baloney." As lieutenant governor, I was chairman of the Legislative Council, which drafted the REA bill that was presented to the special session in 1937–1938. Governor Chandler included REA legislation in a special call to the General Assembly. Ben knows I had something to do with that. The bill which was enacted placed the REA Co-ops under supervision of the Kentucky Public Service Commission. Ben blustered and stormed against that provision.

It was fortunate that REA Co-ops in Kentucky were placed under supervision of the Public Service Commission. This utility regulatory body took a special interest in helping REA get off to a good start in Kentucky. To the Public Service Commission—and not to Ben—is due the credit for fixing the wholesale rate for electricity sold by the private utilities to REA Co-ops at eleven mills per kilowatt. There are few states that have provided REA with a rate so low. The Public Service Commission it was—not Ben—who issued an order that forbids an electric utility from running a spite-line into territory in which formation of an REA Co-op is projected.

John M. Carmody, administrator of the Rural Electrification Administration in Washington, said:

> I am just advised of the order issued by your Public Service Commission, establishing a wholesale rate of approximately 11 mills per kilowatt hour to be made available to rural cooperative projects in Kentucky by seven private utilities. This order, together with the previous recent order of the Commission controlling spite-line construction, represents marked progress and should pave the way for rapid extension of the benefits of electricity to the farmers of your state. The action of your Commission might well serve as a model for other state commissions as representing what they can do as their part in making rural electrification possible on a wider scale.

The Kentucky Public Service Commission blazed a new trail in rural electrification. Other states followed. Yet, Ben tries to deceive Kentuckians to whom the advantages of electricity have been made available through REA by claiming to have brought this convenience to them. That is untrue. We would have had a splendid REA program in Kentucky even if Kilgore had stayed in North Carolina. Under the REA law, the Public Service Commission has supplied the Co-ops, without cost, with technical skill and engineering advice on electric installation problems that has been invaluable to them. Yet Kilgore tells you this and the last administration have taken no interest in rural electrification. The record refutes that statement.

This phony farmer from North Carolina bitterly complains that the "State Administration is playing politics." But no more brazen example of an effort to play politics with a public agency has been revealed than the attempt of Ben to use REA for his own political advancement. Letters are being sent to users of REA service by Kilgore campaigners, telling them that it was Ben who got electric lights for them. Now that this light has been shed upon the deception Ben has sought to perpetrate, I know you will give credit where credit is so richly due and give Ben the rebuff which his deception merits.

The second candidate whom I shall mention is the lieutenant governor who wails so loudly that he is opposed by the "Crown Prince" of my administration. Rodes was anxious to be the "Crown Prince." He thought it was all right for me to support him as the "Crown Prince." He urged it, but he complains when such support was not given him.

The lieutenant governor is doing a lot of bragging about being a veteran of the World War. He would have you believe that he it was who won the war. Let's take a look at the military record of this self-styled veteran. He entered the Student Army Training Corps at Ogden College and Western Teachers College on October 10, 1918, and was discharged December 10, 1918, having served two months in the SATC.

Lyter Donaldson was a married man. They were not drafting married men, but Donaldson volunteered for service. The record in the Adjutant General's Office in Washington discloses that Lyter Donaldson was examined on November 6, 1918, at Camp Taylor for a commission. On November 9, he was recommended by the Adjutant General for appointment as a second lieutenant in the Army Service Corps and ordered to report to the Commanding Officer at Camp Upton, New York, to accompany a detachment of Army Service Corps troops overseas. This commission was not issued because of the cessation of hostilities on November 11, when all pending appointments in the United States Army were suspended.

Rodes is a "promising" young man. He promises more money for everything on the one hand; yet he promises to repeal much of the state's taxes.

The sincerity and honesty of Myers's entire campaign may be judged by his assertion that if he is elected governor, he will give back to the railroad employees of Kentucky the contributions which they made to the unemployment compensation fund. Of course, Rodes knows the truth—but he does not think that you know it.

The Unemployment Compensation Commission of Kentucky, early in 1940, asked the courts to approve the return to the railroad employees [of] their contributions to this fund, since they no longer came under the jurisdiction of the Unemployment Compensation Commission. A suit was filed. The Court of Appeals of Kentucky held that the commission could not legally repay these contributions. And if any doubt exists in your mind as to the correctness of this statement, ask any lawyer to show you the decision of the Court of Appeals in *Unemployment Compensation Commission* v. *Savage*, 283 Ky. 301, decided May 24, 1940. Rodes knows of this decision; now you know about it. Now you can decide whether Rodes can give the money back or not, and you can decide further whether he has any regard for the facts as they actually exist.[1]

In surveying the agencies of the state government in an effort to improve their efficiency, it became necessary for me to replace D. C. Moore[2] as director of the Division of Motor Transportation because I became convinced that this division was not being efficiently conducted. The results prove the wisdom of that action.

Money collected by the Division of Motor Transportation goes into the Highway Fund. In the year 1939 when Moore was director, collections of that division totaled $404,767. Under William Blanton[3] as director, collections have increased each year as a result of more vigorous and diligent activity. In 1942, collections of that division totaled $684,492—an increase of $279,725 over collections the last year that Moore was director. That is an increase of 69 percent.

Moore was demoted to assistant director. He recently resigned to support Rodes Myers. Moore's conscience has been in a coma for three and a half years. Now he asserts that he raised a fantastic sum of money from the motor truck interests for my campaign. He had no authority from me to raise campaign funds. He charges that Mr. Donaldson, my campaign chairman, and I authorized him to promise preferred legislation to the trucking interests. Lew Ullrich,[4] executive secretary of the Motor Truck Club, was present at a meeting Mr. Donaldson attended with truck representatives. He kept minutes of the meeting. Mr. Ullrich says no promise of preferred legislation was made. I tell you no promise was made. I tell you further that no governor ever took the oath of office as completely free from commitments, specific or implied, as I did. No unworthy obligations were made by me as a candidate to any group or special interests. The record of my administration proves that no group or special interests have received any preferred consideration.

Notwithstanding the things which have been accomplished in Kentucky's government, much remains and will always remain to be done. I would not support the candidacy of any man whom I did not honestly believe would bring to the governor's office the highest possible degree of experience, sincerity, and honesty. As governor of your state, I have the deepest interest in seeing the program begun under my administration carried to fulfillment. As a citizen of Kentucky, I think I have as much right as any other citizen to express my preference amongst the candidates.

It is fortunate for Kentucky that Lyter Donaldson seeks the nomination of his party. By experience, by education, and by the sincerity of the efforts which have marked his official life, he is preeminently well qualified for the job. He has not promised more than he can perform.

Under his direction as commissioner of highways, rural highway improvements have reached a new high point of usefulness. He recognizes the need for still greater expansion in rural road building. When he is elected governor, he is pledged to recommend to the legislature that the present $2 million for rural highways be increased to $3 million. He will concentrate his experience and his vast knowledge of road building upon the problem of speeding up the building of "farm-to-market" roads. No greater service can be performed for Kentucky's rural citizens. He is a Kentuckian. He loves Kentucky and seeks to serve her.

He has supported with enthusiasm the rural electrification program, and was most helpful in the passage of the TVA Enabling Act which furnishes the source of cheap power to Kentucky's farms and municipalities.

He is acutely conscious of the need of increased educational facilities and has pledged increased support of public education.

I am anxious, indeed, that Kentucky not turn aside from the high road of progress along which she has advanced in the past eight years toward the elusive goal of good government. Under the leadership of Lyter Donaldson as your governor, she will advance with accelerated pace. He has the ability, the character, and the wisdom to make a great governor.

It has been charged that Mr. Donaldson "is without color!" It is more important that the Democratic nominee have character, than color—and Lyter Donaldson has both. He will build upon the foundations that have been laid. He has an excellent grasp of the state's problems and a clear understanding of the state's needs.

I urge his support by every Democrat in Kentucky on August 7. I confidently predict that the Democrats of Kentucky will nominate him by an overwhelming majority. I am certain that, as the Democratic standard-bearer, he will register a notable triumph over the Republican candidate in November.[5]

---

1. To refute the assertion of Myers, Chairman Vego E. Barnes of the Unemployment Compensation Commission issued a similar statement shortly before this

address by the governor. *Lexington Herald,* July 24, 1943. See also speech from October 20, 1941, in the Health and Welfare section.

2. D. C. Moore (1889–1955), b. Pike County. Director, 1936–1940, assistant director, Division of Motor Transportation, resigned July 1943. Circuit court clerk, Pike County; sheriff, Pike County, for two terms. Telephone interview, Mrs. Carl Hatcher, daughter, Pikeville, September 26, 1978.

3. William Watt Blanton (1904–1966), b. Richmond. City attorney, Paris, 1928–1930; police judge, Paris, 1930–1940; state senator, 1946–1950; state representative, 1952–1954. *Lexington Herald,* June 16, 1966, and interview, Mrs. Thomas J. Smith, sister, Richmond, September 5, 1978.

4. Lew Ullrich (1896–1971), b. Louisville. Managing director, Motor Truck Association; executive secretary, Automobile Dealers Association. Telephone interview, Mrs. L. Ullrich, September 14, 1978.

5. A similar speech was given at the Courthouse, Frankfort, on July 31, 1943.

VALEDICTORY ADDRESS
Frankfort / December 7, 1943

AS has previously been called to your attention, this is the second anniversary of Pearl Harbor. The Republicans today drive the Democrats from the state Capitol just as the Japs made Pearl Harbor untenable. But there are certain fundamental differences between the attack on Pearl Harbor and the attack on the Democratic party in Kentucky on November 2.

The brave defenders of Pearl Harbor were not expecting such a cowardly blow as the treacherous sons of Nippon administered. But we Democrats well knew that a state of political warfare existed between us and the Republicans. We even knew the zero hour for the attack. It was to be 6 A.M. on November 2.

For days, Democratic scouts had reported evidence of growing Republican strength. Their political maneuvering, our scouts reported, was precise and well timed. They appear to have plenty of ammunition. They were observed to be a little hungry looking, but otherwise fit and rarin' to go.

Then, came the dawn! Came the attack! And what an attack! Swarms of well-armed Republicans quickly mounted the offensive against us on every front. Our men fought bravely. We engaged the enemy everywhere he appeared. We fought him on the riverbanks, the mountain passes, and the hills and the hollows, on the streets, the country lanes, and the isolated crossroads.

But still the enemy pressed forward. He brought up fresh reserves at unexpected intervals. He was out to beat the Democrats. And beat us he did! He simply got there "fustest with the mostest!"

I would not be constrained to tears, nor moved to laughter, if it were not for the biblical injunction, "Rejoice with them that do rejoice, and weep with them that weep."

So, my fellow Democrats, I weep with you who are to join me in the temporary exodus from Frankfort. And, my Republican compatriots, I rejoice with you at your hard-won one opportunity to live so short a time in so fine a town as is Frankfort.

Four years ago, in my inaugural address, I said, "The great honor you pay today is not to me, but to the office which I assume and to the form of government which is symbolized by this ceremony. Our celebration is not alone in honor of what we inaugurate; it is principally in honor of what we continue—the succession of power in the hands of the people through their elected representatives." Four years ago, I said, "You inaugurate me as the governor of a sovereign people, and by that act you reaffirm your own sovereignty. My own term is for a fixed period after which I shall step aside, and another shall take my place. But your rule will continue as long as we and our children shall be free Kentuckians and free Americans." That may properly be said on this or any other inaugural occasion.

In my inaugural address, I said further, "I shall try to justify your confidence by diligently endeavoring to make you a saving, thrifty, frugal governor. With the funds available, I shall diligently endeavor to give you a constructive, progressive administration of your state affairs. I will not make you a spectacular governor, but I will try harder than did any of my predecessors to make you a good, honest governor."

I find great satisfaction in the knowledge that I have kept those pledges. I find great satisfaction in the fact that I turn over the reigns of authority to my distinguished successor with Kentucky in better condition than when I accepted responsibility for her government. I find great satisfaction in the fact that as I transmit the authority as governor to my distinguished successor, the Commonwealth is in better condition than ever before in her history.

Eight years ago, I was inaugurated as lieutenant governor with Governor Chandler. Your state government was on the brink of bankruptcy, in debt about $28 million. When I was inaugurated as governor, that debt had been cut to about $7 million, and on March 25, 1942, the last interest-bearing state warrants were called for payment and, today, I have the proud distinction to turn over your government to my distinguished successor with Kentucky completely out of debt and $10,301,799.38 cash in the bank to the credit of the general fund. That bank balance has been temporarily depressed because we have been paying the public school per capita appropriation. This is the largest item in the budget. It is paid in seven monthly installments of about $1.3 million each. We have paid five of the seven installments, and as soon as this heavy drain on the treasury ceases, the surplus will return to a much higher figure before the end of the fiscal year, July 1. Not since the close of Governor Beckham's[1] administration has Kentucky been out of debt. He left office with a surplus of $43,000 in the treasury, and this is the first time since that there has been a surplus in Kentucky's treasury. My purpose in accumulating that surplus had been to make it available for meeting the critical needs of the postwar period and completing the program of rebuilding the long neglected state institutions.

I find great satisfaction in the fact that I turn our state government over to my distinguished successor with the state institutions in the best condition in which they have been for forty years. Within the last eight years, a modern prison has been constructed. Within the last four years, the other prison has been modernized. The hospitals for the mentally ill have been rebuilt, transforming them from foul, hideously frightful institutions into hospitals that are clean and bright, and sanitary and modern. This humanitarian program is approximately 70 percent complete. I am leaving ample money in the treasury to complete this program.

So I take pardonable pride in the fact that I turn the Commonwealth over to Governor Willis in the best condition in her history. I hope that, under his administration, Kentucky will continue to move forward. Prior to my period of public service, I engaged in the publication of a newspaper. I shall again engage in such activity. I have found, after trying it both ways, that it is much easier and simpler and more fun to run a newspaper and tell someone else how to run the state government than it is to run the state yourself. In Kentucky, we swear in a governor and then start swearing at him. Every governor hopes he may escape but none have yet. I hope Governor Willis will escape and prove an exception.

In concluding my brief valedictory, I want to express to the people of Kentucky my appreciation for the opportunity of serving as governor. I want to publicly express my appreciation to the fine citizens of Frankfort for their generally hospitable attitude toward me and Mrs. Johnson and our daughter Judy during our four years residence in the Executive Mansion. So with best wishes to Governor Willis, I make my exit from public service, smiling.

---

1. John Crepps Wickliffe Beckham (1869–1940), b. Bardstown. State representative, 1894–1898, Speaker, 1898; lieutenant governor, 1899; governor, 1900–1903 (became governor when Goebel was killed), 1903–1907. United States senator, 1915–1921. Chairman, Public Service Division; commissioner, Department of Business Regulations, 1936–1940. *Who's Who in Kentucky, 1936*, p. 27.

APPENDIX 1
PRIMARY CAMPAIGN OPENING
Shelbyville / June 24, 1939

I STAND before this throng of militant Democrats as a candidate who does not represent any special interest, and the first promise I make to you is that I will not be controlled by the CIO or bossed by John L. Lewis.[1]

Four years ago the Democrats of Kentucky honored me with the nomination for lieutenant governor. I promised that I would cooperate with whomever you elected governor and help him in every way possible. Although I did not support Governor Chandler in that primary campaign, he was chosen by the Democrats of Kentucky as their nominee. I contributed all I could to his election in the final campaign against the Republicans, despite the fact that the candidate I had supported broke the pledge to support the nominee of his party that he had made in his declaration of candidacy. He not only bolted, but he was so afraid that someone might fail to know that he was bolting that he engaged the radio for the occasion and bolted the Democratic party in a public broadcast. It is true that the bolt he undertook to lead failed miserably, but that was through no lack of effort on his part. It was just a repetition of "Casey at the Bat." "There was ease in Tom Rhea's[2] manner as he stepped into his place. There was pride in Tom Rhea's bearing and a smile on Tom Rhea's face."

But after the election in November 1935, in which I supported the nominee of the Democratic party and he supported Judge King Swope,[3] the nominee of the Republican party, "There was no joy in Mudville, mighty Tom Rhea had struck out."

During the four years I have served as lieutenant governor, I have kept the pledge I made to uphold the hands of the governor and cooperate with him. I have given him the fullest measure of loyalty. That was the promise I made. That was my duty and I performed that duty. I invite you to contrast my loyalty to a Democratic administration with the action of my opponent when Speaker of the House during the administration of Governor Ruby Laffoon.[4]

I ask Kentucky Democrats to endorse at the polls on August 5 the action of a loyal lieutenant governor who tried always to be helpful to the Democratic administration of which he was a part. I submit to you that the loyalty for which I am now assailed provides abundant proof that I tell the truth. It proves that I do my duty and that I keep my word.

In my opening statement[5] I outlined my position on important questions. A demagogic critic asks, "Why did you not do those things while lieutenant governor." Anyone who does not know that, under the law and constitution the lieutenant governor cannot do that which he may do as governor, doesn't know enough to be governor. When I was serving as acting governor, the legislature had already enacted the laws under which the state was to operate and gone home.

As lieutenant governor, I have had exceptional opportunity to become familiar with the state's problems, to learn much about the state government which better qualifies me to serve you as governor. I know the financial limitations of the state as well as her needs. But I am not running on the record of the present state administration. I ask you to choose me as your governor because of the sound, sensible program I guarantee to you.

I know what I am going to do as governor. That is more than my opponent does. I know what the present revenues of the state are. I know that the taxpayers of Kentucky cannot pay increased taxes and should not be compelled to do so. I know that by careful economy and prudent management of the state's business reasonable provision can be made for the essential agencies and functions of the state government.

The governor is inaugurated the second Tuesday in December and the legislature meets the first week in January. The first thing that a governor must do is to plan his budget. The biennial budget measure lists every appropriation for an entire period of two years. Under the law, after the budget is adopted and the legislature adjourns, the governor, no matter how good a promiser or sleight of hand performer he may be, cannot spend any money for any purpose except as specified in the appropriations bill. That appropriations bill specifies the exact sum of money that every governmental agency can spend for two years.

I shall urge the legislature to increase the maximum payments of old age assistance to $30 per month. Revenues of the state are sufficient, with the state debt reduced as it has been in the last four years, to justify an increase in the maximum payments to $30 a month. My opponent's campaign manager, Frederick A. Wallis,[6] said in a speech in Brownsville last summer, "It is ridiculous for any one to believe that the state could pay a maximun of $30 a month to old age assistance." He said, "This would cost the state $20 million a year and mean increased taxation." My opponent pretends to promise $30 a month for every person receiving old age assistance. His campaign manager says it is ridiculous for anyone to believe such a promise. Surely Mr. Brown would not be guilty of duplicity. Certainly one who professes such exalted ideals of public integrity would not try to deceive the splendid, silver-haired Kentuckians who have spent their lives in honorable, useful toil—yet have the misfortune to come to the declining years of life without enough to provide for themselves. These on the old age assistance rolls are splendid men and women. Their labor has contributed to the upbuilding of Kentucky. They were victims of hard luck. It is our duty as Kentuckians to extend them a helping hand. But it is despicable to try to get their vote by promises which the campaign manager of my opponent declares cannot be kept. Since Mr. Wallis has been serving as campaign chairman for my opponent, he said in a newspaper interview that the statement of Mr. Brown that he favored $30 a month old age pension did not actually mean that he proposed to pay everybody $30 a month. It has been suggested that Mr. Wallis and Mr. Brown hold a public debate on the question. Mr. Brown is now taking Mr. Wallis with him everywhere he goes to prevent him spilling the "beans" again and to let Tom Rhea run his campaign headquarters.

The present law requires that, before qualifying to receive old age assistance, one must give the state a lien against what little property may be possessed. This provision in the law was written at the suggestion of a representative of the federal Social Security Board who supervised the drafting of the Kentucky act.

I believe that these old people should be permitted to keep possession of what little they have. The money distributed to these worthy old people should be an outright gift instead of a loan. I favor canceling all existing claims and liens against the property of those who have been receiving assistance under the present law.

The federal and state laws require that cash grants be based on the need of the individual. I shall urge that the appropriation for old age assistance be increased sufficiently to pay the maximum of $30 a month to those most destitute and substantially increase the grants made to all others entitled thereto. I shall be cautious to see that all venerable Kentuckians entitled to aid get a cashable check for a fair and reasonable sum and not counterfeit promises. I shall so conduct the state's business that the old age assistance fund will not be bankrupted and the needy recipients face the tragedy of want because of a "busted" treasury.

It is not the governor's money with which old age assistance is paid. It is money collected from the taxpayers. There is no magic by which money can be plucked from the air with which to redeem extravagant, insincere promises, made for the purpose of deceiving the old people who are in want. If such could be done, it would be very clever.

There comes to mind the story of a magician who was giving a program aboard a ship at sea. Passengers were being entertained as white rabbits were pulled out of a high, silk hat and other mystifying acts performed. The magician held up a bird cage inside of which was a parrot. He said he was about to perform a trick, the like of which had never been seen before. At that instant one of the huge boilers of the ship blew up. The terrific explosion blasted the ship asunder. The wreckage was scattered about the ocean. The bird cage containing the parrot lighted upon a large piece of the wreckage. The magician came floating by, holding to a life raft. The parrot saw him and said, "Very, very clever."

If there be at the helm of the Ship of State a pilot who overtaxes the boilers, pushes them beyond their capacity, the certain result will be an expolsion that will injure every citizen and bankrupt the state government.

As your governor, it will be my purpose to conduct the business of the Commonwealth on a sound, business basis. I learned the importance of thrift in the hard school of experience. As the son of a circuit rider Methodist preacher, the meager income of our family made thrift a bitter necessity. I am thankful that I acquired the habit of being saving with money. I am glad I was taught that it is honorable to pay one's debts and that one should do without many things that are wanted if there is not the money with which to pay for them. I promise to be a saving, thrifty governor—one that will avoid wastefulness. One that will make your money go as far as is possible in buying for you the biggest dollar's worth of public service in old age assistance, public education, public health, and public improvements. You know these desirable services must be paid for with cash and not "phoney" promises—that actual money, taken from the taxpayers is required to meet these obligations.

In order to fulfill the pretended promise of my opponent to pay the full maximum of $30 a month in every case, to every person eligible for old age pensions, it will take approximately $9 million a year or an increase of nearly $7 million in present funds.

The present appropriation for common schools in Kentucky is $12 per child. This is the most generous contribution for public schools in the history of the state. It should be maintained with such increase in the per capita as becomes possible without bankrupting the school funds. In addition, a teachers' retirement fund will add an estimated $750,000 and should be provided for. I favor also the submission of a constitutional amendment to permit an equalization fund which is the only solution to the problem of inequality in distribution of school money.

My opponent in his opening announcement promised an increased per capita of $15 for public schools. There are 792,079 children in the public graded and high schools of the state. That promise will add $2,376,237 to the present appropriation for public schools. This would be a fine generous thing if the money was available. I am going to be honest and say that I do not know where all these millions would come from. My opponent is no more anxious to provide this increased aid for public education than I am, and with the help of the legislature I can come as near doing it as he can.

The institutions of higher education in the state should be adequately supported. I pledge untiring effort to a progressive educational policy.

Our teachers are underpaid, not because we do not appreciate their services, but because loose financial management in years past has laid a burden on the state that they have been forced to suffer from. I shall strive to provide ways and means to increase their pay and to build a sound financial policy for the state government that will make possible for them compensation to which they are entitled and to give to every child in Kentucky, whether in cities or rural counties, good schools, free textbooks, rural roads on which to go to school, and the chance for the greatest gift of this free country, an education.

I have advised the officers of the Kentucky Free Bridge Association that I will work with them in trying to develop a sound and feasible plan for amortizing the existing bonded indebtedness of the toll bridges of the state so that they may be freed in the immediate future. Substantial relief has already been given the traveling public by a cut in toll charges and further relief appears to be possible.

When I read my opponent's speech, I took a pencil and a piece of paper and wrote down the increases which his program will make. I then added the revenue received from the taxes he says he is against. If he does what he says he will do, it will require over $15 million more than the state of Kentucky now has annually to spend. The present annual expenditure of the state of Kentucky is $24,742,131, exclusive of expenditures for highways. It would require a tax of more than $1.41 a hundred on all the real estate in Kentucky to raise this additional money, and the state tax on real estate is now five cents on the hundred dollars of valuation. It would take a 5 percent retail sales tax to raise the $15 million required by the lavish promises of my opponent.

But suppose we do not raise the money. Suppose we just vote the appropriations without passing tax bills to provide the money. That means issuing IOUs, the legal form of which will be state warrants bearing 5 percent interest with no legal provision made for their payment. The state's credit would be so impaired that instead of issuing state warrants at 1.5 percent now selling for more than 100 cents on the dollar, the state would be issuing warrants that would soon be selling for 75 cents or less on the dollar and be bearing 5 percent interest.

The schoolteachers are educated and intelligent. They know that in a year or two this would mean short terms or closed schools, bankrupted funds for teachers' salaries and for retirement. The elderly people of our state whose long lives of usefulness we honor, whose gray hairs we venerate, whose care is our noblest opportunity, know that this would mean for them soon cold checks, broken faith, waiting at the door for the postman to arrive with a check that cannot be cashed because a wild and reckless promiser dissipated the funds with which to pay them.

During some of the previous administrations, the pardoning power has been grossly abused. During the present state administration, the governor has issued no pardons and has adhered to a strict policy with respect to pardons. During those periods of time that I have served as acting governor, I have adhered to that policy. I have felt that it was improper for me to undertake in the governor's temporary absence to nullify or deviate from the policy of his administration. When I am elected governor, I shall determine the policies of my administration for the next four years; and my policy with respect to the pardoning power will be that all applications for executive clemency will be given prompt and careful consideration. Each application for pardon will be fully and carefully investigated and considered, and I shall not hesitate to grant pardons in such cases as the facts and circumstances justify.

On that matter or any other, I shall not be bound by any of the policies of any previous governor. I gave to Governor Laffoon, when he was governor, my loyal cooperation; I gave to Governor Fields, when he was governor, my loyal cooperation; I gave to Governor Chandler my loyal cooperation. I am running now on my own platform and not on the record of any of them.

It shall be my purpose as governor to complete the program so splendidly started for the improvement and modernization of the charitable and penal institutions of the state. I shall complete that program during my administration so that these institutions shall be second to none in the nation. I shall see that they are administered by adequate staffs of competent, trained personnel. These institutions will be so modernized, equipped, staffed and operated that Kentuckians may have a justifiable pride not only in the adequacy of the building, the equipment, and the facilities, but also in the competency of the management, the staff, and in the service rendered.

Now I have told you what I am going to do as governor. Let me tell you what my opponent would do if he were governor. I am not going to get into any promising contest with so reckless a promiser as my opponent. He promises more money for this, and more millions for that, as glibly as though the billions in the gold vault at Fort Knox had been turned over to him. He promises to repeal those taxes which he thinks will get him most votes. Such promises are as fantastic as they are insincere. He evidently has overlooked the fact that most Kentuckians can add and subtract.

While in France with the AEF, I walked along the parade ground one spring evening in front of a barracks in which was quartered a company of colored troops. A dusty Alabama lad was entreating the dice to come "seven." I joined the spectators. "Shoot $500," said one colored doughboy as he caressed the dice. "Shoot $1,000," said the next lad as he got the dice. It sounded like a big game. Then along came a colored Yank from the next barracks. He got the dice and threw down a dime. A mad scramble was set off as a dozen dived for the lone dime. I inquired of a bystander why the "rumpus" over a dime when they had been shooting $500 and $1,000. "Why, sir," he explained, "That dime was the only real money in the game." My opponent is playing for votes of those who may be fooled by promising them millions of the taxpayers' money without any thought of the taxes that would have to be levied to collect the money.

As to what taxes he proposes as a substitute for those he intimates may be repealed, he plans to appoint a "fact-finding commission" to find out what to tax. No "fact-finding commission" can find any painless taxes. There are no facts about taxes that are not already known. And judging from his speeches, he has no regard for facts anyhow. At least he needs a fact-finding commission to get him up some accurate facts to use in his speeches.

No doubt there would be named on his "fact-finding commission" to find taxes the Honorable Thomas Rhea. Last time he served on a tax "fact-finding commission" he came forth with the retail sales tax, and perhaps he still regards it as what Kentucky taxpayers need. We have had plenty of fact-finding in Kentucky. In 1923, there was a careful compilation of facts by the Efficiency Commission. The firm of Griffenhagen and Associates made a survey of Kentucky government and compiled many more facts. John Y. Brown, when Speaker, named a fact-finding committee. It is not facts that would be needed to redeem the extravagant promises of my opponent but cash, cold cash, and millions more of it than taxpayers are now coughing up each year.

Should my opponent be inaugurated governor, if he is not on a sit-down strike, he would appoint a Civil Service Board to examine the thousands to whom Mr. Tom Rhea has promised jobs. Tom Rhea, the chief apostle of political spoils and assessments, is whispering into every ear that he can find, saying, "We will have plenty of jobs if we win. You will be taken care of." Mr. Tom promises all who request it a job. Then my opponent promises to establish civil service so these who have been promised jobs cannot get them. The purpose of his civil service is to find an excuse for not giving the jobs he promised.

Let me predict as to who will compose that Civil Service Commission. Head of it will be Professor Tom Rhea. With what zeal he will hop to that job of purifying politics in Kentucky. With what fervor he will tackle the task of taking politics out of patronage. How slyly he will cook up some clever scheme to get those Logan County jobhunters past the examination so that the hungry hordes of Logan County job seekers, which composed one-fourth of the crowd at the Morganfield opening, may get back in the clover of purified political spoils. What a great day it will be for Kentucky when politics has been purged, dry-cleaned, and fumigated under the guidance of the man, who in 1935, John Brown called a bank wrecker and a corruptionist. Can you imagine an administration dominated by Tom Rhea in which no state employee would be assessed for campaign purposes?

Then, I predict that the second member of that Civil Service Commission will be Sam Caddy, head of the CIO in Kentucky. His chief interest will be as to whether the applicant belongs to the CIO, believes in sit-down strikes, and pays dues regularly to John L. Lewis.

Then, the third member of that commission, designed to purify politics, will be the Honorable Frederick A. Wallis—the one who was commissioner in New York—the one Mr. Brown used to call "Windy" Wallis. He will be content to again qualify to be addressed reverently as Mr. Commissioner. His disposition toward "scatteration" of his activities will often prevent attendance at the purification ceremonies of the Civil Service Commission. But such will not slow it up because he will leave a rubber stamp signature which may be used as required to verify the purifying procedures.

Since the announcement of my opponent that he has been reading the *Richmond Daily Register,* I am surprised that he is not better informed. I hope he will continue to read it. He will find it more interesting, accurate, and informative than his speeches. He found some cartoons in the *Register* which displeased him. The *Register,* like most newspapers, buys its cartoons and comic art from a newspaper syndicate. Artists draw their cartoons and comic strips to reflect humor. President Roosevelt has a keen sense of humor, and I am certain that he would laugh heartily at the cartoons in which he was humorously caricatured, yet of which Mr. Brown complains.

Why, there isn't any finer thing that President Roosevelt has done than to laugh at all the cartoons that have been published about him. He is said to have enjoyed the play, "I'd Rather Be Right," in which George M. Cohan[7] imitated him, more than anyone else in the country. This is a tribute to his greatness, the big heart, the true democracy of a man for whom I have the greatest respect and admiration and with whom I shall cooperate wholeheartedly when elected governor in all matters in which the state and nation have a joint interest.

In the comic strips, I often wish that Jiggs might occasionally get the best of Maggie. I wanted Uncle Bim and the Widow Zander to wed and live on in connubial bliss. I would like to see Popeye get his great strength from eating Kentucky turnip greens instead of canned spinach. But I am not drawing the comic strips or cartoons. That is the job of the artist. Often I wish the cartoon or comic strip had been given a different quirk. But so far as the *Richmond Daily Register's* cartoons reflecting discreditably upon the Great American in the White House that we admire and revere, no thought or intention was farther from the mind of the capable young man who is serving as managing editor of the paper. The *Register* also recently published a story, as did other daily newspapers, quoting John L. Lewis as he made a bitter attack on the Roosevelt administration and declared that the nation needs a "courageous leadership." The story was published as a matter of news, but I do not personally approve of the denunciation of the Roosevelt administration by the chief sponsor of my opponent's candidacy.

My opponent professes great loyalty to President Roosevelt, yet as a member of Congress during the one term he there served, on March 13, 1934, Representative Weideman,[8] Democrat from Michigan, pointed out that "only a week ago he [Brown] was leading a revolt against him [the president]." He referred to the revolt against the use of government bonds to back Federal Reserve notes, legislation which the president favored and requested be passed, yet Brown, the precocious authority on the intricate financial question, refused to follow the president's leadership on this important piece of legislation.

My opponent says a lot of things about me in his speeches. He had the gall to criticize me for changing political alignments. He has the nerve to point the finger at me and say I am inconsistent. He will say many other things about me. May I suggest that you not be greatly concerned about that which he says about me because he has talked that way about nearly everybody in the state. On July 20, 1935, in a speech in Somerset, the gentleman who is my opponent viciously attacked Tom Rhea, now his chief political sponsor. In that speech, Mr. Brown suggested that Mr. Rhea take some of the money he was spending for "burgoo" and pay depositors of a closed bank with which he said Rhea had been connected. In a speech in Louisville, July 27, 1935, my opponent assailed the then governor, Ruby Laffoon, and Tom Rhea as he urged all honest citizens to join the campaign to drive corruption from the Kentucky Capitol. He harshly criticized Governor Laffoon for selling his property to the state for a highway garage at a price he charged was excessive. In a speech in Louisville, August 3, 1935, my opponent declared that Governor Laffoon and Tom Rhea had found special sessions of the legislature necessary in order to buy additional members of the legislature to do their bidding and betray the people who had elected them. In October 1935 he denounced them for bolting the Democratic ticket.

Now these were not very nice things to say about Govenor Laffoon and Mr. Rhea. But those words and many more came from the vitriolic tongue of my opponent. Yet four years hence, we find him curled up complacently in bed with the pair he castigated as corrupt. These about whom he said such harsh things, he now claims as his bosom cronies. These he branded as unfit for public service are now his chief advisers and political connivers. Perhaps he did not mean those harsh things he said about Mr.Tom and Governor Laffoon. Or it may be that he has found it politically expedient to kiss the hands of the pair against whom he unleashed his vituperative tongue. One gets the impression that he is a gentleman of plastic convictions. So I suggest that you do not take too seriously the things he says about me, because it may be that next year when he runs for something else he will change his mind about me too and take back that which he says and go back to "cussing" Governor Laffoon and Tom Rhea.

My opponent gets interested in the farmers every time he gets into a political race, and that is every time an election comes around in which there is something he can run for. The greatest help the state government can extend to farmers is to make the tax burden on them as light as possible. I approve of taking all the tax off farmland and real estate for state purposes, except the five cents which the Court of Appeals ruled could not be removed without an amendment to the constitution.

In 1933 there was submitted to the people for a vote the question of whether they would alter the constitution so as to take all state tax off real estate and farmlands. I favored that amendment and supported it. My opponent, who says he is so "hot" for the farmers, opposed changing the constitution so the state tax could all be taken off farmland and homes. He made speeches against it and contributed to the defeat of the amendment. It is because of that defeated amendment that the five cents tax on real estate is now levied for state purposes. The reckless and extravagant promises made by my opponent as he pledges millions for this—and millions for that—mean that should he undertake to keep those promises he would be forced to raise millions of dollars more in taxes. There are only two sources from which substantial additional money can be raised, and those sources are either a general sales tax, which Mr. Brown says he opposes, or a heavy state tax on real estate and farmlands. I shall, as your governor, vigorously oppose an increase in the state tax on real estate or a general retail sales tax.

Back in 1933, when my opponent was serving his one term in Congress, officers of the Burley Tobacco Growers Association asked him to help other Kentucky congressmen to secure a change in the first Agricultural Adjustment bill, then before the House Agriculture Committee. Effect of that amendment was to raise the parity prices on burley tobacco from ten cents a pound to sixteen cents a pound. My opponent's reply to officers of the Burley Association was, "I am not interested in the parity price of burley tobacco." All other Kentucky congressmen manifested deep interest in the change in the bill, effect of which was to add millions of dollars to the income of burley tobacco growers of the state. The Mr. Brown who was not interested in a vital farm problem in 1933 is the same gentleman who now says he is "hot" for the farmers. Of course, he was not a candidate that year.

I spent my boyhood on the farm. I know from experience the hardships, the uncertainties, and heartaches of the farmer. I own a farm in Hardin County. That farm has been cultivated in complete cooperation with the national farm program. Every phase of the Agricultural Adjustment Act was adhered to. All provisions of the Soil Conservation Act have been complied with on that farm. That should be sufficient proof that I am in accord with the farm legislation and activities of the national administration. I shall as governor cooperate fully with plans for improvement of this program and will give encouragement to it. I am a member of the Farm Bureau Federation in Hardin County. These facts are important only as they reveal that my interest in Kentucky farmers results from intimate knowledge of their needs and trials and problems and that in me, as governor of Kentucky, they will have a sincere, sympathetic friend whose dominant interest will always be for their welfare.

As governor, I shall utilize all available facilities to advance rural electrification development already so well started in Kentucky. I favor establishing a public research laboratory at the University of Kentucky where a staff of competent scientists may devote their full time to efforts to develop profitable new uses for tobacco and other farm products and try to find wider uses for the mineral and agricultural resources of the state. Discovery of new uses for tobacco would increase consumption and result in better prices to farmers for their chief crop and an increase in their income.

I endorse the proposal of the Kentucky Farm Bureau Federation to have the federal government refund 20 percent of the money collected from federal taxes on cigarettes to states having no cigarette tax. This would permit immediate repeal of the state cigarette tax which I would like to see removed as soon as possible.

I have demonstrated my sincere friendship for labor at every opportunity. I shall, as governor, be sympathetic with all reasonable labor legislation which improves the condition of the working man without reducing employment opportunity. Who is the real friend of labor? Is it the man who is their champion because he receives $10,000 a year as their paid attorney and lobbyist, or is it the man who risks his capital and expends his energy in an effort to provide jobs for honest and industrious working men?

I recognize the importance of developing the state park system as rapidly as possible. While I am unwilling to promise everybody a lake at their front door and two ducks on every lake, which would cost about $500 million, I have no hesitancy about giving assurances that it shall be my purpose as governor to cooperate with the National Park Service in an endeavor to develop to the fullest extent the unusual park possibilities in Kentucky, with the aim of making our beautiful state increasingly inviting to vacationists and tourists.

Kentucky has had for governor many eminent lawyers, and they have filled the duties of the governor's chair with distinction. Kentucky has had as governor soldiers whose courage and devotion to their state has been tested under fire. Kentucky has had as governor farmers, called from the field as was Cincinnatus from the plow. But, so far as I know, no lobbyist, actively engaged in lobbying, ever before made a race for governor while still representing any special interest or group. My opponent is a lobbyist in that he is concerned principally with those interests of his client that come before the state government in Frankfort.

Under the present method of operation, the CIO is primarily concerned with the attitude of the state government. In Detroit, it was the chief question raised in connection with the sit-down strikes. In Missouri, when the CIO started organizing farm workers, they staged sit-down strikes on the public highways, a problem directly affecting state government.

Since the shutdown of operations in the Harlan coalfields from which all the state has suffered, including especially the men employed by the railroads, the question has arisen in Frankfort as to whether money paid into the Unemployment Compensation Fund should be distributed to those on "strike" in the form of unemployment compensation. This is a problem directly dealing with the state government, and the CIO sent its attorney, John Y. Brown, to Frankfort to represent it in this matter. This was on June 4, after he formally announced his candidacy for governor, after he had made his opening speech in Morganfield, and after he had filed his declaration papers.

Now, let's figure out what this would mean. With John Y. Brown, the CIO leader in the governor's chair, every strike called by his principal backers, John L. Lewis and Sam Caddy, in the state of Kentucky would be financed from the Unemployment Compensation Fund. The Unemployment Compensation Fund was created by contributions of the workers of the state and their employers—all the workers of the state who are under the act including members of the American Federation of Labor. The money is to pay benefits to those who may become unemployed as a result of business or industrial adversity or for causes beyond their own control.

I am against letting John Brown and Sam Caddy take this money that belongs to all workers of the state, in all kinds of businesses and industries, to pay benefits to men who are unemployed because of strikes that are the result of "bungling" leadership of CIO chieftains. Laboring men certainly should have the right to strike, but it is equally important that they have the right to work. Both are sacred rights and of equal importance.

In a speech in the United States Senate, Senator M. M. Logan said recently that the real purpose of the CIO is to control the food supply of the nation. In McCracken County last year when strawberries ripened and were ready to be picked, a CIO strike was in progress at the plant of the Paducah box factory. Before the strike, the crates in which these strawberries were to be shipped had been manufactured. They had been paid for by the berry farmers and left there in storage. When farmers went to the plant to obtain their own crates, the CIO strikers refused to let them remove them. As the strawberries started to rot, it became necessary to enter the plant under the protection of peace officers and take the berry crates to the field.

My opponent in this campaign says that he is employed by the CIO as an attorney and that he has a right to accept that employment. Of course he has. I do not question that right and I think that the CIO has a right to the same fair treatment as any other party to any other controversy. Mr. Brown says he has represented the CIO as he has represented housebreakers, bank robbers, highwaymen and murderers, banks, and corporations. Surely no one will question the right of any lawyer to represent any client he may choose in the courts. I do say that the people of Kentucky do not want him representing the CIO in the governor's chair.

My opponent is more than an attorney for the CIO. He is a member of it. He has a card in the United Mine Workers, although he has not dug a scuttle full of coal since he has been a member. While the pay of these miners was cut as a result of a strike, their attorney continued to draw his big salary.

There are many splendid men who are dues-paying members of the CIO. I have no word of criticism for them. They are doing the best they can to make a living for their families. But I am against the practices of their dictatorial leaders, leaders that exploit honest working men, leaders which the dues-paying members have no voice in selecting. The CIO is the most undemocratic, dictatorial organization in America. The men whose money supports it are not permitted to choose their own leaders. They do not have a chance to say whether they want Sam Caddy as their district boss or John Y. Brown as their lobbyist or John L. Lewis as their overlord, although money is taken from their pay envelopes to pay the big salaries of these bosses. This is directly opposite the sanely guided American Federation of Labor in which members by vote select their leaders.

I believe that working men should be permitted to join any union they desire and that no dictator should be given power to require them to join the union of which he is the czar and "dues-taker." I know that many of the honest working men of the CIO do not approve of the radicalism of their bosses. I know they do not approve of illegal, ruthless methods they employ. I sympathize with them rather than condemn them.

My opponent in one of his speeches said, "To those who help me much in this campaign I shall owe much." And let me ask you, who is helping him more than John L. Lewis and the undemocratic CIO? Should he be elected governor, he will owe more to the CIO and John L. Lewis than anyone else. Lewis will dominate him as governor and control him to do the bidding of the CIO. I warn you against the danger of letting that happen. I warn you against the peril of permitting the communistic CIO leadership to get control of your state government.

My opponent tries by insinuation to create the impression that his candidacy received the blessing of the great American who occupies the White House. He tells you that he would not be running had not the president said it is all right. I have no doubt he would have told me that it is all right for me to run, but I would not embarrass him by trying to draw him into a state race.

My opponent got into a race for the United States Senate in 1936 without getting the consent of the White House. He ran against Senator Logan, who had loyally supported the president and whose reelection he desired. Yet Mr. Brown ran against him anyhow.

My opponent tells you that, because I supported Governor Chandler instead of Senator Barkley last summer, I am against the president because President Roosevelt was for Senator Barkley. But go back to 1936. The president wanted Senator Logan reelected. I vigorously supported Senator Logan and was on the president's side, when Mr. Brown disregarded the attitude of the president and himself sought to defeat the junior senator from Kentucky whose loyalty to the president justified his reelection. Mr. Brown criticizes me for doing in the senatorial race of 1938 the very same thing he did in 1936, only his action was more out of line with the president's desires in that Brown was himself the candidate who opposed the choice of the president.

The man who occupies the governor's chair should represent the whole people of the state of Kentucky. He should not know any dividing line between any group of our citizens. We are all the same. I look out over the state of Kentucky and I see men and women working in the sun in the tobacco fields where the greatest of skill and care is required to handle that difficult crop. I see men going beneath the surface of the earth where the sun's invigorating rays never reach to dig the resources which nature has stored there. I see county courthouses where honest, frugal businessmen have disregarded their own personal interests and have given long hours to offices to which they have been elected to try to work out the problems of their people. I see boys and girls going to school in buses or walking on the roads where development of the rural road program, enforcement of the safety laws, free textbooks, and better school conditions should give to all the best advantages that the state can furnish.

Here and there are many who need the friendly cooperation of a sympathetic state government. There are farm workers and tenants who are striving to own their own farms and homes. There are men and women of the hardihood and strength of character of their pioneer forebears who have suffered from an economic condition that is not of their own making. There are working men, some at times unemployed, and families from time to time in need. They are our own kinsmen and our people, thrifty, industrious, and upright men and women who will resent any attempt to make political capital of any temporary difficulties they may have encountered.

> Let not ambition mock their useful toil,
> Their homely joys, their destiny obscure,
> Nor grandeur see [hear] with a disdainful smile,
> The short and simple annals of the poor.[9]

I think, indeed, that when the poet wrote this greatest elegy in the English language, he must have had in mind that some day some smart aleck running for office would call them "One gallused guys" and that was why he paid to them such a tribute.

I see teachers in the small schools struggling in that noblest of all professions against difficulties that should be removed. I see farmers trying to take their products in to market needing better roads on which to haul their tobacco and their lambs. I see stores at every crossroads that serve the needs and interests of their people. I see boys that went overseas with me when the nation's destiny was at stake and served, every man alike, side by side with other men, their equals and their friends. All are proud of their citizenship, of the work that they do, and all are joined together in looking to the future of their state. When I am governor, I shall recognize no distinction between any group or class. The proudest boast a man can make, the only title that he needs, the only introduction required by me as governor is to say that "I am a Kentuckian."

We have lived in Kentucky all these years without serious industrial strife and nothing would more seriously hamper the progress of Kentucky than such discord as has been created in other states by the CIO, with its class hatred and bitterness.

My opponent talked about the "psychology of victory" in his opening speech. He claimed it was all on his side. He wrote that speech before he saw the disappointingly small crowd that gathered in his native county for the occasion. Despite ingenious efforts to assemble a big crowd for the event, there was present by actual count 2,765 people, one-fourth of whom were from Logan County hunting for jobs. And when he saw that disappointingly small audience, it was then he realized that "the frost was on his pumpkin." He compared this contest to a football game in which two teams lined up to play in which one had just beat the other by 70,000. This is a different game between different teams. Last year there was a great fullback as a candidate on the team he is talking about. This year that team has a fullback that is a drawback. Last year the best player on the team he claims is his, was a hard-running halfback, whose name was Louisville Democratic Organization. This year that powerful halfback is on the team that is going to win. Many of the best players that were on his team last year refuse to follow the CIO lobbyist. This year he has as his quarterback or campaign chairman, Frederick A. Wallis, who was one of the second string players last year on the other team. Besides Brown might have to stop the game at any time and go out on a sit-down strike. His psychology of victory is just another case of whistling in the dark.

I know that I am not a superman whom Destiny has called to solve all the problems of the Commonwealth, myself. I do not know all the answers. I do know the state's problems cannot be solved with a Big "I" and a little "we." I do know that only as I can obtain the loyal support of the patriotic citizens of the Commonwealth of Kentucky will it be possible to solve its problems. I will "get along" with the people of this state, will confer with them, will invite cooperation and advice. I would like to have all the assistance that I can in the campaign now opening. I shall need all the help that I can obtain to serve you well as governor for four years. I have said before I have no ambition for a political career. I look toward becoming governor with humility, yet with a heart full of hope that there is no problem too big, no task too large, no opportunity too great for the intelligent, upright, courageous citizenship of the state of Kentucky to accomplish.

---

1. John Llewellyn Lewis (1880–1969), b. Lucas, Iowa. Labor leader, AFL organizer, 1911–1917; vice-president, UMWA, 1917; president, UMWA, 1920; organized Committee Industrial Organization, 1935; reorganized CIO, 1938 (Congress Industrial Organization) and entered into competition with AFL. President, CIO, 1935–1940; resigned when President Roosevelt was elected for a third term but retained the presidency of the UMWA. *Webster's Biographical Dictionary*, p. 895.

2. Thomas Stockdale Rhea (1871–1946), b. Russellville. Farmer, attorney. Candidate for several offices, defeated in Democratic primary for governor, 1935. Frequent campaign manager. State treasurer, 1911. *Lexington Herald*, April 17, 1946.

3. King Swope (1893–1961), b. Danville. Unsuccessful Republican candidate for governor, 1935, 1939. Lexington attorney. Judge, Circuit Court, 1931; United

States representative, 1919–1921. *Who's Who in Kentucky, 1936*, p. 391, and *Lexington Herald*, April 24, 1961.

4. Ruby Laffoon (1869–1941), b. Madisonville. Judge, Circuit Court, Hopkins County, 1921–1931. Governor, 1931–1935. *Who's Who in Kentucky, 1936*, p. 237, and *State Journal*, March 2, 1941.

5. Johnson announced his candidacy in a speech at Richmond on May 17, 1939.

6. Frederick Alfred Wallis (1869–1951), b. Christian County. Primary campaign manager for John Young Brown. Commissioner of public welfare, 1935–1939. Supervising editor of *A Sesquicentennial History of Kentucky*. Ibid., 4:2142-45, and *Who Was Who in America, 1951–1960*, 3:886.

7. George Michael Cohan (1878–1942), b. Providence, Rhode Island. Composer, playwright, and producer. *Who Was Who in America, 1897–1942*, 1:239.

8. Carl May Weideman (1898–1972), b. Detroit, Michigan. United States representative, 1933–1935. Circuit judge, Third Judicial District, Michigan, 1950–1968. *Biographical Directory of the American Congress, 1774–1971*, p. 1895.

9. Thomas Gray (1716–1777), b. London, England. *Webster's Biographical Dictionary*, p. 623. The quotation is from "Elegy Written in a Country Church Yard," *The Complete Poems of Thomas Gray*, ed. H. W. Starr and J. R. Hendrickson (New York, 1966), p. 38.

APPENDIX 2
General Election Campaign Opening
Mount Sterling / October 7, 1939

EVERY man, woman, and child in this state is glad today to be a Kentuckian. This grave hour in the history of the world impresses upon us the responsibilities of citizenship. It is not an accident of fate that in our Commonwealth law and order prevail. Here life is safe; property is protected; civil and religious rights and liberties are secure; homes are happy; fear is a stranger; children laugh at their play; they go to schools where improved educational opportunities are provided for them; they travel to country schools in buses over improved rural roads; they cross in increased safety at the street corners. The full resources of the Commonwealth are being mobilized to protect the humblest home from being haunted by the gaunt specter of want. By matching federal funds, the state government joins in sending a check each month to more than 45,000 elderly men and women who otherwise might face despair in the days when the shadows lengthen behind them in the reddening glow of the sunset of life.

The name of the state we love has not been besmirched by any scandal in high places or disclosures of crookedness in public office. The credit of the state is sound. Taxpayers are not burdened with paying interest on an increasing state debt. There is no longer danger of bankruptcy of the state government or the collapse of financial support for any of its essential functions.

The necessary pursuits of business, agriculture, and industry and of peaceful, profitable employment, and the alluring pursuit of happiness are encouraged and promoted. None of these pursuits is threatened by the insidious practices of governmental privateering. There is no terrorism of any kind within our borders. No bitter animosities divide our people. There is no occasion for lasting differences of opinion of the type that bring distrust and hatred. The state is singularly free from industrial unrest. Our cities are not "blacked out" at night through fear of any outside foe. We are also glad that there has been no fulfillment of the dire Republican prophecies of seven years ago that in the event of a return of the Democratic party to power in the nation, weeds would grow in the streets of our cities. We are free to gather together wherever we please. We can express our opinions freely and most of us abuse the privilege, but no governmental agency of any kind places any unfair censorship upon us. We can come together on an occasion like this, which naturally is a very pleasant one to me. If we wish, we can even "talk politics."

It seems to me, however, that politics in the narrow, bitter, and partisan sense should be far from our thoughts today. Free government is threatened throughout the world. Open challenge is being made to democracy and to human liberty and to the rights of men. It was to uphold these things that our forebears carved a pathway for civilization in the western wilderness. It was to uphold them that nearly 150 years ago Kentuckians laid aside all differences and applied for statehood. These critical times demand that we turn our thoughts earnestly and honestly without partisan bias to the continued upbuilding of this Commonwealth.

The great American in the White House—President Roosevelt—has asked for an adjournment of mere partisan politics. To his plea I add my own and ask that the questions of this campaign may be decided upon the proved accomplishments of the respective parties and candidates, upon the programs they advocate, and upon their respective records of ability to serve the people, weighing all these factors by the single test of which will best contribute to the unity, to the welfare, and to the happiness of the people.

I thought everyone in the state of Kentucky knew and understood what was being done by the state government until the Republican nominee for governer made the opening speech of the Republican campaign in Lexington. But do not worry if he is somewhat mixed up about what has been done, is now being done, and about what ought to be done by the state government, because he is a busy man and when he is not running for office pays little attention to the problems of government affecting the people of the state as a whole. He is circuit judge in his judicial district. He must be a good one. He says so himself. The Fayette Circuit Court over which he presides is proclaimed by him to be the largest and busiest circuit court of continuous session in the entire state. Now to preside over that extremely busy court and to make two state campaigns as candidate for the Republican nomination for governor and two state campaigns as the Republican nominee for governor within four years without resigning is enough to overtax the capacity of any man. In addition to being a judge of a court of continuous session, he is also a candidate of continuous session. He has run for governor twice within a six-year term, and I submit that this is a pretty good record for running although his record for winning is not so good.

The Republican nominee for governor in his opening speech at Lexington devoted most of his speech to partisan criticism of Governor Chandler. He proclaimed certain things which he says he will do if elected governor. The Democratic state administration has already done practically every worthwhile thing that the Republican nominee for governor promises that he will try to do if he is elected. His only platform is the safe and easy one of what we already have done. He offers nothing new.

I think it is in tragically bad taste at such a time as this for any political party or candidate to ask for a hearing when coming forward with nothing but criticism, serving nothing but selfish, partisan ambition, offering no semblance of political principle or program, shouting nothing but glittering generalities.

On the morning after our opponents launched their state campaign, I found this description in the first paragraph of the story published by the Lexington newspaper: "The battle-cry of the Republican Party—'Kentucky in 1939, United States in 1940'—rang through the Woodland Auditorium." It was the Republican leaders themselves who thus stated what they consider to be the main issue and who selected the battleground on which they wish to wage their campaign. Put in plain language, the opposition thus presents as its main feature a stark and naked political appetite.

I cannot say that I do not understand such an appetite, because the people of Kentucky and the nation in 1931 and 1932 turned out the sterile leadership of that opposition to feast upon Mr. Hoover's two chickens in every pot. It was a diet upon which they must have gotten hungry. But neither can I forget, nor can you forget, that the whole body of the people got hungry on the same diet. I cannot sympathize unduly because the leadership that plunged the nation into that tragic depression has had to suffer politically while others suffered in the flesh.

But in nature, even the most voracious appetite is wrapped up somehow in skin and bones to hold it together. After noticing this bold parading of a political appetite as the main feature of the opposition campaign, I looked carefully to see what kind of dressing they had wrapped it in so that it might appear with seeming decency in public. I wanted to see whether it wore hair or fur, whether it walked or crawled, and whether it barked or snarled or merely grunted.

But after reading the proceedings of that meeting carefully, as they were reported in the daily papers, I was surprised to find that this appetite exists without benefit of any other organs or bodily functions whatever. It lives only for itself. It does not offer to feed into any program the strength of that which it boasts its intention to devour. In column after column of the description of the Lexington meeting, you can find nothing but criticism, and criticism is only a symptom of this stark and naked political appetite, not a reason or a justification for that appetite.

They gave no indication of understanding that state and national administrations under Democratic leadership have assumed their rightful role of servants to the people.

The Democratic program is specific. There are certain very important progressive undertakings that have been started in Kentucky that should be completed. The first big job of the next four years should be to continue the worthwhile progressive and constructive activities of the state government that are already under way. In addition to these, there are other very necessary steps that must be taken in order that Kentucky may continue to be the best place in the world in which to live. These things are not political in any sense. They are social, civic, economic, and administrative problems. They should be considered as matters of business for the state and as activities that touch the welfare of its people. Here are some of the things that should be done:

1. The state should continue to live within its income and retire the remainder of the state debt without increasing the burden of taxes. We particularly oppose any increase of the state tax of farmlands and homes.

2. Old age assistance should be continued and the maximum old age assistance grants should be increased from $15 to $30 per month, and the law amended so that the grants so made shall be contributions and no lien required on the property of the recipient. Present liens should be canceled.

3. The Public School System and the public institutions of higher learning in the state must be adequately maintained and improved. No backward step should be countenanced or permitted in the educational policy or program of the state. The compensation of teachers must be maintained and increased to the highest standards that the present revenues of the state will permit. Funds should be provided for the teachers' retirement system.

4. The legislature should submit to the people two important constitutional amendments, namely:

a) To permit the state to match federal funds for the assistance of the needy blind and the dependent children of needy families.

b) To permit a program for equalizing educational opportunities so that the less fortunate counties may be afforded those equal opportunities without detriment to the school systems in those counties in which greater advantages and opportunities now prevail.

5. The arterial highways of the state should be improved and dangerous curves and conditions eliminated upon sound engineering principles for safety and durability, with full consideration of traffic needs as shown by traffic surveys which have just been completed by the Department of Highways of Kentucky and the federal Bureau of Public Roads in a joint cooperative program.

6. The rural highway program should be continued and a fair and reasonable amount of money appropriated from the state road fund for the continuation of this program with the cooperation of the fiscal courts

and the WPA so that the rural farm-to-market highways may be improved and maintained as one of the greatest services that can be rendered to the farmers and to the schoolchildren in rural communities.

7. An effective Department of Markets should be established in a revitalized Department of Agriculture to render service to farmers and farm organizations in developing a program to make Kentucky's farm products reach the best available markets and to sell for the best available prices.

8. A study should be made by the College of Agriculture, with a reasonable appropriation therefor, of new uses of tobacco and other farm products with the view of increasing markets for and prices of such products.

9. A commission should be appointed to study the problems of farm tenancy relative to farm ownership to assist farm tenants and farm laborers in the development of a practical program for the purchasing and financing of farms.

10. The program of public health, which vitally affects every individual in the state and which is a cooperative enterprise between the state and federal governments and local health units, should be given full cooperation by the state government and as adequate financial support as the finances of the state will permit without increasing the tax burden.

11. The program of the present Democratic state administration for the construction of modern and adequate buildings, for the installation of modern and adequate equipment, and the complete modernization of the state reformatories and hospitals should be completed, and the present program for increasing the number and improving the standards and qualifications of the staffs, management, and personnel of these institutions should be continued with a determined objective and purpose that the buildings, equipment, personnel, and operation of these institutions shall be second to none in the United States.

12. We favor the protection of labor in all its rights and legitimate aspirations under a policy of "equal opportunity for all and special privilege for none." We favor the continuance of the unemployment compensation act and the continued improvement of the workmen's compensation law. We seek the encouragement of conditions which will provide private employment on steady jobs at regular wages for our people.

13. There should be continued cooperation by both the governor and the legislature of Kentucky in the enactment of the necessary laws and the adoption of the necessary administrative policies and agencies to enable Kentucky to receive all available benefits provided, or which may be provided, by the Congress of the United States under federal laws which require corresponding state legislation and state cooperation. Included in this is cooperation between the state and federal governments in develop-

ing a state park system through the full use of the CCC camps, which will increase tourist attractions and reap for Kentucky an increased share of tourist business.

There are many other things of the greatest importance which time does not permit me to discuss at this time. They were dealt with fully in the primary campaign; our position on them is well known; and I shall discuss them in further detail from time to time.

I do not know whether my opponent, Judge Swope, favors this program or not. You do not know whether he favors it or not. If he knows, he does not specifically say so in his speeches. Instead he criticizes and derides. If he is really for this program, why is he running against me and on the Republican ticket?

Public education in the last fiscal year accounted for more than one half of the state's general fund expenditures. The state's whole expenditure in the last fiscal year for common schools and higher education was $12,696,734, and all general fund expenditures, including schools, totaled only $24,995,000. These figures clearly show the emphasis that has been placed on the school program by the present Democratic administration, a policy which will be continued by your next Democratic state administration.

The per capita school fund is now $12.19, the highest in the entire history of the state. We are pledged to maintain a per capita of at least $12.00 and to increase this amount as much as possible with existing revenues. I ask the people of Kentucky to compare this record with the record of the Sampson and Morrow[1] administrations. Our opponent boasts that "the greatest educational advancement in the history of Kentucky has been made under Republican leadership." The record clearly shows how false that claim is.

In the four school years for which the present administration has made appropriations, the total amount of state funds appropriated to the common school system is $37,597,872.18. In the four years for which the Sampson administration made appropriations, the common schools received $24,778,526.35. In the four years of the Morrow administration, they received $17,255,915.93.

A return to Sampsonism and to this "great progress under Republican leadership," in other words, would slash the common school fund per capita from $12.19 to about $8.00, on the basis of the present school census. A return to the appropriations of the Morrow administration would cut the per capita to about $6.00 on the basis of the present school census. That would mean cutting schoolteachers' salaries or cutting the school terms by a third or a half. That is the "great progress" which our opponent advocates.

The free textbook law was put into effect when a Democratic administration provided for the first time the funds necessary to purchase the books and distribute them to the schoolchildren of Kentucky. The distribution of these books has been extended into a greater number of grades by the present Democratic administration, and your next Democratic administration will continue to extend this service. The claim that Republican leadership is responsible for the free textbook system is refuted by the fact that the law never was put into operation until Democratic administrations provided the necessary funds. The institutions of higher learning have flourished under the same progressive policies of support. We shall continue to give them ample support and help make higher education increasingly available to Kentucky boys and girls.

There is no more important part of the program of government than that which deals with the problems of labor. In the opening speech of the Republican nominee for governor, he said: "The Magna Carta of Labor—that great principle of collective bargaining by labor through representatives of its own choice without interference—is now an accomplished fact, recognized and written into the law, and has been upheld by the Supreme Court of the United States, and is, therefore, the law of the land."

In plain language, what he appears to mean is that a law was passed and it is now the law and, therefore, it is a law. He fails to tell you whether his own party helped put it there or what it will do about it.

Contrast this Republican straddling with the definite accomplishments and pledges of the Democratic party. You know and every laboring man in Kentucky and the nation knows that the Democratic party is the only party that has ever given any fair consideration to the problems of the humble citizen. We remember the fate of labor under Hoover. We know that what progress has been made for the laboring man by legislative action was made by a Democratic Congress under the leadership of a Democratic president.

Here in Kentucky, and I am proud to have had a part in it as president of the Senate, we supplemented labor's Magna Carta with a new Declaration of Independence for the laboring man when a Democratic state legislature passed the deputy sheriff-mine guard bill. That legislation secures to every working man the right to join the union of his choice. The American Federation of Labor and the CIO and all their members are equally given by this legislation the right to live in peace among their neighbors in Kentucky. The peaceful and lawful rights and aspirations of labor were freed from every threat from the system of company-paid deputy sheriffs which this legislation outlawed.

I am pledged to conduct my administration in the spirit and practice of equal opportunity for all and special privilege for none—and that applies not only to laboring men, to labor organizations, but to trade and commerce and agriculture and industry and every other field of human enterprise. No legitimate aspiration or enterprise asks for more than that, and none will receive more than that.

Broad benefits result when the responsible administrators of government clearly proclaim and protect the rights of both labor and industry. There is no such guiding channel marked by our opponent's assertion that "a law was passed and it is now the law and, therefore, it is the law."

My opponent professes to pledge himself to assist in the solution of labor's problems and the amicable settlement of labor disputes. Against this mere promise, I ask you to weigh the record of the present Democratic administration of having brought about peaceful and mutually satisfactory settlements of numerous disputes in which its good offices have been invited.

The present Democratic state administration created Kentucky's first real labor department—the Department of Industrial Relations, and since its establishment a man who carries a union card has been the head of that department and a member of the governor's cabinet. The laboring people of Kentucky are already familiar with how the present Democratic administration put the unemployment compensation law into effect in Kentucky. It liberalized features of the Workmen's Compensation Law and eliminated the "week of waiting" period. I was nominated with the endorsement of the great, patriotic American Federation of Labor. I have made specific pledges to support many improvements in the labor laws, with which pledges the laboring men are already familiar and which I shall discuss in detail at another time.

Your present Democratic state ticket was nominated in a free and open Democratic primary in which I pledged that I would do all in my power to encourage and foster those conditions and policies in government which would encourage trade and industry to flourish or to come to Kentucky, here to provide employment and payrolls and markets for our people.

Safeguarded by the recognition which national and state Democratic administrations have given to the problems and the interests of the humble individual, the encouragement of recovery is the greatest field of service which government may offer to the laboring man. We see about us on every hand the evidence that this recovery is under way.

I recently read an Associated Press dispatch which reported an admission by the *Saturday Evening Post*, a critic of the Roosevelt administration, that one of its current issues carried a new record volume of advertising. The publishers announced that this business was contracted before the outbreak of the European war and that it reflected "normal improvement in conditions."

By the continued efforts of the national administration to insulate this nation against the unsettlement of foreign influences, its assistance in helping the national economy out of the depression in which it was thrust by the Hoover administration, by the enterprise and ingenuity and the honest toil of capital and labor, we shall continue this recovery. In this joint effort by all of us, the state administration will lend every possible help. We shall do this particularly by demonstrating to other states which have been troubled by strife and by oppressive governmental policies that in Kentucky we desire to live together in peace and profit, that we will not discriminate here against any honest enterprise or any legitimate aspiration, and that in our taxation and other policies of government we shall continue to avoid oppression.

I am opposed to any increase of the tax burden. The recovery, that was under way before the outbreak of war, gives me hope that tax rates may actually be reduced. Your next governor is pledged to make you a saving, thrifty, frugal governor, one who will make certain that every cent of every taxpayer's dollar buys the maximum amount of service for the taxpayer.

We cannot say with any assurance at this time whether the dislocation of world trade by war will affect adversely our Kentucky industries, the prosperity of Kentuckians, and the tax revenues of the state. I do promise you that if any reduction of taxes is possible, consistent with the maintenance of necessary public services, the preservation of sound fiscal policies, the payment in cash of teachers' salaries and old age pensions, and the completion of the needed state institutions, then taxes will be reduced in that amount. No reasonable citizen will ask for more, and no prudent candidate, aware of the responsibilities of the office he seeks, can promise more.

The burden of state taxes today rests more lightly on the individual in Kentucky, on the average, than in nearly any other state in the nation. The present Democratic administration is responsible for that happy condition and is pledged to continue to pursue that aim. At the same time we have sought to avoid placing any undue burdens on trade and commerce and industry, and we shall continue to avoid imposing any such burden. Some taxes have already been reduced or repealed when it was possible to do so. The general sales tax was repealed by this administration in accordance with its pledges.

The Sampson administration was the first Kentucky administration to explore the idea of a general sales tax and actually put through the legislature and made law a bill to impose taxes on Kentucky merchants on the basis of the volume of their sales. That legislation was later declared unconstitutional. I recall it to your attention because one of its professed purposes was to provide money to rehabilitate the state's penal and charitable institutions. Much of the tax money was actually collected, but nothing was done for the institutions except a little patchwork.

Since then, the Democratic party has done all the worthwhile things that Judge Swope now says that he will do for these institutions if he is elected governor. What has been done is only a step in the right direction and is only the beginning of what should be done and will be done for the institutions, but still it is more than he says he will do if he is elected. In his opening speech, Judge Swope said there should be better facilities for the care of the prisoners in the state reformatory and that there should be a clinical hospital for the mentally ill. He has been so out of touch with the state government that he did not know that a new reformatory is now nearing completion at La Grange; that a new women's reformatory has been built at Pine Bluff in Shelby County; that the prison at Eddyville is being completely modernized and improved; that a hospital for the mentally ill is now under construction at Herrington Lake; and that these institutions are of the most modern design and construction.

The improvement of facilities, personnel, and administration of the mental hospitals is in accordance with a program recommended by a committee of outstanding Kentucky physicians. This program is still under way and remains to be completed. One of its features which I have repeatedly stressed is the establishment of a diagnostic clinic.

Our opponent also says that there should be more doctors and that there should be trained nurses at the hospitals. Let me point out the fact that in the past year the number of attendants at the state hospitals has been increased until there is now an average of one attendant to each fifteen patients; the number of physicians now serving in these hospitals and institutions is twice the number employed a year ago; three trained, graduate nurses have been placed on duty at each of the hospitals. A trained dietician has been placed on duty at each of the institutions, and a trained social worker has been placed in each one of the institutions. In addition to that, a clinical director has been placed in every hospital in the state, and these directors have charge of diagnosis and psychiatric treatment. There are now three full-time dentists in these hospitals for the first time.

It should make the Republican nominee a very happy man to learn that all these things that he says should be done have already been done, and under the definite plans and program of the present state administration there is constant and progressive improvement of both physical facilities and personnel.

The Republican nominee for governor also says that there should be a law to keep the Department of Public Assistance from participating in politics. Well, he doesn't have to worry about that because there is now on the statute books a law passed by a Democratic Congress which becomes effective January 1, 1940, which provides that the Social Security Board shall require that state Public Assistance and Unemployment Compensation departments "provide such methods relating to the establishment and maintenance of personnel standards on a merit basis as are found by the Board to be necessary for the proper and efficient operation of the plans." The act provides that "personnel standards on a merit basis will be construed by the Board to prohibit pernicious political activity."

This act merely supplements in Kentucky the Chandler-Wallis Act, long ago put into effect by a Democratic state administration for the conduct of the state institutions. We are pledged to continue the policies of this act, but our opponent seems to suggest reservations to it as an entering wedge to destroy it.

I advocate selection of personnel for public service on a basis of competency and do not believe in pernicious political activity, but I would go a great deal farther than Judge Swope has ever gone. I know of no department or branch of either the state or federal government that touches more closely or is more vital to the people in the enjoyment and protection of their personal liberties, rights, and property than the Judicial Department. Of course, no politics should stain the worthy work of welfare and public assistance that was conceived and written into law and executed into action by the cooperative and joint efforts and initiative of Democratic national and state administrations. We can hardly expect, however, that these worthy functions of government would be purified by the political hands of a political judge who has engaged in politics actively and almost continuously while presiding over one of the busiest and most important courts in the Commonwealth.

The Federal Social Security law plainly requires that old age assistance grants shall be based solely on needs. The federal government will not participate in payments based upon any other plan. Your next Democratic administration will increase the maximum old age pension grant from $15 to $30 a month and will pay in cash every month the actual amount of the grants determined on the basis of the individual's needs. My opponent proposes a minimum pension of $10 a month, and it may be expected that his minimum would also be the maximum. Those old people who need the maximum $30 a month should beware of a candidate who pledges that he will give them $10. The old people and everybody else interested in the Social Security program know that the Social Security law will be improved more by those who are its known friends than by those who are its known critics.

Last summer my opponent made speeches throughout the length and breadth of Kentucky bitterly attacking and condemning President Roosevelt and the New Deal. He made it plain then that he would like to oust them both from Washington and return Hooverism to the nation and Sampsonism in Kentucky. These were and still are the Siamese twins of politics. The Sampson administration was closely associated with the

Hoover administration. A political crony of Governor Sampson was the chief political sponsor of Judge Swope's candidacy for governor four years ago and again this year. The chains of mutual interest and profitable political association inseparably bind together the Hoover leadership nationally and the Sampson-Swope leadership in Kentucky.

My opponent first went on the bench as an appointee of Governor Sampson. Before that, he obtained one term in Congress as representative from the old Eighth District—not the district in which we both now reside.

He won that term in the Harding administration, which gave this nation the "Ohio Gang" and the "Teapot Dome" scandal in which the oil reserves of the nation's defense forces were bartered away. Four years ago he aspired to run for governor and came out of the experience with a defeat by nearly 100,000 votes. Fresh from making that record, he is not in this race because of any bright hope of winning. He is only running to be elected the caretaker of the Republican log cabin in the hope that the Republican party may some day win the presidency and that he and the leaders of his faction may have first chance at the federal political plums.

Defeated four years ago by the greatest majority in any general election of state officers in the history of Kentucky, he now boasts that he cannot be shot twice in the same place. Well, that is just twisting the old saying that lightning never strikes twice in the same place.

There's an old answer for that—it doesn't need to. Perhaps the reason he feels so sure he cannot be shot twice in the same place is that he doesn't stand still long enough to be hit by anything less than a barrage. His unwillingness to take a stand anywhere is the best evidence of the lack of political principle presented by his leadership of the opposition. I cannot believe that the Republican party itself is as devoid of political principle as the candidate who now professes to represent it. He is so busy running that he neglects to stand for anything. Four years ago, he ran for a while against one of the candidates in the Democratic primary; then he ran for a while against one of the other candidates; but at no time in that year did he open his mouth in any word of criticism against the New Deal.

The leaders of his own party vainly importuned him to express a viewpoint on national issues. I commend his political sagacity for not undertaking to interpose his partisan obstructionism at that time against the efforts of the New Deal to bring about recovery. But I do say that he showed a lack of political principle by seeking and accepting the support of anti-New Deal voters without daring to say where he stood on the issues in which they were most interested. For nearly four years thereafter he wrapped himself in his judicial robes and engaged in political sniping, but avoided public discussion of his views on state or national problems.

Then came another election year in which he himself might renew his claims to future reward by the Hoover-Sampson wrecking crew. Once again he did not know where to stand but was only certain that he wanted to run. At the Lincoln Day dinner in Louisville, he renewed his attack on a Democratic state administration. It was a different administration and it had a different record from the one he attacked four years ago. It had undone in the intervening years many of the things for which he had criticized its predecessor, but our opponent was unable to keep step with the progress that he himself had advocated. Once again his only utterance was partisan and vituperative criticism.

But his austere and arrogant exterior hid within it a pliable concept of political principles. He did not feel entirely certain who would be the Democratic candidate in November and came to the conclusion that his safest course for the Republican primary was to condemn President Roosevelt and the Democratic national administration. So for week after week he traveled the length and breadth of Kentucky, bitterly attacking and condemning President Roosevelt and the New Deal and all its works. It was the same President Roosevelt and a more nearly completed New Deal than had stood before the people in bold relief four years ago, and the grass of recovery was beginning to grow green over the desolation left by Hoover, but this was the first time Judge Swope found these things of sufficient importance to merit his notice.

When I am elected governor, there is no question in the mind of any person that the full cooperation and assistance of the state government will be accorded the federal program, limited only by the amount of revenues available. I am confident that the people of Kentucky prefer four years of competent Democratic government for the benefit of all the people of the state to four years of uncertainty, of partisanship, and of obstruction.

It is also important that Kentucky elect a governor with whom the legislature can get along. There have been instances in which the legislature could not get along with the governor. That creates a condition that is detrimental to the state and thwarts the progress and proper development of needed governmental function. The next state legislature will be overwhelmingly Democratic in both houses. Democratic legislatures in Kentucky have had unhappy experiences in the past in trying to get along with a Republican governor. Such a situation is hurtful to the state. It creates strife that is subversive of progressive legislation. This reason alone makes unwise the election of a Republican governor.

In looking over the accomplishments of the past few years in Kentucky, it is difficult to separate that which has been promoted and encouraged by the federal government and that which has been developed through the state government. In most cases the two have worked hand in hand, either through federal aid or by cooperation of state departments and of local city and county governments with the federal and the state governments.

Nearly every bank in Kentucky is now a member of the Federal Deposit Insurance Corporation, and the depositors in them are insured by an agency of the federal government against loss from bank failure. That agency was created by the Roosevelt administration. The legislature in the Chandler administration passed, while I was president of the Senate, and Governor Chandler signed the necessary state legislation to make our state banking laws conform to this new system. No longer can the collapse of a major Kentucky bank cast the shadow of economic tragedy over the people and the industries of Kentucky as it did in the Hoover administration.

A recent summary by George H. Goodman,[2] administrator of the WPA, shows that in the first three years of the WPA in Kentucky more than 6,000 miles of roads and streets were constructed, reconstructed, or otherwise improved; 28,500 new culverts were built and 2,300 bridges were erected, replaced, or reconditioned. Much of this was done through cooperation with the State Highway Department. We want the WPA to continue to build roads in Kentucky. We want a state administration that we know is not headed by those who have sought to block and destroy the WPA from its beginning. We want to keep jobs for those who would be unemployed if it were not for the WPA. We want roads built—and new schools. The school system of Kentucky has been enhanced by more than $17 million dollars in actual value by the construction of 142 new buildings, 90 gymnasiums and other recreational buildings, and the modernization and improvement of 653 school buildings, 114 recreational buildings, and 324 institutional buildings. There have been 376 additional public buildings, such as city halls, courthouses, and jails built in the state.

The Democratic party has nominated a strong ticket without any attempt by me through a slate to control the selection of the other nominees that were named in the traditionally democratic way by more than a half million voters.

I deeply appreciate the honor of having been chosen as the Democratic nominee for governor of Kentucky. I fully realize that this distinction carries with it grave responsibilities. I was born and brought up in the humble circumstances of the son of a circuit-riding Methodist minister in Western Kentucky. It was just such a home as those in which many thousands of our sturdy, honest, patriotic but humble citizens live today. No matter what further honors may be given to me by the people of

Kentucky, no matter what change in my circumstances, my heart will always be attuned to the heartthrobs of those who, like myself, were born in the two-room shacks of Kentucky.

I have been cautious about the promises that I have made to the people of Kentucky because it is my determined purpose to fulfill every pledge that I have made and that I may make in this campaign. For that reason I have avoided and shall avoid making any promises concerning which I have any doubt about being able to perform.

I have no resentment toward those Democrats who exercised their right to vote and express their choice for another in the primary. I am grateful for the support and the votes that I received but there is no malice in my heart toward any Democrat or toward any citizen of Kentucky. Now joined together in a common cause, harmony and unity have been established and will be maintained within our party. We shall devote our full attention and concerted efforts to solving the problems of government in a constructive and progressive manner for the welfare of our state and of our citizens. Together we stand; we are not divided and we shall not fall.

The Democrats have named as their nominee for lieutenant governor, Rodes K. Myers of Bowling Green, an able and experienced legislator; for secretary of state, George Glenn Hatcher of Ashland, who has had four years experience as clerk of the city of Ashland and four years experience as assistant clerk of the Court of Appeals; for attorney general, Hubert T. Meredith, a capable and experienced lawyer, who has had three years experience in that important office; for auditor of public accounts, David M. Logan of Brownsville, brother of that distinguished Kentucky statesman, Senator M. M. Logan, whose untimely death has saddened the hearts of all Kentuckians and whose passing was a great loss not only to his state but to his nation; for treasurer, E. E. Shannon of Louisa, who for the past four years was the auditor of public accounts; for commissioner of agriculture, William H. May of Prestonsburg, for several years connected with the Federal Land Bank; for superintendent of public instruction, John W. Brooker of Cynthiana, for the past several years connected with the state Department of Education and whose public life has been devoted to the teaching profession and public education; and for clerk of the Court of Appeals, Charles K. O'Connell of Louisville, who has already served as clerk for almost four years.[3]

These nominees are men of ability and experience, and whose records in public service have received the approval not only of the Democratic party but in several instances of the entire electorate of Kentucky. It is a distinct honor to us to have been selected as we were in an old-fashioned primary election and to have today the support without a single exception, insofar as I know, of every Democrat in the state of Kentucky, and to enter this campaign with the active, aggressive support of a united Democratic party. We are going to have an old-fashioned Democratic victory this year. There isn't going to be any bolting and there isn't going to be any strife. No one is going to ask to what branch or group or faction of the Democratic party anyone has heretofore belonged. We say to every forward-looking, progressive, right-thinking Kentuckian of "whatever gift or persuasion" or party affiliation that there is a great program for which the Democratic nominees in this election stand and from which every Kentuckian will benefit. We ask that you join us to serve Kentucky's best interest now.

A great and far-reaching program that touches the life of all our people has been launched. It is as certain to continue as free government is to live upon this planet. It found its foremost advocates in a gifted friend of ours whose thoughts are with the "Forgotten Man" and who has awakened the conscience of the nation to the need of assistance to all of those who are in distress. We are proud of the accomplishments and the gallant leadership of the great man in the White House, Franklin Delano Roosevelt. It is a source of pride to Kentuckians and to Democrats that in formulating his program for social justice and human welfare and for national recovery, he has had at his right hand an able, fearless, and effective statesman from our own state. When history properly records the story of the New Deal, it will write in large letters the name of Alben W. Barkley, the senior senator from Kentucky. We pay tribute, too, to his associate in the Senate, Senator M. M. Logan, whose unfortunate death brought sadness to the hearts of all of us and whose passing was not only Kentucky's loss but the nation's. We honor and commend the outstanding statesmanship of our eight Democratic congressmen from Kentucky.

The program that has been initiated and partially accomplished by the national administration would have failed, in the main, had it not been supported by the cooperation and assistance of state governments. In nearly all of the outstanding activities that have been launched, federal aid has been granted and is administered through a state department for federal funds are required to be matched by state funds. State legislation has been required in most instances to bring to Kentucky the benefits which have accrued as a result of the program of the national administration. In this state, this program has had no abler champion of the rights of man, no more efficient administrator, and no more earnest supporter than Governor A. B. "Happy" Chandler.

It thrills me to my heart to find this splendid crowd of free and unterrified Democrats gathered together here to open the campaign, exercising your precious American privilege of free speech and free discussion.

It should thrill all of us to our very souls in this troubled time to realize that we are a free people, and that, in this beloved land of ours, the rights of peaceable assembly, of free speech, of a free press, of religious freedom, and of representative government still flourish.

For that precious inheritance, we humbly thank God and revere the memories of the sturdy forefathers who founded and handed on these gifts to us. We are determined that we in turn shall hand them on to our children.

A terrible European war is now raging, which is bound to have major effects upon the world around us and hence upon us, regardless of our determination to stay out of it. A generation ago, wearing my country's uniform overseas as a member of the AEF in France, I, with some of you who are in this audience, saw war closer at hand than did many of the rest of you. Those of you who did not have such a close view of it are happier for not having seen it. Those of us who saw it at close hand do not want to see it again.

There are no winners in war, only losers. It is the ultimate tragedy. Its price is blood and suffering, which is being paid even yet by many who were my comrades-in-arms, still lying today in government hospitals.

We know that much about war. We do not know much else about this war except that it is not our war, that we want to stay out of it, and that we intend to stay out of it unless our own shores are threatened. That is the way President Roosevelt feels about it, that is the way I am sure all of you feel about it, and that is the way I feel about it. In any action I may ever be called upon to take as governor, which might affect this problem in any way, I will be guided solely by the determination that our own peace must be preserved.

We cannot claim to know everything about why this war is being fought. But it is fairly clear, I think, that one of the reasons is the arbitrary use of power when it is entrusted to men who are arbitrary and ill-tempered and dictatorial. That issue is not confined to Europe. We have sometimes had to fight here against the rise into power of men, of groups or of parties who were arbitrary, who were dictatorial, who were careless of the rights of the humble citizens, or who, sometimes, were merely ill-tempered and thus poorly equipped for the responsibilities of authority.

We fight out that issue in America with ballots while other nations fight it out with bullets and blood. The Democratic party is the champion of the cause of democracy in that fight, both historically and today. It was the champion of democracy when Thomas Jefferson founded it as a party; it is still the champion of democracy today when its leader is Franklin D. Roosevelt.

In the battle for democracy, your candidates on the Democratic ticket ask you to join, and in it we shall march shoulder to shoulder toward that peace and prosperity and progress that we all desire, and to an old-fashioned Democratic victory.

---

1. Edwin Park Morrow (1877–1935), b. Somerset. Republican. Soldier, Spanish-American War. United States district attorney, 1910–1913. Governor, 1919–1923. G. Glenn Clift, *Governors of Kentucky* (Cynthiana, Ky., 1942), pp. 120-22.

2. George Hill Goodman (1876–1961), b. Big Clifty, Grayson County. Administrator, WPA in Kentucky, 1934–1941; administrator, OPA, 1941. *Who's Who in Kentucky, 1936*, p. 161, and Louisville *Courier-Journal*, September 23, 1961.

3. George Glenn Hatcher (1903–), b. Bonanza, Floyd County. Resides in Frankfort. City clerk, Ashland, 1932–1936; assistant clerk, Court of Appeals, 1936–1940; secretary of state, 1940–1944, 1948–1952; administrative assistant to finance commissioner to set up state archives, 1965–1972; Purchasing Division, 1972–1974. Interview, March 13, 1978, and telephone interview, September 26, 1978.

David A. Logan (1868–1943), b. Brownsville. Auditor of public accounts, 1939–1943; judge, Edmonson County. Letter, Frank A. Logan, son, Louisville, May 8, 1978.

William Harvey May (1908–), b. Prestonsburg. Resides in Frankfort. Commissioner of agriculture, 1940–1944; appraiser and engineer for Federal Land Bank, Louisville; farmer and real estate, 1945–1958; executive, Brighton Engineering Company, Frankfort, 1958–. *Kentucky Directory, 1940–1941*, p. 145, and letter, W. H. May, October 4, 1978.

Charles K. O'Connell (1904–1957), b. Frankfort. Clerk, Court of Appeals, 1936–1943, 1947–1951; secretary of state, 1943–1947, 1951–1955. *Kentucky Directory, 1954*, p. 150, and telephone interview, Clem O'Connor, Frankfort, August 9, 1978.

APPENDIX 3
Speeches of Governor Johnson

ON RESIGNATION OF CHANDLER AS GOVERNOR, October 9, 1939, Executive Document*

APPOINTS CHANDLER AS UNITED STATES SENATOR, October 9, 1939, Executive Document*

LETTER TO VICE PRESIDENT GARNER, October 9, 1939, Chandler Papers, University of Kentucky*

ON APPOINTING CHANDLER AS SENATOR, October 9, 1939, Statement, *Louisville Times,* October 9, 1939

LA GRANGE PRISON DEDICATION, La Grange, October 9, 1939, Compiled Summary, *Louisville Times*, October 9, 1939, and *State Journal*, October 10, 1939*

MAYSVILLE, October 10, 1939 (stop at Paris), Louisville *Courier-Journal,* October 11, 1939

EIGHTH DISTRICT, October 1939, Governor's Notecards

DEFENDS APPOINTMENT OF SENATOR CHANDLER, Ashland, October 11, 1939 (stops at Flemingsburg, Morehead, Olive Hill, Grayson), Compiled Speech, Louisville *Courier-Journal* and *Lexington Herald,* October 12, 1939

PRESTONSBURG, October 12, 1939 (stops at Louisa, Paintsville), Louisville *Courier-Journal,* October 13, 1939

PIKEVILLE, October 13, 1939, *Louisville Times,* October 13, 1939

HAZARD, October 13, 1939, Louisville *Courier-Journal,* October 14, 1939

LYNCH, October 14, 1939, *Louisville Times,* October 14, 1939

SOMERSET, October 14, 1939, Louisville *Courier-Journal,* October 15, 1939

JACKSON, October 16, 1939, Louisville *Courier-Journal,* October 17, 1939

GEORGETOWN, October 17, 1939, *Lexington Herald,* October 18, 1939

DEMOCRATIC WOMEN'S CLUB OF KENTUCKY, Frankfort, October 18, 1939, *State Journal,* October 19, 1939

SHELBYVILLE, October 18, 1939, Louisville *Courier-Journal,* October 19, 1939

*Address is included in this volume.

CARROLLTON, October 19, 1939 (stop at Warsaw), Louisville *Courier-Journal*, October 20, 1939

ALEXANDRIA, October 20, 1939, *Cincinnati Enquirer*, October 21, 1939

NEWPORT, October 20, 1939 (stops at Cold Spring, Bellevue-Dayton), *Cincinnati Enquirer*, October 21, 1939

DANVILLE, October 21, 1939, MS

CYNTHIANA (radio), October 21, 1939, Louisville *Courier-Journal*, October 22, 1939

LA GRANGE, October 23, 1939, *Cincinnati Enquirer*, October 24, 1939

SHEPHERDSVILLE, October 23, 1939, *Cincinnati Enquirer*, October 24, 1939

DEMOCRATIC WOMEN: THIRD DISTRICT, Louisville, October 23, 1939, Louisville *Courier-Journal*, October 24, 1939

LEBANON, October 24, 1939 (stops at Bardstown, Springfield, Greensburg, Campbellsville), *Cincinnati Enquirer*, October 25, 1939

COLUMBIA, October 24, 1939, *Cincinnati Enquirer*, October 25, 1939

LEXINGTON, October 25, 1939, *Cincinnati Enquirer* and *Lexington Herald*, October 26, 1939

LEITCHFIELD, October 26, 1939, *Cincinnati Enquirer*, October 27, 1939

GLASGOW, October 27, 1939, *Louisville Times* October 27, 1939

BOWLING GREEN, October 27, 1939 (stops at Auburn, Elkton, Franklin, Russellville, Scottsville, Cave City), Louisville *Courier-Journal* and *Lexington Herald*, October 28, 1939

HARDINSBURG, October 28, 1939, MS

OWENSBORO, October 28, 1939 (stops at Morgantown, Beaver Dam, Hartford), *Cincinnati Enquirer*, October 29, 1939

MUHLENBERG COUNTY PARTY WORKERS, October 30, 1939, *Cincinnati Enquirer*, October 31, 1939

MADISONVILLE, October 30, 1939 (stops at Central City, Greenville, White Plains, Nortonville), *Cincinnati Enquirer*, October 31, 1939

MORGANFIELD, October 31, 1939 (stops at Providence, Clay, Dixon, Henderson, Corydon, Sturgis), Louisville *Courier-Journal*, November 1, 1939

THIRD DISTRICT RALLY, Louisville, November 1, 1939, *Cincinnati Enquirer*, November 2, 1939

PADUCAH, November 2, 1939 (stops at Smithland, Marion, Kuttawa, Eddyville, Princeton, Cerulean, Cady, Hopkinsville), MS

FULTON, November 3, 1939, *Cincinnati Enquirer*, November 4, 1939

MAYFIELD, November 4, 1939 (stops at Benton, Murray, Sedalia, Wingo, Heckman, Clinton, Arlington, Bardwell, Wickliffe, Barlow, LaCenter), Louisville *Courier-Journal*, November 5, 1939

RAVENNA, November 6, 1939, *Cincinnati Enquirer*, November 7, 1939

IRVINE, November 6, 1939, *Lexington Herald*, November 7, 1939

CLOSES GUBERNATORIAL CAMPAIGN, Richmond, November 6, 1939, Speech, MS*

STATEMENT ON ELECTION OUTCOME, November 9, 1939, *Cincinnati Enquirer*, November 10, 1939*

YOUNG DEMOCRATS OF KENTUCKY, Louisville, November 12, 1939, Louisville *Courier-Journal*, November 12, 1939

GARRARD COUNTY BABY BEEF CLUB, Lancaster, November 16, 1939, Summary, *Central Record*, November 16, 1939

KENTUCKY MUNICIPAL LEAGUE, Frankfort, November 20, 1939, Summary, *State Journal*, November 21, 1939

ESTABLISHES A BUREAU OF MARKETS, Frankfort, November 24, 1939, Executive Order

KENTUCKY DAM DAY, Paducah, December 4, 1939, Compiled Speech, MS and *Paducah Sun-Democrat*, December 5, 1939*

DEPARTMENT HEADS OF STATE GOVERNMENT, December 8, 1939, Policy Letter, Louisville *Courier-Journal*, December 22, 1940*

INAUGURAL ADDRESS, December 12, 1939, MS*

ASKS LEGISLATIVE COUNCIL FOR BUDGET CUT, Frankfort, December 14, 1939, Compiled Speech, *Louisville Times*, December 14, 1939, and *State Journal*, December 15, 1939

TEACHERS' RETIREMENT FUND, Frankfort, December 19, 1939, Statement, Louisville *Courier-Journal*, December 20, 1939

LOUISVILLE BOARD OF TRADE, Louisville, January 1, 1940, Speech, *Lexington Herald*, January 2, 1940*

STATE OF THE COMMONWEALTH ADDRESS, January 2, 1940, *Journal of the House of Representatives, 1940*, 1:19-42*

STATEMENT BEFORE TEXTBOOK COMMISSION, Frankfort, January 5, 1940, MS*

VETERANS OF FOREIGN WARS, Frankfort, January 6, 1940, Summary, *State Journal*, January 7, 1940*

JACKSON DAY, Louisville, January 8, 1940, Speech, MS*

KENTUCKY FARM BUREAU FEDERATION, Louisville, January 11, 1940, Compiled Summary, MS, Governor's Notecards, and *Louisville Times*, January 12, 1940*

KENTUCKY PRESS ASSOCIATION, Louisville, January 18, 1940, Summary, Louisville *Courier-Journal*, January 19, 1940

AMERICAN LEGION, POST 7, Frankfort, January 24, 1940, Summary, *State Journal*, January 25, 1940

ACCOUNTS RECEIVABLE ASSESSMENT BILL, February 1, 1940, Compiled Speech, *Richmond Daily Register*, February 1, 1940, and Louisville *Courier-Journal*, February 2, 1940

AMERICANISM WEEK, ELKS LODGE, Frankfort, February 20, 1940, Summary, Governor's Notecards

ON HIRING AUDITORS, March 6, 1940, Statement, *Cincinnati Enquirer*, March 7, 1940*

SIGMA ALPHA EPSILON, Lexington, March 9, 1940, Speech, MS

VETO OF BILL TO LEGALIZE LIQUOR SALES, March 13, 1940, *Journal of the House of Representatives, 1940*, 4:4380-86*

EASTERN KENTUCKY STATE TEACHERS COLLEGE FOUNDERS DAY, Richmond, March 21, 1940, Speech, MS*

INDEPENDENT ORDER OF ODDFELLOWS CENTENNIAL, Frankfort, March 25, 1940, Summary, *State Journal*, March 26, 1940

CUVIER PRESS CLUB: KENTUCKY NIGHT, Cincinnati, April 3, 1940, Summary, *Kentucky Post*, April 4, 1940

RED BIRD HIGH SCHOOL GRADUATION, Bell County, April 7, 1940, Summary, *Pineville Sun*, April 11, 1940*

KENTUCKY SCHOOL FOR THE DEAF, Frankfort, April 17, 1940, Statement, *Cincinnati Enquirer*, April 17, 1940*

KENTUCKY EDUCATION ASSOCIATION, Louisville, April 19, 1940, Speech, MS*

AMERICAN LEGION, Lexington, April 20, 1940, Summary, *Lexington Herald*, April 21, 1940

TWO NEW STATE BUILDINGS, April 27, 1940, Statement, *State Journal*, April 28, 1940

STEPHEN COLLINS FOSTER COMMEMORATIVE POSTAGE STAMP, Bardstown, May 3, 1940, Speech, MS

KENTUCKY DERBY, Louisville, May 4, 1940, Speech, MS*

EASTERN KENTUCKY STATE TEACHERS COLLEGE ALUMNI, Richmond, May 25, 1940, Summary, *Lexington Herald*, May 26, 1940[†]

STATE HIGHWAY PATROL, Frankfort, June 14, 1940, Statement, Louisville *Courier-Journal*, June 15, 1940*

DEDICATION OF BRIDGE ACROSS GREEN RIVER, Munfordville, June 21, 1940, Compiled Speech, *Hart County News*, June 27, 1940, and Louisville *Courier-Journal*, June 22, 1940

MADISON COUNTY DEMOCRATS NAME DELEGATES TO STATE AND DISTRICT CONVENTIONS, Richmond, June 29, 1940, *Richmond Daily Register*, July 1, 1940

STATE DEMOCRATIC CONVENTION, Louisville, July 2, 1940, Speech, MS*

STEPHEN COLLINS FOSTER PORTRAIT, Bardstown, July 4, 1940, Speech, MS*

PEACE OFFICERS, Lexington, July 8, 1940, Summary, *Lexington Herald*, July 9, 1940

AMERICAN LEGION, Ashland, July 22, 1940, Speech, American Legion Files*

DEDICATION OF BRIDGE ACROSS KENTUCKY RIVER, Irvine, July 26, 1940, Compiled Speech, MS, Louisville *Courier-Journal* and *Lexington Herald*, July 27, 1940*

EASTERN KENTUCKY STATE TEACHERS COLLEGE: TEACHERS VISIT STATE CAPITOL, Frankfort, July 27, 1940, Welcome, *State Journal*, July 28, 1940

VETERANS OF FOREIGN WARS, Calloway Post 2657, Kingdom City, Missouri, July 28, 1940, Speech[†]

COUNTY AND CITY HEALTH OFFICERS, Louisville, July 29, 1940, Summary, Louisville *Courier-Journal*, July 30, 1940

DEDICATION OF BRIDGE ACROSS OHIO RIVER, Owensboro, July 30, 1940, Speech, MS*

VANDERBILT TRAINING SCHOOL, Elkton, August 15, 1940, Speech, *Todd County Standard*, August 16, 23, 1940

MEETS PRESIDENT ROOSEVELT, Newfound Gap, North Carolina, August 30-September 2, 1940, Article by Governor Johnson, *Richmond Daily Register*, September 5, 1940*

DEMOCRATIC WOMEN'S CLUBS: SIXTH CONGRESSIONAL DISTRICT, Richmond, September 5, 1940, *Lexington Herald*, September 6, 1940

KENTUCKY METHODIST CHURCH CONFERENCE, Wilmore, September 6, 1940, Speech, MS*

[†]Address has not been located.

ADMINISTRATIVE ORGANIZATION OF WELFARE DEPARTMENT, Frankfort, September 7, 1940, Executive Order Number 12*

AMERICAN LEGION AND AUXILIARY UNIT: BLUEGRASS BOY'S STATE, Frankfort, September 14, 1940, Comments, *State Journal,* September 15, 1940

FIRST SUNDAY SCHOOL IN KENTUCKY, Frankfort, September 22, 1940, Compiled Speech, MS, Louisville *Courier-Journal,* September 23, 1940, and *State Journal,* September 24, 1940*

GREAT BRITAIN SUNDAY, Frankfort, September 24, 1940, Proclamation*

LOUISVILLE CONFERENCE OF THE METHODIST CHURCH, Madisonville, September 25, 1940, Speech, Louisville *Courier-Journal,* September 26, 1940

REGISTRATION FOR MILITARY SERVICE, Frankfort, September 25, 1940, Letter, Louisville *Courier-Journal,* September 26, 1940*

LEESTOWN TERRACE DEDICATION, Frankfort, September 26, 1940, Summary, *State Journal,* September 27, 1940

DEDICATION OF PUBLIC SQUARE, Lancaster, October 1, 1940, Summary, *Central Record,* October 3, 1940*

KENTON COUNTY YOUNG MEN'S DEMOCRATIC CLUB, Erlanger, October 3, 1940, Summary, *Richmond Daily Register,* October 4, 1940

DEMOCRATIC WOMEN'S CLUBS: FIFTH DISTRICT CONVENTION, Covington, October 4, 1940, *Kentucky Post,* October 5, 1940

NORTHERN KENTUCKY INDEPENDENT FOOD DEALERS ASSOCIATION, Covington, October 8, 1940, Summary, *Kentucky Post,* October 9, 1940

SOUTH AND CENTRAL AMERICAN ARMY OFFICERS, Fort Knox, October 9, 1940, Welcome, Louisville *Courier-Journal,* October 10, 1940

THOROUGHBRED CLUB OF AMERICA, Lexington, October 10, 1940, Speech, MS*

DRAFT BOARD PERSONNEL, Frankfort, October 11, 1940, Statement, *State Journal,* October 12, 1940*

BLUEGRASS AVIATION CLUB, Lexington, October 17, 1940, Speech†

ESTILL COUNTY YOUNG MEN'S DEMOCRATIC CLUB, Ravenna, October 17, 1940, *Richmond Daily Register,* October 18, 1940

DEMOCRATIC WOMEN'S CLUB, Louisville, October 18, 1940, Louisville *Courier-Journal,* October 19, 1940

ELIZABETHTOWN, October 19, 1940†

WILLIAMSTOWN, October 19, 1940†

DEDICATION OF U. S. 60 BRIDGE ACROSS GREEN RIVER, Rockport, October 21, 1940, Compiled Speech, Governor's Notecards, Louisville *Courier-Journal*, October 22, 1940, *Ohio County News*, October 25, 1940*

URGES STATE EMPLOYEES TO GET OUT THE VOTE, Frankfort, October 22, 1940, *State Journal*, October 23, 1940

KEHOE VIADUCT OPENED, Maysville, October 25, 1940, Compiled Speech, *Maysville Daily Independent* and Louisville *Courier-Journal*, October 26, 1940*

BENTON, October 26, 1940†

MADISONVILLE, October 26, 1940†

SPRINGFIELD, October 28, 1940†

JESSAMINE COUNTY RALLY, Nicholasville, October 29, 1940, *Lexington Herald*, October 30, 1940

RALLY, Newport, October 30, 1940, *Kentucky Post*, October 31, 1940

DEDICATION OF UNDERPASS, MARY INGLIS HIGHWAY, Coal Haven, October 30, 1940, Summary, *Cincinnati Enquirer*, October 31, 1940

BELLEVUE BUSINESS MEN'S ASSOCIATION, Dayton, October 30, 1940, Compiled Summary, *Kentucky Post* and *Cincinnati Enquirer*, October 31, 1940

LOUISVILLE, October 31, 1940†

LAWRENCEBURG, November 1, 1940†

UNIVERSITY OF KENTUCKY HOMECOMING, Lexington, November 1, 1940, Summary, *Lexington Herald*, November 2, 1940

SECOND ANNUAL TOBACCO FESTIVAL, Shelbyville, November 1, 1940, Speech, MS*

RICHMOND, November 4, 1940, *Lexington Herald*, November 5, 1940

CYNTHIANA AIRPORT DEDICATION, Cynthiana, November 11, 1940, Speech, MS*

SOUTHERN MEDICAL ASSOCIATION, Louisville, November 12, 1940, Speech, MS*

FRANKFORT HIGH SCHOOL PANTHERS CELEBRATION, Frankfort, November 26, 1940, Summary, *State Journal*, November 27, 1940

AMERICAN LEGION, Louisville, November 30, 1940, Summary, Louisville *Courier-Journal*, December 1, 1940

KENTUCKY MINING INSTITUTE, Lexington, December 6, 1940, Speech, *Lexington Herald*, December 7, 1940*

MERIT SYSTEM, December 10, 1940, Letter, Louisville *Courier-Journal*, December 22, 1940*

BLUE GRASS DENTAL SOCIETY, Lexington, December 14, 1940, Summary, *Lexington Herald*, December 15, 1940

THE ROUND TABLE CLUB, Louisville, December 16, 1940, Summary, Louisville *Courier-Journal*, December 17, 1940

STATE GUARD CAPTAINS COMMISSIONED, Frankfort, December 17, 1940, Summary, *State Journal*, December 18, 1940*

"BATTLE OF EVARTS" CLEMENCY, Frankfort, December 23, 1940, Statement, Louisville *Courier-Journal*, December 24, 1940

W. A. FROST APPOINTED WELFARE COMMISSIONER, Frankfort, December 30, 1940, Statement, *Lexington Herald*, December 31, 1940*

A. M. LYON APPOINTED DIRECTOR OF HOSPITALS AND MENTAL HYGIENE, Frankfort, December 31, 1940, Statement, Louisville *Courier-Journal*, January 1, 1941*

TRANSYLVANIA COLLEGE CONVOCATION, Lexington, January 8, 1941, Speech, MS*

REFINANCING OF OUTSTANDING WARRANTS, Frankfort, January 9, 1941, Statement, Louisville *Courier-Journal*, January 10, 1941*

HAZARD COAL OPERATORS ASSOCIATION, Lexington, January 10, 1941, Compiled Speech, MS and *Lexington Herald*, January 11, 1941*

INFANTILE PARALYSIS, Frankfort, January 18, 1941, Statement, *State Journal*, January 19, 1941

SALUTE TO NATIONAL GUARD, Frankfort, January 21, 1941, Statement, Louisville *Courier-Journal*, January 22, 1941

VETERANS OF FOREIGN WARS, Frankfort, January 25, 1941, Speech†

CHAMBER OF COMMERCE, Somerset, February 20, 1941, Compiled Speech, *Commonwealth*, February 26, 1941, and *Somerset Journal*, February 27, 1941*

DAUGHTERS OF THE AMERICAN REVOLUTION, BRYAN STATION CHAPTER, Lexington, February 22, 1941, Speech, *Lexington Herald-Leader*, February 23, 1941

GROUND-BREAKING FOR ARMCO BLAST FURNACE, Ashland, March 12, 1941, Speech, MS*

HENDERSON'S INDUSTRIAL REVIVAL, Henderson, March 19, 1941, Compiled Speech, MS and Louisville *Courier-Journal*, March 20, 1941*

HENDERSON-EVANSVILLE BRIDGE BECOMES TOLL FREE, Henderson, March 20, 1941, Compiled Summary, *Henderson Evening Journal*, March 20, 1941, and *Evansville Courier*, March 21, 1941*

HENDERSON-EVANSVILLE BRIDGE CELEBRATION, Evansville, Indiana, March 20, 1941, Speech†

KENTUCKY MASTER BAKER'S ASSOCIATION, Frankfort, March 26, 1941, Summary, *State Journal*, March 28, 1941

ROTARY CLUB: TAXES, Lexington, March 27, 1941, Speech, Governor's Notecards

JACKSON DAY, Louisville, March 29, 1941, MS and Democratic State Headquarters' leaflet

KENTUCKY SOCIETY FOR CRIPPLED CHILDREN, Lexington, April 2, 1941, Summary, *Beattyville Enterprise*, April 10, 1941

KENTUCKY BAR ASSOCIATION, Louisville, April 3, 1941, Speech, MS*

TOBACCO DAY FESTIVAL, Hopkinsville, April 10, 1941, Speech, MS*

MERIT SALES, Mayfield, April 10, 1941, Speech, *Mayfield Messenger*, April 11, 1941

COAL FREIGHT RATES AND WAGE DIFFERENTIALS, Frankfort, April 14, 15, 1941, Telegrams and Statement, Louisville *Courier-Journal*, April 15, 1941*

FOUR MADISON COUNTY FUTURE FARMERS OF AMERICA CHAPTERS, Richmond, April 15, 1941, Summary, *Richmond Daily Register*, April 16, 1941

KENTUCKY EDUCATION ASSOCIATION, Louisville, April 16, 1941, Speech, MS*

BLUE GRASS AUTOMOBILE CLUB SILVER JUBILEE, Lexington, April 22, 1941, Comments, *Lexington Herald*, April 23, 1941

NATIONAL FORENSIC LEAGUE, Lexington, April 29, 1941, Welcome, *Lexington Herald*, April 30, 1941

AMERICAN WAR MOTHERS, Frankfort, April 30, 1941, Compiled Summary, Louisville *Courier-Journal* and *State Journal*, May 1, 1941

NATIONAL ASSOCIATION OF POSTMASTERS OF THE UNITED STATES, KENTUCKY CHAPTER, Lexington, May 5, 1941, Comments, *Lexington Herald*, May 6, 1941

CENTRAL KENTUCKY L & N SURGICAL SOCIETY, Lexington, May 8, 1941, Summary, *State Journal*, May 9, 1941

GEORGETOWN COLLEGE CITIZENSHIP DAY, Georgetown, May 12, 1941, Compiled Speech, MS and *Georgetown Times*, May 14, 1941*

LEAGUE OF KENTUCKY SPORTSMEN, Lexington, May 12, 1941, Compiled Speech, Governor's Notecards and *State Journal*, May 14, 1941*

CHAMBER OF COMMERCE, Danville, May 14, 1941, Summary, Danville *Advocate-Messenger*, May 15, 1941

NEW ENTRANCE TO STATE CAPITOL, Frankfort, May 15, 1941, Speech, *State Journal*, May 16, 1941*

MOREHEAD STATE TEACHERS COLLEGE: I AM AN AMERICAN DAY, Morehead, May 15, 1941, Summary, *Trail Blazer*, May 17, 1941

NATIONAL ASSOCIATION OF COUNTY OFFICERS, Louisville, May 16, 1941, Summary, Louisville *Courier-Journal*, May 17, 1941

KIWANIS, ROTARY, AND LIONS CLUBS, Bowling Green, May 22, 1941, Summary, *Paducah Sun-Democrat*, May 23, 1941

BOWLING GREEN HIGH SCHOOL GRADUATION, Bowling Green, May 22, 1941, Speech, MS*

TO THE CABINET, Frankfort, May 23, 1941, Address, MS*

UNLIMITED EMERGENCY PERIOD, Frankfort, May 28, 1941, Statement, State Archives, May 28, 1941*

MOUNTAIN LAUREL FESTIVAL, Pineville, May 30, 1941, *Lexington Herald*, May 31, 1941, and *Pineville Sun*, June 5, 1941

COUNTY TAX COMMISSIONERS' ASSOCIATION, Lexington, June 3, 1941, Summary, *Lexington Herald*, June 4, 1941

KENTUCKY MILITARY INSTITUTE, Lyndon, June 3, 1941, Summary, *Kentucadet*, June 9, 1941

EASTERN KENTUCKY STATE TEACHERS COLLEGE COMMENCEMENT, Richmond, June 4, 1941, Speech, MS*

NATIONAL ASSOCIATION OF TAX ADMINISTRATORS, Lexington, June 9, 1941, Welcome, *Lexington Herald*, June 10, 1941

LIONS CLUB, Frankfort, June 10, 1941, Summary, *State Journal*, June 11, 1941

KENTUCKY STATE COLLEGE COMMENCEMENT, Frankfort, June 10, 1941, Welcome†

PAROLE OFFICERS ANNUAL SCHOOL, Frankfort, June 11, 1941, Summary, *State Journal*, June 12, 1941

4-H CLUBS JUNIOR WEEK, Lexington, June 12, 1941, Speech, MS*

AMERICAN LEGION PREPAREDNESS PARADE, Frankfort, June 16, 1941, Summary, *State Journal*, June 17, 1941

MAMMOTH CAVE NATIONAL PARK, Frankfort, June 21, 1941, Statement, Louisville *Courier-Journal*, June 22, 1941

KENTUCKY LEAGUE OF WOMEN VOTERS, Louisville, June 30, 1941, Speech, MS*

IRREGULARITIES IN THE DIVISION OF PURCHASES, July 1, 1941, Letter, Louisville *Courier-Journal*, July 2, 1941*

REDEDICATION TO AMERICANISM, Lexington, July 4, 1941, Speech, MS*

STEPHEN COLLINS FOSTER BIRTHDAY CELEBRATION, Bardstown, July 4, 1941, Speech, MS*

STATE HIGHWAY PATROL EFFICIENCY, Frankfort, July 12, 1941, Summary, *State Journal*, July 13, 1941*

KIWANIS CLUB, Frankfort, July 17, 1941, Summary, *State Journal*, July 18, 1941

COAL FREIGHT RATES, Louisville, July 21, 1941, Speech, *State Journal*, July 22, 1941*

AMERICAN LEGION, Lexington, July 22, 1941, Speech, American Legion Files*

FANCY FARM ANNUAL PICNIC, July 30, 1941, *Mayfield Messenger*, July 30, 1941

DEDICATION OF LEXINGTON AIRPORT SITE, Lexington, July 31, 1941, Speech, *State Journal*, August 1, 1941

MERCER COUNTY FAIR AND HORSE SHOW, Harrodsburg, July 31, 1941, *Lexington Herald*, August 1, 1941

BEN WILLIAMSON MEMORIAL BRIDGE BECOMES TOLL FREE, Ashland-Coal Grove, August 5, 1941, Speech, MS*

DIVISION OF PUBLIC ASSISTANCE, DEPARTMENT OF WELFARE, Frankfort, August 6, 1941, Speech, MS*

DAVIESS COUNTY FARM BUREAU, Owensboro, August 7, 1941, Speech, *Owensboro Messenger*, August 8, 1941*

FUTURE FARMERS OF AMERICA, Louisville, August 8, 1941, Comments, *State Journal*, August 9, 1941

YOUNG DEMOCRATIC CLUBS OF AMERICA, Louisville, August 21, 1941, Speech, MS*

FUTURE FARMERS OF AMERICA DAY, STATE FAIR, Louisville, September 11, 1941, Comments, *Richmond Daily Register*, September 12, 1941

MOSE GREEN CLUB, Louisville, September 17, 1941, MS

DEMOCRATIC WOMEN'S CLUBS: SIXTH CONGRESSIONAL DISTRICT, Harrodsburg, September 18, 1941, MS

CONSTITUTIONAL LIMIT ON SALARY, September 19, 1941, Statement, Louisville *Courier-Journal*, September 26, 1941*

INDIANA DEMOCRATIC EDITORIAL ASSOCIATION,French Lick, Indiana,September 20, 1941, Speech, Governor's Notecards

OUT-OF-STATE TRIPS, September 23, 1941, Statement and Letter, *State Journal*, September 26, 1941*

KENTUCKY STATE MEDICAL ASSOCIATION, Louisville, September 30, 1941, Speech, MS*

NAVAL GUN MOUNT PLANT, Louisville, October 1, 1941, Summary, *Louisville Times*, October 1, 1941

BURLEY TOBACCO SHOW, Paris, October 2, 1941, Summary, *Lexington Herald*, October 3, 1941

HOUSES OF REFORM, GREENDALE, Frankfort, October 3, 1941, Compiled Statement and Executive Order, *State Journal*, and *Lexington Herald*, October 4, 1941*

NATIONAL SOCIETY OF CRIPPLED CHILDREN, Lexington, October 5, 1941, Welcome Speech, *Lexington Herald*, October 6, 1941

REHABILITATION OF STATE HOSPITALS AND OTHER INSTITUTIONS, Hopkinsville, October 16, 1941, Compiled Statement, *Daily Kentucky New Era*, October 16, 1941, and *State Journal*, October 17, 1941*

RALLY FOR W. A. FROST, Mayfield, October 16, 1941, Compiled Address, *Mayfield Messenger*, *State Journal*, and Louisville *Courier-Journal*, October 17, 1941*

WESTERN STATE PENITENTIARY, Eddyville, October 17, 1941, Compiled Speech, Governor's Notecards and Louisville *Courier-Journal*, October 18, 1941*

FEDERALIZATION OF UNEMPLOYMENT COMPENSATION, Frankfort, October 18, 23, 1941, Letters*

DEMOCRATIC WOMEN'S CLUB OF KENTUCKY, Louisville, October 23, 1941, *State Journal*, October 24, 1941

AMERICAN LEGION AUXILIARY, Louisville, October 27, 1941, Speech, MS*

CHANGES FOR HOUSES OF REFORM, GREENDALE, Frankfort, October 30, 1941, Compiled Statement, *Kentucky Post* and Louisville *Courier-Journal*, October 31, 1941*

UNIVERSITY OF KENTUCKY FIELD HOUSE, Lexington, October 30, 1941, Compiled Summary, Governor's Notecards, Louisville *Courier-Journal*, October 31, 1941, and *Kentucky Kernel*, November 4, 1941

CONSTITUTIONAL AMENDMENT ON SCHOOL FUND, October 31, 1941, Speech, MS*

KENTUCKY CONFERENCE OF SOCIAL WELFARE, Louisville, October 31, 1941, Welcome, Louisville *Courier-Journal,* November 1, 1941

JEFFERSON COUNTY RALLY, Louisville, November 1, 1941, Louisville *Courier-Journal,* November 2, 1941

JUSTICE BRANDEIS MEMORIAL SERVICE, Louisville, November 6, 1941, Speech, MS*

NEWPORT-CINCINNATI BRIDGE BECOMES TOLL FREE, Newport, November 11, 1941, Speech, MS*

FARM TENANCY COMMISSION REPORT, Frankfort, November 12, 1941, Statement, *Lexington Herald,* November 13, 1941

KENTUCKY YOUNG DEMOCRATIC CLUBS, Louisville, November 14, 1941, *Cincinnati Enquirer* and Louisville *Courier-Journal,* November 15, 1941

JOHN R. DEMOISEY APPOINTED GREENDALE SUPERINTENDENT, Frankfort, November 19, 1941, Statement, Louisville *Courier-Journal,* November 20, 1941*

MESSAGE TO LEGISLATIVE COUNCIL, November 24, 1941, Address, *Lexington Herald,* November 25, 1941*

DEMOCRATIC WOMEN OF KENTUCKY, *Democratic Women's Journal,* December 1941*

VIRGINIA AVENUE TOBACCO WAREHOUSE, Lexington, December 2, 1941, Comments, *Lexington Herald,* December 3,1941

WORKMEN'S COMPENSATION, Frankfort, December 3, 1941, Statement, Louisville *Courier-Journal,* December 4, 1941

KENTUCKY MINING INSTITUTE, Lexington, December 5, 1941, Compiled Speech, *Lexington Herald* and *State Journal,* December 6, 1941*

PEARL HARBOR, Frankfort, December 7, 1941, Telegram, *Kentucky Post,* December 8, 1941

WAR PROCLAMATION, Frankfort, December 9, 1941, State Archives*

TIRE RATIONING BOARDS, Frankfort, December 20, 1941, Statement, *State Journal,* December 21, 1941*

TIRE RATIONING BOARDS, Frankfort, December 29, 1941, Speech, *State Journal,* December 30, 1941*

SESQUICENTENNIAL YEAR, Frankfort, January 1, 1942, Proclamation*

LOUISVILLE BOARD OF TRADE, Louisville, January 1, 1942, Speech, *Board of Trade Journal,* January 1942*

DAY OF PRAYER, Frankfort, January 1, 1942, Address, *State Journal,* January 2, 1942*

STATE OF THE COMMONWEALTH ADDRESS, Frankfort, January 6, 1942, *Journal of the Senate, 1942,* 1:19-46*

LEAGUE OF KENTUCKY SPORTSMEN, Frankfort, January 13, 1942, Summary, *Kentucky Post,* January 14, 1942

KENTUCKY SOCIETY OF PROFESSIONAL ENGINEERS, Lexington, January 23, 1942, Summary, *Lexington Herald,* January 24, 1942

TENNESSEE VALLEY AUTHORITY BILL, February 11, 1942, *Journal of the Senate, 1942,* 2:1933-44*

CALL FOR REDISTRICTING, March 3, 1942, *Journal of the House of Representatives, March 5, 1942, Extraordinary Session, 1942,* pp. 4-5*

ADMINISTRATIVE ORGANIZATION OF REVENUE DEPARTMENT, Frankfort, March 5, 1942, Administrative Order*

EXTRAORDINARY SESSION OF THE GENERAL ASSEMBLY: LEGISLATIVE REDISTRICTING, Frankfort, March 10, 1942, *Journal of the House of Representatives, March 10, 1942, Extraordinary Session, 1942,* pp. 11-16*

LEGAL SERVICES, March 20, 1942, Compiled Letter and Statement, Louisville *Courier-Journal,* and *Lexington Herald,* March 24, 1942*

CENTRAL STATE HOSPITAL WARD BUILDING, Lakeland, March 24, 1942, Compiled Speech, MS and Louisville *Courier-Journal,* March 25, 1942*

EXTRAORDINARY SESSION OF THE GENERAL ASSEMBLY: LEGISLATIVE REDISTRICTING, March 30, 1942, *Journal of the Senate, March 30, 1942, Extraordinary Session, 1942,* pp. 166-76*

MEMBERS OF THE SENATE, April 2, 1942, Proclamation, *Journal of the Senate, April 2, 1942, Extraordinary Session, 1942,* pp. 211-12

VENEREAL DISEASE, Frankfort, April 3, 1942, Statement, *Louisville Times,* April 3, 1942*

JEFFERSON DAY, Morehead, April 11, 1942, *State Journal,* April 12, 1942

KENTUCKY EDUCATION ASSOCIATION, Louisville, April 15, 1942, Speech, MS*

JOHN GILL WEISIGER MEMORIAL STATE PARK DEDICATION, Danville, April 20, 1942, Speech, MS*

OPTIMIST CLUB, Lexington, April 24, 1942, Summary, *Lexington Herald,* April 25, 1942

MURRAY STATE TEACHERS COLLEGE, Murray, April 28, 1942, Speech, MS

KENTUCKY DERBY, Louisville, May 2, 1942, Speech, MS

INSTALLATION OF HERMAN LEE DONOVAN, Lexington, May 6, 1942, Speech, Inaugural Booklet, University of Kentucky*

CUMBERLAND FALLS STATE PARK LODGE, Corbin, May 9, 1942, Speech, MS*

KENTUCKY FEDERATION OF WOMEN'S CLUBS, Lexington, May 13, 1942, Summary, *Lexington Herald*, May 14, 1942

DEDICATION OF POLIN NATIONAL GUARD ARMORY, Springfield, May 20, 1942, Speech, MS and *Springfield Sun*, May 21, 1942*

MADISONVILLE HIGH SCHOOL GRADUATION, Madisonville, May 22, 1942, Speech, MS

REYNOLDS METALS COMPANY, Louisville, May 23, 1942, Speech, MS*

CENTRAL STATES PROBATION AND PAROLE CONFERENCE, Louisville, May 26, 1942, Compiled Speech, Governor's Notecards and Louisville *Courier-Journal*, May 27, 1942*

MINE INSPECTORS INSTITUTE OF AMERICA, Lexington, May 27, 1942, Summary, *Lexington Herald*, May 28, 1942

DEDICATION OF SIGNAL CORPS DEPOT, Lexington, May 29, 1942, Speech, MS*

AMERICAN LEGION, Lexington, May 30, 1942, Speech, *Lexington Herald-Leader*, May 31, 1942

WAR BONDS, June 5, 1942, Speech, MS*

BOONE DAY, Frankfort, June 6, 1942, Speech, *Register of Kentucky Historical Society* 40 (July 1942): 227-28

KENTUCKY SCHOOL FOR THE BLIND CENTENNIAL, Louisville, June 8, 1942, Speech, Louisville *Courier-Journal*, June 9, 1942*

CIVILIAN DEFENSE SCHOOL, Murray, June 14, 1942, Compiled Summary, Governor's Notecards and *Murray Ledger and Times*, June 15, 1942

FLAG DAY, Murray, June 14, 1942, Speech, MS*

ANNIVERSARY OF HARRODSBURG, Harrodsburg, June 16, 1942, Speech, MS*

LEGALITY OF 1942 APPROPRIATIONS, June 17, 1942, Compiled Statement, *Richmond Daily Register* and *Lexington Herald*, June 18, 1942*

INTERSTATE OIL COMMISSION, Lexington, June 19, 1942, Welcome, *Lexington Herald*, June 20, 1942

SUPPORTS SENATOR CHANDLER AND JUDGE THOMAS, Frankfort, June 25, 1942, Louisville *Courier-Journal*, June 26, 1942

ASSESSMENT OF STATE EMPLOYEES FOR CAMPAIGN FUNDS, July 2, 1942, Compiled Statement, *Lexington Herald* and Louisville *Courier-Journal*, July 3, 1942

CHARGES ATTORNEY GENERAL SOUGHT DEAL, July 16, 1942, Statement, *Cincinnati Enquirer*, July 17, 1942

FARMS AT STATE INSTITUTIONS, Frankfort, July 27, 1942, Statement, *State Journal*, July 28, 1942*

SUPPORT OF SENATOR CHANDLER, Louisville, July 29, 1942, Speech, MS*

KENTUCKY REVISED STATUTES, July 30, 1942, Statement, Louisville *Courier-Journal*, July 31, 1942

JOINS CHANDLER ON ELECTION EVE, Versailles, August 2, 1942, *Lexington Herald-Leader*, August 3, 1942

NATIONAL GUARD ARMORY DEDICATION, St. Matthews, August 8, 1942, Summary, Louisville *Courier-Journal*, August 9, 1942

KENTUCKY FIREMEN'S ASSOCIATION, Danville, August 11, 1942, Summary, *Danville Advocate-Messenger*, August 11, 1942*

ANNIVERSARY OF THE BATTLE OF BLUE LICKS, Blue Licks State Park, August 19, 1942, Speech, MS*

STRIKE AT REYNOLDS METALS COMPANY, Frankfort, August 19, 1942, Telegrams, *Louisville Times*, August 19, 1942*

KENTUCKY JERSEY CATTLE CLUB, Lexington, August 20, 1942, Summary, Louisville *Courier-Journal*, August 21, 1942*

NAVAL TRAINING SCHOOL, Morehead, August 21, 1942, Compiled Speech, MS and *Morehead Independent*, August 27, 1942*

ARMCO BLAST FURNACE, Ashland, August 24, 1942, Speech, MS*

LOUISVILLE MENTAL HYGIENE CLINIC, Lakeland, August 26, 1942, Compiled Summary, *Lexington Herald* and Louisville *Courier-Journal*, August 27, 1942

APPOINTMENT OF G. LAWRENCE TUCKER AS LEGAL COUNSEL, August 27, 1942, Statement, Louisville *Courier-Journal*, August 27, 1942*

KENTUCKY ACTIVE MILITIA, Frankfort, September 1942, Message, *Kentucky Militiaman* 1 (September 1942)

PARADE AND MUSIC FETE, Paris, September 2, 1942, Summary, *Kentuckian Citizen*, September 4, 1942

STATE CENTRAL AND EXECUTIVE COMMITTEE, Frankfort, September 5, 1942, *Lexington Herald-Leader*, September 6, 1942

ALEXANDRIA FAIR, Campbell County, September 6, 1942*

NATIONAL YOUTH ADMINISTRATION, Richmond, September 9, 1942, Summary, *Lexington Herald*, September 10, 1942

TWELFTH ARMORED DIVISION ACTIVATED, Hopkinsville, September 15, 1942, Speech, MS*

FIRE MARSHALS AND INSPECTORS TRAINING SCHOOL, Frankfort, September 16, 1942, Summary, *Louisville Times*, September 16, 1942

STATEWIDE DRIVE FOR SCRAP METAL, September 17, 1942, Compiled Speech, Louisville *Courier-Journal*, September 18, 1942*

CELEBRATION OF KENTUCKY'S SESQUICENTENNIAL, Louisville, September 18, 1942, Speech, MS*

MARINE DAY, Glasgow, September 22, 1942, Speech†

OFFICIALS OF STATE INSTITUTIONS, Frankfort, September 22, 1942, Statement, *State Journal*, September 23, 1942*

KENTUCKY MUNICIPAL LEAGUE, Mammoth Cave, September 24, 1942, Speech, Louisville *Courier-Journal*, September 25, 1942

HONORS CAPTAIN GEORGE (ED) KISER, Somerset, September 25, 1942, Speech, MS*

CAMP KNOX, Adair-Green County Line, September 27, 1942, Summary *Adair County News*, September 30, 1942

DEMOCRATIC WOMEN'S CLUB: SIXTH DISTRICT ANNUAL MEETING, Danville, September 30, 1942, Governor's Notecards and *Danville Advocate-Messenger*, September 30, 1942

KENTUCKY STATE MEDICAL ASSOCIATION, Louisville, September 30, 1942, Compiled Summary, Governor's Notecards and Louisville *Courier-Journal*, October 1, 1942

SCRAP METAL DRIVE, Louisville, October 2, 1942, Address, MS*

OFFICERS CANDIDATE SCHOOL GRADUATION, Fort Knox, October 3, 1942, Speech, MS*

RALLY FOR CHANDLER, Frankfort, October 10, 1942, *Kentucky Post*, October 11, 1942

NAVY RECRUITING DAY,Louisville, October 11, 1942, Speech, MS*

ADDRESS TO STATE WORKERS, Frankfort, October 13, 1942, Speech, MS*

MASON COUNTY HEROES, Maysville, October 13, 1942, Speech, *Maysville Daily Independent*, October 14, 1942

370TH COMBAT TEAM ACTIVATED, Henderson, October 15, 1942, Speech, MS*

FOURTH DISTRICT RALLY, Elizabethtown, October 19, 1942, *Hardin County Enterprise*, October 27, 1942

DEMOCRATS OPEN FALL CAMPAIGN, Richmond, October 24, 1942, MS

NAVY DAY, Louisville, October 27, 1942, Summary, Governor's Notecards and Louisville *Courier-Journal*, October 28, 1942

ORDER OF THE EASTERN STAR OF KENTUCKY, Lexington, October 27, 1942, Summary, *Lexington Herald*, October 28, 1942

FIFTH DISTRICT, Newport, October 28, 1942, *Kentucky Post*, October 29, 1942

DEMOCRATIC WOMEN'S CLUB, SECOND DISTRICT, Owensboro, October 29, 1942, MS

URGES ELECTION OF CHANDLER, Frankfort, October 30, 1942, *State Journal*, October 31, 1942

DEDICATION OF HOSPITAL FOR MOTHERS AND BABIES, Oneida, Clay County, November 1, 1942, Speech, Louisville *Courier-Journal*, November 2, 1942*

PADUCAH AIRPORT DEDICATION, Paducah, November 8, 1942, Speech, MS*

AMERICAN LEGION, Lexington, November 11, 1942, Summary, *Lexington Herald*, November 12, 1942

COVINGTON-CINCINNATI TOLL BRIDGE, Frankfort, November 12, 1942, Executive Order*

TOBACCO PRICE CEILING, Frankfort, November 19, 1942, Telegram, Louisville *Courier-Journal*, November 29, 1942*

EASTERN KENTUCKY STATE TEACHERS COLLEGE GRID DINNER, Richmond, November 24, 1942, Summary, Governor's Notecards and *Richmond Daily Register*, November 24, 1942

UNIVERSITY OF KENTUCKY ALUMNI HONORS THE WILDCAT SQUAD, Lexington, November 30, 1942, Summary, *Lexington Herald*, December 1, 1942

AVON SIGNAL CORPS DEPOT GRADUATION, Avon, December 4, 1942, Speech, MS

PEARL HARBOR ANNIVERSARY, Frankfort, December 7, 1942, Speech, *State Journal*, December 8, 1942

AMERICAN FLAG PILGRIMAGE, Frankfort, December 11, 1942, Tribute, MS

FARMER DEFERMENTS, Frankfort, December 14, 1942, Telegram and Comment, Louisville *Courier-Journal*, December 15, 1942*

UNIVERSITY OF KENTUCKY SUPPORTERS OF CLYDE JOHNSON, Lexington, December 15, 1942, Summary, *Lexington Herald*, December 16, 1942

AWARD TO TUBE TURNS PLANT, Louisville, December 18, 1942, Speech, MS*

CLOSE OF SESQUICENTENNIAL YEAR, December 27, 1942, Speech, MS*

COUNTY JUDGES, SHERIFFS AND ATTORNEYS, AND COMMONWEALTH ATTORNEYS ASSOCIATION, Louisville, December 29, 1942, Speech, *Louisville Times*, December 29, 1942

ON KENTUCKY'S SOLVENCY, January 19, 1943, Guest Editorial, MS*

KENTUCKY RETAIL LUMBER DEALERS ASSOCIATION, Louisville, January 20, 1943, Summary, Louisville *Courier-Journal*, January 21, 1943

CHILD WELFARE SCHOOL, Louisville, January 30, 1943, Compiled Speech, Governor's Notecards and Louisville *Courier-Journal*, January 31, 1943*

WAR BONDS, Mayfield, February 13, 1943, Speech, MS

COVINGTON-CINCINNATI CHAMBER OF COMMERCE, Covington, February 17, 1943, Compiled Speech, *Kentucky Post* and *Lexington Herald*, February 18, 1943

SAVE TIN, GREASE, AND HOSIERY, Frankfort, March 3, 1943, Speech, MS*

DAUGHTERS OF THE AMERICAN REVOLUTION, KENTUCKY SOCIETY, Lexington, March 10, 1943, Speech, *Lexington Herald*, March 11, 1943

UNIVERSITY OF KENTUCKY CONVOCATION, Lexington, March 12, 1943, Compiled Speech, MS and *Lexington Herald*, March 13, 1943*

AWARD TO COCHRAN FOIL COMPANY, Louisville, March 16, 1943, Speech, MS*

AWARD TO PORCELAIN METAL CORPORATION, Louisville, March 17, 1943, Speech, MS

AWARD TO STOKES INDUSTRIES, Covington, March 26, 1943, Speech, Governor's Notecards

CANCELLATION OF LAUNDRY CONTRACT, March 29, 1943, Statement, *Cincinnati Enquirer*, March 30, 1943*

RICHARD G. WILLIAMS APPOINTED HIGHWAY COMMISSIONER, Frankfort, April 1, 1943, Statement, Louisville *Courier-Journal*, April 2, 1943*

MIDWAY HIGH SCHOOL, Midway, April 2, 1943, Speech, *Lexington Herald*, April 3, 1943

SOIL CONSERVATION, Frankfort, April 3, 1943, Letter, *State Journal*, April 4, 1943*

JEFFERSON DAY, Ashland, April 13, 1943, Speech, MS

CITATION OF MERIT FOR CIVILIAN DEFENSE COUNCIL, Lexington, April 14, 1943, Summary, *Lexington Herald*, April 15, 1943*

HEALTH INSTITUTE, Frankfort, April 14, 1943, Summary, *State Journal,* April 15, 1943

AWARD TO KELLY-KOETT MANUFACTURING COMPANY, Covington, April 15, 1943, Speech, MS*

DEPARTMENT OF CONSERVATION, Frankfort, April 23, 1943, Executive Order*

GUEST OF PRESIDENT ROOSEVELT, Fort Knox, April 28, 1943, Article, *Richmond Daily Register,* April 30, 1943*

KENTUCKY DERBY, Louisville, May 1, 1943, Speech, MS

IMPLORES MINERS TO RETURN TO WORK, Frankfort, May 2, 1943, Telegrams, Governor's Notecards*

KENTON COUNTY AIRPORT, Boone County, May 3, 1943, Summary, *Kentucky Post,* May 4, 1943

MOTHER'S DAY, Frankfort, May 9, 1943, Speech, MS*

UNION COLLEGE, Barbourville, May 11, 1943, Speech, MS*

CONSTITUTIONAL AMENDMENT ON $5,000 SALARY LIMIT, Frankfort, May 18, 1943, Executive Order, May 18, 1943, and *Lexington Herald,* May 19, 1943*

WAAC CLASS GRADUATES, Richmond, May 19, 1943, Speech, MS

BIG SINGING DAY, Benton, May 23, 1943, Speech, *Paducah Sun-Democrat,* May 24, 1943*

HENDERSON COUNTY PUBLIC HEALTH DEPARTMENT, Henderson, May 24, 1943, Speech, MS*

NAVAL AIR CADET TRAINING CENTER, Henderson, May 24, 1943, Summary, *Henderson Morning Gleaner,* May 25, 1943

TRANSFER OF FUNDS TO GOVERNOR'S EMERGENCY FUND, Frankfort, May 25, 1943, Executive Order*

ALLOCATION OF EMERGENCY FUNDS, Frankfort, May 25, 1943, Executive Order

MASONIC HOME JUNIOR HIGH SCHOOL GRADUATION, Louisville, May 28, 1943, Summary, Louisville *Courier-Journal,* May 29, 1943

UNITED VETERANS MEMORIAL ASSOCIATION, Covington, May 30, 1943, Summary, *Cincinnati Enquirer,* May 31, 1943

KENTUCKY COUNTY TAX COMMISSIONERS ASSOCIATION, Frankfort, June 7, 1943, Summary, *State Journal,* June 8, 1943

RESIGNATION OF INDICTED STATE EMPLOYEES, Harlan, June 15, 1943, Written Statement, *Richmond Daily Register*, June 15, 1943*

AMERICAN LEGION, JESSE M. DYKES POST, Richmond, June 17, 1943, Speech, Governor's Notecards

AWARD TO NAVAL ORDNANCE PLANT, Louisvile, June 22, 1943, Speech, Governor's Notecards

CIVIL DEFENSE COUNCIL, Hazard, June 29, 1943, Summary, *Lexington Herald*, June 30, 1943

MOREHEAD STATE TEACHERS COLLEGE, Morehead, July 1, 1943, Summary, *Lexington Herald*, July 2, 1943

AMERICAN LEGION, ST. MATTHEWS, July 4, 1943, Summary, Louisville *Courier-Journal*, July 5, 1943

LIONS CLUB, Richmond, July 8, 1943, Summary, *Richmond Daily Register*, July 9, 1943

200,000TH KENTUCKIAN ENTERS ARMED SERVICE, Louisville, July 8, 1943, Speech, MS

KIWANIS TRAIL AT CUMBERLAND FALLS, Corbin, July 10, 1943, Speech, *Corbin Times*, July 11, 1943*

CENTRAL STATE HOSPITAL BUILDING DEDICATION, Lakeland, July 12, 1943, Speech, MS*

CATLETTSBURG-KENOVA BRIDGE BECOMES TOLL FREE, Catlettsburg, July 15, 1943, Compiled speech, MS and *Ashland Daily Independent*, July 16, 1943

AMERICAN LEGION, Louisville, July 21, 1943, Speech, American Legion Files*

OPPOSITION OF BEN KILGORE TO REA, Frankfort, July 23, 1943, Statement, *Lexington Herald*, July 24, 1943*

KENTUCKY INDUSTRIAL SAFETY AND HEALTH CONGRESS, Louisville, July 28, 1943, Compiled Speech, Governor's Notecards and Louisville *Courier-Journal*, July 29, 1943*

STATE EMPLOYEES, Frankfort, July 28, 1943, *Cincinnati Enquirer*, July 29, 1943

SUPPORT OF J. LYTER DONALDSON, Louisville, July 30, 1943, Speech, MS*

SUPPORT OF J. LYTER DONALDSON, Frankfort, July 31, 1943, MS

DECLARES KILGORE IS INSINCERE, Shelbyville, August 4, 1943, Louisville *Courier-Journal*, August 5, 1943

SAYS DONALDSON'S FOES STOOP TO GUTTER, Frankfort, August 5, 1943, Louisville *Courier-Journal*, August 6, 1943

STANFORD METHODIST CHURCH ANNIVERSARY, Stanford, August 8, 1943, Speech, MS

EASTERN STATE HOSPITAL BUILDING DEDICATION, Lexington, August 24, 1943, Speech, MS*

HOME FRONT PLEDGE, August 26, 1943, Speech, MS*

UNDERGROUND WATER SUPPLY, Frankfort, August 31, 1943, Executive Order*

STATE CENTRAL DEMOCRATIC EXECUTIVE COMMITTEE, Frankfort, September 1, 1943, MS and Louisville *Courier-Journal*, September 2, 1943

LABOR DAY, Western Kentucky, September 6, 1943, Speech, MS*

KENTUCKY LAMB VERSUS NEBRASKA HOG, Frankfort, September 9, 1943, Statement, *Lexington Herald*, September 10, 1943*

BURLEY TOBACCO PRICE CEILINGS, Frankfort, September 19, 1943, Letter and Statement, Louisville *Courier-Journal*, September 20, 1943*

THIRD WAR LOAN BOND RALLY, Owensboro, September 24, 1943, Speech, *Owensboro Messenger*, September 25, 1943

SURPLUS OF STATE FUNDS, Madisonville, September 25, 1943, MS

STATE EMPLOYEES AND OFFICIALS, Frankfort, October 1, 1943, *State Journal*, October 2, 1943

DEMOCRATIC WOMEN'S CLUB OF KENTUCKY, Louisville, October 5, 1943, *Richmond Daily Register*, October 6, 1943

LANCASTER, October 9, 1943†

PLEDGES KEPT, Danville, October 9, 1943, MS

FEES FOR SUMMER TEACHER TRAINING COURSES, Frankfort, October 11, 1943, Executive Order*

ADMINISTRATION LEAVING OFFICE DEBT FREE, Carlisle, October 12, 1943, *Lexington Herald*, October 13, 1943

CALLS WILLIS TALK MISLEADING, Frankfort, October 19, 1943, Louisville *Courier-Journal*, October 20, 1943

NORTH END DEMOCRATIC CLUB, Louisville, October 19, 1943, MS

INTERSTATE CONFERENCE OF EMPLOYMENT SECURITY AGENCIES, Louisville, October 20, 1943, Summary, *Louisville Times*, October 20, 1943

KENTUCKY MASONS, Louisville, October 20, 1943, Summary, Louisville *Courier-Journal*, October 21, 1943

BRENNAN DEMOCRATIC CLUB, Louisville, October 21, 1943, MS

TUBERCULOSIS SANITARIUM, HAZELWOOD, Louisville, October 22, 1943, Speech, MS*

DEFENDS MANAGEMENT OF OLD AGE ASSISTANCE, Campbellsville, October 23, 1943, Louisville *Courier-Journal,* October 24, 1943

SPEAKS WITH SENATOR CHANDLER, Bardstown, October 25, 1943, MS and Louisville *Courier-Journal,* October 26, 1943

DENIES STATE PAYS RENT FOR UNEMPLOYMENT COMPENSATION BUILDING, Frankfort, October 26, 1943, Louisville *Courier-Journal* and *State Journal,* October 27, 1943

JEFFERSON COUNTY RALLY, Louisville, October 28, 1943, Louisville *Courier-Journal,* October 29, 1943

DENIES CHARGES MADE BY WILLIS, Winchester, October 30, 1943, MS

URGES ELECTION OF J. LYTER DONALDSON, Richmond, October 30, 1943, *Richmond Daily Register,* November 1, 1943

GOVERNOR AND SENATOR CHANDLER, Versailles, November 1, 1943, Louisville *Courier-Journal,* November 2, 1943

METALLIC MINERALS DEPOSITS, Frankfort, November 10, 1943, Executive Order

ON CONVENING A SPECIAL SESSION FOR INCOME TAX REPEAL, November 19, 1943, Letter, Louisville *Courier-Journal,* November 20, 1943*

PADUCAH-BROOKPORT BRIDGE BECOMES TOLL FREE, Paducah, November 24, 1943, Summary, *Paducah Sun-Democrat,* November 24, 1943*

KENTUCKY GOVERNMENT, 1939–1943, November 27, 1943, News Release, Tom Underwood Papers, King Library, University of Kentucky*

CALHOUN-RUMSEY BRIDGE ACROSS THE GREEN RIVER, Frankfort, November 27, 1943, Statement, Louisville *Courier-Journal,* November 28, 1943*

MENGEL COMPANY, Louisville, n.d., Speech, MS*

WEST KENTUCKY VOCATIONAL TRAINING SCHOOL, PADUCAH, Frankfort, December 3, 1943, Executive Order*

VALEDICTORY ADDRESS, Frankfort, December 7, 1943, Two Records, WHAS*

INDEX

www.ingramcontent.com/pod-product-compliance
Lightning Source LLC
Chambersburg PA
CBHW020944310726
48980CB00001B/53